VICTOR HERBERT

VICTOR HERBERT

A Theatrical Life

NEIL GOULD

FORDHAM UNIVERSITY PRESS New York 2008

Library of Congress Cataloging-in-Publication Data

Gould, Neil, 1943–
    Victor Herbert : a theatrical life / Neil Gould.—1st ed.
        p.   cm.
    Includes bibliographical references (p.   ) and index.
    ISBN-13: 978-0-8232-2871-3 (cloth)
    1. Herbert, Victor, 1859–1924.   2. Composers—United States—Biography.
I. Title.
ML410.H52G68   2008
780.92—dc22
    [B]   2008003059

Printed in the United States of America

First edition

Quotation from H. L. Mencken reprinted by permission of the Enoch Pratt Free Library, Baltimore, Maryland, in accordance with the terms of Mr. Mencken's bequest.

Quotations from "Yesterthoughts," the reminiscences of Frederick Stahlberg, by kind permission of the Trustees of Yale University.

Quotations from Victor Herbert—Lee and J.J. Shubert correspondence, courtesy of Shubert Archive, N.Y.

"Crazy" John Baldwin,

Teacher, Mentor, Friend

Herbert P. Jacoby, Esq.,

Almus pater

CONTENTS

 ACKNOWLEDGMENTS

In the course of researching and writing this biography it has been my good fortune to make the acquaintance of many friends of Victor Herbert. These colleagues, I discovered to my delight, form a kind of unofficial fan club whose only bond was forged by the fact that each provided support and encouragement for this project above and beyond his professional responsibilities.

First among these is Herbert P. Jacoby, chairman of the Victor Herbert Foundation, whose generous support, constant encouragement, and wise correctives were invaluable. It was at his suggestion that I began the seven years of challenging work that have proven uniquely rewarding. To Arthur G. Adams, friend and unofficial editor, who read the manuscript in development and made many insightful contributions, I am equally grateful.

Librarians from London to Hollywood, from Chicago to Austin, whose enthusiasm led me to much information I might otherwise have missed, are the real heroes of this study. Ray White of the music division of the Library of Congress is a name well known to afficionados of acknowledgments sections of countless musical studies; his helpfulness and that of his staff are beyond praise. Librarian Raya Then provided entree to the many hidden treasures of the Buffalo and Erie County Public Library's collection. Her warmth and personal attention, her provision of scores and recordings, her generosity of time and spirit proved a welcome antidote to the Sturm und Drang of early November, 2000. Lewis Hardee, fellow Lamb and historian of our club, guided me through ancient archives open only to initiates. To Miles Kreuger and the Institute of the American Musical I am indebted for generous hospitality and invaluable materials not available elsewhere.

Three unpublished memoirs provided personal commentary on the fabric of Herbert's life. These are "Yesterthoughts," from the Gilmore Music Library at Yale University; the recollections of Charles Dillingham; and the autobiography of Werner Janssen. I am grateful to Richard Boursy, archivist of the Rare Book and Manuscript Division at Yale, to the New York Public Library and to Mrs. Christina Jenssen for making these resources available.

Boston was a main focus of Herbert's activity. Annette Fern of the Pusey Theater Collection at Harvard University provided guidance and wise counsel. I am also grateful to the staffs of the Loeb Music Library at Harvard and the Boston Public Library for their valuable assistance in accessing the papers of Richard Aldrich and the Brown Collection, respectively.

The research librarians of the following institutions expeditiously responded to my many exacting inquiries: the Newbury Library, Chicago; the American-Irish Historical Society of New York; the Columbia University Oral History Collection, New York; the Margaret Herrick Library of the Academy of Motion Picture Arts and Sciences, Los Angeles; and the Rare Book and Manuscript Division of Princeton University, Princeton, New Jersey. The Peabody Conservatory and the Milton Eisenhower Library (Levy Collection), both of the Johns Hopkins University; Cathy Logan of the Carnegie Library of Pittsburgh; the Manuscript Division of the University of Texas at Austin; the Vassar College Archives; David Sanjik of the BMI Archives, New York; Reagan Fletcher of the Shubert Archives, New York; Robert Kimball for his ASCAP anecdotes; and Sarah Hartwell at the Rauner Library at Dartmouth College, Hanover, New Hampshire; and "Chris in the library" at DCC—to all of these my sincerest thanks and respect.

In London the archivists of the Honourable Society of the Middle Temple and of Lincoln's Inn were able to help me finally determine the facts of Herbert's paternal lineage. At the Portsmouth, New Hampshire, Public Library I found invaluable information on the "Bostonians" among the papers of Henry Clay Barnabee. Timothy Doyle, Dean of Lawrenceville School, Lawrenceville, New Jersey, an historian himself, kindly made available information about the academic career of Clifford Herbert, which made it possible for me to gain insight into the family life of the Herberts.

John Privatera supplied me with the court transcripts of *Herbert* v. *Musical Courier Co.*; this material was not easy to come by. To my friend and attorney Richard J. Miller, Jr., for his pro bono service to the Herbert cause "with heart and with voice," my deepest appreciation. To Drs. Brent Petty and William Brieger of the Johns Hopkins School of Medicine I am indebted for guidance in my discussion of Herbert's medical condition and his care under a homeopathic physician.

Bernt and Ruth Schlesinger were of invaluable aid in transliterating Herbert's early letters from *Frakturschrift* to modern German calligraphy.

And to Florence Graff, my long-suffering computer genie and some-time copy editor, I express my thanks for her perseverance and patience.

Finally, to the directors and editors at Fordham University Press, Saverio Procario, Bob Oppedisano, Mary Beatrice Schulte, Mary Lou Pena, Nicholas Frankovich, and Aldene Fredenburg, I am indebted for encouragement and above all patience, as we traveled this long and winding road together.

 PREFACE

In 1992, the year the Victor Herbert Festival was established at Saratoga Springs, New York, I was standing in front of the Adelphi Hotel, the last survivor of Saratoga's Gilded Age (the hotel, not me). A large poster announced, "Victor Herbert Returns to Saratoga"; it referred to a cabaret entertainment I was producing in the old ballroom at the Adelphi, in honor of the hundredth anniversary of Herbert's first performances with his orchestra at the Grand Union Hotel.

I was testing the waters—was there still an audience for the Herbert repertoire? As I busied myself positioning the poster, two teen-aged girls stopped to look.

"Victor Herbert! Who's that?" one asked.

"Oh," said the other, pulling her friend along, "he's dead."

Well, I thought, at least she knew *that*. It's a start.

And it was, and not just for the girls. I had not grown up with any particular love for Herbert myself, although my work as a stage director specializing in light opera and operetta had led me around his traces. I had first been bitten by the operetta bug at a series of D'Oyly Carte performances, and during my years of work in Switzerland, Austria and Germany, by a combination of good fortune and osmosis, I had absorbed what the old routined chorus members of provincial theaters referred to as *"Der echte Operettenstil"*—genuine operetta production style. Those old guys in the chorus of the Landestheater Salzburg had been young chorus boys in the original productions of Lehar and Kalman operettas. They tolerated the young American *regisseur* with good humor, and after evening performances, over strong Romanian wine, they taught me the right way to do things.

Herbert's earliest stage works came out of that same middle European tradition, but I had never seen them performed on the stage. The only Herbert material I had seen were films from the 1930s: *Naughty Marietta*, *Sweethearts*, and *Babes in Toyland* with Stan Laurel and Oliver Hardy. Those films seemed hokey and ridiculous; I wondered how such entertainment could ever have found a following that allowed Herbert to become a major force in the American musical theater. Were audiences that naive, more easily satisfied, or just plain dumb? Something must be missing from the picture, I felt. And so I read the three extant biographies.

The earliest, by Joseph Kaye, has the advantage of being written by a contemporary of Herbert's. While by no means scholarly, it has balance. The book's anecdotes have the ring of truth, since many are not complimentary. The second, by Claire Lee Purdy, appears to be one of a series of books on composers for young readers. The picture Purdy provides touches the highlights of Herbert's career and includes some valuable material about his youth that is not available elsewhere.

The third book, *Victor Herbert: A Life in Music,* is the recognized standard biography of Herbert, written by Edward Waters, who served as assistant chief of the music division of the Library of Congress in the 1950s. His work is that of an exacting scholar and Herbert devotee, and has all the strengths and weaknesses that this approach implies. The volume contains immense detail of use and interest to the music historian, as well as cast lists and other production details invaluable for the specialist.

As for the weaknesses, while it would be incorrect to describe Waters's work as hagiography, the fact is that one is hard-pressed to find any negative comments in this volume about anything Herbert wrote or did. Though his critical conclusions are a product of informed taste, they are, of course, open to honest dispute. But there are passages in Waters in which the facts are colored or slanted to support his evaluations. For instance, despite what the author has written about the reception of Herbert's cantata "The Captive," the work was not a success with either the audience or the critics at the Worcester Festival.

There is also limited material presented in the Waters biography about Herbert's persona. "Give us the man," Waters's editors at Harcourt urged, to which he responded that if the editors knew the constraints under which he had to work, they would understand the omission. One "constraint" was named Ella Victoria Herbert Bartlett, Herbert's daughter, who consistently defended her father's reputation and controlled much of what Waters was able to write about Herbert's personal life. She also had a track record of threatening libel suits. Rather than criticizing Waters for what he could not do under the circumstances, perhaps it is better to appreciate the excellent positive aspects of his achievement.

The present work is not a replacement of, but rather a supplement to, Waters's work. There can be no doubt that, whatever else he did, Herbert's significance is as a man of the theater. This book is a picture both of a man of the theater and of a theatrical man.

I have made no attempt to deal with his orchestral compositions simply because, lovely as some of them may be, they are musically insignificant.

Again, the focus here is on the man, his personality, his life, and his achievement in the theater.

Herbert was more than a great stage composer. He was an ideal subject for a biographer—by turns litigious, bellicose, short-tempered, loving, faithful, collegial, patriotic, indulgent, generous, frustrated—in short, a great character. He left us a storehouse of wonderful musical theater treasures worthy of the revival that is slowly gaining momentum; it is my hope that this book will do him and his work the justice too long delayed and denied. May it encourage many to revisit, or to visit for the first time, his wonderful world, a world of princesses and politicos, of pilsner and perfumed waltzes—a theatrical world whose image and essence was Victor Herbert.

VICTOR HERBERT

HERBERT—LOVER FAMILY TREE

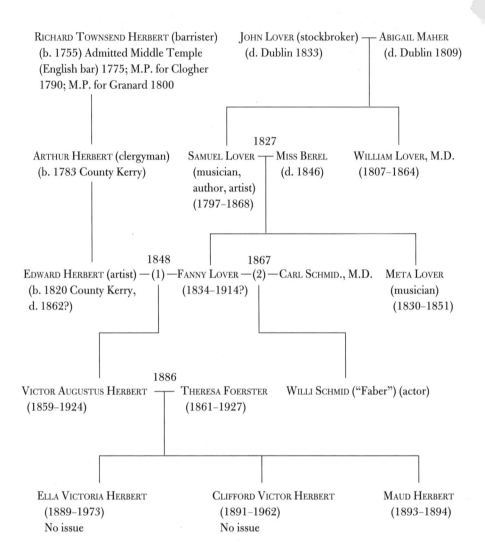

RICHARD TOWNSEND HERBERT (barrister)
(b. 1755) Admitted Middle Temple
(English bar) 1775; M.P. for Clogher
1790; M.P. for Granard 1800

JOHN LOVER (stockbroker) —— ABIGAIL MAHER
(d. Dublin 1833)　　　　　　(d. Dublin 1809)

1827

ARTHUR HERBERT (clergyman)　　SAMUEL LOVER —— MISS BEREL　　WILLIAM LOVER, M.D.
(b. 1783 County Kerry)　　　　(musician,　　　(d. 1846)　　　(1807–1864)
　　　　　　　　　　　　　　author, artist)
　　　　　　　　　　　　　　(1797–1868)

1848　　　　　　　　1867

EDWARD HERBERT (artist) —(1)—FANNY LOVER —(2)—CARL SCHMID., M.D.　META LOVER
(b. 1820 County Kerry,　　　(1834–1914?)　　　　　　　　　　　(musician)
d. 1862?)　　　　　　　　　　　　　　　　　　　　　　　　　　(1830–1851)

1886

VICTOR AUGUSTUS HERBERT —— THERESA FOERSTER　　WILLI SCHMID ("Faber") (actor)
(1859–1924)　　　　　　　　(1861–1927)

ELLA VICTORIA HERBERT　　CLIFFORD VICTOR HERBERT　　MAUD HERBERT
(1889–1973)　　　　　　　(1891–1962)　　　　　　　　(1893–1894)
No issue　　　　　　　　　No issue

CHAPTER 1

IRELAND, MY SIRELAND (1859–1886)

If Victor Herbert was not the greatest of composers, he was certainly a great human being. He was tolerant and fair, but strongly tenacious of his own convictions and devoted to the ideals in which he believed. Cheerful and sophisticated, his humor ever-present, he had the rare faculty of drawing others to him. To be happy he had to give play to the tremendous mental and physical energy that carried him, at top speeds, to the very end of his life. He touched people in many extra-musical ways: with his generosity and encouragement; with the example of his enormous capacity for enjoying life and work; with his enthusiasm for personal and political justice; and with his patriotism—Irish, German, and American. As he once said, "I dream of the old sod of Ireland; I love the fatherland, but a yoke of oxen couldn't drag me from the States."[1] The brilliance of his talent for composition, approaching but not truly reaching genius, illuminated the world of musical theater of which he and his art remain a vital part.

To say that a composer is not a genius in no way belittles his contribution. Puccini, almost Herbert's exact contemporary, famously remarked that he felt God had touched him with His little finger and told him to write for the stage. If God had indeed touched Puccini with His little finger, then He had, perhaps, touched Herbert with His finger tip.

But that was sufficient. That light touch provided the essential element. Herbert had what the Germans call *Theaterblut*, a sense of what works on stage. Without that instinct, composers of the caliber of Beethoven and Schubert, whose purely musical gifts were far greater than Herbert's, failed in the theater.

This genius for the stage shows itself in the method, the technique, the instinctive appreciation of what will and won't work, the skillful adaptation of musical means to theatrical ends that permitted Herbert to achieve success in the composition of operettas, even if his specific gifts were not of the highest.

But, for Herbert, that was not enough. If Puccini accepted his fate, Herbert never really did. Where other artists might have accepted their limitations and rejoiced in their strengths, Herbert never could—at least with good grace. Beneath the jovial exterior there lay a feeling of discontent, of frustration that surfaced in explosions of temper and bursts of passion that punctuate the story of his career and, in many cases, shape it as well. His cutting remarks during rehearsals, for example:

> I used to know a musician who had played with Victor Herbert. He told me that Herbert used bristling Swabian dialect when he got mad, such as *"Des isch jo zom Schwanz raussreissa."* (That makes me so angry I could tear my dick off!)[2]

or his self-described, passionate Irish identity:

> Blood will tell, especially Irish Blood. I'm a grandson of Samuel Lover and was born in Dublin myself, and it should not seem strange that an Irishman could and should write Irish song, or an Irish rhapsody. A real Irish song has to come from the soul . . . and an Irish soul by preference.[3]

or his famous tears:

> The first thing Fritzi Scheff did when she got back from her European junket was to hunt up Herbert and hand him a photograph she had stumbled upon in an old curio shop in Dresden.
>
> The picture shows members of the court orchestra at Stuttgart
>   in 1885, including Victor Herbert at the age of 25.
>   In the photograph he is lean of face and of compact frame.
>
> The composer first laughed—and then cried at the sight of
>   the familiar faces in the picture.[4]

and this:

> My mother told me that she only saw Victor Herbert cry once. She was visiting him in his studio at Willow Grove Park where he presented summer concerts; and he told her he was upset because his opera, *Natoma*, had not been a success.[5]

This, after *Natoma* had a run of twenty-four performances, more than any other American opera at that time.

This illustrates something else about Herbert: he was absolutely honest in his self-appraisal. He knew what his limitations were. That motive force drove him to attempt ever greater achievement. He was convinced that *Natoma* was as good as *Madame Butterfly*, he once said; but he knew better. And the discontent that grew from the disparity between his dreams and his results is a key to his personality.

But there is rich irony here, for in the arena in which Herbert found earliest distinction, he proved a genius of the first rank: he was a natural adept as a cellist. Victor Herbert played in his first concert only eight weeks after he first held a bow in his hand, and after only two years of study with the virtuoso Bernhardt Cossmann, during which he did not practice very much,[6] he began a career as a concert cellist in Europe and the United States, a career which, had it been sufficient for him, might have placed him among the outstanding instrumentalists of all time. We have the recordings and the reviews, including this from *Metropolitan Magazine*:

> The depth and sweetness of Victor Herbert's tone upon the violoncello has never been exceeded, if equaled, by any of the cello virtuosos of this country or Europe.[7]

But acclaim was not enough. This was a man to whom much was given, but who expected much more of himself, a man self-condemned to a life of striving for what he felt was not attainable: a place with the immortals.

When Victor Herbert was born in Dublin on February 1, 1859, the musical-theatrical world he entered was dominated by the figure and spirit of composer Richard Wagner. Wagner, recogzined as a musical genius, was aesthetically divisive, but it was impossible to ignore his influence. Wagner redefined the role of the artist in society, as Beethoven had before him. Where Beethoven had emancipated the artist from the role of servant and elevated him to a place with the nobility, Wagner demanded for the artist a central place in societal hierarchy. He pressed his art into the service of issues far beyond the aesthetic: politics, racial advocacy, mythology, national destiny—no area was exempt. Herbert often remarked that Wagner was his inspiration. A large portrait of the master dominated his study, and although Herbert's own musical palette only briefly reflected Wagnerian influence, largely in his unsuccessful early cantata, "The Captive," in his first extant operetta, *Prince Ananias*,[8] and in the compositional technique he adopted in *Mlle. Modiste*, the image of composer as political-social advocate, with a responsibility to speak out in all areas of concern, remained a model for Herbert all his life.

But a formative force existed much closer to Herbert: his maternal grandfather, Samuel Lover, artist, author, composer and entertainer. Lover was born in Dublin on February 24, 1797. He was versatility personified: a songwriter, novelist, painter, dramatist, entertainer—and successful at all. At age thirteen he entered the office of his father, a stockbroker, but very early gave evidence that he was fonder of the arts than of business, and was soon banished from the paternal home—and not without violence. In Victor Herbert's home he kept an old mirror, an inheritance from his grandfather. "My grandfather dexterously stepped behind that mirror," Herbert reported in an interview,

> when my great-grandfather in righteous, conservative indignation aimed a nearby missile at his head. Desirable as was the feat of breaking my grandfather's noggin—which seems to have been fairly hard at that—my great-grandfather was as yet unwilling to bring further and eternal misfortune on his household with the awful curse of a shattered looking glass; thus, his lifted hand was stayed. The mirror sheltered my grandfather from immediate damnation. He went on to a distinguished career. But deep in his heart he may have felt terribly remorseful.[9]

Perhaps. Or perhaps Victor was tipping his own hand with that remark. In many ways his own career paralleled that of his grandfather, and though never banished from the paternal roof, the fact is that neither his grandfather nor his mother ever imagined a career as a musician for him. He was expected to follow the profession of his stepfather, a physician. And though Victor achieved great success as a musician, one wonders if he somehow carried with him some of that remorse he attributes to his grandfather. Herbert's lineage was strictly upper middle class, and while he chose to follow his muse, he may have carried with him a late-nineteenth-century attitude that artists were, no matter how proficient, somewhat declassé.

At any rate, Samuel Lover spent the years from 1814 to 1817 studying marine and miniature painting in Dublin, supporting himself by making anatomical illustrations. He was very gifted, and by 1826 his portraits were on exhibition at the Hibernian Academy of Arts and, after 1832, at the Royal Academy of Arts in London. His fame spread so rapidly that, shortly before her elevation to the throne, Lover had been asked to paint a miniature of Victoria, Duchess of Kent. The commission went to a more established court painter named Hayter, which led the Dublin wags to remark that the new queen's portrait might have been painted by a Lover instead of a Hayter. In any event, the young queen did not forget Samuel Lover. After he moved to London in 1835 and continued his career with several portraits selected for the National Portrait Gallery, the queen awarded him an annual stipend of 100 pounds "in recognition of his various services to art and literature."

The reference to literature recognizes his authorship of two great classics, *Handy Andy* and *Rory O'More*, both farcical, racy tales of Irish life. Their wide popular success made both his fortune and his reputation. Along with these novels he produced the words and music for two operettas, *The Greek Boy* and a satire on Rossini, *Il Paddy Whack in Italia*. He also penned two libretti for his friend Michael Balfe.

At this point in his career Lover had become synonymous with things Irish, and personal correspondence reveals that he was an intimate of famed Irish-American showman, P. T. Barnum. At Barnum's request he had put together an entertainment of Celtic songs for a protégée of Barnum's, a Miss Williams, "The Welch Nightingale." Following up on this connection, Lover arranged an evening called "Ireland in Song and Story," in which he sang in his "sweet, true small voice"[10] the songs of Ireland, and related and acted out tales of the Old Sod.

Lover first came to the United States in 1846 and spent two successful years there, touring the northern and southern states and Canada. The American tour was so successful that when he performed in Washington, D.C., the room was so full of U.S. senators it looked like an adjourned meeting of the Chamber. When he returned to England, he turned the experience on its head and used his adventures in the New World to create an entertainment to amuse his English audiences.

Fresh from triumph and flush with new wealth, he moved from his former home to a new establishment in Sevenoaks, variously called Vine Cottage or the Ivy. The move may have been occasioned by the loss of his first wife while he was touring the U.S. He settled in with his daughter, Meta, now his companion and comfort. After she died suddenly in 1851, Lover took another wife, Mary Waudby, who later became the only grandmother Victor ever knew. Seasoned by a spectacular success and chastened by fate, Samuel Lover set up shop at Sevenoaks to rebuild his personal life.

Fanny Lover, Samuel's elder daughter, was Victor Herbert's mother, and the individual who had the first, greatest influence on the young boy's life. Victor was a late talker, and Fanny might have felt concern over this had there not been other evidence that the baby was far from abnormal. Since the age of ten months, young Victor sang almost continually—with accuracy and true pitch. The tunes, Irish folk songs sung to him by his mother, appealed to the young boy, and by the time he was two years old he knew many of these. Years later, he reminisced, "I rejoice that the memories of my earliest childhood are inseparable from the Irish melodies sung over my cradle by my mother."[11]

Fanny herself was very musical, a fine pianist and very much her father's daughter, and was apparently attracted to a man of similar talents. She married Edward Herbert, Victor's father, in 1848. Although from a long line of barristers, he has been described in some sources as an artist.[12] Victor Herbert himself remarked that he was fortunate to have artistic forebears on his father's side of the family:

> I am forced to admit that my heredity and environment have been somewhat above average. My dear old mother, now in her 80th year, writing to me from Stuttgart on the 10th anniversary of the production of my first opera (1904) remembered with maternal partiality, "I will not, however, be so unjust as not to add that you also probably inherited your precious gifts from your own father and even from his father and grandfather. They were all gifted and distinguished men and thorough Irishmen."[13]

Tragically, in 1862 Edward Herbert disappeared during a trip to Paris, never to be seen again. While there is no documentation of his death, it is presumed that he died while in Paris. There is also scant documentation about Victor Herbert's siblings. According to two unidentified clippings in the Library of Congress, Fanny and Edward had three children, and a photo[14] exists in the collection, of Victor at age four, with a younger girl identified as his cousin, at his grandfather's home. The child in the photo is more likely a sister; if in fact the girl was his cousin she would have been the daughter of Fanny's sister Meta. But Meta died, unmarried, in 1851 at the age of twenty-one. The photograph, taken in 1863, makes a cousin relationship impossible. If Victor was the eldest of the children, the siblings would have necessarily been born in 1860 and 1861.

Fanny Lover, undoubtedly very hurt by the death of her husband, reacted by setting forth with her children on a constant round of travel to the Continent. Vivid, independent, energetic and to some extent eccentric as well, she caused a mild sensation, Herbert recalled, when she arrived at a city with a passport signed by Lord Russell and two portable bathtubs packed in her luggage. Her eccentricities grew with the years, and in 1910, when she visited her now-famous son in New York, the papers marveled at her taste for smoking cigars.[15]

Fanny Herbert spoke fluent French, German, Italian and Spanish and saw to it that her son became proficient in these languages as well. As the little family traveled, Fanny engaged private tutors to give the children instruction in the essentials. Victor Herbert could hardly remember a time when he was unfamiliar with German and French. A week before he died, as he sat for a portrait by Enid Stoddard, he remarked, "I owe everything to my mother."[16] If not everything, then certainly much, including the cosmopolitanism that was one of his defining characteristics.

After her traumatic loss and somewhat desperate wanderings about the Continent, it was to the Ivy at Sevenoaks, a Kentish suburb of London, that Fanny brought her dear son Victor and his two siblings. The loss of Edward Herbert, so seemingly destructive to the family's well-being, may have actually proven to be a blessing to the future musician. His mother's urge to travel and his stay at the home of his grandfather, Samuel Lover, exposed the boy to influences that he would scarcely have experienced had he been reared in Dublin.

After the personal losses suffered by Victor's mother and grandfather, it is easy to understand that they both looked upon the boy to fill a void in their shattered lives. The handsome, charming, talented child reveled in their love and attention and that of the coterie of artists who made the Ivy a daily destination—for the place had become a magnet for celebrated writers, artists and musicians of the day. An old autograph collection compiled by Herbert's grandmother shows letters of Byron and Balfe; a figure study by Millais; a line of music signed by Mendelssohn; a couplet signed by Thomas Moore.

Samuel Lover took congenial comfort in the presence of Victor during the boy's stay at Sevenoaks, and in the hours that the two spent together in the garden, Lover busily painting as Victor kept him company. As Herbert recalled,

> How the days in my grandfather's household used to fascinate me. I would stand perfectly still for hours at a stretch watching him paint. I must surely have been quieter, more dreamy, more reflective at that stage of my life than I was destined to be a very, very few years later.
>
> His painting I adored. The music they made of afternoons or evenings when singers or violinists or pianists dropped by for a little social time

of it filled my soul with deep, peaceful satisfaction. There was, I recall a cellist named Piatti. Oh his music was the supreme thing for me! Nobody in all the universe seemed quite so wonderful as he; nothing quite so glorious as his cello. I don't suppose I said much about it at the time. But the longing to play a cello was lodged then and there in my soul. It took root and awaited its time.[17]

It was not yet time for Herbert to pick up the cello; that would come later. Meanwhile, his grandfather's influence shaped the boy in yet another area—Lover was an indefatigable worker. That same capacity for work Herbert saw as his own saving grace; he absolutely had to hammer away at an idea until the thought took on material shape. He always felt that he deserved no credit for his stupendous aptitude for work—it was stronger than he was: "No sooner is an opera completed and produced, than the morning following the first performance I am at work again at something else," Herbert said of his own work habits.[18]

During his idyll at the Ivy, Victor had grown into a happy, laughing lad. But both his mother and grandfather saw that the time had come to enter Victor upon a formal course of education. Private schooling in England at that time was prohibitively expensive and public schooling limited and rudimentary. Fanny and Samuel decided that Victor, already fluent in German, should continue his education on the Continent. Fanny and her family took up residence at Langenargen, a small village on the shore of Lake Constance. There Fanny met and fell in love with Dr. Carl Schmid. After their marriage they moved to Stuttgart, where the doctor might have the opportunity to expand his medical practice through a connection with the medical faculty at the University of Tübingen. The newly married couple also thought that Victor might benefit from schooling in a larger community.

The young man who arrived in Stuttgart was now a rambunctious adolescent. He still had his charm, but he had added to it an element of pugnaciousness that was to characterize him through all the adventures of his incident-rich life. Victor was full of the physical; in the course of his boyhood he "broke everything he owned"—he broke his legs, his arms, his shoulder blades, his nose (twice) and his jaw. "I would have broken my ears, if they had been breakable," Victor said.[19]

The Germans had a cure for such rambunctiousness: the classical Gymnasium, or secondary school. Its curriculum, designed to put a crimp in the high animal spirits of adolescents, included Greek and Latin, differential calculus, and physics and chemistry labs. The plan was that Victor become a barrister or a physician. But fate willed otherwise.

The arts were not neglected at the Gymnasium. The school orchestra had recently lost its piccolo player and the muses, having an odd sense of humor, ordained that Victor should be chosen by his classmates to master the instrument. His first assignment: the nine-note solo in the overture to Donizetti's "Daughter of the Regiment." This requirement is not as outrageous as it seems, for the solo consists of only two pitches, C and F, alternating. Daily practice preceded the performance. Here Victor takes up the story: "I do not claim that I was a piccolo virtuoso by any means. But I do insist that any player might have had the same trouble with that spot that I did. Any experienced player might have messed the thing just as I did. Besides, I had a sudden attack of dizziness when I got to it."[20]

This defensive account was given to an interviewer over thirty-five years after the event. It's clear that his embarrassment was still strong; that there was something in Victor Herbert that could not tolerate imperfection. His reaction to the contretemps at the time was equally typical: he threw the instrument in the garbage. Again a defense: "I didn't throw the piccolo out because of that [his poor performance]. What really annoyed me was the smell of the oil required to clean and polish the ebony woodwork. You had always to be cleaning and polishing. It was an untidy business. I made up my mind to chuck it."[21]

The tendency to have violent reactions when embarrassed in public was one that stayed with Victor all his life. In this case it led to a positive outcome for, soon after, Herbert took up the cello. His fluency was so immediate that he joined the section of the school orchestra after only two months. His genius for the instrument was so obvious that plans for him to follow a career in medicine or the law were abandoned, and he began study with Bernhardt Cossmann in Baden-Baden. He was the virtuoso's only pupil and had been accepted because of his prodigious talent. "The day I first held a cello in my hands was a day of destiny," Herbert said. "From a student of promise at the Gymnasium, who had won his share of honors, I became indifferent and lazy. I was possessed of but one enthusiasm—to become a cellist."[22]

Herbert's graduation picture from the Gymnasium shows that he had a strong face, his very determined expression relieved by the twinkle in his merry brown eyes, with their interesting, slanted lids. (He had not yet acquired the famous mustache.) At about this time, the family suffered financial reverses; Samuel Lover had died in 1868, and the lawyer for the estate ran off with the money. It was time for Victor to use his God-given talent to make his own way in the world. For four years Herbert played engagements with concert orchestras all over Europe, finally landing a position with the Edouard Strauss Orchestra in Vienna. He remained on the Danube for an entire year, and his experiences added richly to his education. He familiarized himself with the capabilities of all the orchestral instruments, and learned firsthand the subtleties of orchestration for which he was to become justly famous.

Setting off on his own as a concert cellist, he soon found himself stranded in Montreux—without work. He tried to convince authorities of his plight, but no one believed him; they regarded with suspicion a musician, supposedly homeless and out of work, dressed in evening clothes and carrying his cello through the streets. He played the cello so well, the Swiss refused to believe he was dead broke. "It looked phoney," recalled Herbert.[23]

Eventually a musician had pity on him and took him in. This was Gustav Klemm, a man whose generosity paid off in many ways. Years later Herbert, who never forgot a favor, brought Klemm to the United States to play in the Pittsburgh Orchestra he was then conducting. Historians also have reason to be grateful for this association, for it is the Gustav Klemm scrapbook in the Library of Congress that has provided much of the source material on Herbert's career as a conductor.

With Klemm's help, the young Herbert got back on his feet and resumed his touring. During an engagement at Dresden, an incident occurred that set him on the road to composition. He had come early to the theater to practice and, seated at the piano, began to improvise. Another cellist in the orchestra expressed his enthusiasm for Herbert's improvisation and suggested he study composition. When, shortly after, he returned to Stuttgart to play at one of the Liederkranz concerts, he was offered a position in the Royal Court Orchestra. He accepted because this gave him the opportunity to study with the conductor, Max Seyffritz, a friend of Wagner, Liszt, and almost all the great composers of the period. He studied harmony, orchestration and counterpoint. Seyffritz advised him to "Do your counterpoint here [with the orchestra]; but at home begin to compose; write for your cello." Herbert remarked later, "That only shows what the teacher can do. Deprived of the lighter muse of my Irish heart I might have done nothing but lose myself in counterpoint."[24]

Herbert's first published works were arrangements of Swabian folk songs, but his first great success as a composer was the Cello Suite (Op. 3), which he composed for the Royal Court Orchestra. It was quite a triumph for the young composer, and the papers praised the work as well as the cello concerto he composed the following year.

> Mr. Herbert, whose excellent suite for cello and orchestra was received with great acclaim last winter has composed a cello concerto which is equally praiseworthy. It displays the same characteristics as his suite: it is fresh and sensitive with a fine sense of melody. The concerto is much more technically challenging but these challenges were easily overcome by the composer who is a master of his instrument.[25]

Professor Ferling, oboist in the orchestra, recognized Herbert's talent and gave him an interesting piece of advice: "Get away while there is still time." Exactly what the professor meant by that can only be guessed. One might think that he wanted to encourage the young man to escape a life as a secure but undistinguished pit musician, but he might have had something else in mind. Herbert had established an extra-musical reputation by this time; he was known as an admired figure in Vienna, a gay blade in Berlin, and as "the playboy of Stuttgart." The handsome and gifted man-about-town was considered a "catch" by the ladies. As yet the "catch" had enjoyed his bachelorhood to the fullest. Handsome, witty, immensely talented, he had never been truly smitten. And then one day, at the end of August 1885, as rehearsals for the new season at the Court Opera began, a young woman walked onto the stage and changed his life.

Theresa Förster was a dramatic soprano who had already made a name for herself in Vienna and Dresden. Newly engaged for Stuttgart to sing Senta in *The Flying Dutchman* and Valentin in *The Hugenots*, she was "tall and striking, with a perfect hour-glass figure."[26] She immediately caught Victor's eye.

Stuttgart, September 1, 1885

Dearest Mademoiselle!

I've learned from Mr. Luria that you need an accompanist for your role preparation and I allow myself to tell you that it would be a very special pleasure for me . . ."

Her response was short: "No, thank you, Herr Herbert. An accompanist has already been engaged."

My dearest Mademoiselle!

The thought that after all it will not be possible for you to get rid of your piano accompanist—since he has already been engaged—leaves me no peace. Therefore I would like to make another suggestion.

Perhaps you will graciously permit me to pay my respects to you (because I can make my case by word of mouth more effectively).

In this most pleasant hope (it's unfortunately my *last*) I am with respect

Your most obedient servant,

Victor Herbert

At some point Theresa's curiosity was aroused. Who was this cellist who spoke German with a brogue—and who also wrote verses to her when the rumor went around that she was going to Berlin to sing in "The Tales of Hoffmann"?

As I sat at the Stammtisch
At "Louie's" Tavern dear
Some news arrived to plague me
Such as I would not hear:
Theresa, who had just arrived
To join our company
Was leaving for Berlin to sing
In "Hoffmann" that same day!

If "Hoffmann" were the devil
No greater my despair
Would be, to hear that not just she
All Försters would go there.

Now in Berlin there reigns supreme
An angel, bright and fair
Who speaks: "That's just the devil's work.
A rumor. Nothing more."

And now you're here among us
Theresa, good and kind.
May all good things await you!
The words I cannot find

To tell you all my gladness
My happiness and bliss.

Stay here and dwell among us all . . . but . . .
Save for ME your kiss!
                          VH

Obviously between September 7 and the verse from "Louie's," a relationship must have blossomed. As the colleagues became lovers the muse
did not abandon Victor. He memorialized a trip the two took to the
suburbs to have their photos taken, and showed not only his affection but
also good humor.

It was a lovely day in Spring
April, a Thursday, newly green
And Victor Herbert being there
Theresa, his beloved, fair
Said, "Let us go to Degerloch."
"A fine idea," said her betrothed.

So they set off with horse-drawn rig
And soon were at the railroad head.
And they enquired, one and both,
"What time's the train for Degerloch?"

"You've got a half an hour to wait,"
The stationman said. "Don't be late."
Theresa said, "Impatient I'm,
What shall we do to pass the time?"

Then Victor said, to her surprise,
"Look over there and use your eyes."
What did she see, alas alack?
A photo shop stood near the track.

The cameraman was standing there
Ready to shoot the handsome pair.
They paid one mark, that was his fee,
And posed for an eternity.

The print was one you'll never see
For it was a monstrosity!!

Part of the responsibilities of artists was to go on tour to spread the reputation of their home theaters. So Victor and Theresa were frequently separated. Victor early formed the habit of using local beer halls as studio and office, not only for letter writing but also for musical composition, a practice he continued when he arrived in the United States. Here Victor writes from out of town:

Saturday evening, 7:30 at Hiller's

My sweet and only Theresa,

This is the first time I've had to sit down since I arrived and I want to write to you immediately, because, unfortunately, I've had to make music all day, you know? I don't wonder because of the great, I might say blissful excitement in which I lived yesterday, I could only sleep a few hours on the train.

Write me my darling If you're arriving Monday at one PM. I hope you're coming, because my longing borders on depression.

Well, now to business!

Yesterday you sang so beautifully and you touched my heart as never before. I was so happy when I thought, "The one singing there is your dear, sweet Theresa" and my heart leapt with joy and if I ever in my whole life felt how much I love you—you enchanting darling—then it was yesterday.

Oh dear! That wasn't very businesslike, was it?

But now, if you only knew how your voice sounded and if you could only hear it—not for a moment would you be nervous—you shouldn't be—and you must promise me that tomorrow evening you will be very, very quiet. Soon your rehearsal will be over and no doubt you have been as enchanting as Valentin as you were as Senta . . . and tomorrow the applause will go on and on.

Tomorrow . . . stay calm. You can. You must, because it's certain you will have a great success.

With 1,000.000.000 kisses—your

Loving, burning

Victor

Is it possible that shortly before that letter was written, Theresa had said "Yes"? It seems so, for the letters that Victor writes from Heilbronn come fast and passionate.

My sweet Theresa,

The concert is over and we're all sitting around—enjoying. When I'm feeling happy and relaxed naturally I think of you continually and I need to write you a couple of words simply to say how immensely I love you.

Good bye my sweet darling.

Good night.

10000000000 kisses.

Your,

VICTOR

There were other chatty letters dealing with professional backstage matters; but even in these the musician was soon replaced by the lover, as the number of hugs and kisses multiplied geometrically:

In your imagination have you kissed me? If you could only feel my kisses how your mouth would ache. . . . Well good night my adored darling.

1,0000000000000000 hugs and kisses from

Your yearning

Victor

And then they were married . . . in Vienna . . . on August 14, 1886. At this time, S. J. Bendiner, owner of a prosperous pharmacy in New York City, who was to play an important role in the young couple's future, was visiting relatives in Vienna. There he met Victor, who had married his stepbrother's daughter.[27] A wedding photo preserved at the Library of Congress shows the newlyweds, Theresa's father, her sisters and Mr. Bendiner.

When the couple returned to Stuttgart they were surprised to meet Frank Damrosch, brother of the newly appointed Director of the Metropolitan Opera Company, Walter Damrosch. The Met was about to begin its fourth season and it was felt that a new direction was needed to improve the financial status of the fledgling company. Damrosch decided to present a season of German opera (which included *Aida* in German) to attract the large German-speaking population of New York, and his brother traveled to Europe to audition singers. He heard Theresa, and offered her a contract to open the season of 1886–87 as Goldmark's "Queen of Sheba." She was also to sing Aida. The young soprano insisted that she would not leave her husband. Only by offering her a joint contract,[28] one clause covering the prima donna's singing, the other the cellist's playing, was the Met able to bring the talented diva to New York. Although many accounts say that Victor was hired as first cellist of the orchestra, no evidence exists to support that distinction. Clearly, at this stage of their careers, Theresa was the star.

Before the couple left Stuttgart, Theresa's Royal Opera colleagues presented her with this valedictory, which she preserved among her personal papers to the end of her life:

A Poem to Remember Us By
for
Theresa Förster

The artist finds a home in all the world.
His art's the country that ties him to us.
His magic circle binds all things
Embracing all that's noble in the human soul.

Too soon your genius leads you far from here.
Great fame and honors shall your art adorn.
So, as you part, receive this final word
To take with you: a tribute from your friends.

When you've achieved high happiness and honors
And wrung from fate the laurels that she lends
And all your dreams have come to sweet fruition
We pray you, don't forget old friends.

The friends who truly cared about you
Even while mild privations brought you down
Will follow your career with great rejoicing
As, surely, art bestows its nob'lest crown.

From his colleagues there was no poem for Victor. But from his mother, there was this:

Remembrance

(A song for my Vic to compose if he likes)

What by day was long forgotten
Comes to me in dreams again

All that once my heart so treasured
Ancient rapture! Ancient pain!

Then I wake, my heart appeasing
With the thought: "All this is o're!
Yet a secret yearning fills me
For the joys and griefs of yore."

How many joys and griefs they had shared! And now the cello genius, the charming man-about-town, the budding composer and happy-go-lucky Irishman, with a huge head and an ego to match, was off to conquer new worlds.

CHAPTER 2

IN OLD NEW YORK (1886–1891)

Seen from the deck of the steamship *Saale*, Battery Place—a speck of green surrounded by a few buildings, backed by the spires of a few churches—was the setting for some thrilling theatrical spectacle.

The New York to which Victor Herbert came, which he saw and conquered, was never beautiful by the standard of Paris or Rome. Too many of its buildings were glorified chimneys. It was the titanic energy of the city that gave it its shape, and a kind of beauty defined by a new esthetic: ambition.

The scene of Victor Herbert's eventual triumph was the Great White Way, then as now a slippery, glittering region—"the kingdom of light and lies"—of mediocre theater, indigestion, katzenjammer and tenuous morality. But before that he frequented the great houses of Fifth Avenue and the nightclubs of Second; the cavernous watering holes of 14th Street and environs: Lenau's, Werle's, Lüchow's and Jenssens's; the grand hotels: the old Waldorf, the Astor, the Ritz; and the concert halls: Steinway, Chickering and Carnegie.

He lived everywhere: on Union Square, on Irving Place, on 14th Street and on Park Avenue. But he settled on the uplands that commanded a view of his field of battle. From his studio on the fifth floor of 321 West 108th Street, from 1906 until his death in 1924, Herbert strove to create what he named American operetta.

> If you write for musical comedy you are confronted with the difficulty of combining simplicity with originality. You cannot hope to write a "Pinafore" which would please the American public. That public, essentially sentimental, demands musical comedy of sentiment, charm, warmth. It will not grasp the satirical verse, the sarcastic dialogue of thrust and parry with the foibles and politics of the day. It is the country's loss—musically; but melting sugar makes the best musical comedy music; the piquant sauce of satire would be tasted but not relished. Further, I have a deep-rooted dislike of all attempts to feed the public salacious theatrical bits. I recently told a producer, who

wished me to write music for a piece of questionable character that I would not write music for that for less than a million dollars a note.[1]

The New York awaiting Victor Herbert was surprisingly familiar. In 1886 German was the second-most-common language heard in the United States, and New York was in many ways a German city. The Germanic influence in politics, the arts and social life was very strong. Germans of all classes made their homes in what was known as *Kleindeutschland*— Little Germany—the area bounded by 17th Street to the north, Grand Street to the south, Union Square to the west and, to the east, the East River. German women and children populated the sidewalks and stoops; the streets and sidewalks were filled with carts, their vendors selling seed cakes and German bread; hardly a street sign in English could be seen. One might spend a day wandering the streets without hearing a word of English spoken; even the policemen on the beat were required to know some German.

Twice daily at *Brotzeit*, 10 A.M. and 3 P.M., boys would carry well-filled beer cans and thick salt pretzels strung on long poles through the streets for the refreshment of workers in the shops lining the alleys south of 14th Street. Horse cars were still common in those days, and it was impossible to keep the city clean. The overpowering barnyard smell mingled in some areas with the scent of cheap cigar smoke. It was not an odor one would soon forget.

Life was comparatively simple for a newcomer who had not yet established himself. Men would stroll down Broadway and take the opportunity to become better acquainted with each other—there was ample time to stop and chat. Walking was the most reliable way of getting about in those days, and Herbert became and continued to be, until the final year of his life, a great walker.

New York's cafés were filled with clever men who welcomed the recently arrived musician to their company. Francis Neilson, Herbert's first librettist, remembered:

> Almost any day of the week between the hours of 11 and 1, men connected with the drama, literature, music and the fine arts might be found in the barrooms of the city; they were generous souls who spent it when they had it and loved life and lived it for its own sake. What raconteurs they were![2]

The greatest of these, a man who had come to New York just a few months before Herbert, and who was ultimately to have an immense and lifelong influence on the young man, was James Gibbons Huneker.

Huneker had just returned from Paris. The handsome and talented pianist, a multifaceted man of the arts and perhaps the greatest critic of music and literature New York was to see for many years, was arch and sophisticated, a worldly-wise bon vivant who was both astute and generous. Infallible in his judgment of men and the arts, he

> breathed an atmosphere of ozone charged. The idols of my youth were there. William Steinway, Theodore Thomas, Anton Seidl, Lilli Lehmann. . . .
>
> The East Side was in those hardy times still virginal to settlement workers, sociological cranks, impertinent reformers, self-advocating politicians, billionaire socialists and the ubiquitous newspaper men.
>
> It was still the dear old dirty, often disreputable, though never dull East Side.[3]

Mencken and Woollcott were Huneker's progeny; Herbert, his favorite son. Huneker introduced Herbert to the life of the city and to the strata of American society reflected in its varied populations, an experience central to Herbert's ability to create music that appealed to a wide and diverse audience. The following broadside from Teddy Roosevelt, which Herbert preserved in one of his scrapbooks, makes it clear that the young composer was determined to assimilate.

> A tangle of squabbling nationalities, an intricate knot of German-Americans, Irish-Americans, English-Americans . . . each preserving its separate nationality, each at heart more in sympathy with Europeans of that nationality than with the other citizens of the American republic. The men who do not become Americans, and nothing else, are hyphenated-Americans and there ought not to be room for them in the country.[4]

What a panorama of types and institutions there were! At Justus Schwalb's café, across from Tompkins Square, the broad-shouldered, six-foot Boniface, with his large head and flowing blonde hair, played patron saint to socialistic, anarchistic refugees from the Old World. No one went hungry or thirsty. There were no bombs, but plenty of Nietzsche and beer. Joe Kasper's at 72nd Street and First Avenue, brewed a wonderful pilsner, served across genuine bohemian tables where fashionable slummers sipped champagne to the banging and scraping of fake gypsy orchestras.

But the center of New York's artistic life was 14th Street and Union Square. Tammany Hall, the Democratic Party headquarters, shared a roof with Tony Pastor's Music Hall. The Academy of Music, Steinway Hall and Piano Factory, and the Hotel Hungaria Café stood across from the imposing German Bank building. The original R. H. Macy store was there, as were Tiffany's and Brentano's Literary Emporium. At the northwest corner of 14th and Broadway stood Miss Spengler's Institute for Young Ladies. Every morning these very pretty girls walked, two by two, around Union Square, then enclosed by a high fence.

Farther up Broadway were the music shops of Schirmer and Schuberth, Herbert's first publisher. There, one was likely to run into singers and pianists trying out new works, long before there was a Tin Pan Alley. Adjoining Schirmer's was the studio of Sarony, the photographer. Seemingly, every visiting celebrity had his picture taken there. The proprietor, Napoleon Sarony, was one of the many picturesque figures who gave the area its special character. Dressed in plaid trousers tucked into high boots, his head covered in all sorts of weather by a huge astrakhan hat that provided him the stature nature had denied him—he was no more than five feet tall—he stood in the door of his shop like a cigar-store Indian, greeting the famous and infamous alike with his trademark, "Ho! Neighbor."

A building on the north side of the square was the original home of the Union League Club; adjoining it was the office where *Century* magazine was making literary history. Completing this fertile ring of the arts, sculptor Augustus Saint-Gaudens had established his studio next to the Academy of Music.

But the crown jewel of the area was Lüchow's Restaurant at 110 East 14th Street. From its earliest days the story of the restaurant was bound up with music, and had it not been for the kindness of William Steinway, there would have been no Lüchow's at all.

August Lüchow began his career as a waiter at Mehlbach's Restaurant, and dreamt of owning the place someday under his own name. When Mehlbach announced his intention to retire in 1882, Lüchow had not yet put enough money aside for the $1,500 asking price. He went across the street to see one of his best customers, Steinway, and asked him to go in with him as a partner. Rather than become a partner, Steinway decided to lend the needed funds, and promoted the place to his acquaintances—at which point the restaurant began its legendary history as a popular meeting place for luminaries of the concert hall and stage. All the notables of the music professions met after concerts to enjoy the excellent Würzburger; more criticism was to be found there than in all the newspapers put together. Lüchow's was to become Herbert's throne room, where he officiated at his Stammtisch almost daily; and it was at that table that he oversaw the creation of the American Society of Composers, Authors and Publishers (ASCAP).

Not far to the east of Lüchow's, Irving Place intersects 14th Street. Named for the author Washington Irving, who had a residence at number 49, the street held rows of modest three-story buildings and comfortable boarding houses, the most famous of which, Werle's, was "a joyous place, full of bohemians, with excellent cooking and wine brewed after the German method."[5] The Irving Place Theater, at number 9, was managed by Heinrich Conried, who later provided management for the fledgling Metropolitan Opera. Here his Deutsches Theater provided plays and operas for a German-speaking audience.

This was the exciting and stimulating creative environment in which both James Huneker and Victor Herbert spent their salad days; fortunately these days are preserved in the writings of both men, and illuminate both the times and the men. From Huneker:

> There I sat me down with Victor Herbert and others. I buried the lower half of my face in a huge seidel of pilsner and discussed the tempi of a Beethoven symphony, the orchestration of a Richard Strauss tone poem or the technique of Walter Damrosch's new cellist. Then I hear why Seidl conducts "Tristan" better than any living conductor, and why Victor Herbert's harmonies are Irish.[6]

Isidore Witmark, Herbert's friend and publisher, was present at one of these evenings, when Huneker expressed his opinion that no one could write good music unless he had some Jewish blood in his veins. Now Victor Herbert, in his cups at the time, was in no way anti-Semitic, but he nevertheless bridled at the suggestion. "I'm Irish," he proclaimed, "of Irish descent. My mother was Irish. My grandfather, the illustrious Samuel Lover, was Irish!" "That proves it," Huneker replied; "Now I'm convinced more than ever that the Irish are one of the ten lost tribes of Israel."[7] Such was the banter that many years later Herbert fondly recalled in this letter to Huneker, who had just presented him with a copy of his latest book, *The Pathos of Distance.*

Lake Placid, New York
July 27th, 1913

My Dear Jim:

Do you remember the old allnight taverns around 14th Street and 3rd Avenue, sheltering us often after friend Lüchow had bidden us good night?

"The pathos of distance!!"—How your book made me think of those "Thousand and one moments," when your wonderful imagination was spinning shining threads, sparkling, as it were, with the beads of that golden bohemian brew!

Ibsen is surely wrong when he says that all truths sicken and die about every twenty years.

The thousand and one truths you uttered in those bygone small hours, *over* twenty years ago are still the same, your exceptional ability of illuminating them even more brilliantly than *then*, being the difference.

You, dear Jim, have not only held, but have given us *more* than you promised! Your books, all so *different* (the only sign of true genius, to my mind) but all the *same* in the glittering brilliancy of your all-embracing knowledge and astounding versatility, are today's living monuments to one of this country's most brilliant and interesting men, thank God *again* a man of *Irish blood*—to my mind the best "Ding an sich" in the world. [The implication here is that the basis of Huneker's achievement is that he is of Irish descent.]

Blessings on you, Jim and all your future work! I am proud to be numbered by you whenever you give birth to a new work and I thank you most heartily for your latest book. Let me assure you that no one could have devoured all the good things in it more interestedly and more lovingly than your old friend.

Victor Herbert

My compliments to Mrs. H.[8]

This letter is fascinating as a self-portrait in miniature of the author. First, it reveals that Herbert inherited from his grandfather a talent as a wordsmith. The diction of the letter itself, written in an offhand manner, reflects the depth of Herbert's mastery of his native language. Then there is the obvious sincerity of his compliment, a sincerity that shines through every line and reveals the basis of his talent for friendship. Of course we see the man who enjoys life's gustatory pleasures, not only in the metaphorical image of Huneker's achievement "sparkling with the beads of golden bohemian brew," but also in his choice of the verb "devour" to describe the gusto with which he attacked the book. Finally, his comment about things Irish completes the picture of Herbert, the eternal Celt.

The musical and theatrical scene that existed in the United States when Herbert arrived was vibrant. In many ways it was more varied and more participatory than that which we know today. One statistic gives insight into the level of interest that characterized the so-called "frontier nation"—with all the low level of sophistication that term implies. Between 1824 and 1888, thirty-five periodicals devoted solely to musical matters were published and thrived. They varied in technical level and were aimed at different audiences. The *Musical World and Times* (1850), *Trade Review* (1875) and *Orpheus* (1862) were general-interest magazines. *Music and Voice* (1879) and *Choral Advocate* (1850) offered the obvious emphases. The *Musical Courier* (1880), *Music and Drama* (1883) and the *Musical Critic and Trade Review* (1878) were the most technical and aimed at readers of higher sophistication. All featured extensive advertisements for musical merchants, schools and instruction. Boston, even more than New York City, was a hub of musical publishing. Between 1821 and 1880, twenty-two periodicals appeared, of which *Dwights's Journal of Music* (1859), the *Boston Musical Gazette* (1846) and the *Euterpiade and Musical Intelligencer* (1821) were outstanding examples.

The church was an obvious center of musical activity, and shared with the concert hall a taste for large choral performance. These choral activities would not have been possible without a population that not only appreciated music, but also actively participated in performances; this means that musical education was at least at a level where musical literacy by the masses was a fact. Participation in music, whether in massive choral festivals or around the parlor piano, was the rule, and it wasn't until the advent of the Victrola and the radio that music making gave way to passive "appreciation."

The great symphony societies of New York and Boston were dominated by superstar conductors of German descent. The most famous of these, Theodore Thomas and Anton Seidl, at different points became mentors to the up-and-coming Herbert. However, the dominant musical organization of nineteenth-century America wasn't the symphony orchestra, but the band. Originally a cornet band, it had its genesis in the second and third decades of the century as an adjunct to political activities. The band grew tremendously in popularity as the result of the establishment of regimental bands during the Civil War. Later, during the final decades of the nineteenth century, under the great band conductors John Philip Sousa and Patrick Sarsfield Gilmore, the band attained its highest level of influence. It was as Gilmore's successor that Herbert first achieved the status of a musical superstar; in those days the great musical figures were vocal and instrumental soloists, conductors and bandmasters; Herbert was to shine in all three categories.

Despite all the musical interest and ability increasingly displayed by Americans, the leadership and membership of professional musical organizations remained firmly in German hands. There was in the musical world a palpable anti-American prejudice, deeply rooted in the educational establishment. Americans had been brainwashed into believing that if it didn't have a Teutonic accent, it couldn't be any good.

A letter from Professor Heinrich Haas to Professor F. L. Ritter of Vassar College clearly expresses this view:

> I flatter myself to share in a measure your sentiments about American musicians. I think to have discovered among them a great deal of superficiality coupled with pretense and arrogance in music, to say nothing of not infrequent glaring ignorance and in their character a mercenary spirit, as well as one of envy and jealousy.
>
> The American musicians ought to remember that *Germany* has for them, as for the whole world, produced the masterworks in music and has also been to them the mediator and interpreter of all the excellent foreign music. American musicians, although as such hardly weaned, as yet waddling infants, strike at their nurse and consider themselves fully emancipated from their preceptors. I say they have to learn a good deal yet.[9]

In the 1880s the musical life of New York was divided between what we might call the professionals and the not-so-professionals. Theodore Thomas and Leopold Damrosch were the rival symphony conductors on the concert scene. Thomas conducted the orchestra of the New York Philharmonic Society, an organization whose membership was by invitation only, where the players chose the conductor, footed the bills and divided the profits. Thomas also led the Theodore Thomas Orchestra at the Academy of Music. Damrosch conducted the New York Symphony and Oratorio Society at Steinway Hall, just down the street. They were rivals on a scale unheard of in our day. In 1881 Damrosch mounted a choral-orchestral festival in New York that featured 1,200 singers and 300 instrumentalists. Not to be outdone, Thomas produced a festival the following year with 3,000 singers and the "standard" orchestra of 300.

The world of opera was likewise characterized by rivalry, based not so much on personality as on repertoire. The Academy of Music was the scene of Colonel Mapleson's operatic forays into the Italian canon. The limited number of boxes at the Academy prevented newly rich parvenus—among them Vanderbilts and Schoenbergs (later Belmonts)—from attaining that entree to social acceptance, "a box at the opera." So a few disaffected millionaires set up shop at the corner of 39th Street and Broadway, founding the Metropolitan Music Hall (later Opera House) in 1883 with an Italian repertoire similar to that offered at the Academy. After three seasons the solons decided to adopt a German program, specifically emphasizing Wagner, and they brought his amanuensis and disciple, Anton Seidl, over (on the same boat as Victor Herbert) to lead the band.

> Every lover of the Bayreuth master who could beg, borrow or steal a ticket had rallied to the flag to swear devotions to the cause of Wagnerian music and breathe curses on the obnoxious Latins. After a performance of *Meistersinger*, Emil Fischer, the Sachs, addressed the assembled capacity audience: "I hope I may live to sing again in this place and on this stage—in German!"—which brought down the roof.[10]

A glimpse of concert hall activity is provided by the *American Musician*:

> Vocalist Miss Anna Russell [No!] at Steinway Hall with assisting artists as follows: Miss Ellen Parepa, a "light soprano" from Boston; Mrs. Bertha Webb, the charming little Violiniste; Miss Emma Cummings "whose mannerisms caused merriment" sang the air of the "Barber of Seville." Later, Mrs. Harriet Webb presented a 25 minute recitation, "The Chariot Race from Gen. Wallace's 'Ben Hur.'"[11]

In the evening the annual concert of the Gaelic Society offered selections from the works of Irish composers, among them Samuel Lover. Uptown at Chickering Hall, Lillian Russell was singing one of her great hits, "The Silver Line," in aid of the Institute of Holy Angels of Fort Lee, New Jersey.

This account of a private musicale is representative of the not-so-professional scene.

> Mrs. William Tosterius' spacious parlors on West 18th Street were well filled with guests for a "voice-evening." The assemblage was a brilliant and critical one, if somewhat uncertain as to what it was to hear.

Promptly at 8:30 all conversation ceased and the program began with Mr. Frank M. Stephens leading a whistling solo, "Sweet Sixteen Waltz." The tone of the whistle was clear and crisp as a bird's and his execution remarkable for ease and delicacy of sound. This was followed by Mrs. M. E. Muller, a lady of pleasing personality and physique who recited: "John Maynaird, The Hero of Lake Erie." Then, as grande finale, Miss Pictou, the soprano of the choir of the Dutch Reformed Church sang, "In Old Madrid."[12]

New York's theatrical scene was likewise divided between the "haute" and "not-so-haute." You could experience the artistry of Ada Rehan as Viola, Duse as Camille, Thomas Keene as Othello; or *The Mulligan Guard's Ball* at Harrigan and Hart's Theater, *The Corsican Brothers* at the Grand Opera House, *The Gondoliers* at Daly's, a *New Hebrew Play—Isabel* at the Fifth Avenue Theater. Lillian Russell's Opera *Comique* held forth at the Garden Theater and Barnum was in full flower with *The Greatest Show on Earth* at Madison Square Garden, while uptown on the shores of the Harlem River, at the Polo Grounds—in a tent—his new production of *Nero* roared forth like the lions of classical Rome.[13] Mrs. M. G. Van Rensselaer, whose very name is imprimatur for her commentary on "things New York," has left us a vivid description of the theatrical scene through the eyes of one who was there and seems to have seen it all:

And our theaters? The finest of these are much like fine theaters everywhere in the world, except they are more comfortable, better ventilated—uptown. But visit our less aristocratic quarters and the theaters will seem as strange as the people themselves.

There are rows of them, big and little, along the bowery. With some exhibitions that it could not profit your morals, and some that it would disgust even your curiosity to witness. They offer you others well worth contemplation. Here the variety-show may be seen at its worst; but also sometimes at its best because, while its "acts" are good of their kind, you could not feel, as you must uptown, that the audience ought to care more for "acts" of some other kind.

There is blood and thunder melodrama which your grandfather enjoyed in his youth; there is the modern drama which tries to be up to date, reproducing "To-day" in its figures and happenings with a realism so unselfconscious you would be foolish to judge it by the standards of art at all. These witnesses to life in New York may be taken in the same spirit as the voice of the newspaper, which likewise makes no pretense to be an artistic form of speech.

Almost as characteristic are the German dramas, adapted to the soul of New York but played in the language of Germany.[14]

This, then, was the musical-theatrical world that awaited Victor Herbert.

In 1886 newcomers to America from Germany did not land at Ellis Island. The North German Lloyd steamships docked at Hoboken; from there, a carriage brought passengers to a ferry that shepherded them across the icy North River to Castle Garden at the lower end of Manhattan.[15] It was there that Theresa Förster and her husband were met by relatives from the Bendiner family. They were first brought to the family's pharmacy, where Mr. Schlesinger's memoir picks up the story.

> Mrs. Herbert was a tall, striking type, with an hour-glass figure. She spoke only German. Victor Herbert spoke English with a German accent. He was elated at being in America and during the afternoon, which I spent with him, he told me of his experiences on the ship.
>
> Mr. Bendiner placed the couple at the Hotel Hungaria on Union Square, where Klein's store now stands [the northeast corner of the intersection]. There was a Weinstube [a café serving wine, beer and pastries] on the ground floor and the rest of the building was the hotel. They occupied a large room on the first floor.
>
> Every Tuesday morning it was my duty and privilege to take over $50.00, advanced as a loan. After two years here, Herbert became known and recognized and with his first money he repaid the loan.
>
> Paying my weekly visits I got to know him quite well. He was about 5′10″ in height, rather heavy and very demonstrative. He would embrace me and volunteer to play for me. He played the cello and composed his music on that instrument, while his wife played the piano. He had an unusually large head and wore a size eight hat.
>
> At this time we took him to Lüchow's on 14th Street to entertain him, a weekly occurrence. He was a voracious eater and invariably ate three or more sandwiches with his beer. He told wonderful jokes and he was a good listener as well.

As his fame grew his visits became less frequent—but he never forgot me. He always sent me concert tickets and stayed in touch until his death.[16]

Victor's fame grew slowly and sporadically; Theresa's was immediately established. A reporter from the *New York Herald* tracked her down for an interview the day after she arrived. His description of her agrees with that of Schlesinger: "A young, statuesque German type with an abundance of blonde hair, blue, luminous eyes and delicate features." He wrote that she would make a beautiful Queen of Sheba. "Yes," Theresa replied, divaesque, "that is the part that has been chosen by the management for my debut. I have never sung it before. How I should like to have sung Aida instead. It will be my second role here. I have been engaged in Dresden and Stuttgart where I have sung Wagnerian parts and the dramatic repertoire generally."[17]

She soon busied herself with preparations for her opening night appearance in Goldmark's opera. Victor was, as always, trying to make music and money. Although he had been hired to play cello in the Met orchestra, the salary was a mere sixty dollars per week, and he needed more. Fortunately, on the voyage from Bremen he had made the acquaintance of Mr. Koster, a proprietor of Koster and Bial's Music Hall. Impressed by Herbert's personality and experience, Koster engaged him on the spot as leader of the orchestra for the music hall, which was often referred to as a "tingle-tangle." Herbert was free to accept the engagement, since in those days the Met performed only four times a week, on Monday, Wednesday and Friday evenings, with a matinee on Saturday.[18]

The story of Herbert's first professional engagement in the United States is highly characteristic. Herbert would jump at any chance to make money, even if he didn't know what he was getting into. Just as quickly, he would exit a situation he found embarrassing. He certainly did not know what a tingle-tangle was, or that the "tingle" referred not so much to the music as to the patrons' state of consciousness, and that the "tangle" referred to their relationships. He was soon to learn.

Koster and Bial's Music Hall and Cork Room[19] was one of only three theaters that imported European acts. John Koster and Adam Bial began their careers as partners in a successful brewery, and when they established their entertainment business at 114 West 23rd Street the purpose was to push beer sales; entertainment was secondary. The partners decided that Bial would manage the Music Hall and Koster the brewery.

Herbert was already starting off on the wrong foot, since he had been hired by the brewer to work for the producer.

When the Music Hall first opened it featured a Viennese orchestra of fifty men playing light classical music[20]—a perfect fit for Herbert. But it soon became obvious to the partners that the audience for such a program was not the audience for beer. By the time Herbert arrived, the establishment had a huge clientele. It had become a pick-up place, with a mix of imported and domestic beers and blue acts featuring women who stripped down to their tights.

Koster and Bial's was built to resemble an English Music Hall: a balcony ran all around the spacious room, and featured private boxes that served as the scene of the most private kinds of activities. The New York City Municipal Archives' "Reports on Concert and Variety Halls"[21] contain a letter charging K and B with violation of the Blue Laws on Sunday closings; another document mentions incidents of prostitution; in a third, K and B vow to conduct a serious cleanup, including "glass doors on the boxes to prevent illicit assignations" as well as "bars on objectionable persons and ladies without male escorts."

On the main floor the buzz of voices was deafening. At least a hundred tables were crowded together, with all sorts and conditions of men and women drinking the night away. David Mannes recalled the scene: "At the age of eighteen I was playing for an audience of harlots and pimps, hard faced, bitter eyed women and overdressed young fops swigging quarts of champagne in an atmosphere of cigar smoke, stale drinks and sweat."[22]

By the time Herbert arrived, typical variety hall "orchestras" varied in size from one piece (a piano) to seven or eight, consisting of violins, cornets, trombones, piano, bass, and drums. Bial was nothing if not creative. He introduced operetta afterpieces as his grand finales and interspersed them with satirical travesties on grand operas such as *Orfeo* and *Traviata*. But his masterpiece was "An Affair of Honor," an act in which two women duelists stripped nude to the waist. When this piece was presented there was invariably a police raid and a brawl, after which artists and customers alike wound up in police court.

But Koster and Bial's is most fondly remembered for its famous "Cork Room." Located to the right of the stage, this small enclave, about 15 by 20 feet, served only vintage champagne. After a bottle was opened its cork, signed by the purchaser, was affixed to the wall as decoration. If you stopped buying you were asked to leave. Years later, when the hall closed, the corks were placed in tiny coffins and presented to the regulars as a souvenir of happy times, now gone forever.

This, then, was the scene of Herbert's first employment in America. His elation at having the good fortune to find a job even before he left the ship soon turned to dismay. Herbert was by no means a prude, but obvious displays of overt sexuality and drunkenness were not to his taste. He was certainly a man, but he was also a gentleman, with a strong sense of what was appropriate. He could not endure the behavior of patrons who pounded their beer glasses on the tables, keeping time with his music. On the third night he dropped his baton and walked out. Later on, defending his actions to Schlesinger, he explained, "I was not impulsive—but I could not stand it!!" The short fuse blew again. The piccolo player still lived!

In the meantime, November 8 dawned bright and clear, and Theresa made her debut at the Met. Four days later she sang *Aida*. That first season her roles included Elsa (*Lohengrin*), Irene (*Rienzi*) and Elizabeth (*Tannhauser*). The reviewers* were ecstatic. W. J. Henderson of the *New York Times* said of Theresa's portrayal of Sheba,

> She has a fine stage presence and a dramatic soprano voice of great beauty and power. She was in every way suited to the role. Her rendering of the great dramatic scene was most effective and the success she gained during the evening leads us to look forward with pleasure to her appearance in other great dramatic roles.

while the *Telegram* reported that "She acted with rare intelligence and has a soprano voice of good range and power which she uses with consummate skill." Of her performance of Aida, A. Steinberg of the *New York Herald* said,

> She is a singer of excellent accomplishments and holds a front rank among primme-donne. Her voice is one of uncommon strength, endurance and brilliancy. She sings with feeling and seems to have admirable vocal training, as was seen in the use of mezzo and sotto voce effects. Her success with the audience was complete.

And Theresa was making big money. The size of salaries for Met stars in this period is fantastic. To grasp the largesse of the company, we must

*Reviews were published without bylines in this period; these were the major critics for their respective newspapers and the presumed authors of the reviews.

bear in mind that the factor that corrects 1900 dollars to 2000 dollars is 20.6. The following salaries were paid for a single performance:

Adelina Patti:	$5000 (= $103,000!)
Marcella Sembrich:	$1500 (+ hotel bills of $1400 per month)
Christine Nilsson:	$2500
Jean de Reszke and Eduard de Reszke:	$2000 (for both)
Francesco Tamagno:	$2500
Victor Maurel:	$600[23]

Even if Theresa was paid only $1,000 per performance, that would be the equivalent of $20,600 in today's dollars. Victor made sixty dollars a *week* as a pit musician, the equivalent today of $1,230.

Soon both artists had business cards printed up. Theresa's read, "Theresa Herbert-Förster; Metropolitan Opera." It reflected the present. Victor's read, "Victor Herbert: Solo cellist of the royal orchestra of His Majesty the King of Wurtemberg." It reflected the past.

The unequal balance of income and recognition placed a strain on the relationship. There is preserved in the Library of Congress one of Herbert's business cards. It is enclosed in an envelope addressed, "Theresa Herbert-Förster, Metropolitan Opera House, New York." In a strong pencil scrawl, with double underlinings and double exclamation points, it reads: "Zweimal hierbei gekommen!! Wutend dass Du fort bist!!" ("Been here twice!! Furious that you're out!!") A far cry from "With 1,000,000,000 kisses your Loving, burning Victor." Burning? Yes. Loving? Maybe.

Unfortunately, Victor Herbert was not the only Met employee watching Theresa. Lilli Lehmann was the thirty-eight-year-old queen of the German dramatic repertoire. She had been one of Wagner's original Rhinemaidens and had a distinguished international reputation. But she was not queen of the Met. That distinction belonged to Adelina Patti. Lehmann was "sick to heart" with jealousy of Patti, and once left the Opera House in the middle of one of Patti's performances. A *Herald* reporter noticed the exit and asked Patti what she thought of this discourtesy. With child-like simplicity Patti replied, "I do not know Miss Lehmann and was not aware that she had been in the theater, or that she had left it."[24]

Still, within her realm of German opera, Lilli felt she reigned supreme. In her memoirs[25] she reflects this attitude: "Although Fides *(La Prophete)* belonged to me alone, like all the dramatic roles, I gave up the first production of it to Marianne Brandt, and made claim only to the second performance of it."

The Lehmann repertoire was an exact duplication of the roles for which Theresa had been engaged: The Queen of Sheba, Aida, Irene, Elsa. What was not generally known was that Lehmann's attitude was contractually based.

> I had been installed at the Metropolitan Opera House at New York *in a confidential position and my artistic advice was asked concerning occasions of special engagements, opera productions, or appointments* [italics mine].[26]

In other words, she had control over casting. Lehmann read of Theresa that "she holds a front rank among primme-donne." For her first, triumphant season in 1886–87 Theresa sang fourteen performances of five major roles. For the season of 1887–88, the beautiful, youthful 25-year-old sang one performance of Elsa, on Valentine's Day, 1888. It was her last appearance with the company.

Theresa was not Lehmann's only rival. The great Anton Seidl's wife, Mme. Seidl-Kraus, also had the misfortune to specialize in the German dramatic soprano repertoire. In January 1887 she appeared as Eva in a brilliant *Meistersinger* production.[27] Shortly thereafter, it was announced that Mrs. Seidl had given up a promising operatic career in order to "devote herself entirely to the care of her beloved husband."[28] He was to die twelve years later of ptomaine poisoning.

Although Mrs. Seidl-Kraus never again appeared before the public, Theresa was made of sterner stuff. During the summer of 1887, Mme. Herbert-Förster returned to Europe to sing at the Vienna Opera, accompanied by her husband. On her return she was engaged for the opera season at the Thalia Theater, where she sang Valentine in *Les Hugenots* and Leonora in *Il Trovatore*. Once again the reviews were triumphant. This from Steinberg of the *New York Herald*: "She sang superbly as Valentin. Her fine presence, her impassioned delivery and intelligent acting were well worthy of the recognition they received from the large audience."[29]

An equally enthusiastic—if, for Victor, somewhat unsettling—review greeted her Leonora: "Mme. Herbert-Förster with her handsome face and ample figure proved a charming Leonora. She sang with great beauty of tone and vocal strength and acted admirably. With her Manrico, Heinrich Boetel, both were very effective and successful as a stage couple."[30]

There can be no question that, with his wife's career continuing to blossom, Herbert felt tremendous pressure to produce. When she left the Met, the decrease in income was a blow. Herbert confided to a friend that "he was hard-pressed to pay their rent, but he was proud to be head of his family in every sense of the word."[31]

He tried everything. In October of 1887, he placed an advertisement in the *Musical Courier,* stating that he was "ready to accept a few cello pupils and also that he was available for concert and solo work."[32] He took odd jobs as an arranger. A letter in the Harvard Theater Collection, written after Herbert moved from the Hotel Hungaria to 212 East 14th Street, gives us a glimpse of that activity.

Wednesday

Dear Mr. Smith

I think I might be able to score the Bizet number for next Sunday, if you will let me have the piano score as soon as possible.

The scoring (on the orchestral part) would cost you about $15.00—I should say.

If you want it done, don't lose time in bringing me the score, as time is very short.

Yours truly

Victor Herbert

The letter is typical Herbert. Whether dealing with matters of employment or collaboration, the workaholic was always urging his colleagues on to beat the clock. Time *was* money for this man, and his attitude would bring him as much frustration as it did remuneration, for few if any of his coworkers were as highly motivated as he to get on with the job and move to the next project.

The question of why Theresa, a major talent with a brilliant career underway, retired from the stage has often been raised. Some answers have already been offered: the opposition of Lilli Lehman was surely one factor contributing to Theresa's leaving the Met. But perhaps more important, a conflict arose within her relationship with her husband, born of her success and Herbert's delayed recognition in the United States. Herbert was a man of his time, and he no doubt found it difficult to play a supporting role in the family drama. Further insight into this attitude is available if one examines the role James Huneker played in all this. When Herbert first met him on the café circuit, the "poor man's club," as he called it, "the stamping ground for men of talent," Huneker knew Herbert only as the husband of "that handsome Viennese woman, who sang with a sumptuous voice."[33] But among Huneker's papers at Dartmouth, in a folder devoted to Victor Herbert material, there exists a draft copy of a tale he later developed into a story variously titled "A Tale of Old Irving Place" and "The Husband of Madame." One can imagine the great raconteur spinning this cautionary tale for Herbert, lubricating its message with pints of golden brew.

The Husband of Madame

I usually walked around Union Square for daily exercise. On summer evenings it was a favored promenade for residents of the vicinity.

For several years I had noticed a lady of a certain age, fantastically attired, escorted by a tall, elderly man. It was the celebrated singing teacher, Mme. Miramelli-Mario. The man was M. Mario, ex-baritone. She had a studio on Irving Place. She was invariably addressed as "Madame" by her students.

I got to know M. Mario as we shared many glasses of wine at the various bars around Union Square. But no matter his whereabouts, at 7 o'clock every evening he could be seen piloting his heavy wife around Union Square—she fatigued though voluble, he, melancholy and taciturn. They did not give the impression of being well-matched.

One day when I had occasion to call on him the little maid-servant who opened the door shrewishly responded to my question: "Is M. Mario at home?" with "You mean the husband of Madame?" That threw some light on their domestic relations, and when I saw him shoveling snow, carrying bundles or market baskets, or running errands, I realized his subaltern position in the artistic partnership. M. Mario was educated and a linguist. His clothes were fashionable and neat. He did take a drop too much and too often, though I'll swear I never saw him the worse for it.

One night returning very late from the opera I saw him sitting on a Union Square bench, his head in his hands—and I saw that he had been weeping. Oh, these ancient prima donnas and the tyrannical airs they display to their suffering husbands. The husband of Madame! It was a little tragedy; his.[34]

Joseph Kaye, Herbert's first biographer,[35] feels that as a vain man Herbert was jealous of his wife's success and induced her to give up singing. That seems a simplistic answer. It might have the ring of truth if Herbert had ever shown jealousy in any of his relationships; but that was not the case. He had too much self-respect and too much self-confidence. It might be a sustainable position if he, himself, had never known success. But his career in Europe had been triumphant. True, he must have felt frustration that his success in the United States was delayed. But he loved Theresa very much. He had rejoiced in her European successes. As a husband he continued to love her, and the children they had together. (Herbert's friend and associate, Gustav Klemm,[36] informs us that Herbert had five children, only two of whom survived.)

In 1888 Victor began a series of tours as a solo cellist. By 1889 he was often on the road. His letters home continue to express his affection, and concern, for Theresa.

St. Nicholas Hotel
Decatur, Ill [October] 1889

My Dear sweet little wife,

I've just sent you a telegram since, when I arrived, there was no letter from you and I haven't any word of you since Friday.

I hope to God that you are well and that because of some mistake on your part the letter you intended to send me got taken to the post office too late.

Well, I hope to have an answer in a couple of hours because it makes me very uneasy to have no letter from you.

Victor

Why was Victor so nervous, so upset, so anxious?

Galt House
Louisville, Kentucky
[October] 1889
Thursday

My sweet beloved wife,

My deepest, most affectionate congratulations on your successful delivery and my deepest thanks for the beloved little daughter [Ella Victoria] which you have presented to us both. I'm really burning up with excitement in anticipation of seeing you and our little dear one; how awful it is to have to be so far away you can possibly imagine.

I only have a little time to write. I've just cabled mama, who no doubt will send a telegram to father [i.e. Theresa's father] at once—or would you rather have me send a cable to father? Now Mrs. Lenkow [the midwife] must write and tell me how the little girl looks and everything—

Did you have much discomfort? Tell me everything—I'm dying with excitement.

Now to the main thing. With all my heart I pray you take care of yourself. Don't make a move—don't even think about it!—follow the orders of the doctor and the midwife exactly! Not a move!

It seems possible, from the urgency of Herbert's text, that Ella may not have been their first child. He is very concerned about Theresa's health. At this time it was not typical to have both a doctor and a midwife in attendance at a confinement, unless there had been previous medical problems. In any event, Herbert's loving concern for his wife shines through the correspondence. This is not the letter of a jealous man.

Why, then, did Theresa retire? Alice Nielsen, one of the singers who made a career starring for Victor Herbert, probably comes as close to the truth as we ever shall. She was interviewed in the *New York Times* on May 30, 1924, four days after Herbert's death.

Victor Herbert's devoted wife "created" Victor Herbert. Mrs. Herbert discovered me. I can hear her voice, with foreign pronunciation: "You are the girl to be Victor's Yvonne. No one else will do."

She would have had the same manner if she'd discovered an overcoat that was right for him—the man whom she so loved. She put no sentiment into it—made me no complimentary speeches. I was the type that was needed—she must have me.

Theresa Förster unhesitatingly gave up her career on the opera stage, feeling her talent to be the lesser and his career the one thing that mattered. She studied him and worked for him until she became his other self. She knew his abilities and needs better than he—and he realized it. They were true mates. If Victor had had for a wife a less devoted and less competent woman I doubt if he would have been so great. As it was he had his struggle.

Victor Herbert was her creation![37]

And that is why Theresa retired. She chose to. She had more important things to do.

🙠 Burdened with the responsibilities of a growing family, Herbert redoubled his efforts to supplement his income. Many private musical conservatories existed in New York City in those days that provided employment for instrumentalists. One of these, the "Grand Conservatory of Music of the City of New York," had no official connection with the municipality. Located at the corner of Fifth Avenue and 15th Street, a "central and delightful neighborhood,"[38] it offered degrees from Bachelor's to Doctor of Music and boasted a faculty of over sixty professionals who gave instruction in all instruments; one course offered students the opportunity to study with K. Zschronwomski, Professor of Zither. These were money-making organizations, and they advertised in music journals right alongside ads for WC&W Scarfs and Suspenders, O&O Tea, and the Central Park Riding Academy.

Almost unique[39] among these organizations was the National Conservatory of Music, created and supported by Mrs. F. B. (Jeannette) Thurber, wife of a millionaire grocer. Mrs. Thurber's idea was to establish a conservatory, with an eminent musician as its director, that would offer instruction to students for little or no cost. Her feeling was that with a musician of international eminence at its head, the director's reputation would reflect credit on the institution. Her plan was also to enrich the wider cultural life of the community by providing a series of free public concerts.

Thomas Quigg, editor of the influential *American Musician*, describes her self-sacrificing spirit and indomitable will: "Surrounded by every luxury that wealth can command she refused to pass her time in the frivolous enjoyments of fashionable life; she devoted it together with her talent and wealth to a serious endeavor to accomplish something substantial for art."[40]

The *Chicago Tribune* gives us a vibrant portrait of this remarkable patron.

She is a slight woman, with white, nervous hands and a very mobile face. Her eyes are dark and a mass of brown hair lies tumbled back from her forehead in a daring, graceful fashion. She speaks rapidly, breaking her sentences into small fragments as though she were writing a book in one syllable words for young readers. In short, a charming woman with brains.

She was a strong believer in the cultural potential of the American people:

> Musical America has been discovered and will surely be developed. There is a quantity of fairly cultured talent in this country wanting an opportunity to be heard, and many rough gems are ready to be cut, polished and set. There are also enough patriotic Americans, who are tired of absolute dependence upon foreign countries for our music, who will contribute toward this development.[41]

She spent over one million dollars on the National Conservatory, giving a free education to hundreds of young Americans, many of them female and black.[42] The National Conservatory, located at 110 East 17th Street, numbered among its faculty:

Piano	J. G. Huneker; Rafael Joseffy
Violin	Leopold Lichtberg; Camille Urn
Cello	Victor Herbert; Fritz Giese
Organ	Horatio T. Parker

Mrs. Thurber chose Antonin Dvorak as director of the school. The composer's relationship with Victor Herbert makes an interesting footnote to the story of Herbert's activities in the late 1880s. Dvorak was not born to be a teacher. His personality, a mixture of naivete and hot temper, did not auger well for success in the classroom. He was a "child of nature, little spoiled by culture."[43] His face was homely and covered with warts, and there was something earthy and peasant-like in his features, but his "genius shone in his wonderfully expressive eyes."[44]

Dvorak was a difficult character, and a mixed blessing for the Conservatory. He took great interest in Herbert's pupils, since he wanted to include them in his school orchestra. This presented something of a problem for Herbert, who felt that the orchestra was not very good, and that Dvorak was less than brilliant as a conductor. Furthermore, there were incidents. One of Herbert's pupils, "a charming girl," used to faint, for example, whenever Dvorak got excited at rehearsals.

But Dvorak could be very kind to those he liked. H. T. Burleigh, a black student who went on to a successful career as a composer, arranger and choral conductor, was one of his favorites. The two were often seen walking down Broadway, deep in conversation. It was Burleigh who supplied Dvorak with many of the themes he used as the basis of his symphony "From the New World." Concerning the Burleigh-Dvorak relationship, Herbert himself provides an interesting postscript in a letter from Herbert to Dr. Ferdinand Louis Ritter, professor of music at Vassar College, who was engaged in preparing a history of music in the United States. Ritter had written to Herbert, asking him his recollection of Dvorak at the National Conservatory.

> P.S. Dear Doctor,
> Mr. Harry Burleigh (one of Dr. Dvorak's best pupils in composition) probably knows much about him, than I do [this last stricken]. I have asked him to send you a "résumé" of his recollections.
> Burleigh (a Negro) was thought much of by Dr. Dvorak and has written many beautiful songs, etc. etc.—showing the Dr.'s judgment was right.
> Wishing you success—
> Yours
>
> VH[45]

Dvorak could be very disagreeable to people he did not like. One of these, unfortunately, was Anton Seidl. The great composer and the great conductor were both fond of a coffee house called Fleischmann's. Located at the corner of Broadway and 10th Street, near Grace Church, Fleischmann's served the best coffee and pastries in New York. Like Lüchow's, it was a magnet for artists. Huneker, Herbert, Seidl and Dvorak were often seen there. Seidl, known to his friends as "der grosse Schweiger" [the great silent one], had a shell that was difficult to pierce, but once it was pierced his friends found a very warm-hearted human being.[46] For some reason, perhaps because of jealousy of Seidl's conducting prowess, Dvorak had an antipathy toward him. Nevertheless, Seidl was in the habit of seating himself at Dvorak's table every day, only to be completely ignored. Here they sat, opposite one another, one with his newspaper, the other with a long, thin cigar, without exchanging a word. Herbert and Huneker, amused but disturbed by this situation, suggested that the four of them go on a tour of local bars. They began at Black's, a boite located on Broadway, just below Houston Street, famous for introducing the Manhattan cocktail, which had taken the city by storm.

Dvorak had an immense capacity for pilsner, but expressed curiosity about the American libation. The four of them started out on a tour of local oases. Twenty Manhattans later, Dvorak was calling for a sixth round while Herbert, Huneker and Seidl stared at him in disbelief.[47] But the ice had been broken. When the *New World Symphony* premiered it was by the New York Philharmonic Society under the direction of Seidl, with Herbert as cello soloist. When the work received a tremendous reception, Dvorak acknowledged Seidl's genius. And when Herbert's second cello concerto was premiered by the same organization, Dvorak stormed the green room after the performance, threw his arms around the composer before the members of the orchestra, and cried, *"Famos! Famos! Ganz famos!!"* [Wonderful! Wonderful! Absolutely wonderful!]. Then he went home and composed his own cello concerto, which has become one of the greatest contributions to the literature.

Although Herbert's activities at the National Conservatory brought him some income and kept him in contact with many of the leading musical personalities of the day, this alone did not provide real career advancement. He thought of himself as a composer; he had yet to establish himself as a conductor. Seidl had been generous in employing him as an assistant, but it seemed a long way from the occasional stint on the podium to a role as a successor to the great maestri of his period. Thomas, Seidl, Damrosch and Zerrahn all acknowledged the musical value he brought to their orchestras as an instrumentalist, but none of them was prepared to grant him a real opportunity as a conductor.

It was work as a concertizing cellist, the activity through which Herbert had achieved his European success, that seemed most promising. He made his New York debut as soloist with the New York Symphony Society at the Metropolitan Opera House on January 8, 1887. The conductor was Walter Damrosch; his co-soloist was pianist Adele Aus der Ohe. Krehbiel, writing for the *Tribune*, took note.

> Herbert, a violoncellist, presented himself for the first time to a New York audience in the dual capacity of composer and soloist. . . . Frau Aus der Ohe ranks with the very best of pianists heard in this country. Herr Herbert's triumph was hardly less emphatic than [hers]. The "andante, serenade and tarantelle" from a suite of his own, show not a little invention and are distinguished by good writing. As an executive artist he made an impression such as but few violoncellists have done before him. For his style is infinitely more easy and graceful than that of most 'cello players, just as his tone is more liquid, more melodious and of a more noble quality, simply because he never forces the tonal capacity of his instrument beyond its natural limits.[48]

This was a "money review"—one you could take to the bank. At last Herbert had recognition to match Theresa's. When he appeared as soloist with Seidl's orchestra at Steinway Hall on December 1, 1888, Krehbiel's evaluation of his Serenade for String Orchestra was muted—but still positive: "Less interesting for its melodies (some of which have familiar faces) than for the manner in which they are handled. [There are] vivid and varied dashes of color—most effective especially in the 'Love Scene' movement."[49]

Herbert built his reputation by appearing as a guest with other organizations. The *Buffalo* (N.Y.) *Tribune* for January 22, 1892, reports on his performance of the "Andante and Tarantella" from his cello suite as well as performances of the Gabriel-Marie "Klage" and Davidoff's "An der Quelle." The review reflects the growing esteem in which he was held:

> The soloist was the cello virtuoso Victor Herbert of New York. He is a master of his instrument. Many much prefer the sound of his cello to that of the violin because of the soulful tonal quality he achieves. His playing was elegant and artistic. He mastered all technical difficulties with an ease which pleased his listeners completely. They rewarded him with two calls for encores. . . . After his first group of selections he joined the ranks of the orchestra and played in the cello section. Mr. Herbert can be sure of always receiving a hearty welcome from our contemporary music lovers.[50]

This from the German-language press. The *Daily Courier*, writing for the English-speaking audience, was no less unstinting in its praise.

> Victor Herbert, the cellist par excellence of this country, was a concert all in himself and one which was delightful throughout. He played beautifully. The tarantella bristled with difficulties, but he surmounted them so easily that it seemed the simplest thing in the world to play the cello. . . . The Klage—lament—was truly a heart-breaking wail, while the "spring" laughed and bubbled and tossed itself about with unrestrained joyousness. He scored a most decided triumph.[51]

Many of these reviews comment on the apparent ease with which Herbert mastered the difficulties of his material. The Italians have a word for this highest level of artistry: *sprezzatura*. The word literally means "scorn," in this case scorn for technical difficulty. The artist who achieves *sprezzatura* moves beyond technique to the level of true mastery, which shows itself in the apparent ease with which he triumphs over his material and lifts it to a level unique to genius. That was the playing of Victor Herbert.

The money was finally starting to roll in and Herbert, from the days of his earliest success, was ready to share his good fortune. "Easy come—easy go" might have been his motto—and he lived by it. Many musicians were the beneficiaries of his largess. Still, he had a way of responding to requests for support that spared those down on their luck any embarrassment; he had the knack of making them feel they were doing him a favor by allowing him to help. Dressed to the nines—morning coats in the daytime, formal wear in the evenings, turned out in grey kid gloves and spats—he would stroll down Broadway, his pockets stuffed with twenty-dollar-bills, an easy touch for his fellow artists who did not share in his Irish luck. "He was a wonderful, wholesome man. His politeness to everyone was an expression of his kindness of heart."[52]

If someone met him on the street, he made it seem like an occasion. He would take the individual in hand, buy him a drink and then, if need be, help him out. The memory of his generosity, largeness of spirit and lack of affectation survives to this day.

Herman Brinkmann was sales manager for Tams-Witmark Publishers and a good friend of Herbert's. Brinkmann's daughter recalled in October 2001:

When I was born Herbert sent my father fancy filagree gold pins as a present for the little girl to wear. I still use them. I remember father telling the story of meeting Herbert on East 37th Street. He was going West and Herbert was going East. Herbert grabbed him and said, "Come into this restaurant!" Father responded "I've just had lunch. I'm not hungry" to which Herbert replied, "Never mind that. I have to take a shit!"

He was full of the old nick. That was the Irish in him. He never said much about the ladies. He was very circumspect. But he was a great cutup. He liked to have fun.[53]

Mary Ellis, the actress who introduced his last theater song, "Heart O' Mine," in *The Merry Wives of Gotham* (January 1924), remembered him in a telephone interview in 2001: "Everyone was in awe of him. He was a lovely man with a fine sense of humor."[54] And jazz musician and composer Eubie Blake revered Herbert. When Blake used to enter the ASCAP offices in New York, where a great meeting room, dominated by

Herbert's picture and piano, is dedicated to his memory, Blake would bow down before Herbert's picture and say, "If it weren't for that man I'd be out in the street: 'Tote that barge! Lift that bale' "[55]

Songwriter Harry Ruby, when Herbert's name was mentioned, summed up the feelings of a younger generation:

> Victor Herbert? Oh, but wait a minute—now you're talking about a part of the business that was so beyond us. We only heard of his name. We didn't know Victor Herbert. We knew of him, but we did not come into his atmosphere or level or background. If he walked by we just held our breath—"There goes Victor Herbert," we'd say. We weren't on the same level with him.[56]

The awe that people felt toward Herbert is only one side of the story. He was also very much one of the boys—a great man with the heart of a boy, and his talent for fun and games opened the door to close, lifelong friendships. The *Aschenbroedel Verein*—a society of orchestral musicians—had a clubhouse that boasted the longest bar in New York. At all hours of the day beer and whiskey, gossip and business mixed with jokes and laughter and gave this social club a special place in the clubby world of the city. One member remembered the night when Herbert, dressed in a gigantic fake beard, entertained with a comic baritone solo.[57] Another recalled that Herbert was not above practical joking. Once he told a group at the bar that if you put a wine glass down so that all of the bottom touched at once the glass would smash to pieces. He was challenged to try it, since it seemed impossible. Herbert did it, and the glass snapped at the stem. Five times he was asked to repeat the feat, until someone noticed that a whole set of valuable glasses was being destroyed. The glasses broke, not because they had been set down straight, but because Herbert had snapped the stems between his powerful fingers.[58]

Herbert's personality, a rare mix of kindness and power, energy and a touch of Irish pigheadedness, made him unique. The respect in which he was held brought him to the point where the endorsement of Victor Herbert was enough to stamp anyone as an excellent musician. The crowning evidence of Herbert's acceptance into the highest level of musical reputation was his invitation to provide music for the famed Bradley-Martin Ball on February 10, 1897. Not until Truman Capote's famous "Black and White" ball seventy years later was there anything comparable in the history of New York Society.

If ever in the social history of the American people one particular event stood out above the rest for the advance speculation it evoked or for the sensation and notoriety that followed in its wake it was the Bradley-Martin Ball. There were pages of reportorial description and editorial comment which compared it to the days of Roman extravagance at its worst.[59]

It was also the best PR Victor Herbert ever received. No single event so catapulted him to the heights of popular attention than did the Bradley-Martin Ball. What an evening it was! The guests—Livingstones, Astors, Rhinelanders—were dressed in Louis XIV costumes to match the decor of the Waldorf Ballroom. As they arrived they were announced by a liveried major-domo and bowed and curtseyed before their host and hostess. Mrs. Bradley-Martin, on a raised dias, was weighted down with over a million dollars' worth of jewels.

The musicians' gallery was garlanded with pink roses and clematis imported from the South. Supper was served at 125 tables, and the dancing lasted until dawn. A total of 107 quarts of wine and bottled water and 32 small glass carafes of brandy were served. And the bill? Corrected for 2000 dollars it would come to a grand total of $186,512. Victor Herbert earned $13,581.12, not including "beer and wine for the musicians," which came to $897.84.[60]

 It was customary in this period for concert programs to feature two contrasting soloists. One of Anton Seidl's favorites was the Vienna-born but American-trained soprano Emma Juch. A real prodigy, Juch began her career in London as a member of Mapleson's opera troupe at the age of seventeen, and by the time of her appearances with Seidl she had established her reputation in America as the founder of the Emma Juch Opera Company. This was no small beer. The *American Musician*[61] reports that the company featured 20 principals, a chorus of 45, an orchestra of 35, and a stage complement—carpenters, property men, etc.—of 25. Juch worked on tours with Seidl, singing Elsa and Sieglinde in his Wagner concerts; on the same tours Herbert appeared as cello soloist. Juch was a beautiful and ambitious woman who was fond of touring; Herbert was a handsome young genius who enjoyed life with great gusto. Whether the relationship between the two amounted to anything more than a musical synthesis can be left to the imagination. However, soon after the Seidl tour, Juch created a new organization, "Emma Juch's

Concert Artists," featuring Victor Herbert as musical director, piano accompanist, and cello soloist. One song that was frequently programmed was a translation ("by a friend," as Miss Juch demurely put it) of French verses. "Mr. Herbert, my musical director, has set them to music, and it is one of my nicest encore songs."

The Silent Rose

When all on earth is silent
And stars in heaven shine,
I'd be thy little rose, love,
And on thy heart recline.

My heartfelt love, my secret
I'd give thee in a kiss,
For in my soul I feel it:
To bloom for thee were bliss.

I will not question further,
What future shall be mine
Content to be thy rose, love,
And on thy heart recline.[62]

The song was "dedicated to Miss Juch by the composer Victor Herbert."[63]

The Concert Artists program offered a first section of various solos. On February 5, 1889, the company appeared at Vassar College in Poughkeepsie, where a student, in a personal memoir[64] written years later, pronounced Herbert a "romantic figure." He undoubtedly was.

At the same time that Herbert was developing his career as a soloist, he also continued his work as a chamber music artist. His colleagues and his critics were united in their praise of his "exquisitely poetical refined playing,"[65] a quality that was, apparently, inherited from his studies with Cossmann. At first his cello work was largely with the New York String Quartet. The *Sun*,[66] while remarking that the members of the quartet played well together, mentioned that they lacked precision in their playing. The *Tribune*[67] makes reference to the leader's want of breadth.

It is important to note that when Herbert joined the quartet he replaced Fritz Giese; the circumstances of the substitution are not known. Both men served on the faculty of the National Conservatory and, soon after, Giese moved to Boston to begin a career as that city's premier cellist. A rivalry existed between the two men that, for the time being, was put to rest by Giese's exit from the New York scene. But it wasn't long before Herbert's activities led him to the Boston area and his personal rivalry with Giese surfaced in the press.

One might be willing to consider any bad feeling between the two an aberration in a career in which Herbert was seen by both colleagues and press as a "genial friend and companion."[68] But a dark side to the story of his chamber music work shows him in a less than favorable light. Two elements of this story make it believable. The first is Herbert's remark—already quoted—that during his study with Cossmann he didn't practice very much. His natural gifts may have betrayed him now that he had entered the close and exacting world of quartet playing, where precision, preparation, and communal give-and-take are the sine qua non of successful achievement. Second, when we inspect the programs that Herbert chose to play as a soloist with symphony orchestras, we notice that the same few pieces are offered again and again; even the larger solo work is confined to the concertos of Raff and Rubinstein and, of course, his own first and second concertos. This very limited choice of solo repertoire may reflect an unwillingness to devote his time to serious preparation for chamber music performance—time that he may have seen as better spent producing income in other, more fruitful areas. One of his colleagues mentions that Herbert had trouble with the final movement of the Beethoven Quartet in A-minor, and that, during the break before the performance, the other players saw Herbert take "three swigs from a bottle of whisky which he carried in his pocket."[69]

Of all the areas in which Herbert was active, his string quartet career was the one in which he was least secure and least successful. In this arena he may have displayed certain personality traits that seem uncharacteristic. The quartet Herbert is brusque, arrogant, manipulative and difficult.

The Schmidt-Herbert Quartet, organized by violinist Louis Schmidt, gave its first concert on December 9, 1891.[70] The debut was auspicious and the *New York Sun* enthusiastic. It called the playing "truly a revelation with respect to the tone, sonority, precision and energy of the ensemble." But the career of the quartet was a stormy one. If Schmidt is to be believed, the story does little credit to Victor Herbert.

Because of Herbert's reputation as a cellist, Schmidt shared profits equally with him. This was unusual, for it was customary for the first violinist, by whose name a quartet was identified, to take the lion's share.

Schmidt also served as manager and booking agent for the group. Herbert became dissatisfied with both the financial arrangements and with the name under which the quartet was advertised. "Of any quartet," Schmidt remembered, "the cello is the tail, but Herbert wanted to be the head."[71]

Herbert became difficult. He demanded that he be consulted on engagements. He told Schmidt that he could make $75 or $100 for a solo appearance, and since the quartet only received $150 or $200 for its concerts, he was, in effect, working for half-price. Still, Herbert saw the potential for gain for himself; but it would have to be on his terms. He insisted that the bookings be placed with his personal manager, Henry Wolfson. Schmidt agreed. It seems that Herbert felt that Schmidt was not aggressive enough for booking work. He made fun of Schmidt's "kid glove" approach to selling the quartet. Early on in the quartet's career, Schmidt had arranged a large number of bookings. Pleased with his achievement, he hunted Herbert up and found him in the bar of the Lenox Lyceum. Schmidt showed Herbert the list; Herbert dismissed his achievement with a sarcastic, "The first day is always the easiest." That was his whole reaction. It seemed as if Herbert was out to make trouble. Herbert, Schmidt and Wolfson had a meeting that resulted in a stalemate. Afterward, Herbert became even more difficult. When Schmidt found a booking, he couldn't close a deal without Herbert's approval, and Herbert saw to it that he was difficult to locate. When Schmidt found him to check to see if the booking would fit Herbert's busy schedule, Herbert would reply, "Why bother me?"

The next season, 1892, without consulting Schmidt, Wolfson began to advertise the ensemble as the Herbert-Schmidt quartet. Schmidt wrote to Herbert asking why the name was changed. "Herbert sent back a letter, I wish I had kept it as a curiosity. Every other word was an oath—he could swear!"[72] Herbert finally told Schmidt that it was Wolfson's fault, and suggested the changed name remain for the season. Schmidt agreed, but when the same thing happened the next season and Herbert didn't seem to care, the quartet broke up.

This is not a pleasant story; it does not reflect credit on Herbert. But it is credible, a picture of an egotistical artist under financial and professional pressure, especially from the technical musical demands put on him by the quartet literature. He was a man who, as the Irish say, was capable of "hanging up his fiddle behind the door" on occasion. He was, after all, human and not a paragon. One can believe that when the quartet broke up, Herbert heaved a sigh of relief. Perhaps that was what he wanted all along. Herbert was a wonderful team player—so long as he was captain of the team.

$\backsim$ If some of the foregoing seems to paint Herbert in an unfavorable light with respect to his focus on earnings, it is important to remember that, beginning in 1893 and lasting until roughly 1897, the United States economy suffered a serious contraction. Even though J. P. Morgan was able to ameliorate the situation temporarily in 1894 through the purchase of government bonds, the entire period was one of extreme financial stress. For a musician who was the sole support of his family and who was determined to achieve a well-to-do lifestyle, a focus on the economics of his profession was clearly understandable. His was a materialistic age, and he played his role within his profession in the same way that the idols of his age—the Carnegies, Vanderbilts and Rockefellers—played theirs. He shared with these titans the quality of clear vision and the ability to seize events and opportunities in a way that led to his own increasing wealth and power. There was nothing wrong with that, although for some reason when such attributes are associated with an artist instead of an industrialist, some tend to look down their noses.

$\backsim$ When Victor Herbert came to America he saw himself first as an instrumentalist and second as a composer of serious orchestral music. But the path that led him to expand his career into the areas where he would achieve greatest distinction, as a conductor and theater composer, was surprisingly direct. Three great conductors, Anton Seidl, Theodore Thomas, and Carl Zerrahn, were to prove decisive influences. It is important to know something about the personalities and careers of these artists, for each had a mentoring relationship with Herbert. He learned much more than conducting from them.

$\backsim$ ANTON SEIDL

Anton Seidl and Herbert shared a veneration for Wagner—Seidl because he had worked one-on-one with the master as copyist, musical assistant, and conductor, Herbert because of his genuine appreciation of the immense changes the Bayreuth master had wrought in the shape and structure of musical-theatrical composition. Whether this admiration for Wagner helped form a bond between the two men, the fact is that a warm fellowship developed between the two men, and when Seidl formed his own orchestra he chose Herbert to be his first cellist and conducting assistant.

Herbert's experience with Seidl told him that there were greater opportunities for him as a conductor. He had all the requisites: personality, musical scholarship, emotional force and interpretive ability. At the end of Herbert's employment at the Metropolitan season of 1888, Seidl invited him to join an orchestra he was organizing to play a series of concerts at Brighton Beach. A typical format for the Seidl concerts was a series of overtures, novelties, and American works, interspersed with performances by various solo artists. Herbert later copied this formula for his summer programs at Saratoga and Willow Grove Park, Pennsylvania, a formula that remains a model for summer "pops" concerts to this day. It was Seidl who requested that Herbert compose a typically American piece for the orchestra. Herbert came up with a medley of patriotic tunes, ending with the Star Spangled Banner—à la Wagner. This became a perennial crowd pleaser—"The American Fantasy." According to the *New York Sun*, "It was Victor Herbert's 'Fantasy of National Airs' that drove the audience fairly wild. The sound of those well-known airs carried the vast audience off its feet."[73]

For those who only know Brighton Beach from Neil Simon's theatrical memoir or, more recently, as a thriving community of Russian immigrants, it is hard to picture the Brighton Beach or its neighbor, Manhattan Beach, as they were in the 1880s. Both sites were favorite destinations for all classes of society seeking relief from the sweltering New York summer. Day trips became very popular, and the railways provided transportation to the sea at intervals of fifteen minutes. This presented problems for the concerts: "Not so agreeable to the ear was the puffing, blowing off steam, whistling of the elevated railroad engine at the rear of the music hall."[74]

Brighton Beach had taken its name from the then fashionable British seaside resort and was a step above its Manhattan Beach neighbor, both with respect to facilities and programming. "The poorest German laborer takes his holiday in the summer and is likely to be found at one of the resorts on Coney Island. . . . Sausages, lager and sauerkraut served in little booths on the sea sand make his heart glad and he lounges on the beach smoking his pipe in perfect contentment."[75]

Music at Manhattan Beach was provided by Gilmore's Band, an organization that Herbert was later to lead. Brighton Beach boasted a really grand hotel along the lines of the great institutions of Saratoga, and music of a higher order. As Seidl remarked, "My chief aim is to attract to the concerts the music loving masses who wish to cultivate their taste. For years Mr. Thomas has worked in the same direction. Why retard the progress of what has been accomplished by giving light and frivolous music simply because Brighton Beach is a summer resort?"[76]

Why, indeed? Nevertheless, Seidl did program popular fare along with his signature Wagner. By the second season of concerts, which were held in a specially constructed music hall separate from the hotel, Seidl had attracted a group of ladies known as "Seidl's 400." Organized by a Mrs. Laura C. Holloway, they would hold private dinners—for ladies only—before the concerts. After dinner, in the parlor of the hotel, a few selected males were permitted to pay their respects to Mr. and Mrs. Seidl—and Mrs. Holloway, of course.

In addition to the "American Fantasy," Herbert performed a few of his own smaller works; a "Berceuse, Polonaise and Bagatelle and Scherzo" were frequently programmed. But his conducting work was limited, and doubtless his satisfaction with the arrangement was minimal, for he never returned to Brighton Beach after that first season.

The intense respect and real affection that Herbert felt for Seidl is reflected in the tribute he paid to him after Seidl's untimely death. It also reveals how much Victor absorbed from his mentor.

When I came to the United States I had known Seidl by his reputation as a Wagner disciple. He was thoroughly imbued with both the general conception and smallest detail of each opera. He bustled with energy. His thorough knowledge enabled him to make incredible progress with both players and singers. . . .

To his soloists he was always anxious to accord full measure of praise. . . . Seidl was universally admired and loved by the members of his orchestra. His players were his companions, his helpers—he was simply one of them. It was through this strong bond of fraternity that he came to acquire personal influence over the instrumentalists which was entirely distinct from the musical magnetism exerted in rehearsals and performance.[77]

Seidl's influence is also significant because of his encouragement of Herbert's work as a composer. He programmed Herbert's pieces as they were completed—a great opportunity for a fledgling composer to get his work before the public. In 1888, at the first of the symphony concerts given by Seidl at Steinway Hall, Herbert's Suite for String Orchestra—now becoming a signature piece—was programmed. When the moment came for the Suite to be played, Seidl gracefully handed the baton to the composer[78]—a gesture that was to prove as prophetic as it was symbolic. A contemporary description of Seidl at work with this orchestra gives us a picture of the model Herbert chose for himself.

> In his temperament he presents a striking example of strong emotional susceptibility and a certain brilliant nervous virility almost magnetic in transmutability—qualities which make him a truly remarkable conductor. He has the power to transmit his conception to his performers and at the same time drawing from them faithful and spontaneous expression of his purpose.[79]

Victor closed his own valedictory of Seidl with a personal note.

> We all loved him, he was so kind and affable—his great, big, beautiful eyes radiated warmth and such childlike sympathy and naturalness. When he left us we lost not only a great master musician whose presence had marked influence on musical activities in New York, but a most amiable, lovable friend.[80]

THEODORE THOMAS

"Amiable and lovable" were hardly the adjectives chosen to describe Theodore Thomas, another of Herbert's mentors. A critic for the *American Musician* had this comment:

> The Theodore Thomas orchestra was a means of glorifying the fame and advancing the career of Mr. Thomas. For twenty years it has been used as a pedestal upon which Mr. Thomas has posed as the musical discoverer of America. It moved around the country crushing the life out of local orchestras. Thomas has been successful in educating the American public to an appreciation of the works of the great masters but he never failed to take care of his own personal interests.[81]

By the time this broadside was leveled at Thomas he had been the dominant force in American classical music for over twenty years. The following year *Mapleson's Music Magazine* joined the fray and jumped all over him for his populist tendencies: "Thomas in order to cater to public attention is continually baptizing his orchestral concerts with new and would-be striking names—popular concerts, young people's concerts, symphony soirees, request programs—but some 'society people'—or pianoforte manufacturers have generally to foot the bill."

By 1888 Herbert was ensconced as the first cellist for Thomas. He learned from the master four abiding truths of the concert world: first, that a conductor's podium is a platform for self-aggrandizement; second, that the "education of the masses" is a popular mission that brings forth substantial financial support; third, that ego is not a block to successful conducting; and finally, that popularizing of the repertoire is no sin. Whatever the harpies of the press might write, Thomas remained the giant of American classical music.

Born in Hannover, Germany, in 1835 of a professional musical family, Thomas emigrated to the United States in 1845 and began a career as a young violin prodigy virtuoso. By 1852 he was conducting German and Italian troupes featuring such major artists as Jenny Lind and Henrietta Sontag. Between 1855 and 1869 he championed the cause of chamber music as principal of the Mason and Thomas quartet, which had a dominating influence in the chamber music world. In 1861 he abandoned his theatrical work for good, and the next year began his twenty-year service as conductor of the Brooklyn Philharmonic Society. He soon formed the sixty-man Theodore Thomas Orchestra for the express purpose of touring the States to educate and elevate the musical taste of the public. He had a talent for building programs that attracted a wide and diverse audience. Although the result of this was great renown, he never sacrificed art to gratify personal ambition.

The *New York Tribune* presents a favorable side of the picture:

He has labored for twenty years to place his concerts on the highest plane of excellence, not wishing to lower his standards. The classics were not crammed down the throats of the people, but by careful selection from the lighter pages a taste and capacity for better music was created—but he has been disgusted by the fact that his encores have been more applauded than his entrees.[82]

Here, indeed, was a lesson for Herbert. The crowd-pleasers were what was wanted. When he formed the Victor Herbert Orchestra, they became the basis of his programming.

As a conductor Thomas's beat was described as graceful; his collegial style was far from that. Neither soloists nor audiences had a chance when Thomas was in charge. Lilli Lehmann recounts with relish the story of an oratorio performance under Thomas's direction for which Patti had been engaged as soloist. Patti was given to taking liberties with the musical text in order to show off her superb voice. At one point Patti demanded her own way, as she was the prima donna. Thomas exclaimed, "Excuse me, madame, but here *I* am prima donna!"[83]

At another concert, Liszt's "Mephisto Waltz" was interrupted by whistles and hissing from the audience. Thomas took his watch in his hand, enforced quiet, and turned to the audience with the following words: "I give you five minutes to leave the hall; then we shall play the waltz from the beginning to the end. Who wishes to listen without making a demonstration may do so; I request all others to go. I will carry out my purpose if I have to remain standing here until two o'clock in the morning—I have plenty of time." The audience remained and listened to the whole waltz. Thomas triumphed.[84]

The attitude demanding complete control of all musical aspects of a situation was so characteristic of Herbert that we can assume that, whatever his natural proclivities in this direction, he was certainly encouraged to follow them by his experiences under Thomas's leadership.

Herbert's relationship with the Theodore Thomas Orchestra was extensive. He played his first cello concerto under Thomas at Steinway Hall on December 10, 1887. The reviews were positive, but nowhere near as enthusiastic as those it had received at its premiere in Stuttgart.

> The soloist of the afternoon was Mr. Victor Herbert who played an original concerto. [His] work, though far from being profound, contains many good ideas and some delightful instrumental effects. Mr. Herbert plays well, and his interpretation of his own composition was decidedly commendable.[85]

J. T. Jackson in the *World* found the work "admirably written—a very interesting concerto. Herbert played with much beauty of tone and skillful and brilliant execution."[86]

But in the *Herald*, Krehbiel's evaluation was a far cry from his earlier enthusiasm. He makes reference to this in his review: "Victor Herbert had been heard earlier to better advantage. As for the concerto it is neither meretricious nor commonplace in thought or workmanship."[87]

Damning with faint praise? Why? Krehbiel, the dean of the New York critics and its most influential voice in musical matters, was not above pettiness. A fascinating exchange of letters exists between the critic and his sometime friend, Professor Ritter of Vassar College,[88] in which Krehbiel, in response to a query from Ritter as to whether he is still employed at the *Tribune*, remarks that yes, he is, and in all likelihood will maintain that employment, although he is not surprised that Ritter asks the question. Krehbiel maintains that since he published a negative review of a Thomas performance, "T. Thomas and his lackey, Herbert" had been spreading the rumor that Krehbiel's tenure at the *Tribune* was in jeopardy. Herbert, just beginning a career in New York, would have been foolish to tempt fate by alienating a major critic. It is doubtful that he did. But he was so closely identified with Thomas that the notoriously thin-skinned Krehbiel saw him as an enemy.

It was not the only time that Herbert was to suffer from critical enmity. He was an attractive young genius and a lightning rod for envy, especially from critics and professors who fancied themselves composers. Herbert was also an aggressive promoter of Herbert among the critical fraternity, and this aspect of his persona could be off-putting. The archives of the Peabody Institute of the Johns Hopkins University contain a letter from Herbert to William Lines Hubbard, music critic of the *Chicago Tribune*, written while Herbert was on tour with the Thomas orchestra.

Chicago, July 20, 1889

Dear Sir

A composition of mine, a Serenade for string orchestra which has been performed with success at the Berlin Philharmonic Concerts and one of Anton Seidl's concerts in New York will, by courtesy of Mr. Theodore Thomas, be played at next Monday's concert.

I would respectfully request you to hear and pass your opinion on same.

Very respectfully yours,
Victor Herbert
Cello soloist of the Theodore Thomas Orchestra

Herbert did not leave success to chance.

Critics are fond of rivalries, and there was a competition between the Symphonies of Boston and New York that anticipated the famous Red Sox–Yankees rivalry. It was a commonplace for critics to feast on invidious comparisons. They read each other's commentaries and did not hesitate to balance the scales and settle old scores when opportunity arose. The rivalry between the municipal orchestras became focused on the comparative strengths of their star cellists: Fritz Giese of Boston and Victor Herbert of New York. Herbert's sharp tongue did nothing to ease matters, especially when it was noised about in musical circles that he was in the habit of referring to the Boston Symphony as the "Viennese Ladies Orchestra." Things came to a head in February of 1888 when, on consecutive nights, the BSO and the Theodore Thomas Orchestra presented back-to-back concerts in New York—each featuring its star cellist. Giese played the Schumann concerto and Herbert the Rubinstein. The New York papers gave the palm to Herbert, remarking that "Mr. Victor Herbert acquitted himself much better than the player of the previous evening. . . . He surmounted obstacles with a fine command of technique and played with good tone and no little expression." This was, of course, not the final word. The following year, when Herbert began a three-year association with the Worcester (Massachusetts) Festival, the Boston critics were ready for him.

The *New York Times'* W. K. Henderson probably takes the measure of Thomas best: "Whatever advance this country has made in musical culture during the past quarter century is due almost entirely to Mr. Thomas' leadership. He has kept steadily before the public the highest standard, and has allowed no consideration, pecuniary or otherwise, to swerve him from his loyalty to his art."[89]

CARL ZERRAHN

If, from Seidl, Herbert learned the importance of personality for musical success with an orchestra, and from Thomas, the decisive role that popular programming played in building an audience, from Carl Zerrahn he learned that the indispensable element for success was work, work and more work. Of course Herbert had never been a sluggard; quite the contrary. But after seeing the example of Zerrahn he never stopped working on music until the day he died.

Born in 1826 in Melchow (Mecklenburg-Schwerin), Carl Zerrahn emigrated in 1848 as first flautist with the Germania band. He toured extensively in the Northeast and eventually settled in Boston, where he became one of the city's most eminent citizens. In 1854 he became conductor of the Handel and Haydn Society and of the Harvard Symphony Association. By 1856 he was conductor of the following organizations: the Worcester Festival Chorus; the Salem Oratorio Society; the Lynn Choral Union; the Lowell Choral Society; the Taunton Beethoven Society; and the Exeter (N.H.) Choral Union, all in the evenings. During the day he served as professor of conducting, harmony and composition at the New England Conservatory; on the side he took private pupils. During the summer he was conductor of the following festivals: Worcester, Gardiner,

St. Johnsburg, Burlington, Vermont, and Concord, New Hampshire. A program from the Worcester festival describes Zerrahn's technique: "When Zerrahn raises his baton he is as calm as the everlasting hills. Every wave of his magic wand indicates careful preparation."[90]

One wonders when this sense of calm set in. Zerrahn taught Herbert how to work but, unfortunately, not how to relax; for Victor Herbert was never, ever "calm as the everlasting hills."

In 1889 a new opportunity presented itself. Zerrahn hired Herbert as pianist, soloist and assistant conductor for the Worcester Festival. During the last decades of the nineteenth century monster music festivals featuring huge choral forces were popular throughout the country. They attracted immense audiences hungry for great performances of classical music. The Worcester Festival was one of the most outstanding events, boasting a chorus of five hundred and an orchestra of sixty.

Herbert was thirty when he first appeared at Mechanics Hall. Worcester had heard of him through his expanded solo activities. He was hired as assistant conductor to Carl Zerrahn, and his contract called upon him to also provide piano accompaniment at chorus rehearsals and to appear as cello soloist. During his first season, in 1889, Theresa was also contracted, as soloist. At the opening concert matinee she sang the duet from *The Flying Dutchman* and "Ozean, Du Ungeheuer." That evening Emma Juch sang the letter aria from *Figaro* and her signature "Act Two of *Faust*." Herbert played a few untaxing salon pieces, notably Servais' "Fantasie Characteristique: Souvenier de Spa," a Bach "Saraband," "Melodie" by Massanet and his own "Fairy Dance." After that first season Theresa no longer appears in the program, her place being taken first by Clementine DeVere and later by Lillian Nordica. Herbert's contributions to the 1890 Festival as soloist were performances of his Serenade for String Orchestra and a few lighter pieces: "Adagio" by Bargiel, "Spanish Dance" by Popper and a new "Petit Valse" of his own. The 1891 season saw his farewell performance as soloist in the Saint-Sans concerto and the premiere of his Cantata, "The Captive."

The Worcester *Spy* paints a familiar picture of Herbert at work: "He was here, there and everywhere. He was always affable, worked hard for the success of the festival at the expense of personal comfort. He stayed up late nights, gossiping and was up early for rehearsal."[91]

And to no one's surprise, he was a hit with the ladies.

Nobody who did not see it would have imagined that a Worcester audience of ladies could have been aroused into such a state of enthusiasm. They clapped their gloved hands and they stamped with their feet and they rattled their parasols on the floor.

To many of the ladies in the hall the cello selections were the event of the afternoon. Herbert played three selections and was a thorough master of his instrument. The cellist's own composition ("Petit Valse") trifling, flimsy as it was, appeared to be a favorite with the audience. It was full of flowing, understandable music.[92]

The *Worcester Telegram* reports on Zerrahn's reaction: "It was delightful the way Carl received Herbert's success in his cello performance. The veteran conductor was not content with clapping his hands. He followed his assistant half over the stage and clapped him heartily on the back for doing so well."[93]

The *Telegram* goes on to mention Herbert's "air of confidence which indicated he knew his own powers," and calls him "an ornament to the Festival Association." The critic goes on to remark, "He has succeeded in making friends with everybody, from the ladies in the chorus, most of whom are now worshiping at his shrine, to the artists and the orchestra."

That was the set-up. Then this: "People will differ on the question of his being a greater cellist than Giese, but certainly he is more of a man."[94]

One wonders if the lady critic (one assumes it *was* a lady critic) was speaking from personal experience. There was, apparently, plenty of hanky-panky at the festival: "One of the soprano soloists had stirred up a nasty scandal involving a member of the orchestra. The audience had its eyes glued on the poor fellow most of the time, and he was sort of sneaked in and out of the hall by some of his sympathetic colleagues."[95]

By this time Herbert had become something of a matinee idol. His status is confirmed by a short note that he wrote in response to a friend's request for autographs:

December 16, 1891

Dear Mr. Wissman—
Enclosed please find the autographs for your lady friends.
I hope they will find them allright.
Victor Herbert[96]

At any rate, by Herbert's second season, the bloom was off the rose. The *Evening Gazette* reports: "Compared to his reception of the previous year, Victor Herbert was received as solo cellist with far less enthusiasm in the 1890 Festival."[97]

And the *Telegram* was similarly disaffected:

Mr. Herbert's "Petit Valse" was trivial and quite below the festival standard. It showed Mr. Herbert's tone, his light touch and his clever execution, but *Boston has several cellists who outrank him in all these respects* [italics mine].[98]

At about the same time, local music lovers were reading this review of a performance by the Boston Mendelssohn Club:

Giese was the most capable artist of the ensemble who not only delighted the public, but also moved up his fellow musicians to fresh enthusiasms every evening. Although he never took his instrument from its case between one concert and another, his playing was masterly in every respect as to tone, technique and phrasing. I have never heard his like.[99]

Now the pressure began to build. A critic discussed Herbert's conducting style and compared it unfavorably with Zerrahn's: "His short, snappy method is in direct contrast to the wide, decisive sweep of the baton which characterize Mr. Zerrahn's method of work."[100] And the *Telegram* critic took Herbert to task for his handling of extra-musical events. A Mrs. Ford had been singing a Mozart concert aria when ". . . a youngster in the audience didn't like the performance and set up a terrible wail. The singer would have gone on trolling, but Herbert brought things to a grinding halt.

"Bad as was the infant's yell Mr. Herbert seemed to make the matter worse. He is such a pleasant chap that it is unfortunate that it should be necessary to speak of the matter."

The high point of the 1891 season was to be the premiere of Herbert's Cantata, "The Captive." From every standpoint, it can only be viewed as a disaster. The most favorable review gives a picture of a performance in disarray.

The chorus did not do him wholly justice and it looked as if the orchestra would have to be prodded with a stick; but the work is a good one. . . . The chorus did not seem sure whether it would be better to sing the next chorus sitting or standing. Several desperate waves of Mr. Herbert's hand finally got them up.[101]

It was the critic of the *Gazette* who delivered the coup de grace.

The concert was too long by just about the length of Mr. Herbert's dramatic cantata, "The Captive," which it would have been wiser to omit, in spite of promise and expectation, when the rehearsals had proved that it could not be adequately performed. Wiser, we mean, for the sake of Mr. Herbert's reputation and for the pleasure of the audience.

The cantata is to illustrate a German Ballad which recounts how a young prisoner meets his death. The cantata fills 90 pages and occupies nearly an hour in performance. This is a treatment too extended and ambitious for such a subject, which should be treated as the ballad which it is and not elaborated like a tragic drama. There will be, we believe, many serious strictures upon the work, but the most difficult to meet will be upon the frank and ingenuous Wagnerism which pervades every page. This overweighs ideas which ought to have an untrammeled flow with tremendous chords and ponderous instrumentation or perplexes them with idle and unmeaning dissonances—devices apt for only the most intense and massive emotions and the mightiest actions. The poem and the musical manner do not belong together—it is cupid loaded down with the armor of Mars and the club of Hercules.

On the other hand Mr. Herbert shows a distinctively poetic treatment in his writing, invention and technical acquirement in the use of his means and the art to work up a climax, gigantic at least in volume of sound and nervous influence. Whether he has not been "breaking the butterfly on the wheel" in this instance and whether his cantata will be ultimately found to have value and endurance, can not now be said. We have our doubts, but we suggest them with reserve.

The performance was unequal. Mr. Herbert could not bring the choir within hailing distance of the great central scene and its part had, therefore, to be cut out bodily, leaving nothing between the soprano solo and the orchestra. At this very juncture, too, being anxious and excited, Mr. Herbert apparently forgot that only one woman was singing and urged the orchestra into such a tremendous fortissimo that hardly could the voice of a Lehmann have been heard above its tumult. Mrs. Ford had the soprano part which can not by any stretch of good feeling for the author be called interesting, significant, or fair to the singer. There were to be heard some bravos and personal calls for Mr. Herbert, who certainly deserved them for his persistent and elaborate work, even though his results were not all that he or the audience could wish.

But then, in a final paragraph, the critic provided a road map for Herbert, a vade mecum that, with brilliant if painful insight, set the composer's feet on the proper path. Humiliated by the experience of the premiere, Herbert left town the next day. But these final words of the *Gazette* critic must have been ringing in his burning ears:

> Of one thing however, we are firmly convinced. When next he writes, he will do well to get out of the musical atmosphere in which he has been steeped so long, free his brain of the influences with which it seems to be saturated, and use his poetic feeling and his cultured talent independently along new lines of work.[102]

That was the way to a brilliant future. But it was not yet to be. Herbert needed time to lick his wounds.

CHAPTER 3

OH, MY NAME IS VICTOR HERBERT—I'M THE LEADER OF THE BAND (1891–1895)

The central railroad station in Worcester, Massachusetts, looks very much today as it did in September 1891, when Victor Herbert boarded the train for his return to New York City. Restored to its former glory, it shocks the observer and holds his eye—a gleaming, riveting white behemoth set against the faded facade of the old industrial town, a lonely monument to its glory days.

A feeling of faded glory was very much what Herbert must have experienced as he reflected on his three summers at the Worcester Festival and on his disappointment with the critical reception of "The Captive." The mercurial ups and downs for which this Celt was famous were never more in evidence than in his reaction to the Worcester experience. He had arrived heralded as the golden hope of American music and left under a cloud. With two exceptions, he never again attempted serious choral composition. The minor cathedral anthem "Christ is Risen" and "The Call To Freedom," a patriotic ode for which he supplied both music and text, were both unsuccessful.

Waiting for him at his new residence at Park Avenue and 90th Street were Theresa, eight months pregnant with their son, Clifford Victor; Ella Victoria, a nursemaid for the children; and a cook to realize the Viennese specialties for which Theresa had become famous as hostess to Victor's growing complement of friends. Theresa had by this time gained weight, lots of it, and the transformation from diva to hausfrau may have taken a toll on the Herbert relationship. Lionel Barrymore, then a young matinee idol just beginning his career, recalled that "everybody knew Victor Herbert but nobody knew much about him."[1] Victor was circumspect about his extramarital intimacies, and the evidence that there were any is largely indirect. We have the long tours with Emma Juch and the songs dedicated to her in Opus 15. This is not conclusive, since Herbert was in the habit of dedicating many of his compositions to friends and colleagues. Then there are stories of off-hand remarks. After a particularly trying rehearsal,

Victor and his musical assistant Harold Sanford were relaxing in a bar when a group of pretty chorus girls from the show descended upon them. Their manner made it obvious that any one of them was Victor's if he had made a move. Herbert refused to take the bait, and the ladies retreated. He remarked to Sanford, "Can't do that anymore. I'm too well known. They'd all point their fingers."[2] It's clear that a man with Herbert's huge appetite for work and food and drink did not restrict himself to Theresa for companionship. But, given a choice and given the satisfaction he derived from his children, given his background as the scion of a loving and nurturing family, it is easy to conclude that, despite any transitory dalliances, Herbert lived a life of frustrated marital fidelity.

This frustration is reflected in the way he is reported to have spoken of Theresa to his friends, sometimes even in her presence. He referred to her as "Dumme Theresa," stupid Theresa. Whatever else she may have been, Herbert's wife was not stupid. She was completely devoted to her husband and his career, and did whatever she could to advance his fortunes. When he died unexpectedly after almost forty years of marriage, she fell into a state of collapse and followed him in death less than two years later. Some said she died of a broken heart. "Of a broken heart— and diabetes," Dr. Emmanuel Baruch, the family physician was heard to remark. Whatever it was, Theresa was devoted to him completely. The fact that Ella and Clifford had been born only two years apart is evidence that, between Victor's out-of-town trips, the couple was sexually active. There were three other children born to them, a daughter, Maud, who did not survive, and two more who were stillborn. Ella, though an attractive child, shared her parents' tendency to gain weight easily and was lame. Only Clifford was what we might call completely normal. He became his parents' favorite, a dynamic that was to shape Ella's development and activity as she grew to become first her father's confidante, then his business manager and, after his death, the keeper of the flame. If Theresa had become depressed because of the loss of three children and the frequent absences of her husband, this could only have added to the strain of the relationship.

This then, in brief, was the family situation that awaited Herbert. As the train thundered through the sweltering Massachusetts September he had time to reflect on his career. Boston had not yet become a good town for him, although as a conductor he got his first real start there. His work as assistant to Seidl at Brighton Beach had been limited to the leadership of his own compositions. Even then it is doubtful if it was a significant conducting experience, since the orchestra was apparently capable of playing without any conductor at all.

> Seidl sometimes passed his baton over to Herbert and he also had the queer habit of letting the orchestra play without a conductor. At these times I noticed that the orchestra often seemed to follow the glance of Herbert [as first cellist] rather than the concert-master, and I began to divine the power of this handsome artist, whose vivid personality contributed so much to the popular success of the organization.[3]

In Boston, a Festival Orchestra had been organized by George Washington Stewart (1855–1940). Stewart was a fascinating impresario who rose from humble beginnings in upstate New York to become the musical commissioner of the St. Louis and San Francisco World's Fair expositions. In its first incarnation the Boston Festival Orchestra was managed by Stewart and conducted by the former concert-master of the Germania Orchestra, Emil Mollenhauer. Both men had left the Germania to form the Festival Orchestra. It wasn't long before Stewart made the orchestra an institution, since its purpose was to supply orchestral accompaniments for the choral festivals ubiquitous throughout the eastern parts of the United States and Canada at the end of the nineteenth century. For twenty-five seasons (1889–1913) it toured from Memphis to Halifax; guest soloists included artists of the first rank: Sembrich, Schumann-Heink, Nordica, Ferrar, Fritz Kreisler and Victor Herbert. Carl Zerrahn conducted the first tour with Herbert as cello soloist, and later as conductor, in place of Mollenhauer.

> Many an argument he [Mollenhauer] had in his time, and when he and Herbert clashed it was a case of "an irresistible force meeting an immovable object."

> On an early tour [1890] Stewart gave Victor Herbert his first chance to conduct, sharing the honors with Tchaikovsky. Many are the names of famous musicians who owe their fame and fortune to the foresight and great musical judgment of Stewart.[4]

Herbert was not one to miss an opportunity. The notoriety that Tchaikovsky had brought the orchestra (the press avidly chronicled every aspect of the maestro's discontents) enabled Herbert, the following year, to form an organization of his own, the "Majestic Orchestre Internationale."

Imagine a symphony orchestra featuring "40—INSTRUMENTAL-ISTS—40" promoted and programmed in the best tradition of P. T.

Barnum and Tony Pastor, and you will come close to understanding this unique creation.

The program featured

HERBERT—the eminent European conductor and cello soloist to His Majesty the King of Wurtemburg. . . . The Boston Trombone Quartet . . . a popular dramatic contralto (her first appearance in this city). . . . The Swedish Male Quartet (in their picturesque national costumes) . . . a New York Casino favorite—a charming young prima donna famous for her personal beauty and her delightful, thoroughly-trained, bird-like voice.[5]

The program featured a "Salute to America" (a march by Herbert) and ran the gamut from "The Lost Chord" to the "Funeral March of a Marionette." Herbert appeared as soloist in the Goltermann Concerto Andante; he also premiered a new waltz (now lost) called "Honeymoon." The finale? "Ponchelli's [sic] Dance of the Hours."[6]

Well, it was a living, and its "pop" quality created the format preserved in summer concerts at Boston to this day. But the orchestra was a temporary episode, and Herbert soon returned to New York to resume his work as solo cellist for Seidl and Theodore Thomas. At one of the Thomas concerts Herbert was called upon to take the place of an ailing soloist, and he performed his first Cello Concerto. The critics found the work "admirably written and interesting," and his playing was recognized for its "beauty of tone and brilliant execution."[7] Also on this program was the *Meistersinger* overture, and the critic's discussion of the performance under Thomas is important because it directly compares Thomas's conducting with Seidl's. Since these maestri were Herbert's mentors and models, it is important to examine their distinctive approaches:

Mr. Thomas's rendering of the Meistersinger Vorspiel was an exceedingly interesting performance for many reasons. It was as different as the one we are accustomed to from Seidl's orchestra as could possibly be imagined. It was more pedantic, more scholarly in the sense of being clear-cut and carefully polished. There was less of enthusiasm, of buoyancy, of elasticity, less swing than Seidl gives. On the other hand every theme was brought out with the most painstaking exactness and distinctiveness, every thread of the wonderful fabric was shown from beginning to end. A more perfect example of Mr. Thomas's extraordinary ability to cause his own conception to be precisely interpreted by the members of the orchestra even to the smallest detail could not be had than was afforded by the performance.[8]

Thus Seidl as Dionysus and Thomas as Apollo both shaped the virile enthusiasms and perfectionist demands that were to characterize Herbert, the conductor.

Conductor—but of what? Round and round, he went touring as a soloist, playing with small chamber groups, arranging other composers' music, teaching, continuing his work with Seidl and Thomas. And then on September 24, 1892, fate took a hand in the matter of Victor Herbert: word came of the death of Patrick Sarsfield Gilmore, leader of the most famous concert band in America. The news sent shock waves, not only through the musical community, but through all of America. To understand the reaction of what can only be described as national mourning, it is necessary to examine the role that concert bands played in the fabric of nineteenth-century American civilization. Band directors were the superstars of their day. Herbert's acceptance of the leadership of Gilmore's Band was a direct bid for the limelight. There were some who said he did it for the money. The wife of his good friend James Huneker felt that his career move was a "step down" from his orchestral activities. She is quoted as saying that Herbert had said to Huneker, when questioned about his motivation, "You can keep your ideals, Jim. I wish to make money."[9]

But it was more than that. Something much more basic was at work here. Even before Herbert set foot in America, a movement was developing to promote American musical artists. Theodore Thomas had initiated a season of opera "sung by Americans" at the Academy of Music in 1886. The operas were sung in English.

> It has been deemed not only desirable, but it has been felt to be just, that a broadly American spirit should animate the direction of the movement which has resulted in the announcement we have made. The plan upon which it is based is so thoroughly national, and its execution so thoroughly American, that its most bitter opponents will scarcely decry it as being tainted by foreign influences.[10]

An article published in anticipation of the company's first performances expresses the idea that one of the purposes of the project was to "show Americans how needlessly *unpatriotic* it is for them to bow down to singers of foreign origin."[11] In short, as the *New York Tribune* proclaimed on January 7, 1886, "The American eagle has screamed for over a century. Now it is time for it to sing."

This nationalist outcry was not limited to the field of music; it was part of a general cultural awakening that sought to promote all things American as equal, if not superior to, anything foreign. The objective of the opera project was first to train American artists and then to encourage the composition of American opera. With a chorus of one hundred and a ballet of eighty, with the Thomas orchestra in the pit, this was a major commitment by the leaders of American society. The trustees of the project included Mr. and Mrs. August Belmont, Andrew Carnegie and William K. Vanderbilt. Herbert was determined to become a leading spirit in this movement. It is why he composed patriotic music and why he joined the National Conservatory.

The United States, whose entire musical history had been largely shaped by European influence, was flexing its muscles. A decade before Teddy Roosevelt's Great White Fleet sent its clear message abroad, Theodore Thomas was sending his own: America was ready for a native expression of its artistic spirit. Victor Herbert read the signs and rushed to shed his European image. He took the best of his talent and training and determined to make himself one-hundred-percent American. What better way to Americanize his image than through association with the musical tradition that was most typically and fiercely American: the brass band?[12]

"The important part that military bands have taken in the development of musical knowledge in America can not be overstated," Herbert wrote in 1895. "In this land of the free a musician can seek engagements where he will, and is not compelled to accept enforced service." This remark refers to the fact that originally bands were associated with regiments, as was Gilmore's 22nd Regiment Band. They were supported by the military authorities and controlled by them. Even before the Civil War, during which time bands became symbols of patriotism, a few musicians formed independent bands that later became identified with the names of their leaders. This tradition persisted well into the twentieth century, with the Edwin Franko Goldman Band the most notable example.

During the Civil War the participation of musicians in the events of the war (for example, the New York State National Guard 71st Regiment Band at the Battle of Bull Run) made band music the most popular kind of music in America, and in the postwar period the number of specialty bands increased. Along with concert bands and regimental bands were black bands (Scott Joplin, the father of ragtime, played cornet in the Queen City Band in Missouri); club bands (Herbert's beloved Lambs Club Band often fielded an ensemble of sixty-five players); service bands (such as the U.S. Marine Corps Band, which Sousa directed); circus bands (the overtures to Ringling Brothers performances featured Herbert selections); industrial bands (the Charlevoix Cigar Company Band, for example); and specialty bands such as the Eskimo Band, the Utopian Ladies Band, and the Redmen Band. In short, there were more bands than you (or any conductor) could shake a stick at.

Band concerts became vehicles, not only for entertainment, but for education as well. Herbert continued,

> Today we have bands bidding for the appreciation and support of music-lovers of every degree of culture. . . . The bands of the present day interpret the works of the greatest [composers]. . . . To Patrick Sarsfield Gilmore belongs most of the glory. Mr. Gilmore knew men and music, and through his knowledge of both he held the masses and led them [to become] better men musically.[13]

And everybody knew Gilmore. From his beginnings as leader of the Boston Brigade Band in 1856 he was dedicated to expanding the capabilities and repertoire of the ensemble. He performed monster celebratory concerts featuring thousands of singers and instrumentalists. He began his association with the 22nd Regiment Band in 1873, and his regular summer concerts at the Manhattan Beach Hotel were visited by Herbert. Herbert was well known to the members of the Gilmore Band, and when Gilmore died it is not surprising that Herbert succeeded him. It was not unusual for band directors to divide their time with engagements at theaters or with symphony orchestras; when Herbert decided to work in both the worlds of symphony and band, and later in the theater, he was not "abandoning art" at all; he was merely following a tradition long established in the professional music world.

The succession was not without complications. At first Gilmore's assistant, Charles W. Freudevoll, attempted to carry on, but he lacked the charisma needed to replace a leader loved and admired as much for his humorous remarks to his audiences as for his outstanding musicianship. One faction of the orchestra then suggested the celebrated bandmaster D. W. Reeves.

At the time, David Wallis Reeves was conductor of his own organization at Providence, Rhode Island. The Reeves Band had possibly the greatest musical reputation of any marching band extant. "All the musicians knew the marches by heart; not faking a 2nd, 3rd, or 4th part. Each man had played what Reeves had written. No one who ever heard the Reeves Band ever can forget the solidity of tone as the men marched in perfect rhythm to the music of Reeves' marches."[14]

Reeves conducted the Gilmore Band for only one season. It is possible that the discipline he demanded contrasted too much with the easygoing approach of his predecessor. At any rate, Reeves returned to Providence, and Herbert was chosen by the membership to succeed him.

> To the band Herbert brought an interpretation hitherto unknown to band music: a crisp, raspy, snarling style of conducting and wit, romance, and powerful imagination to his interpretations. He brought drama in place of refinement. Liszt's Hungarian Rhapsody #2 is a good example. There is a passage for clarinets where Herbert made the instruments imitate the gurgling of an old pump being primed until the water came rushing out of the spout. The wail of the gypsy was as obvious as his reckless abandon. In "Panamericana" the band played a long vamp heavily—coarsely and very roughly—indicating a "shuffle" and then launched into "Dixie."[15]

Not that Herbert's job was an easy one. The Gilmore organization was not without its critics, most prominent among them John Philip Sousa. Sousa had been criticized in an editorial in the *American Musician* for not programming more American music. The editor remarked, "If Pat Gilmore had had the making of that program it would have bristled all over with American airs." Sousa replied to the editor with a stinging critique of Gilmore.

> Do you, high priest, in your judgment seat, believe that American art is elevated when the majestic Star Spangled Banner is converted into a heel-and-toe polka, the martial Hail Columbia is hammered into a Ballroom Glide [a dance often burlesqued in vaudeville acts]? Knowing that many people look upon dancing as wicked, do you demand that our patriotic melodies shall change the content of their present purpose and masquerade as purgatorial polkas, sun-steeped schottiches, Mephistophelian mazurkas, vicious valses, and God-forsaken gallopedes? Do you believe the progress of musical art is going to be accelerated in this country by twenty trumpeters standing in a row, triple tonguing The Young American Polka with more or less

faulty articulation, with red fire rondos, Roman candles and rhapsodies sent forth in a heterogeneous mass, or presenting to our public the standard compositions of worthy composers of all countries of all time?[16]

Not to be outdone, H. L. Mencken in *Heathen Days* recalled with characteristic tartness a performance in the Baltimore of his youth.

Bands were then at the height of their popularity in the United States, and every trolley park had one. They all began with one of the more deafening Rossini overtures and ended invariably with The Star Spangled Banner, played a couple of tones above the usual key of Bb to show off the trumpets. . . . There were two great set pieces that were never missed: one was the Sextette from Lucia di Lammermoor, done with all the trumpets and trombones lined up on the apron of the platform, and the other was the Anvil Chorus from Il Trovatore, with a row of real anvils in the same place, and a series of electric wires so arranged that big blue sparks were struck off as the gentlemen of the percussion section clouted the anvils with real hammers. For this last effect, of course, the lights were always turned out. It had been invented years before by the celebrated Patrick Sarsfield Gilmore, the greatest of all American bandmasters.[17]

The tradition that Herbert was inheriting was that of the "show band"—a vehicle for popular entertainment—and if some educational benefit was incidentally thrown into the mix, then so much the better.

Herbert began by rebuilding the ensemble. In the period of uncertainty that followed Gilmore's death, many of the best instrumentalists had been tempted by offers to join the newly forming Sousa Band. Sousa, the great leader of the United States Marine Corps Band, had recently been decommissioned and was busily building an ensemble that he hoped to make the finest in America.

Herbert set to work to improve the Gilmore sound, and his stringent demands soon brought the men of the 22nd to a level of perfection not associated with his predecessor. In rehearsal he ruled with an iron hand, but the moment rehearsal was over he was ready to associate with his new colleagues on a basis of equality—a true democrat. This characteristic earned him the enduring admiration—perhaps love is not too strong a word—of the men who played under him here, and later with the Pittsburgh and Victor Herbert orchestras. Henry Eichendorfer, a member of the ensemble, tells of the birth of a tradition that persisted throughout Herbert's career.

It was the habit of musicians working with Victor to serenade him on his birthday. The custom grew out of his term as leader of the 22nd Regiment Band. . . . He liked the blare of brass and the uniform of a bandmaster. Idolized by the musicians under him, Herbert each February 1 was summoned by buoyant band music to show himself at the front window of his residence and receive the acclamations of devoted associates celebrating his birthday. The collations Mrs. Herbert served on these occasions following the speech of the bandmaster were something to inspire song.[18]

For Herbert, a man never satisfied with the status quo, a successful debut in a new area of music making was essential. This represented his first prominent outing as the leader of his own ensemble, and he made sure that the world was watching. His new manager, John Mahnken, orchestrated an extensive promotional campaign, which included sending boilerplate releases to the New York English- and German-language press; the story was covered as widely as Indianapolis, Buffalo and Washington, D.C. The following release was printed, word for word, by most of the New York papers.

Mr. Victor Herbert, who has been elected conductor of Gilmore's famous band, has succeeded in reorganizing and increasing the strength of the same to the standard it had under the leadership of the late P. S. Gilmore. The New York public will be given a chance to judge Mr. Herbert's ability as a conductor of a military band at the first Sunday concert to be given November 26, 1893 at the Broadway Theater, at popular prices.[19]

Other releases discussed the specific conditions of his election to the leadership, and the fact that he would continue his career as a soloist with the band. The *New Yorker Herald* remarked that "for the first time Herbert's Irish and German female admirers [*Bewunderinnen*] would have the chance to see him in regimental uniform"—and these were new uniforms, specially designed for the occasion. The *Staats-Zeitung* remarked that, rumor had it, Herbert looked so handsome in his uniform that "it was no wonder that Lillian Russell is longing to appear in a comic opera he is writing [*La Vivandiere*]".[20]

Some sour notes were inevitable. A snob at the *New York Home Journal* wrote,

> There is some comment upon the announcement that Victor Herbert has accepted the position as leader of Gilmore's Band. Mr. Herbert was formerly 'cellist of Seidl's orchestra, which he occasionally conducted. The abilities he has displayed as 'cellist, leader and composer have given the impression that his labors should be devoted to more serious work than that of conducting a popular band.[21]

The *Musical Courier*, sounding the first notes in a campaign of subtle vilification that was to culminate in a legal confrontation a decade later, turned up the heat:

> This concert will create great interest as it follows immediately the concerts given by the foreign military bands, which happening will undoubtedly lead to comparisons in regard to the abilities of the leaders and their respective orchestras.[22]

Herbert's competition for audience and critical attention on the day of his debut was formidable. The de Reszkes and Emma Eames were performing *Faust* at the Met. An orchestral concert under Damrosch featured Anton Hegner, a world-class cellist. At Brooklyn's Columbia Theater, Sousa's Band was about to premier one of his greatest marches, the "Liberty Bell," known to contemporary audiences as the musical theme of "Monty Python's Flying Circus."

There were other pressures as well—pressures that affected not only Herbert but all of American society. On May 6, 1893, the stock market had collapsed, sending the national economy into a depression. National Cordage, a favorite stock for speculators, crashed soon after having declared a 100-percent dividend. Other stocks followed. Small businessmen ran to make withdrawals from local banks in which they had little faith—the Federal Reserve System was twenty-five years in the future—and soon the economy was in ruins. In June the British Government suspended the coinage of silver, and a monetary panic hit Wall Street. Banks called in outstanding credits—call money was at 75 percent. In the West, hundreds of thousands of workers lost their jobs in mines and factories. Four hundred million dollars that had been put in circulation in 1890, and supposedly backed by specie, were now supported by less than 12 percent because of a gold drain. Railroads ceased to pay dividends to stockholders, and by 1895 169 railroad companies were in receivership.

The railroads were the Enrons of their day—the famous Atchison, To-peka and Santa Fe was found to have overstated its income by seven million dollars (144 million in year-2000 dollars), and the phrase "take a ride on the Reading," made famous in Parker Brothers Monopoly game, the product of a more recent depression, took on a new meaning: the Reading had a capitalization of forty million dollars and debt of 125 million. The public lost faith in the markets—a death knell to any economy.

And yet—the band played on! For Herbert, in this atmosphere of economic uncertainty, it was absolutely necessary that he enjoy a success. Neither press, public, nor his muse abandoned him. From the *New York World*:

A Fine Leader
The New Conductor of Gilmore's Band Proves He Is an Artist

"The King is dead; long live the King!"

The Gilmore Band has a conductor who will preserve the organization from the oblivion into which it was fast drifting. When Victor Herbert stepped upon the stage of the Broadway Theater last night he had no doubt about his hold on the affections of New York music lovers. The great violoncello virtuoso, in the becoming uniform of the 22nd Regiment Band, bowed his thanks to a great audience, largely composed of familiar faces.

The band, under its new conductor, played with great elan and brilliancy, and with a finesse which showed the careful drilling of Herbert. . . . Herbert's "Badinage" a cleverly composed and scored gavotte brought down the house. Mr. Herbert's cello soli were played with the rich, sonorous tone and fluency which we are accustomed to in this artist's work.

Mr. Herbert is a great success as a conductor. His beat is firm and spirited. He led a rousing march by himself, dedicated to the men of the 22nd Regiment.

Anton Seidl sat in a box with Mrs. Seidl and Mrs. Victor Herbert (both ladies were celebrated several years ago in the operatic world). Gilmore's Band has again another Irishman at its head, and no fear for its fortunes now.[23]

Fresh from this triumph, Herbert immediately set out to bolster his reputation through charitable activities. The *New York Music Times*, on

November 11, 1893, noted that Gilmore's Band would tender a grand complimentary concert at the Lenox Lyceum on Thanksgiving Eve, November 29, to the newly organized Band of the New York Letter Carriers' Association, to enable them to purchase musical instruments. Shortly thereafter, both Seidl's Orchestra and Gilmore's Band shared the honors at a grand benefit concert at Madison Square Garden in aid of the *New York Herald*'s Free Clothing Fund. Seidl led 155 performers—without a rehearsal!—in Wagner's "Kaisermarsch" and Prelude to *Tristan und Isolde*. When Herbert took the podium to succeed his mentor it was a defining moment for him, a true rite of passage for the thirty-five-year-old musician. Standing beside his mentor and sharing the ovation of the crowd, it was the moment when at last he became a completely independent conductor. The reporter from the *New York Herald* recreates the moment.

> The reception vouchsafed to Mr. Herbert was not one whit less enthusiastic than that accorded to Mr. Seidl. He was kept busy bowing and smiling in a very charming way for quite a time, until he took up the baton and plunged into a performance.
>
> The band played under the new conductor's direction in a musicianly way, which demonstrates most emphatically what a powerful artistic influence Mr. Herbert has already exerted over the organization. That such fine performers would produce a good tone from their instruments is a matter of course. But the delicate way in which all the quiet points in the music were brought out, the promptitude of attack, the broad phrasing, the way one passage was contrasted with another by an infinite variety of shading, all proclaimed Mr. Herbert's fitness for the post of conductor of such a world famous military band as Gilmore's. . . .[24]

Herbert now set off in search of greater glory. After his first successful outing with Gilmore's Band there followed a series of performances in New York City and on tour that served to spread his reputation as a conductor into venues that had previously only recognized him as a virtuoso. As was the custom, his concerts featured instrumental and vocal soloists to provide contrast to the otherwise unrelieved palette of martial sound. In March of 1894, he leavened his offerings with the voice of a Signor Campanari, Baritone ("Toreador Song," "Largo al Factotum") and Miss Ida Klein ("Pace, Pace mio dio!"). Herbert himself was a frequent soloist. The band offered a program of light classics (the *Tannhauser* overture was a favorite), as well as ethnic and patriotic selections (Godfrey's "Reminiscences of Ireland" and the "American Salute").[25]

In May, Herbert was contracted to appear at El Dorado, a pleasure park located on the crest of the Palisades, directly across the Hudson from Manhattan Island. As Herbert premiered his "El Dorado—1894 March," a great throng made its way to the wooded heights. The grounds were reported to be in fine condition—"a charming pleasure resort." The Rhine (wine) castle dispensed potables to thirsty masses, and the broad piazzas and cool walks drew thousands from the turmoil of city life. Herbert's programs followed the much-encored "El Dorado March" with his potpourri of folk tunes, the "American Fantasy." The engagement called for concerts every Sunday from 3 to 7 P.M. and again from 8 to 10 P.M. Weekday concerts were performed at 3 P.M. and at 10 P.M. after a performance of a theatrical spectacle, "Banamela—A Midsummer Night's Dream," for which Herbert provided original incidental music.

Herbert followed this engagement with several weeks at the Manhattan Beach Hotel's music pavilion. The Gilmore Band was not the only attraction, however. Sousa's Band also performed there. And every night there was "A Pyrotechnic Dream: Lalla Rookh," with the inevitable whine and pop of Roman candle salutes providing an obligato to the Band's signature "Anvil Chorus." Gilmore's Band had been engaged at the hotel after a season's absence at the request of many of the guests, who wanted to hear the old favorites again. During that summer Herbert invited Dan Godfrey, whose "Reminiscences of Ireland" was a favorite program item, and his band as his guests one afternoon, when a program made up of English and Irish selections was performed and heartily enjoyed. "The English bandmaster Godfrey embraced the Irish conductor and complimented him upon the excellence of his band."[26]

An interesting item was announced for the concert of October 7, a march, "The New York Sun," by Monroe H. Rosenfeld. It was "dedicated and respectfully inscribed to a forceful writer and fearless editor, Charles A. Dana, Esq." H. L. Mencken, in his memoir, mentions that such dedicatory pieces were often a ruse intended to gain space and notice in local papers for coverage of band concerts. He himself had been the target of advance men for touring ensembles, and he noticed that frequently old, dog-eared manuscripts were re-titled, depending on which publication was being approached. "The New York Sun March" was, by contrast, the genuine article. The October 6, 1894, edition of the *Sun* published an advance notice that "Victor Herbert will introduce his new two-step dance entitled 'The N.Y. Sun March.' This arrangement has been specially made for the occasion by the bandmaster himself, who will introduce in its production several novelties which will add to the musical effect of the composition." The *Sun* did not specify what novelties there might be, but the *New York Times* on October 7 scooped the *Sun* as follows: "He will include several novel effects including the aligning before the audience of his trombones, who will render the Trio of the march as a sextet in unison."

In any event, the *Sun* came through for Herbert on October 8 with a cut of the bandmaster resplendent in tunic and heavy silver lace epaulettes.

The Sun March a Beauty
Fit for the Battlefield and for the Dancing Floor

Monroe H. Rosenfeld's Stirring Composition as Played Under Victor Herbert's Leadership finds Instant and Enthusiastic Favor with the Audience at the Academy of Music.

A new march was brought out at the Academy of Music last night where the second Sunday concert of Gilmore's Band was given under the leadership of Victor Herbert. It was a stirring rhythmical piece of music, and as a politician in the audience remarked, it was the kind of a tune that a Democratic torchlight procession could march all night to and never get tired. Perhaps that is what the composer had in mind when he named it "The Sun March and Two-Step," and dedicated it to Charles A. Dana.

Whatever the purpose of the music it met with the instant and enthusiastic approval of the audience who demanded a repetition before they would allow Mr. Herbert a rest in the intermission, the march being the last number of the first part of the programme.

There followed a detailed musical analysis of the composition. And then the reporter continued:

Victor Herbert, who arranged The Sun March was very pleased with it. "It is a very fetching piece of music," said he. It has splendid rhythm, and the melody is original and catchy, a combination rarely found.

The following week the *Sun* again noticed the band's repetition of the eponymous masterpiece and then added this populist slam: "The march will be played by Gilmore's Band tomorrow evening and will *form a happy relief to the more pretentious compositions of the evening*" (italics mine).

This demand in the press for programs dedicated completely to the popular taste was not unique to the *Sun*. The *New York Mercury* remarked on October 13, 1894, that "It was a wise decision on the part of Victor Herbert to confine his repertoire to popular airs and eschew classical."

Herbert was not one to ignore the popular taste or the popular press. He did indeed eschew classical items in his programming for the immediate future. On October 24, 1894, the *Musical Courier* reports on a concert featuring a "Fantasia on Annie Laurie" for autoharp, a "full four octave instrument whose sweetness of tone pervaded the house from pit to dome."

Success followed success. On October 10 the *Evening Telegram* announced that the concerts were "likely to become a permanent thing at the Academy of Music" and that arrangements had been completed "to continue the entertainments [not concerts!] throughout the winter months." Although there was no way Herbert could have known it, these successes with the masses were to have a dark side. It was not long before his enemies in the New York press, and later in Pittsburgh, where he was to become conductor of the Symphony, used this very popularity against him in attempts to denigrate his stature as a serious musician.

At the end of October the ensemble left on a brief tour to Newark, New Jersey, and Rochester, New York. The *Rochester Democrat and Chronicle* remarked on November 2, 1894, that "many went to the concert with misgivings, but they came away with far different conceptions and their misgivings [about the ability of Gilmore's successor] happily dispelled." The critic then offered some perceptive commentary:

> As much interest was centered in the new director as in the performances of the band, and it may be said that while Victor Herbert is not Gilmore, he is Victor Herbert, and as such is destined to just as great a career as his predecessor enjoyed. Mr. Herbert is a master, and it is a delight to watch his leading and mark his emotions, to notice how they are imparted to his musicians, to see how quickly they get his inspiration and interpret his desires. He is not an emotional

director, but he leads his players from the softest melodies to the grandest climaxes with but little display.

These comments about his conducting style are something quite new. One has only to think of the description of the desperate sweeps of his arms during the premiere of "The Captive" to wonder if he had consciously adopted a less sanguine style. However, if we turn to the notice in the *Rochester Herald* on November 2, 1894, we find that, after remarking that Herbert does not possess the "humorous personality" of Gilmore and that he is nevertheless "possessed of a magnetic musical personality," the critic makes these fascinating comments, especially so when we remember that Herbert spent a year in the Eduard Strauss Orchestra.

> While watching Mr. Herbert wield his baton the audience is reminded of no one so much as Edouard Strauss. Like his German [sic] contemporary, Herbert throws his whole soul and body into the composition he interprets. At times his entire figure moves in sympathy with the rhythm, arms, shoulders, head and even toes participating in the beat.

One must wonder if the critics attended the same performance.

It wasn't long before the great world beckoned. A grand tour had been arranged for the spring of 1895, to introduce the ensemble and its new conductor to an audience of long-standing enthusiasts. Gilmore had fronted the band for twenty years; now it was time to reestablish and burnish its reputation.

Herbert always seemed to be at his best on tour, at the top of his form as man and artist. He loved the road and the camaraderie that went with it: the ever-changing audiences and venues, the chance to make new friends and greet old supporters. Most of all he loved to solidify the bonds that grow when a large cohort of artists faces the challenges and vicissitudes of travel. He used every minute of his waking hours while on tour in creative activity. When not rehearsing or performing, he was composing. When not composing, he was glad-handing the press and the local underwriters of his tours. Using his robust charm, his ready Irish ribaldry, his enthusiasm, which equally embraced his art and his fellows, he created a world that, centered on the lodestone of his magnetic personality, proved an irresistible force and drew thousands of Americans to his concert halls and bandstands.

What better time and place to start such a tour than St. Patrick's Day in our nation's capitol where, some forty years before, Victor's beloved grandfather had enchanted the members of the Senate with his signature "Ireland in Song and Story"?

"Gilmore Band Played Green. Such melodies predominated in its programme—Crowds at both concerts"—the Washington press still identified Herbert as "the great 'cellist,' " but went on to praise his new role:

Mr. Herbert's style is one of intense enthusiasm and corresponding action. He plays on the baton as he plays on the violoncello. His activity on one instrument is as visible as on the other. He cannot conduct a spirited rendition by his band of "Dixie" or "Marching Through Georgia" with the self control and composure of Sousa, Damrosch or Seidl. He is carried completely away by the emotion his music and musicians produce. . . . He carried his audience along with him irresistibly—and the audience was large.[27]

Baltimore was next, and greeted "Professor Victor Herbert," one of "the leading musicians in this country," with equal enthusiasm.[28] The *Baltimore Herald* noticed the changes the new director had wrought.

The organization, while not numerically so strong as in former days is comprised of finished instrumentalists, and in the program presented showed to a great extent the higher aims of Victor Herbert, as well as a decided diversion from many of the old methods for which it became noted.

Not only were the selections of a greater depth from a musical standpoint, but the novelty of their construction was extremely interesting—so much so that the meaningless and flippant encore renditions which, it seems, must be given to please the public grated harshly upon the classical ear and, as a whole, seemed decidedly out of place.[29]

Herbert determined to put his stamp on the organization early on. While remaining faithful to the tradition that his audience demanded, he slyly added to the gravitas of the programming. He was probably wise to restrict these novelties to the tour; in the programs for the Broadway Theater he did not challenge his audiences (or critics) with repertory changes.

Knoxville reported that hundreds of souls were thrilled by Herbert's music, but also reported on a rather odd addition to the mise en scene.

In other selections where a number of dancing melodies were given some artists in the rear of the band cleverly imitated the shuffling of feet on a sanded floor, the clogs, etc., to famous effect. In this number, too, the Salvation Army was represented with artistic effect, and a number of the musicians sang a parody of the Salvation Army Song in which the members of the band sang falsetto to mimic the women of the army in their street parades.[30]

The *Atlanta Constitution* declared on March 21, 1895, that "Victor Herbert has captured Atlanta," and praised his versatility as soloist and conductor as well as his "willingness to respond to the reasonable demands of those in the audience who preferred less profound and more sprightly compositions." The *Atlanta Commercial* remarked that "in spite of Lenten prohibitions," nearly every amateur and professional musician of the city was there."[31]

The *Roanoke Times*, on March 20, 1895, found the selections "of a high order" and remarked that "Herbert seems to have imparted the ability to produce more spirited and graceful results than were achieved with Gilmore."

At Augusta, Georgia, there occurred one of the most surprising and moving events of the tour. While Herbert was chatting with a reporter from the *Augusta Herald* in the parlor of the Arlington House Hotel, one George A. Oats appeared and introduced himself as a friend of Herbert's grandfather. Many years before, when Oats was in England, Lover had presented him with the manuscript of his most famous song, "The Low Backed Car." Oats had preserved it through all the years and now presented it to the young composer. "Mr. Herbert was overjoyed beyond expression at the receipt of what (to him) could be no more valuable a gift," the reporter wrote. "His thanks and his gratitude can not be told in cold print. He pressed the precious paper to his heart and happiness and joy lit up his every feature."[32]

Seeing the composer in a good mood, the reporter returned to his interview.

"What success did you have in Atlanta?"

"We had very encouraging houses and all three of our performances in Atlanta were complimented with oceans of flowers."

"Isn't the music rather loud for the opera house?"

"No, indeed. We can play as softly as a string orchestra when the occasion demands, and then when we choose, we can make the rafters ring. We always play loud when we play 'Dixie,' especially in Georgia."

Mr. Herbert then casually remarked that he greatly preferred playing to Southern audiences, as they were more enthusiastic, more appreciative than the Northerners. "They are warm hearted people and have music in their souls."

Thus having displayed his genius for public relations he quipped, "Now, treat me right—and don't write a criticism of the music until you hear the band." Then, with a grand smile and a wave of his hand, he ended the "brief but pleasant interview."[33]

The *Jacksonville* (Fla.) *Citizen*, on March 25, 1895, tells the story of Herbert—the democrat. When it became evident on a leg of the journey that no sleeper accommodations were available, the bandsmen were able to find one for their exhausted leader. Herbert graciously said that he would travel in the day coach, just like his men. Although he was their leader, he was "always one of them."[34] The article quotes one of the bandsmen as expressing the feelings of all.

He is one of the finest men that I have ever met; he never thinks he is above any of the other members of the band. We do not feel as though we are working when we are playing. It becomes a positive pleasure under his leadership. He is so enthusiastic that the time passes rapidly and we forget all about being tired. He knows how to get all the music there is out of the players. If there is any music in a man it has got to come out—he couldn't keep it back if he wanted to.[35]

The tour continued through Savannah, Columbus, Montgomery, Binghamton and Americus, Georgia, then south to New Orleans for a five-day stay, where nothing but plaudits were heaped upon the organization and its new leader. The deeper south they moved, the more ethnic the program became. The hit of the Louisiana concert series was "The Darkie's Jubilee," a "breakdown" featuring special solos on the "bones" (xylophone).

Then, in April, in the midst of all the triumph, everything ground to an unexpected halt. "ENJOINED!" screamed the headline of the *Helena* (Arkansas) *World* on April 8, 1895. The coming of Gilmore's Band was looked upon with as much anticipation by certain segments of the population as would have been the advent of the anti-Christ. The Protestant ministers of Helena descended upon the town council and demanded that steps be taken to prevent the coming desecration of the Sabbath. Gilmore's Band and Victor Herbert, conductor, were coming to Helena for the purpose of violating the law by accepting money in payment for a concert performance on a Sunday.

Sunday dawned. Special trains had been chartered and low rates advertised to secure a huge crowd for the two performances scheduled. The Midland, Iron Mountain and Valley railroads discharged hundreds of passengers. Crowds of expectant masses milled through the streets, and the rumor spread that there would be no performance. The assistant prosecuting attorney for the town appeared with the sheriff, prepared to issue a restraining order to stop the concert.

Promptly at 2 P.M. the whistle of the Gilmore Special sounded and the crowd migrated to the depot. The band marched to the Opera House and the crowd moved along with them. Gilmore's Band had never had such a reception. The box office opened; at once the sheriff appeared and served a writ on the owners of the Opera House. Herbert and his manager, John Mahnken, huddled in conversation and then announced that the performance would be offered—free of charge. The immense crowd, amid cheers and rejoicing, stormed the facility.

The concert was, of course, received with great enthusiasm. Then, at the request of several members of the audience, an opportunity was given the people to contribute something to the band's treasury. The audience responded liberally as the ushers passed the hat. The scene was repeated at the evening performance, and the entire sum was then handed by Herbert to the chief of police, with instructions to spend it in the interests of the poor and needy of the city. Herbert's good will and good humor triumphed over the mean-spirited provincialism of a few Arkansas blue stockings; he had turned what might have been an ugly confrontation into a personal triumph.

On to Sioux City and St. Paul, where Herbert took the opportunity to praise American bands at the expense of their German counterparts, which, he said, contained "a good many poor musicians" in contrast to American bands where "a man is hired because he is an expert musician."[36]

Minneapolis, Duluth and Milwaukee praised his complete mastery. Then, in Chicago, the critics were somewhat muted. They found the band to be "less scintillant and brilliant than under the director who gave it name and fame, but still admirable in many ways."[37] Herbert *was* recognized as a thorough musician, and it was anticipated that "In time

[he] will impress his personality upon the band, just as Mr. Gilmore did, but at present it is in a transition period and ranks neither so well as it may when it becomes more thoroughly settled."[38]

But the Chicago critics were alone in their tempered praise. Kalamazoo found that Herbert had "carried the band far beyond what Gilmore ever did and made it the most admirable organization of its kind."[39]

The tour was completed at Buffalo and Toronto on a high note with the *Mail*, on May 1, 1895, proclaiming that "Herbert has quite won the esteem of the music-loving public and when he returns he will be warmly welcomed."

The 1895 tour established Victor Herbert in the public imagination as *the* American conductor. Sousa was the great bandmaster; Seidl a vigorous classicist; Thomas the perfectionist who had done most to raise America's musical consciousness. But it was Herbert who marched to the drumbeat that drove the American spirit—the spirit of independence, bonhomie, verve and optimism. And in this sense—in the sense that it provided him with the image that enabled him to achieve the successes of the rest of his career—it can be said that, more than Herbert did for Gilmore's Band, Gilmore's Band did for Victor Herbert.

CHAPTER 4

PITTSBURGH—HEAVEN AND HELL (1898-1904)

*My idea of heaven is to be able to sit and listen
to all the music of Victor Herbert I want.*
—Andrew Carnegie

Andrew Carnegie can go to hell!
—Victor Herbert

When the wind rose through Pittsburgh in mid-December of 1897, it picked up the chill of the ice-bound rivers that, then as now, cut a channel between the bottom land on which the city rests and the Allegheny Mountains, and swept six men through the dark, icy streets. It was with no little relief that they entered the Farmer's Bank boardroom to begin a process leading to six years that Victor Herbert would recall as the most musically satisfying, and personally frustrating, of his life.

The meeting of the Orchestra Committee of the Art Society of Pittsburgh was chaired by a new man, William Nimick Frew, a wealthy attorney and associate of Andrew Carnegie, shortly to become Chairman of the Board of the Carnegie Institute and trustee of the Carnegie Corporation. To his right sat Henry Clay Frick, the giant whose domination of the fields in which coke was mined—in coordination with Carnegie's Iron Works—had made possible the establishment of Carnegie Steel, the foundation of Pittsburgh's prosperity and prominence. The others present were men of like stature who, having brought Pittsburgh to a level of industrial prominence hardly equaled elsewhere in the United States, were now determined to bring to their city a cultural eminence to rival that of Boston and New York.

The Art Society had been founded in 1873, the same year Frew had entered Yale. Andrew Carnegie had, in the early 1890s, presented to his city a unique institute: an art museum, library, music hall and center of natural history—a complex of buildings that brought together, in one physical location, a depository and laboratory of the arts and sciences.

Here in 1895, after many hours of devoted work, the Orchestra Committee founded an orchestra and placed it under the direction of Frederick Archer, English organist and conductor. Archer had been imported to give Pittsburgh an ensemble that, if not ranked with those of Thomas, Seidl, and Damrosch, at least would be looked upon by all classes of citizens with pride and affection.

The committee supported Archer for three years, and had enlisted a group of guarantors to underwrite the financial deficits that all recognized would be inevitable—certainly in the fledgling years of an organization that, in Pittsburgh, had no predecessor. But for all his gentlemanly graces, Archer had proven musically deficient, and now, amid the paneling and plush, the committee had come to discuss the successor candidates.

The only man present who was not a member of the committee was George H. Wilson, manager of the orchestra. Mr. Wilson had distinguished himself as a man completely devoted to the goal of his employers: the promotion of the good reputation of the Pittsburgh Orchestra.

His attitude is open to conflicting evaluation. To his detractors he was like a dog, faithful to its master; to his supporters he was merely a dedicated employee. Wilson never thought of himself as an artist; he was a thoroughly typical middle-class professional with a wife and two daughters, both of whom were musically gifted instrumentalists. If Wilson was somewhat awed by the company that fate had brought him to serve, he might well have been. Not Wilson alone, but a whole generation of Americans born after the Civil War, had grown up in a time when the great heroes of the age were the captains of industry. Chance had given Wilson the opportunity to work in concert with such men; this was an opportunity not to be belittled. Wilson loved his job, and dedicated his life to the interests of the Pittsburgh Orchestra. He delighted in the company of Frew, Frick and Carnegie, and to promote their agenda was a satisfying goal for a man who considered himself fortunate beyond measure to have the opportunity to do so.

Wilson has been described as "finicky," and commentators have drawn the contrast between Wilson's and Herbert's personalities as the source of a conflict that eventually led to Herbert leaving the orchestra. Wilson was always correct, always gentlemanly, as might be expected of any ordinary man working in such a rarified atmosphere. Whatever conflicts arose—and there were several after the initial years of Herbert's service—Wilson did not have the power to destroy Herbert's career with the orchestra. Whatever authority Wilson had was a derived authority. To suggest that a mere apparatchik could sway or mislead the likes of Frew, Carnegie and Frick is ludicrous.

The key to understanding the difficulties Herbert had with the Pittsburgh Orchestra organization may be found not in personality, event, or even in questions of musical achievement or repertoire. It can be found in a statement Frew made to the guarantors of the orchestra on the occasion of Herbert's election as conductor on February 10, 1898. In discussing the motivation of the committee, acting as "trustees for you and the many patrons of the orchestra," Frew writes,

> They [the committee] have been actuated by the belief that the orchestra, as an institution, as a most powerful factor in the growth of the higher life of our city, *should be regarded as of first importance*, and that, if it is to take a permanent place among the great symphony organizations of our country, *individuals, as such, must be assigned a secondary place.*[1]

Frew clearly states his position from the outset. That he did not communicate that position to Victor Herbert is regrettable, but understandable, for there had been as yet no incident to occasion such communication. Still, if the committee had been more insightful they might have had an inkling that Herbert would prove a mixed blessing. In any event, things came to a head after Frew resigned to lead the Carnegie Institute, and it was left to his successor, James I. Buchanan, to deal with the heightening conflicts and tensions of the last years of Herbert's employment.

Herbert's abilities were well known to Pittsburgh. At the time of the city's 1889 May Music Festival, he had appeared as cello soloist and assistant conductor with Seidl's orchestra. Likewise the Gilmore Band, now billed as "Victor Herbert's 22nd Regiment Band," had been well received there. These appearances, as well as Herbert's work with the Thomas Orchestra, led to his consideration for the vacant post.

Of a field of fourteen candidates, Herbert was the only one who had not actively expressed an interest in the position. He was securely established with the band, and by 1898 had already composed six successful operettas, the most recent of which, *The Fortune Teller*, would move him to the first rank of American stage composers.

When Frew wrote to his friend Philip Hale, a leading Boston music critic, to ask for possible nominations, he apparently received two: Emil Mollenhauer and Victor Herbert. Both were associated with the Boston Festival Orchestra, though their personal relationship was not positive.[2]

Frew and Wilson both proceeded with due diligence to vet the candidates, but the surviving correspondence relates only to Herbert. Wilson contacted S. C. Haysleys, of the Cincinnati Conservatory of Music, who responded, "Lost $650.00 on Herbert's 22nd Regiment Band in 1897; my kind regards to Mr. Herbert just the same."[3] This response was balanced, reflecting two aspects of Herbert's career that were to play out in Pittsburgh: he made himself money even at the expense of his employer, and, in spite of that, remained well liked.

In mid-January Herbert came to Pittsburgh, and the committee interviewed him. On January 31, Frew sent him a standard option letter, telling him that the committee would arrive at a decision within a week, enclosing two copies of a contract with a place for Herbert's witnessed signature, with a request that both copies be returned. "Leave the date blank. It will be filled in and the contracts signed by the Orchestra Committee, in case you are selected as conductor."[4]

There followed a series of urgent letters from Frew to Thomas and Seidl, requesting a confidential evaluation of Herbert; Frew wrote to Thomas on February 1 and to Seidl the next day. When, by February 5, in spite of the fact that Frew emphasized the urgency of the situation, Thomas had not replied, Frew, at Wilson's suggestion, contacted Daniel H. Burnham and asked for his assistance in urging Mr. Thomas's reply. Burnham, an eminent architect who had designed the buildings for the 1893 Columbian Exposition at Chicago, was a generous patron of the Thomas Orchestra, and answered immediately. From Frew's response to his letter we may infer that Burnham may have expressed unsettling comments. In his reply, Frew wrote to Burnham: "It had not occurred to me that any special reason could exist why Mr. Thomas should decline to give us his opinion. If such is the case, however, of course we could not expect you to go any further."[5] Frew asked Burnham to try once more to secure Thomas's opinion of Herbert, but received no reply. The implication of Thomas's silence is subject to conjecture; but on March 25, 1891, in an interview in the *New York Herald*, when a reporter raised the question of his standard for hiring personnel, Thomas is quoted as saying he was ready to hire musicians for the Chicago Exposition, "provided they satisfy his standard as musicians and as gentlemen." Of course, Thomas had hired Herbert in the past, long before his candidacy for the Pittsburgh Orchestra arose, but at this point had not worked with him for several years. In any event, between Burnham's response to Frew's letter and Thomas's silence, there were indications that Herbert might prove a problem.

However, Seidl must have forwarded his strong recommendation and, as Frew remarks in the letter to Burnham, "the name of Victor Herbert has been urged by many of his friends in this city."[6] In his correspondence to the guarantors of the orchestra, Frew claims to have obtained "the views of a large number of musical people," and that "the great conductors and the ablest musical critics located in other cities have been consulted with. . . . Their names would be laid before you, were it not that such action might in some cases involve a breach of confidence."[7] That may merely reflect the careful statements of a lawyer and gentleman. But a search of the orchestra society's correspondence reveals no evidence of such widespread activity. Not as many prominent conductors were active at that time as his comment suggests, and to assume, for example, that Damrosch, Seidel, Zerrahn, Thomas and others had been requested to discuss the qualifications of fourteen prospects is not reasonable. Furthermore, how sharing the names of prominent musical experts—without giving their specific recommendations or comments—would breach a confidence is not easy to understand. We may conclude that either Frew destroyed all the correspondence related to the search, or that it either never happened or did not involve the extensive activity he implies. In any event, the Orchestra Committee voted to hire Herbert on a one-year contract for two thousand dollars.

At this point it might be useful to take a step back and view the situation from Herbert's point of view. His career had brought him prominence as a soloist, bandmaster and stage composer. He was well established and respected in New York musical circles. He had a good income and a growing family. He spent summers at the Lake Placid club. He had been commissioned to provide the band music for the inauguration of William McKinley. Who needed Pittsburgh?

Herbert was probably responding to the two elements that consistently motivated him: a new artistic challenge and the opportunity to add to his income. New directions always appealed to him, and since the Pittsburgh season was limited to fifteen weeks, there was plenty of opportunity for him to continue his band and theatrical work. Originally he had no intention of moving his base of operations to Pittsburgh. He sought a rental apartment for his family, and only later leased a lavish home on Aiken Avenue in the then fashionable East End.

Herbert's early activities in Pittsburgh were tentative, a fact reflected in his first contacts with Frew. The chairman was anxious to get Herbert to come to Pittsburgh to begin preparation for the new season, but Herbert did not respond to Frew's requests. He chose to remain in New York. By mid-March, Frew was expressing the possibility that someone other than Luigi von Kunitz might be hired as concertmaster—all the while paying lip service to the idea that such decisions must remain Herbert's responsibility. Kunitz was an old friend of Herbert, and had served the orchestra as concertmaster and occasional soloist. Separately, Frew approved Herbert's dates for the next season, but with some trepidation, "always reminding you that you must be responsible for what seems to the committee a very short period for preliminary rehearsing."[8]

One can see the hair rising on Herbert's thick neck as it became clear that non-musicians were not reluctant to make strong recommendations on purely musical matters; no wonder Herbert was not rushing to the Alleghenies!

When the news of Herbert's appointment was announced, it was not a cause for rejoicing in the streets of Pittsburgh. Herbert had made it clear that he had no intention of relocating his permanent residence;[9] this met with an unpopular reaction.

Then the *Musical Courier* chimed in, underlining its continuing animus with a broadside that said, in part, that Herbert's projected rehearsal schedule would be a departure from the previous practice, under which Archer's frequent rehearsing had been a "watchword" of the orchestra, stating that any change in such an approach would cause "retrogression." The *Courier* then brought out its heavy artillery and placed Frew, his new conductor and the city of Pittsburgh firmly in its sights:

> In the selection of Mr. Herbert we cannot conscientiously congratulate the chairman of the Art Society, nor indeed Pittsburgh. Herbert is anything you like but a good conductor. He is not even a successful band conductor, as his recent tours have proved. And he has absolutely no experience with symphony orchestra conducting, indeed with any orchestra.

> As a cellist he was proficient before he stopped practicing, and he is a highly successful composer of comic opera. Personally, we have not the slightest fault to find with this Irishman [How *that* must have resonated with a man who sought to be recognized as an American], but to put a raw man—in the sense of a conductor—at the head of a well-equipped symphony orchestra seems a pity.[10]

The *Courier* goes on to describe Herbert's conducting as "wild and amateurish" and accuses him of lacking "personal magnetism."

Marc Blumenberg, the editor of the *Courier*, was only four years away from a landmark lawsuit in which Herbert successfully sued him for libel. The miracle is that Herbert held his temper for as long as he did. Still, at this juncture, it must be admitted that Blumenberg was merely expressing his opinion. That opinion was given wide and damaging notice when the *Pittsburgh Herald*, the *Pittsburgh Leader* and the *Pittsburgher Volksblatt* reprinted the *Courier* article.

The *Pittsburgh Press* attempted to outdo the competition, not only by excerpting Blumenberg's invidious diatribe but also by quoting, under the headline, "Bim-Boum and Pilsner," the soi-disant "dean of music journals," the London magazine *Music* as lamenting Herbert's "vulgarity" as a composer and "his absorbing passion for the effects produced by a big drum." The *Press* also quotes the *Criterion* as believing that Herbert's chief distinction lies in his being "the only living Irishman who drinks Pilsner."

Herbert responded to all this in a measured letter, published by the *Leader* and the *Post* on February 22.

> My operas and other work have made me independent financially, and it was not money that brought me [to Pittsburgh.] It was my ambition to make the orchestra second to none in the world. I shall retain the leadership of the 22nd Regiment Band, N.Y. Half the year I shall be a New Yorker, and the other half a Pittsburgher.

To which statement the *Musical Courier* replied, "That is, symphony in Pittsburgh and 'All Coons Look Alike' in New York."[11] When Herbert wrote to the *Pittsburgh Times* that concerts should be made as attractive as possible to everyone, the *Courier* reacted with an unprecedented outburst of sarcasm:

> That is the best scheme of all. "Heavy" music must not be played to those . . . who are not able to understand it. The only way we can reach an understanding of Bach and Beethoven is by playing "pieces of simpler construction."

Blumenberg then produced a facetious

Program for Next Fall
Overture—Wizard of the Nile   Herbert
Serenade from "The Serenade"   Herbert

Cello solo	Herbert
By Victor Herbert	
Symphonic Poem, Prince Ananias	Herbert
Fantasie, The Idol's Eye	Herbert
(Obligato on the voice: Frank Daniels)*	

In case of an encore of Herbert's cello solo he will accompany himself on the piano.[12]

The *Courier* kept up its unremitting attacks, constantly referring to Herbert as the "brass band conductor" and "the bandmaster." Undaunted, Herbert arrived on his own schedule and took up residence with his family in a suite in the Schenley Hotel. These living arrangements were not what the Herberts had requested. On September 26, Mrs. Herbert had asked W. B. Clayton, Herbert's secretary, to write to Wilson to ask if he could secure "a small home or good size flat, furnished, in a healthy part of the city. Her object is to give Mr. Herbert all the comforts of home which a hotel cannot furnish." The Herberts arrived on October 3 and found that Theresa's request had not been acted upon.[13] This was the first of a series of delays and miscommunications that eventually became a serious problem.

Herbert was used to moving at his own pace and expected his agenda to be followed. For the first time in his life, he was dealing with men who had the same expectations—both Frew and Wilson were forces to be reckoned with. So was Victor Herbert. From the very beginning, beneath the politesse and formality of the correspondence, one could detect the roll of distant thunder.

On February 11, the day after his appointment, Frew had notified Herbert of his election: "Allow me to assure you most heartily that every assistance possible will be rendered you by the Orchestra Committee to make the next season a notable success." So? Where were the suitable living accommodations? This was the single personal request that Herbert had made. Frew continued: "If it is possible I hope you will come to this city before long. The plans for next season should be mapped out well in advance. Hoping to hear from you soon. . . ."[14]

Herbert's response was silence. Perhaps Frew's attempt to shape Herbert's schedule rubbed him the wrong way. In any case, a week later

---

* Frank Daniels, a popular stage comedian who had starred in *The Idol's Eye* was, famously, a poor vocalist.

Frew wrote again. His second letter reveals that he had little sensitivity to Herbert's personality, for he not only repeats his requests of the first letter but goes on to deal with personnel matters in a manner that could only have inflamed Herbert:

> Dear Sir—
>
> I wrote you Friday last, notifying you that you had been elected conductor of the Pittsburgh Orchestra for the season 1898–99, and enclosing a signed copy of the contract. So far I have heard nothing from you in reply.
>
> It seems to me very necessary that you should come to Pittsburgh for a few days for consultation. A great many things must be talked over, and our policy decided on at an early date. A number of members of the orchestra are still in the city, and all seem to be anxious to know what chances they have for next season. While a good many could be improved upon, there are some we would be very glad to have retained, both on account of their years' service in the orchestra, and because the quality of their work justifies it.
>
> You know our policy has been to employ Pittsburgh musicians as far as possible, and the public prefer to see old faces in the orchestra year after year. I hope you can arrange to come at once. Be kind enough to let me hear from you without delay."[15]

So, here we have a high-powered attorney virtually commanding Herbert's presence, and letting him know that the Committee policy favors local musicians because of their loyalty and the fact that they have faces familiar to the audience. Frew also passes judgment on the quality of their musicianship. Apparently letters crossed in the mail, for the next day a somewhat mollified Frew writes with a touch of attempted humor, rare in this correspondence: "I am this morning in receipt of your note of February 16, 1898. Not having heard from you for nearly a week, I was afraid you had gotten lost, strayed or stolen. Glad to hear you will be in Pittsburgh on Monday next. I will be in the city and will give you all the time necessary."[16] On the same date Frew prepared a draft policy directive, possibly to serve as a basis for his discussions with Herbert. It proposes shortening the season from fifteen to thirteen weeks, saving $1,430 in orchestral salaries, and using the funds for "strengthening the orchestra." Herbert descended on Pittsburgh and the original season dates were restored. A few weeks later, Frew wrote to Herbert to discuss the development of a standardized contract under which instrumentalists might be employed. In this letter he makes specific recommendations concerning which soloists might be used, and encouraging Herbert to get busy and take care of the legal business so men can be hired. These are all legitimate business requests, and Frew's comments on soloists were merely attempts to give Herbert insight into how certain performers had been received by Pittsburgh audiences. Herbert remained unresponsive. On September 10, while he was appearing at Manhattan Beach with the band, Herbert received this from Frew:

> Dear Sir—
> I requested Mr. Wilson a few days ago to get from you the amount you have contracted to pay to the eleven players whose contracts we had not then seen. We have received three, I believe, of these contracts, but he says you did not give him the salaries of the other eight players.
>
> Please let us have this information without delay, as it is necessary for us to know definitely the cost of the season before deciding as to the amount of the other expenditures.[17]

A perfectly legitimate request, and Herbert was not being fair to his new employers by his tardy responses. Obviously Wilson had written to him, and it became necessary to bring Frew into a matter that should have been handled at the manager-conductor level. Herbert was a busy man. So was Frew. So was Wilson. Herbert may have resented the intrusion of nonprofessionals into his musical affairs. If so, Frew's postscript did nothing to improve Herbert's mood.

> P.S. The committee hopes that you will make every effort to examine and obtain any new works of interest and merit that may come out, for presentation during the orchestra season.

This reference to "new"—and for "new" read "American" and, further, "native Pittsburgh compositions"—was the first shot in a battle that was to engage Herbert for most of his Pittsburgh years. At this point it is fair to characterize the Herbert-Frew relationship as cordial but mutually insensitive. Frew was a formal gentleman who expected the common courtesy of prompt reply to his communications. He expected his wishes to be, at the very least, acknowledged. Herbert was a touchy artist who had no patience with amateurs who presumed to interfere in the sphere he rightfully considered his own. This was a tentative relationship, at best. When Herbert arrived at the Carnegie Music Hall to begin work, waiting for him was this from Frew:

October 3, 1898

Dear Sir—

I have just been informed that those in charge of the Knights Templar Conclave, which assembles here next week, are to make an effort to secure the services of yourself and band to play the dance music at the ball to be given on Tuesday, October 13th. If my information is correct, I sincerely hope that, without mentioning the Orchestra Committee or myself in the matter, you will tell the Conclave people that it will be impossible. I think it would very seriously handicap our orchestra season if you were to appear as the conductor of an orchestra giving dance music.[18]

The trouble begins! Even before the first concert the anti-band snobbishness of the Pittsburgh haute monde emerges as an interference with Herbert's activities. Nothing in his contract with the Orchestra Committee, or indeed in any of the contracts he executed throughout his career in any capacity, provided for exclusive service. To the very end of his life, in his last contracts as a conductor (for the orchestra at William Randolph Hearst's Cosmopolitan Theater) he always was scrupulously careful to avoid exclusive service provisions. He did, indeed, play the dance music for the Knights. Thus he began his first rehearsals with the orchestra under a cloud. It was not by chance that, for his first formal communication with the men, Herbert chose to write on the stationery of "Victor Herbert's 22nd Regiment Band." The touch was not lost on Frew.

Pittsburgh
October 12, 1898

Dear Sir—

You are hereby notified that the first rehearsal of the Pittsburgh Orchestra, of which you are a member, will be held in Carnegie Music Hall, October 24, 1898, at 10 o'clock sharp.

Please be prompt.

Victor Herbert[19]

During the period from March to October 1898, while Frew was establishing his relationship with Herbert, manager Wilson was careful to maintain a strict, businesslike correspondence with Herbert and his representatives. His letters restrict themselves to orchestra business, especially to matters of planning extra concerts. One of the proposed dates that Wilson was trying to arrange was an appearance at the Omaha Exposition, where the Thomas Orchestra was scheduled to perform. An appearance by the Pittsburghers would not only bring extra revenue to the organization; it would hopefully add to its reputation. Herbert contacted friends in the Thomas Orchestra to determine if it would be wise for the Pittsburgh Orchestra to play there.[20] He concluded that since only thirty-five men of the Thomas ensemble would be appearing "it would only injure the dignity of the Pittsburgh Orchestra to accept an engagement there. I would not consent to take only a part of the Pittsburgh Orchestra," he wrote to Wilson. How taking a cut-down orchestra on tour, standard practice at this time, would be "injurious to the dignity" of the orchestra is not easy to understand. It is more likely that Herbert was anxious to avoid a situation where critics would have the opportunity to compare his work with that of the man universally recognized as the best conductor in America. We can only imagine what Blumenberg's *Musical Courier* would have made of that opportunity. The result of Herbert's reply was to dampen Wilson's efforts to book extra concerts, for the time being.

Herbert's next communication from Wilson, dated May 1, 1898, is friendly and personal. There was continuing discontent on the part of the Orchestra Committee with his work with the band, although this time it was couched as a concern that he might be called to the colors with his regiment, since war with Spain had erupted on April 24.

> Mr. Frew wishes me to ask you to write him at once if your connection with the local militia of New York will make it necessary for you to hold yourself personally in readiness to obey any order to attach yourself with the troops either in New York or elsewhere for a shorter or longer period.[21]

Herbert responds that "according to the latest developments there is not the slightest likelihood of my being called out." Then, in a more personal vein, he continues, "I had a fall with my spectacles last week and broke my nose; therefore the delay in answering; the fall did the nose good, however. It's almost straight now. Please remember me to Mr. Frew."[22]

By August 17 Herbert was taking care of business, enclosing contracts and program information. At Wilson's request he also includes an updated curriculum vitae, which is fascinating, not so much for what it contains as for what it omits, and for the corrections made in Herbert's hand. The original C.V. was written for release in New York City, and Herbert's editorial additions are significant. They are indicated by square brackets; his deletions are indicated by parentheses.

Victor Herbert was born in Dublin, Ireland, in 1859, and is a grandson of Samuel Lover, the famous Irish novelist. (When only seven years of age) [At the age of seven] he was sent to Germany to begin his musical education and (he since that time) [since that time he has] continually and assiduously devoted his life to the acquirement of a thorough knowledge of all branches of his chosen art. His first position of prominence was that of (solo) [principal] cellist in the Court orchestra at Stuttgart, and he (played) [worked] in many important concerts [throughout Europe] before accepting in 1886 an engagement as solo 'cellist in the Metropolitan Orchestra (in this city) [in New York]. (Since that time he) [During the twelve years of his residence in the United States, Mr. Herbert] has been prominently connected with the best orchestral organizations (in New York), and as soloist and conductor he has become favorably known in many of the principal cities throughout the country. He was [for a number of years] connected with Theodore Thomas' orchestra, and more recently with that of Anton Seidl, in which he was soloist and (second leader.) [assistant Conductor.] (He is at present leader of the famous 22nd Regiment Band of New York.) Mr. Herbert has also won distinction as a composer having written concertos for the 'cello, some charming numbers for orchestral instruments both solo and concerted, and many delightful songs. Among his most ambitious works is an oratorio, "The Captive," which won marked approbation at the Worcester Festival, for which it was written. His music in all his works is characterized by exquisite daintiness, and while it is extremely melodious, it is always written with musicianly skill. (His operas, "Prince Ananias," "The Wizard of the Nile," "The Idol's Eye," and "The Serenade" have met with great success, while his latest opera, "The Fortune Teller," written for Alice Nielsen, is expected to even surpass the works mentioned above.)[23]

The first thing we notice is that Herbert is reacting to the pressure from Frew, the Orchestra Committee and the *Courier* as being known as a bandmaster and stage composer. Although these were, to date, two of the areas in which he had achieved greatest distinction, he chooses to omit them from the résumé submitted to Wilson for inclusion in the program book of the Pittsburgh Orchestra concerts.

Second, in emphasizing what can be called the "serious" aspects of his career, he emphasizes his European experience, tacitly acknowledging the fact that for this period the imprimatur of European training and experience was the sine qua non of acceptance as a serious musician in the United States. It is also significant that while he specifically characterizes his work with Seidl as soloist and assistant conductor, his work with Thomas is described as a "connection." Finally, the mischaracterization of "The Captive" as an oratorio (even the printed score calls it a cantata), and its reception proves that Herbert was not above misrepresentation of events of his career.

This document, with its redactions, reveals more than it conceals. It is a picture of a musician who needs to pump up his confidence at a time when he is entering a field of activity that is for him the least secure of all the areas of his experience. This insecurity may explain the tentativeness of his contacts with Frew and Wilson. In all the other areas of his life, if something went awry he could cover himself by telling a funny story or standing the company another round of drinks. Frew and Wilson were not susceptible to such diversionary tactics, and Herbert knew it. They wanted and expected a first-class performance of his duties. This Herbert was able to deliver in full measure; but at this juncture, neither they nor he was certain that all would be well in Pittsburgh.

Herbert's subsequent correspondence with Wilson focuses on program building ("Wouldn't put Brahms on the program—Mr. Frew knows why"), and reflects Herbert's insistence that the selections chosen reflect a balance between serious and lighter works. ("We must leave some room for novelties.")[24] Throughout all this Wilson maintains a tone of helpful collegiality.

> I told Mr. Frew yesterday that if you were having a delay in getting Pittsburgh musicians to meet your terms that perhaps I could be of service to you by seeing some of them personally and settling matters at the rate you want, at least I should be very glad to help you if you would like me to make the attempt; I know most of them personally and probably would have some influence.[25]

Wilson once again raises the issue of orchestra bookings and asks for names and addresses of important people in places where Herbert is known, and where and when he thinks the orchestra could be placed. He concludes, "I may look in upon you in New York in early July, but meanwhile command me in any way that I can be of help."[26]

A few months later there appears an interesting corollary to this matter of bookings. Under discussion was a popular concert at Homestead Hall, a venue seating 1,500, with tickets to be sold at 25 cents each. This price would only be feasible if Herbert were willing to waive his guarantee of $100 for extra concerts. Wilson is offering Herbert the opportunity to be a team player, since a concert at popular prices might add to the orchestra's audience base. Herbert answered in the affirmative, for Wilson writes that "referring to our telephone conversation this morning I would say that I have arranged for a concert by the orchestra in Homestead."[27]

It is certainly fair to say that at this point Herbert and Wilson are working together as a team, each with his own area of responsibility and expertise. Wilson writes in September, making suggestions for soloists in the most cordial tone. "Were we to add Burmeister and Carrano to our list it would make it very fine. What say you?"[28] Later, he informs Herbert that "by vote of the Orchestra Committee" a box had been reserved for the use of his family"—a nice gesture.

Shortly before the opening of the season, it came to Herbert's attention that one of the major New York critics, Mr. August Spanuth of the *Staats-Zeitung*, had been omitted from those invited to attend the premiere. His letter to Wilson reflects his respect for the manager's ability to handle the potentially touchy situation:

> Spanuth has accidentally learned that the other boys in New York have been asked to come and he may feel hurt if we do not invite him. I know that you can tactfully arrange it, so as to smooth his ruffled feathers in case Mr. Spanuth should be disappointed, and indeed, an invitation now would hardly be too late.[29]

And so, as the day of rehearsals approached, while all concerned were on edge, it seems as if the leadership team of Frew, Wilson and Herbert was pulling together.

We are fortunate that one of the members of the Pittsburgh Orchestra, Fritz Stahlberg, took the time and trouble to compose an extensive memoir of his many years with Herbert. He has left us a picture of his first interview with the man who became his mentor and friend. Stahlberg was a violinist who had joined the Stuttgart Orchestra in the years after Herbert had left it. He had made Fanny Lover Schmid's acquaintance, and she had recommended him to her son.[30] Here he is, after the long journey from Stuttgart, waiting for his interview.[31]

While I waited my feelings were a mixture hard to describe. Meeting the Kapellmeister is not an easy thing for a young musician. Would things work out as I hoped? I wondered. Would he like me? Would I like him?

Then I heard quick, heavy steps. A moment more and I was looking into the kind face of Victor Herbert. As if it were only yesterday this first view of him comes back to me. He greeted me in his friendly fashion and buoyantly began to talk in fluent German, asking me about my trip, about his relatives and old friends in Stuttgart. About this, and about that. He almost made me feel that I was doing him a favor by answering the questions he put to make me feel at home. I have always noted that Mr. Herbert had that great gift of making utter strangers feel as if they were good friends of his.

Nothing was said about passing an examination. Mr. Herbert casually mentioned that if I wanted to play for him after I had become acclimated he would be glad to listen to me. . . . When the interview was over I reflected what a different matter in America this meeting of Conductor and musician, employer and employee, was. In the old country the young musician stands trembling with awe at the feet of the Olympian heights the Kapellmeister (supposedly) stands on. And here, this man with his genius for friendliness, had made me more than welcome.

This personal account of Herbert's talent for friendship reinforces a portrait we already know: Herbert-Jeckyl. Stahlberg goes on to describe Herbert-Hyde: the Conductor!

Victor Herbert during rehearsals was an entirely different proposition. He was a fine drill-master, untiring in rehearsals, and very strict. With all his good humor, he could become very severe and sarcastic. . . . Often he was pronouncedly sharp, going to the point of hurting people.

Somehow the sound of music seemed to change him; his face had a different expression, and was easily irritated when matters did not go as he wanted them to. The musician who, either through laziness or inability, was unable to meet his musical demands came in for a thorough scolding. So, as he weeded out the lesser talented ones, at times he felt sorry to have to do so, but as he once said, "Kindness alone won't build a fine orchestra."

The *Pittsburgh Press*, in the fall of 1898, provides a more detailed picture of Herbert in rehearsal:

Attired in a negligé shirt, minus both the tie and collar, the whole surmounted by an old band coat [!], his feet encased in a pair of slippers, he looks anything but the well-groomed man we instinctively look for.

One or two raps on the desk, a remark or two in some jovial strain, another rap, and we are ready to commence. "Now, then, the Symphony," and away it goes. Not far does it proceed, though. A series of sharp raps on the desk are the signals for a sudden halt. "What's the matter with the wind instruments?" "Not so loud." "Now this passage should go thus: rat-a-tat-ta." "Now, all together with me. Al-so. . . ." Always the invariable, 'Al-so,' before each attack.

Another start is made, but scarce another minute elapses until there come some more raps. "Four bars before A-i-t-c-h isn't it marked pianissimo? So. . . . Well, why don't you play it, then? You play forte."

It is with a sigh of extreme satisfaction that the intermission is greeted. Herbert squats down on the director's platform for the much-needed rest.[32]

So, pushing, persuading, laughing, insulting, demanding, commanding, Herbert made his way to the eve of his premiere.

On the afternoon of his first performance Herbert received a memo from Wilson, relaying detailed instructions from Frew:

Mr. Frew, being disappointed at not seeing you within a day or two and finding it unlikely to see you before the beginning of the concert tonight wishes me to say for him:

That the Orchestra Committee very much hope there will be no encores allowed during the season except occasionally with the soloists under extreme enthusiasm, that tonight there will be no orchestral encores at all.

That you adopt the custom of former years of having the entire orchestra on the stage by at least thirteen minutes past eight o'clock, and that at quarter past exactly you come on the stage and take your position.

The committee earnestly recommend that you announce to the players that they are not, during the intermission or before the concert, to leave the assembly-room: in other words that they are not to go into the hall proper during the concerts; afternoon or evenings.[33]

The first orchestra concert under Herbert's direction was the climactic event of "Founders' Day," a whirligig of society events structured to honor Andrew Carnegie. The hall was filled to the last seat with the crème de la crème of Pittsburgh's elite. Carnegie himself sat in the upper box to the left of the stage accompanied by his wife, her brother, and Mr. and Mrs. Frew. Theresa and her children sat opposite them at stage level, directly in line with the conductor's stand. The audience was tense with anticipation and, as the orchestra members took their places at exactly 8:13, the concertmaster, Luigi von Kunitz, appeared, carrying his beloved Amati, and very hearty applause broke out spontaneously. Apparently he was a great favorite with the Pittsburghers, and conflict with Archer had eliminated him from the ensemble the previous year. The reaction of the crowd when he walked onto the stage was a vindication of his talent and the trust Herbert had placed in his friend when he decided to bring him back in spite of Frew's recommendation.

The storm of applause greeting the concertmaster must have taken Herbert by surprise. He appeared somewhat nonplussed at his entrance, according to press reports, for he naturally expected that the wave of applause would not break until he appeared.

Mr. Herbert exhibited just the slightest degree of embarrassment as he first faced the vast audience, but its reception was so cordial that he quickly recovered his composure.[34]

The program presented was one familiar to his audience:

Leonore Overture #3	Beethoven
Aria: "Non piu andrai"	Mozart
Sig. Campanini	
Symphony #5	Tchaikovsky
Symphonic Poem "Le Rouet d'Omphale"	Saint-Saëns
Aria "Dio posente"	Gounod
Sig. Campanini	
Vorspiel, "Die Meistersinger"	Wagner

Much of this program is theatrical music. Consciously or not, Herbert was leading with his strong suit.

In spite of Frew's strictures, there were encores, three of them, for Sig. Campanini was a great favorite with Pittsburgh audiences. The *Pittsburgh Press* review comments, in passing, on a local custom that gives us insight into why Frew discouraged orchestral encores. "A large audience . . . filled the hall and remained to the close of the concert, so intense was the interest in the work of Conductor Herbert and his players."[35] Apparently the practice in past seasons may have been a thinning of the ranks after the intermission.

The anti-band prejudice of haute Pittsburgh is reflected in another comment from the same article: "He [Herbert] looked so much better in evening dress than in the hitherto unconventional attire of a military band conductor that he seemed almost a different being. He looked taller and more commanding."[36] There followed a single sentence of musical criticism, positive in nature. Then, "Space will not permit extended comment at this time on the work of the orchestra." The writer liked the strings, but found the brasses "ragged. The entire brass section needs toning down." Since many of the new men Herbert had engaged were brass and wind players from the loathed band, could this have been another subtle slam? Whatever agenda the *Pittsburgh Press* may have had, its carping was swamped by the comments of the rest of the critical fraternity. A few excerpts will suffice.

> Mr. Herbert's directing is never dry. The Beethoven classic he reads with perfect understanding. The Saint-Sans tone poem he interprets with the daintiest finesse. . . . The ensemble was perfect, the wind and strings balanced. . . . Herbert is a broad-shouldered, powerful man, and he injects all his powers into his work. Not only his hands and arms, but his head and body move in rhythmic sway to the music. His method is to lead, literally, conducting ahead of his players by the fractional part of a second. An orchestra is seldom seen so perfectly under the control of its leader. . . . He has a magnetism for his men that makes their music the all important center of attraction.[37]

The *Pittsburgh Leader* rated the concert a "brilliant achievement," and noted that the players displayed "fine discipline, distinct rhythm, delicate shading and characteristic tone color. The softer passages were most like a breath, the fortissimo climaxes were rounded and evenly balanced."[38] Then there followed a comment that must have given Herbert the greatest satisfaction. Speaking of the Tchaikovsky Symphony, "Certain it is that the work last evening was far more satisfactorily interpreted than it was on the same stage by the Theodore Thomas Orchestra."[39]

After the concert Carnegie rose and addressed the audience from his box. He expressed his inner contentment that the concert had been so well received by a full house, "including the balconies, where the music lovers sit." He went on that he fully believed that the performance could be favorably compared with the best Europe had to offer, and remarked that the achievement of the orchestra had been for him and his wife a rare pleasure. "My idea of heaven," he concluded, "is to be able to sit and listen to all the Victor Herbert music I want."[40]

Herbert received hundreds of congratulations after the performance, several from New York by wire:[41]

"Go on, Victor, make another hit, make one for life. We have them standing up"—Paul Steindorff [Musical Director of *The Fortune Teller*]

"Your success is well deserved, and we wish you still more."—Edward Schuberth [Herbert's publisher]

"The Fortune Teller predicts that your symphony concerts will be box office symphonies as well."—Frank Perley [Producer of *The Fortune Teller*]

"One more hit can not make you more famous. Strike Hard."—Alice Nielsen [Star of *The Fortune Teller*]

Three days later the official word of approbation arrived:

November 7th, 1898

My dear Mr. Herbert—

Now when the excitement of the past week has worn away and we have had time to collect our thoughts, allow me to congratulate you again most heartily on the very great success, musically and socially, of the Orchestra concerts of Thursday night and Saturday afternoon, both of which I heard. There is but one opinion, and that is, that you have achieved a most decided success and we look for even greater things next Friday.

I would like, on behalf of the Orchestra Committee, if you do not object, to say a word or two of encouragement and praise to the members of the Orchestra, and for that purpose will be on hand tomorrow morning at the Hall at ten o'clock, at which hour I believe the rehearsal begins. It will, I think, be gratifying to you to learn that the Saturday afternoon receipts, while not as large as they should be and will be, break all the records for three years.

Wishing you all manner of success,

I remain,

Very truly yours,

W. N. Frew.[42]

The season rolled on, and Herbert went from strength to strength. Ovation followed ovation, and the support of the guarantors was such that after the second pair of concerts it was announced that the size of the orchestra had been increased from fifty-three to sixty-eight. The soloists Herbert had chosen were enthusiastically received, and the addition of string players seemed to the critics to have given the entire organization a new ensemble, which was the needed quality.

In January of 1899 Herbert accepted a second year's contract, and the concert season was lengthened to eighteen weeks. In a press release Frew compliments Herbert on the artistic success of the season, and even goes on to mend an old fence by acknowledging "with great pleasure the excellent and conscientious work of the concert master." Frew proclaimed the season of 1898–99 "the most successful in the orchestra's history."[43]

This era of good feeling was based on more than Herbert's accomplishments as a musical director. It was also based on his willingness to always go the extra mile to promote the fortunes of the orchestra. In late December Wilson wrote to Herbert about a problem. The scheduled soloist, the bass Pol Plançon, had telegraphed his regrets; he would not be able to appear. Frew asked Wilson to inquire if Herbert would be willing to fill in as soloist. Wilson's letter is addressed "My dear Mr. Herbert," and is uncharacteristically signed "Very truly yours, Manager G."

Herbert, of course, agreed to play his 2nd Concerto and reaped some of the finest reviews of his career. The unanimous praise noted that he had not been heard as soloist in Pittsburgh since his days with Seidl, and that he had lost none of his touch. Pittsburgh was thrilled to experience this triple-threat artist—composer-conductor-performer—and pulled out all the stops in its praise. Proof that the city had taken him to its heart is found in the *Press*, which points out the competition the orchestra faced that evening:

Neither the subscription ball at the Pittsburgh Club nor the horse show at the riding academy seemed to have any perceptible effect on the attendance at the concert last night. It had been a three-cornered competition between the ball, the horse show and Victor Herbert as to which was the best attraction of the evening and Herbert won.[44]

But it is the *Pittsburgh Times* that shows how complete Herbert's victory had been:

Mr. Herbert felt the glow of the kindly hearts that warmed to him and responded to them feelingly and artistically. He was not the stranger, not the guest. He was the Pittsburgher.[45]

There was, however, a nasty counterweight to all this triumph in the person of Professor Doktor Adolf Foerster, a local musical eminence and self-styled composer. The story of his relationship with the Orchestra Committee and later as a constant nemesis for Herbert begins long before Herbert came on the scene.

In February of 1898, shortly after Herbert's appointment as conductor had been announced, the following letter appeared over Foerster's signature in the *Musical Courier*:

The Pittbusgh Situation

Editors of the Musical Courier:

I am sorry that our orchestra affairs do not receive unbiased treatment at the hands of your correspondent, anonymously signing himself "X." This person is evidently a rabid partisan of the clique that has quietly kept up a crusade against Mr. Archer.

Mr. Archer made marked progress as a conductor, against whom I have but one complaint to make,—that of cutting movements too frequently. In the making of programs, interpretations, and general wariness Mr. Archer has given considerable satisfaction. An earnestness and artistic atmosphere has always prevailed at the concerts of the past two seasons, and the last one in particular. . . .

My record with reference to the orchestra has been anything but sympathetic, until I was convinced that things were conducted honorably and free from political motives. I regard this change of conductorship absolutely useless in the manner of its solution.[46]

Who was this man Foerster, and what did he want? Foerster was several things. First, he was a Pittsburgher with pretensions as a composer. Second, he was a "professor" of vocal art at the local conservatory, an institution that was a center of the supporters of Archer. Third, he was a person who had, despite his pretensions, been excluded from the inner circle of the Pittsburgh Orchestra. When Archer's contract with the orchestra was not renewed, Foerster determined to make as much trouble for the organization as he could. Foerster became the *Courier*'s unofficial Pittsburgh correspondent. Blumenberg relished any opportunity to blacken Herbert's reputation, and Foerster was, for him, a gift of the gods. Foerster kept up his campaign until the Committee felt constrained to issue a press release in response to a "series of venomous articles" that appeared in the *Courier*, "purporting to come from a Pittsburgh correspondent." These "libelous screeds" were written anonymously and represented a "frantic attempt to hold up to public derision Mr. Herbert, the Orchestra, the Committee, the press and the people of Pittsburgh." While Foerster is not named as the author of the anonymous correspondence, he is certainly a candidate. So is Marc Blumenberg, who was not above printing unsigned articles directed at the objects of his personal animus. It may be that Foerster had developed a close relationship with Archer and had looked forward to having his own works played under his direction. A march and a tone poem of Foerster's had already been performed in earlier seasons by Archer, and no doubt the ambitious composer looked forward to more of the same. His capacity for self-deception was immense. In spite of all this private and public turmoil in the press, he had the effrontery to write to Wilson and ask him to arrange for a performance of a new original orchestral work featuring a vocal solo to be performed by one of his own voice students! Herbert would have nothing to do with Foerster or his pupil, and for the time being the case was closed. The season proceeded to a peaceful conclusion with Herbert, Wilson and Frew content that, in spite of gadflies like the professor, it had been the most successful in the orchestra's history.

The season ended, Herbert lost no time in returning to New York and his pursuits with the band and in the theater. *The Fortune Teller* had proven his greatest success, and he set to work at once on the composition of an adaptation of Cyrano de Bergerac—a subject that was to inspire him to produce some of his most effective stage music—although because of its failed dramaturgy the piece was not successful. The next spring brought another engagement at the Manhattan Beach Hotel and, before that, at the Lambs Club, to whose membership Herbert had been elected. The Lambs were preparing their annual "Gambol," a fund-raiser touring production featuring many of the outstanding theatrical personalities of the day. Herbert was scheduled to compose the music and conduct the orchestra for the production, "Hula Lula," until problems arose involving a complaint lodged against him by the Musical Protective Union of New York that resulted in the temporary suspension of his union membership. Seventeen members of an orchestra Herbert had conducted at a concert of the Mozart Club in 1896 complained that they each had been paid $5.00 for the concert, when the Union scale was $7.00. Herbert's position was that it was not his responsibility to pay the musicians; rather it fell to the Mozart Club to remit the money. He was reinstated by the Union on June 11, 1899, but before that there were some very nervous Committee members back in Pittsburgh:

April 6, 1899

My dear Mr. Herbert—
I enclose a clipping from this morning's Dispatch. What is the explanation of this, and what is to be the outcome?
Very truly yours,
W. N. Frew[47]

As was his habit when faced with a contretemps, Herbert ignored the whole thing. By June, however, Frew was pressing—and expressing his legitimate concern:

June 5th, 1899

My dear Mr. Herbert—
The members of the Orchestra Committee feel that they should be informed by you as to your present status with the Musical Union, and just what your plans are for relieving yourself of the complications in regard to it. We certainly feel that it would be unwise to make contracts with a lot of musicians if there is a possible chance of your being prevented from acting as conductor. You have always treated the matter very lightly, but the Union seems to have been strong enough to have interfered with you on several occasions. [Herbert had not been allowed to conduct the Gambol.] Mr. Wilson is working on several out-of-town contracts and these we would not feel safe in going on with, if the Musical Union matter is not settled some way or other. Kindly let us know just what your plans are, and *how* you expect to

get out of the complication. I understand it to be a very unfair move on the part of the Union, but unfortunately we are obliged to admit their strength.

Awaiting your reply, I remain,
Very truly yours,
W. N. Frew[48]

There can be no doubt that Herbert's habit of placing himself incommunicado did little to reassure the Orchestra Committee of his sensitivity to their needs or feelings. On June 10 Herbert let Frew know that there was nothing to worry about, and that the matter had been settled. This was correct, technically, but lawyer Frew was not comfortable with Herbert's assurances:

June 12, 1899

My dear Mr. Herbert—

I am just in receipt of yours of the 10th, and am glad to learn that you feel so sure of having your complications with the Musical Union settled. I enclose you a clipping from this morning's Dispatch which presents a different view of the case. According to it, if you will notice, the reason given by the Musical Union for reinstating you is the fact that they did not give you sufficient notice and hearing, and are advised by their attorney to recommence the proceedings in a way that will bring about a result that cannot be upset by the courts. In fact you are quoted as saying that this reinstatement does not by any means settle the trouble between you and the Union and that the matter now stands exactly where it did some time ago and before you instituted your legal proceedings. Shall we take your letter or the newspaper quotation as the correct statement of the case.[49]

Thus Frew is holding Herbert's feet to the fire. He sees that the settlement mentioned in Herbert's letter is merely a legal tactic to assure that the courts will not vacate any decision on procedural grounds. Frew calls Herbert's bluff, and although things were eventually settled in Herbert's favor, this exchange must have been the beginning of a feeling of suspicion concerning Herbert's straightforwardness. Although Frew was always willing to give Herbert the benefit of the doubt, doubt was now clearly established in his mind and in the minds of committee members less inclined to Herbert. It had not been that long since Thomas had refused to respond to their request for a recommendation of Herbert's candidacy. No doubt in Frew's mind little clouds were gathering.

July of 1899 was especially hot. Frew went on vacation to the Jersey Shore; Herbert led the band at Manhattan Beach; Wilson worked away at business matters. By the end of September, Herbert was happily ensconced at the Placid Park Club, enjoying a vacation, prior to packing up his household for the move to Pittsburgh. Arrangements for Herbert's second season with the orchestra had been completed, and all concerned anticipated great things to come.

5:55 A.M., Wednesday, October 19, 1899: The scene is the sidewalk in front of the C. C. Mellor and Company store on Fifth Avenue, not far from the front steps of Carnegie Music Hall. Sixty-five "big boys, little boys, full grown men smoking corncob pipes, colored men, youths swapping stories of their winnings at craps"[50] were lined up to hold the places of Pittsburgh music lovers, willing to pay handsomely so that at 8 A.M. on the 20th they could take their places in line to purchase the few remaining tickets for Herbert's second season. The scene was reminiscent of film premieres in New York City at the Radio City Music Hall in the 1940s, when crowds would fill the streets to be the first to enjoy the Hall's new spectacular entertainments. But this was Pittsburgh in 1899, and the offering was classical music. Nothing can convey more the star quality that Victor Herbert brought to the orchestra than this scene of popular approbation. Not all the scribbling of Foerster, Blumenberg or other critics reprinted in the sensation-loving press, nor the continued carping of local malcontents, could dampen the wild enthusiasm with which the Pittsburghers greeted Herbert's second season. The *Dispatch* commented that "a decided improvement" had been made over the first season. "Perhaps the most noticeable of these improvements is the toning down of the brass contingent. . . . The strength of the First Violin corps is excellent from any standard."[51]

The soloists chosen were universally praised and one, Cecile Lorraine, writing to Herbert's daughter in 1938, recalled her experience with a mixture of affection and awe:

Dear Miss Herbert:
In the year 1899 I sang two concerts with the Pittsburgh Symphony orchestra, your father the conductor.
When I arrived for rehearsal . . . I was given a seat on the stage and when the orchestral number was terminated your father came over to bid me welcome and repeated, "Lorraine—Lorraine—French?" "No,"

I replied, "Irish!" Whereupon he gave me a good hearty handshake and told me I was thrice welcome.

When I stood up to sing it was discovered that a mistake had been made in the orchestral score sent from New York; Filine's aria instead of Ophelia's Mad Scene from Hamlet.

I was terribly disappointed because the latter aria was my "Cheval de Bataille" but I said I would make the best of it. To my amazement, he volunteered to write the orchestral score for that evening. A tremendous task, there being at least 14 pages. I don't think any other conductor in the world would have taken on such a task and I would like the world to know, besides being such a genius, what a wonderfully generous soul he was.[52]

This story of Herbert's facility and speed in providing a new or substitute score has been repeated so often and in so many contexts that, incredible as it seems, it must be credited. He is said, among other things, to have written an original piece for Galli-Curci at the last minute for a concert at the Brooklyn Academy of Music and to have composed new numbers during dress rehearsals for *Mlle. Modiste* ("The Nightingale and the Star") and *The Red Mill* ("I Want You to Marry Me") in a matter of minutes!

The warm reception from public and press seemed to augur well for the new season. But December, 1899, brought with it expressions of discontent from both the ranks of the orchestra and from the Orchestra Committee. Out-of-town touring contributed considerably to Herbert's income—he received $100 for each extra concert—and he naturally encouraged Wilson to expand the number of engagements. A few of the members of the orchestra were unhappy with the tour conditions. They claimed not to have been treated in a "manner fitted to their calling."[53] Some said that they had been "treated as so many sheep or pieces of luggage." Others denied the charges: "The idea that we were ticketed with numbers is absurd. People must think we are a menagerie or a lot of Zulu savages. Each man can take care of himself and doesn't need to be ticketed."[54]

Some complained that they were handed only 25 cents apiece for dinner (the equivalent of $5.00 in current value). Some objected to the quality of the hotel accommodations provided. Von Kunitz, the concertmaster and Herbert's good friend, acknowledged that there was some discontent, but also added that it was unreasonable. He noted that first-class accommodations were not to be had in some of the "one-horse towns" where the orchestra had been booked, and that "you can get a pretty good meal for a quarter." In short, although there were a few chronic complainers, the general feeling was that "the management did all it possibly could for our comfort."[55] These kinds of problems are to be expected in any large organization. There was another problem, reflected in this letter from Frew, that was not.

December 29, 1899

My dear Mr. Herbert—

During the last few concerts I have noticed a relaxation of the discipline of the Orchestra. . . . This morning, the proprietor of one of the important morning newspapers tells me that two ladies with whom he is well acquainted, were made very uncomfortable last Friday night by the evident determination on the part of Mr. Burck to compel them to recognize him. The ladies were very much incensed and were anxious that the matter should be made public, but the proprietor of the paper thought that the matter could be remedied in this private way. A few words from you to the members of the orchestra will I know have the desired result, and I hope you will speak to them before the concert tonight.[56]

We should not make too much of these complaints. That problems of discipline and murmurings in the ranks existed cannot be denied. It is important to remember that while discipline was Herbert's responsibility and easily managed, there was little Wilson could have done about tour conditions: he did not set the budget, nor did he build the hotels. He had to accept engagements where and when they became available; the orchestra contracts specifically obligated those members chosen to tour to play at the sites arranged by the management. It is also important to note that not all members of the orchestra went on tour. They were chosen for their excellence, but also by seniority, since touring meant extra income. Thus, those who went and complained had no basis for their criticism. Commentators have sought to lay blame for the tour conditions at Wilson's door, concluding that it was these sorts of problems, combined with a disparity of personality, that eventually led to a serious rupture in the relationship between Herbert and his manager—and from this, to Herbert's ultimate departure. This seems a stretch. Herbert knew the problems of the road intimately and was pleased that Wilson had arranged for an increase in the number of concert dates. His correspondence with Wilson from this period reflects only continued cordiality.

Dear Wilson—

Don't forget to get the repertoire from the different singers we will have this winter, in time, so that I can select fitting numbers for the hall. I don't want to have such noisy selections such as Bispham and Plançon sang last year.

How are you?

Yours,

Victor Herbert[57]

If we want to find the reason for Herbert's leaving the orchestra, we will have to look beyond his relationship with Wilson, which did in fact deteriorate, but not to such an extent that it can be said to be the determining factor.

From a musical standpoint, the highlight of the second season was the appearance of the orchestra at Carnegie Hall in New York City. For these concerts Andrew Carnegie was the sole guarantor. The program was demanding: Berlioz ("Roman Carnival"), Tchaikovsky (Symphony 5), and Liszt ("Mephisto Waltz"). New York society, led by Carnegie and Frew, were in attendance and the critical reception was largely positive. From the *New York Herald*, we have this:

> Mr. Herbert surprised many of us. He showed a good understanding of the famous Russian composer. . . . He surprised us by his skill in bringing out what Tchaikovsky demands from the lower instruments, to which are given so many strong themes. He might have had the Russian at his elbow constantly reminding him of the national regard for basses and baritones, vocal and instrumental, and still have provided no better result than he did through the exercise of his own gifts.

> Mr. Victor Herbert has proven his right to be classed with prima donna conductors. A fine body of men Mr. Herbert has got together. You can see that they are full of enthusiasm and have unbounded confidence in their conductor. They follow his every movement, and the entente between them and him is well nigh perfect . . . precision, sureness of attack, clean phrasing, admirable dynamic gradation characterize the playing.[58]

And from the *New York Tribune*:

> The Pittsburgh Orchestra distinguishes itself particularly by the readings which it gives its numbers under Mr. Herbert. . . . Last night's

concert demonstrated that Pittsburgh is entitled to rank with the foremost cities in the country in respect to orchestral music.[59]

The *New York Times* was more restrained, remarking that the performance was "not one to call forth expressions of ecstacy, but it was one to call for the conveyance of felicitations to Pittsburgh." Even this, however, was high praise, compared with this notice from the *Musical Courier*. Although it is unsigned, the diction is pure Blumenberg: "The Pittsburgh Orchestra is in its make-up by no means an ideal organization. In every department is there cause for critical disapproval. The wind is mediocre, the strings mediocre, the brass mediocre—excepting the first hornist—yet the band plays like a house on fire."[60]

The thin-skinned Herbert was evidently put off by those members of the critical fraternity who had shown themselves less than enthusiastic. On January 13, he wrote to Wilson: "I am not in favor of announcing through the press the second New York programme (February 27th) for several reasons. One in particular is because the critics would begin to analyze and pick to pieces the different numbers. You may, however, announce the fact that my new suite will be played." Unfortunately a look at the program reveals that Herbert's "reason" does not hold up. The major work was to be the Mozart "Jupiter" Symphony. To imagine that professional critics like Henderson, Krehbiel, and Aldrich would have to prepare a special analysis for a war-horse like this is just not tenable. They could have analyzed it in their sleep. Herbert was really gun shy after the first concert, as apparently he might well have been. It seems fair to say that, while the Pittsburgh critics were definitely interested in booming the orchestra, even if no formal agreement with the Art Society was in place, the preponderance of New York criticism was only mildly enthusiastic.

Shortly after his return from New York, Herbert was treated to one of the most delightful evenings of his life, a stag party given in his honor by the Caribou Hunters, an exclusive social organization of prominent Pittsburgh citizens, dedicated to fun and games. The host, Emil Winter, had arranged a sumptuous feast featuring eight vintage wines, plus cognac and liqueurs, and the courses to go with them: oysters, puree of game, fillet of sole, Caribou steak, terrapin, canvasback duck and omelette soufflé.

As a special treat, an orchestra of fifteen players, hidden behind curtains in the parlor, had been engaged to play the evening's program. As they began the march from Meyerbeer's "Prophet," "Mr. Herbert's delicate ear" might have been offended, according to reports of the evening. He remarked, "Do you know, there is something in the sound of that music like the tones of a familiar voice. Those are not any of my boys, are they, Mr. Winter?" Winter assured him they were not as the orchestra began its second number, the Overture to *William Tell.* Here the faults of execution were more glaring. Herbert bit his lip. Now false notes and a lack of unison began to fill the hall. The dinner went on, and no one dared look Herbert in the eye. When the orchestra struck up a medley from Herbert's own "The Serenade," everyone held his breath. The orchestra began bravely. "Suddenly there was a hesitation, a trembling, a pause, a fresh start, a wavering, a wild frantic screech. The guests looked at each other in consternation. Herbert sprang from the table without a word and drew aside the curtains, disclosing to the view of the guests fifteen laughing men, the pick and choice of the Pittsburgh Orchestra." It took but an instant for everybody to catch on to the practical joke. Herbert, who was himself a great practical joker, had been completely fooled. No one enjoyed the joke more than he, and the evening was filled with laughter, merriment, shouting and wholesale fun.

But that was not the end of it. Before long, a quartet appeared and sang this tribute to Herbert, set to a melody from *The Singing Girl.*

> In New York the music critics used to snub us
> Mere tyros and provincials they would dub us.
> But Herbert now has made them understand
> That, guided by his very skillful hand,
> Our city has a jewel of a band.
>
> Unto Victor they must bow
> There's not a chance to doubt it.
> He's first and foremost now
> There's no argument about it.
>
> When the orchestra from Pittsburgh
> Goes abroad and shows its skill
> The voice of jealous rivalry
> Must instantly be still![61]

Wishful thinking! Herbert now ran smack into a new attack from the Pittsburgh cabal. This time the message was his putative aversion to programming the works of American composers. A long article in the *Pittsburgh Leader* claimed that there was a "concerted movement upon the part of Pittsburgh symphony musicians and composers outside the personnel of the Symphony to create sentiment in favor of such works."[62]

There followed the expected campaign of letter writing to the press, inquiring as to why the works of Foerster, Zitterbart and other local musicos had not been included in Herbert's programs. Letters were also directed to Wilson and the Orchestra Committee. One, signed by a local attorney but inspired by the usual suspects, is loaded with ridiculous claims: that a "very large" contingent of concert goers was demanding American music; that the orchestra management had ignored a list of "superb compositions"; that "Mr. Herbert's unfortunate, though unaccountable, antipathy to American orchestral works was exciting a great deal of unfavorable comment." The suggestion was then made that the final concert of the season be composed of works by Pittsburgh composers, and that the orchestra be conducted by the composers themselves.[63]

In reply to this nonsense, Frew, Wilson and Herbert formed a united front, each backing the other and refuting one by one the malicious accusations. Frew responded that "compositions by Mr. Foerster and Mr. Zitterbart were performed by the orchestra last season" and that "Mr. Herbert is not so greatly opposed to rendering works by American musicians as you seem to think."[64] Then Wilson made it clear to the press that "the arranging of programs is not my province. I have nothing to do with it. Mr. Herbert is the sole judge of what compositions shall be selected. I believe, however, that the orchestra is doing something along the lines suggested in the letter I received, for we have one of the Hadley symphonies on this week's program.[65]

At first Herbert's reaction to the charges was measured, for him. "I have no personal feelings at all against any native composers, Pittsburghers or others and the statement that I entertain an unaccountable antipathy to American orchestral works is not true." He went on to say that his aim in making selections was to program "the best obtainable. Artistic merit must rule—no other. In the United States there are not more than six or eight composers who have written works for orchestra of the best artistic quality. . . . It will not do for a great symphony orchestra to play merely good selections, they must be artistic as well . . . only the best should be given."[66]

In making these statements Herbert fell precipitously into his enemies' trap, for he was faced with a "catch 22" situation. If he defended quality—as he had to—he was, as a consequence, forced to negate the native

American product. "America has as yet produced no works equal in originality, treatment, or technique to the compositions of European masters," he wrote. True enough at the time; but the statement was a lightning rod for those who wished Herbert ill. This was a period when American society was again in the throes of one of its periodic infatuations with nativism. McKinley was in the White House, and Teddy was not far behind him. Anti-immigrant fervor infected not only the upper classes; it was rife in the blue-collar world where the AFL Craft Union movement looked upon newcomers as a threatening source of cheap labor. A perfect expression of this mood is found in a letter sent to Wilson: "Here is a great orchestra in an active American city, managed by a native American, supported by American guarantors and patronized by American citizens at whose concerts world-famous orchestral works by native Americans are tabooed."[67] And, of course, the unspoken implication, tabooed by a conductor-composer who is a foreigner. As Herbert warmed to his subject in response, he eloquently made the case for art—but, before that, he finally turned his attention to his Pittsburgh enemies.

> For some time persons in this city desirous of having their compositions played by the orchestra, have by devious and round-about ways tried to influence me through friends to include such compositions in the repertoire. This I cannot accede to unless the work were up to an artistic standard which I am given the full power to judge. I resent the public or individuals trying to teach me how my programs should be made up. My years of directing bands and orchestras and playing in the best organizations in the country, and also hearing the best orchestras in Europe interpreting the highest forms of musical art fit me to judge orchestra compositions.

> Anybody that has any artistic work, no matter who he is or who he isn't will get a hearing; but there is no use in anybody's trying to foist works on the orchestra that do not come up to my requirements. There is no pull or influence about it. It is all pure merit. I recognize art as belonging to the world—as universal—and will be only too glad to give native composition a hearing.[68]

Herbert's stirring defense of his program was given strong support in the press: "We want the best of music as we want the best of everything else and we take it wherever we find it without imposing any arbitrary limitations. This is Mr. Herbert's method and it is the method of every competent orchestra leader under the sun."[69] Naturally the nativist contingent was not satisfied. Nothing Herbert said or did could have accomplished that. But now they had his own words concerning the present state of American orchestral composition to use against him. His enemies would bide their time.

A few weeks before the orchestra's second appearance in New York, Herbert premiered his "Suite Romantique" at Pittsburgh. His friend James Huneker reviewed it favorably in the pages of the *Musical Courier*(!), praising both its musical materials and their treatment. "The opening theme lifts one up by the very hair of the head; the composer rushes in with a brain full of flaming eloquent phrases. . . . The serenade is delicately indicated—one's nerves recover balance. The third movement is the crowning stroke of the composition . . . at the close one feels the entire gamut of passion has been exhausted. . . . The closing 'Fete nuptuale' is vivid and highly colored. . . . Herbert knows his orchestra from tympany to piccolo. . . . Opulent in color, rich in rhythmical life and fairly boiling over with rude vitality, this Suite Romantique is sure to become a favorite. It is just the sort of work as a modern audience delights in hearing."[70]

The New York reception for both the piece and the orchestra was sobering. Typical was this February 27, 1900 report in the *New York Times*:

> There is no attempt at elaborate form, and the composer has made no efforts in ingenuity in his working out. His four movements are simply rhapsodical color pieces and they are light in both thematic matter and general style. The recent labors of the composer in the field of light opera have shown him the easy path to popular approval, and he has not been slow to tread it. The third movement, a compound of Wagner and Tchaikovsky in style, is the best.
>
> The work of the orchestra was in none of its essential features different from that heard at the first entertainment. The instrumental body, as we said then, lacks distinction of tone, and in this matter there is room for a great deal of improvement. The performance of the "Jupiter" symphony could not be characterized as other than rough. Perhaps smoothness will come in time, but at present the claims of some enthusiastic Pittsburghers for superiority of their orchestra over that of Boston will not produce anything but smiles.[71]

Nevertheless, in his annual report to the guarantors, Frew remarked on the "splendid musical results" of the season just completed and predicted that "the receipts will grow as they have in the past."[72] The guarantors responded with enthusiasm and cash. Herbert was unanimously re-elected conductor for the 1900–01 season, the committee declaring itself "extremely fortunate in again being able to enlist the services of the distinguished conductor and composer—now a resident of Pittsburgh."[73] Wilson was elected to a third consecutive year as orchestra manager, and "Mr. W. E. Clayton was appointed advance agent to give personal attention to the promotion of concerts in other cities."[74]

Previous commentators seem to have misunderstood the role Clayton was to play. His experience prior to his appointment had been as private secretary and librarian to Herbert. It is a misinterpretation to understand his appointment as an attempt to alleviate the road problems that had arisen the previous year. His task is specifically defined as "promotion of concerts"; that is, he was to serve as advance press agent to beat the drum for the orchestra. Nothing in his contract suggests that he was to act as company manager, dealing with accommodations, meal tickets and the like. Those with a suspicious turn of mind have seen his appointment (and later advancement to assistant manager) as part of a campaign by Herbert to get rid of Wilson.

There is no evidence to support this. Both Orchestra Committee and conductor were anxious to build the attendance at road concerts in order to increase the orchestra's income. This is the reason for hiring Clayton. What is more, his presence in Pittsburgh provided Herbert with a part-time private secretary at the orchestra's expense. Not a bad deal for Herbert. Finally, the evidence that Clayton was not being groomed as a replacement for Wilson is clear. When, later on, Herbert did indeed seek to replace Wilson, he supported another man for the position.

For the new season, Herbert accepted a contract salary of $3,000 ($61,800 in today's equivalent), an increase from the $2,700 for the previous year. The season was to last eighteen weeks, and his $100 stipend for extra concerts was maintained. An interesting stipulation in the contract reflected the history of Herbert's entanglement in petty local jealousies: "During the term of this engagement the party of the second part [Herbert] agrees not to connect himself or allow his name to be used in connection with any similar organization in the City of Pittsburgh, or any musical school or conservatory in said city, without the consent of said orchestra committee."[75] This paragraph was included to prevent Herbert from associating himself with any other local rival musical organization. Why Herbert might want to establish a relationship with his adversaries is unclear. Archer had been lecturing at the conservatory, which was a hot-bed of anti-orchestra agitation. With respect to the first restriction—

that forbidding Herbert to allow his name to be used in connection with any similar organization (i.e. orchestra), Frew was prescient. Perhaps the chairman was thinking of Herbert's tendency to attach his name to entities with which he became associated. Not long after taking the leadership of the 22nd Regiment Band he began to advertise it as "Victor Herbert's 22nd Regiment Band"; and then there was the "Herbert-Schmidt" String Quartet episode. Was it possible that he would contemplate establishing a "Victor Herbert Orchestra?" Not on Frew's watch.

Summer arrived with a relaxation of tensions. The Herbert who writes to Wilson from the Pines, his new home at Lake Placid, is bantering and outrageously punning, while still taking care of business. He is collaborative in areas where previously he had shown himself to be rigid and flexible on the subject of American programming—altogether warm and friendly and collegial.

June 9th, 1900

Dear Mr. Wilson

Yours of June 7th at hand. As to the Buffalo Exposition*—4 or 5 weeks would be very acceptable. It would be best to get September or October time in one way; on the other hand if the Exposition is not a great financial success it is much better to get time in the early part of the affair; you're sure of your money then. I have had experience of this kind.

As to St. Louis, I personally hope we will not get it, it's so hot there, but, for the rest of the band, alright, here goes.

I think you are quite right about what you say about Gabrilowitch and the Everett piano,** I guess we'll pass him untouched.

I enclose letter from Whiting. I think it would be nice to have an American composer and soloist for a change. I saw his Fantasy—a very

---

* The Pan-American Exposition to be held between June and October 1901 at which William McKinley was assassinated in the "Temple of Music," where Herbert and the orchestra played less than a month after the event. Although Herbert seems concerned with the ability of the sponsors to meet their financial obligations, in fact he need not have worried. Although the nation went into official mourning for thirty days, the gate receipts at the fair held up very well throughout the period. As a matter of fact the site of the assassination proved a great attraction!

**Ossip Gabrilowitch objected to playing anything but a Steinway. In spite of this he became Herbert's good friend and neighbor at Lake Placid.

good work. As to the second part [of the program]—numbers *all Brahms—no*. If Mr. Frew is in favor of having him [Whiting] will you please communicate with Whiting, telling him that I turned the thing over to you now, and that we must have selections of a popular or brilliant character in the 2nd part of our program. Tell him that we don't believe in forcing the Brahms-pills down an audience's throat as long as we can give them pleasant and more exhilarating doses of morphines (pronounced MORE-FINESSE!) Ha! Ha!

To be serious, Whiting is certainly one of the best American composers and a fine pianist. . . .

I am having a great time here. Come up soon, it is simply divine.
With best regards to everybody
Truly
Victor Herbert[76]

August brought an unsettling letter to Wilson from a Miss Katherine S. Parsons, Director of the Tuesday Musical Club of Akron, which had sponsored an appearance by the orchestra the previous year.

> August 21, 1900
> There is also another matter of consideration—the unfortunate reputation of the Pittsburgh Orchestra in Akron. I was not here last year, but I am told that several of the orchestra were somewhat under the influence of liquor, when they played here, and that the comments of the press upon their performance were unfavorable. . . .
>
> Now the club understands that the Pittsburgh Orchestra is a fine one and can do good work under its own director, Mr. Herbert. But the public does not understand this. It would be to your interest to wipe out this unfavorable impression.[77]

This communication, which we can assume Wilson shared with Frew, cannot have done anything to put to rest the lingering doubts concerning the problems of orchestral discipline.

As the new season drew near there was an increase in correspondence, Herbert urging Wilson to nail down engagements ("Don't let up on Atlantic City! Better go there yourself! What about Willow Grove?")[78] and agreeing to appear at the Merchant's and Manufacturer's Exposition at Boston in October,[79] as well as to appear, gratis, as conductor at a benefit for the Police Protective Association of Pittsburgh ("All right if you

[Frew] and the Orchestra Committee consider it good policy to give concert in question. As far as I am personally concerned the police are always welcome to any protection they need").[80]

The first appearance of any possibility of tension between Herbert and Wilson surfaces in an exchange of letters concerning the program for the appearance of the pianist Fanny Bloomfield Zeisler on October 26. Zeisler had written to Herbert suggesting that she play the Schumann A minor concerto as well as the Chopin Andante Spianato and Polonaise. At the bottom of the letter, as a guide for Wilson's reply, Herbert scribbled: "Liszt's E-flat. A and B [i.e., the Chopin selections] OK. You were so great last year."[81] These notations would leave one to assume that Herbert was anything but annoyed with Zeisler's suggested concerto. Whatever Wilson read into Herbert's note, his letter occasioned this response from Zeisler:

> My dear Mr. Wilson—
> At last your letter has arrived. I am very sorry that Mr. Herbert should be "annoyed" and that I should be the innocent cause. If I would have been informed some time ago that he wished a particular concerto, when there was still time to prepare it, I should have been glad to comply with his wish, but as I do not play the Liszt Concerto, I cannot get it ready in so short a time.[82]

She then goes on to suggest several concertos and requests an immediate response, by wire. Herbert scrawls a response at the bottom of her letter: "Ms. Bl.Z. St. Saens C minor all right. Am not as badly annoyed as you may think."[83]

Perhaps not anymore. Herbert, famous for mercurial shifts of mood, may very well have given Wilson the impression that he was annoyed with the pianist's suggestion. Or he may just have been having a bad day. At any rate Wilson's letter, justified or not, had given what to Herbert seemed the wrong impression. Herbert's notes, constantly urging Wilson to get on the ball and set concert dates, become more urgent. We remember Schmidt's remark that Herbert was not impressed with his bookings and felt that he had not been aggressive enough in his approach. It might be that Herbert felt no personal animus toward Wilson—just that, as we have seen, when a personality got in the way of his income stream he began to look for ways to fix the problem.

Herbert's third season opened not in Pittsburgh, but in Boston. It was a sign of the growing importance of touring in the life of the orchestra, and of its growing reputation. The week-long engagement at the Merchant's and Manufacturer's Exposition was not uneventful. Somehow, several newspapers throughout the country had been informed that "The music loving people of Boston did not take to the classical music usually played by the orchestra and had made a special request of Mr. Herbert that he give the people ragtime selections." Herbert responded:

> This is a lot of bosh. I do not play ragtime with my Pittsburgh Orchestra. I wish it distinctly understood that while in Boston not one piece of the so-called ragtime air was played. The Pittsburgh orchestra does not play such light, frivolous stuff. . . . We have no time for such nonsense. The whole story was the invention of a single enterprising reporter on a Boston paper who knew nothing whatever about music![84]

Not exactly. The author of the article was Philip Hale, critic of the *Boston Journal*. This was the same man whom Frew had consulted when seeking candidates for conductor. Hale's article[85] is strangely reminiscent of Blumenberg's earlier diatribe in the *Musical Courier*—even to the choice of ragtime title cited! "There will be no more of the bing bang boom of Wagner's Tannhauser, but from now on the lickety split and hammer-de-bang of 'All Coons Look Alike to Me' propounded by the famous Pittsburgh Orchestra."[86] Coincidence? One wonders. In any event, Clayton saw the potential in the story and proved himself a clever flak, winning national coverage for the orchestra and its conductor.

Returning to home base, the orchestra still had one obligation to fulfill before its opening concert at the Music Hall. This was the police benefit concert at the Duquesne Garden. The Garden was an elaborate pleasure dome decked out with clusters of multi-colored incandescent lamps and a virtual forest of potted palms and aspidistra. Three thousand Pittsburghers of all stations and classes thronged to the Garden to sip lemonade and fill the air with manly cigar smoke.

The concert began with Wagner's "Huldigungs March." It was a rough house. Somebody threw graniteware about and kept beautiful time to the music. The bang and crash was interrupted by the arrival of the police, and "just as the gang was being lifted into the patrol wagon there was an earthquake from the orchestra and the house came down."[87]

Shortly before the beginning of Herbert's third season, Frew was interviewed by the *Pittsburgh Post*. "Much of the credit for the satisfactory state of affairs as regards the Pittsburgh Orchestra is due to the Orchestra Committee and its dignified methods. Its President, W. N. Frew, is intensely enthusiastic and more than pleased with present and prospective conditions."[88]

The formal season opened, once again, with a Founder's Day tribute to Carnegie. Herbert had the orchestra play "Auld Lang Syne" when he appeared, reducing Carnegie to tears. The audience thundered its respect and thanks with sustained applause, and Herbert coaxed thunder from the tympani to add to the ovation. Ex-President Cleveland was in the audience and proclaimed that "The fame of the Pittsburgh Orchestra is spreading to every section of the country. A splendid performance of the evening is the best evidence of the truth and justice of this statement."

But it wasn't long before a concert was the occasion for Herbert to display his "short fuse" to the Pittsburgh public for the first time. Weber's "Invitation to the Dance" was the concluding number on this program. The piece contains a false cadence that precedes the exciting finale. When the orchestra reached the cadence, the audience rose and rushed for the exits. Herbert finished the piece, turned, and shouted at the retreating backs of the "music lovers," "Now it's over!" The press had a field day!

The orchestra continued its out-of-town trips, and from the road Clayton reported to Wilson that things were improving, but

> I found everything quite satisfactory with the exception of a large dog in the audience which annoyed Mr. Herbert very much and I believe Messrs. Wise and Stanley were recipients of Mr. Herbert's wrath in consequence.
>
> Leroux would not sleep on a cot in the same room with Laurendeau.
>
> Lovely letter, this.[89]

Toward the middle of November Frew hosted a birthday party for Carnegie. As a surprise the orchestra appeared and played a short program featuring "The Blue Bells of Scotland" and Herbert's newly composed "Punchinella." Carnegie and Frew were both very pleased. "A sweeter compliment to any man could not be conceived," the steel baron remarked, and Frew added his thanks to the orchestra: "I realize the effort it must have cost you all, coming back from a wearisome trip and after a day of rehearsing."[90]

Another new orchestral number that Herbert created in this period of fertility was slated to be premiered at the upcoming Buffalo Exposition.

Dedicated to President McKinley, the new piece, "Panamericana," was, according to the composer,[91] "a morceau characteristique of the more popular order. The first part is supposed to be 'Indian,' the second part 'ragtime' (modern America) and the third 'Cuban' or of Spanish character."

December was a busy month for the orchestra. After the Pittsburgh premiere of his new suite, "Woodland Fancies," an evocation of Adirondack moods, Herbert subjected the orchestra to increased discipline and drilling, hoping that its upcoming appearance in New York would result in more positive critical evaluation.

January saw the most important events of Herbert's third season: the world premiere of his tone poem, "Hero and Leander," and the New York premiere of "Woodland Fancies." With respect to the latter, the *New York Tribune* praised the orchestra for its "high energy" but remarked on its "lack of euphony," a comment seconded by the critics of the *World* and the *Staatszeitung*. "Hero and Leander" is Herbert's most ambitious orchestral composition—an evocation of the Greek myth of lovers frustrated by fate, challenged by event and destroyed by the whims of the gods. After the premiere at New York's Carnegie Hall, Herbert's redoubled efforts with the orchestra were acknowledged by the critics:

> It is a pleasure to be able to record the marked improvement in the efficiency of the Pittsburgh Orchestra [wrote the *New York World*]. A high degree of precision has been attained. . . . He [Herbert] has drilled his men carefully, assiduously and intelligently, and he has kept them stimulated with his buoyant, optimistic nature. . . . What the orchestra lacks and must obtain before it can be placed in the class which its patrons and supporters, unduly moved by local pride, claim for it now, is what time and time alone can bring. . . . Rome was not built in a day, neither do orchestras attain perfection in a season.[92]

Another critic then turned his attention to a discussion of the conductor and his achievements.[93] The bottom line amounted to an evaluation that saw Herbert as earnest, hard-working, and inspiring but essentially lightweight.

> Mr. Herbert is an admirable man, for his place. He believes in himself and in his men and they believe in him. He is a thorough musician, perhaps a little too impulsive and not reflective enough, perhaps *disdaining intellectuality in musical interpretation and preferring*

superficial brilliancy of execution [italics mine], but he is intensely earnest, an indefatigable worker, amiable and magnetic.[94]

This is probably the fairest, most cogent and accurate evaluation of Herbert as a conductor that he was ever to receive. New York noted his "Hero and Leander" with tempered acceptance. No one was overwhelmed.

Frew responded to both of these critiques in confidential correspondence that gives great insight into his agenda for both Herbert and the orchestra. These letters show how closely aligned Frew and Wilson were in their points of view.

1/1/01

Mr. F. N. R. Martinez
Dear Sir—
Although personally unknown to you, allow me to express my appreciation of your criticism. . . . I feel that for much of the improvement shown in the orchestra . . . we are indebted to the friendly, honest criticism of writers who . . . recognize that a sincere, honest effort is being made to present to the people the best examples of music *in its higher forms* through the medium of proper interpretation.

I fear you do the "patrons and supporters" a slight injustice in stating that they claim for the organization a position to which it is not entitled. Probably you have formed this opinion by reading the criticism of some of the local [Pittsburgh] newspaper men. They are very willing but not always able to discuss the work of the orchestra in a judicial manner, and in many cases, I feel sure, find it easier to award praise without discrimination or judgement. Much of the comment by the Pittsburgh critics has been amateurish or even absurd. . . . In Mr. Herbert we feel we have a conductor of very great promise, who, *as he separates himself farther from the lighter forms of music*, will develop to an even greater extent the refinement and delicacy that will form a fitting complement to his virility and earnestness.

Requesting you to regard this communication as confidential, I remain
W. N. Frew

In this letter Frew is playing Queen Victoria to Herbert's Arthur Sullivan. Once again a composer whose greatest strength lies in his lighter compositions is unrecognized for his true area of genius. Sullivan, having already composed "Pinafore," was famously encouraged by his Queen to attempt more serious stage composition. "You would do it so well," she remarked. How wrong both she and Frew were!

And to Henry T. Finck, critic of the *New York Evening Post*, Frew wrote in a similar vein:

> February 4th, 1901
>
> In Mr. Herbert, we feel that we possess a conductor of rare promise, and although you express a hope that he will not desert the field of operetta, we are convinced that the more completely he separates himself from the "band" and the study of music in its lighter forms, the more thoughtful and serious he becomes and the better he fits himself to interpret the works of the great masters, with not only virility and earnestness, but with refinement and delicacy. Requesting that this communication may be regarded as personal
>
> I remain,
> Very truly yours,
> W. N. Frew
> Chairman, Orchestra Committee

In mid-February the orchestra returned to New York for a second concert, and on that occasion Carnegie expressed the great pleasure he took in the orchestra's progress: "I have always built air-castles but never a dream of an air-castle has approached its realization."[95]

With such enthusiastic support from Carnegie, it can come as no surprise that the third season concluded with the announcement of Herbert's election as conductor on an extended contract for the three years ending March 15, 1904. In the same announcement Wilson came in for special praise: "The committee takes pleasure in recording its appreciation of the enthusiastic and faithful work of Mr. Wilson in a trying and laborious position, noting especially the ability displayed by him in the preparation of the program books, the educational value of which is of first importance."[96]

In addition, Clayton was elected assistant manager of the orchestra. Ironically, it was immediately after Herbert had been signed to a long-term contract that the era of good feelings began to unravel. The tensions associated with the production of a concentrated musical season began to surface in connection with the orchestra tour, which was managed by Wilson and Clayton. But Herbert, now feeling his oats as a popular favorite in the theater and with a three-year contract in his pocket, began to press his luck, with the result that he managed to alienate both Wilson and Frew in the space of a few months.

The post-season tour was the most ambitious attempted by the orchestra. It included a western trek as far as St. Louis and a southern journey to New Orleans. The programs are significant because they became a model for the programs of the "Victor Herbert Orchestra," an organization born out of this tour. They would generally begin with classical selections and follow with an overture or symphony, with a soloist performing between the two. The second half consisted of lighter music, often featuring the works of Herbert himself. Frequently, in more rural venues, such as Terra Haute, Bloomington, and Columbus, Indiana, the orchestra played to poor houses. This may have been the fault of the serious programming—or because of unfortunate local competition.

> Victor Herbert probably learned one thing which other fine artists have learned of Richmond [Indiana] before this—and that is not to come here and buck a circus. We are musical, yes, but it seems to be absolutely imperative that we take the children to the circus, and we can't afford both. So, in order to see the elephant walking "round and round," we have neglected some of the finest talent in the United States.[97]

Herbert could not have been pleased with the empty halls, and the easiest thing was to blame Wilson for not scheduling concert dates free of conflicts.

As the tour continued, a critical pattern emerged: in the smaller cities the critics praised the performances and lamented the small houses; in the larger cities the concerts were well attended but the criticism was more severe. There were frequent comments on "balance" problems of the orchestral choirs.

This first extended tour is most important, because it is the period when Herbert solidified his good relations with the men of the orchestra. Without the feeling of camaraderie that he took pains to build, he would not have been able to establish the Victor Herbert Orchestra, the organization that was to support his reputation as an orchestral conductor long after his Pittsburgh connection had ended.

Despite tensions with management, nothing was able to dampen Herbert's spirit. He loved to play games with names—especially the names of his first-chair musicians. Luigi von Kunitz, his friend and concertmaster, came in for special treatment. "Kunitz . . . Kunitz. . . . The name comes from 'Kann Nichts'—which means 'Knows nothing,'" Herbert teased. This was especially amusing, since everyone admired Kunitz's erudition.[98] Herbert never ceased ragging his friend. In those days every Pullman car carried a special name on its side for identification purposes in ticketing. Herbert had learned that the one assigned to the orchestra was named "Darius." While the orchestra was waiting to board, Herbert pointed to the name on the car. "Darius," the scholarly von Kunitz remarked, "King of the Persians." "Yes," Herbert replied nonchalantly, "King of the Persians, son of Hystapes, born 550 BC and died 485—the founder of the Persian Dynasty, etc. etc." Von Kunitz, very much impressed by this display of learning, did not know then what Herbert told the boys afterward—that he had looked the whole story up on the morning of the trip, and had memorized as much as he thought necessary to dumbfound Kunitz with his knowledge.

Herbert always considered himself "one of the boys," and it was that attitude more than any of his achievements that endeared him to them. There was a time when, traveling on "Darius," Herbert uncharacteristically went to his berth early while the others stayed up drinking pilsner. Fritz Stahlberg, trying to climb into his upper, missed the support and fell heavily on someone in the lower berth. There was a deep "Ooooff!!" and then silence. He feared he had trampled on forbidden ground. The next morning, when the lion awoke, he stuck his disheveled head between the curtains. Stahlberg innocently inquired if Herbert had slept well. "Rotten," Herbert grumped, using his favorite adjective. "Some son-of-a-bitch walked around on my stomach!" Stahlberg never confessed to being the guilty pedestrian. There were limits to Herbert's good will.

A concert in Greencastle, Indiana, was also significant. It is the first time that the press describes the ensemble as "The Herbert Orchestra." Whether this was the result of Clayton's press agentry or merely an editorial mistake, the notice touched a nerve back in Pittsburgh. When, after the tour, Clayton made the mistake of showing Frew new stationery that Herbert had arranged to be printed, reading "Victor Herbert's Pittsburgh Orchestra," Frew finally lost his cool:

> Mr. Clayton showed me yesterday the letterheads you are having prepared. I speak only as an individual member of the Orchestra Committee, the others being out of town, but I feel sure that the wording as you have prepared it would be very distasteful to the committee. If the Pittsburgh Orchestra *belongs to anyone*, it is to the

Art Society or the guarantors who have spent $100,000 in making the name of value. If you have definitely decided to branch out for yourself next Spring [i.e. of 1902] *and are desirous of keeping in friendly touch with the Orchestra Committee*, I think it would be wiser for you to omit the word "Pittsburgh" altogether from your letter heads, prospectuses and advertisements.[99]

Herbert had finally pushed Frew too far. But it was not merely the idea of his attaching his name to the orchestra that had rankled the chairman. The press, ever eager to report trouble, had carried stories that Herbert was dissatisfied with the railroad arrangements made by Wilson and was attempting to have him dismissed. Frew issued a statement that the rumor was untrue. Although Herbert may well have been disgruntled by the arrangements and may have been unhappy to play to small houses, these events in themselves were not sufficient reason for him to seek to have the manager replaced. But the fact that these matters had made their way into the press—via Herbert's man Clayton—must have annoyed Wilson.

Then there were other matters. The spring tour had been followed by a triumphant series of "pops" concerts at the Duquesne Gardens. For these evenings Herbert chose very accessible, lighter works and filled the house. For Wilson, the spectacle of his orchestra being led down a primrose path of easy virtue for the sake of a popular triumph was not easy to take. Wilson, like Frew, had always wanted the orchestra's success to be based on a firm foundation of classical achievement. This pandering to the popular taste could not have been to his liking.

Wilson was more than just manager of the Pittsburgh Orchestra. He was also manager of the Carnegie Music Hall and, as such, he had arranged for a concert of "high class" music to be performed on the very night of Herbert's opening at the Garden.

Music lovers had their choice of the classics or the popular airs last night, for while the Kneisel Quartet of Boston exploited old and modern masters at Carnegie Music Hall there was a crowd at Duquesne Garden listening to Victor Herbert and his [!] orchestra in a programme of popular variety. . . . The Kneisel Quartet appeared under the auspices of the Art Society. It is a marvelous ensemble, not surpassed by any similar organization. . . . As a program maker Victor Herbert is something of an artist.[100]

Herbert could not have been pleased with Wilson providing competition. This was added to his displeasure with the travel arrangements. But these were all events, and events can be ignored if a basic empathy between individuals has been established. For three years the two men had worked together as colleagues, but never as friends. Herbert had rightly felt that Wilson was never a member of his team; Wilson had always clearly shown his loyalty to the Orchestra Committee. But there was more to it than that. Herbert must have felt that Wilson had always been closer, in both temperament and in his vision of what the orchestra was to become, to Archer, his predecessor, than he was to him. This was more than a feeling on Herbert's part. Archer's reputation, before he had been chosen first conductor of the orchestra, had been as an organist. Soon after he was replaced as conductor, Wilson had hired him as "Pittsburgh City Organist" to provide music for special occasions and free organ concerts on the impressive instrument that in those days dominated the stage of the Carnegie Music Hall. Thus Wilson and Archer remained in close contact. They were in fact good friends. When Archer appeared at the Music Hall for a lecture on "the Modern Orchestra" and leveled an indirect attack on the Orchestra's work under Herbert, the fat was in the fire.

ARCHER'S SLAP AT HERBERT

Frederick Archer, the city organist, created a mild sensation at Carnegie Music Hall last night. He delivered a lecture on "The Modern Orchestra" and what he said about Boston and what he didn't say about Pittsburgh was what set tongues a-wagging. His remarks were generally interpreted as a slap at Victor Herbert and the local orchestra:

"The only properly balanced orchestra in this country is the Boston Symphony organization. The *brass is here properly subordinated* and its tone is rich and sonorous because it is unforced. *Its present conductor is a man of refinement and culture* and his reading of classical works is alike reverent and sympathetic"[101][italics mine].

A slap, indeed—at the old "brass band" leader and an ad hominem attack on Herbert's well-known "hale-fellow, well-lubricated" reputation, to boot.

Herbert responded, lamely, "I think Mr. Archer has been misunderstood. He cannot have intended to criticize the Pittsburgh Orchestra, because to the best of my knowledge he has never heard it." Everyone knew this was untrue. Five months later the Archer-Herbert animosity ended with the death of the city organist. But the damage had been done. The combination of all these events was enough to motivate Herbert to try to replace Wilson.

In July, articles appeared in the press stating that Frederic M. Ranken, the librettist of Herbert's most recent operetta, *The Ameer* (a poor imitation of *The Pirates of Penzance* set in Afghanistan!), would replace Wilson as orchestra manager. Apparently Herbert had written to Frew requesting such a change.

Frew sent two letters in reply. In the first he expresses his sorrow that "violent differences of opinion" had arisen, but explains that the committee has a firm contract with Wilson and cannot "abrogate that contract without making ourselves liable to Mr. Wilson for the amount of his salary."[102]

The second letter, a reaction to articles in the *New York Times* and the *Baltimore Sun*, is a testy and serious warning to the composer to quit playing games with the committee.

> My dear Mr. Herbert—
>
> I enclose a clipping from this morning's *Times* which will explain itself. I have already been approached by three newspaper reporters who told me that it had been given out in New York that Mr. Ranken was to be the manager of the orchestra for the coming season. . . . Evidently someone in the East has given this information to the papers, and a serious mistake has been made.
>
> You can readily see the confusion that is going to result. Mr. Wilson is the regularly elected Manager of the Pittsburgh Orchestra, and no one else at present is entitled to call himself such. If you have definitely determined to cut loose entirely from the regular management of the orchestra for the proposed Spring Tour [1902] I want to suggest to you this early in a most friendly way and yet most earnestly that you as Conductor of the Pittsburgh Orchestra in promoting a Spring Tour must not do anything that will detract from the interest in our regular out-of-town business.

In other words, Frew sees Herbert's decision to go it alone for the postseason tour as potentially harmful to the bookings Wilson will arrange. Frew continues with a warning:

> I most earnestly recommend and urge caution in the treatment of this matter. You can see from the clipping enclosed how eager the newspapers are and will be to assist in bringing about an unpleasant state of affairs, and we none of us have the right to do anything that will interfere in the slightest degree with the success of the regular season of the Pittsburgh Orchestra.

And now the attorney issues a "cease and desist" order:

If Mr. Ranken is holding himself out as Manager of the Pittsburgh Orchestra, it should be stopped at once.

I hope you will take this warning in the friendly spirit in which it is offered you, and that we will all work in concert to make the coming season even more successful than the last.[103]

On July 21 it was announced that the Pittsburgh Orchestra would tour in the spring of 1902. Herbert himself would be the guarantor. It would be a private enterprise, directed by Victor Herbert and managed by Frederic Ranken. Thus began the long, painful and troublesome gestation that eventually led to the birth of the "Victor Herbert Orchestra." The tensions between Herbert, Wilson and Frew were out in the open and the gloves were off. Three years later Herbert was replaced.

During the summer of 1901. Herbert was busy establishing himself as a semi-permanent resident of Lake Placid. After several years as a guest at the Lake Placid Club, he decided to purchase a camp for himself and his family on the shore of the lake. The area was "divine" and a blessed retreat from the Sturm und Drang of his Pittsburgh activities. This home, eventually christened Camp Joyland, was substantial and typical of Adirondack "cottages" of the period: heavy wood rafters and beams, large stone fireplaces, wheel-shaped chandeliers, well-bolstered furnishings. From this mountain eyrie Herbert surveyed the coming season with enthusiasm and apprehension. He was still concerned with his prospects at the Pan-American Exposition at Buffalo. He wrote to Wilson:

I hope you will see that we get all the advertising we ought to have there *before* we arrive and when *we get there.* I know that the Buffalo Expo people are *very hard up* and that several of the organizers had the devil's own time to collect the money due them. They are perfectly honest alright enough, but they don't seem to have it! I hope however they will do some business from now on and that we will *have no trouble of that kind.* . . . Let me know when you are going to get out the new, revised orchestra list. I want it to come out without a mistake this time.[104]

Even after the engagement, Herbert was smarting from comments made comparing him with Sousa.

I wish you would give Mr. Hennssler a few points on the difference between the Pittsburgh Orchestra and the beloved and great Sousa. If he says *plenty* of people ordain first honors to Mr. Sousa he is speaking of *himself* as the *plenty*. Both Hennssler and Landy felt sore about our tremendous success because they had opposed us before. Sunt illae lacrimae!"*[105]

Herbert needn't have worried about Buffalo. In spite of the assassination of President McKinley on September 6, the attendance at the fair continued to grow. Herbert's orchestral appearance had been preceded by what in effect amounted to a Victor Herbert Festival. An examination of the programs of the many bands and orchestras that had performed from June through September reveals just how popular Herbert's compositions were. "Gems," "scenes," "selections," and "excerpts" from most of his operettas, plus the perennial "Badinage" appear; by the time Herbert stepped to the podium on October 14 a good deal of his theater music had been heard.

Although many of his own selections replicated much of what had gone before, he took pains to present new material. Fritz Stahlberg's memoir takes up the story:

> We played in the Temple of Music which four weeks earlier had been the scene of the McKinley tragedy. (During the concerts the hall space was taken up with seats, except for a fenced-in square in the center of which was a golden star marking the spot where the President was standing when the assassin's bullet struck him.) On the first program was Mr. Herbert's "American Fantasy," and since we played the number often it had not been rehearsed. To heighten the effect of the climax the drummer was supposed to shoot off a revolver, and as we came to that place I wondered if Mr. Herbert was going to recall to the audience the tragic moment of not so long before. But there was no shot, and after the concert the drummer told me that Mr. Herbert had personally told him to omit it.

> It was for this engagement that Victor Herbert wrote "Pan-Americana." We played it with great success, and after that it appeared

* Herbert occasionally sprinkled his correspondence with Latin phrases. Here his reference is to the famous remark of Aeneas, when he saw a depiction of the Trojan War on a temple wall in Carthage: *Sunt lacrimae rerum et mentem mortalia tangunt.* This line is difficult to translate in its original form. Herbert may be equating the "tears of things" (lacrimae rerum) that Aeneas shed with the sorrow experienced by his opponents, beholding his success.

often. And how often! The orchestra men got so tired of it that it was easy to read their feelings by their expressions. One day when he announced it, one of the men muttered, "What . . . again?" Mr. Herbert, overhearing him, said, "Of course. . . . I'll get fat on my own cooking!"

Years later we spoke of the fact that he played the same encores so often, but his argument was that that was what the people wanted. "They're like children. When you finish telling them a fairy tale, the first thing they say is, 'Tell it again!'" And, to be perfectly fair, he only played what was requested.[106]

Herbert's correspondence with Wilson from this period is formal. He is, as always, concerned with the financial success of the tours being developed: "As to the Baltimore concerts . . . be sure to let me know when you intend starting the subscription list so that I can advise my friends there of the fact and make them push the thing along.[107] A lady in the club here [Lake Placid] asked me if we could possibly give a concert in Montclaire. . . . Please answer the question."[108]

Even Herbert's reaction to the assassination is focused on the business implications of the event: "The deplorable death of the President will certainly settle the matter of our playing an extra week in Buffalo. Under the circumstances we can't expect to get it. They are certainly getting it *in the neck*."[109]

As Herbert got deeper into the details of planning the new season's tour, memories of past events brought old resentments to the surface.

For Oberlin [sight of a famous music conservatory] suggest the following program . . . this program is almost *too long* again. So far all our concerts in Oberlin were a perfect *disgrace*! We had to get through an enormous program in about one hour. Will you please look up the last criticism about our concert there if Mr. Rice [the Director of the Conservatory] wants a longer program.[110]

As I say, *the concert had to be given in a disgraceful hurry*. Dinner at the hotel there was terrible also. I think you might ask them to give us a *simple* but *substantial* meal (if we have to dine there,) say *Roast Beef, boiled ham, potatoes and vegetables* and a cup of coffee, but *enough of it*! That wouldn't take long and would satisfy the boys better. It is very hard to work with an empty stomach. Will you kindly bear this in mind when you make arrangements in that *terrible little place*."

If Herbert felt that Oberlin was terrible, Oberlin returned the compliment. In a confidential letter to Wilson the director of the Conservatory compares Herbert's reading of the Tchaikovsky 5th Symphony unfavorably with those of Thomas and Seidl given in previous years. He discounts the argument that time pressure was the reason for the weakness of the performance, and in doing so reinforces Wilson's prejudices vis-à-vis Herbert:

> I do not believe Mr. Herbert can sustain himself as a good conductor and at the same time spend his vacations in writing the poor stuff that he does. A good conductor must have a high ideal,—one so high that he cannot let himself down to the low level that is necessary for that kind of writing.

> I wish Mr. Herbert would give up this foolish kind of business—that I suppose he engages in for the ducats—and give himself earnestly to the higher work of preparing himself to do the best possible work with the noble orchestra that he has. He will never rise to the height of his opportunities until he does it.[111]

Herbert continues his commentary, *molto agitato.*

> As to Akron I don't see how I can make a program without knowing *what numbers* that singing society is going to sing! (Anyway, who conducts those two numbers?) Is it that same woman of two years ago? If so, remember that *Mr. Frew* said (at the time) she should never have had the chance to conduct the orchestra. Am I to share the honors on that occasion with that lady? Would you think of offering Mr. Theodore Thomas or Mr. Geirike a like partnership? Is *anybody* good enough to stand up before an orchestra like the Pittsburgh?!"[112]

One of the major concerts of the tour was planned for Cleveland. It had been arranged by Wilson and Adela Hughes, a woman who was a powerful force in the musical life of Cleveland and who had been a champion of Herbert and his career ever since her days as a Vassar undergraduate, where she had favorably noticed his appearance with the Emma Juch company.[113] The soloist at the performance was to be Lillian Nordica, the great Wagnerian soprano. "I would like Nordica to sing the 'Liebestod' in the second part. Then I would like the second part all Wagner, perhaps.[114] If we receive the music for Mme. Nordica's aria *in time to rehearse it here* [Pittsburgh] we will certainly *not need* a rehearsal with her in Cleveland. Mme. Nordica knows me and will without doubt *not insist* upon a rehearsal."

In this, Herbert was very much mistaken. Adela Hughes now takes up the story and reveals another possible source of the growing conflict between conductor and manager.

> Mr. Herbert agreed to a piano rehearsal with the soloist at her hotel because of the tight orchestra schedule. Nordica, however, refused to sing without an orchestral rehearsal. Victor Herbert arrived at the station.

> I knew my gentleman, and didn't give him a chance to start talking about his troubles, but began commiserating with him about how terrible it was for a soloist to demand an orchestral rehearsal with such a prominent conductor.

> So, early in the morning I thought we both needed something to pick us up. Mr. Herbert thought the pick-up an excellent idea, and so he and I drank champagne cocktails together before 9 A.M.. His good humor after that was infectious.

> Herbert's bubbling Irish wit and gaiety made him a popular guest everywhere, but he could get mad at his manager. He complained bitterly that George Wilson took up most of the space in their publicity in praising the guarantors and directors of the orchestra association, and didn't devote nearly enough space to him. "I *am* the orchestra," said he.[115]

There were three important events that occurred during Herbert's fourth season with the orchestra. The first was a disappointing recapitulation of the past; the second, the first steps to a brilliant future; the third, a decisive shock that turned out to be fatal to Herbert's Pittsburgh career.

In December the orchestra played two concerts at the Chicago Auditorium, bearding the Thomas lion in his lair. The writer for the *Chicago American*[116] reflects in his notice the critical view of New York:

> Well, we have heard Victor Herbert's Pittsburgh Symphony Orchestra and—we like it. The erstwhile 'cellist and brass band leader and his musicians did all in their power. The evening was worthy of serious attention.

> Those who expected in Herbert a second Thomas or Nikish were disappointed. . . . The rounded, fully-developed precise orchestral

conductor was not observable in the man from Pittsburgh. Greatness is not within reach of Mr. Herbert. Proficiency, exceptional talent, yes, they are his, and having these qualities he will certainly add to them. Just how far Mr. Herbert will advance will remain to be observed.

The Pittsburgh Orchestra is unseasoned, underdeveloped, and while it has the elements of a serious, weighty organization, it has still a good many steps to climb before it can reach the Chicago or Boston Orchestras.

Following the close of the regular season the orchestra set off on an extended spring and summer tour. This was the first outing for the Victor Herbert Orchestra. The ensemble traveled to Ohio, Michigan, Indiana, Illinois and Kentucky and finished up with two weeks at Duquesne Gardens, three weeks in Baltimore, two weeks in Buffalo, eighteen days at Willow Grove Park outside Philadelphia, and eight weeks at the Grand Union Hotel at Saratoga Springs. These last two venues were to become annual sites of pilgrimage for those who loved Herbert and his music. As tensions had risen with respect to the circumstances of the regular season, Herbert must have looked forward with increasing anticipation to these post-season sojourns, where he was in complete control of all elements of the situation: program, personnel, bookings and advertising.

Herbert continued his businesslike relations with the orchestra management. He also continued his habit of performing end-runs around Wilson, preferring to deal directly with Frew on purely day-to-day matters. It was in this connection that in May, while on tour, he sent Frew some information on salaries for the coming season. He must have been shocked by Frew's response:

May 20th, 1902

My dear Mr. Herbert—

Your letter of recent date in regard to salaries for some of the players was duly received. I have resigned from the Orchestra Committee, but handed your letter to the President of the Art Society who will give it to the new Orchestra Committee when appointed on Thursday of this week.

I am very glad indeed to learn from the newspaper clippings that you are having such fine success.

Very truly yours,

W. N. Frew

Frew had had enough. This is the briefest of notes to a man with whom Frew had worked for almost four years. There is no retrospective;

no reflection on the work of the past. Frew had come to the conclusion that the fight to shape Herbert to the goals that the committee shared was futile. The loss of the support of this dedicated and fair-minded individual would prove fatal to Herbert's future at Pittsburgh. But it is doubtful whether Herbert—in the throes of a tremendous success with his own orchestra and on the verge of his greatest decade as a composer, a decade that would witness the creation of *Babes in Toyland*, *Mlle. Modiste*, and *Naughty Marietta*—realized the importance of Frew's departure; or if he did, whether he cared.

The Orchestra Committee that presided over the final years of Herbert's tenure was, with two exceptions, composed of new members. J. B. Shea was Frew's immediate replacement as chairman, but James I. Buchanan soon took the reins, and it fell to him to deal with the problems of Herbert's last years with the orchestra.

The season of 1902–03 was distinguished by two important events, one positive and auspicious for the future, one providing ammunition for Herbert's detractors. In December, Fritzi Scheff, the "Viennese firecracker," who was one of the most popular stars of the Metropolitan Opera, appeared as soloist. She sang the two Cherubino arias and a selection of Viennese lieder for her second group. "There has never been a singer at Carnegie Music Hall to whom the audience took a more enthusiastic fancy," raved the *Dispatch* on December 6, 1902. Fritzi caught Victor's eye with a delightful combination of theatrical verve and musical expertise. It was after this concert that Herbert began a campaign to convince Scheff that her future lay in the world of operetta. He wrote some of his strongest works for her. The first, *Babette*, marked her Broadway stage debut. This was quickly followed by *Mlle. Modiste*, whose score contains Herbert's most popular vocal composition, "Kiss Me Again," a number that became associated with Scheff through a career that lasted fifty years. In the 1950s, on a special radio series devoted to the history of the American musical theater, she sang it beautifully for her interviewer, Mike Wallace. When he asked her why she had moved from the Met to Broadway she replied with a chuckle, "That's an easy question. Mr. Dillingham paid me $1000 a week. It was the money!"[117]

Herbert's relationship with "his boys" continued its comradely course, with the exception of a squeaky wheel, the cellist Gaston Borsch. Borsch was another of the interesting characters Herbert seemed to attract during his career: a competent instrumentalist, but a man lacking financial responsibility and who fancied himself a potential successor to Herbert as conductor! At one point he wrote to Wilson[118] about his financial troubles, complaining that he was stranded in Indianapolis, with no money for transportation to reach Pittsburgh in time for rehearsals, while at the same time recounting tales of his success as a conductor in Lausanne. It is with this background in mind that we read his letter of March, 1903, resigning from the orchestra. The letter is important, not so much for its content—although the charges contained are substantial and believable—but because the letter made news in the national press under such headlines as: "SAYS HERBERT IS VULGAR" and "CONDUCTOR OF PITTSBURGH ORCHESTRA IS TOO VULGAR."

In the letter to the Orchestra Committee Borsch claims that he had said before coming to Pittsburgh that he would not be interested in a season of just twenty weeks. He states that he auditioned for Herbert and was offered the position of second solo cellist. He continues:[119]

> Herbert induced me to take that position telling me that it would mean much longer engagement, as he intended to take a larger part of the orchestra on a concert tour after the Pittsburgh season, and I, as second solo cellist, would be sure to continue my engagement as long as the orchestra was together.

> These were the conditions on which I accepted the position. Since the beginning of the season Mr. Herbert has, for personal reasons, changed his mind, and without giving me any notice has made other arrangements amongst the cellists for his Spring tour. He has thus broken his agreement with me.

Borsch then proceeds from the legal to the personal:

> Mr. Herbert treats the members of the orchestra in such a rough and vulgar way that the Art Society will find the orchestra to be less good every year, instead of improving—as no musician that is good enough to do something else would submit to Mr. Herbert's ungentlemanly manners and personal insults. I, for my part, find it impossible, and Mr. Herbert, as the Art Society's representative in this question having broken his agreement with me, find I am not bound to stand his treatment and I refuse to work with him.

> If Mr. Herbert has personal reasons to insult me, his position as conductor of the orchestra does not entitle him to do so during rehearsals and concerts.
> Yours very respectfully,
> Gaston Borsch

The reaction of the orchestra was immediate. The personnel issued a statement branding Borsch's charges "absurd and malicious."[120] They further asserted that "Mr. Herbert always has been gentlemanly and has treated us more as friend than as employer." Herbert's only public comment was that Borsch was not up to the standard of the organization and that a better man had been procured.

What are we to make of this? Perhaps that Herbert was, indeed, vulgar in his comments during rehearsals and performances; there is just too much anecdotal evidence to deny this. That Herbert played favorites? We know he did. Now, it is possible that Borsch auditioned and played well enough for Herbert to be assigned second chair, and that his playing deteriorated during the season to the point where Herbert dropped him from the tour. Shall we give Herbert the benefit of the doubt?

Unfortunately there is more going on here; but this information did not surface until after Herbert left the orchestra. On May 31, 1904, shortly after Herbert's departure, Wilson received a letter from Borsch after Emil Pauer had been announced as the new conductor of the orchestra. In this letter Borsch reveals his agenda: "I had hoped there would be a competition for the position of Director—but an unknown man has but little chance in this country. It is the great names people want!!—and what there is in a man never gets a chance to show off."

In spite of this outburst, Wilson brought Borsch back to the orchestra. In a letter of June 4, 1904, Borsch accepts a contract as cellist, commenting: "I hope to have better luck this time!!" Thus we have the two parts to the puzzle. Borsch wanted a chance to conduct, and he was clearly a friend of Wilson. These are two very good reasons Herbert might have wanted him removed. All of this is significant because it throws light on the unstable situation growing during Herbert's penultimate season.

The reviews from the road tours of the orchestra reflected the combination of positive critical reception and poor attendance that had characterized the previous season's reception. Following the conclusion of the regular season tour, Herbert again took selected members of the orchestra on his own outing, advertised under the name "Victor Herbert's Orchestra." On some of the stops of this tour the newspapers reported, with no little horror, that beer was served while the orchestra was playing. Writing from beery Baltimore, Herbert defended the right of sponsors to serve any beverage they chose.[121]

It had become more and more obvious to the Orchestra Committee that the concerts of the Victor Herbert Orchestra, programmed to cater to the popular taste, were proving far more successful than the classical offerings of the Pittsburgh Orchestra. In fact, what was happening was what Frew had feared and tried to prevent through the contract language he had developed the year before: the Victor Herbert Orchestra was providing the most competition the Pittsburgh Orchestra had known. Herbert had become the Art Society's worst enemy.

The story of Herbert's final season at Pittsburgh should be read in the context of his other activities. He had already created two of his greatest stage works, *The Fortune Teller* and *Babes in Toyland,* and was firmly established as the outstanding American composer of musical entertainments of his time. Although the works of George M. Cohan and Harrigan and Hart were as popular, the artistic level that Herbert brought to his achievement was unique and recognized as such by his contemporaries. Further, the success of the Victor Herbert Orchestra, both on tour and in sit-down engagements at Saratoga and Willow Grove Park, was unmatched by any other American musical organization, with the possible exception of Sousa's Band. In short, Herbert was at the height of his considerable powers. With this record of achievement he was not inclined to tolerate the petty problems of the Pittsburgh scene. Nevertheless, the fact that even after his resignation he offered to remain with the orchestra—albeit on his own terms—shows that he was hesitant to relinquish the role of symphony conductor. That role still held a challenge for him, and he realized that the music critics who pointed out his weaknesses had their point. Herbert never ran from a challenge. Had the Orchestra Committee met his terms, he would have been pleased to hone his conducting skills at their considerable expense.

The conflicts of personality and agenda that separated Wilson, the Orchestra Committee and Herbert did not abate. In late March, 1903, Wilson received a letter from an associate in Cleveland enclosing an article from the *Cleveland Press* in which the writer vigorously lauds Herbert's recent performance. "Such things are not pleasant to read," Harrison Gravely writes, firmly placing himself in the anti-Herbert camp. He then proceeds to delegitimize the encomiums by mentioning that "The writer showed such external evidences of friendship with the conductor he booms, as keeping company with him in a local Rathskeller 'till 3 A.M."[122] This sort of communication supports the evidence that Wilson and Co. were, in fact, bluenoses. This characteristic might not have been important in itself, but combined with Herbert's tendencies toward popularization of the repertoire and self-promotion, it added fuel to the flames.

On November 26, Thanksgiving Day, in a letter to James I. Buchanan, Herbert detonated his bomb.

> I enclose a letter addressed to you as Chairman of the Orchestra Committee, conveying my request that I not be considered as conductor of the orchestra after this season.
>
> I have written this early for two reasons: first, that the Committee should have ample time to select my successor; and next, that I should be in a position to announce in New York my intention of returning to that city, where important matters are dependent on my decision.
>
> With kind regards.[123]

Enclosed with the cover letter was the formal letter of resignation. It mentions that Herbert had told Wilson in August that he could not continue with the orchestra "unless the Committee could see its way clear to pay me a straight salary of $10,000.00." This represents a doubling of Herbert's compensation. He goes on to say that "the demands of my profession have become so many and so varied that I do not feel that I can afford to sacrifice them." He remarks that his decision is "based upon the broadest view I can take of my professional future and not upon any small or local considerations. The difficulties I have met have been the ones usually inseparable from the task of establishing a new orchestra in a new place, and it has been a labor of great interest and pleasure to me to overcome these difficulties."[124] Herbert attributes that "pleasure" to the fine orchestra, to the loyal support of the Pittsburgh public, to everything done by the Committee and to the support of the Press; to everybody but Wilson.

The Orchestra Committee lost no time in acknowledging Herbert's letter.[125] Both "regret and surprise" are expressed at Herbert's "positively determined" decision. The situation is "reluctantly accepted" and the Committee "unanimously tender their "gratitude" for his "splendid work" and conclude, "Wherever your future may lead, you will take with you the good will of ourselves and that also of the entire cultivated public of this community."

That should have ended the matter. But nothing in Herbert's career was that simple. The exchange of letters was released to the press and in an interview with the *Leader*, Herbert made it clear that it was his career as a stage composer he referenced when mentioning the "demands of his profession."

My comic opera successes, coming coincidental with contracts to furnish three elaborate compositions next year, necessitates my residence in the metropolis. My attention has been so steadily directed to the Pittsburgh Orchestra that I have had no opportunity to give the proper time to my composition.[126]

Wilson, contacted by the *Dispatch*, "refused to talk at any length upon Mr. Herbert's resignation," but he released the Orchestra Committee's acceptance letter as self-explanatory. Seen at his home that evening Herbert confessed that he had "been desirous of retiring from the orchestra for some time past and had only remained as long as he had as a matter of sentiment, to the detriment of his business interests."[127]

Sentiment was the order of the day when Herbert acknowledged to the men of the orchestra that the rumors of his departure were in fact true. "Tears came to the eyes of many of the musicians, for to them all, Herbert was more of a friend than a conductor."[128]

Soon the rumor mill began to churn out its dross. Herbert had requested $18,000.00 worth of acoustical improvements in the Hall; when the Committee turned him down he resigned. Carnegie had promised to underwrite a European tour for the orchestra. When he changed his mind, Herbert resigned.[129] The press had a field day, and was present in full force at Herbert's first appearance with the orchestra following the publication of his letter of resignation. He is described as being "in tears" at the concert. In a curtain speech he is quoted as desiring to follow the promptings of his heart, "but my head dictates this move. Even my wife and children almost weep at leaving the home and friends they have made here and you see how deeply I am moved by what has occurred this evening."[130] He went on to praise the Pittsburgh musical public for its "keen discrimination and cultured musical intelligence."[131]

The period from January to April 1904 was one of constant turmoil, characterized by an unceasing chorus of rumors and counterrumors: Herbert had resigned; the orchestra had begged the Art Society to urge him to reconsider his position; the guarantors were fed up with him; the guarantors were willing to continue their support—but only on condition that Herbert remain as conductor; Wilson was leaving; Wilson was completely in charge and the Committee had become disengaged from the process; the problem was that the programs were too high-brow; too low-brow. The press reported every thrust and parry with equal emphasis.

Was Herbert sincere in his letter of resignation, or was it only a ploy in a subtle campaign to restructure the situation to his advantage? Was

Herbert a master Machiavellian manipulator of people and public opinion? These questions need to be answered, because the answers will tell us something essential about Herbert. If, indeed, he had become manipulative, this would be something new. The Herbert we know is bluff and gifted, personally vastly appealing to many, musically by turns demanding and insulting, secure and insecure, hot-headed and sentimental, an easy touch and a tough negotiator when it came to money matters. This package of contrasts and contradictions could be off-putting, but it was always honest. What you saw was what you got. Herbert was anything but a games player.

The best evidence we have that Herbert had not changed is found in a private communication to his old friend Ludewig Schenk. Schenk, a former colleague of Herbert's in the New York String Quartet, was at this time in residence at Rochester, New York. He was a private teacher who would soon join the original faculty of the Eastman School of Music. On January 23, Herbert writes:

> My dear Ludewig!
>
> Okay. Try to bring us [the Victor Herbert Orchestra] to Rochester (maybe in the 3rd week in May.) It should be easy for you to find sufficient "guarantors."
>
> Next winter I'm going to New York, (I have resigned here, that is after the expiration of my contract) and if you want to go back there (to New York City) wouldn't I be delighted if we could make music together again. Naturally I will have my own orchestra and I'll be in control of all matters [*nach wie vor bei den Spitze sein*].
>
> With warmest greetings
> Your [dein]
> Victor Herbert[132]

This private, personal letter to an old friend reveals two important things: first, that Herbert was completely sincere in his announced intention to leave the orchestra; second, that he really was fed up with having to trim his sails to the windy whims of committees and administrators. He wanted to do things his own way and had had enough of "team playing." This is the Herbert we know!

Shortly before his resignation, Herbert seized an opportunity to rid himself of his old gadfly Professor Foerster. Foerster had sent him the score of his latest masterwork, "At Twilight." Herbert responded with a devastating technical musical critique, the sort of thing a first-year student of harmony and orchestration might have received from a demanding master.

Dear Sir—

I cannot find enough merit in your "At Twilight" to give it a place on one of the Pittsburgh Orchestra programs. The orchestration is much too thick and boisterous for a piece of such character.

There are also quite a number of offenses against clean harmony in the piece; for instance [there follow several musical examples of poor orchestration and incorrect harmony].

In view of these facts I cannot comply with your request and herewith return your manuscript.[133]

Foerster withdrew from the field of combat.

It wasn't long before the Committee's mail box began to fill with conflicting communications. Soprano Lillian Blauvelt offers her free services at any concert honoring the departing conductor. Her letter is chock full of positive comments on Herbert, the orchestra and Pittsburgh. On the other hand, there was this from James B. Oliver, President of Oliver Iron and Steel, a major patron of the orchestra, expressing long pent-up dissatisfaction with the programs. The letter also provides new insight into the valuable role Wilson played in mollifying the guarantors.

I have been thinking over the matter of the Pittsburgh Orchestra next year, and I have decided that I will not be a guarantor. I have not enjoyed these concerts, either last year or the year before. I spoke to Mr. Wilson about the music that Herbert was dishing up to us a year ago, and told him it was not acceptable to me and lot of others. I would have drawn out last year if it had not been for Mr. Wilson.

Possibly a change will be beneficial, but while it is going on I will stay out, and have my family go to the afternoon concerts if they want to. I simply would not be bored going out to the East End and listening to the kind of music Mr. Herbert has been giving us. No doubt it is high class, but it has never been pleasing to me.[134]

On February 14, Gustave Schlotterbeck, critic of the *Post*, provided a two-sided valentine, praising Herbert's contribution ("This Hercules of the baton has not been given the consideration his merits fairly deserve") and balancing the scales thus: "Mr. Herbert has his decided weaknesses: he is not always the perfection of diplomacy and often does he permit a red-hot temperament to override his coolness of judgement."

The press commentary was as muddled as the orchestra situation; rather than providing perspective and insight, it added to the problem.

The next day the Committee received a letter "on behalf of the members of the Pittsburgh Orchestra," signed by Henneberg, Mertz and Burck. The letter misfired. While praising Herbert and his achievement and asking for the Committee's aid in an appeal to Herbert to reconsider his decision, it clearly contains a veiled threat: "His withdrawal from Pittsburgh might involve some changes, possibly more than a few, in the permanent personnel of the Orchestra, and a consequent impairment of its efficiency."[135] With this letter was enclosed a copy of one to Herbert, expressing the orchestra's regret, praising his achievement, mentioning their reverence and admiration, his genius and grateful personality, begging him to reconsider his decision.

A note from Wilson to Buchanan from Detroit, where the Orchestra was on tour, did nothing to aid Herbert's cause:

> Detroit
> 2/17/04
>
> There has been only one blot on this trip, the persistent vulgarity of Mr. Herbert, which has continually made me ashamed. I wrote Mr. Smith [E. Z. Smith, acting chairman of the Orchestra Committee] yesterday of this freely.[136]

On February 26 Wilson received anti-Herbert ammunition of another sort. Arthur W. Tams, owner of one of the great international music libraries, refused to send the Pittsburgh Orchestra any more music. His letter to Wilson places the reason for the cutoff squarely at Herbert's door:

> I note what you say in regard to Mr. Herbert continually finding fault with the orchestra scores furnished by my library, and I am glad of the opportunity of saying, that if Mr. Herbert is correctly quoted by numerous artists, he continually finds fault with my music; and I expect this, as I believe his sympathies are with another concern [Isidore Witmark] naturally where he publishes his music; and while I value the business that you send and the business from the Pittsburgh Orchestra, if Mr. Herbert is correctly quoted, I am not at all anxious to send any music for his use, as I do not want to give him an opportunity of finding fault with music that receives nothing but praise from other directors in this country; and there are others besides Mr. Herbert, in which, I believe, you will agree with me.[137]

Thus, Herbert's badmouthing of the Tams library to all and sundry had come home to haunt him.

In the midst of all this, relief was provided by the arrival of Dr. Richard Strauss and his wife, Pauline de Ahna, as guest conductor and soloist with the orchestra. After a warm-up concert in Cleveland on March 10, the great composer led the orchestra in a concert of his tone poems and lieder. The Strausses were house guests of the Herberts, and the master signed Ella's autograph book, "in remembrance of the most delightful evening spent in your parents' beautiful home in Pittsburgh."[138]

One of the more amusing events of this otherwise tense period occurred when, before the first concert, photographers appeared to memorialize the great event. As Strauss mounted the podium it was noticed that one of the bass players was missing from his position. Herbert sprang into action, ran to the back of the orchestra and placed himself behind the instrument, bow in hand, where he is pictured for posterity. Then in a moment of antic humor worthy of the composer of "Till," Strauss ran to the bass stand and replaced Herbert among the orchestral troops. Herbert picked up his cue and mounted the podium in Strauss's place. Thus we have the only photograph of Herbert conducting Strauss, famous bass fiddle virtuoso. After the Strauss episode the members of the orchestra strove to regain the atmosphere of sport and fun that had surfaced all too rarely in recent days. Knowing how Herbert loved jokes, they tried to restore his good humor. It had been decided before one rehearsal on March 17 that, instead of playing the overture to *The Flying Dutchman*, they would surprise him by playing "The Wearin' of the Green." Herbert came to the stand—a frown on his usually friendly face. "Overture," he called, lifting his baton. The full orchestra intoned the Irish tune. Expecting to hear the strains of *The Flying Dutchman*, he angrily stopped conducting. Then, immediately recognizing the familiar tune, he conducted it enthusiastically to the end. Everybody was laughing, including the conductor.[139]

The next day, articles in the press noted that the orchestra contracts were due to expire on March 19, and speculated that the best members of the ensemble would no doubt scatter to the four winds in search of more secure employment, thus destroying the body of the seasoned orchestra. There were calls for a delegation to Herbert to attempt to induce him to remain. There was a rumor that Damrosch had been offered $15,000 by Wilson, and that now it would be impossible to retain Herbert for less than that sum. All this gloom and doom was countered by reports that new guarantors, led by Frew, were coming out of the woodwork ready to see to it that the orchestra would not collapse, and that a groundswell of pro-Herbert sentiment was rising in the town. Then Herbert pulled a Sherman:

> I will not remain in Pittsburgh. I made up my mind to leave last Fall. I gave my landlord notice that I would relinquish the lease on my house. I have resigned from the local clubs. I have looked up the freight rates to New York. Does this look as if I intended remaining in Pittsburgh? Does it give any basis for the rumors that I would open negotiations with the Committee and consent to a contract for next year?
>
> I am ready to go immediately upon the close of the concert series. I have received no offer, formal or informal, from the Committee. I certainly shall make no overtures myself. The story published about my choosing to remain here is ridiculous. It is trash.[140]

Then, two days later, there was this:

> In a letter written to the Pittsburgh Orchestra Committee I said that $10,000.00 was the salary I asked for my services. More money than that will now be necessary to retain my services, but I can be induced to remain in the city.[141]

The Orchestra Committee read these conflicting statements and shook its collective head. It had issued a general appeal to the public and to the guarantors for a commitment for the new season of $40,000. It decided that no further action was possible until that amount had been unconditionally pledged. Friends of Herbert had made their pledges, totaling $16,000, conditional upon his retention. The Committee responded that such conditional pledges were not acceptable.

In the meantime, Wilson had been actively attempting to find a replacement for Herbert. The Committee claimed that it had no knowledge of a $15,000 offer to Damrosch. The conductor then showed the written evidence to Schlotterbeck at the *Post*, who published the information that he had seen the documents on March 6. It was reported at the same time that Felix Mottl and Alfred Herz had been approached by Wilson and that he had cabled Henry J. Wood, a prominent conductor in London, with an offer. The Committee claimed to have no knowledge of this. But the impression was given that the new Orchestra Committee had given

Wilson carte blanche to find a replacement and that "There was only one head" on the Committee—and that was Wilson's. Now all the old stories about the Herbert-Wilson animosity were trotted out; the pressure grew, and on March 16 Buchanan transmitted the following memo to Herbert. It constitutes a litany of official grievances, and is hardly calculated to change the conductor's determination to exit the scene:

> Standard of programs at out-of-town concerts to be as high as those of Pittsburgh. Very few encores at out-of-town concerts. "No use of Pittsburgh Orchestra name on so-called 'Spring tours'" or anywhere outside the control of the Committee.
>
> No competition for business between the "Spring tour" management and the management of the regular season: The regular season management to say what field or cities it will not visit in a given season. Conductor to exercise control of all encores of singers.
>
> While the Committee welcome occasionally compositions by its conductor, it does not approve of the general use of his compositions, in either the home programs or those abroad.
>
> The Committee requires fewer if any encores by the orchestra.
>
> The Committee to exercise supervision over all musical matters whenever in their opinion it becomes necessary.[142]

In other words, stop playing low-brow stuff out of town; cut the encores; don't associate us with your private enterprises; we have first refusal on all out-of-town dates and venues; stop playing so much Victor Herbert music; and, by the way, we have final say in all musical matters. One wonders why they bothered.

Where did this manifesto come from? Not, apparently, from the Committee, although it was transmitted to Herbert from them. The copy in the Carnegie Library archive contains a crayoned note: "Proffered to V. H. on March 16, 1904, by Mr. Buchanan," with the signature "Hall" at the bottom of the page. "Hall" was Robert C. Hall, investment broker, and generous guarantor of the orchestra who had written to Buchanan as follows:

> As a guarantor please allow me to write you a personal letter commending your businesslike and dignified position in the Pittsburgh

Orchestra situation, both of yourself, and of the Committee. I am perfectly content to leave the matter in the Committee's hands, and I know a right decision will be made.

Personally, I prefer a change of conductors as I think we are all tired of Mr. Herbert, and that the whole situation will take the new interest with a new leader, but as I said before I am willing to leave this matter to the judgement of the Committee.

In the event of absolute failure staring the Committee in the face I would be one of five or ten to double my guarantee rather than see the orchestra fail, although I don't feel able, at the present time, to incur this expense, unless absolutely necessary, but you may count on me in an emergency."[143]

At this point Herbert had not yet received the Committee "offer," because he was in Philadelphia to speak at a meeting of the Clover Club. His topic was "True Art." In his speech he responded to a report in the *Dispatch* that "It is understood that the assurance of Manager Wilson to the Art Committee was that if given full rein he would bring the season to a close next year with a profit instead of a loss."[144]

True Art must be supported. It must be placed above the mere level of business opportunity and the box office receipts. It is to the public and the education of the public that we must turn for aid. Men must be taught to have ideals. The man that has not an ideal is a pig! That is the truth![145]

And so the gloves were off at last as Herbert mounted the podium for the final concerts of his Pittsburgh career. The pair of concerts that concluded his tenure were the scene of an out-pouring of affection and respect from the guarantors, the general public and the orchestra. There were presentations after each number—a huge silver and gold loving cup inscribed, "To Victor Herbert from his many Pittsburgh admirers," huge bouquets of flowers that Herbert distributed to all the members of the ensemble, a five-minute standing ovation at his first appearance, "Auld Lang Syne" sung by all present at the end of the concert. At the afternoon concert there was a spontaneous improvisation begun by the organ, joined by the strings and then the rest of the orchestra, of Handel's "See the Conquering Hero Comes." At both performances speeches were demanded. At the evening session there was a brief expression of gratitude in which Herbert thanked all those to whose appreciation he said the success of the orchestra was due.[146] But after the final concert, which ended with a rousing performance of "Triumph" from his "Columbus" Suite, he was unable to speak. "He could only stammer out his desire to speak as he felt, but that his physical condition was such that he felt unequal to the task and beyond a few thanks and a tear-stained face, the leader could do no more."[147] The finality of the situation had grasped him. As the audience once again rose with the orchestra to sing "Auld Lang Syne," "Herbert's smile suddenly melted and he walked from the stage with bowed head."[148]

In his dressing room after the concert the previous evening, Herbert and his soloist, Ernestine Schumann-Heink, had given a remarkable joint interview: "There is nothing for me to say about the orchestra situation," he began. "With the concert of tomorrow afternoon my connection with the organization known as the Pittsburgh Orchestra ceases, though as the Victor Herbert Orchestra it continues."[149]

Here Herbert was spelling out just what his intentions were. He would, at his own risk, literally take the orchestra on tour and perhaps co-opt its membership for his purposes back in New York. His letter to Ludewig Schenk had stated clearly that course as his intent, but the fact that he tipped his hand publicly is truly amazing. Was this an attempt to shock the Orchestra Committee into moving in his direction in fear of losing its ensemble to him? Perhaps, because he continues with an opening to the Committee:

> I would be without a heart and without feeling if I were not touched by what has occurred. They say that some of the guarantors have conditioned their subscriptions on my continuing as conductor. Solicitations have come to me personally and by letter at my home expressing deep regrets that my departure should be considered. I am not heartless. These things influence and sway me. I can sincerely say I would like to stay in Pittsburgh.[150]

To which "the Heink" added:

> I do not know what the difficulty is relative to Mr. Herbert and the orchestra. But it is quite a pity that he should be allowed to leave. He is a great musician and a fine artist.[151]

At the conclusion of the evening performance, Schumann-Heink and a number of Herbert's friends celebrated the successful evening informally at his home. At the same time, another group of friends gathered at the Hotel Schenley and decided to appoint a delegation to consult with the conductor to find out just what they might say to the Art Society when they "took the stand that the public is demanding that he stay at the head of the orchestra."[152] The group then joined the party at Aiken Avenue, as it was at this meeting and over the course of the next week that a list of Herbert's demands was developed in response to Buchanan's recent memo. The response acknowledges the influence of Herbert's friends, but is couched in terms of a personal expression from the composer. It was forwarded to the Orchestra Committee on March 25th.

At the urgent request of friends Mr. Herbert has decided to say to the Orchestra Committee that he is willing to abandon other plans formed and remain as conductor provided existing conditions are changed.

1st. Mr. Herbert would require the present manager to be superceded by another satisfactory to both the Committee and himself.

2nd. Salary to be fixed at $10,000 for the season to consist of 20 weeks and pro rata for extra four or five weeks.

3rd. The right to engage players for 25 weeks instead of 20 weeks.

4th. The use of the name "Pittsburgh Orchestra" to be entirely under the control of the committee.

5th. Standard of out-of-town concerts must be left to the judgement of the conductor.

6th. Will agree that there shall be no competition for business between the Spring Tour management and the management of the regular season. The lowest price for the orchestra to be fixed by the committee. The regular management to say what fields or cities it will not visit in a given season. The conductor will exercise control of all encores of soloists when made part of contracts with soloists.

7th. The conductor will welcome frequent meetings with the committee to discuss plans to enlarge the money making scope of the orchestra and other features, but reserves the right to settle all artistic questions.[153]

The Committee responded immediately in the following memo:

To the guarantors of the Pittsburgh Orchestra, 9th Season, 1903–04.

We received on 11/26/03 a letter from Mr. Victor Herbert, requesting us not to consider him a possible conductor of the Orchestra after the expiration of his contract on 3/19/04 on account of the demands of his profession in another direction, which he could not afford to sacrifice. In reluctantly accepting the situation the Committee unanimously tendered to Mr. Herbert their gratitude for his splendid work. Subsequently, at the urgent request of his friends, Mr. Herbert decided to say to the Committee that he was willing to abandon his plans and remain as conductor on *conditions to which we are unable to accede.*[154]

Soon someone leaked Herbert's demands to the press. Wilson had been in New York on business and, on his return, in response to an article maintaining that his problems with Herbert were the main reason for the resignation, denied that friction existed between himself and Herbert. He was then asked, "If Victor Herbert would consent to remain conductor on condition that you resign, would you resign?"

Wilson responded, "I would not for a minute stand in the way of the success of the Pittsburgh Orchestra. If the Art Society asked me to resign I would certainly do so. I have too much personal pride to remain if it were wished that I were out. I have the best interests of the Pittsburgh Orchestra at heart, and will be guided in my future actions with the steadfast desire to relieve the present most trying situation."

At this point another story appeared in the press that hurt the fundraising campaign badly. Apparently Frew had approached Carnegie unofficially to ask him to guarantee $20,000 per year for three years to preserve the orchestra. "It would be lamentable to have the report go abroad that Pittsburgh was no longer able or willing to maintain the orchestra," Frew was quoted as having cabled Carnegie.[155]

Carnegie turned him down flat: "It would indeed be lamentable, but it would be more lamentable to have the report go abroad that Pittsburgh was only able to maintain its orchestra by the assistance of outsiders resident in New York."[156]

On several occasions, when Carnegie learned that there had been financial need for some Carnegie Institute purpose, he had been quoted as asking, "Why did you not let me know about this?"[157] What had happened?

Apparently, Herbert's temper had once again worked to his disadvantage. During the previous few weeks while the resignation controversy was raging, Carnegie had come to Pittsburgh on business and had scheduled a noon luncheon with Herbert. The great man arrived at the institute that bore his name while Herbert was still rehearsing the orchestra. The rehearsal was, as usual, closed, and Carnegie was forced to cool his heels in the grande foyer. Herbert continued his rehearsal. At one point he was informed that Carnegie had been waiting for him for thirty minutes. "Andrew Carnegie can go to hell!" Herbert shouted.

Carnegie's short fuse was as volatile as Herbert's. When the conductor appeared in the foyer at last, he found that Carnegie had left, taking with him any hope of Herbert having a future in Pittsburgh.[158]

In the shadow of the continuing problems of conductor, committee and manager, financial revelations came to light. The success of the orchestra under Herbert may have been debatable from an artistic point of view, but from the standpoint of a committee of hard-headed businessmen, it was anything but successful. No one expected the orchestra to be self-sustaining. But the trends that were now revealed were troubling. In an attempt to appeal to a wider public for funding guarantees, the Committee released the following information: The yearly deficit during Herbert's tenure ranged from 22 to 29 thousand dollars. The deficit for the current season had grown to 32 thousand dollars, an increase of almost 30 percent over the previous season's average. Subscription sales had fallen from 25,000 in 1901 to 17,000 for the season of 1903–04, a decrease of 25 percent.[159]

The appeal was successful, and on March 25 it was announced that the required guarantees had been subscribed. On the same date Herbert forwarded his demands to the Orchestra Committee and announced plans to take the Pittsburgh Orchestra on an extended tour as "Victor Herbert's Orchestra." He announced, laughingly, that he planned to have an orchestra of his own in the fall and that "many of my Pittsburgh players are to accompany me to New York."[160]

On March 26, the Orchestra Committee chose Emil Paur as Herbert's successor. Immediately, Wilson provided a private memorandum on personnel and repertoire that is a catalogue of his long-pent-up discontents:

> Outside of Pittsburgh, it is unavoidable to play music of the lighter kind; but discrimination should be used and the orchestra should never descend so far from its level as to give renditions and encores from, e.g. "Dolly Varden," "Florodora," "Mr. Dooley," and the like, as has been done before—although under a conductor like Emil Paur, there will not be any danger of that. . . .
>
> As for the Pittsburgh programs, only works of real merit should be selected.

He goes on to evaluate certain members of the orchestra, with special reference to Herbert's favorites:

> Henri Burck—Undesirable, since he owes his position and title "second concertmaster" only to a long standing personal friendship with Victor Herbert.

A couple are labeled "undesirable for reasons known."

> Second Trumpet—Otto Kegel. Mr. Herbert's valet and as such scarcely desirable.
> Tuba—Mr. Herbert's faithful servant. As a player not of much merit.[161]

Wilson received this, from W. J. Dunham in Buffalo:

> I have laid very low and kept watch and have heard a good deal, but said nothing. I know that the large-headed gentleman was extremely anxious to remain in Pittsburgh and I think it was the disappointment of his life that he did not down you and stay there. I congratulate you and the Committee.[162]

This last communication is highly creditable, since it comes from a man who was an intimate of Hobart Weed, a Buffalo publisher and close friend of Herbert. Herbert had dedicated his Cathedral Anthem, "Christ is Risen," to Weed and had been in Buffalo for the premiere in early April of 1904. This expression of Herbert's private feelings no doubt occurred during his visit.

Emil Paur proved to be a poor choice for Pittsburgh. He was "an egotistical and overbearing man who succeeded in wrecking the Pittsburgh Orchestra."[163] Ironically, because of extreme conflicts with Paur, Wilson resigned at the end of the 1905–06 season but remained manager of the Concert Hall until his death in 1909. The orchestra predeceased him. In an interview with *Musical America* in 1906, Herbert, looking back on this troubled history, confided the real reason why he dispensed with the services of the guarantors of the Pittsburgh Orchestra: "they wanted me to play "Annie Rooney" instead of Beethoven and Wagner."[164]

Perhaps we should conclude with the comments of two eyewitnesses. Fritz Stahlberg, Herbert's protégée recalled, "In leaving Pittsburgh for New York to devote time to the composing of lighter music and the giving of concerts of a more popular character, Mr. Herbert was only doing the inevitable thing. He could hardly have gone on with his talent swinging like a pendulum from Symphony to Comic Opera and back again."[165]

But the conductor Wallace Munro, a Pittsburgh friend and admirer of Herbert, sums it up best: "If Herbert had an enemy in the world—it was himself."[166]

CHAPTER 5

CODA BRILLIANTE—THE VICTOR HERBERT ORCHESTRA (1901–1924)

The story of the remarkable organization known as the Victor Herbert Orchestra began in the last three years of Herbert's residency at Pittsburgh. Immediately after announcing his resignation, Herbert openly declared his intention to form his own orchestra in New York City. "Victor Herbert Coming Here," headlined the *New York Times*.[1] "Will organize an orchestra and he intends that it shall be the foremost musical organization in the country. 'I expect to die in harness,'" is the way Herbert expressed his continuing commitment to the role of conductor. The article notes that Herbert will conduct a spring tour, with sit-down engagements at Willow Grove Park, near Philadelphia, and at Saratoga Springs, New York. On-the-road touring and his performances at Willow Grove and Saratoga encompass almost all the activities of the orchestra from the time of its establishment in 1901 until Herbert's death in 1924. There were early engagements in Buffalo from 1901 to 1904 and in Baltimore from 1901 to 1905; but Willow Grove, between 1901 and 1923, was the venue with which the orchestra became associated in the mind of the public, and it was the place where Herbert was happiest in the role of conductor. Because Herbert's activities with respect to each of these venues were somewhat different, it will be useful to discuss them separately.

SARATOGA: CONDUCTOR AND BON VIVANT

Herbert's association with Saratoga Springs began a decade before he arrived with his own ensemble in 1902. From 1892 through 1894 his Buffalo friend, John Lund, conducted a small ensemble, of which Herbert was a member. The group appeared at the Grand Union Hotel, the greatest of the many elaborate hostelries that lined Broadway in those halcyon days.

> At all hours of the day the piazza is a favorite resort of hotel guests, who here linger in *dolce far niente* to listen to the sweet strains of the hotel orchestra—not a mere band of music makers, but a gathering of

trained artists, playing selections of highest merit, and conducted by a director of national reputation.[2]

Now, years later, every day at 10 A.M. on the broad piazza facing Broadway and again in the evening under the elms of the hotel court, surrounded by fountains playing softly under colored lights, Herbert's own orchestra continued a musical tradition that had been described by an observer of the Saratoga scene a half-century before: "Music flows toward us from the ballroom in languid, luxurious measures, like warm, voluptuous arms wreathing around us and drawing us to the dance."[3]

Writing in the *Saratogian* in 1952, the mayor of Saratoga mourned the passing of this last of the great ladies of hospitality, and especially one particular adornment of her finery:

> It would be remiss not to speak feelingly and fondly of the popular Grand Union Café and Bar as it was conducted in those days. Here of a summer evening might be seen prominent horsemen, top-liners from the theatrical profession, book-makers, politicians, musicians and bon vivants. At one table would be Eddie Foy and Lew Fields. . . . And of course promptly following the evening concert, Victor Herbert with some of his cronies would take possession of his reserved table, where a lengthy session would ensue over their pilsner.[4]

Music publisher Edward B. Marks, a friend of Herbert, picks up the story:

> Herbert's throat was unquenchable. One night the bartender walked over to Herbert's table and asked, "How are the pilsners tonight?"
>
> "Perfect," replied Victor. "Couldn't be better."
>
> "Victor, my boy," said the bartender, slapping the cellist on the back, "we two have studied our professions."
>
> "By God, you're right," said Herbert, appreciative of the correct temperature and foamed collar of his beer.[5]

As fortunate as Herbert was with his music, the scales were balanced by his ill luck at the track. He loved to bet, but had no talent for it, and the rumor was that despite the astronomical fees he commanded for his music, he never took a cent home from Saratoga. One evening he entered the bar and proclaimed, "I will play Wagner no more!" Then, to the astonished musicians assembled, he revealed that "Wagner" was a horse on which he had lost a whole week's salary. It was the only time his favorite composer let him down. After that he refused to place bets himself, and sent others to pick the winners for him. "I know you'll do better for me," he said, "because no one could do worse."[6]

Saratoga provided a beautiful respite for Herbert, especially during the tension-filled final years at Pittsburgh. It was a place of healing and restoration. Monty Woolley eulogized it best: "There was in those days a wonderful slow tempo to life. Even the weather was warmer. God, what a lovely time it was to live."[7]

WILLOW GROVE PARK: ENTERTAINER AND EDUCATOR

Once upon a time, a short distance from Philadelphia, there stood a lovely park, "Philadelphia's Fairyland—the Music Lover's Paradise." "The Grove," as the locals called it, was created in the first years of the twentieth century by the Philadelphia Traction and Rapid Transit Company to make money. Some things don't change. Today, where once fountains played in the "Garden Spot of the World which rivals the magnificence of the Arabian Nights,"[8] where thousands escaped the oppressive heat of the city and strolled by willow-shaded reflecting pools, there stands one of America's great shopping malls, where piped Musak and recycled air immeasurably enrich the lives of modern Philadelphians. But back in those benighted days of Victor Herbert, the "highest class music in the world" was heard there, including the ensembles of Herbert, Sousa and Damrosch. In fact, Walter Damrosch had conceived the idea for a pavilion seating 4,000, and the great bandmaster Frederick Innes had drawn up the plans. The acoustics were said to be perfect.

The Transit Company reaped great revenues from the fares of thousands who flocked to the free concerts. Every day there were four: two in the afternoon, two in the evening, each lasting forty-five minutes. At times as many as 15,000 people could be accommodated on the vast lawns surrounding the pavilion. One newspaper report recorded 50,000 people gathered to hear a performance in 1905. There were Grand Opera nights and Wagner matinees. Every Thursday was "Herbert Day." On those occasions the audience was treated to premieres of the composer's latest compositions. Willow Grove heard "The March of the Toys" and "Toyland" before Broadway, and the enthusiastic reception given to those works told Herbert that he had another hit on his hands. But it was not only the Herbert canon and the works of famous composers that found a prominent place on his programs; American composers were given every opportunity for a hearing. The works of Harold Sanford, Victor Kolar, Henry Hadley, George W. Chadwick, Ethelbert Nevin and the man Herbert considered America's finest composer, Edward MacDowell, were regularly featured.

Herbert's Willow Grove agenda was to entertain and educate the American public, and the huge attendance he attracted was a large factor in his satisfaction with the enterprise. "It's a wonderful place," he remarked to a reporter who interviewed him in the special studio he occupied over the band shell. "With an enterprise like Willow Grove Park, which has no counterpart anywhere else in the country, the setting up of a healthy musical force may be assuredly looked for, if not, indeed, prophesied as an inevitable outcome."[9] With the exception of a two-year hiatus, Herbert led his orchestra at Willow Grove for almost a quarter of a century. At the time of his death in May 1924, he was busily preparing the programs for the summer season. It was an enterprise very dear to his heart—love at first sight for Herbert and the Grove—and he expressed his feelings as early as his inaugural season in an interview that is almost unique, since it contains a rare overtone of self-criticism. His remarks on impatience in an artist reflect a maturing of his personality and a growth of his self-knowledge, based on the Pittsburgh difficulties he was then experiencing:

> [At Willow Grove] all classes of people can unite with a delightful outing a baptism in art. . . . My programs are arranged with a regard to the cosmopolitan character of the audiences. *I sometimes think that artists are not sufficiently tolerant. Themselves trained to the highest standards they sometimes show impatience to those not up to their standards. This is a mistake* [italics mine].

> The artist [should not] give Bach and Wagner to those who enthuse over simpler music. The great object of the artist should be to furnish entertainment and education for every type of mind and every degree of development. Therefore I make it a point in my programs here to accomplish this. . . . I have noticed also that those less cultivated very rapidly show by their applause an appreciation of the classics. It is solely a question of furnishing good music, simple to some, classic to others, in the same program, finally to have a thoroughly appreciative cosmopolitan audience. . . .

> Nothing gives me so much delight as the intelligence and hearty response of the people who come here. I am sure that I am accomplishing a lot of good at Willow Grove.[10]

Although Willow Grove provided Herbert with relief from the high-tension life he had chosen, the work of performance and composition never ceased, and he used every spare minute to fulfill his commitments for the coming theatrical seasons. He once told the composer Deems Taylor that he "made it a practice to try to write at least one melody every day— which accounts for the fact that he left behind him a thousand pieces of music."[11]

Above and behind the band shell, Herbert had a private sanctum to which he retreated after each concert. A short, dark stairway led to the studio. Shedding his sweat-drenched clothing as he bustled up the stairs, he would fling collar, coat and trousers about haphazardly. They found their resting places on the music-strewn upright piano, the writing table, the sofa or the ice-box that completed his furnishings. His shirt he draped over the whirring electric fan in hopes that it might dry somewhat before the next performance.

Herbert's messy studio was well supplied with Turkish towels. With these he would vigorously dry his face, head and arms. Then, pouring himself a whiskey and soda, he would light up one of his specially made "Victor Herbert Cigars" and, seated comfortably with his chair tipped backward against the piano, his legs resting on the writing desk, he would finally relax. The Willow Grove studio was one of the few places that anyone ever saw him completely at ease. Then his good humor bubbled to the surface.

"You look quite comfortable, Mr. Herbert," one of his musicians remarked to him one day.

"There's only one drawback to this outfit, Fritz—the confounded hot ashes from my cigar drop down where they shouldn't!"[12]

In this atmosphere Herbert did some of his best educational work. He loved to talk. His manner of expression was unique—almost stenographic. Many important points were made through his use of gesture and grunts. In the studio, surrounded by men from the orchestra who dreamt of becoming composers or conductors, Herbert would lead informal seminars and share his vast experience with his "boys." This was another expression of his generosity, for his time was precious, and every hour spent mentoring was an hour torn from composing, from turning cheap sheets of music paper into thousand-dollar-bills.

"After playing a new work, he would always tell us frankly what he thought of it," Gustav Klemm recalled.

His knowledge of orchestration was second to no one's, and many were the profitable hours we spent with him, going through scores, his quick eye and vast knowledge suggesting various changes.

He conceived everything orchestrally. This was a "flute figure," that a "cello melody." He urged us always to "think orchestrally," not as a pianist:

"The trouble with the writer of today is that he relies too much on the piano. It has been said that every composer should play the instrument fluently. A fine idea, but beware of the pernicious influence it exerts on the creator. Upon writing for orchestra, he thinks only in terms of the piano. His piano technique is evidenced in the various figures appearing here and there in the score. When a youngster shows me his score I say: Where's your pedal?

"The successful composer for the orchestra must think in terms of the orchestra. Then and only then will he achieve effects that impress the listener. Of course I often make sketches and develop them at the piano—which I play only fairly well—but the ideas arrive invariably 'scored' and it is in their orchestral guise that I constantly hear them."[13]

Sometimes he would turn his attention to the tricks a music director uses to get his effects. In his remarks on conducting technique it is not surprising to find the lasting influence of Herbert's grandfather. We recall the image of the six-year-old Vic standing in the garden of the Ivy watching Samuel Lover paint. We can see the example of the artist transformed into the technique of the conductor:

Everything is in the eye, my boy. You must make everybody on the stage think you are looking straight at them all the time. Notice, for instance, a well painted portrait. Let a dozen people look at the picture from all sides and everyone will declare that the eyes of the portrait are looking straight at them; that is because the sitter looked right at the artist when the portrait was painted. So with conducting. Look at everybody at once. It's not so easy, but it's the only way.[14]

All too soon these sessions were interrupted.

"We're ready," Mr. Herbert's manager announces.

"Yes, yes," Herbert replies. "All right, my boy. I'm coming. Just tell me when the concert master finishes combing his hair."

And he pulls on his clothes and hastens away to conduct the next concert.[15]

The length of Herbert's engagements at Willow Grove varied from year to year. His first season was for two weeks, his last, for three. In between were years when the orchestra was engaged for five weeks, and two years, 1911 and 1912, when his commitments resulted in the cancellation of his appearances altogether. The selections for the programs were always chosen from the light classical repertoire, Wagner's "Huldigungsmarsch," a Mendessohn Overture ("Ruy Blas" or "Calm Sea and Prosperous Voyage"), popular operatic instrumental interludes ("Dance of the Priestesses" from *Samson and Delilah*), and novelty numbers that antedated PDQ Bach by several generations. Siegfried Ochs prepared a series of variations on the German folk song "Es kommt ein Vogel geflogen," in the style of composers from Bach to Wagner, that achieved great popularity. But far and away it was Herbert's own compositions that brought the audiences to their feet, and not only numbers from the operettas. His "American Idyll," with the famous English Horn solo "Indian Summer," was premiered in 1919.

TOURING: THE JOLLIEST AND BEST OF FELLOWS!

There have been greater orchestras than the Victor Herbert Orchestra—more polished, more intense, more sophisticated and refined. But there never was, and has not been since, an orchestra that was more fun to listen to, or to play in.

> Everybody loved Herbert. There was a boyish enthusiasm about him which captured all hearts. When he personally conducted one of his own works the joy was unbounded. He was able to compose music that was popular and yet thoroughly artistic, abounding in catchy tunes and happy details.[16]

During his first post-Pittsburgh season in New York, Herbert was showered with honors by the musical establishment and the public at large. He was the only American artist invited to conduct the New York Philharmonic during its season of guest conductors, and the *Times* saw the engagement as the "logical outcome of the five years of hard and successful pioneering work in driving high class music into the heads of the Pittsburgh public."[17]

Herbert relished the success of his orchestra's Sunday night concerts presented at the Majestic Theater, at Daly's Theater, and later at the New

York Theater. At the end of the season he arranged for a "request concert." He extended an invitation to patrons to send letters to his home containing suggestions for the program. The results of this survey yield insight into the musical taste of the New York audience, circa 1906. Topping the list were demands for selections from his own recent works, *It Happened in Nordland, Babes in Toyland,* and *Babette.* Following close on their heels were:

Overture to *Poet and Peasant*	von Suppé	1647 votes
Overture to *William Tell*	Rossini	1439 votes
Introduction to Act III *Lohengrin*	Wagner	1006 votes
March from "Leonore Symphony"	Beethoven (?)	924 votes
Melody in F	Rubinstein	804 votes
Scenes Neapolitans	Massenet	839 votes[18]

More significant than the naive quality of the selections is the number of responses. Literally thousands of New Yorkers stood up and were counted as avid Herbert fans.

Herbert's good humor hardly ever failed him. Many of his programs contained inside jokes that reflect his taste for putting things over on both public and critics. The writer for the *New York Telegraph* was taken in (4/1/07) by a program item on April 1, 1907—April Fool's Day.

> The name of Cavaliere Enrico Burck, a distinguished Venetian composer, appeared in the list of things offered.

> The Cavaliere has composed a gracious thing entitled, "The Gypsy" and it secured marked approbation.

A cursory glance at the orchestra personnel list would have revealed that the "Cavaliere" was our old friend Henry Burck, second concertmaster of the orchestra. "The Gypsy" was a set of variations on Herbert's own "Gypsy Life," from *The Fortune Teller.*

But Herbert was always doing things like that. On another occasion, he was scheduled to play a concert for "a certain ladies' association." Many of the pieces he suggested for the program were rejected out-of-hand by the music committee. He then offered to play the famous "Spanish Rhapsody" of Sibinghi. There was no such composer—but the ladies had to accept his suggestion, since they had no grounds for rejecting it. The musical matrons then were treated to something of Herbert's own concoction.

Herbert's humor was not just directed at others. He loved a good joke, even if he was the butt of it. Like so many truly great artists, he took only his work seriously, not himself. One day, on tour, the subject of his older compatriot Michael Balfe came up. Herbert remarked that it was a pity he had gone to study in Italy, for he felt that Balfe had lost the Irish quality of his music. He went on to wonder aloud what might have happened if he himself had never left Dublin. One of the men, taking his life in his hands, responded that "Instead of being a conductor, like the rest of the Irish you'd be a cop standing on a New York street corner!" Everybody laughed, but Herbert laughed the most.[19]

And then there were the jokes going around about his personal appearance. One of these was so ubiquitous that it even made the pages of the *Philadelphia Record*:

> Two chorus girls attended a Victor Herbert concert.
> "My" exclaimed one with a glance at the program,
> "Hasn't Mr. Herbert a tremendous repertoire?"
> "Well, I wouldn't exactly say that," replied her friend, "but he *is* getting pretty fat."[20]

Herbert seemed to take jokes about his weight in good spirit. He often remarked, when criticized for programming so much of his own music, that he enjoyed "getting fat on my own cooking." If that is what he had in mind, his extended tours were the scene of much musical and gastronomic excess—and success. For these tours he chartered three special railroad coaches and a dining car provided with all the specialties he enjoyed, including barrels of his favorite Würzburger Hofbräu. He also had one of the coaches fitted out as a work studio for himself, so that no opportunity would be lost for continuing creative activity.

The 1911 tour was typical. It covered 12,000 miles, with stops for afternoon and evening concerts at Washington, D.C., Richmond, Louisville, Atlanta, Mobile, Memphis, New Orleans, San Antonio, Oklahoma City, Des Moines, and points in between. His concerts featured Wagner, selections from his newly composed *Natoma*, and three war-horse overtures (*Tannhauser*, *1812*, and *Leonore* III). Large audiences turned out at every stop to greet the man acclaimed by the press as the "Greatest American Composer and Orchestra Leader."[21]

Added to his usual company of instrumentalists were six prominent New York vocal soloists frequently called upon to perform ensembles (the

Rigoletto Quartet, *Meistersinger* Quintet and *Lucia* Sextet), as well as solos from the ever-expanding Herbert operetta repertoire. John Finnegan, tenor soloist of St. Patrick's Cathedral was a Herbert favorite. As was his custom after a tour, Herbert took time to send personal letters of thanks to all his soloists. One to Finnegan is especially warm, and reflects the fact that he and Herbert shared many an afterglow:

> It is my desire to tell you how much I enjoyed your thoroughly artistic work on our concert tour through the South-West.
>
> The rare quality of your voice and the most artistic rendering of your numbers have been a delight to all of us and I wish you all success in the future.
>
> "More power to your elbow," dear John![22]

Another member of the ensemble who became a beloved feature of the Herbert concerts was Henry Boewig, librarian of the New York Philharmonic and the Victor Herbert Orchestra tours. Boewig developed a system that made it possible for the concerts, with their many encores, to be played without interruption. Many concertgoers looked forward to the appearance of this "dear old white-haired gentleman who would arrange the new music on Herbert's stand between numbers."[23]

Love is not too strong a word for the relationship that Herbert shared with his men. One of them commented on the personal interest he took in each of them that was the basis of their affection: "He's big—and he's great. Oh, what a man! Never does he forget that I have a wife who is sick and two little ones. 'How is the wife, John?' he says each day. Oh, so kind. It makes me feel good, and my wife also when I tell her. And I would play my soul out for him."[24] Of course, since this was Victor Herbert, there were events on the tours that caused the old temperamental prima donna maestro to surface. On one such occasion, Governor Hooper of Tennessee became the object of his wrath. At a concert in Memphis the Governor and his party were starting to leave during the last number, when Herbert stopped the orchestra cold. Turning to the audience, he addressed Hooper: "It will take ten minutes to play this piece, Governor. If you are in a hurry to leave you perhaps better go now." The Governor and his party resumed their seats. Herbert resumed his concert.

But these incidents were relatively rare, and the tours can be counted a series of triumphs. None was greater than the triumph of the 1911 tour, which was crowned by the announcement that Herbert was to be honored

Wedding party, Vienna, August 14, 1886. Victor Herbert standing second from right, his bride, Theresa, in center; members of her family. (Library of Congress)

Publicity photo, 1887. (Library of Congress)

Caricature of Herbert by Enrico Caruso, Herbert's favorite, because "He didn't draw me as fat as others." (Library of Congress)

Herbert as leader of the 22nd Regimental Band, U.S. National Guard, 1898. (Library of Congress)

Theresa (star of the Met) and Victor (pit cellist), 1887. Theresa, diva divina, opened the Met's 1886–87 season as the Queen of Sheba. Three days later she sang the Met's first Aida, in German. Victor left a note for Theresa at the stage door of the Met: "Been here twice—furious that you were out!" (Library of Congress)

Each summer, the Victor Herbert Orchestra gave free public concerts from the porch of the Grand Union Hotel in Saratoga Springs, New York (1899). (Library of Congress)

"Frisky" Fritzi Scheff in *Mlle. Modiste,* 1905. (Library of Congress)

To celebrate his twenty-fifth wedding anniversary (1911), Herbert, seen here (at left) with singer George Hamlin, held a "pow-wow" for 200 friends at Lake Placid. (Library of Congress)

Above: In the Adirondacks, preparing for the production of Natoma. From left: Herbert, son Clifford, singer George Hamlin, and Hamlin's accompanist, Charles Lurvey. (Museum of the City of New York) Below: Escaping summer heat in New Orleans during a Victor Herbert Orchestra tour, 1907. (Library of Congress)

by Villanova University with an honorary Doctor of Music degree. This was the first and only official recognition of his achievement by any American college. The citation called him "the greatest musician of this century" and noted that "he has done more for the American music-loving public than has any man in years."[25] The *New York Telegraph* noted the honor. "Mr. Herbert is the pride of American musicians and composers. He stands all alone in a class by himself, the greatest of living composers, the Offenbach of America. . . . All honor to the master."[26]

But there were triumphs even sweeter than official recognition. Herbert and the orchestra were invited to perform at the Pittsburgh Exposition. His reception might be understood as sweet revenge, if a taste for revenge had been part of his makeup—which it was not. "The old saying that absence makes the heart grow fonder was proven when Victor Herbert was welcomed by thousands of his old friends," the *Pittsburgh Post* reported. "A cheer and a round of hand-clapping went up when he appeared. With difficulty he was permitted to proceed with the opening number. There followed two hours of enchanting music."[27]

But perhaps the sweetest triumph of all was the following commentary on his work with the orchestra:

A man is known in the musical world by his musical deeds and Victor Herbert's musical deeds are the basic element of the fame which he has deservedly won and now so properly enjoys.
[As to] his mastery of the baton: his exuberant temperament chastened by scholarly sobriety, warm imagination tempered by dignified musicianship, and a fine perception of the most subtle musical niceties of phrasing, orchestral combination and instrumental shading and coloring reveal the powers without which no conductor can hope to be great. . . .

With all these advantages Victor Herbert seems to be the logical choice as permanent conductor of the New York Philharmonic society. . . . [He is] a favorite of the people (as evidenced by his Sunday night concerts at the Majestic Theatre where crowds flock to hear him conduct,) and one of the best experienced, best equipped musicians in this large country. Victor Herbert is the man for the job.

His work at Pittsburgh is too well remembered to need repetition at this moment. Herbert trained and developed the raw material which he found in Pittsburgh and laid the foundation for the finished work which the Pittsburgh Orchestra is able to accomplish.

The source of this accolade? The cover story of the November 29, 1905 issue of the *Musical Courier*.

Omnia Vincit Victor!

CHAPTER 6

PATERFAMILIAS (1889-1924)

My father, like many other public figures, presented an
unaccountable paradox of being well known and at the same time
having little known about him or his personal life.
—*Clifford V. Herbert, in the* Philadelphia Gazette-Democrat,
July 13, 1934

Although perhaps unaccountable in his son Clifford's eyes, the fact is that this situation was exactly what Victor Herbert wanted. He was a public figure who reveled in the persona which he chose to display to the world—a gregarious, generous disciple of the jovial; quick-witted, prodigiously productive, mercurial in mood, devoted to his art, his Celtic heritage and his family; the trencherman gourmand who refused to discuss business at table, since such discussion would distract his attention from the real business at hand: the enjoyment of his beloved pilsner and the delectation of mountains of Teutonic cuisine.

"Immaculate and fastidious,"[1] decked out in Chesterfield overcoat and grey fedora hat, carrying the inevitable walking stick, Herbert would move through the crowds on Broadway, his bouncy short-legged quick-step a magnet to every eye. "There goes Victor Herbert," the people would say. Victor Herbert—on-stage every moment of his public life. Entering the theater to conduct a performance, he would doff this exterior and stride from the rear of the theater down the center aisle to the podium, resplendent in white tie and tails, acknowledging the applause with genial bows to the right and to the left. At home receiving guests, and even working in his study, he favored morning cutaway coats and striped trousers. This was the public Victor Herbert.

Variations on these familiar images were fueled by pithy public pronouncements. Herbert was always good for a headline or a feature story, for to the end of his days he was never chary of biting commentary on the world in which he moved:

Prohibition was brought about by fanaticism and hypocrisy. Do you know the reason the laboring man is not happy? Is not contented? He does not have his beer! You cannot take away something from people that they actually want. Why, 200 years ago in Russia the punishment for smoking was to have one's nose cut off. But it didn't stop smoking, did it? Prohibition is one of the greatest farces of today.[2]

Thus spake the public Herbert. It was the private man, the father and husband, that Clifford was referencing in his remark. Years later Lionel Barrymore, who knew Herbert from their salad days at the Player's Club, made an astonishingly similar comment: "Everybody knew Herbert but nobody knew much about his personal affairs."[3] Understandably, Herbert chose to hold his personal cards close to his chest. According to his own comments, extramarital affairs were limited to the period before he achieved great celebrity. In the early years Herbert would squire young women about town. He would meet them for lunch and invite another of his associates to join them as a beard for the assignation.[4] If there were any love letters among his papers, it is certain that his daughter, Ella, destroyed them. She devoted her life, after her father's death, to the promotion of his work and the burnishing of his image. During examination of the papers of Harry B. Smith, one of Herbert's most frequent collaborators, a letter from the composer to the actress Frances Starr was discovered. Although written on Lambs Club stationery, its return address is listed as 140 West 57th Street, which was the address of Carnegie Hall, where Herbert maintained a business office. The salutation is unique for Herbert, and the diction of the text, as well as the complimentary close, leave no doubt that this was more than a fan letter:

Dear Sweet!
I must write a short line before I go home. I could not possibly remain still when I am so full of emotion.

I thank you with all my heart for one of the most exquisite evenings I have ever spent in the theatre in all my life. There is nothing to say about your performance; it is beyond praise. Every line, every value, the unfailing tenderness and beauty and humor too, all combine to make a performance that I will remember all my life.

The play is a gem, a rare one and everyone who loves Beauty will see and love it. I cannot thank you enough for the joy you have given me.

Ever your devoted
Victor H[5]

That being said, it must be noted that Herbert's amours are not an area of major significance. In no way did they affect Herbert's devotion to his wife or his children. There is, however, an area of Herbert's relationship with women that is significant, and that will be explored in the discussion of the creation of his stage works. In his selection of leading ladies for the operettas and in his choice of librettos, he invariably selected individuals whose physical appearance and dramaturgical characteristics mirrored those of his mother. All the great Herbert heroines are petite, independent, feisty, quirky characters. Mlle. Modiste, Naughty Marietta, the Only Girl, the Fortune Teller, Sylvia (in *Sweethearts*) are all sisters and inspired Herbert's greatest musical characterizations. Herbert was not so much unfaithful to Theresa's type as he was devoted to the image represented by his mother. This was Herbert's real affair, his only significant infidelity.

Six A.M. in the Herbert home. Herbert is singing. His voice, with its slight accent (no one knew whether it was German or Irish), a famous "composer baritone, a kind of muted trumpet tone with all too frequent cracks,"[6] caroled through the house with great gusto: little comic songs which he sang to the delight of his children and anyone else who would listen. These were followed by chords and runs on the piano and perhaps selections from *Algeria*.

> Of all his works I believe he liked "Algeria" the best. I know that he
> would frequently play the score through for his own amusement,
> chuckling over the notes and nodding his head in appreciation through
> some of the more subtle passages.[7]

Then came calisthenics. "I always take plenty of physical exercise to keep myself in trim," Herbert is quoted as saying. "If a man uses his brain and does not use his muscles he becomes morbid and gloomy."[8] Whether in residence in New York or Pittsburgh or at his summer home at Lake Placid, part of his routine was to walk five or six miles a day, a practice he continued until the final year of his life. At Placid he added to the repertoire of his activities. Logs were rolled, trees cut down, swimming exercises indulged in, horses ridden, trout fished! The big, enthusiastic, vigorous Herbert needed some kind of recreation or else he could not stand the strain on his nerves that work imposed. Herbert was not much of a gamesman; billiards was the only such recreation he enjoyed, but he enjoyed it enough to have a billiard room installed in the attic of his residences at Pittsburgh and New York City.

Along with exercise and song, alcohol played a large role in his life. It was ever-present in his home. In his studio, he kept a vat filled with ice and stocked with varieties of wine. In one year, when he produced three operettas, he drank Mosel while working on the show with the German setting, Valpolicella for the Italian piece, and white burgundy for the French. He favored champagne cocktails laced with Worcestershire sauce drizzled down the edge of the glass (his secret formula for lifting not only his spirits but, once, those of an entire theatrical company after a disastrous dress rehearsal of *The Red Mill*). He carried a flask and nipped from it before playing demanding string quartets. He had large regular shipments of imported pilsner sent to his home from Lüchows.

We have seen that he was given to mood swings. With all this, the question naturally arises: was Herbert alcoholic? Probably not. Although at 250 pounds his weight was high for his 5′10″ frame, he was not a fat man. He was muscular and powerful, physically active, prodigiously productive. He no doubt had a great capacity for liquor and, like all other aspects of his life, he enjoyed it hugely both in public and at home, but by no means did it affect him in a negative way. He was not one of those who, as the Irish say, "Hang up their fiddles behind the door when they come home." "He could not stand to see folks downcast and he would always try to cheer them up."[9] Alcohol was part of this effort, but only part. He was a "raconteur par excellence," and could tell "killingly funny stories, and could even take mediocre jokes and make them seem funnier than they were."[10] One of these jokes survived him in the memory of John Fitzsimons, a member of the Friendly Sons of St. Patrick, whose glee club, founded by Herbert, still concertizes regularly in New York. Mr. Fitzsimons recalled this, one of Herbert's favorite stories: "Two Irishmen were drinking. After twenty rounds one of them fell off his bar stool and passed out. His companion turned to the bartender and said, 'I admire that. I like a man who knows when to quit!'"[11] Alcohol was ever-present in Herbert's life, but as a welcome, invited and helpful guest.

⌒ Victor and Theresa always shared wine at dinner, usually his preferred Bernkasteler Doktor. Before dinner there were martinis, although these were eliminated at Placid. "Now, mother. I just think we don't need martinis up here. The air is so wonderful," Victor is quoted as saying.[12] Conversation between the two was frequently in German, since Theresa was more comfortable with her native language. Even though she preferred to speak German, Theresa had mastered English and, when pressed, could write respectably. As their son Clifford's seventeenth birthday approached, she wrote to the headmaster of his prep school, Lawrenceville:

Dear Dr. McPherson,
My son Clifford's birthday is on October the 20th and it would make me very happy if he could spend the day at home. If you think it best for him to stay at school, I shall, of course, be content, but you would be conferring a happiness to me if you let Clifford come home. Hoping this favor may be granted and thanking you for your kindness.
I am sincerely yours,
Theresa Herbert
Mrs. Victor Herbert[13]

A few grammatical glitches, but not so many as to justify accounts of Theresa's lack of English facility.

Theresa was by nature a homebody, and was content to focus her life on her family and on her husband's career. The fact that Herbert often addressed her as "mother" serves to emphasize the mutually nurturing quality of their relationship. From the earliest days she showed great concern about his health. She was unhappy with his preference for big, black cigars—a fondness he had learned from his mother(!). Theresa made a habit of substituting lighter smokes for Herbert's preferred cheroots, and the composer "submitted to her mothering"[14] with as much good grace as he could muster.

Theresa was a noble cook, and when she didn't do the cooking herself she supervised her staff minutely in the preparation of Herbert's culinary favorites, which included:

Tafelspitz (boiled brisket of beef) with horseradish and Weinkraut
Broiled veal chop with butter
Beef ragout with mushrooms
Hamburger steak (medium rare) with beef marrow fried in butter
Planked veal steak with cauliflower, peas, beans, asparagus and mushrooms
Double bouillon with parsley
Onion soup
Boiled haddock with mustard butter

Fried sole
Sturgeon steak with potato salad
Kaiserchmarrn
Krautstrudl

Between courses Victor would always drink water—laced with claret. He refused to drink plain water under any circumstances. Considering what is known today about nutrition, it is a tribute to his constitution that Herbert survived this culinary onslaught to the age of sixty-five.

Theresa's contribution to the home extended to the area of decoration, with some input from her husband. "One of the things that one noticed as one climbed to his study was that the house was largely decorated from top to bottom in shades of green. Herbert was very proud of his Irish national color."[15] The exception to all this greenery was the drawing room. This was decorated in tones of red, white and red—a reflection of Theresa's Austrian heritage. There were red walls and a red Persian carpet under a large grand piano, a piano that dominated the room and gave it more the aspect of a music than a drawing room. It was in fact a salon, designed to encourage artistic inspiration, for both in Pittsburgh and New York it was the scene of much distinguished music making. One typical "at home" began with string quartet playing, followed by a sumptuous dinner, then billiards and cigars, and finally more quartets. On one such occasion the impromptu quartet featured Fritz Kreisler (Violin 1), Henry Burck (Violin 2), Luigi von Kunitz (Viola) and Herbert (cello.)

Herbert's study was always located on an upper floor in order to afford him the utmost privacy. There stood the upright piano on which he tried out his compositions. In the corner his beloved red Amato was stored, wrapped in an old blanket. To one side stood the famous writing desk at which he worked out his orchestrations. In New York the room commanded a fascinating view of the Hudson River through a wide bow window. There was a complete music library on shelves that lined three sides of the room, a library supplemented by volumes, in English and German, on physics and metaphysics. The walls were lined with pictures, not only of classic composers—Liszt, Wagner and Schubert—but with miniatures painted by his grandfather, Samuel Lover. There were photographs of scenes from productions of his operettas. Mementoes of his illustrious career were scattered throughout the house: the bust of Beethoven, batons from the band days, medals won in competitions, laurel wreaths, loving cups, signed photographs of world-wide celebrities. And everywhere music was scattered. The piano was loaded with it, the settees covered with it. Even the brackets on the walls were used as improvised music stands. The whole scene was a living witness to Herbert's vibrant career.[16]

Theresa and Victor had five children. Two were stillborn; one, Maud, died in infancy. Two survived: Ella Victoria and Clifford Victor. A letter that Victor sent from the road on the occasion of Ella's birth in October of 1889 (see pp. 36–37) reflected his concern for Theresa's well-being. A similar sentiment is reflected in his comment to Fritz Stahlberg when he learned that Stahlberg was about to become a father:

> My boy, you must now be especially kind to your wife. You know, a woman in that condition sometimes has strange whims, but humor her—always let her have her way. She might even want to eat the paper off the wall—let her. Mrs. Herbert can advise her. I'm sure she would, gladly.[17]

Max Reinhardt, the great theatrical producer, once remarked that the secret of artistic success was for the artist always to keep "a little bit of his childhood hidden in his pockets."[18] There was never an artist of whom that was a more accurate description than Victor Herbert. Some of his most charming and successful music was inspired by sentiments directed at children. *Little Nemo*, based on a comic strip adventure, *The Lady of the Slipper*, a modern Cinderella, *Alice and the Eight Princesses* (*Wonderland*), and *Babes in Toyland* were all creations especially close to his heart. In his everyday life this childlike quality was a facet of his personality that surfaced only in the relationship with Ella and Clifford. He loved to play, and he played like a child.

> He adored his children. He fairly idolized them. In the middle of a composition he would stop to have a romp. He was never too busy to answer a childish question—never too occupied to join in a game. Many a time I'd see him scrambling on the floor making believe he was an animal or playing "engine."[19]

But even when playing with his children, Herbert tried to dominate the action. "Once he got so interested in laying a miniature track and running the trains that he kept pushing his small son Clifford out of the way. At last the baby got mad and set up a howl—the only way he could get a chance at his toy."[20]

"Clifford was the favorite," Ella complained. "They never scold Clifford."[21] Perhaps it was natural for Ella to feel that way. She was lame[22] and physically favored her father, not necessarily a plus for a young girl. Her handicap might have caused her to feel that she held second place in her parents' affections, but she was certainly not unloved. Clifford also was handicapped: he spoke with a slight lisp, not exactly an advantage for a young boy.

The dedication to Ella's autograph book, written when she was eleven reads,

> To my dear little Ella from her loving father. Pittsburgh, December 4, 1900.

This is followed by musical excerpts from "In Dreamland," "Badinage," and a section of the overture to *Prince Ananias*, Herbert's first-extant stagework.[23]

The entries in Ella's autograph book give us a glimpse into the level of artistic activity at the Herbert home. It is almost as if he tried to recreate the atmosphere he had experienced at his grandfather's home in Kent. It is a veritable honor roll of the arts in Herbert's time:

Composers and Instrumentalists:
Dr. Richard Strauss (with incipit of "Till Eulenspiegl" and the note "Zur freundlichen Erinnerung an den hoechst gemuetlichen Abend in dem schoenen Elternhaus." [In friendly remembrance of the most pleasant evening in your parents' beautiful home.]
Cecile Chaminade
Montemezzi
Fritz Kreisler
Paderewski
Pablo Casals
Eugene Ysaye
Mischa Ellman
Rachmaninoff

Singers:
Sembrich
Schumann-Heink
Lilli Lehmann
Louise Homer

Nordica
Jeritza
John McCormick
Scotti
Mary Garden
Frieda Hempel
Caruso ("After dinner with Vic. Il caro ed affetuoso amico" with
sketches of Herbert conducting)

Conductors:
Felix Weingartner ("Der Tochter meines Freundes und Kollegen
Victor Herbert zum Andenken an die Tagen in New York.") [To the
daughter of my friend and colleague Victor Herbert in memory of the
New York days.]
Walter Damrosch

Actors:

David Warfield	Richard Mansfield
Otis Skinner	Blanche Bates
Elsie Janis	Lillian Russell
Eleanor Robson	Forbes-Robertson
Digby Bell	Sarah Bernhardt
Wilton Lackaye	Charlie Chaplin (with a sketch of the tramp.)

John Drew ("A sketch of John Drew by his nephew John Barrymore.")

Playwrights:
David Belasco
John Luther Long
G.B.S. ("I don't usually . . . but for Handy Andy's sake here goes—just
this once.")

And this delightful verse from Henry Blossom, Herbert's most gifted
collaborator:

ELLA (AN ACROSTIC):
Eyes that beguile with an innocent smile,
Lips that were made to be kissed,
Lovely brown hair and a skin that's fair
As . . . . but this isn't *half* the list.
Your sincere admirer.

Cartoonists and Illustrators:
George MacManus (with a sketch of Jiggs)
R. F. Outcault (with a sketch of Buster Brown)
A picture of Ella by Howard Chandler Christy
And one of a "girl" by Charles Dana Gibson.

Miscellaneous prominent persons:
Andrew Carnegie
Theodore Roosevelt
George Ade
Thomas Lipton
Edison
W. H. Taft
Jack London
W. Wilson
Warren G. Harding
J. G. Huneker ("With regards from Jim.")
Mark Twain
Herbert Hoover

Certainly an atmosphere to make any little girl feel special.

But just as there is a special relationship between fathers and daughters, there is an equally special relationship, if different in quality, between fathers and sons.

> It is a rather strange sensation to sit in the music room in the morning with Herbert, watch the door open and see Herbert's daughter enter, to be greeted with a handshake and such a pleasant, "Good morning, my dear." Or to be back stage at an orchestra concert and hear Herbert greet his son with a cheery, "How are you, my child?" and shake his hand just as though they were a pair of friends who had not met for weeks, but had a deep and lasting love for each other.[24]

It was true that Herbert favored his son, but that indulgence early proved to be a very mixed blessing for both of them.

Herbert's childlike quality also revealed itself in his devotion to the 22nd Regiment Band. He loved to march at the head of his troop dressed as a drum major; sometimes he had Clifford join him dressed in a uniform that was a miniature version of his own. As Ella and Theresa watched them pass in review, it is easy to understand why Ella felt that Clifford held first place in her father's affections. This feeling caused her to redouble her efforts to please him, and lay at the root of her resentment of her brother. "She never had a good word to say about him."[25] Part of the trouble lay in the timing of the children's births. Ella was born on October 28, 1889, Clifford almost exactly two years later on October 20, 1891, a less than ideal developmental placement for siblings.[26] Neither child was baptized. Theresa was Roman Catholic, Victor Anglican. Perhaps they had not been able to agree on which communion their children would join. For some reason the children, at the ages of ten and eight, were suddenly hustled over to St. Agnes Chapel of Trinity Parish, Episcopal, and there, in the presence of their parents and their sponsors, Charles and Ellen M. Lellman, were welcomed into the body of the one, holy catholic and apostolic Church on August 7, 1899. (It is important to remember the name Charles Lellman. At this time he was an attorney representing the Musical Courier Company and a man whose purported remarks, cited at Herbert's landmark libel suit, may be impeached by his evident close friendship with the composer, a fact that was not brought out at trial.)

As they matured it was inevitable that both children were set to the study of music. For those who hold that environment may to some extent compensate for lack of natural artistic ability, the case of Ella and Clifford Herbert comes as an irrefutable rebuke, for never were two less gifted children born to more talented parents.

At Pittsburgh both began the study of violin and piano. At first, Fritz Stahlberg was piano master and Henry Burck gave the violin lessons. Since both men were close friends as well as employees of Herbert, the situation was not without its tensions.

> Ella was a good little student, but Clifford had different ideas. When I would call for him after Ella's lesson, he would have to be coaxed into the home from some neighbor's yard where he had been busy playing. My reluctant scholar was a real boy and after his play sessions his hands always bore witness to the fact. So, before the lesson Clifford would obediently trot out to wash, but would only come in again when firmly required to do so. By that time 15 minutes of the half-hour piano lesson would be gone.
>
> Henry Burck, who gave the violin lessons and I brought the children far enough so that for their father's birthday they could play a little

duet, "The Low Backed Car," a song written by their famous great-grandfather Samuel Lover. Mr. and Mrs. Herbert, Henry Burck and I were the audience. We found it hard to keep straight faces during the rendition. There was one part near the end of the song where Clifford rose to dramatic heights; he seemed to lay in wait for that part, promptly pouncing on it and pulling it out of his fiddle with great vehemence. Needless to say that tickled the Herbert sense of humor and nothing would do but to have the performance repeated.[27]

When the family returned to New York, Herbert himself tried his hand at Clifford's musical instruction, but with little success. "Out on the slopes of Riverside Park a battle royal of snowballs was in progress and as soon as the lesson ended Master Herbert used his happy freedom to join the battalions."[28]

Still, there was another area in which the children contributed to the Herbert musical legacy.

These two children are Herbert's most stern musical critics. They and the mother hear everything that is given to the public before the public has an opportunity to hear it. If they like it, well and good; if they don't it ends right there. Probably it's a superstition of Herbert's, but it's nevertheless a fact that nothing, not even his symphonic poems goes out to the world without their passing judgement on it.[29]

The children had no illusions about their musical abilities. "As a musician I am nil," Clifford remarked in an interview some years later.[30] As for Ella, Herbert pronounced his judgment. "Yes, she plays the piano with great style, but you should hear her rattle on the typewriter!"[31] The maestro meant no harm by the remark, but he was capable of slaying with the truth. Oddly enough, that typewriter was a key to the strong bond that eventually developed between Herbert and his daughter, for during the last fifteen years of his career Ella made herself his indispensable amanuensis, serving as her father's secretary, driver and representative and, after his death, managing director of all things Herbertian.

The bonds between Herbert and his children were really forged during the family vacations at Lake Placid. The Herberts made the annual trip with car and chauffeur, bringing the New York servants with them. Herbert acquired two camps, Joyland and Sunset, just above Paradox Bay. He also purchased the adjoining Camp Woodland so he could have complete privacy. But his never-ending search for tranquility was unsuccessful even amid the pines and the hemlocks. One summer a neighboring family decided to keep a cow staked out across the road from Camp Joyland. The cow birthed a calf that was sold for veal, and the bereft mother "bawled day and night." Finally Theresa, who was always trying to provide peace and quiet for Victor, approached the neighbors. "She pleaded in her rich Viennese accent, 'You have to do something because that cow moos and moos, and my Victor can't make his moosic.' "[32]

"He composed in the morning and at night until 2 A.M. One little room on the Northeast corner of the second floor, bare except for a piano and desk, was his workshop."[33] Between work sessions there was time for the children. Ella recalled the long walks she took with her father daily. "He always carried a little notebook and jotted down tunes as they occurred to him."[34]

It is said that it is the dream of every Irishman to own a boat. Herbert was no exception. He acquired his first in 1905 and named it "Handy Andy," after his grandfather's novel. There followed "Handy Andy II," "Rory (O'Moore) I," "Rory II" and "Natoma" in quick succession. Why all these boats? Why an armada? The answer, in a word, is Clifford. By all reports the boy had inherited his father's sunny, buoyant disposition, but his luck with boats was as poor as his violin playing.

In the summer of 1907, just before Clifford was scheduled to enter Lawrenceville School, Herbert bought him his first vessel. Two speedboats made their appearance on the lake that summer. One was Clifford's "Victoria," named for his sister. It was built like a racing shell. The clutch was installed to the rear and, on its trial run, to Clifford's delight, a young lady whom he had invited to take a spin got her long skirt caught in the clutch and lost it as Clifford set the boat in motion. Victor and Theresa ordered their son to cover the clutch at once, as the story of the skirtless maiden spread through the village like wildfire. Soon Clifford challenged the owner of the other speedboat, the "Theanogran," to a race. Clifford lost. Disgusted and upset, he immediately sold the "Victoria" to a friend. He had inherited his father's short fuse.

That was not to prove an asset as summer turned to Indian summer and Clifford set off for Lawrenceville. He had studied at the Horace Mann School in New York for two years, and then transferred to the less demanding Cutler School, where his record was mediocre. Herbert enrolled "his boy"[35] in the classical course of study to prepare him for matriculation at Princeton. This was ambitious, and the acting headmaster of

Lawrenceville, responding to Herbert's letter of application, makes it very clear that Clifford was being admitted with some trepidation.

June 15, 1907

Mr. Victor Herbert
Lake Placid
Dear Sir:

Clifford seems to be qualified to enter our Fourth Form. I note that he is to enter the "Classical" course at Princeton. As you know, that course includes Greek, and your son has not studied it. . . .

Mr. Cutler has not made a very full statement in regard to your son's studiousness and school record. The statement is made that his mental capacity is "good," and his moral character is "good."

I am glad to accept the application in the understanding that Clifford will work hard and do his best to maintain a good standing in the school.[36]

On June 24, Herbert responded that Clifford "will take a course in Greek with a private tutor during the summer." How many Classical Greek tutors were resident at Lake Placid in the summer of 1907 is unknown, but Herbert seems to be hedging his bets as he continues, "Is it possible for him to enter the Fourth Form and take Greek in the Third? [where Greek study was normally begun at Lawrenceville] if he should be deficient in his Greek examinations? Clifford assures me that he will be very studious and work very hard during his course at your school." He then went out and bought Cliff the "Victoria."

Assistant Headmaster Raymond was a wise and experienced bird— with fathers as well as with sons. He responded immediately that the school "shall endeavor to accommodate Clifford in Third Form Greek," but immediately added, "The more progress Clifford can make, the sooner he will catch up with the class reading Anabasis."[37] As the Greek armies beat a miraculous retreat from the clutches of the armies of Persia, Clifford passed his days carnicular in pursuit of teen-aged girls and racing victories. Both eluded him.

The summer over, the family returned to New York City and Clifford went off to study Bible, Elocution, German, Geometry, Cicero, English and his beloved Greek. He arrived on October 1. One month later Raymond sent an internal memo to Clifford's housemaster.

Clifford Herbert is reported as having after Penal [a forced study hall detention] 79 marks [demerits awarded for various deficiencies and infractions]. This puts him in great danger of suspension—and that very soon. Won't you see him about this and issue him a definite warning?[38]

The following month Dr. McPherson, the headmaster, sent a memo to Raymond.

Herbert says that he appreciates now how "awful bum" [wretched, shiftless] he has been and asks for "another chance." You know the case better than I do and I venture to refer it to you.[39]

Soon a private tutor from Princeton was engaged to help Clifford pass Bible. It helped—but not much. At the close of his first year Clifford had passed 13 hours, but failed 10, including German, the language of his home. Of this record his housemaster wrote, "The above [record] is a *great* improvement for Clifford. If he can get any two conditions [almost passing] off by Saturday, May 9, I think he deserves his Boston trip. He is now tutoring 11 hours."[40] As a result of the tutoring of Mr. McIlvane of Princeton, Clifford passed to the Fifth Form. With pride he wrote to the headmaster from Camp Joyland,

July 4, 1908

My dear Doctor,
I enclose you a slip from Princeton, on which it says I passed Algebra—A, English—A, and German—A. This report is exceedingly gratifying to me as I flunked German three times straight and English two times.
The reason my third term report was so bad was that I did so much tutoring for the Princeton exams, that I had to neglect my school work.
With best wishes to you and your family for a happy summer.[41]

Dr. McPherson's reply was not what Clifford expected. He congratulates him on his grades but criticizes the "methods by which you were enabled to pass" as "poor, for it amounted practically to cramming. You neglected your regular work for them. Your string of conditions in school is wretchedly long." He goes on to recommend that Clifford "settle down to steady hard work, not to spasmodic work such as you have done heretofore." Dr. McPherson then delivers the coup de grace. He describes Clifford's work as "disgracefully poor" and reprimands him for his delinquency marks, absence from recitations and misconduct "by far the greatest number of misconduct marks by any boy in your form." He then concludes,

"Let me know what you are doing this summer by way of study" and asks Clifford to "show this letter to your father and mother."[42]

Clifford shared the contents of the letter with his parents. They chose to focus on the Princeton report and to ignore Dr. McPherson's clear caveat. Clifford's reward for his achievement was the "Rory I," a new supercharged speedboat. For himself Herbert bought the "Handy Andy," a putt-putt vessel good for trout fishing and quiet evening glides across the lake.

Clifford lost no time in challenging his rival to a rematch and, though it seemed the "Rory" would win in a walk, the "Theanogran" repeated its triumph of the previous season. Clifford took it out on the "Rory." The poor thing lasted only one season. One day the boy had trouble starting the engine in the boathouse. He removed the cover from the gas tank and, smoking a cigarette, started to tinker with the mechanism. He flipped his cigarette away and it landed in the tank. The explosion threw Clifford into the lake, and the resulting fire destroyed both "Rory" and the boathouse. Not to worry. "Rory II" was soon launched, but now the long-suffering father warned his boy the boat would be his last if he did not make good with it.

Whatever suffering Victor and Theresa endured from Clifford's antics during the summer of 1908 was nothing compared to what lay ahead for them when he returned to school in the fall. In the meantime, Herbert had his representative, Robert W. Iverson, send a note to Lawrenceville. In the light of the summer's events—even in the light of Herbert's indulgence of his son—it seems incredible:

> Dear Sir:
> Mr. Victor Herbert directs me to send you the enclosed check toward a check account for his son, Clifford. Further, he wants me to state that he has given Clifford permission to smoke.[43]

The fall term began inauspiciously with an excuse for absence, not from Clifford, but from his father, who cabled Dr. McPherson from New York, "Clifford not well. Doctor thinks he should stay here till tomorrow."[44] That was the first request for special treatment. The second was Theresa's request to allow her son to come home for his October birthday, to which the headmaster replied that he regretted the request had been made, since Clifford was doing poorly in his work, which he characterized as fitful and irregular. Less than one week later there was a follow-up note to Theresa, reporting the results of a conference held with his masters:

I think his fundamental fault is a combination of carelessness and self-indulgence of a comparatively useless sort. I regret extremely that his career at Lawrenceville should end this way and that his required withdrawal from the school must impose sorrow upon Mrs. Herbert and yourself.[54]

When the letter and Clifford arrived on the doorstep on 108th Street, Theresa collapsed and took to her bed. Victor hit the roof. Clifford was handed pen and paper and told to find an excuse for his behavior that might ameliorate the situation. Clifford wrote:

December 10, 1908

My dear Doctor:—

I am absolutely heartbroken at my indefinite suspension, and now I fully realize, what an awful fool I have made of myself, and how poorly, and how wickedly I have been to my parents. I pray to God with all my heart, with all my soul that I will be able to return to dear old Lawrenceville.

I beg of you, dear Doctor, that you will give me a trial after the Christmas holidays. If I ever get another chance at Lawrenceville, I will do my very best to make my name a name to be respected for having made good.

My poor, dear mother is very ill, and this abominal [sic] conduct of mine, makes her suffer simply awfully. If you will only give me one trial. Please, oh please give me a chance. I am sure that it is in me to make good, and I will try to bring out every good quality there is in me. If you allow me to return I will study every vacant period in the big study with the underforms.

I beg of you again please let me back and give me a chance to redeem myself before my family, and the school.[55]

To all of which Dr. McPherson replied, devastatingly:

December 12, 1908

My dear Clifford:

I was touched by your letter of December 10th. I cannot help but feel, however, that in your own interest you should go to a smaller school. We certainly gave you every chance that we could during the Fall term, as well as last year, and your course, while in a few senses bad, was yet invariably unsatisfactory.

I was informed last night that besides the paper written by your tutor and rejected by Mr. Warren and Mr. Thompson, you had handed in another paper as your own, and yet not written by you, and that it had gone through.

I cannot help feeling that while your intention is to be truthful, you do not always tell the truth; but this is not the reason for my decision. It is rather that you were so consistently careless and so frequently frivolous, and accomplished so little work. The school has been of very little use to you, and your influence, without any unconscious intention on your part, has been demoralizing on the school because you have never persistently worked with regularity, but so far as I have learned, have only worked by fits and starts. You will always have my good will, but I think it altogether wiser for you to go to some other school and begin over.[56]

Here endeth the Lawrenceville lesson; but not the academic career of Clifford Herbert. With private instruction, he was able to enter Princeton with the class of 1912. Halfway through his sophomore year he dropped out, but managed to gain entrance to Cornell, where he graduated with a degree in mechanical engineering with the class of 1915.

The Lawrenceville experience served as a wake-up call for father and son. In 1914, in the summer before his senior year, Clifford went to Detroit as a summer intern to work at Ford for $6.00 per week. His celebrity dogged him even there, and a reporter for the *Detroit News* caught up with him.

My father has warned me that I must be prepared to assume the responsibilities and I am taking the first step. A motor appeals to me far more than a piano does. I communicated my desire to be a mechanical engineer to my father. I would rather don overalls and crawl under an auto than stand up and direct an orchestra.

Many people think it strange that a young man whose father is wealthy should seek hard labor. I think he should seek any kind of work that appeals to him. True, I have always been accustomed to the best, but this must end when I return to Detroit to take employment. I will then seek some little apartment and live on less than I earn.

If one would acquire wealth you must certainly work and deny yourself. Other young men with wealthy fathers have gone to work so why should I be exempt?[57]

This was the voice of a new and independent Clifford. In order to mature, he needed to get out from under his father's shadow. Clifford worked for Ford for many years. During World War I he brought pride to his family by joining the Coast Artillery as a First Lieutenant, Ordnance, and served with distinction at the battles of the Argonne and at Chateau Thierry.

Thrice married, he left Ford and took up cotton planting in Louisiana where, with a final bow to the Victor Herbert tradition, he received his mail and daily held court as a popular figure at the Kickapoo Café in Gloster, Louisiana. He later took up ranching at El Paso. Winters were spent in Los Angeles, where he supported the programs of the Boy Scouts at Palm Springs and at Redlands. In 1959, ill health forced him to retire. He moved to El Paso, where he died on New Year's Day, 1962. He was laid to rest at Forest Lawn Memorial Park, Los Angeles. Ella, from whom he had been estranged, flew out for the service. As is so often the case, jealousy and hurt end only at the tomb.

For Clifford, a wealthy and famous father had proven a very mixed blessing. He only found his way by separating himself from his family. The story of Ella and Theresa, in contrast, is so closely merged with that of Victor, and their work and influence so important, that it must be considered in the context of the discussion of Herbert's theatrical career.

As the years passed, Victor and Theresa grew closer. August 14, 1911, was their twenty-fifth wedding anniversary, and the day was celebrated at Lake Placid. There was a reception and a garden party in the evening with an "Indian" motif—Herbert referred to it as his "pow-wow." Two hundred guests from various parts of the country attended. Scores of congratulatory messages and many gifts were received from all over the world. Herbert remained the fixed star, with Theresa and Ella his faithful satellites.

But for Clifford, the role of satellite would never do. He was to become a comet, an offshoot of the star, with an erratic trajectory all his own.

CHAPTER 7

OYEZ! OYEZ! OYEZ! (1902–1924)

"I broke my arms, my legs. . . . I would have broken my ears, if they had been breakable."[1] Thus Victor Herbert recalled his fighting spirit as a young man at school. He came by his pugnaciousness naturally: it was one more thing he inherited from his famous grandfather, Samuel Lover. And, of course, he was Irish.

As Herbert added to his activities as concertizing cellist and conductor the role of theatrical composer, the scene of his conflicts moved from the schoolyard to the courtroom. He was fiercely protective of his reputation and the rights to the properties he created.

During the period of his important compositional activity, there were many changes in the area of copyright law. In 1894, when his first extant operetta was produced, if a composer wanted to be sure to protect his property it was necessary for him to arrange for a performance to take place physically in the country for which copyright was sought.

Gilbert and Sullivan were outraged by the number of pirated productions of *H.M.S. Pinafore* that took place in the United States immediately following the London premiere. Henry Clay Barnabee, a leading producer and actor with the "Famous Bostonians" company responsible for one of the earliest of these stolen *Pinafore* productions, admits in his memoirs that he attended the world premiere production in London and took extensive notes, on which he based the Boston staging. Soon after, when *The Pirates of Penzance* was created, the official premiere was held at the Fifth Avenue Theater in New York City in order to protect the authors' rights for the United States, while a semi-staged production was held in the British Isles a week earlier to protect the copyright for the U.K. Gilbert, a barrister by training, archly reflected all this legal hodge-podge in his lyric for Richard, the Pirate King:

> Away to the cheating world go you
> Where pirates all are well-to-do.

Victor Herbert, like Gilbert, was nothing if not litigious. He came by that naturally, for his paternal great-grandfather had been a prominent barrister and M.P. for Clogher and Granard. Herbert's most famous lawsuit involved a libel controversy with his old adversary, the Musical Courier Company, but the range of the litigations in which he became ensnared, both as plaintiff and defendant, is astounding, involving copyright, theatrical, and personal injury law.

It is a fascinating coincidence that, three years before Herbert's birth, his mother's father, Samuel Lover, was engaged in an intellectual property suit in Chancery Court in London and in a libel conflict with that city's leading arts publication, the *Atheneum*. The substance of these conflicts anticipates those of the famous suit that Herbert brought against the *Musical Courier* and its editor, Marc Blumenberg, almost a half century later.

The *Atheneum*, in discussing two newly published songs "by Samuel Lover," remarked:

> Mr. Lover comes by some of his melodies as others across the water
> [i.e. in Ireland] came by theirs. Some one good turn (to adapt the well-
> known proverb) suggests another, and the phrase of some wandering
> peasant's ditty . . . being imperfectly remembered comes out . . . newly
> dressed as "The Angel's Whisper," or "The Low-backed car" [two of
> Lover's most popular compositions]. . . . The number of tunes *that
> grow* is legion; the list of tunes that have been born would be shorter
> than the alphabet.[2]

Lover hastened to court to protect his interest in "The Low-backed Car," for a week later the *Atheneum* reports:

> Mr. Lover's "Low-backed Car" has been into court again—and he has
> established his right in the song, with a forty-shilling verdict against
> those who have attempted to interfere with it on the ground of the
> song having been published in America. In the course of his evidence
> Mr. Lover naturally and honourably deposed to the source whence he
> has derived his airs;—his deposition being so identical with our
> speculations of last week, that we may call attention to the testimony.[3]

The writer for the *Atheneum* levels at Lover a charge similar to the one Herbert successfully litigated; that is, as H. E. Krehbiel, critic of the *New York Tribune*, remarked on the occasion of the premiere of Herbert's *Suite Romantique*, ". . . some of these melodies have familiar faces."[4] The essential issue was the nature of originality and how closely that characteristic could be constructed without defaming a work or its creator. Lover, having once established his right in "The Low-backed Car," preferred to pursue the issue in the pages of the *Atheneum* and the London *Times*, wisely avoiding the legal three-ring circus to which his grandson subjected himself. Herbert was fully justified in resorting to the courts, for the charges leveled against him in the pages of the *Courier* by its editor were more ad hominem and reflected greater personal animus than anything Lover had suffered.

Lover's letter to the *Atheneum*[5] references the question of his originality by stating that the comment might have been "more accidentally, than intentionally disparaging," and as the result of the "manner of your musical critic, rather than supposing it to be ill-naturedly leveled against me." But he continued, when the *Atheneum* claimed to have its position vindicated by Lover's own testimony at trial,

> It is evident that the criticism . . . was *purposely* written to underrate and discredit me. . . . That testimony your critic falsifies; he says, "Mr. Lover naturally and honourably deposed to the *source whence he derived his airs*, his deposition being identical with our speculation of last week." Here is a sweeping assertion in the plural—"his airs." Now I only deposed to the air of one song—yet my honourable testimony as to *one* is venturously perverted to rob me of all, and my honour into the bargain—for I hold picking and stealing to be quite as dishonourable in literature or musical composition as in other things, though not legally punishable.

Lover concludes his letter with the statement that he never claimed musical authorship of "The Low-backed Car," "The Angel's Whisper," or "Rory O'More," and that "all the rest have been a twin birth of words and music; and the twin claim of authorship is publically made on their title-pages. Yet it is insinuated I 'derive' my airs from other sources than my invention." He concludes with a challenge to the critic to "look up evidence against me, if he can."

The *Atheneum*, after publishing Lover's response, thought to have the last word:

> There can be no objection that Mr. Lover should be angry at any complimentary and good-natured notice of his songs—there can be no objection to his not comprehending the passage, "The number of tunes that grow is legion:—the list of tunes that have been born would be shorter than the alphabet."[6]

It mentions a preceding article in which "unconscious borrowings" by Clementi, Beethoven, Mozart and Rossini were discussed, thus placing

Lover in excellent and nonexclusive company with respect to the general subject of authenticity and originality. It concludes with the screed that if the three songs that Lover admits were not original with him are removed from the catalogue of his musical compositions, "what remains of Mr. Lover's fame as a melodist?"

Despairing of fair treatment in the *Atheneum*, on July 5 Lover had recourse to the pages of the London *Times*.[7] After remarking that the *Atheneum* had edited his response and perverted his argument, he appealed to the "chivalrous spirit which characterizes the *Times* as the champion of the wronged," and proceeded to declare that with respect to the illustrious company in which the *Atheneum* placed him, "I have no ambition to be renowned in the musical martyrology of the *Atheneum*." He repeats that he never claimed musical authorship of his three most famous songs. "I am content with the fact of having written these words, as it was my words that gave celebrity to airs before unknown." He concludes by mentioning several popular songs on which his reputation as a melodist depends.

The issues raised in this dispute, the nature of originality, the extent and significance of "unconscious borrowings" and the motivation for a published criticism lay at the legal heart of *Herbert* v. *Musical Courier Company*.

Before we can understand or evaluate this action, it is important to examine the background and interests of the personalities involved. "Personalities" is not a word lightly chosen, for this case was driven as much by personal animus as by any issue at law. Herbert may be summarized as a hot-tempered genius whose achievement had placed him in the forefront of American musicians. His warm and attractive persona drew legions of men and women to him, and his generosity of spirit had become a basis for broad public popularity. A dedicated and demanding professional, he was not a man to suffer personal insult or professional defamation lightly.

Marc Blumenberg was no less a dedicated professional. The *Musical Courier*, founded in 1880 "as a magazine for the piano, organ and sewing-machine trade,"[8] had been built by the owner-editor into a publication that dominated the American musical scene by the time Herbert arrived in 1886. Blumenberg had a fine head for business. In this, as well as in his encyclopedic knowledge of the arts, he resembled his millionaire cousin Otto Kahn.[9]

The period in which Blumenberg flourished was one in which American musical activity was driven by a conscious desire to place indigenous musical achievement at the forefront of world culture. At a time when the country's phenomenal industrial development, and the excesses of display that characterized the activities of some of her wealthiest citizens, caught the attention of the world, there arose a desire to destroy the image of philistinism with which European critics sought to censure American civilization: Americans might be inventive and rich, but they were culturally immature and given to tasteless excess.

Marc Blumenberg's *Courier* embodied a virulent opposition to such blanket indictment. It championed what it felt was the brightest and best of American musical art; in the service of this work, Blumenberg employed a coterie of talented writers, most prominent of whom was James Gibbons Huneker. Huneker was a young Philadelphian who had spent some time in Europe studying piano and absorbing the heady romantic atmosphere of the Continent. He was a supporter of the Chopin-Wagner-Liszt school and brought to the *Courier* not only an insightful advocacy but also a chatty insouciance, captured in his weekly column, "Raconteur." Since he was an unknown quantity, Blumenberg picked him up cheap when he first joined the *Courier*, a fact that caused the critic no little rancor when he eventually left the magazine under an Herbertian cloud. But the fact is that Blumenberg launched his career, gave him his break, and did so because his instinct told him Huneker was the right man for the job.

The content of the *Courier* was wide-ranging. There were reviews, reportage of significant musical events of local and national interest, and book reviews and articles in translation from Europe, where the *Courier* maintained active bureaus in London, Berlin, Dresden, Leipzig, Paris, Florence and Milan. There were personal items of gossip (where artists were living, what new works composers were creating), correspondence, even poems. And, of course, there were editorials. It was an editorial that precipitated the Herbert suit.

These, then, are the positive qualities associated with the editor-in-chief: dedication, intelligence, energy, business acumen and humor. Naturally there were negatives. Blumenberg stood at the head of his profession—as did Herbert of his—and like any prominent figure, he had enemies. These fell into two camps: musical artists whose work had been sharply criticized in the pages of the *Courier*, and the editors of rival publications, who were delighted to aid Herbert in his effort to blacken

Blumenberg's reputation and thus, weaken his publication. Jealousy was behind much of the negative publicity the *Courier* and its editor received during the trial—the positive aspects of Blumenberg's character, such as his "generosity to needy music teachers,"[10] were studiously ignored. There can be no doubt that the diction of the editorial content of the magazine was vitriolic. That was part of the attraction. A certain portion of the general readership of arts publications has a highly developed taste for Schadenfreude, and the popularity of the *Courier* was to a certain extent based on its catering to that perverse palate.

The substance of the allegations against Blumenberg may be summarized as follows: he was malicious, and his critical faculty was "for sale." His opprobrium could be influenced by the willingness of an artist to purchase advertisements in the pages of the *Courier*. Not far below the surface of these money-related charges lurked the fact the he was Jewish.

It must be stated immediately that Herbert was no anti-Semite. His actions with respect to the exclusion from membership in the Lambs Club of his friend and publisher, Isidore Witmark—he resigned from the club—and his rejection of a libretto prepared for him by Huneker in which Jews were used as a source of fun and ridicule, prove beyond a doubt that Herbert was above such pettiness. But the America of 1880–1920 was a country in which the seeds of prejudice germinated easily in a nativist soil nourished by annual waves of immigration. In the world of arts publications, Blumenberg was a rare figure in those days: a prominent man of Jewish extraction. It would be as incorrect to place too much stress on this subject as it would be to omit it. In this period, if you were a Jew, it was a factor, if only because a Christian world made it one.

How justified are these charges of mercenary interest? The Huneker archive at Dartmouth College[11] contains several items that substantiate the charges, the most significant in Blumenberg's own hand. In a series of notes to his secretary, dated January 1, 1901, he writes:

> If Geppert has not replied to Rosel he can send a letter to say that it was a matter of accommodation to us in the printing of the paper due to the holidays and that we however will or did *arrange to meet their demands. I do not wish them to think that the sale of a front page would induce us to neglect them* [italics mine]. Tell them that I am West and you had no time to submit the matter to me. *I do not care to know about it*" [italics mine].

The obvious interpretation of this memo is that a client had purchased a notice for the front page of the *Courier* and that because of production problems at the holidays, the favor had not been granted. This pretty much proves that the front page was, indeed, "for sale." Blumenberg's comment that he "does not want to know about it"—on the record—underlines his reluctance to be officially associated with such activity.

In dealing with some relatively unimportant clients, Blumenberg displays an indifferent attitude:

> Will you please look up on our sub [scription] list the address of Mrs. Carrie Jacoby somewhere on West 147 Street and write her that M.B1. is West and that he received her letter but could not reply because she had no address in it. Tell her I may be absent a few weeks. *See? I don't want to be bothered*" [italics mine].

Most damaging to Blumenberg is an extended passage in which, in full tilt, he reveals the extent to which he attempted to use the editorial pages of the *Courier* to affect the careers of artists. At this time Huneker had added to his activities work as a contributing editor for the *New York Sun* and had written favorable notices of artists who were on Blumenberg's blacklist. While crediting the editor's desire to improve the general state of musical activity in America, his list of "no goods" is so obviously the result of personal prejudice, since it constitutes a pantheon of high achievers, we can only maintain support of Blumenberg's motives with the greatest difficulty. The bottom line is this: in general his influence was positive, but he was guilty of allowing personal pique to cloud his judgment and editorial decision making. Whether in fact this pique was activated by personal animus, aesthetic judgment or, as claimed at trial, by financial considerations is a key question here. It is a question of motive.

> I don't understand, Driggs, [Secretary and Vice President of the *Musical Courier*] why you are afraid to incur any opposition from Jim [Huneker]. Why don't you tell Jim straight out what you tell me of his dam [sic] foolishness in booming our enemies. I told him once but I don't know if I will tell him anymore because *it is no longer my funeral.* It is his. If you are a true friend of his you can tell him that you cannot be fooled by his statement that he has *orders* from the *Sun* to boom Gadski as he did or
> W. Damrosch or
> F. Damrosch or
> Kneisel or

Franks and Lichtenberg or others who are *no good. None of these people are any good. If they were great artists it* might *be excusable, but they are all fakes. When Herbert comes in* [with the Pittsburgh Orchestra] *Jim will boom him and he is also a fake.* [italics mine].

As I say, I don't care and I shall not even read the criticisms in the Sun having stopped reading Jim's column after he boomed Gadski last week. I shall pay no attention to what he does in the Sun anymore. But if you are a friend of his you might as well show him this because I'll give you my word that Jim's course in the Sun is his death as a valuable man to any newspaper on the subject of *music*. Already he has proved that he has *no* say on the Courier. That is very bad for him. The idea of an intelligent man like Jim not knowing *when he is committing moral suicide* [italics mine] to put himself right in the ranks of the other musical critics and strengthening the opposition to the M.C. instead of helping to smash it! *I see now that if he had had his own way on the Courier there would be no Courier"* [italics mine].

Along with a penchant for morbid metaphor ("death . . . suicide . . . funeral") that we will leave for the psychiatrists to plumb, we see reflected in the tone of this private memo Blumenberg's sincere identification of his concept of the *Courier*'s mission as a moral crusade. Further, we feel his passion, as well as his perception of the "them versus us" nature of the world of professional music journalism. We also feel his sense of betrayal by a protégé of fifteen years who has gone over to the side of the boomers of "no goods" and "fakes." Still, by any objective standard, the editor's list can not be supported. Gadski et al. were great artists. Unless we are to assume that the marvelous press they received was bought and paid for, his is an untenable position. Why did this intelligent and gifted man assume such a position, even in a private memo? It was a point of view obviously reflected in the pages of his magazine. Blumenberg's was the decisive voice for, as he remarks, he did not allow Huneker (or anyone else) to "have his way."

The editor gives voice to the crux of his complaint at the end of the memo: it is his fear that his enemies, now regretfully including Huneker, would destroy the work to which he had devoted his life, by supporting Herbert's suit for $50,000 damages (approximately one million dollars in current value). A loss would be enough to ruin the *Courier*.

If he booms Herbert in the Sun and *thereby makes the Courier ridiculous* [italics mine] I am afraid I shall ask him to stick to his

Raconteur for $25 a week and let the rest [the criticism] go. I will then engage a big man (maybe Krehbiel) to write the editorials and then show you and Jim how I will get the Tribune over on our side [against Herbert].

Thus Blumenberg feels that even a great critic like H. E. Krehbiel was open to the blandishments of a *Courier* paycheck, that everyone was for sale, and that he could shape the editorial policy of the *Tribune* with his money. Warming to his subject, Blumenberg follows a fanciful trajectory. With the *Tribune* once safely in his pocket

Charley Steinway would want nothing better and that would also bring in the Novello [publishing] business; other business, too. *I refuse to be made ridiculous by Jim in the Sun in the Herbert case* [italics mine].

All this as of January 1, 1901. By October 1902, the month for which the trial date was scheduled, Huneker had resigned, not only from the *Courier*, but from all music criticism, anywhere. In his letter of resignation to Blumenberg he writes:

The main thing is that I am out of music journalism for good and all and I am glad of it. I am leaving for the reason that I expect to earn more money elsewhere. . . . I have been grievously underpaid by the MC during the past five years. . . . The Courier could have claimed my entire time by paying me enough money. But you can't blame me for being practical, at last, can you? For coming out of my idealistic "trance."

He then turns his focus on the behind-the-scenes world of the *Courier* and his own treatment in its columns:

I am not in sympathy with the personalities in the Courier, personalities that you lay at the door of the critics of the dailies. On this your logic is sadly defective though more than counterbalanced by your sense of humor.

The way my name has been banded [sic] about in a paper that I wrote for has been, and is excessively distasteful to me. Only in the last issue am I deliberately insulted in two different parts of the sheet.

I am heartily weary of the atmosphere of petty intrigue, personalities and futile bickerings that disgrace the profession of weekly musical journalism.

And this from a man who had devoted fifteen years of his life to the development of a publication that he felt to be a repository for his idealistic activity.

This background information serves to substantiate Herbert's characterization of Blumenberg at trial. Unfortunately, none of this material was available to Herbert's counsel, and the case made in court to paint Blumenberg in a negative light in the minds of the jury was based on hearsay and unsubstantiated testimony, admitted by the trial judge under strenuous exception taken by Blumenberg's attorneys, Howe and Hummel.

Motivation is always an issue at any trial for substantial damages and, as background for establishing any malice Blumenberg may have felt toward Herbert, there is one small but fascinating detail that surfaces in an article from the *New York Times* dating from 1887, the period when Herbert was touring with the Emma Juch company.

> In Mr. Herbert Miss Juch has an invaluable assistant. His accompaniments are faultless in their intelligence and taste. His violin-cello solo showed a degree of mastery not often met among the few who attain excellence upon that far too little cultivated instrument.
>
> Taking Louis Blumenberg as the standard American player Mr. Herbert may be said to equal him in finish, to surpass him in adherence to musical interpretation and to be inferior to him only in a slight coarseness of tone at times.[12]

This article reveals a personal angle that may have colored Blumenberg's attitude toward his relative's rival.

The fact that during the period when Herbert was developing his career as virtuoso and composer of classical works, the pages of the *Courier* had nothing but praise for him, is not as damning as Herbert's counsel would have it.

One of the suggestions made at trial was that the tone of the *Courier* comments in re Herbert had changed when Herbert stopped advertising in its pages. The *Courier* had indeed praised Herbert in 1891 ("The Captive"), 1892 ("Irish Rhapsody"), 1897 ("The Serenade"), 1900 ("Suite Romantique"), and 1901 ("Hero and Leander"). What Herbert's counsel neglected to include in his argument is that all of these positive notices were written by Herbert's close friend Huneker—not by Marc Blumenberg. What is more, they were not included in the editorial content of the paper, but in Huneker's "Raconteur" column, a popular feature that everyone knew expressed the critic's personal opinions rather than the editorial position of the paper. Thus, nothing had changed with respect to Blumenberg's opinion of Herbert. At no time had he been a "boomer" of the composer. The putative relationship between advertising and positive notices was nonexistent in Herbert's case.

In the pages of rival publications it was said that the musical world at large held the *Courier* and its editor in contempt. But W. J. Henderson, critic of the *New York Times*, is quoted as believing that professional musicians themselves were responsible for the success of the *Courier*.

> I remember one musician who came to me with a long tale of woe about the Courier and its wickedness. I had chanced to see his portrait on the cover . . . together with one of those nice, fat articles inside, and I said to him, "Don't you talk to me about the Musical Courier, for I know that you want it. You want praise and you've got to have it. You can't earn it and you can't buy it in the daily papers, but you can buy it in the Courier, so you must have the Courier." . . . These people want that paper; they will stand by it and pay for its praise. They will themselves be dishonest in order that they may get dishonest praise before the public.
>
> I recall one instance when a lady whose daughter had appeared as a violinist the night before, came to the Times office and asked me, "Where is the good notice that my daughter was to receive in the Times this morning?" "What good notice were you to receive?" I asked. "Why," she answered, "I paid Mr. Blumenberg $300.00 and he promised that he would get me good notices in all the New York dailies."
>
> Supposing that young woman had played well and we critics had said that she played well. Mr. Blumenberg would have gone to that woman with the clippings from our papers in his hands and said, "See, I did as I said I would."[13]

This testimony was presented not at trial, but at a testimonial dinner held to celebrate Herbert's victory at the close of the initial phase of the litigation. One must consider the source of this report: the *Concert Goer*, a rival publication out to blacken the image of the *Courier* in the public eye. Henderson was, of course, a respected figure in the world of music journalism. But one must wonder, with all the cadre of professional musicians called to testify in Herbert's behalf—Otto Weil, the manager of the Witmark publishing house, Frederick Ranken and Kirke LaShelle, two of his librettists, Henry Hadley, a composer of some note in that period, Walter Damrosch, conductor of the New York Symphony Society—that not one shred of evidence was introduced at trial along the lines of Henderson's anecdotal comments. Where was Henderson? Where was the aggrieved mother? Where was the musician who complained so bitterly of the *Courier*'s "wickedness"? Their absence at trial speaks volumes. We may well ask what caused Henderson to speak so virulently at Herbert's celebratory dinner. Was this catalogue of infamies occasioned by the occasion itself? The length and detail of Hendeson's remarks prove that no little preparation went into the presentation.

The truth is that the critic had recently taken up a new post at the *New York Sun*, which promised to publish his name as author of his articles. This was a groundbreaking event in music journalism, since the custom of the period was to publish unsigned critiques. Just a week before, Blumenberg had unleashed a brilliant, sarcastic commentary on this event. He began by revealing that the *New York Tribune* had issued a circular and mailed it to potential advertisers, that the mailing list had been culled from the list of *Courier* advertisers, and that the mailing offered to publish advertisements in the *Tribune* at lower rates than those charged by the *Courier*. Blumenberg recognized this as a "legitimate business proposition" and went on to comment that, obviously, the *Tribune* felt it could reach a greater number of potential advertisers by copying the *Courier*'s list than by offering advertisements only to the readers of its own pages. The conclusion was evidently that more people read the *Courier* than read the music items in the *Tribune*.

> We confess that a circular issued by a newspaper indicates that its circulation does not cover the ground as effectively as a circular can; ergo, why should people advertise in such a paper?

Blumenberg then turned to Henderson.

> The advertisers list of the Musical Courier has also been personally requisitioned by W. J. Henderson, of the Sun, in circularizing the following card:
>
>> Mr. W. J. Henderson begs leave to announce that he has accepted the musical editorship of the New York Sun. Mr. Henderson will make a feature of his Sunday articles in the Sun and will comment daily in its columns on all current performances.

This, Blumenberg wrote, constituted

a digression in the etiquette of the profession, a new departure, for it [a signed article] constitutes an advertisement, and music critics have hitherto not advertised themselves directly. If Mr. Henderson desires to reach hundreds of thousands of readers on music his advertisement, as issued, is no comparison to a card in this paper [the Courier] which is read by the universe of music.

Both Henderson and Blumenberg recognize, the editor continued, the legitimate nature and value of advertising. He then invites Henderson to publish an ad in the *Courier*, for that is a "Far, far better, more practical and more comprehensive method of advertising than a circular sent through the mails." Then the coup de grâce: if everyone were to adopt Henderson's practice

Then there would be no newspapers and then there would be no music critics, because they could not exist without the newspaper existing first. . . .

Men who get their living out of newspapers should be the first to advocate advertising on principle because they subsist on it, and out of it comes the profits which enable the newspapers to pay such eminent writers as Mr. Henderson.[14]

Thus, with succulent and brittle sarcasm, Blumenberg demolished the pretense of his enemies—that they were above the commercial fray—and showed them to be the hypocrites they were when they accused him of motives from which, by implication, they were exempt.

The precipitating event that caused Herbert to take action was the publication of Blumenberg's editorial of July 17, 1901. We know from the internal memo already quoted, and from the unrelenting barrage of invective directed at Herbert's work in Pittsburgh, that Blumenberg had made up his mind that he was "no good" and a "fake." Herbert's complaint states that the editorial contained the following "false and defamatory matter":

1. A cablegram from London states that Victor Herbert's "Fortune Teller" made a most lamentable failure at the Shaftsbury Theatre.

2. The "Fortune Teller" had no merit whatever. All of Victor Herbert's "written to order" comic operas are pure and simple

plagiarisms; there is not one single aria, waltz movement, polka, gallop or march in these operas that has touched the public's ear, and the street pianos and organs have ignored them—the best evidence that the people do not find them palatable. The whole Sousa repertory is alive and pulsating; the whole Herbert repertory is stone dead . . . an agglomeration of puerile piracies.

3. Everything written by Herbert is copied; there is not one original strain in anything he has done, and all his copies are from sources that are comic or serio-comic.

4. The great symphony conductors are not drafted from the ranks of composers of shoddy American farce operas, alias leg shows, nor are they taken from the leaders of parading military bands.[15]

Herbert maintained that these statements were false and defamatory and, further, that they were written and printed maliciously and with a wrongful intent of injuring him in the community and in his profession. He demanded judgment of $50,000, plus costs.

Blumenberg responded that there was no evidence of actual malice on his part, and that Herbert could not prove any special damage, i.e., loss of income. Further, the alleged "libel" was made up partly of statements of fact and partly of privileged expressions of opinion.

There were true facts in the editorial. The statement that the telegram was sent was, of course, true. The information contained in the cable was opinion. In any case the *Courier* was merely repeating what the London critics had said. It was beyond dispute that in the field of symphonic conducting, custom placed "at its interpretive head" only those closely identified with the pursuit of classical music. Expressions of opinion in the article were justified as a matter of musical criticism, and therefore privileged. The balance of Blumenberg's critique was made up of such criticism as would likely appear in any musical journal. Blumenberg stipulated that he had written the editorial, and satisfactorily explained why he had criticized Herbert's compositions. He fully justified every opinion expressed by him.

Asked as to the grounds of his opinions that "The Fortune Teller" had no merit whatever, and that all of Herbert's written-to-order comic operas were pure and simple plagiarisms, Blumenberg gave this explanation:

a. that music written to order (i.e., to a prepared libretto for the purpose of public entertainment) is not classical music—art music in any sense.

b. that such music may be grammatically correct, but it is not original, i.e., it has no creative character. It is commonplace, in order to reach the taste of the public, which is not educated in classical music.

As to why he wrote as he did, Blumenberg continued

c. that the purpose of the *Musical Courier* is to educate the people in classical music and *to discourage* "this kind of music that Mr. Herbert has written."

He further explained that

It was only after he got into the business of writing music to order that he fell from that high stand [i.e., of classical music composer], and for that reason the paper protested that a person who lives in the atmosphere of comic opera music cannot legitimately aspire to do that which men do who devote themselves to classical music.

Referring to the passage of purple prose that claimed Herbert's music to have been rejected by the general public and constituting an "agglomeration of puerile piracies," Blumenberg responded:

This may be a somewhat extravagant manner of stating well-known facts, and the adjectives used may be strong, yet it falls within the line of fair criticism. . . . Mere rhetorical expressions are not sufficient to constitute libel per se.

Not only did it constitute fair criticism, it was the sort of diction that was in common use in that period. For example, in 1901 Huneker had added to his work at the *Courier* by accepting the position of associate music editor of the *Sun*. One of his earliest reviews discussed the premiere of *Tosca* at the Met. This piece is important because it contains phrases that directly relate to Blumenberg's criticism of Herbert: "Puccini's themes are *neither original* nor generally expressive. . . . His writing is all top and bottom, the inner weaving *puerile*"[16] [italics mine].

The significance of this passage is that it supports Blumenberg's concept of originality. Taken by themselves and examined from the perspective of a century past, Blumenberg's definition of originality and use of the word "puerile" seem on the one hand tortured, and on the other extreme. But placed in the context of Huneker's review from the same period, and remembering that Huneker had been part of the *Courier*'s team and shared the paper's vocabulary and style, it is possible to read Blumenberg's comments in a light more favorable to the editor's cause.

With respect to the issue of Herbert's originality and his definition of "copied music," Blumenberg explained that he did not mean to imply that Herbert deliberately and consciously copied mechanically, note for note, but that his music lacked originality in the sense that it was reminiscent and contained no themes or motifs that were original with him. At this point the issues replicated the case that Samuel Lover had brought against the *Atheneum* fifty years earlier.

> Copied music that is taken from preceding sources is not necessarily copied mechanically. A musician carries any quantity of airs in his mind and recalls at once phrases or musical themes. . . . There is no original air in the Herbert compositions. Much of the music Mr. Herbert has written is good music, legitimate music, honest music; but not original. It is copied music.

> Copied music is copied very frequently unconsciously. By stating that a musician copies music or is not original in his composition is no reflection on him whatsoever, because the great bulk of musicians copy unconsciously. . . . But if you compare [their work] with other works you will find that they have taken melodies and harmonic sequences from other works. Hearing it so many times these things impress themselves upon their minds and they unconsciously copy it. That is the difference between real genius and other musicians.

This, then, was Blumenberg's somewhat tortured defense: his opinions may be mistaken, but there was sufficient ground for them to redeem them from the charge of deliberate libel. With respect to the issue of his borrowings we have one brief statement from Herbert himself: "It's no disgrace to borrow folk-melodies. The greatest composers have done it."[17] This statement was made long after the suit was settled, but it gives us insight into Herbert's attitude, and lends credence to Blumenberg's position that he was not above writing "copied music."

Malice is a function of motivation, and it was in this area that Blumenberg's defense seemed to falter. The real issue was not so much the definition of originality or the strength of Blumenberg's prose, but whether the article complained of was a malicious libel or a candid musical criticism expressing the honest opinion of the writer. In an attempt to prove that Blumenberg's motivation was related to the fact that Herbert had discontinued advertisements in the *Courier*, Herbert's counsel entered into the record several advertisements for the 22nd Regiment Band that appeared in 1896 and 1898. These contained a picture of Herbert and, as such, were accepted, over strenuous objection, as evidence that Herbert had personally advertised in those years. No attempt was made to examine the source of funding for the ads, whether they came from Herbert or from the Regiment itself.

Entered into the record were several passages from the *Courier* that lavishly praise Herbert as a musician, even at one point referring to him as the "Irish Wagner." It was never mentioned that these passages were by Huneker, writing in a non-editorial capacity.

Counsel then engaged in the following colloquy with Blumenberg:

Q. Did you at one time have a lawyer by the name of Lellman?

A. Yes.

Q. He was your lawyer during the years 1898 and 1899.

A. Mr. Lellman had charge of some legal business of the paper.

Q. Did you ever authorize Lellman to say to Mr. Weil if Herbert would pay you $2000.00 you would stop pounding him?

A. I never used such language in my life to anybody.

Q. Did you ever say to Mr. Weil in the latter part of 1898 that you admired Victor Herbert and you believe him to be a good musician, but that your criticisms were because of the business of the transaction?

A. Never remember it.

Q. Did you ever say that to him?

A. No, sir.

Q. Do you remember that?

A. I don't remember speaking to Mr. Weil more than half a dozen times.

Q. Do you remember Mr. Weil coming to you and telling you he had a conversation with your lawyer?

A. No, sir.

Q. And you say you never did say to him that Victor Herbert was a good musician, that you admired him, but that you pounded him as a matter of business?

A. No.

Q. Or words similar to that?

A. Never.

Herbert's counsel was attempting to prove through this line of questioning that the negative treatment Herbert received in the editorial was a result of his failure to maintain his advertising in the *Courier*. Otto Weil, manager for Herbert's publisher Witmark, had testified earlier at trial that he had known the Herberts since their arrival in the United States in 1886, and that he was a personal friend of Mr. Herbert and his family. What he did not mention in his response was that he had been a schoolmate of Theresa in Vienna. His relationship with the Herberts was of longer standing than their arrival, a fact that may have colored his testimony. In any event, Weil never testified to the conversation that Herbert's counsel imputed to him in this questioning. The purpose was obviously to plant in the mind of the jury the idea of a mercenary basis for the article.

Even more revealing is the issue of Lellman himself. At the time of the trial Lellman was deceased, and therefore any putative conversations with him could not be directly substantiated. Lellman is mentioned as the source of the "pounding" statement, a statement that, if accepted by the jury, could constitute malice. The implication is that Lellman, as an employee of the *Courier*, never would have made a statement so potentially damaging to his employer, if it had not been true.

In fact, however, Lellman was much more than Blumenberg's attorney. The baptismal records of St. Agnes Chapel of Trinity Parish reveal that at the time of the baptism of Herbert's children on August 7, 1899, Herbert had chosen Charles Lellman and his wife Ellen to be godparents to his children as their sponsors at baptism. This is a sure indication that Lellman was as close to the Herberts as can be imagined. The relationship was not brought out at trial, as it would have served to impeach any purported comments Lellman might have made in support of Herbert's claim of malice. The fact that Lellman was deceased, and that nevertheless potentially damaging indirect testimony was admitted to the record over counsel's strenuous objection, is typical of the bias of the court. The jury returned a verdict in favor of Herbert, but reduced the amount of the award from his requested $50,000 to $15,000, plus costs of $158.40. On appeal the Appellate Division further reduced the award to $5,158.40. The order of the court stated in effect that if Herbert agreed to the reduced judgment, then the Appellate Division affirmed the modified sum. If Herbert did not agree, then the judgment was reversed and a new trial ordered. One justice dissented on the grounds that the judgment of the trial court should be reversed. In other words, you get $5,000, take it or leave it. Herbert, on advice of counsel, took it—as a triumph.

When the jury brought in its verdict Herbert felt vindicated, in spite of the fact that the reward had been greatly reduced. Fritz Stahlberg recalled, "There has been much said about Victor Herbert's drinking, but in the many years I knew him I saw him in somewhat higher spirits only twice. The first time was at Lüchow's after he had won his suit against the *Musical Courier*."[18] This must have been an informal gathering of cronies who repaired to Herbert's favorite haunt immediately after the verdict came in. The formal celebration was organized by Walter Damrosch as a tribute to the composer by "Friends of Music." This banquet was attended by the leaders of New York's musical world, eighty men culled from the ranks of music critics, instrument manufacturers, managers, publishers and patrons. The committee included Krehbiel, Weil, Alexander Lambert, director of the New York College of Music, and August Spanuth, critic of the *Staats-Zeitung*. All the witnesses who had testified on Herbert's behalf were present. The only prominent member of the musical fraternity who was conspicuous by his absence was Huneker. Although he expressed his disapproval of Blumenberg's remarks privately,[19] his loyalty to the editor was such that he chose not to associate himself with the public celebration.

The after-dinner toasts began with Damrosch's remarks. He praised Herbert for having "done more to break the miserable power of the *Musical Courier* than anything that ever happened. This gathering," he continued, "shows that the better element of the musical profession is determined to suffer no longer the attacks of this disreputable sheet." Damrosch, caught up in the moment and infatuated with the echoing tones of his famously booming baritone, referred to Herbert as "the courageous man who with one blow defeated this dragon, this hydra. Hoch soll er leben!" And at this the crowd stood as one and, with glasses raised, sang the beerhall refrain: "Ein Prosit! Ein Prosit der Gemütlichkeit!"[20]

Herbert was not a confident public speaker, and usually restricted himself to a few modest remarks on such occasions. Here he uncharacteristically spoke for ten minutes. He recognized the celebration as a victory in which he "chanced by circumstances to be the conqueror" and declared his happiness that the opportunity was given to him to "punish a common foe for all musicians." In discussing the effectiveness of Damrosch's testimony, he declared, "So clearly and singly did he show up the falsity of the charges, that even a policeman had tears in his eyes—and a Irish policeman at that!"[21]

This bit of levity changed the tone of the evening, which had been filled with condemnation of Blumenberg and his publication in the worst possible terms. ("We must one and all agree that there shall be no more blackmail possible," Frank Damrosch declared.) As a final coup de thé-âtre, a response had been prepared to Blumenberg's charge that "not even the street organs had taken up his music." The revelers produced a hand organ that ground out a series of Herbert melodies.[22] The following Saturday the *Concert Goer*, the rival music publication that billed itself as "the Dependable Musical Weekly," reported that Blumenberg had used "strenuous efforts to intimidate men who had planned to attend this banquet," and further that their attendance demonstrated that "the sentiment against his paper was stronger than any fear for the revenge that he is expected to take upon those who identified themselves as his opponents." The *Concert Goer* then proclaimed popular satisfaction over the fact that "this vicious journalist had at last been successfully brought to the bar of justice."

Those remarks were not enough for the *Concert Goer*. In its next issue it continued its negative attacks:

> The abnormal egotism of Mr. Blumenberg has enabled him to weather
> many a storm of indignation, and he has bobbed up serenely after
> rebuffs that would cause a man of ordinary sensibilities to seek
> isolation from his fellowman. But it is difficult to conceive of a manner
> of man who can withstand the avalanche of condemnation that has
> been let loose by the incident of Blumenberg's prosecution by Mr.
> Victor Herbert.[23]

As much as his enemies would like to have seen Blumenberg defeated, defeat was the furthest thing from the editor's mind. In the first issue of the *Courier* published after the jury's verdict, Blumenberg wrote an editorial detailing its implications for the profession of criticism at large. He began by asserting the basic incompetence of a lay jury adjudicating matters requiring highly technical expertise. (This is a ploy frequently used by the losing side in any litigation. All juries are to some extent technically unsophisticated; it is the responsibility of counsel to clarify the issues.) When Blumenberg moved to the business side of publishing, he was on firmer ground. "If lay juries are to determine the value of a grievance in dollars and cents then the whole world of music publishing is threatened—since no one will invest in a paper whose liability to such suits is established in law."[24] If this were to happen, Blumenberg concluded, the whole world of music publishing would be threatened, since not only would no one invest in a critical organ so threatened by potential litigation from anyone who felt himself aggrieved by its commentary, but no new papers would be established, since they could not raise the capital needed to protect themselves from such litigations. The other alternative, equally dangerous to the profession, would be for critics to write nothing but innocuous articles. In either instance critical function would be seriously impaired.

> Our music critics have prejudices, and prejudices are motives. . . . So there is always at the bottom of a critic's statement some motive . . . when it comes down to the very concrete criticism of a person or the nature of his composition, particularly when it is an aggressive—a strong and powerful criticism that expresses decided opinions . . . such criticism is now subject to a libel suit. . . . The question is whether it is not necessary for the time being to abrogate criticism altogether. The situation will discourage the publication of any article which may elicit grievance and thus damage the profession.[25]

This is *ruductio ad absurdum*. The fact that one jury in a single instance had returned a verdict for damages in a libel suit in no way invalidated the critical process for any and all situations. Nor did it damage the profession of musical criticism or stem the proliferation of writers on music. The best argument against Blumenberg's position comes from the man himself. He continued to attack his enemies with equal doses of vitriol and sarcasm until his death in 1913. His portrayal of W. J. Henderson as a man of business, not above advertising himself, was just one instance of Blumenberg's undiminished critical activity.

In the issue of November 5 he published this disclaimer:

> The criticisms of musical performances, of musical works and the productions of musical authors will continue to be published in this paper on the basis of its attitude during the past twenty-odd years, and if any musicians feel themselves aggrieved it would be an excellent idea for them to express to us the nature of the grievances so that we may be led to an intelligent understanding as to the justification.

> Every aggressive paper necessarily invites hostility, but its existence and its prosperity are evidence in themselves that its expressions on the average must be satisfactory.[26]

Blumenberg's coverage of the celebratory dinner is amusing in its refusal to name names or even to identify the purpose of the event: "The committee that has been appointed for a dinner to be given next Monday night for the purpose of something or other consists of the music critics of the Tribune, of the critic of a German paper, of the conductor of an orchestra in this city and of a clerk in a sheet music house uptown."[27] He then suggests that the sole purpose of the dinner is commercial, a "scheme for advancing the business of a sheet music house. . . . Why was it not possible to organize a committee that was free from all pecuniary and business interests and that really represented a sentiment? Because *there is no sentiment against the Musical Courier* [italics mine]. There are some individual prejudices and there are certain personal interests opposed to the Musical Courier, but otherwise there are no SENTIMENTS OF ANY KIND OPPOSED TO THIS PAPER—and even if this were the case it would not amount to anything anyway, because this is a universal publication that goes all over the globe, and is not merely a local enterprise."

This is a defensive disconnect from reality worthy of Captain Queeg. But Blumenberg wasn't finished, for he had found a new arch enemy in the person of Henderson, to whom he turned his attention in the issue of November 26. He printed a letter from the *Courier*'s Berlin office that recounted how a young, aspiring music critic arrived with a letter of introduction from Henderson.

> While Henderson was preparing his hostile and unwarranted
> speech—a speech in which he mentioned something he cannot
> prove—the machinery of this business and the influence of this paper
> were being used to his interests, for the letter of introduction from him
> to our Berlin correspondent must prove of some direct or indirect
> benefit to him. This very music critic did not hesitate to use us, while
> within his mind he was nourishing abuse of us, which he poured forth
> with vitriolic violence at a dinner given ostensibly to honor a man, but
> in reality to make a demonstration against this paper.[28]

Blumenberg described the dinner as a "humiliating fiasco" and characterized the whole activity as an attempt by the critics of the major New York dailies to injure the *Courier*. How foolish this was, for

> They [the critics] have actually posed as interested litigants who were
> through a libel verdict given against a newspaper. That is to say they

have encouraged libel actions. . . . The critics place the dailies at a disadvantage and at considerable financial risk since the music budget of the daily papers is a source of loss and not profit, hence libel cases against the papers must end the critics, for the stockholders of the corporations of the daily papers will not suffer the cost and consequence. . . . The music writers who attended that so called demonstration against the *Musical Courier* must see—unless they are actually as dense as is usually assumed—that they were engaged in digging their own graves. They were endorsing all kinds of schemes to promote libel cases against music criticism, and that puts a conclusive conclusion to music criticism in the daily papers. . . . [The celebratory dinner] seems after all to have been a modern Belshazzar's feast.[29]

In 1904, on appeal from the decision of the appellate division, the Court of Appeals upheld the verdict in the amount of $5,000 plus costs. Both editor and composer went on to greater triumphs than those provided by *Victor Herbert* v. *The Musical Courier Company*.

The White-Smith Music Publishing Company v. The Apollo Company

On November 28 and 29, 1887, in Chickering Hall in New York, a benefit reading for the American Copyright League took place and here, before large and enthusiastic audiences, appeared the chief representatives of American literature: James Russell Lowell, Oliver Wendell Holmes, John Greenleaf Whittier, Samuel Langhorne Clemens among them.[30]

One of the most attentive members of that audience was Victor Herbert. As a fledgling composer he had a vital interest in the copyright issues. As recently as 1884, Congress had failed once again to protect the interests of American artists. Since under the current law American producers and publishers were free to gain from the creative output of Europeans without paying a cent, native creators were placed at a disadvantage. Why should anyone pay royalties for a Victor Herbert work when one by a European composer could be produced here without payment of royalties? From the earliest days of his American career, Herbert was personally involved with issues of copyright and the protection of the interests of American artists.

Harry B. Smith, Herbert's most frequent librettist, writing in the *American Mercury* shortly after Herbert's death,[31] pointed to the great profits earned by the manufacturers of mechanical instruments for reproducing sound performances, at the expense of composers who had created the material. With hyperbolic enthusiasm he referred to "The recent death, in absolute destitution, of a man whose writing gave pleasure to American theater goers for many years and whose songs are known to hundreds of thousands of people."

Herbert did not die a pauper. He was generous during his lifetime, but what the man chose to do with his money was his own business; the restrictions the law placed on his potential income, Herbert *made* his business.

There is a famous photograph taken in February, 1924, in front of the National Press Club in Washington. Here are pictured most of the great creators of American popular music: Herbert, Berlin, Smith, Kern, Sousa, and many, many more had descended on the Senate to testify in favor of liberalization of copyright laws. It wasn't the first time they had appeared before the Congress, but it was the last time they would enjoy Herbert's leadership. Questioned before the Senate Committee on Patents, Herbert testified that he had earned $500 per day making phonograph records as conductor of the Victor Herbert Orchestra. That sounded like big money to the Senators.

After the hearing, a senator approached Herbert. "Sir," he began, "you should not expect to be paid for your music. God gave you your talent and your work belongs to the world. You should be proud to have your songs sung by the people. You should be above asking for payments for them." To which Herbert replied, "Fine! And I am to be fed by ravens, I suppose?"[32]

The anecdote sums up the attitude of many politicians toward the interests of creative artists versus those of manufacturers. This was Washington, of course, and then, as now, money talked. What were the chances of musicians opposed to the interests of businessmen? Those who would have bet against Herbert in the contest would have been foolish indeed. In 1907 his interest in promoting a just copyright law was such that he instructed his attorney, Nathan Burkan, to file an amicus brief with the Supreme Court of the United States in the matter of *White-Smith Music Publishing Company* v. *Apollo Company*, a manufacturer of piano rolls, recording cylinders and disks. These perforated purveyors of parlor performances filled the homes of middle America with song—much of it by Victor Herbert. The substance of Herbert's brief stated that he suffered great loss and injury by reason of the unauthorized use made of his copyrighted compositions by persons and corporations engaged in the sale of perforated music rolls and other devices adapted to the automatic reproduction of music. The copyright statutes then in effect had been drafted long before machines for the automatic reproduction of music had been invented. Herbert determined that a new law was needed, and with that in mind he put together a posse of creative artists, including Julian Edwards, John Philip Sousa, George Ade, Gustav Kerker, Henry Blossom, Reginald de Koven, George Hobart, Harry B. Smith, Gustave Luders and Glen MacDonough, to lobby Congress for change. These men formed the Authors and Composers Copyright League of America, of which Herbert was elected President.

It is a measure of the importance of the copyright issue to the composer that he accepted the presidency. In later years he always refused to serve as president of the many clubs and societies of which he was a member, since such responsibility would rob him of time better spent in composition. When ASCAP was founded he would only serve as vice president; he accepted election only as "boy" of the Lambs [vice president]; he also served as vice president of the Friendly Sons of St. Patrick.

In 1907, Senator Alfred Kittridge submitted a bill to extend copyright to mechanical recording devices. After creative artists had done their best and publishers had spent time and money to bring the work before the public, if a song proved popular, as one songwriter said, "Then the mechanical and talking machine sharks come in. Like their slimy brothers of the deep they smell from afar the blood of their victim and gather around the helpless prize. They seize the musical child of the composer's brain and devote it to their own selfish purposes."[33]

Naturally the "sharks" had no intention of allowing Kittredge's bill to pass. They enlisted Representative Frank Currier on their side. Currier attempted to rush through the House his own revision of the copyright law, which contained a paragraph fatal to creators' interests. Copyright was

> To include the exclusive right to print, reprint, publish, copy, arrange or adapt a musical work, provided that the words to rearrange or adapt, if it be a musical work, shall not for the purpose of this act be deemed to include perforated rolls used in playing musical instruments, or records used for the reproduction of sound waves, or the matrices or other appliances by which such rolls or records are made.[34]

When he saw the text of Currier's bill, Herbert exploded:

> Mr. Currier's bill deliberately aims to discourage the American composer. For it expressly sanctions the confiscation of his works by corporations engaged in the manufacture of phonograph records and perforated rolls. . . . [These] are rapidly supplementing sheet music. The endeavors of the musician to have his rights protected led the President [Theodore Roosevelt] to urge a change in the copyright law, after which Mr. Currier introduced a bill which omitted all references to mechanical devices.[35]

This, Herbert stated, was done in anticipation of the decision in *White-Smith* being favorable to composers, with the aim of nullifying such a decision. Herbert then revealed Currier to be the lackey of the manufacturing trust, since

> The very provision that Mr. Currier has incorporated in his new bill was proposed [at hearings on the copyright revision] in almost identical words by the attorney for several of these corporations. . . . The enactment of this provision would be a staggering blow to the art of music and the cause of intellectual labor. Never in the history of American legislation has any bill been passed deliberately depriving intellectual labor of the protections it has been entitled to.[36]

Herbert then proceeded to an issue that had often caught Teddy Roosevelt's attention: he painted the activities of the manufacturers as those of a monopolistic trust.

> What will Congress say to a bill that permits these corporations, which by secret agreements have managed to keep the entire market to themselves, to exploit and appropriate the intellectual creations of the composer: that will enable them to thrive and wallow in wealth while the composer must see his name and that of the offspring of his brain emblazoned on the management shop windows of the trust, announcing that thousands of records of a masterpiece have been sold, for which he has been paid not a penny.[37]

Senator Kittredge, presiding at the hearings of the joint committee on patents, remarked that the committee had been moved to a sense of natural justice by Herbert's testimony, and that the position of the manufacturers was manifestly selfish. Thus Herbert returned from Washington anticipating a victory in the court and continued his war on what he termed "mutilated melody" in the press. The Copyright Association rapidly expanded its membership to 5,000, and the leaders engaged in a lobbying blitz that included a visit to the White House by composer Charles K. Harris. He made the point that his hit, "After the Ball," published before mechanical reproduction had been developed, sold 1,500,000 copies, but his later song, "Break The News To Mother," a sentimental ballad of the Spanish War period, had sold only one-third as many copies because of the activities of the talking machine companies.

Unfortunately for Herbert, the Supreme Court was bound by the existing copyright law, and therefore decided the issue in favor of the manufacturers. Mr. Justice Daw, writing for the Court, declared that perforated rolls were not "copies within the meaning of the act." Mr. Justice Holmes concurred, but wrote an opinion strongly suggesting the need for copyright revision in favor of the rights of composers.

In March of 1909, Herbert et al. again descended on Washington and went head-to-head with the representatives of the manufacturers. Herbert's testimony, the arguments of his counsel Nathan Burkan, and the strong implication of Justice Holmes's decision tipped the scales in favor of Herbert's cause, but only slightly. The law was amended to provide the specific royalty of two cents per mechanical copy to the creator. Herbert had won a moral victory in law, although he was much dissatisfied with the statutory amount. In this he was certainly justified, for the two cents plain award, which went into effect on July 1, 1909, was still bitterly complained of in Harry Smith's article of August, 1924. Such riches as followed from Herbert's efforts would flow only to his heirs.

 Herbert v. *Shanley's Restaurant Corporation*

In this old town,
where e're you go,
The Very Best
Is SHANLEY'S show.

New York's Greatest Restaurant
Broadway—43rd and 44th Streets

The world's Wonder Cabaret
From 7 P.M. Until 1 A.M.
20 ACTS[38]

In 1917 Herbert brought ASCAP its greatest triumph. Were it not for the outcome of this litigation, it is questionable whether the organization would have continued to exist. Because of the decision, composers who had only one source of income—the sale of sheet music—acquired the right under federal law to royalties for public performances of their work for profit, to phonograph royalties, and later, by extension, to royalties from radio, television and film use of copyrighted works.

The battle was not an easy one. At one point ASCAP was ready to throw in the towel. It was only Herbert's persistence that brought the matter to the Supreme Court, the scene of his eventual triumph under the benign eye of Mr. Justice Holmes, who had earlier ruled against Herbert's interests, being hamstrung by the then existing copyright law. It is almost as if Herbert knew that Holmes was waiting for the opportunity to interpret the statute to protect the interests of creative artists.

Shanley's Inc. operated three large restaurants in New York, two on Broadway and one on Sixth Avenue. The scene of the alleged copyright infringement was a cavernous emporium on the ground floor of the block between 43rd and 44th streets. The dining room, dominated by huge crystal chandeliers and famous for the ministrations of a liveried waitstaff, featured a huge round table reserved for the leading personalities of the theatrical world. This Stammtsich was the forerunner of the Algonquin "round table" of the 1920s, which was a focus for literary rather than theatrical artists. From noon to 2 P.M. at luncheon and in the evenings from 7 till 1 A.M. a cabaret was presented for the entertainment of the 2,500 patrons who daily filled the room. This was not a cabaret in the Parisian sense, a series of quasi-theatrical song and dance numbers alternating with acrobatic acts, magic turns and the like. The Shanley cabaret was restricted to musical performances. The repertoire was varied: there were light classics, operatic arias, popular songs of the day and numbers from successful Broadway entertainments. In offering this program Shanley's was far from unique. Live performances were featured in all restaurants that could afford them; they were a standard addition to the ambiance of fine dining

In his suit, Herbert and the co-creators of the operetta *Sweethearts* charged that one of the songs performed there on April 1, 1915, was the title song of that work. This constituted a public performance of a dramatic work for profit and as such was a violation of Herbert's copyright. This seemed a simple, straightforward assertion, but it flew in the face of a recent decision that placed such a claim in legal jeopardy.

In the case of *Church* v. *Hilbert Hotel Co.* (U.S. Dist. Ct. for the So. Dist. of NY, 1914) the publisher of a Sousa march claimed that it had been performed at the hotel dining room in violation of copyright. The trial judge had found in favor of Sousa and his publisher, remarking that the hotel would not have paid the musicians to play if it didn't stand to gain from the performance. This decision was reversed on appeal to the 2nd Circuit. There the judge reasoned that people go to a restaurant primarily to eat and drink, and further that "they pay for what they order and not for the music. . . . We are not convinced that the defendants played music for profit within the meaning of the words of the copyright act."[39]

ASCAP, which had contributed money to the costs of the litigation, was devastated by the decision. But Herbert's brilliant attorney, Nathan Burkan, was not. For the Shanley's suit he prepared an argument based on an aspect of the issue unexamined by the previous litigation. The copyright law grants to the owners of a dramatic work the exclusive right of public performance, irrespective of whether profit is involved. Burkan argued that the operetta *Sweethearts* was a dramatic work and thus protected, not only in whole, but also in part. Thus, the performance of the title song violated this aspect of copyright. Further, Burkan maintained that the purpose of the performance was to attract patrons, and that the musical cabaret was mentioned in the restaurant's advertisements. The wrongful performance caused great injury and damage to the business and profits of Herbert et al., because they were "deprived of the exclusive right to publicly perform and represent the said dramatico-musical composition *Sweethearts* and to grant to others the privilege to publicly perform and represent the said composition in the payment of royalties."

To all this Herbert added his own affidavit. He maintained that the situation damaged him in other ways than the purely financial ones addressed in Burkan's brief. Since the value of his copyright depended on his exclusive right to control public presentation, then the regular theatrical performances being given nightly in "hotels, restaurants and places of public accommodation," even if no direct charge is made for the performance, caused a "diminution of attendance" at licensed performances of the operetta *Sweethearts*. He was further deprived of the power to prevent inferior renditions of his works, and the injury to the artistic reputation of the work that would result from inferior representations.[40]

Shanley's admitted to performing *Sweethearts*, but claimed the performance was not for profit. It also denied that the performance could be characterized correctly as "dramatic," for there was no stage, no curtain, no special lighting, no costumes, and further, the young woman who performed the song was not an actress. Shanley's maintained that the musical presentation was incidental to its business, and that the price charged for food and drink would have been the same, with or without music. All of this argument was secondary to what followed, a devastating position: "The song, 'Sweethearts' . . . is published as a separate musical composition by Schirmer in the form ordinarily known as sheet music and is published as a complete musical composition in itself."[41] Thus, it was not part of a dramatic-musical work. Here Herbert was faced with the Church precedent. His reliance on the fact that the song was part of the score of *Sweethearts* and therefore qualified as a dramatico-musical work was shaken by the fact that the song had been published separately—and with a separate copyright.

The trial court issued its decision on May 1, 1915. The judge was Learned Hand, at the beginning of what was to become one of the most distinguished careers in the history of the American bench. The jurist relied on the Church precedent (music in a public place was not, per se, a performance for profit); further he agreed that a performance of the song "Sweethearts" *as part of a score* would have constituted an infringement of Herbert's right to control its public dramatic performance. But, he reasoned, since the individual song had been both published and copyrighted separately from the complete score and had been performed from the sheet music, Herbert had lost his protection of the dramatic rights in it. In sum, Herbert could not have it both ways. "There can be no justice in preserving dramatic rights at the expense of the public's rights arising from taking out a musical copyright. Had they (Herbert et al.) wished to retain a complete dramatic monopoly, they had it in their power to do so."[42]

On appeal, the same judge who had rendered the decision in Church accepted Judge Hand's reasoning and reaffirmed its previous decision, that the public performance of music is not for profit "when no admission fee is charged," specifically for the music.

Composers, authors and publishers saw the decision as a complete defeat. But not Herbert. He was not about to be defeated by a technicality. He entered an appeal to the United States Supreme Court, and the Court accepted the case. On January 22, 1917, Justice Holmes, writing for the Court, destroyed Shanley's argument that the music provided was a free benefit for patrons. After briefly summarizing the arguments of the lower courts Holmes lowered the boom:

If the rights under copyright are infringed only by a performance where money is taken in at the door, they are very imperfectly protected. Performances not different in kind from those of the defendants could be given that might compete with and even destroy the success of the monopoly that the law intends the plaintiffs to have.

There is no need to construe the statute so narrowly. The defendant's performances are not eleemosynary. They are part of a total for which the public pays, and the fact that the price of the whole is attributed to a particular item which those present are expected to order is not important.

It is true that the music is not the sole object, but neither is the food, which probably could be got cheaper elsewhere. The object is a repast in surroundings that, to people having limited powers of conversation or disliking the rival noise, give a luxurious pleasure not to be had from eating a silent meal.

If music did not pay, it would be given up. If it pays, it pays out of the public's pocket. Whether it pays or not, the purpose of employing it is profit, and that is enough.[43]

Herbert's persistence had won a signal victory far beyond his own parochial interests. Holmes's decision had established ASCAP as a viable force in the battle for the preservation of intellectual property rights. Generations of authors and composers then unborn, many of whom may not know the name of Victor Herbert, nevertheless stand deeply in his debt.

Herbert v. Broadway
(Including, but not limited to Joe Weber; Lee and J. J. Shubert; Irwin Rosen et al., etc. etc. etc.)

"The kingdom of light and lies." This was Jim Huneker's characterization of the world of Broadway theater. He made the statement long before Herbert entered the lists of creators of popular entertainments, but no more reliable witness could be called to testify to the truth of the statement than Herbert. Although the most significant aspects of his litigious activities were concerned with issues of libel and copyright, he was no slouch in defending his own interests elsewhere. Nathan Burkan's legal genius had successfully served him since the *Musical Courier* days and stood by him through countless forays in the courts. Scarcely a season passed that did not see Herbert involved in some legal brawl, and the hyperbole that characterized his public pronouncements provided a constant source of amusement to readers of the New York dailies.

Nor were Herbert's suits frivolous. Some of the wrongs that he contested are so egregious that, even in this era of corporate fraud and shenanigans, they retain their power to shock and awe. For example:

⤳ Herbert v. Weber

Joe Weber was famous as half of the team of "Weber and Fields," one of the premier dialect comedy acts in vaudeville. Weber was a smart operator. He knew the big money was in theater ownership and production, and he successfully operated his own house, "Joe Weber's Music Hall."

In 1906 Weber produced a new Herbert work at his theater, *Dream City* and *The Magic Knight*. It ran from December 1906 until June 1907, a respectable run for that period. It was the aftermath of this production that sent composer and producer to the courts.

Dream City was an ambitious satire on the activities of real estate developers on Long Island. These hoped to hoodwink the local hayseeds into selling their land cheap in return for promising their wives entrée into "society" by the construction of a grand opera house in the middle of one of their potato fields. After two acts of such nonsense, the show actually represented the opening night of the opera—a delicious-send up of *Lohengrin* and the Wagnerian ethos. This piece, *The Magic Knight*, is probably the earliest full-blown Wagner parody we have, if we except the sly Tristan/Walküre moments of Gilbert and Sullivan's *Iolanthe*.

Herbert had a contract with Weber that granted him 3 percent of the gross receipts. The show ran for twenty weeks, and Herbert earned $5,500 in royalties. After the initial run he leased the touring rights to Weber for one year at the same rate. Weber requested Herbert to consider reducing the percentage, but Herbert refused. Weber then attempted an end run. He dropped the *Lohengrin* satire completely and hired his house composer, Maurice Levi, to supply a new score for Edgar Smith's libretto. Weber felt he had a separate and distinct agreement with the composer and the librettist, and was therefore within his rights to drop either one. He purchased Levi's score outright, thus eliminating his obligation to pay him royalties; since he had eliminated Herbert's music, he paid the composer nothing.

The scene shifts to Weber's Music Hall, September 21, 1907, where the dress rehearsal for a new college musical, *Hip, Hip Hooray*, was in progress. Weber was on-stage directing a scene satirizing the vicissitudes of fraternity hazing when Burkan appeared, accompanied by a burly associate, marched down the aisle, and served Weber with the preliminary papers in an action to enjoin the touring production he had arranged. Weber had leased the touring rights to a subcontractor, and the show had opened the previous week in Asbury Park, New Jersey, advertised as "Direct from Weber's Theater, NEW YORK!" leading the public to believe that it was the same piece that had played there, i.e., a Victor Herbert operetta.

Herbert's Supreme Court brief maintained that Weber and Smith had "usurped his rights" by substituting a new score, and asked for an injunction, since the advertisement traded on the New York success to which he had contributed. As a result of the collaboration, Herbert claimed, the music was "incorporated and merged into and became part and parcel of" the operetta; the music "being so thoroughly adapted to the book and lyrics became invaluable in the show's production and absolutely useless and valueless without them."[44] Further, Weber had represented to Herbert that he had an agreement with the publisher Charles K. Harris to publish all the scores of musicals presented at his theater. Herbert agreed to such publication in return for a flat fee of $1,000—which had not been paid. Herbert claimed that the production violated his contract with the purpose of cheating and depriving him of his royalties, and that the action did him "irreparable injury." Nevertheless, he was willing to attempt an estimate of the damages in real money.

On October 21, 1907, Justice Seabury of the Supreme Court of the State of New York recognized Herbert's request for a restraining order, and the tour of *Dream City* came to an abrupt end in the pine barrens of New Jersey. Significantly, Seabury noted in his opinion that "the contract between Weber and Herbert provides that the music is not to be dissociated from the lyrics." With that as an indication of what might happen in a full-blown trial, Weber wisely decided to settle out of court—for an undisclosed sum.

Herbert v. Shubert Theatrical Co.

There are some instances in which the original evidence speaks more aptly than critical commentary. The following correspondence between the Shubert Brothers and Herbert's representatives concerns the original production of *The Duchess*, the last of a series of starring vehicles Herbert wrote for Fritzi Scheff.

This record of recrimination, delay, temporizing, threat, and cupidity is not without equal in the annals of the Broadway Theater. To anyone who has been there it's simply "business as usual." The real miracle on 39th–51st Street is that anything is produced at all![45]

J. J. Shubert–Nathan Burkan
My dear Mr. Burkan:
With reference to Mr. Victor Herbert's contract, I hardly think that Mr. Herbert would ask for the fulfillment of a contract which was rendered impossible. Mr. Herbert is familiar with the indifferent success of his play, and the moneys that we expended in trying to make the play a success. We did everything we possibly could—we tried it out last season and again this season, but the public would not have it, and I think in lieu of the fact that this show has cost us thousands of dollars, and also in view of the fact of the caprices of the star, that he will realize we could not continue any longer.
I am sure that Mr. Herbert will not lose anything by being lenient in this respect, as we may get some other play in the near future which may recuperate our losses and which will make up for the unfortunate conditions which resulted in our not being able to keep this play on tour as contemplated. I wish to state that I have written Mr. Herbert on the subject, as he is more familiar perhaps with the conditions.

Nathan Burkan–J. J. Shubert
Mr. Herbert instructs me to say to you in answer to your letter of the 22nd inst. addressed to him respecting the operetta "The Duchess" that he does not consider that he should change the terms of the contract because of what you say in regard to your great expense in making the production for this play. He insists that you carry out the stipulations of the agreement.

J. J. Shubert–Nathan Burkan
                                                                Feb. 1st, 1912
I have your letter of Jan. 31st, and note what you say in reference to Mr. Herbert's statement. Mr. Herbert does not say that he gave us a great operatic score like he gave "The Enchantress." I think the failure of the play was due to a combination of circumstances, and I am surprised that Mr. Herbert would want to take advantage of conditions for which he is as much responsible as anybody else. Had Mr. Herbert

worked in co-operation with us and given us as much time as he has given to his other operettas, perhaps we would have a different story to tell. I am only citing this as I do not think that Mr. Herbert is treating the matter fairly.

Nathan Burkan–Lee Shubert

Sometime ago I took up with your brother, Mr. J. J. Shubert, the matter of the claim of Victor Herbert against the Shubert Theatrical Company, for the stipulated royalty of $150.00 a week for each week less than twenty that the "DUCHESS" was produced during the present season.

A number of communications passed between your brother and myself, and between your brother and Mr. Herbert, but Mr. Herbert after considering the matter informed me Sunday last that he would not relinquish his claim, but that he would insist upon the payment of the stipulated royalty for each week that the operetta has not been performed, in accordance with the terms of the contract entered into between himself and the Shubert Theatrical Company in December, 1910.

Before starting any suit, I wish to lay the matter before you for whatever action you may deem fit, in accordance with my promise to you some time ago.

Internal Memo: J. J. Shubert–Lee Shubert

There is nothing else that I can do as I wrote both Mr. Burkan and Mr. Herbert, and I do not know what more to do about it. In the first place he cannot collect until the end of the season as we have a certain period in which to produce the play. I return you the letter.

Robert W. Iverson [Herbert's secretary]–Lee Shubert

Mr. Victor Herbert directs me to write to you that he is willing to waive the payment of $2000.00 in the "Trilby" matter but that he insists upon the settlement of "The Duchess" according to contract.

Internal Memo: J. J. Shubert–Lee Shubert

L.S.

You better take this up with me.

Although Herbert had given the Shuberts ample time to settle the matter amicably, the continuing delay forced him to instruct Burkan to file suit against the Shubert Theatrical Co. during the spring of 1912. The Shuberts then were moved to suggest a face-to-face meeting.

Nathan Burkan–Lee Shubert
I had a long talk with Mr. Herbert Saturday night, regarding his case against the Shubert Theatrical Company.
Mr. Herbert cannot see the utility of a conference between you and him regarding the matter, and he insists that the case be carried through. . . .
He cannot see why he should waive any provisions of the "Duchess" contract. He carried out his contract in full, wrote the score, and if the opera was not a financial success, it was no fault of his.

Then the matter was adjudicated in the Supreme Court of New York (the state of New York's trial court) in Herbert's favor. But it is one thing to win in court and another to bank the victory.

Nathan Burkan–Lee Shubert
Mr. Victor Herbert telephoned me today and asked me why the check for $500.00, the first installment due under the settlement in Herbert against Shubert Theatrical Company, was not made.
Kindly let me have your check by return mail, and oblige.

The holidays came and went. Herbert's birthday came and went. Shortly before St. Patrick's Day, an associate in Burkan's firm wrote to Lee Shubert.

H. Greenberg–Lee Shubert
In re Herbert.
Mr. Herbert insists on a definite arrangement on or before this coming Saturday, otherwise he demands payment of the sum of $500 which was due on March 1st, 1913.

Burkan had agreed to a schedule of payments to Herbert of $500 on October 1 and another on March 1. Now the Shuberts requested that a new schedule be set up.

H. Greenberg–Lee Shubert
I have submitted your proposition to Mr. Herbert, and he is disinclined to wait for the payment due him, as requested, to wit,

October 1st, 1913. He says that this amount should have been paid to him long before this time, and insists upon an immediate payment of the same. I will therefore ask you to kindly let me have a check by Saturday for the unpaid balance of the sum of $1000."

Burkan followed up with a phone call to Shubert and agreed to another postponement.

Lee Shubert–Nathan Burkan

Confirming our conversation over the telephone, it is understood that you are to wait until my return from Europe, which will be on or about July 1st, 1913, for the payment of the $1000 due to Mr. Victor Herbert.

Shubert had a fine working vacation in Europe and returned to New York at the end of June, rested and ready to continue the battle.

H. Greenberg–Lee Shubert

I was to get a payment in the following matter by July 1st, 1913:
Herbert v. Shubert, balance due—$1000.00
Please let me know whether you can give me this payment by the end of this week.

The following memo, dated September, reveals that Herbert's treatment was not unique.

Nathan Burkan–Lee Shubert

The following matters are still open and un-disposed of:

Herbert v. Shubert, balance due	$1,000.00
Hopwood v. Shubert, " "	12,000.00
Witmark v. Shubert (Merry Countess)	762.50

Will you kindly send me your check in the above matters in order to close same, and oblige."

Surprisingly, Burkan received an immediate reply—but no money.

Lee Shubert–Nathan Burkan

Your favor of the 12th to hand. As soon as the season is underway, I will take care of the matters referred to.

Six weeks later Burkan had run out of patience.

Nathan Burkan–Lee Shubert

I cannot permit the unpaid balances in the following matters: Victor Herbert, Avery Hopwood and M. Witmark & Sons—to remain in this fashion and to be carried on indefinitely. All these matters should have been paid up a long time ago, and apparently you have taken advantage of the fact that I have extended you the courtesy of permitting these payments to be made in installments, coupled with promises that the full amount would be paid up by the next promised date.

Unless these matters are paid up in full by the 1st of November I shall be obliged to enter judgment in the Herbert case and re-open the Hopwood case.

The Shuberts provided a partial payment. Burkan sent them a friendly reminder.

Nathan Burkan–Lee Shubert
This is to remind you of your promise to clean up the following matters by December 1st:

Victor Herbert, balance due	$450.00
Avery Hopwood	950.39
M. Witmark & Sons	512.50

Please give these your immediate attention, and oblige.

The next day Lee Shubert sent a memo to the treasurer of the company authorizing further partial payments on the accounts.

Lee Shubert–J. A. McMartin
Send me down the first thing tomorrow checks in favor of Nathan Burkan as follows,

$200 on account of Herbert
$150 on account of Hopwood
$150 on account of Witmark

The new year dawned. Germany, France and England prepared for war. The Balkans, the powder keg of Europe, were set to explode—and so was Herbert.

Nathan Burkan–Shubert Theatrical Co.
There is long overdue my client Victor Herbert from the Shubert Theatrical Co. the sum of $250.00.
If I am not in receipt of a check for that amount by return mail I shall be compelled to enter judgment against you for that amount.

As a birthday present for Herbert, Burkan hired a special courier to retrieve the final installment.

Nathan Burkan–Mr. Lee Shubert
> This is to remind you that there is due to-day $200.00 on account of Hopwood vs. Shubert, in accordance with your promise, and $200.00 on account of Herbert vs. Shubert Theatrical Company.
> Will you please give bearer your check for $400.00 on account of these two items, and oblige.

Lee Shubert authorized the final payment on a matter that had been in negotiation for over two years. J. J., who had been silent on the matter for some time, now had the final word in an internal memo to the company treasurer.

J. J. Shubert–JAM (office)
> When you send this money to Mr. Burkan, be sure to get the proper receipt from him.

And they say lawyers don't earn their money!

Irwin Rosen v. *Harry B. Smith, Victor Herbert et al.*

This case involving the musical play *Angel Face*, which Herbert wrote with Harry B. Smith (book), and Robert B. Smith, his brother (lyrics), is a sad chapter in the story of his theatrical adventures, since it placed a strain on an old friendship. The show was produced in 1919 by Erlanger and Powers. The original production contract contains a clause that is not typical of Herbert's agreements, to wit

> The authors and the composer agree that they will at their own expense defend any suit based upon a claim that the book, music or lyrics are an infringement upon the material of any other play, music or lyrics. . . .

Herbert, even with his sensitivity to issues of copyright, may not have known the background to this clause—or he may have dismissed it as just so much legal boilerplate. He had worked with Harry Smith for decades; they were friends and neighbors on Riverside Drive; there had never been an issue of copyright infringement with respect to their common work, although Smith had a history of unofficial "borrowing" that extended as far back as their work on *The Serenade*. *Angel Face* was a case of the chickens finally coming home to roost.

One Irwin Rosen, in February 1915, had acquired "all rights, title and interest of the Estate of Harry B. Harris." That estate had exclusive right, privilege and authority to produce a play entitled *The Elixir of Youth*. That work, produced as *Some Baby*, had been the basis of Smith's book for *Angel Face*. Rosen brought suit against Herbert, his collaborators and producers for infringement of his right in the property.

The matter was amicably settled for the sum of $2,500, paid to Rosen equally by all the defendants, on August 18, 1920. Although this was a clear public embarrassment for Herbert, it did not lead to a break in his long friendship with Smith.

Theresa Herbert v. *Turner*[46]
Victor Herbert v. *The American Gypsum Company*[47]

When Victor Herbert purchased his vacation home at Lake Placid he also purchased the properties on either side of Camp Joyland. He had good reason. During the first year at Placid he was surprised to discover that his neighbors to the north and west considered themselves musicians. In the summer, before the age of air conditioning, all windows stood open, and Herbert had the greatest difficulty concentrating on his composition as the children of his neighbors struggled with the challenges of "The Happy Farmer" and "The Spinning Song."

About the same time he purchased the country properties, Herbert moved his family to 321 West 108th Street, a five-story private residence where he lived until the end of his life. Today the building looks very much as it did when he lived there. It bears a plaque identifying it as his former residence. The inscription claims that it was in this house that he composed *Naughty Marietta* and all the rest. That claim is open to dispute, since the quiet that Herbert required for composition was easier to achieve at Placid than on Riverside Drive. Herbert's search for tranquility led him and his wife to the courts and through the labyrinth of New York City Municipal statutes, a terra incognita which even the bravest souls enter at their peril.

The story begins simply and amicably. Soon after the Herberts took up residence, they discovered that their neighbors to the west at number 323 had a musical daughter. The young lady was accustomed to practicing her Czerny for three hours each morning—about the same time that Herbert loved to compose—it was his habit to sketch new compositions in the morning when he was fresh and to spend the evenings orchestrating what he had written that day. The young lady's music penetrated the wall of Herbert's studio and disturbed his routine. Theresa, who had made a career of protecting her husband's interests, was soon at the neighbors' door. She introduced herself and explained the problem, and it was agreed to change the daughter's schedule. Herbert would compose mornings and the Czerny would fill the afternoon hours, while the composer was out and about. Thus, tranquility was achieved.

Still, Herbert was apprehensive. Riverside Drive was changing. The lovely bridle path that ran along the Hudson River embankment was being paved so that automobiles (and their horns) could have easy access to the area. With the growth of population came street vendors, hurdy-gurdys and carousels. Herbert hit upon a solution. He hired the American Gypsum Company to construct a soundproof studio on the fifth floor of his home. A special design was developed. At great expense concrete walls were installed, and between the double layers a baffle of sea grass was placed. This special feature was to stop not only noise, but vibrations as well. When the installation was complete, the Herberts were delighted. Not only was Czerny bound and gagged, but when Victor himself was at the keyboard not a sound could be heard in any part of the house. They no longer had to concern themselves with the neighbors; or so they thought.

The story now moves to the Cincinnati Conservatory of Music. Dr. Fery Lulek, a professor of vocal art whose studio had attracted many charming and ambitious young women, suddenly severed his connections with the Conservatory and decided to move his base of operation to New York City, where his charges would have a better chance of making a career. When the news got out that Dr. Lulek was moving to the big city, a violiniste and two pianistes as female artists were then known joined eight vocalists, and, together with Mrs. Mary Turner as chaperone, and her daughter "Miss Jean" as piano coach, landed on 107th Street. Soon after, when 323 West 108th Street became vacant, the whole bunch took over the house next to Herbert. What better location for a music school chock full of career-hungry young females than three steps from the front door of America's most famous composer? As Victor and Theresa watched in disbelief, in they came: eight chirping sopranos, four Steinway pianos (one for each floor) and a pubescent Paganini.

It wasn't long before eleven geniuses were making music all at the same time. Victor retreated to his eyrie, but to no avail. The sea grass and concrete had worked well enough against a single piano, but they were no match for lusty young lungs, sky-high tessituras and the battery of keyboards. Victor resorted to his secret weapon. He sent Theresa to visit the new neighbors.

Theresa discussed the problem with Mrs. Turner and her daughter. They agreed to move the pianos to the west walls of the house, as far from Herbert's studio as possible. They even agreed to move one piano from the top floor—all to no avail. The sounds still penetrated the sanctum. Theresa hinted broadly that the newcomers might consider moving. This they declined to consider. Theresa and Victor then decided to lay the matter before the courts.

Municipal Magistrate Patrick McGeehan was the lucky jurist who faced Theresa, Turner and the girls. The charge was "disorderly conduct." Theresa testified in her highest Viennese hauteur: "Such technique, such awful method, such attack, such rendition of scales! It is terrible. Never have I heard such singing. I was a prima donna in my day, a high soprano. I sang Wagnerian roles and I know singing. I have heard many poor singers in my day—but this—what they call singing, these girls!" Amid muted sniffling from the young ladies, Mrs. Turner rose to defend her charges. Speaking sweetly, but not without a touch of vitriol, she testified: "We are sorry if we annoy the Herberts, but what can we do? We have moved the pianos. We do not practice all the pianos at one time, as Mrs. Herbert said. No doubt the Herberts do not enjoy the music. It is quite likely that they do not appreciate our music. Thank heaven, it isn't the kind of music Mr. Herbert writes. We play classical music!"

The decision was clear. No law had been violated; there had been no disorderly conduct by any stretch of the statute. So Theresa tried another tack. The music constituted a "public nuisance." Under Section 285 of the Penal Code of the State of New York such a nuisance is defined as

A crime against the order and economy of the State, and consists in unlawfully doing an act . . . which act . . . annoys, injures or endangers the comfort, repose, health or safety of any considerable number of persons.

But the law, as construed, defines a "considerable number" as "more than one household or a whole neighborhood." On this point Theresa's suit was dismissed.

Still, if Herbert could not silence his neighbors he could at least get his money back. He sued the American Gypsum Company in the 9th

District Municipal Court for breach of contract. He claimed that the faulty soundproofing constituted such a breach, but because he was absent from court (at the out-of-town tryout of *The Lady of the Slipper*) judgment went against him in the amount of $220.55. He vowed an appeal, and eventually prevailed.

Victor and Theresa are long gone. Riverside Drive and West 108th Street are much changed. But not completely. There is still, to this day, a music studio at 323 West. And the spiritual great-granddaughters of Herbert's neighbors still study there and dream of great careers upon the New York stage.

Some things never change!

CHAPTER 8

A THEATRICAL MUSICIAN AT WORK (1894–1924)

Musical theater is a living social event. As such it is subject to change that reflects the changes in society. It is the position of this study that Victor Herbert was significant as a creative artist, not only for his time, but for our time as well. In order to justify this position it is useful to view Herbert's works as part of a continuum, to describe what musical theater pieces were like before Herbert made his contribution and how his work affected contemporary and later composers and the American musical in general, if indeed it did. Was there a clear developmental line from Herbert to Friml to Romberg to Kern to Rodgers to Sondheim and Lloyd-Weber? If there was, does he live on only through influence? Finally, whatever the answers to these questions may be, are they significant for our evaluation of Herbert's works and their potential for a future life in the theater?

Bruce Kerle suggests valuable guidelines for dealing with this agenda. He "distrusts linear, text-based historiographical approaches to the Broadway musical," as well as the "absolute autonomy of text and score." He insightfully remarks that "performance style and elements must be considered in any valid discussion," and warns against value judgments when comparing various types of musical shows. Indeed, Edith Borroff's examination of the literature references twenty-nine separate and overlapping show types and clearly demonstrates that the distinctions historians have drawn, qua distinctions, yield little meaningful information. As to the subject of influences and their possible significance, she writes, "Metaphors of descent and derivation are false. A creative person is influenced by his or her predecessors, potentially by everything he or she has ever experienced; the process of selection remains mysterious, but certainly is not genetic."

The discussion of Herbert's works in the chapters devoted to the last three decades of his life contains much detail related to the performance style of the original productions. The purpose of this approach is, first, to reflect that the text and score are not the only source of or knowledge of these works. Second, the attempt is made to create for the reader the full piece: music, text, performances and production values. There is no implication here that this information should be used as a guide for creating an "ideal" production. As Kerle reminds us, "New productions will inevitably adapt to new cultural moments and to new audiences. . . . New productions take on lives of their own." Such new productions would, ideally, "meld contemporary performance style with the flavor of the original to create something new and relevant" for contemporary audiences. Thus the discussion of the Herbert works is an attempt to provide for contemporary readers and producers as complete a picture as is possible of the originals as first produced, to provide a valid starting point for new imaginings.

There is, however, an element of these original productions so integral to them that contemporary stagings violate it at their peril. The reference here, of course, is to questions of musical style. Every significant composer has a recognizable style, and whatever may be done to book or production values, a violation of musical style can destroy the only legitimate reason for reviving these works. For example, since much of Herbert's greatness was based on his genius as an orchestrator, reorchestrations essentially destroy the validity of his achievement. Further, violations of tempi, incorrect realization of his special type of rubato, or the interpolation of songs from his other operettas into his finished scores are aesthetically invalid choices. There *are* limits.

Although the various types of musical productions that preceded Herbert or were contemporary with his work in the theater are far from works of genius, it is important to describe them briefly, because Herbert and his librettists were influenced by these creations, for better or worse. This discussion will be followed by an analysis of Herbert's style—those factors that set him apart from his contemporaries and may have influenced them—and that distinguished him as an artist whose creations are historically significant and capable of providing beauty and humor for contemporary audiences.

Victor Herbert's works had cultural prestige because of their close links to European models. As he strove to become more American, he and his collaborators moved further from these European roots. As the subject matter became increasingly Americanized, his musical style absorbed contemporary influences. When the setting was fantasy-based— *Babes in Toyland*, *Little Nemo*, *The Lady of the Slipper*, *Wonderland*—his Continental style was as appropriate to the subject matter as any other.

When the texts focused on purely American subjects—*Dream City*, *The Only Girl*, *The Girl in the Spotlight*—his palette attempted to incorporate the colors of post-war dance music. If the setting of a work was exotic— *The Wizard of the Nile*, *The Idol's Eye*, *The Rose of Algeria*—his musical choice produced scores combining faux "oriental" effects with popular song forms tailored to the specialties, and often limited vocal abilities, of the comedians for whom these works were created. Finally, scores driven by unabashedly romantic themes—*The Enchantress*, *Naughty Marietta*, *Mlle. Modiste*, *Sweethearts*, *The Fortune Teller*, *Eileen*—written for prima donnas with operatic-quality voices, called forth his strongest melodic gifts and yielded his most artistically satisfying achievements.

Although Herbert's librettists provided texts of varying quality, these contributions gave Herbert the opportunity to compose in a wealth of styles. It has become a commonplace in the literature to blacken the reputations of Herbert's co-creators with snide deprecations. Still, the fact remains that their librettos fostered the creation of a body of work that, in its day, held and dominated the American musical stage. Herbert and his librettists created memorable moments in the theater and in theatrical history; of equal importance, they created an audience for high-quality entertainment, significantly raising the level of audience expectations of what music theater should and could be.

"High-quality" is not the adjective of choice one would apply to much of the musical theater as it developed in the United States between the end of the Civil War in 1865 and Herbert's earliest theatrical ventures in 1894. These three decades saw a broad division of theatrical types, into those uniquely American and those reflecting European origin or influence. Among the former were minstrel shows, with their eccentric song and dance, pun-based broad humor and racial stereotyping; spectacular entertainments, characterized by elaborate scenic effects, physical comedy and lots of music strung together by the thinnest of plot lines; the farce comedies of Harrigan and Hart, whose simple songs and plots—with "heart"—focused on everyday subjects and characters drawn from the events of the Irish immigrant experience—twenty-four shows between 1878 and 1893; and what were sometimes called "musical comedies," entertainments whose plots barely held strings of songs together. All these were American in that they shared the high energy and optimistic point of view that characterized and distinguished American society from European, at least in the minds of America boosters of the period.

There were hits that seemed to run forever. *Evangeline*, a send-up of Longfellow's 1847 poem by John Cheever Goodwin and Edward E. Rice, held various stages for eighteen years. Charles Hoyt and Percy Gaunt created the very popular show, *A Trip to Chinatown*. This middle-class subject was basically a spoken play with simple, strophic songs. "Reuben, Reuben, I've Been Thinking" and "The Bowery" lacked both originality and any attempt at integration into the plot. They were stand-alone events meant almost as interludes in the telling of the story, opportunities for comedians or soubrettes to show off their specialities. "The Bowery" was a typical show-waltz number: a series of comic verses with refrain that was much imitated thereafter, and had superior reincarnations in Herbert's "Streets of New York" (*The Red Mill*—1906) and Cole Porter's "Brush Up Your Shakespeare" (*Kiss Me, Kate*—1948). The comedian Frank Daniels starred in several of Hoyt's productions and provided a direct link to Herbert's early exotica. *The Wizard of the Nile*, *The Idol's Eye*, *The Ameer*, and *The Tattooed Man* were all written as vehicles for Daniels.

Burlesque and vaudeville were ubiquitous offerings in the years when Herbert worked, although at first burlesque was not the type of entertainment associated with naked ladies and low, salacious sketch comedy. Early burlesque was farce comedy, a combination of "songs, dances and snappy patter." The patter was based on events of the day and depended for its success more on topicality than wit. Think late-night television-host monologue set to poor-quality music and aimed at a family audience, and you have it. The great vaudeville team of Weber and Fields, both when they worked together as dialect comedians and later independently as producers, provided star vehicles for the great ladies of the period musical stage, Fay Templeton and Lillian Russell. Chorus lines of pretty girls were a staple of Weber and Fields' shows. The subject matter was as often as not clever parodies of current Broadway hits.

The superior production values associated with these entertainments were a large part of their allure. Both men worked with Herbert as producers and stars (*Old Dutch* and *Dream City* and *The Magic Knight*) and brought many elements of their shows to the Herbert repertoire.

The contribution of George M. Cohan to the Herbert works is indirect. The only similarity between the two creators lay in a shared pride in their Irish heritage and their super-patriotism. These characteristics run through the most successful of Cohan's works. For Herbert, Americanism was expressed in his attempt to add to the operetta style the energy and vivacity that he read as typically American. Cohan's works were aimed straight at the heart of his blue-collar audiences. It was the dominating talent and presence of Cohan, his eccentric dancing, and high-energy delivery of simple but effective songs that were the unifying factors in his shows. The other element, almost absent from other types of popular entertainment of the period (except operetta), was romance. Strong, patriotic plot lines and good, believable characters and dialogue produced hit after hit from *Little Johnny Jones* (1904) through *Hello Broadway* (1915). This was Cohan's golden decade and almost directly paralleled Herbert's: *Babes in Toyland* (1903) to *Sweethearts* (1913).

The number-one stage attraction of the period was the "Revue." Between 1907 and 1914, approximately one hundred of these were produced. George W. Lederer's "Passing Show" of 1894 and Florenz Ziegfeld's "Follies" and "Midnight Frolics" best typified these entertainments. They were unified only in the sense that all the editions had similar elements: top comedy acts, fabulous stars, elaborate settings, costumes and special effects, and dance styles ranging from tap to ballet. The best composers were engaged to provide the music: Irving Berlin's syncopated numbers alternating with Herbert's ballets; and everywhere the beauty of the female form was apotheosized.

All these attractions brought to the theater a largely working-class audience, with an admixture of upper-middle-class and wealthy patrons out "slumming." This latter constituency as a rule patronized its own level of theater, a repertoire that played to the snob appeal of what was perceived as the more elevated product of European society—the operetta.

Opera had been available to American audiences since the eighteenth century, but operetta made its successful invasion of the American stage immediately after the Civil War. Since 1867 the opéra-bouffes of Offenbach had been popular with American audiences. A good deal of the salacious or social satire of the Second Empire may have been lost on this audience, since the performances were in French; but the fact that *La Belle Hélène* and *La Vie Parisienne* were Continental was enough to insure their success. When the generation of French composers who followed Offenbach added the element of romantic sentimentality to the brittle mix, the way was paved for the entrance of the Victor Herbert operetta.

In 1879 the first production of *H.M.S. Pinafore* in the United States began the American love affair with the works of Gilbert and Sullivan. Here was unsurpassed social satire presented in a package that combined the highest quality libretto and song lyrics with sensitive, humorous theatrical music, brilliantly orchestrated, the work of highly skilled, thoroughly trained, richly gifted creators that set a new standard for light opera not yet surpassed. Suddenly every operetta librettist became a would-be Gilbert. In vain, composers attempted to imitate Sullivan's unique scores. Even a composer of Herbert's gifts briefly fell under Sullivan's spell. *The Wizard of the Nile* contains a love duet that could seamlessly have been inserted into the score of *The Pirates of Penzance*, and *Cleopatra's Wedding Day* is clearly *The Flowers that Bloom in the Spring*, redux. Reginald de Koven and Harry B. Smith created the first successful American operetta (*Robin Hood*—1890) that combined the influence of Gilbert and Sullivan with the Viennese school, especially von Suppé. John Philip Sousa attempted to master the form, but lacked the theatrical spirit necessary for effective stage composition. Viennese opera productions introduced frivolity and contemporary settings through the influence of Johann Strauss, Jr., and soon an operetta craze was at hand. By 1894, when Herbert's first operetta was produced (*Prince Ananias*) there were fourteen operetta companies touring the United States.

During the first decade of the twentieth century a group of composers of middle European descent produced a repertoire unabashedly foreign in both style and subject matter. These men were good musical technicians, but on the whole, compared with their European models and Herbert's creations, their works seem uninspired. Ludwig Englander, Gustav Kerker, Karl Hoschna and Gustav Luders basked in the shadow of the star of operetta's silver age, Franz Lehar. The vogue that his *Merry Widow* created in the United States was an early example of pop-cultural fads that seemed to characterize American society with regularity during the twentieth century. Couture, slang and dance all aped the *Merry Widow* style and, in the theater, much operetta created in the decade before World War I followed Lehar's lead, focusing on contemporary subjects and offering less elaborate scores.

Contemporary with the last decade of Herbert's work (1914–1924), three gifted composers rose to prominence. Two of them, Rudolf Friml and Sigmund Romberg, worked largely in the classical operetta format. The third, Jerome Kern, was a seminal force in the transformation of the musical stage. Because these three composers rose to prominence during the period when Herbert was still an important force, it is sometimes assumed that he influenced them. Although both Friml and Romberg were capable of creating the kind of arched arioso romantic melody we associate with Herbert, each produced a body of work that was clearly his own. The books of the Friml and Romberg operettas were quasi-integrated with the musical numbers, and there was an element of the exotic in some of their settings. But Friml's melodic style, securely based on the pentatonic scale, and Romberg's graceful adaptations of American dance rhythms, gave each an individuality that stamped him as his own man. Romberg remained faithful to the operetta format until mid-century; Friml, seeing the handwriting on the wall, gave up composition in the 1930s. By the time Romberg quit the stage, the best compositions of both men ("The Firefly," "Katinka," "Rose Marie," "The Desert Song," "The New Moon," "The Vagabond King") had become historical artifacts.

Not so the work of Kern. He was the only one of the three to success-fully incorporate American rhythmic elements into his music in a natural, unself-conscious way. His melody was non-florid, his harmony so sophis-ticated and original that it not only supported the dramaturgy of his shows (*Show Boat*—1927), but was so attractive as to become a contribu-tion to a whole new chapter in American musical development, a har-monic basis for jazz improvisation from the be-bop of the 1940s and 1950s through the cool West Coast styles of the 1950s and 1960s. Contemporary jazz repertoire still contains Kern creations as "standards" ("All the Things You Are"). Kern among the late-Herbert generation shared Her-bert's *Theaterblut*.

But Kern was influenced by Herbert in one significant way. Kern raised the level of musical comedy music as Herbert had raised the level of popular operetta. When we examine the relationship between Herbert and Kern, we find it was more a question of Herbert's example, rather than any specific aspect of his musical style, that unite the composers. Each took the conventions of his time and raised them to new heights.

Victor Herbert was a craftsman, a highly trained adept who knew all the techniques of creating musical effect that supported lyrics, charac-terization, and dramatic situation. He had, like Sullivan, his bag of tricks that he varied expertly to create musical moments. Orchestration was only the most obvious of his strengths. In examining Herbert's style—what is distinctive about his use of harmony, rhythm and melody—we find one element underpinning all these discrete aspects and that is at the root of his uniqueness: the element of surprise.

It is the element of surprise that makes a theatrical work exciting. Whether in text, decor, movement, or plot, it is the unexpected event that distinguishes the memorable from the cliché. As a composer with a highly developed sense of the theatrical, Herbert used surprises that delighted the audiences at his premieres, and that continue to delight. His melodies contain turns of phrase, especially in the introductions and transitions, that contain unexpected intervals and temporary modulations. The key focus in his harmonic structures changes suddenly within a measure or a short phrase. It is these small-dimensional shifts of harmonic centers that give life to even his most pedestrian melodic passages. In songs in standard popular style, with a series of verses that tell a story and a refrain in contrasting meter, he suddenly presents the refrain in a series of new and unexpected keys. His use of rubato style, for instance, is special. The technique, which features variations in rhythm, many times contrasted with an accompaniment with a steady beat, was common to operettas composed and performed during Herbert's career. Herbert, however, used a unique approach in his compositions employing rubato. In a song with several stanzas, rather than using rubato in parallel sections of the phrases, he varied its occurrence with each iteration, and sometimes omitted it once he had set up his listeners to expect it.

Special effects were typical of his orchestrations. "Buttons," or sudden sforzandos on the final chord of a piece, were standard in his percussion parts, but were not universally used. His use of bassoon and horn doublings with lower string instruments written in their higher registers produced a humorous acoustic inversion that underlay humorous lines of text. And a general use of all instruments in extreme ranges resulted in a sound structure that kept his audiences' ears alert for the unexpected.

There were other special musical effects. The texture of the orchestration of "The Stonecutters' Chorus" from *The Wizard of the Nile* is highlighted by piano and xylophone. The galloping horses' hooves in the percussion accompaniments to the "Postillion's Song" in *The Serenade* and the "Vaquero's Song" in *Natoma* drive these pieces forward with irresistible abandon. To secure these effects, Herbert's production contracts demanded orchestras with a minimum of thirty-four pieces for touring productions and fifty players in first-class venues. He essentially created a new theater orchestra for his operetta productions. In all these ways he provided a new musical sound that supported theatrical moments of his shows and paved the way for the great theatrical orchestrators of the future, Hershy Kay and Robert Russell Bennett.

Musical characterization was one of Herbert's greatest gifts. Many of the plots of his works revolve around the experiences of two contrasting couples, the romantic and comic pairs. Herbert typically chooses long-drawn arioso phrases and triple meters for his romantic types and simple, strophic song forms in duple meters, as well as ragtime in his later works, to portray the comic couple. Comic characters sing polka-based rhythms. Schmalz's "I Wish I Were an Island in an Ocean of Girls" from *The Princess "Pat"* is the sort of song Eddie Cantor made famous with his own "Ma, She's Makin' Eyes At Me." There were also imitations of English music-hall ballads such as "I'm Captain Cholly Chumley of the Guards." Comic heavies like the Count de Mar in *Mlle. Modiste* reflect their rigid, demanding personalities in heavily accented marches such as "I Want What I Want When I Want It!" Romantic characters, whether in contemporary or fairyland settings, invariably waltz gracefully through their scenarios: "Kiss Me, Again" (*Mlle. Modiste*), "The Princess of Far Away" (*The Lady of the Slipper*).

Like many of the greatest composers for the stage, Herbert wrote his music to suit the capabilities of his singers. Gifted coloratura sopranos were provided with show-stopping numbers: "The Nightingale and the Star" (*Mlle. Modiste*), "The Italian Street Song" (*Naughty Marietta*). A more recent echo of these can be heard in Bernstein's "Candide" (Glitter and be Gay). Dramatic divas sang in stately, quasi-operatic style: "The Land of My Own Romance" (*The Enchantress*), "The Song of the Danube" (*The Singing Girl*). Vaudeville stars with limited vocal gifts were provided with numbers whose effectiveness was based on rhythmic, rather than soaring melodies. "The Streets of New York," written for Montgomery and Stone in *The Red Mill* is a "Bowery Waltz" typically associated with the city, and introduced at a point in the story where the expatriot Americans are longing to return home. "A Little Girl at Home," the duet for Cindy and her Prince in *The Lady of the Slipper* is a soft-shoe number perfectly suited to the strengths of his vaudeville star, Elsie Janis.

Exotic scene painting was another of Herbert's strengths. The opening pages of *Wonderland*, in its original format as *Alice and the Eight Princesses*, contains some of Herbert's most glorious music, a portrait of London on Christmas Eve with a gamin heroine roaming the streets in search of shelter. It is one of his most affecting settings. "The Entrance of the Brahmins," from *The Idol's Eye*, plays to his use of instruments to create "Oriental" flavor. This technique, coupled with heavy percussive effects, anticipates the "Siamese Children's March" in *The King and I*. The opening scene of *Naughty Marietta*, with its singing flower girls and shouts and cries of street vendors, paints an indelible picture of morning in "Little Paris," an atmosphere paralleled many years later in the "Who Will Buy?" street scene from *Oliver*. Act Two of *Naughty Marietta* is the occasion for Herbert to use contrasting dance rhythms to depict the several populations of New Orleans. A quadroon song, a Spanish waltz, and the perky rhythms of the melodies given to the French girls contrast with the more stately music of the Ladies of San Domingo. Not since the first finale of *Don Giovanni*, where Mozart employs three dance orchestras to depict the various classes gathered at the Don's house party (a minuet for the upper classes, a duple-meter dance for the peasants, and 6/8 meter for the rest) have we had a comparable musical-theatrical tour de force.

One of the most subtle achievements of the composer is his ability to portray both character and setting in a single number. " 'Neath the Southern Moon" (*Naughty Marietta*) begins with a verse for Ada—a quadroon—in a dark-colored register. The mood is mysterious and has almost the same atmosphere as Carmen's solo in "The Fortune Telling Trio." Like that passage, the refrain is in major and in a higher register, a love song that rises in tessitura as hope rises in the text and then, in the final measures, crashes in despair to the original mood, reflecting that Ada's dream is a matter of hoping against hope. The music not only supports the plot; it anticipates it. In a similar way the verse and refrain of "The Gypsy Love Song" (*The Fortune Teller*) alternate moods. The verse reflects the loneliness of the forest and its creatures, with which the singer identifies; then the refrain, in major, expresses his longing for his "little gypsy sweetheart" to come and end his loneliness. Here hope is encouraged by the new tonality, and in fact the choice of key anticipates a happy ending in the scenario.

An examination of the score of *The Red Mill* reveals how Herbert uses various musical styles to characterize his actors as well as to shape the action of the drama and comment on it. "Mignonette," a solo and chorus for a young girl dreaming of a career on the stage and the freedom it represents from her oppressive family situation, is all optimism and coquettishness. By contrast, "You Never Can Tell About a Woman," which follows, is a stiff duet in duple meter full of double-dotted rhythms for the Sheriff and the Innkeeper Father, two types that represent the stiff, establishmentarian older generation—pillars of law and order and tradition who oppose young dreams of career or love. "The Beautiful Isle of our Dreams," for the lovers, is a simple, romantic duo in slow triple meter and close harmony. It could be a period sentimental parlor ballad. By contrast, "Because You're You," a "love" duet for a somewhat superannuated couple (the Governor and Auntie Bertha) is in duple, halting, alternating lines, parallel echoing phrases, which don't come together until the final phrase, "Because you're you." What better way to reflect in music the difference between young, romantic, impetuous love and experienced, cautious age?

"Moonbeams," the solo for the heroine (Gretchen), is another exercise in characterization and scene painting. Gretchen is imprisoned in the mill and longs for her lover to come and rescue her. The first section reflects sweet longing and contrasts with the urgent fear of the middle section, fear that her lover may abandon her. Finally the lyric returns to the longing hope of the first section. The accompaniment of this piece is similar to that which Schubert uses in his famous setting of "Gretchen am Spinnrade"—Gretchen at the spinning wheel, an ostinato in 6/8 meter that depicts the turning of the wheel. Herbert uses the same device to portray the turning of the arms of the mill in which his Gretchen is imprisoned. Is this portrayal of the two Gretchens perhaps one of the great musical puns in the literature?

"The Legend of the Mill" that opens the second act introduces a new color. Bertha recounts the horrible tale of the spooky events associated with the mill. Here Herbert's music references both Saint-Saens' "Danse Macabre" and the Ghost Scene of *Ruddigore*.

"Every Day is Ladies' Day to Me," the governor's song that introduces us to Holland's philanderer-in-chief, is a pure music-hall romp with a verse in duple and a refrain in triple meter that bounces along in the same mood as "The Man Who Broke the Bank at Monte Carlo."

The finale to Act One is illustrative of Herbert's gifts both as a scene painter and musical dramatist. Constructed in three contrasting sections, the first ("An Accident") is dominated by gallic pique and the excitement and turmoil it creates—all scurrying string passages, choral shouts and interjections, punctuated by the blasts of antique automobile horns. The second section ("When You're Happy") is a calm, madrigal-like expression by the young people of their confidence that all will be well if only order can be restored. The third section, as night falls, is the rescue of Gretchen from the mill. Here Herbert uses ever-increasing tempi and rising tessitura to drive the action to a breathtaking conclusion.

Still another aspect of Herbert's theatrical gifts is his use of parody. In "Rock-a-Bye Baby" (*Babes in Toyland*) he apes the style of both Donizetti and Sousa. In "Hula-lula," composed for a Lambs Club Gambol, he writes in a comically exaggerated "South Sea" style. In his greatest parody, *The Magic Knight*, a take-off on grand opera and *Lohengrin* in particular, he writes both with admiration and humor. You have to know the score, or at least the leitmotivs, to get all the musical jokes, but this is truly, as Hoffmannsthal said of his "Ariadne," "*ein Leckerbissen für kulturelle Feinschmecker*" (a sweetmeat for cultural connoisseurs).

One aspect of Herbert's talent often overlooked is his work in choral composition. He loved to write for men's chorus. Anthems for both the Lambs and the Friars, as well as for the Glee Club of the Friendly Sons of St. Patrick, are still used regularly, but some of his greatest choral writing was reserved for his theater pieces. "Tramp, Tramp, Tramp" (*Naughty Marietta*) and "The Hussars' Chorus" (*The Fortune Teller*) are two of the best male marching songs in the operetta literature. Similarly stirring moments in works by later composers ("Come Boys" and the "Drinking Song" from *The Student Prince*, the "Riff Song" from *The Desert Song*, and even "There is Nothing Like a Dame" from *South Pacific*) owe something to Herbert's example. One of the most effective uses of male chorus for scene painting is the opening of Act Three of *Cyrano*, "In Bivouac Reposing." This is a passage of breathtaking beauty, unmatched in operetta literature.

Equal to his gift as an orchestrator was Herbert's genius for melodic creation. The variety he brought to his lines was inspired by his sensitivity to the dramatic situation. Long-drawn phrases are typical of his romantic Irish settings, e.g., "Barney O'Flynn" (*Babes in Toyland*), "Thine Alone" (*Eileen*). He was just as effective creating their opposite in mood, such as the yodeling choruses from *Old Dutch* and *The Singing Girl*. His waltz melodies could be plaintive and tender when assigned to a character of simplicity and innocence, e.g., "I Wonder" (*Cyrano*). When a more complicated romantic scenario was called for, he added unexpected but still gracious chromatic intervals to his lines (*The Princess of Far Away*, *The Lady of the Slipper*). If a playful quality was demanded, he supplied large skips, more chromaticism on accented beats, and a wider vocal range (*Sweethearts*).

Actions on stage were sometimes underlined by melody; for example, the alternating rising and falling passages in the "Bowling Chorus" (*Babette*). Changing moods of a character were delineated by the choice of melodic and rhythmic type. In "If I Were on the Stage" (*Mlle. Modiste*), Fifi's audition aria, her portrayal of a simple country maid, is supported by a folklike strophic setting; her miming of an upper-class grande dame by a stylish mazurka. Finally, her portrayal of an incurable romantic combines Herbert's most famous waltz melody with his typical extreme rubato.

As a final example of Herbert's melodic dramaturgy, the first and second love duets of *Naughty Marietta* provide a striking example of his sensitivity to the demands of developing relationships, here between Captain Dick and Marietta. The first duet is a duettino, "It Never, Never Can Be Love." The harmony is simple and supports an almost chaste melody. This could almost be a setting for the innocent children in *Little Nemo*. The final duet, based on the dream melody "Ah, Sweet Mystery of Life," is both passionate and at the same time strangely virginal, probably the only grand love duet based on double-dotted rhythms, sung and played very slowly. As the famous sequential melody develops, it rises not so much in pitch as in increasing intensity. As true romantic love is revealed to be the thing "the world is seeking," Captain Dick's passion blends with Marietta's innocence in a unique musical dramatic statement.

Dance rhythms drive many of Herbert's most colorful compositions. Several numbers reflect his fondness for Spanish-style music: "In Fair Andalucía" (*The Serenade*), "It's a Way We Have in Spain" (*Babette*). Herbert frequently introduced "Gypsy" numbers—"Romany Life" (*The Fortune Teller*)—that combine a first section of slow, meandering quality with a second, driven by highly accented Magyar rhythms blended to a whirling, driving climax. These are the most obvious of his interpolated rhythmic styles. But he was capable of much more. For example, a waltz rhythm is the basis for "Live for Today," the quartet and ensemble that represents the musical high point of *Naughty Marietta*. Ensemble and solos characterize both individuals and couples in this piece. Two major waltz styles, lyric and understated, maestoso and stentando, are alternated and build to a stunning climax culminating in an exchange of the triple meter for a short, stretto passage in duple meter that combines new dynamics with the new rhythm and accelerating tempo. As the passion of the scene increases, the frequency of changes in harmony increases in tandem with the rising tessitura of this masterpiece of dramatic musical portraiture.

An anonymous critic writing long ago in the pages of the *New York Post* commented, "Victor Herbert at his worst is better than most of his rivals at their best." True enough for his time. But can his shows work for audiences in our time? Is there still an audience for romantic melody? Ask Andrew Lloyd-Weber. Is there an audience for satirical farce-comedy? Ask Mel Brooks. Is there an audience for fantasy and innocence? Ask Disney Theatricals.

CHAPTER 9

ACT ONE (1894–1900)

It is symbolic that the discussion of Victor Herbert's work in the theater should begin roughly halfway through his biography, for although his popular image rests on the contributions he made to the musical theater, he did not begin that work until the second half of his life.

The popular image of Herbert's operettas, like all cultural clichés, is comfortable but, on examination, faulty. What is that image? Simply, that all of the Herbert librettos are impossibly poor; that it is Herbert's musical contribution that made for such success as he enjoyed in the theater; and finally, that the subject matter of these plays is largely the gossamer world of romance, of fey royals waltzing gracefully through labyrinths of mistaken identity, a custom and device so devoid of attraction for our postmodern sensibilities that they are properly relegated to the dusty shelves of music libraries, a passing footnote to the history of operetta, and nothing more.

This image is as pervasive as it is false. But it is so well established in the popular mind, and in the canon of professional musical literature, that it has led to the cheapening and commercial exploitation of music of sensitivity and beauty: e.g., Mel Brooks in *Young Frankenstein*, chose "Ah, Sweet Mystery of Life" as the birdsong warbled by Madelyn Kahn after her night of ecstasy in the arms of the monster; the same selection was recently chosen as the background music for a supermarket commercial featuring a video scan of shining fresh fruits and vegetables. The 1940s gave us the promotion of a hair treatment to the tune of "Toyland":

Dream girl, dream girl,
Beautiful Luster-creme girl
You owe your crowning glory to . . .
A Luster-creme Shampoo.

Herbert's keen sense of humor might have relished such things—so long as the royalties were paid. What he most definitely would *not* have countenanced is this: the latest edition of *Die Musik in Geschichte und*

Gegenwart (*Music, Historical and Contemporary*) with the *New Grove's Dictionary of Music and Musicians*, the most authoritative and complete encyclopedia of music, in its article on operetta, does not even mention Victor Herbert. Even given the editorial bias toward the Germanic in subject areas that Teutons deem their own turf, such an omission is inexcusable, especially in the light of other composers included in the entry.

What is wrong, then, with the image of Herbert's works? There are three myths that need to be exploded. The first is that all of his works are so old-fashioned and burdened with such poor books that they are virtually unproducible. Among the forty-two (!) works Herbert created for the stage, not counting editions of the *Ziegfeld Follies* and the grand operas, there are fifteen with workable original librettos and effective scores that can hold their own with such other light opera works produced today.

The second is the idea that Herbert was unconcerned with the quality of the librettos he set; that he had such musical facility that he could have set the telephone directory if he had been so inclined. Facile he was; unconcerned and uninvolved he was not. We have ample evidence that Herbert was vitally concerned and intimately involved with every facet of the creative process. He constantly badgered his librettists to get on with the work, making specific suggestions for improvements, urging his collaborators to do their best. This is a pattern that persists from the earliest days of his theatrical work to the end of his career. To get a bit ahead of the story, here is Herbert in 1921, writing to his longtime collaborator, Harry B. Smith:

> Camp Joyland
> Lake Placid
> Sept. 9, 1921

>   Dear Harry
>   I am glad you have decided to "stay right on the job"—as you say—until the piece is right. Both Nicolai and Dreyfus have been served so badly by their former partner that they really deserve an *extra effort* on the part of the authors.
>   If only I had a suitable lyric I would gladly write a new song for the 2nd Act. "Badinage" is too well known, I think, to allow of an imitation by *myself*, although it has often been imitated by others.

I agree with you that two waltzes shouldn't be so close together. We must find something—and the little woman has a good voice.

Let me hear from you as soon as possible.

With regards

Your

Victor Herbert

There are several bad spots in the "Girl in the Spotlight." I wish you would find some time to run over to Phil[adelphia] one evening—it isn't quite right yet.

V.H.[1]

Concerning the third myth—the image of Herbert shows as romances set in cloud-cuckooland—the truth is that fewer than a third of them fall into that category. The majority of his shows were children's fantasies, farce comedies and social satires.

If the image is faulty, what is the true picture? The answer is long in detail, rich in anecdote and humor, sometimes explosive in event and of charming dénouement. But this is a story that cries out for the telling, for once told it may serve to restore Herbert to his rightful place among the very few masters of the musical-theatrical comic genre, and may grant to new generations an inheritance too long denied them, the treasure of theatrical fun and musical beauty that was Herbert's legacy to all who love the operetta.

That being said, there is a criticism of his purely musical efforts that, on the surface, rings true.

> He seems indifferent to the quality of his musical inspiration, to the specific value of the musical material he uses. He seems too easily satisfied with what first occurs to him; he seems not to sift or criticize. All his ideas appear to him good—or good enough—and he relies on his technique in orchestration to make it all seem worthwhile.[2]

It is doubtful if Richard Aldrich, the author of this passage, had the opportunity to examine Herbert's manuscripts. But an examination of the work papers that survive from every period of his activity reveals almost no "reworkings" of material. If something did not please him or did not work as the development of a show progressed, Herbert drew heavy blue pencil lines through the material and wrote "out" across the score; he then began something new. So Aldrich was instinctively on the right track, but it was not that Herbert did not care. His lyric facility was so rich that it was easier for him to try something new rather than rework a clumsy idea. He wrote quickly and was as impatient with himself as he was with his librettists to get the job done and move on to the next. He wrote prodigiously, if not reflectively. Whatever he did and however he did it, we are the richer for it.

Fortunately, Herbert rose successfully to his own defense. In a revealing series of interviews printed in the *Etude* and the *New York Telegraph*[3] when he stood at the pinnacle of his career, Herbert effectively dealt with the critical strictures laid upon his works and then discussed his philosophy of theatrical composition, the problems of librettos, the influences on his work of light opera in Austria, France and England, and his efforts developing the form for America. These statements are seminal and, as such, invaluable for our understanding of Herbert's work as a theatrical composer. Here, then, is Herbert on Herbert:

> It is very hard to be patient with the musical hypocrites who affect to see nothing good in any music that is not of the most serious kind. . . . We need more comedy in life. . . . The world is hungry for something to rob our everyday life of too much of its seriousness. . . .

> I have never been able to look upon the music I have written for my own light operas as music demanding less thought, or less skill, or less careful detailed attention than the music I have written for the so called serious works. I have always held before me the motto "Always do the best you can no matter what the work may be!" There is a great deal in that. It is one of the best mottos for the young musician to adopt. Many young workers complete a work with the—"That is good enough. I'll let it go at that"—spirit. They do not demand the best that is in them.

> This is the attitude I have always felt toward my comic operas: Everybody knows that I could write fugues if I chose to do so. The work upon a comic opera is no less exacting in a way, but of a different kind. When I look back upon the actual labor which my comic operas have necessitated, I can assure you that I have a most wholesome respect for them. . . . It is often far more difficult to write a good piece of light music than a bad symphony. I know, for I have written both.

The reporter noted that Herbert made this last remark with a special earnestness. He then turned his attention to the subject of the libretto.

The American public is entitled to the best. For a time, some musical entertainment with an extremely good libretto—that is, good from the standpoint of popular drawing qualities—may succeed in drawing large audiences, even though the music may be mediocre or even very badly done. However, such pieces usually draw large houses for a comparatively short time while works based upon a good plot, and accompanied by good music are played for years and then frequently revived with gratifying success. To endure, both libretto and music must be good.

With this statement Herbert goes on record recognizing that his music alone would not have been sufficient to achieve long-term success. Thus it is clear that the composer was vitally concerned with finding quality librettos.

It is one of the hardest things in the world to get a good, strong, clean libretto. There are only a very few men who seem to have the gift of writing fine librettos. The story is continually being thrown aside for the music. It is a task which taxes the most skilled dramatist. It is almost impossible for the composer to rise above a bad libretto. I have read dozens before deciding upon a likely one. . . .

Herbert then turns his attention to the influences that shaped his style.

It was my good fortune to have known the Viennese composers Strauss, von Suppé and others. . . . I played in the orchestra in Vienna when some of the Strauss pieces were at the height of their success. Von Suppé was much more of a musician from the sense of craftsmanship than Strauss. Some of his operas are really grand operas in the higher sense of the word. I played under him also.

The light operas of the standard French composers of the past show a kind of polish which makes them inimitable and which is extremely hard to describe. My own inclinations are decidedly toward the French school, although I have tried to create a style of my own. Offenbach is, of course, regarded as a Frenchman, although he was a German Hebrew. He was the inventor of the Opera Bouffe, those musical dramatic satires which poke fun at serious things.

During this period, superficial characterization of national styles was in vogue and Herbert's remarks can be understood properly only in the light of that characterization. "The Future of Our Opera," an article by Professor Louis Ritter of Vassar College, provides a succinct summary:

> German music means highly developed harmony and rich instrumentation as contra-distinguished from the homophonic melodic style of Italy or the preponderance of rhythm in France. Music in America must strive for an ideal in which the impulses and feelings of the American people can feel expression.[4]

Thus, when Herbert inclines "toward the French school," he means that he strives to emphasize the rhythmic element. When he mentions the influence and craftsmanship of the Viennese school he is referencing his emphasis on rich instrumentation. When, later, he speaks of creating "American operetta," he works toward the expression of American impulses and feelings.

> In England the spotlight of comic opera celebrity seems still to be focused upon the works of Gilbert and Sullivan. The fact that they are frequently revived is sufficient testimony to their worth. Time is, after all, the great judge in matters of this kind. The late W. S. Gilbert was such a master of his craft as a librettist that he stands alone among the librettists of all countries. There was never such a man on the continent and the combination of Gilbert and Sullivan was inimitable. I have learned a great deal . . . from the wonderful workmanship of Sir Arthur Sullivan, whose scores are marvels of symmetry and soundness.

> *There* was a workman whose technique never fell away from the severe rules of harmonic sequence. The Sullivan model never struck a note of anti-climax. He wrought far too cunningly ever to touch a higher note in progressing toward a finale than he struck in his musical climax. Yes, indeed, as a model "Pinafore" and "The Golden Legend" and all the operas which lie between these two poles of achievement have been a high school for ambitious composers ever since he founded the brilliant school of English composition.

Finally Herbert turns his attention to the light-opera situation in the United States.

> I do not think that Americans suffer for want of good light opera, even though many of the successes have leaked out of the end of my own pen. I think that the best American comic operas will stand comparison with the best that come over the seas. [To be successful]

there must be a natural feeling for the dramatic. The composer must feel and understand what music is best to enhance the dramatic effect in a certain situation. . . . The feeling for dramatic color is partly innate and partly cultivated. . . . Success most frequently comes at the end of a road lined with many failures. . . . If you have the right stuff, confidence in yourself, you will keep your eyes on the goal and march fearlessly down the road to success.

For Herbert that road was long, but success was not long in coming. When he finally turned to his métier, fortune showered him and his audiences with the richest rewards.

In the last decades of the nineteenth century, European operetta was a strong player on the musical stages of America. In 1886, the year Herbert arrived in America, Jacobowsky's *Erminie* had a great success and began a period when the works of Englander, Luders, Kerker and their contemporaries became so popular that only the spoken drama outnumbered the light opera in numbers of performances. But as the United States began to rise in prominence in world affairs commercially and militarily, it was only natural that the European flavor of the operetta, once a strong point in the minds of those who patronized the theater, started to seem a weakness to the new audience created by rising American affluence.

The story of the development of the American musical theater during the period of Herbert's participation is the story of a dual development to suit the tastes of a dual audience. Those who still dominated society by reason of wealth and prestige demanded from their entertainment the eccentricities of the European model just as they aped European royals in every other way: "Following the big Paris exposition of 1900 many affluent patrons [of the New York theater] . . . who had seen what European capitals had to offer wanted to enjoy a bit of Paris or Vienna on this side of the Atlantic."[5]

The new major players in American society, the newly moneyed professionals, demanded a theater more to their own taste: the musical comedy. Charlie Hoyt's *A Trip to Chinatown* (1891) was a play in which the simple songs were merely incidental to the plot. This format also characterized the popular "immigrant" comedy of Harrigan and Hart, the musical farces of the Yiddish theater, and eventually the first great musical comedy, *Florodora* (1900). There were also productions (not musicals) that featured "the largest number of women in the smallest number of garments."[6]

Rather than one supplanting the other, these two styles, operetta and musical comedy, nurtured one another, a development that finally found its culmination in the greatest creations of Kern, Gershwin and Rogers.

The musical comedy form stressed, at first, the *comedy* more than the musical element. The topical effusions of Harrigan and Hart replaced for the new audience the wit and brilliance of Gilbert and Sullivan. The subject matter of the musical comedy books was more American, the music simpler, if cheaper. DeWolf Hopper, one of the great musical stars of the period, well defined the difference between the operetta and the musical comedy:

> In opera in any form the music helps the story; the story suggests the music. It is the artful blending of the two. In musical comedy the story and the score often were as friendly as the North and South of Ireland. Either they ignored each other, or the story was kept leaping from the cane fields of Louisiana to Greenland's icy mountains, to India's coral strands, and back to a Montana ranch by way of the Bowery, to keep up with the changing costumes of the chorus. The peasants and soldiers, having rollicked a Heidelberg drinking song, gave way for a moment to the low comedy of the Cincinnati brewer and the English silly ass in love with the heroine, and were back as cotton pickers, cakewalking to the strain of the Georgia Camp Meeting, the story arriving badly out of breath in its dash from Mitteleuropa.[7]

This passage neatly sums up the elements perceived as "American" in the popular musical theater: a chorus, brilliantly clad; vaudeville comedy; laughs at the expense of anything "foreign"; and musical imitations of minstrel-show numbers. With all these disparate elements in play, the story of Herbert's creation of what he called "American Operetta" can be seen as an odyssey of three decades, during which, by trial and error, he gradually blended the European models that had shaped him with American musical comedy elements. This blending yielded, when most successful, his finest creations: *Mlle. Modiste, Babes in Toyland, Naughty Marietta, The Red Mill, Sweethearts* and *The Princess "Pat."* This process was shaped not only by Herbert, but by the tastes and talents of his librettists, as well as by the demands of his producers, who were ever-mindful of the changing preferences of the American audience as the United States developed from a nativist society focused on its domestic agenda to one that reluctantly assumed a dominant role on the international stage. It is one of the ironies of American cultural history that, as the country became more and more international in its concerns, its musical theater became increasingly focused on native atmosphere and subject matter. The Grover Cleveland audience held fast to European models; the audience of Teddy Roosevelt's time demanded domestic subjects still clothed in the waltz and polka rhythms of a more secure age; the America of the internationalist Wilson finally rejected the operetta and demanded a higher form of musical play. This is the development that had its finest flowering in *Show Boat, Porgy and Bess* and *Oklahoma!* It is not by chance that these products of the American genius focused in both text and music on national style and subject matter. The more the country became international, the more national her music theater became.

Herbert's stage works fall roughly into three periods: 1894–1901, when he largely wrote European operettas; 1902–1912, when he created his strongest works by blending the European model with American subjects and styles; and 1912–1924, when he adapted American dance and popular music to balance the influence of the European operetta element, which he transformed, in turn, into simpler, if not less telling, musical utterance.

How was it that Victor Herbert came to write for the musical stage? There are several answers to this question, and it was a confluence of events that set him on the road to theatrical glory.

In the beginning, Herbert was experienced in the world of the concert hall but a naïf in the ways of the theater. Late in his career he was still smarting from these early experiences. From the days of his first successes, he was besieged by would-be collaborators.

N.Y. City
1126 Park Avenue
Dec 16th 94

Mr. G. A. Townsend
Dear Sir
I would like to see your libretto very much.
Will you send it on to the above address or are you coming to this city shortly? I have been out of town concertizing and didn't get your letter in time.
Sincerely yours
Victor Herbert[8]

He was unfailingly polite to these unknowns. It was typical of him to encourage young artists with whom he came into contact. Yet he was wary of getting involved in uncertain adventures. Referring to many of the unsolicited manuscripts that each day's mail brought, he remarked

> It's so much trouble returning the things. Many of them are very good, but unless the author has them placed with a producer, my labor is often apt to be in vain. The producer, having certain scenic effects in mind, certain combinations of principals, has his book written to order and attempts to cover all the requirements. If the composer and author labor over a work and merely fit it to visionary characters, their chances of having it mounted are slim, indeed. I have two scores written under such conditions and—well, I still have them.[9]

The two works Herbert referenced were his first for the stage—works that were never produced, *Columbus* and *La Vivandiere*. Each of these has a fascinating history, but the impetus for his becoming involved with the theater was largely financial: "We were all passing through difficult times owing to the financial panic and recession of 1893. Everybody was hard up. Herbert had only the work of the philharmonic and the Brooklyn society [Herbert was cellist for Theodore Thomas] to keep him going."[10] Herbert's friend, the critic H. T. Finck, also reports, "He once explained to me how, since there was no demand in America for serious home-made compositions, he chose the field of comic opera."[11]

By 1893 Herbert also had the responsibility of a wife and two small children. Theresa, who had retired from the opera to devote herself to her husband's career, now took a decisive hand in the matter: "It was only at my mother's insistence that he associated himself with Francis Neilson, an ex-newspaper man. Between the three of them they turned out 'Prince Ananias' for the Bostonians."[12]

But the association of Herbert and Neilson was not his first theatrical venture. Neilson reports:

> Herbert told me he was at work on a great spectacle being devised by Steele MacKaye for the Columbian Exposition [1893] in Chicago. The work was based on the discovery of America and Herbert had already set much of it to music. This was a big idea; there was to be a special theater built for the production. However, there were certain things about the spectacle, written by MacKaye, which Herbert did not like and he asked me if I would look it over and suggest alterations. I told him I could not do that without the consent of MacKaye.[13]

This was not the only occasion when Herbert would attempt to run a libretto that did not satisfy him by a second librettist. He tried the same tactic, sending Neilson's work on *La Vivandiere* to Harry B. Smith—with the same result. There may not be honor among thieves, but there was honor among librettists of the period—at least with respect to doctoring each other's work.

The *Columbus* production fell through. Herbert later recycled much of the material as his "Columbus Suite," so his effort was not a total loss. He soon agreed to go to work on a libretto that Neilson had "concocted" for him. This was *La Vivandiere*, the first complete operetta book Herbert set to music.

Neilson chose his words carefully when he stated in his memoirs, "I concocted the scheme for the libretto of 'La Vivandiere.'"[14] He does not claim original authorship. The book was apparently an excellent piece of work, as well it might have been, considering its provenance.

In 1859 Jaime and DeForges created a one-act opera bouffe, *Les Vivandières de la Grande Armée*, which Offenbach set with considerable success for his Bouffes-Parisiens. W. S. Gilbert knew the piece and, after his early success at opera parody, *Dulcamara*, he produced a parody of the Offenbach as *La Vivandiere*, in 1868. By the time the material came to Herbert via Neilson, it had already had a spectacular development at the hands of Offenbach and Gilbert. Not a bad pedigree for a fledgling work. What Neilson provided was apparently first-rate, as Huneker testified in the pages of the *Musical Courier*:

> I spent an afternoon chez-lui and heard his opera "La Vivandiere."
> The music will surprise you all. I am sure I always knew that his Celtic
> blood dowered him with a dainty bright touch, but I was not prepared
> for so much humor and enthusiasm. The book is clever, and Mr.
> Neilson has told his story concisely and clearly. I fancy that Miss
> Russell will do the piece. There is a solo for soprano in the first act
> which is a gem and I need not tell you that it will be orchestrated
> inimitably.[15]

The Russell mentioned in the account was, of course, Lillian Russell, leading beauty and diva of the New York operetta stage and favorite of Diamond Jim Brady, among many others. Neilson takes up the story:

> Herbert and I went to see Lillian Russell about our work. She lived in
> a beautiful house on Central Park West, where she received us
> graciously and heard the whole work. I read the libretto and Victor
> played the music. Occasionally she stood at the piano and sang some
> of the songs at sight. When the run-through was over she told me that

perhaps the part was not quite big enough for her and asked me to strengthen it. I soon submitted a new libretto with an additional musical scene. But the lady became entangled in another matrimonial experience and lost interest in our venture.[16]

It is one of the most frustrating coincidences of operetta history that the first works for the stage of Offenbach, Gilbert and Sullivan, and Herbert have been lost. In Offenbach's case it was *Pascal et Chambord*. Since it was the composer's practice to recycle material, we can assume that the best pages of this debutante work are preserved. Likewise, Sullivan's *Thespis*, his first collaboration with Gilbert, is gone. We have "Little Maid of Arcadee," published separately as a solo, and the chorus, "Climbing over Rocky Mountain," in *Pirates*, lifted directly from the earlier score. The finish and perfection of that chorus only serves to whet our appetite, for it shows Sullivan to have been a fully mature artist at the time of the writing of *Thespis*.

One wonders why, when Russell abandoned *La Vivandiere*, Herbert did not attempt to place it elsewhere for production. There is a clue in an interview given by Francis Wilson, a reigning star of the light opera, who later created the title role in Herbert's *Cyrano*.

> Comic opera as produced in Paris is not up to the standard required to suit American taste. The moral taste of the American public demands the purification of nearly every French opera that is transplanted here. . . . It is unfortunate for an adaptation that the French dramatist does his cleverest work when illustrating risky situations and writing double entendre.[17]

If we credit Wilson's comment, as it seems reasonable to do remembering that we are talking about the *operetta* audience and not the musical comedy audience, we can see that the stage was ready for the emergence of a "native" composer who could write "that bright, jingling kind of music" that his public was ready to patronize—so long as it was wedded to books free of "risky situation and indelicate suggestion," to borrow Sir William's utopian phrase.

In any event, before *La Vivandiere* was finished Neilson was hard at work on a second book, *Prince Ananias*. This was to prove the first Herbert operetta produced. "The speed at which he set it was remarkable. Day after day we met at his apartment and worked. 'Prince Ananias' was finished and I urged him to take it to The Bostonians."[18]

The premier organization producing light opera in the United States was The Bostonians. It was the direct descendant of a company organized in 1878 by the artist's manager, Miss E. H. Ober, and a Mr. Foster, with the purpose of providing a showcase for the concert artists under Ober's management. The initial season—December 23, 1878 to March 10, 1879—offered *Daughter of the Regiment, Fra Diavolo, The Bohemian Girl, Carmen*, and something called *Victor, the Blue Stocking*!

When the news of the unprecedented success of *H.M.S. Pinafore* in London reached Boston, the company reorganized as Foster's Ideal Opera Company, with the purpose of producing an "ideal" production of the Gilbert and Sullivan masterpiece.

This was no small undertaking. With first-class soloists and a chorus of fifty, the company toured the United States in a repertoire that included not only *Pinafore, The Sorcerer, Boccaccio, The Elixir of Love*, and even *Figaro*.

The company's leading spirit was Henry Clay Barnabee. Barnabee, who had seen Gilbert's original production and who copied the author's dramaturgy for the Bostonians, was an outstanding performer with an established reputation. Described as "a born mimic with a mastery of the art of grimacing, he talked with a decidedly Yankee twang."[19] His "Down East" Sir Joseph must have been something to behold.

> Gifted by nature with a noble bass voice and with a keen sense of the comic side of human nature, he happily blends artistic nicety with humorous expression. . . . He is a true musical comedian, his artistic qualities lifting him far above the level of the buffoon. . . . His songs and sketches never hint of anything but the purest fun. The temptation to provoke a laugh at the expense of good taste is never yielded to.[20]

Likewise, the company he led exhibited those characteristics that the American audience for operetta demanded.

> Mr. Barnabee and his associates stood for the higher ideals of comic opera. When the stage was given over to empty and vulgar "shows" in which the staple was the profuse and immodest display of feminine charms, the Bostonians held firmly to the older and better traditions. They did their best to raise the public taste, and offered the best light operas they could get.[21]

For a time the company prospered as the Boston Ideals, but it was not long before new management launched an economy drive. Now there arose a new prima donna over the company, who knew not Sir Joseph. In 1887, after two middling seasons, the major soloists withdrew and formed their own company. This was The Bostonians, whose roster included Barnabee, the bass Eugene Cowles, the gifted mezzo Jessie Bartlett Davis, baritone William MacDonald and tenor Tom Karl.

Although these individuals were the leading lights of the new company, the motive for the reorganization was more than a matter of personalities and finances. There was an aesthetic agenda as well. The Bostonians were to be an ensemble company along the lines of the D'Oyly Carte, with an anti-star system. In this they also distanced themselves from the musical comedy companies of the period, much of whose success was based on the drawing power of star performers. With The Bostonians, the star was to be the material. This approach would work only if the material was of the highest quality. The company was often hardpressed to find such material. They revealed their crown jewel during the season of 1889–90, with the premiere of *Robin Hood* by Reginald de Koven and a new young librettist—Harry B. Smith. *Robin Hood* took America by storm. It was the most popular piece ever produced by the company, eclipsing even *Pinafore*. Part of the reason for its success was that it was written by Americans. This appeal to an audience that demanded a home-made product should not be underestimated as a factor in The Bostonians' success. It shaped the future of the company. The Bostonians "waved the star-spangled banner of native art."[22] And though it was a long time before they found a work to match *Robin Hood*'s popularity, they were the first company to encourage native compositions. These included *The Knickerbockers*, *The Ogallalas*, and *The Maid of Plymouth*. Such works were only moderately successful; and it became clear that even if a new public discriminated in favor of American art, poor-quality material, no mater how sumptuously produced, would not lead to success.

It was at this point, in the spring of 1894, when The Bostonians were at a low point in their fortunes, that Herbert met William MacDonald, and the composer found himself in touch with light opera of the best kind. The association launched Herbert's stage career, and over the next few seasons the company produced *Prince Ananias*, *The Serenade*, and *The Viceroy*.

One secret of The Bostonians' success was not lost on Herbert, and may easily have appealed to him. The controlling spirits of the company, MacDonald, Barnabee, Karl, and manager Kirke LaSchelle were men of business ability with a personal knowledge of the public's taste and its musical desires. "They catered to that taste and filled that desire."[23]

Herbert, badly burned by his recent theatrical disappointments, negotiated a contract with The Bostonians that was signed on June 26, 1894. It provided for the payment of $500 at the signing and another $500 on delivery of the book and score, both sums as an advance against royalties of 5 percent of the first $8,000 of gross receipts and 6 percent of all receipts above that sum, the percentages to be divided equally between the authors. Further, Herbert and Nielson agreed to rebate $1,500 of initial royalties against production costs. Author and composer preserved their rights to supervise the production and their right of approval of any text or musical alterations. Herbert agreed to conduct the opening; the authors retained copyright.

The score and libretto being delivered to The Bostonians in a timely manner and rehearsals being conducted without serious incident, the curtain rose on *Prince Ananias* on November 20, 1894, at the Broadway Theater in New York City.

PRINCE ANANIAS

Type of work: Comic Opera—Farce
Premiere: November 20, 1894
Theater: Broadway, New York

Cast (Major Players):

Boniface	George B. Frothingham
Cedric	William Castleman
Killjoy	Peter Lang
Louis Biron	W. H. MacDonald
George Le Grabbe	Eugene Cowles
La Fontaine	Henry Clay Barnabee
Felicie	Josephine Bartlett
Mirabel	Mena Cleary
Ninette	D. Eloise Morgan
Idalia	Jessie Bartlett Davis

Major Musical Numbers*: "It Needs No Poet"; "The Hamlet of Fancy"; "I Am No Queen"; "Amaryllis"; Ah! Cupid, Meddlesome

* For a complete listing of all musical numbers for each show, please see appendix A.

Boy!"; "Ah! List to Me"; "Love Is Spring"; "An Author-Manager
Am I."

Plot: An itinerant theatrical company arrives at court to find a monarch
who has lost the ability to laugh. They are told they must make him
laugh—or die trying. Their production is a flop but Louis (the "Prince
Ananias" of the title) is so inept that he causes the king to laugh in
spite of himself and all turns out well for the company, the kingdom
and the pairs of star-crossed lovers who manage to sort themselves out
by the final curtain.

The libretto Neilson provided was neither the strongest nor the weakest
with which Herbert was to wrestle. Neilson clearly shows his debt to
Gilbert and the Victorian popular stage. Before his immigration to the
United States he had been associated with Dion Boucicault, and much of
the stagecraft of *Prince Ananias* shows the stylistic influence of that popular figure. The lyrics are unabashedly Gilbertian, as is the plot device of
a company of strolling players at odds with the local populace of some
principality. Gilbert used these elements in *Thespis* and *The Grand Duke*.
They ran a close second to his beloved "magic lozenge" plot. Sullivan
managed to quash both, mostly, but Herbert was only beginning. It is an
odd coincidence that the very month in which *Ananias* was produced
Gilbert wrote his first scenario for *The Grand Duke* that, in its original
form, presents similar situations to those Neilson developed.

Presented with what turned out to be a huge text, Herbert had not
hesitated to bring out his blue pencil. The proof copy from which he
worked contains extensive cuts: "Prelude out." "Prelude to dance too
long." "Shorten the whole thing." The comments are not limited to musical texts. "Too long" is written beside dialogue scenes as well. He even
demands a "different ending" for the text of a duet. Louis, "a vagabond
poet and adventurer," was provided with the following as an opening
song:

Oh my specification
I herewith unfold,
On the list you will find virtues many.
The personification
Of morals of gold,
when most people are born without any.
My head is all brain, on top you will find

Intellectual bumps without number;
You never could guess the size of my mind
Phrenologically I'm a wonder.

I'm not such a bad sort of fellow,
Though I've a peculiar way;
Though sunshine or tempest may bellow,
You will find me the same every day.

Not Gilbert quality, perhaps, but not bad. Herbert found this unsuitable for the love interest for he wrote in the margin, "New song—with his 'not such a bad sort of fellow' kept." Thus, for better or worse, Herbert was very involved in textual matters.

We should not leave the subject of the quality of Neilson's versification without offering a fortunate comparison. Both *Prince Ananias* and *The Grand Duke* have theatrical managers as leading comedians. And each has a song in which he introduces himself. Here is Neilson:

La Fontaine
An author manager am I
Of a company artistic;
Some say the apple of my eye
Is the ultra-realistic!
I try to humor every class
For which the press say I'm an ass—

Players
To which we all agree!

La Fontaine
The compliment I oft return,
In language hot enough to burn;
But phoenix-like they seem to be
When e'er a play's produced by me
If I did not to plays give birth
There'd be no critics on the earth.

Players
Or actors such as we!

La Fontaine
I am the most original
Of authors termed dramatical,

My brain is large and whimsical
Oh! It's acting all the time.
Some say I'm aboriginal
In everything, dogmatical
In me there's nothing flimsical
I'm distinctly super fine."

And here is Gilbert, two years later:

Ernest Dummkopf
Were I a king in very truth
And had a son—a guileless youth—
In probable succession;
To teach him patience, teach him tact.
How promptly in a fix to act,
He should adopt, in point of fact
A manager's profession.
To that condition he should stoop
(Despite a too fond mother)
With eight or ten "stars" in his troop,
All jealous of each other!

Oh, the man who can rule a theatrical crew,
Each member a genius (and some of them two),
And manage to humor them, early and late,
Can govern this tuppenny state!

The point of this extensive comparison is this: although Neilson was no Gilbert (neither was anyone else), his work was far from terrible. The diction and humor of his versification, while not as confident or polished as the master's, still is not of such poor quality that it can be blamed for the modest success *Ananias* enjoyed. To carry the point a bit further, if Nielson was no Gilbert, Herbert, at this point was no Sullivan. The score he produced for Nielson's slight whimsy was overwrought, loaded with heavy orchestration and complicated concertized finales. It is the contribution of a gifted but inexperienced stage composer who was so anxious to make a hit that he brought out his entire arsenal of orchestral weaponry, which threw the whole piece out of balance. As his friend and admirer James Huneker wrote in the *Musical Courier*:

If I am to be critical it is on the score of his want of repose. He gives us an embarrassing amount of riches; his music needs attenuating. . . .

There is little rest in "Prince Ananias." One sprightly rhythm crowds out another. If Herbert and Neilson are strong in nerves and not too enamored of their creation, they will perform the necessary operation known as phlebotomy on it.

An interesting description of the production comes not from the critics, but from Barnabee himself. In his personal, annotated copy of the score, which is in the Barnabee archive at the Portsmouth, New Hampshire, Public Library, there is a note signed by "Fontaine" and "Ninette" (Barnabee and Eloise Morgan, the soubrette). It is dated February 7, 1916, two decades after the premiere, and not intended for public scrutiny, but was written to accompany the gift of a photograph of the two principals.

Prince Ananias

The comic opera of the above title, was the first effort, in that line, of the beloved Victor Herbert, and to The Bostonians fell the honor of exploiting it. We felt moderately sure of it, for the music was beautiful from the beginning to end and, according to the ambitious young Englishman, who posed as an author, the libretto was intensely interesting in the story, melting in the love scenes, perfectly "killing" in humor but, alas! he seemed to be the only one who could observe its manifold beauties, without a pathfinder guide.

If there was a plot, it was so absolutely hidden and concealed under a heap of beautifully costumed young ladies, that it seemed to be their principal business to occupy the attention of the audience to the extent of making it forget there was any intention of story. In the many times we played it, no one found out, even where it got the name "Ananias." The entire attention of the characters, composing the ensemble, seemed to be concentrated in making a smileless king laugh, though what he was to laugh for, or what was to come of it no one could ascertain, or even the librettist tell them.

It, however, gave the orchestra an opportunity to cry, and they improved it, every mother's son of them. Did you ever hear an orchestra cry? No? Well, then, you should have heard Victor Herbert's aggregation weep during the song of the smileless king; the drums, the trombones and the cellos moaned; the reed instruments actually sobbed, and the trumpets cried out in pronounced anguish. It was the most effective offering I ever heard. The smileless king was not in it.

I rather liked my part. It was of an actor-manager, who was continually quoting lines which seemed to bear upon the situation and gave me an opportunity to show the public what I might have been had I turned my attention to the strictly "legit."

I have given this brief epitome of "Ananias" as a "prologue to the swelling theme" of exhibiting the picture [a picture of La Fontaine and Ninette is attached], to which it is an introduction, rather than any dramatic or musical purpose. It represents one of the "hits" of the opera, if not *the* "hit."

It was characterized by the charming prima-donna as one of her fondest memories when "we danced a few fantastic steps together." They were not only fantastic but artistic. If the entire opera dramatically, had been of the same quality, the libretto might have been saved from being a stumbling block, and the close of the season witness a substantial profit instead of a partial treasury wreck. Never mind! The scene was saved from the general demolition, and here it is with the compliments of La Fontaine and Ninette."

Barnabee is of course entitled to his opinion. And from the vantage point of two decades, it was much easier to blame a librettist who never made much of a career than a composer who, at that point, was at the top of his form. Neilson, however, has a different recollection:

A blizzard raged on the night of the first performance at the Broadway Theater in New York. The operetta went well enough, but the streets were almost impassible for about ten days, and the receipts were so small that there was some doubt about keeping it on for the rest of the season. They had to fight both the elements and the depressed state of mind of the public, suffering economic hardship.

The piece made some money on the road and for a time Herbert and I were in clover. On the day we got our royalty checks we met at Brubacher's in Union Square, ate, drank and made merry with our friends.[24]

Some of the professional critics praised Herbert's score as a success. Though no masterwork, the libretto was commended for its "clever de-tails, new jokes and facile versification."[25] The *World* was not impressed by Neilson's work but praised Herbert as a "clever musician, especially versed in striking orchestral effects. The trick of musical jokes, the trick

Sullivan has used so effectively in Utopia, Limited has caught the fancy of comic opera composers. Mr. Herbert has tried his hand at the game, and has been quite successful."[26] The critic then turned his attention to Barnabee and gave some insight into a weakness of the production beyond the libretto: "H. C. Barnabee is seldom letter perfect in his lines. As Fontaine he made no exception to the rule."[27]

Another critic was more inclusive in his condemnation of the production:

The Bostonians were not ready for the work, and there was evident lack of preparation throughout. H. C. Barnabee was unfamiliar with lines and music. . . . The performances of this company are likely to lack vitality, and this was true of their work last night.[28]

The most balanced notice ran in the *Tribune*:

The Bostonians had a famous opening and "Prince Ananias'" fun is always bright and its hits strike home every time. The libretto is not a great achievement but it deals quite happily with familiar material and attains its purpose, merriment. Mr. Herbert's music is rather above the average comic opera level. It is tuneful and jolly and almost too good to catch the common ear. The music is varied in style as well as superior in quality, includes some excellent solo and concerted features and some very strong choruses. There is a great deal of dreary dance music running through the score, and this is accompanied by dancing that is graceful.[29]

The critic of the *New York World*, not much impressed with Neilson's dramaturgy, nevertheless was guardedly enthusiastic about Herbert's contribution and specific in his praise:

He is also happy in the fitting of his music to the lyrics. A good instance of this is the song of La Fontaine, the rhymes of which have a click which finds an echo in the pizzicato of the stringed instruments.

In melody the score is not rich. But in rhythms it abounds. The scoring of his march and waltz measures carry [sic] conviction and produce [sic] the effect of tunefulness. There are two waltzes that set heads to swaying and as many marches that set feet to beating time. One of the marches . . . is destined to become public property.

The workmanship of the score is its chief artistic quality. Mr. Herbert uses devices that are usually not found in comic opera. Full orchestra obligati, broken accompaniments to recitative, unaccompanied vocal cadenzas, duets sung in unison, bits of what used to be called melodramatic music [underscoring] and many other clever little ideas give color and character and above all individuality to the score.[30]

How strange it seems to hear Herbert's music criticized as lacking in humor and melodic quality, the two characteristics that, along with masterly orchestration, were the basis of his success. But the weakness was noted not only by the New York critics but also by the Boston commentators. An examination of the score shows them to have been correct.

One extremely valuable comment was contributed by an astute Boston critic for the *Advertiser*. He alone put his finger on the real weakness of Neilson's libretto. It was not a matter of the quality of his plot, or even of his lyrics. It was a structural defect.

The librettist fell into a very common error. He tried to tell his story in the lyrics. Instead of telling a portion of his story and then having a song sung about it he introduced the songs and then told the story incidentally. The result is that the hearer is at times at a loss to follow the thread.[31]

As perceptive as the critics were, they neglect to mention the aspect of Herbert's music that is most characteristic and that was responsible for the "head swaying" and the "feet beating time." It is his inheritance from the Vienna tradition: the rubato. Rubato style is one of the most difficult musical effects to achieve, because it demands that both conductor and ensemble possess an underlying and unfailing sense of rhythmic pulse against which the rubato is executed. Most frequently, musicians who attempt rubato wind up playing a rallentando followed by either an accelerando or a sudden à tempo. No more accurate description can be found than that given by Fritz Stahlberg, a man who played under Herbert and served as his conducting assistant.

The rubato style was almost unknown in our American music before the arrival of Victor Herbert. While practically all of his music was written to be played rubato, "Badinage" and "Absinthe Frappé" are perfect examples of this style which is so graceful and piquant when controlled by good musical taste.

Rubato means, literally, robbing; instead of playing a melody in strict time, one note or phrase is slighted or played more rapidly than written, the time stolen from this original phrase being added to the following notes or phrase. A sort of "Robbing Peter to pay Paul."

The great difficulty with rubato is that while the tempo is free, it must not be exaggerated, and this requires a very fine sense of rhythm,—a quality not as often found in musicians as one would suppose. Mr. Herbert would drill into the orchestra how he wanted every little phrasing, but after a time, in their effort to do it as desired, the boys would begin to distort or caricature the *rubato* until cautioned by their composer-conductor.

"Go and listen to a negro band," he used to tell us, "—then you'll hear rhythm!"[32]

If the rubato style was the characteristic that made Herbert's music piquant, another eyewitness–participant to the productions of the period has left us an insight into an aspect of the libretti that is equally valuable, for it explains why some of the texts, which today seem rather dull, worked effectively in their original productions. The celebrated comedian Digby Bell, who never appeared in a Herbert operetta, discusses the contribution of the lead comic performer. He remarks that when he played in Gilbert and Sullivan he merely had to study the part written by Gilbert—but that when working in other shows, it was up to the comedian to provide the topical humor and gags the audience expected. He reports scanning the morning papers for the latest events. which he could work into his performance as gags, and even mentions adjusting story lines to suit the exigence of the daily news. Critics who complain of librettists who interjected topical humor into shows were placing unfair strictures on the authors; their complaint was against the style of the period, a style that was accepted and eagerly anticipated by the audience.

In any event, Nielson's libretto for *Ananias* provided neither the structure and witty situations of Gilbert nor the opportunity for Barnabee to exploit topical humor. The result, though flawed, was successful enough that the Bostonians took it on the road as a companion piece to *Robin Hood* and played it for two years; not a bad beginning.

Before the company left New York, a bit of a backstage flap occurred that, had they existed at the time, would have made the front pages of the *Star* or the *Enquirer*. By chance two of Broadway's lights, Jessie Bartlett Davis and Lillian Russell, were playing in adjacent theaters. Russell was mightily offended when she read that two humorous elements of *Ananias* were getting laughs at her expense. It was alleged that the gowns worn by Miss Davis in each act were imitations of those worn recently by Russell in *La Cigole, Apollo* and *The Grand Duchess*. Further, since Neilson's libretto relied heavily on backstage humor and Davis's character, Idalia, is described as having been married and divorced three times, an obvious reference to Russell's situation, la Russell was mightily offended.

> Miss Davis was shocked last Friday when she tore open an envelope, sweetly scented, and found enclosed a newspaper clipping referring to the costumes, across which, in a bold hand Miss Russell had hastily written, "Thanks, awfully."

Miss Davis penned an indignant reply—a very indignant one—and Miss Russell sat down and did likewise. Davis admitted to having designed her own costumes for the production but asserted they were not copies of anything Russell had worn. The spokesman for The Bostonians saw the whole matter as an "elaboration of mere coincidences" and asserted there was no intention of "burlesque of a prominent singer's private affairs."

Perhaps not, but the box office receipts swelled appreciably after this press coverage.

THE WIZARD OF THE NILE
Type of work: Exotic Farce
Premiere: September 26, 1895
Theater: Grand Opera House, Wilkes-Barre, Penn.
Casino, New York (November 4, 1895)

Cast (Major Players):

Kibosh	Frank Daniels
Abydos	Louise Royce
Ptolemy	Walter Allen
Simoona	Mary Palmer
Cleopatra	Dorothy Morton
Ptarmigan	Edwin Isham
Cheops	Louis Casavant

Major Musical Numbers: "Pure and White Is the Lotus"; "Star Light, Star Bright"; "Stonecutter's Song"; "Cleopatra's Wedding Day"; "My Angeline"; "If I Were a King."

Plot: Egypt is suffering still another plague—drought. A wandering fakir—Kibosh—has stolen the royal barge, is captured and is about to lose his head when he remarks what a pity it would be to kill a wizard who could end the drought. Pharaoh spares him and—to his own surprise a storm comes up. But the storm now inundates Egypt. Only the tops of the pyramids are visible and the second act is played in the tops of palm trees and on rooftops. The king condemns the wizard to be buried alive in his own tomb, but good fortune, a crocodile and a chorus of mummies save the day. Most lovers pair up, but Cleopatra decides to wait for "an Italian fella" she's heard about.

The circumstances that brought Herbert into contact with Harry B. Smith and that resulted in the creation of *The Wizard of the Nile*, his first great hit and the work that catapulted him to international renown as a composer of comic opera, are generally agreed upon. The details of this first collaboration are debatable. They are significant for our understanding of the relationship and the process by which Herbert's works with Smith were created.

In association with Smith, Herbert produced more stage works—fourteen—than with any of his many collaborators. While this relationship was fruitful, it resulted in the creation of only one of Herbert's greatest pieces, *The Fortune Teller*. The term "association" is carefully chosen. Although the men worked well together, they could not be described as friends. Herbert's natural gregariousness was not a characteristic that Smith shared. Bookish and intellectual, Smith was phlegmatic and preferred to keep his professional associates at arm's length. Although Smith and Herbert owned homes on adjacent blocks off Riverside Drive, they never socialized. When they met it was for work, amicably to be sure, but in spite of Herbert's attempts to warm the relationship, Smith remained "strictly business."

Harry Bache Smith was, by his own count, the most prolific librettist ever to work on Broadway. He produced over 300 books, or "stage pieces," as he preferred to call them. In addition he provided the lyrics for 6,000 popular songs. He made more money from "The Sheik of Araby" than from any of his stage works. He was the first American lyricist to have a published book devoted to his own lyrics.

The title of his autobiography, *First Nights and First Editions*, is an allusion to his taste for collecting valuable literary items, including manuscripts and first editions of Dickens, Tennyson, Byron and Keats. If ever Herbert met his match as a prolific artist, it was Smith.

A native of Chicago, Smith had teamed with his fellow Chicagoan, Reginald de Koven, to produce The Bostonians' greatest hit, *Robin Hood*.

This was the first of many collaborations, which included not only Herbert, but also an "A" list of Broadway composers, Kern, Berlin and Romberg among them.

Kirke La Shelle had known Smith since the days when both were associated with the Bostonians, LaShelle as business manager and Smith as librettist for *Robin Hood*. Sometime after the premiere of *Ananias*, La Shelle had a falling-out with his colleagues and determined to strike out on his own as an independent producer. Together with his friend Arthur Clark, he had contracted with the famous comedian, Frank Daniels, to present a new operetta.

Theatrical history remembers Daniels for his contributions to the operetta, but at the time he signed on for *The Wizard* (as the piece was then called), he had never before appeared in operetta. He had become famous as the star of Charlie Hoyt's musical farces and amazed audiences with his outrageous characterizations, which relied for their effect on physical comedy and rubber-faced grimaces.

> Mr. Daniels has gone in heavily for the grotesque and the whimsical, without whatever regard for human conditions. He no longer acts characters; he presents absurd monstrosities. The modern type of the court jester is the low comedian of eccentric personality and mirth provoking mannerisms.[33]

Daniels had great success in *The Wizard*, which doubtless led to less inspired Herbert works in which he appeared: *The Idol's Eye*, *The Ameer*, and *The Tattooed Man*.

LaShelle contacted Smith with an offer to write the book for the new work. Smith recalled:

> I offered LaShelle a story for an operetta and both he and Daniels approved it. The Question arose who was to compose the music. LaShelle suggested Herbert. No one else enthused over this idea, as "Prince Ananias" had been a costly failure, in spite of a clever libretto by Francis Neilson.

> LaShelle was persistent in urging that Herbert be the composer of the new piece. "Finish an act of the book," he said, "and let Herbert write it." In accordance with this suggestion, I wrote the first act of "The Wizard of the Nile," and within a fortnight after it has been given to Herbert, he notified us that he had completed the composition of the music and invited Daniels, the managers and myself to hear it.[34]

At this point it is logical to wonder, if the act of the book was first written as a try-out for Herbert, how LaShelle and Daniels could have approved the project, before the book was written. Smith provides the answer in a Boston interview when *The Wizard of the Nile* was on tour there. Discussing his method of working, he said:

> First I concoct my story. In some cases it starts as a bare incident from which I have to work up to the body of the plot. At other times the whole story seems to develop at once. Then I write it, not as an opera libretto, but as a story, in the form of a novel. I divide it into chapters and work the scenes and situations out as though putting it on the stage were the idea farthest from my mind. This done, I am ready for the opera. In other words my book written, I dramatize it. I find this a very easy and practical way of doing it, for by having the thing complete before me and reading it as if it were someone else's work, I can pick out its weaknesses much more easily than if I wrote the opera in opera form first.
>
> My first work in that direction is the lyrics. These I write and turn them over to the composer. With each lyric I suggest the situation and the context but the dialog is the last part of the work. In building up each character I have a certain actor in mind, not with a view to his playing the part, but because it enables me to make it more lifelike when I can see it being played in my mind's eye.
>
> I can also see every scene. "The Wizard" is purely comic opera, while I have been devoting myself to the romantic style for several years. I believe the public wants comedy with its music and the success of this opera has proved it to me.[35]

Harry Smith must have transmitted only the lyrics for the first act of *The Wizard* to Herbert. Since *Ananias* opened on November 20, 1894, and Herbert signed his contract for *The Wizard* on January 16, 1895, the time available for Smith to get the material to the composer and for Herbert to score the lyrics was very short. Herbert finished his work in two weeks and auditioned it for the star, the librettist and the producers at his home. All agreed that a winning team had been formed.

Earlier accounts of this process have made it seem as if Herbert had composed the entire first act in this time. There are also apocryphal accounts of his breaking away from his work, on tour with the 22nd Regiment Band, to work on the score half-naked and bathed in the sweat of an Atlanta summer. The evidence paints quite a different picture.

Between the signing of the contract in January, 1895, and the opening of *The Wizard* in Wilkes-Barre, Pennsylvania, on September 26, 1895, Smith and Herbert were hard at work. We can assume that Herbert had set elements of the first act as his "audition" piece. That would naturally have included the opening scene. Whatever he had written, the following undated letter to Smith from Herbert's summer home in Woodbury, New Jersey, shows that the work was undergoing a thorough revision.

144 Euclid Street
Woodbury, N.J.

Dear Harry

I have composed Casavant's new song, but I have some trouble with the opening chorus. LaShelle said he wanted something bright or at least something lively for the opening, while the verses, good as they are suggest something "misterioso" like.

It strikes me it would be a good thing to have the curtain rise on a wild scene with FF music, something like the enclosed from 'Norma?'

The first part of this chorus scene would be in minor and end up with a strong major part, the crowd rejoicing over the prospect of Cheops' coming decapitation.

This would also be a good contrast to Cheops' song, which is rather good natured.

Anyway the rhythm of the opening chorus as it stands now is very irregular and difficult to handle and I am positive I can't make it brilliant. Let me know what you think of it. If you don't want to change the *whole thing* please give me other verses until "so out with him, out with him, let him make preparation!"

Yours
Victor[36]

The references in this letter are all to numbers in the first act. One wonders exactly what Herbert had prepared for his audition piece. It throws the entire saga of the audition in doubt. The letter is also valuable as evidence of the detailed involvement of both producer and composer in the development of the libretto and score. As an aside, we notice how lucky it was for Herbert that this letter did not surface during the libel trial, for Blumenberg's assertion that Herbert's music was "written to order" and "copied" seems pretty well substantiated.

As for Herbert's working on the score while on tour with the 22nd Regiment Band, that is true. The next letter, written on the stationery of the Cotton States International Exposition Co., is dated two weeks after the show opened at Wilkes-Barre, Pennsylvania. It shows that *The Wizard* was constantly being revised on the road. Thus, the accusation that Herbert did not revise is misleading. He may not have revised individual pieces, preferring to replace them rather than rework them, but he constantly revised his shows as a whole when they were in development.

Atlanta, Ga. Oct. 10th

Dear Harry

I sent you today the Quintette and Waltz song for Morton. If they seem to answer the purpose, telegraph me at once and I'll score them immediately.

I think they are both good numbers.

You might improve the refrain of the waltz a little, if you think it necessary; the refrain of the waltz ought to be very graceful and suggestive, and perhaps also more so in the text.

Don't forget to wire me immediately if they suit. Everything must be tried before one can say a thing is no go; the artist does not deserve the name if he does not work on a thing.

Many numbers in "Prince Ananias" get three and four encores now, when The Bostonians first were ready to call them no good.

I'll bet you a new hat, that the marriage madrigal would get an encore if I conducted it. How would it be, to make another duet, instead of "If I were a king?" I mean something light and graceful, with Dorie's waltz to follow it? This would create the desire for something more solid.

Well, we'll see. So far we don't need to trouble. Evidently the thing is a big, big hit.

With my regards to all.

Yours,

Victor[37]

Herbert was right. "The thing" was a big, big hit. In Pittsburgh, in Buffalo, in Detroit and in Chicago.

Pittsburgh: "The opera undoubtedly made the most positive kind of a hit, the laughter being almost continuous. The music is exceedingly pretty, and was encored persistently."

Chicago: "The libretto of the 'Wizard of the Nile' is a tribute to the skills of Mr. Smith who has produced the best comic-opera books placed to the credit of Americans, and who has happily blended his happy sense of the comic, the humorous, and the ludicrous with the legitimate in sentiment, writing happy, effective and wise dialogue with lyrics above the average.

"Mr. Herbert's music is versatile; it fits the various phases of comedy and sentiment, and in this instant variety of the numbers lies much of the composer's success. Save in a few instances when the music is soothing and languorous, it is spirited, effervescent, brisk and ever changeful and the repeated inclination to the martial style gives it much zest and vigor. He is one of the very few comic opera composers who consider the orchestra as a distinct and important factor and the orchestration is of a very high order. Sunday evening every number had as much applause for the encores as it did for its first offering."[38]

Naturally there were nay-sayers. The critic of the *Chicago Daily News* dipped his pen in vitriol and produced the following schizoid material:

Mr. Herbert struggles again under the inconvenience of an inferior libretto. Herbert's music in "The Wizard of the Nile" is cheap and disconnected in comparison to his even more promising score furnished for "Ananias."

There are several dainty madrigals, a duet—very pretty and well written, and one soprano solo with chorus refrain which are quite in the composer's happiest vein. The most seductive number in the piece is a waltz movement set with exceedingly ordinary comic words. The waltz is "Angeline." [My Angeline]

But then, the critic finished with this: "Mr. Herbert's music may be dismissed as considerably below the standard of that unusually talented composer." Turning to Smith, we read, "If Mr. Herbert was unhappy in his collaborateur in 'Ananias' he is still more so in the handicap put on him by Mr. Smith's book. . . . It is shapeless and incongruous—though some songs are pretty and some rhymes clever, some lines peppery and some repartee crisp and amusing."[39]

On November 4, 1895, at the recently renovated Casino Theater in New York, the crowds climbed the shining marble stairway to the auditorium, luxuriated in newly upholstered plush, and filled the hall to overflowing as Herbert strode down the center aisle to echoing applause and entered the pit as the curtain rose on his first major theatrical success.

The setting of *The Wizard of the Nile* is the Egypt of Ptolemy II, father of Cleopatra. Sometime before the action begins the Pharaoh had been induced to invest in desert property, with the guarantee that when the Nile inundated the land, it would become fertile and greatly increase in value. Unfortunately, for the first time in history the Nile refused to inundate, and Pharaoh stood to lose a fortune. As a result, the royal weatherman, Cheops, was scheduled for beheading. As he is about to be executed, Cleopatra's barge appears, manned, not by the princess but by Kibosh, a bogus wizard and his assistant, who had "borrowed" the barge for a ride up the Nile. Accused of larceny, Kibosh is also scheduled for beheading, to the great rejoicing of the crowd at the prospects of a "double-header."

As the axe is about to fall, Kibosh remarks that it is a pity—since his secret of how to cause the Nile to rise will die with him. Pharaoh and his wife practically kill themselves stopping the execution and promise the wizard untold riches and Cleopatra as wife if he can raise the Nile. Unfortunately, the only trick the wizard has mastered is the old amateur parlor trick of producing a hard-boiled egg from the mouth of an unsuspecting victim. Ptolemy orders Kibosh to perform magic and he obliges— producing an egg from the Pharaoh's mouth and uttering a phrase, "Am I a Wiz?" that became as ubiquitous as had "What never?" "Well, hardly ever" for the *Pinafore* generation. Pharaoh is not amused, and demands the promised miracle. The wizard indulges in an incantation and, to his surprise, a cloud appears, rain falls, and the Nile obliges. Kibosh is loaded with honors and the curtain falls amid general rejoicing.

As act two begins the wizard is again scheduled for beheading. The Nile has risen too far, and all of Egypt is under water, including the Pharaoh's investments. The company is discovered living on the roofs of their buildings. Kibosh arrives in a small boat—chased by an enormous crocodile. As the croc is about to finish him off he saves himself by producing a huge crocodile egg from the creature's mouth. The beast is so astounded it dives into the Nile, and Kibosh escapes to the shelter of a convenient palm tree. Secreted in the tree he observes Cleopatra and two of her suitors, one of whom is Kibosh's apprentice. Since she is only sixteen years old and "knows nothing of love," she rejects their advances. Furious, Kibosh's assistant blows up her palace and blames it on Kibosh. Pharaoh, in a rage, condemns the wizard to be buried alive in the family pyramid. The act ends with an amazing send-up of a Verdian finale.

The final act takes place in the pyramid. The Pharaoh has come to gloat over Kibosh's fate and gets sealed up in the pyramid with him. Now the mummies leave their resting places and terrorize the pair. "Do something!" shouts the king. The wizard produces an egg from his mouth. "I wish you'd learn another trick" says the Pharaoh. "If mother could only see me now!" responds Kibosh, uttering another phrase that entered the common vernacular of the period. Just then the wizard's assistant, feeling great remorse, appears from a secret passage and leads the two from the tomb. Good news awaits on all fronts. The Pharaoh's property, since the Nile has receded, is worth a fortune. Cleopatra has learned the meaning of love, but will allow her suitors only to make love to her on even days of the calendar, since she's seen a picture of a Roman named Anthony Marc or something, and she's saving the odd days for him. Kibosh sails off into the sunset, loaded with gold in search of new honors, and perhaps a new trick or two.

The reception the New York critics gave *The Wizard of the Nile* was heartening. Although there was not unalloyed praise, the level of enthusiasm was such that it can be summarized as unanimous that Herbert's second produced effort was a huge improvement over his first.

> Victor Herbert undoubtedly learned a lesson from his first operetta. "The Wizard of the Nile" is a distinct improvement over that early effort [Ananias]. This time he has evidently written for the best popular taste and has succeeded well. While "Prince Ananias" was full of musicianly work, it was not of a character calculated to please the hearers, as it was too heavy for the average opera-goer and was lacking in that feature which commands popularity—catchy airs. "The Wizard" has plenty of jingle and vivacity. It is full of bright lively music which is entirely original and is marked by an almost entire absence of waltz movement. . . . There are no songs lugged in to display the abilities of the soloists, and there is a swing and dash from the rise to the fall of the curtain.[40]

In *The Wizard of the Nile* Herbert consciously avoided the musical style most closely identified in the public mind with the European model. He toned down the ambitious musical effusions that characterized *Ananias* and played to his melodic and rhythmic strength. In other words, he was true to himself rather than to a style he admired and to which he had aspired. He determined that 2/4 and 4/4 were the natural American meters and leaned heavily on those elements in his score. At the same time,

Smith made sure that every musical number was generic to his scenario. In this way Herbert and Smith created a template to which they were to return time and again, whenever they worked together.

Smith's libretto also came in for high praise: "A really funny comic opera is 'The Wizard of the Nile.' . . . There is not a dull moment in it. The music is light and at the same time good. The story is a clever one, well worked out, and the dialogue is bright."

Another critic described Smith's book as "facile and ingenious," with dialogue that "provokes smiles and even some gales of laughter." Still another called his work "the best thing Harry B. Smith has ever done."

There was some disagreement about the originality of Herbert's contribution. Thus, this question was not one that was restricted to Marc Blumenberg's editorials in the *Musical Courier* of almost a decade later. The question had been in the air for some time, and had been raised by many voices.

> Artistic is just the term to apply to Victor Herbert's music. He has no special gift as an original composer, but he is a clever imitator. He is thoroughly versed in harmony and orchestration and his score is pleasing and melodious throughout.

> As for the star, Daniels wasted none of the opportunities provided by his part and earned all of the applause he received.

> A comedian who has not to exert himself in order to be funny is always a treasure . . . he just goes along and is funny. Nature has endowed him with a nimble pair of legs, a voice that enunciates clearly and the funniest set of misfit facial features now on the comic opera stage.

One of Daniels's opportunities for merriment occurred at the premiere, and illustrates how his legendary talent for ad-libbing added to the success of the production.

During the second act, in the scene where the wizard is abused by the Pharaoh and his court, a large black cat walked calmly down the west aisle of the theater, to the amusement of the audience. Daniels, spying the creature, turned to the company and threatened to use his magic to "turn you all into mice and call the cat!" This remark was made in such a quick and humorous way that it created a ripple of laughter through the audience—although the members of the company had no idea what he was talking about. The cat obligingly bounded on stage, and since cats were considered "gods" in ancient Egypt, Daniels fell to the floor, paid obeisance to it . . . and demanded that the astonished company follow suit. Herbert looked up from the pit in obvious amusement as the *Wizard of the Nile* company welcomed a new member . . . or at least a mascot.

After a successful New York run the company moved on to Boston, where it met a friendly reception from critics and public alike. The piece became a special favorite along the banks of the Charles, and was revived in 1896, 1898, and again in 1899. Each time the piece received a hearty welcome.

The Wizard of the Nile was also responsible for Herbert's international celebrity. The book was translated into German and arrangements were made for a production at the Carltheater in Vienna. Herbert was delighted and anticipated a big success. Smith wasn't so sure. He offered to sell his rights in the production to Herbert but the composer would have none of it.

> Dear Harry. . . .
> I wouldn't buy your European rights for the Wizard for any amount. I want you to make piles of European cash after a successful Viennese production. If I should make that all alone the money would burn in my pockets. No, no. You must not sell your rights.
> I am delighted with the idea of having a great success at one of the finest European court Opera Houses.[41]

As it turned out, Smith's instincts were better than Herbert's.

> Royal Imperial Carltheater
> Management Franz von Jauner
> Vienna
>
> December 4, 1896
>
> My Dear Sir!
> You have made me very happy by sending me the picture of your band with you conducting and I thank you most sincerely for your kind courtesy.
> "The Wizard of the Nile" has received an enthusiastic reception here in Vienna. However the state of affairs in Vienna is a nightmare for all of Vienna's theaters. Therefore the receipts were not outstanding. Nevertheless I will include your "Wizard" in the repertoire for the Christmas holiday season.[42]

"Not outstanding" is something of an understatement. After subtracting the 10 percent commission for the translation and another 10 percent for the European agent, there was next to nothing left for the creators. The Vienna production toured to Prague and then, in a surprising turn of events, the German version had a premiere, as *Der Zauberer vom Nil* at the Terrace Garden in New York. Even without Frank Daniels, the piece, with Herbert conducting, was a hit with the large New York German-speaking audience. This production, without a comedy star, brought the humor of Smith's book into focus and even "lifted the music, which belongs to the best Mr. Herbert has written."

On September 6, 1897, *The Wizard of the Nile* was produced at the Shaftsbury Theater with a cast of London favorites. The critical reception was generally favorable, even allowing for snooty remarks, viz: "A good deal of the American humor does not appeal to a British audience at all. For example, a satire of the financial honesty of politicians, whatever point it may have on the other side of the Atlantic is quite without meaning here."

Pooh! Bah!

More balanced was this:

Mr. Smith's book has a strong and compact first act and his dialogue is usually bright and sometimes witty, the cloven hoof of "American humor" being now and then obtrusive.

Piquant melody is by no means the only characteristic of Mr. Herbert's music, which is exceedingly good for its introduction of Egyptian colour. Mr. Herbert has also done clever work in some parodies of old fashioned opera. The prospects of this "new and original comic opera" should be reasonably good.[43]

Although Smith was present for the opening, Herbert was too busy to attend. It's a good thing. From the critic of the *Stage* comes this: "Pretty, but not otherwise remarkable, is the duet specially written by Mr. de Koven for Cleopatra and her music master."[44]

Since Reginald de Koven was one of the very few figures in the theater whom Herbert despised, it is unreasonable that he would have permitted the interpolation of a duet written by him into this scene, had he known of it. Such interpolations were very common in this period, but for that very reason Herbert specifically forbade them in every one of his contracts. If he ever had learned of this, the explosion would have been the second American "shot heard round the world."

As a final footnote to the story of the London production, it is interesting to note that the dances for *Wizard* were arranged by Jean D'Auban.

He was the much-neglected choreographic genius who had staged the dances for most of the Gilbert and Sullivan premieres. An unsung hero of the Savoy tradition, his membership in the production team must have been a strong contribution to the *Wizard*'s success in London; a success, by the way, that the *Musical Courier* reported to be a failure.

Herbert soon became a focus for many would-be producers. All sorts of no-talents thought they could produce a hit. As one of the popular vaudeville jokes of the period had it, two men, down on their luck, met on Broadway. "Say, I know what we can do," said one. "We'll write a musical." "How's that?" "Well—I can hum a tune—and you know a joke!" That may seem extreme, but for this period it was not far off the mark.

THE GOLD BUG

Type of work: Political Satire
Premiere: September 21, 1896
Theater: Casino, New York

Cast (Major Players):

Lotta Bonds	Virginia Earle
Hon. Willit Float	Max Figman
Wawayanda	Molly Fuller
Penn Holder	Frederick Hallen
Lady Patty Larceny	Marie Cahill
Doolittle Work	Henry Norman
Constant Steele	Robert Fisher
Lingard Long	Charles Wayne
The Mysterious Stranger	Harry Kelly

Major Musical Numbers: "Gold Bug March"; "One For Another"; "The Owl and the Thrush."

Plot: A former Indian Agent has, by hook and crook, wangled an appointment as Secretary of the Navy. With such social distinction his daughter has become a Vassar graduate. Imbued with suffragette ideals she descends on D.C. and, aboard the (HMS?) *Gold Bug* she blackmails her snooty dad into permitting young lovers to get together.

The first proposition to reach Herbert was an offer from Thomas Canary and George Lederer to provide the score for a musical farce, "The

Gold Bug." This travesty, set in Washington, D.C., was distinguished for two reasons: it marked the Broadway debut of the black comedian Bert Williams; and it brought together for the first time Herbert and librettist Glen MacDonough, a man who was to supply the books and lyrics for some of Herbert's strongest works, among them *Babes in Toyland, It Happened in Nordland,* and *The Rose of Algeria.*

Sensitive and tragic, MacDonough suffered all his life from nervous disorders and depression. Still, at the top of his form he could escape to a world of fantasy, humor and romance that most perfectly suited the composer's strengths. Sadly, MacDonough ended his days in a sanitarium, memorialized only by Herbert and his fellow members of the Lambs Club.

THE SERENADE

Type of work: Romantic Comic Opera
Premiere: February 17, 1897
Theater: Cleveland, Ohio
Knickerbocker, New York (March 16, 1897)

Cast (Major Players):

The Duke of Santa Cruz	Henry Clay Barnabee
Alvarado	W. H. MacDonald
Romero	Eugene Cowles
Gomez	George Frothingham
Colombo	Harry Brown
Yvonne	Alice Nielsen
The Mother Superior	Josephine Bartlett
Dolores	Jessie Bartlett Davis

Major Musical Numbers: "With Cracking Whip"; "The Funny Side of That"; "The Serenade"; "The Singing Lessons"; "In Fair Andalusia"; "The Monk and the Maid"; "Woman, Lovely Woman"; "The Angelus"; "Cupid and I"; "Don José of Sevilla"; "Dreaming, Dreaming."

Plot: Alvarado loves Dolores. Dolores loves Alvarado. Yvonne also loves Alvarado. The Duke hates everyone and slaps Dolores in a convent. Romero, a bandit with a conscience, hies to a monastery, conveniently located next to the convent. It all works out, believe it or not!

While he was working on *The Gold Bug* and touring with the 22nd Regiment Band, Herbert was contacted by the Bostonians. Although *Ananias* had proven a disappointment, the huge success of *The Wizard of the Nile* led Barnabee and MacDonald to turn to Herbert and Smith in their never-ending search for a successor to *Robin Hood*. With the work that resulted, *The Serenade*, they added to their repertoire a piece that sustained the company for five years, and at the same time contributed to its eventual downfall. *The Serenade* proved to be a gilded poison pill.

Barnabee was all enthusiasm at the prospect of working with Herbert and Smith.

> We found another "Robin Hood" in "The Serenade." The piece was a sparkling vehicle for the various talents of the company (Smith was familiar with them from "Robin Hood"). The Bostonians enjoyed five "fat years" with its repertoire strengthened by the addition of "The Serenade." The whole opera was a dream of the loveliest music combined with an interesting story. In this delightful creation Messrs. Herbert and Smith handed us an artistic financial atonement for the false-throated "Prince Ananias" in what I regard as the best American contribution to genuine comic opera as distinguished from musical comedy, which I consider "Robin Hood" to be, up, to now, revealed.[45]

Smith was, indeed, familiar with the talents of the Bostonians. He was also aware of their weaknesses—one of which was that, with the passage of time, the company had inevitably become somewhat long in the tooth. In the case of Barnabee that was no problem for, as he aged, he added new dimensions to his comic personae, and his performances were all the better for that when he eventually got off-book. As for the female star, Jessie Bartlett Davis, time had not been kind to her physical attributes, although her voice had held up well. It had become increasingly clear to Barnabee and MacDonald that new blood was needed. They found it while on tour in San Francisco.

When the Bostonians arrived at the coast they discovered the Tivoli opera company in residence. The star of the organization was a twenty-year-old miracle from Nashville, Tennessee, Alice Nielsen. "She started as a little street singer in Kansas City, ended with a huge career in the great opera houses of the world. Opera was her second career. She was first a star in Victor Herbert's comic operas. He wrote three for her, 'The Serenade,' 'The Fortune Teller,' and 'The Singing Girl.'"[46]

Barnabee attended a Tivoli performance and hired her on the spot to tour as Enita in *Mexico*. The following season she appeared as Annabel

The music is all important. In fact, the second act, like that of "Robin Hood" is simply an excuse for a concert in costume.

Miss Alice Nielsen, one of the youngest members of the company, was the only one who did herself real justice. She is an admirable mixture of soubrette and leading (!) soprano. Throughout her work was dainty and naive, and her singing was most effective.

Mr. Victor Herbert was the hero of the evening. He wrote the music, supplied most of the comic element, conducted in person, and kept an eye on everyone on stage. The only fault to find with his score is that there is too much of it. In his anxiety to give every one in the company a fair opportunity, he has written about one song too many for each singer, and the second act especially must be ruthlessly curtailed.[52]

Along the same lines, the critic of the *Chronicle* remarked that "by the third act one is apt to have indigestion."[53]

These comments were right on the mark. Herbert's score, like that of *Ananias*, though more theatrically sensitive, is again too long and too elaborate for the frivolous nature of the subject matter. Herbert had not yet mastered the technique of writing music that not only was responsive to the characters and situations of the libretto, but that also reflected the ambience of the dramaturgy as well. In the case of *The Serenade* the book is a conflation of comic-opera clichés as old as eighteenth-century intermezzi: the aged noble who seeks to wed his young charge; the young troubadour who woos her with a signature serenade; various comic types who try to promote or frustrate the amorous schemes of noble and lover for various worthy or nefarious purposes. All of this played out over the course of an attenuated evening which, with encores, lasted some three and a half hours.

Still, other Chicago commentators found the music a "brilliant success," the libretto "in Mr. Smith's best vein," the lyrics "graceful and neatly phrased" and "uncommonly clever."

The publicity attendant to the New York opening all focused on Alice Nielsen, the new girl in town: "A smile becomes her round and dimpled features as the sunshine does a flower garden; her eyes are dancing with merriment and when she laughs she throws back her head and a free and unrestrained and happy laugh comes rippling out like a robin's note."[54]

During an interview, Nielsen mentioned that one of her favorite roles was Yum Yum in *The Mikado*. Apparently a good part of that character's personality was natural to the soprano, for modesty was clearly not one of her attributes. "One lucky night," she remarked, "lucky for Mr. Barnabee, I mean, he happened to hear me sing in *Lucia* and invited me to join The Bostonians. I don't mind telling you that Mr. Barnabee is a very discerning gentleman who knows a good thing when he sees or hears it. . . . Light operas and character roles with humor in them are most suitable to me, I think."[55]

Even when looking back on her career years later, Nielsen remained true to herself: "I could have done with a little more diplomacy and a little less of the gamin, but then I should not have been Alice Nielsen."

The addition of this new member to the company, whose conceit and self-confidence were propped up by the reviews, did little to strengthen her popularity with the other female members of the ensemble. But Nielsen had a happy-go-lucky heart and a thick skin that saw her through the tough times just ahead.

> No female member of the company was in any danger of being popular with Jessie Bartlett Davis, but she liked me a little less than the others and the fault was largely my own. The Bostonians were as magnificent physically as artistically. Large people, deep of chest, wide of hip, inclined to develop chin upon chin. . . . And I was small, petite, the eternal ingenue, a singing soubrette. My legs, my ankles, my feet had won elaborate praise. . . . Davis' antipathy was not founded wholly upon physical envy. But she was annoyed by my pertness and the habit of the writers of comparing my lack of tonnage with my Amazonian associates.[56]

Not all the pressure came from the critics. There was a scene in the second act in which Nielsen's character proposes to Davis's that they exchange clothes. During one performance in Chicago a voice cried out, "Take her up on it, Jessie. I'll get you a shoehorn!" The audience collapsed in laughter, and, backstage, Davis lost it and accused Nielsen of arranging the incident.

The New York critics reviewed *The Serenade* favorably. There was praise for both the score and libretto, but there were also legitimate reservations.

> The play achieved a decisive success. Mr. Smith's book, while not written in what can be deemed a fine intellectual tone was often bright with colloquial wit, and broke out sometimes in right good humor. . . .

There was a great deal of tomfoolery in the action, and some of it was foolish without being funny. . . . Of dignity there was even less than is sometimes found in professedly comic operas and it did seem something of a pity to see the artistic Bostonians engaged in a performance of an almost altogether ridiculous piece.

The score is bright, melodious and effective, and if not distinctly brilliant at any point from a musician's standpoint, it is sufficiently tuneful and pretty to thoroughly please the popular fancy. [The book] is not screamingly funny, but it is bright and serves its purpose excellently.[57]

When the reviewers turned their attention to the personnel they were, unfortunately, unanimous. Davis had no doubt been feeling the sting of competition from her younger colleague, and the "shoehorn" incident had done nothing to sweeten her disposition. She had therefore arranged for a little surprise on opening night. The surprise backfired.

Jessie Bartlett Davis is both fortunate and praiseworthy in her part, but she was permitted by a bad lapse in management to make an impudent flower show. A dozen floral pieces were handed to her across the footlights, thus delaying the performance and affronting the real enthusiasm of an assemblage whose admiration she had gained. Mrs. Davis is too fine an artiste to behave so.

Contrastingly modest was the demeanor of Alice Nielsen, who represented the other of the two heroines. Miss Nielsen is very young, very pretty, a novice in acting, but a charming singer, with a fresh, light, clear true soprano voice. She was a revelation and a surprise to the audience.[58]

The *Mail and Express* was less gallant.

Jessie Bartlett Davis, who labors under the handicap of physical proportions scarcely suited to a young girl in her teens, would have been forgiven her weight had she done nothing more than sing "The Angelus" as she sang it. Still, to the lithesome Alice Nielsen must be accorded the hit of the evening if comparison must be made.[59]

And then there was this.

The Bostonians have needed new blood for some time. The infusion has been made in the form of a pretty, slender girl, with a clear, fresh voice of agreeable quality. She sings with fluency and is not afraid to attempt a cadenza with flute obligato. Her name is Alice Nielsen, and she has a future. Jessie Bartlett Davis revels in the most grateful part she had had in years and sings as pleasantly as ever.[60]

With reviews like these the Bostonians continued in New York for several months. The atmosphere was icy, and even a roaring box office could not make up for the discomfort the company experienced. For by now it had split into two factions. After Davis had accused Nielsen of paying a flak for the "shoehorn" remark, Barnabee and his wife, Clara, had come to Nielsen's defense. The lines were drawn between the Barnabee Nielsen and MacDonald/Davis factions. To add to the backstage fun, it was rumored that MacDonald had begun an affair with Davis—not the best situation for a company whose survival depended on a long and successful run for *The Serenade*.

By September the Bostonians were again on the road, first to Providence, then to Hartford, where one critic for the first time, discussed the musical composition on which the show's plot hinges—the serenade itself: "The serenade is not good enough to justify all the fuss made about it. For this it should be an incisive number. It is simply a good, sentimental serenade, one of a dozen."[61] And here the critic put his finger on the key to the weakness of the work. Although far and away superior to the run of the mill pieces offered the public in this period, there is not a page in the work that can be called inspired. The music is workmanlike, as is the dramaturgy. But in every aspect, in both the humorous and sentimental numbers, it lacks that spark of genius that characterizes the strongest pages Herbert wrote. Think *Meistersinger* with a second-rate *Preislied*, and you have it.

On September 21, the Bostonians returned to their home country as prophets without too much honor: "It is the foolish season when fool things are popular, and in hopes for its fortune we pronounce 'The Serenade' to be the foolishest fine entertainment in town."[62] As usual, Herbert's orchestration was unanimously praised, though the critics found much of the score reminiscent. Still, "Mr. Herbert is too clever to plagiarize and too capable not to find his own phrases."[63] But spontaneity was absent, as was romantic beauty of melody and grace of expression. The *Globe* thought that Smith and Herbert had "never done better work,"[64] although the "immense amount of music"[65] was noted. Importantly, for the first time the critics praised Herbert's work in the choral sections of the piece; this was a recognition long neglected.

Among the performers, Nielsen again carried off all the honors. More than a star, she "scintillated like an entire constellation."[66] As a result of her contribution the Bostonians were pronounced "rejuvenated. The stodginess of middle age has been cast aside." Smith's book was declared excellent, rising to a high plane of comedy. And there were the by now almost obligatory nods to Davis, Barnabee, MacDonald and others.

In 1898 the company took the production on tour. The critics were less than gracious about Smith's "forced humor." The man from the *St. Louis Star* gave this example:

> When someone says to the Duke that Colombo was once a sweet *singer*, the worthy replies that he is only a *light-running domestic*. [Singer and Domestic were the leading manufacturers of sewing machines.] This is a joke that puts stitches into the sides of those who have need for them, but whose number is limited. Such punning quite overcomes the poetic quality of the score.[67]

An examination of the original prompt book for *The Serenade* shows no such dialogue. Evidently the leading comedians of the Bostonians were adding "improvements" to Smith's text—and not to his credit. The *Globe-Democrat* found the music "heavy" and observed that it was as if Herbert were trying to say, "I could write grand opera if I tried. If you don't believe it, just listen."[68]

Davis was treated more gently. She sang with the "beauty that made her famous"; but then "It is the custom to mention the physical development and changes in favorites like Mrs. Davis, and for this reason all reference thereto is here omitted as extraneous and for the most part ungallant, if not downright impolite."[69]

In August the company paid a special visit to Manhattan Beach, swept by ocean breezes, where Herbert was concertizing with the band. It was a gala occasion.

MANHATTAN BEACH

presents

THE BOSTONIANS

in

THE SERENADE

(Evenings at 9 PM)

TOMORROW EVENING AUGUST 29TH

500TH PERFORMANCE OF THE SERENADE

Victor Herbert's 22nd Regt. Band Daily 3:30–7 PM
Sun 3:30–8 PM

In 1899 the company embarked on a nationwide tour that was un-eventful, until one disastrous evening in Los Angeles. The *Record* head-lined the event:

MACDONALD WAS MAD

The popular baritone of The Bostonians was sorely tempted to stop the performance.

Unwarranted interruptions from a stage box.

Mr. C. Porter of New York and some friends tried to jeer at MacDonald and Jessie Bartlett Davis in the famous love duet.

After the first act MacDonald sent for the manager of the theater and notified him that he would stop the performance if there were any repetitions of the interruptions that disgraced the first act. The manager tried to make peace but MacDonald was stern and unyielding. Jessie Bartlett Davis shook her chubby fists and said that she would like to get even. If Mr. Porter's locks had come within a radius of five yards of the chubby fists of Mrs. Davis, there is no question there would have been some hair straggling down somebody's back.[70]

The "chubby fists" and the unrelenting comparisons of Nielsen and Davis finally did their work. By the time the Bostonians set off on their third season of "serenading," Davis had left the company. The press noticed: "Miss Marcia Van Dresser, who has succeeded Jessie Bartlett Davis, leading contralto, is a young woman of very attractive personality. Her speaking voice is extremely musical, but her singing voice is disap-pointing. It lacks depth, and the notes in high register seem artificial and impotent."[71] Miss Van Dresser was obviously not hired for her vocal accomplishments. Eugene Cowles, a company stalwart, now resigned. And what of sweet Alice Nielsen, whose stellar performance had saved the company? She had long since departed to form the "Alice Nielsen Opera Company." It was for this organization that Herbert and Smith created one of their greatest triumphs, a work that featured the first two of Herbert's immortal compositions, "The Gypsy Love Song," and "Romany Life." This was *The Fortune Teller,* written to showcase the immense talent of Herbert's first great prima donna, Alice Nielsen.

As for the "Famous Bostonians," they hung on bravely until 1904 when, their vogue finished, their day closing and despairing of finding another *Robin Hood,* they bowed to the inevitable and gave up the ghost.

THE IDOL'S EYE

Type of work: Exotic Farce
Premiere: September 20, 1897
Theater: Rand's Opera House, Troy, N.Y.
Broadway, New York (October 25, 1897)

Cast (Major Players):

Abel Conn	Frank Daniels
Ned Winner	Maurice Darcy
Jamie McSnuffy	Alf. C. Whelan
Don Pablo Tabasco	Will Danforth
Corporal O'Flannagan	Sinclair Nash
Chief Priest of the Temple of the Ruby	Newton Westbrook
Damayanti	Norma Kopp
Maraquita	Helen Redmond
Bidalia	Belle Bucklin
Lieut. Desmond	Claudia Carlstedt

Major Musical Numbers: "Entrance of the Brahmins"; "I'm Captain Cholly Chumley"; "Song of the Priestess."

Plot: Two rubies, one bestowing the gift of love, the other the curse of hate to the possessor, are passed around between rival lovers (and haters), with attendant mishaps. Shakespeare did it better in *A Midsummer Night's Dream.*

But before *The Fortune Teller* there was *The Idol's Eye,* a second vehicle for Frank Daniels. The comedian had made such a triumph with *The Wizard of the Nile* that a huge demand had arisen for a sequel. Smith and Herbert put their heads together and quickly produced a farce that kept the Frank Daniels Opera Company busy for several years.

Set in India during the raj, it provided Herbert with the opportunity to compose the "exotic" music at which he excelled. But there was much more to this score than such numbers as "The Entrance of the Brahmins" and an a capella chorus that framed the first act and called forth unanimous praise from the critics. The burden of the plot hinged on an old custom that provided that if anyone should save a suicide from self-destruction he would be held responsible for all the man's past and future actions. In this case Daniels's character, Able Conn, is an "aeronaught" who travels about India in a hot-air balloon in search of adventure. The would-be suicide he rescues turns out to be a kleptomaniac with a penchant for singing British music hall songs such as "I'm Captain Charlie Chumley of the Guards." His most recent theft is a certain "ruby of love," the idol's eye of the title, which he has lifted, since whoever possesses the gem becomes irresistible to women. As the raja's police close in, he secretes the ruby in Daniels's pocket, with the expected complications.

There are two parallels to *The Wizard of the Nile*. In place of the famous egg trick, every time the suicidal character shouts "Hoot man, Hoot!" Daniels drops his trousers. And the comic's big number, "The Tattooed Man," is a sequel to *The Wizard*'s big hit, "My Angeline." In this song the human snake gets her comeuppance.

The possibilities for farcical complications, especially when the action moves to the temple of the juggernaut—where once every year the idol (in the guise of Daniels) comes to life—were endless, and Smith and Herbert gleefully rang changes on all the comic possibilities. The composer was in his best satirical vein and, inspired by the thump and blow of his continuing brass band connection, he carried that atmosphere of fun and games into his setting. This is not to say that he completely neglected his romantic side. The waltz-quintet, "Star Light Star Bright," proved especially effective, perhaps because it provided a graceful contrast to the two-beat quality of the rest of the score.

When Herbert tried least to be consciously artistic, he often came up with a crowd-pleaser. Perhaps the critics picked up this spirit and themselves relaxed. Whatever the reason, from the day of its premiere on September 20, 1897, at Rand's Opera House in Troy, New York, *The Idol's Eye* led a charmed life. It filled theater after theater with lighthearted mirth as it filled the bank accounts of its creators.

One other aspect of the production is unique. Fresh from the rigors of the Davis/Nielsen wars, the creators made a wise decision. There is no prima donna role in the piece. Three attractive ladies were promoted from the chorus to comprimario roles that satisfied the demands of the plot; but here was a show that focused on Daniels—the star. And it worked. *The Idol's Eye* played seven weeks in New York City and then toured, peacefully, for several years.

The New York critics found the comedy bluff and elemental, well suited to the star; they commented on the "immoderate" laughter of the audience. The *Evening Post* called it "the best work of its kind produced in New York in several years," with "hardly a dull moment in it." Commenting on the music, it proclaimed Herbert "at the head of the American school. All of the ungainliness of his first works has disappeared; the flow of melody is easy and spontaneous and the choral writing 'thrillingly dramatic.' "[72]

The Boston critics were supportive if subdued. Typical is this notice by Philip Hale, dean of the critical fraternity:

> Mr. Herbert's music is in certain ways far above the level of that of the ordinary musical farces or comic operas relished keenly by men who have dined well and are inclined to unbutton their waistcoats. I fear that some of the music is too good for this class of amusement seekers. . . . Mr. Herbert's harmonies are often ingenious; his orchestration is pleasing, although at times his late acquaintance with a military band has led him to undue admiration for brass and percussion instruments; and he is tuneful without losing his musical self-respect.[73]

One of the Boston critics took to task colleagues who often accused Herbert of writing beneath his capabilities. This corrective was long overdue.

> He has composed for Daniels, but no amount of 'writing down' can weaken his rich orchestration for which Mr. Herbert is mildly famous. He has a knack of getting at and retaining, in his music, the atmosphere of the scenes to which it is fitted and he clothes his graceful tunes in tasteful, varied vestments which no amount of incompetent vocalism can rend.

> It is easy enough, in short, to decry Herbert's music, but it is possible to name very few men in his line who possess the breadth, abundance of resource, and the exquisite finesse displayed by him.[74]

THE FORTUNE TELLER

Type of work: Romantic Comic Opera
Premiere: September 14, 1898
Theater: Grand Opera House, Toronto, Canada
Wallack's, New York (September 26, 1898)

Cast (Major Players):

Musette/Irma	Alice Nielsen
Fresco	Richard Golden
Count Berezowski	Joseph Herbert
Sandor	Eugene Cowles
Captain Ladislas	Frank Rushworth
Boris	Joseph Cawthorn
M'lle Pompon	Marguerite Sylva
Vaninka	Marcia Van Dresser

Major Musical Numbers: "Always Do as People Say You Should"; "Romany Life"; "Czardas"; "Gypsy Love Song."

Plot: Musette, a fortune teller, has a double, Irma, a budding ballerina. (Both roles were played by Alice Nielsen). A hussar loves the ballerina, a gypsy musician loves the fortune teller. The heavy, a sort of bush league Paderewsky (virtuoso, composer and politician) messes things up but Irma (Musette) straightens things out.

The Fortune Teller is the most important score Herbert created during the first decade of his work as a stage composer. Everything that came before it seems a preparation for this achievement, and the scores that immediately followed it pale by comparison.

At the time he and Smith were creating the work, the composer was still busy with the band and was preparing for his first season as conductor of the Pittsburgh orchestra. He was in residence in New York, spent summers with his family at Lake Placid, and still managed to produce a score that featured three of his most successful compositions, "Always Do as People Say You Should," "Romany Life," and "The Gypsy Love Song."

The book that Smith produced is perhaps the most complicated series of mistaken identity events ever developed for the stage: two heroines who resemble one another (both played by Alice Nielsen); one of these heroines with a twin brother (also played by Nielsen); the first heroine also an heiress—unknown to herself; a tenor slated to wed a prima donna; two suitors for the hands of the heroines—one a penniless count who is also a piano virtuoso, the other the head of a band of Hungarian gypsies who, of course, is musical.

With such a collection of tangled personalities and the plot lines that Smith developed to bind them together, Herbert's music serves as the only unifying element that makes it all work. Faced with such a challenge to his technique, Herbert relied on his usual strengths. The gypsy music presented opportunities for exotic settings. The prodigious vocal abilities of his cast allowed him to write "up" to his best form. The scenes inspired him to create both gentle and stimulating waltz movements, archly witty solos, and rich chromatic-harmonic lines evocative of the Magyar spirit.

If this were all he did, we might say that in *The Fortune Teller* Herbert repeated his previous successes on a higher level. But there is more here—much more. It stems from the fact that the female chorus represents the corps de ballet of an opera house as well as a roving band of gypsies; the male chorus is a thumping, prancing band of hussars as well as a collection of gypsy musicians. Each of these character choruses plays an essential dramatic role in the action; they are not merely singing props as they are in so many operatic works. This called forth something new from the composer: a score in which the dance plays an important structural role. It is dance movement that supplies the energy that binds the scenes, that illuminates the dark corners of Smith's drama and frames it in a robust series of movements that capture the listener from the first bars of the overture and do not release him until the third finale. There were waltz movements, of course, but also mazurkas, polkas, furiants, czardases and march movements that seem, through syncopations and surprising turns of melody, to drive on and on in breathtaking sequence. Here is a score so tightly focused on the rhythmic element that it contains a shock: the only Herbert finale that ends pianissimo! And that finale, because of the subtle rhythmic pulsation that proceeds it, is one of the most effective pieces of theatrical music Herbert ever created. This is a score that could be excerpted for a brilliant ballet. And that is the secret of Herbert's success here; that is what is new. For the first time Herbert is able to balance all the elements of theatrical music in a fresh and original way. There is not a single isolated dance movement in the entire score. The whole operetta dances as few stage works do. *Carmen*, perhaps, shares this characteristic; it is fascinating that it is also built on a gypsy theme. In *The Fortune Teller* Herbert's genius shines forth as it seldom does. It is the first of his "dance operettas," a direct descendant of *Fledermaus* and *The Gypsy Baron*, and a contrast to the vast majority of his works, which are "number operettas," works consisting of contrasting set pieces. Some of his most successful dance operettas, *The Rose of Algeria* (his personal favorite), *Naughty Marietta*, *Sweethearts*, *The Princess "Pat,"* and *The Dream Girl* are in a class by themselves and have a resonance that makes them unique.

After a brief tryout in Toronto, *The Fortune Teller* opened in New York on September 26, 1898, to a tremendous reception. On the opening night, at the conclusion of the second act, the audience demanded a curtain speech. Smith was nowhere to be found. Herbert, always a reluctant public speaker, rose from his seat in the front row and bowed. The audience refused to be satisfied, and Nielsen asked Herbert to take the baton from the pit conductor and lead the company in a reprise of the march-finale. This he was pleased to do, and the house came down.

The critics fell in love with Alice Nielsen and with Herbert's score, and after a short run of five weeks the company set out on a national tour that lasted almost a year. Frank Perley, the manager of the company, had arranged for the tour prior to the New York opening, and once the reputation of the piece reached the hinterlands it had been impossible for him to get out of his commitments. Everyone wanted *The Fortune Teller*.

In 1901 Perley took the show to London.

> The opera made the most characteristic hit that has recently been recorded in the annals of English stagedom. All morning Mr. Herbert has been receiving cable and telegraphic congratulations. Here is the first one and the best one received:
>
> "Cheers and applause tremendous for the opera.—Alice Nielsen."

From other sources come cablegrams stating that the English almost went crazy over the music of *The Fortune Teller*. . . . From the representatives of Herbert's new publisher (Witmark) came word of the wonderful success last night: "Hurrah! Hurrah! Hurrah! You must have hit our English friends hard. Opening was wonderful!"[75]

Asked for a comment on all this, Herbert had an odd reaction. He remarked that he was glad to hear that his music had made a hit with the English, but he refused absolutely to be quoted on the record, for he said he did not know whether he was being gold bricked (swindled) or not.

Herbert, very much the Irish patriot, had no love for the English and had made no secret of it in previous public statements. He had had nothing to do with the London production—it was strictly a venture by Nielsen and Perley and, deep in the turmoil of his third Pittsburgh season, he may have been wary of making public pronouncements . . . and suspicious of everyone and everything.

The London production lasted three months. In July Nielsen became a victim of the summer heat and shut the production down. Under such circumstances *The Fortune Teller* bid adieu to London, but not to the British Empire. One Musgrove, the leading theatrical producer of Australia, had seen the London notices and negotiated with Herbert and Smith for a production down under. It opened in Melbourne in February, 1903, and made a tremendous hit there and at four other sites. Musgrove cabled Herbert to forward production materials for *The Serenade* so that he could alternate the works on tour.

Herbert was forced to admit that, despite his personal animus for the English, thanks to their enthusiasm, it could now be said that the sun never set on the British Empire, or on *The Fortune Teller*.

CYRANO

Type of work: Romantic Comic Opera
Premiere: September 11, 1899
Theater: Academy of Music, Montreal, Canada
Knickerbocker, New York (September 18, 1899)

Cast (Major Players):

Cyrano de Bergerac	Francis Wilson
Christian de Neuvillette	Charles H. Bowers
Ragueneau	Peter Lang
Captain Castel-Jaloux	John E. Brand
Count de Guiche	Robert Broderick
Montfleury	A. M. Holbrook
Roxane	Lulu Glaser

Major Musical Numbers: "Since I Am Not for Thee"; "I Wonder"; "In Bivouac Reposing"; "Balcony Scene."

Plot: Rostand reduced to light opera format.

In December 1897, one of the great plays of the French theater premiered in Paris. Rostand's *Cyrano de Bergerac* was an almost perfect drama, full of honest emotion, pathos, humor, dramatic movement—all the elements that, one would think, would lend itself to musical adaptation. The play was so good that, as it turned out, music had nothing to add. Indeed it seemed only to detract from the power of the original. As Harry B. Smith, who provided lyrics for Herbert's version, later remarked, "Rostand's play is too fine to have musical interruptions."

New York knew the original. It had been produced to great acclaim in October 1898. Francis Wilson, one of the period's great comic-opera personalities, saw in it an opportunity for a starring vehicle. Wilson was not only a competent performer, he was also a master of sword play. The Cyrano role proved irresistible. Compared to Frank Daniels, Wilson's work was on occasion relatively more refined: "His comic opera work is . . . full of droll turns and quaint fancies which stamp the comedian as an original creator. He tries to lift comic opera out of mere buffooneries. His productions are always carefully staged and costumed. In his acting he appeals to the sense of the droll instead of the vulgar."[76]

Wilson approached Herbert and Smith with a proposition to produce and star in a musical adaptation. Smith agreed to provide lyrics, but passed on revising Rostand's original. This ungrateful job fell to Stuart Reed, a journeyman librettist who jumped at the chance of working with Herbert.

Cyrano is a play with both humor and romance. The original balances these elements in a masterful way. Reed, working with Wilson looking over his shoulder, was at a loss to strike this balance in his libretto. A subtle decision was needed. It was easy enough to alternate contrasting scenes. The problem was how to present the character of Cyrano; was he to be a figure of fun or one of sympathy? Reed and Wilson never made up their minds, and the figure of Cyrano was never presented in a convincing way. With a weakness at the pivot of the plot, the fact that the rest of the cast was chosen for their dramatic rather than their musical strengths did nothing to promote the prospects of a musical production. Herbert, inspired more by Rostand than by Reed, produced challenging music, much beyond the capabilities of his cast. The result opened in Montreal on September 11, 1899. One week later it premiered in New York.

> The opera is a decided abridgement of the play. It is more than that; it is a burlesque of it. Little effort had been made to retain any of the beauty or poetic grandeur of M. Rostand's original, but Mr. Wilson and the other comedians have been supplied with topical gags and a liberal sprinkling of "damns" without which Mr. Wilson's productions apparently would be incomplete. To say that these interpolations are a shock to any admirer of the original Cyrano is to put it mildly. It is sad to see a mutilated vulgarized version of a work so great put on the stage.

Mr. Wilson seemed to be uncertain whether to attempt to play his role in his customary clownish matter. To make sure—he did both. At times he was the same Francis Wilson with whom we are familiar, winning laughs by buffoonery and low comedy tricks. Again he appeared to be striving to give some dignity to the character and here he was hopelessly out of his element. Not for a moment did he show the real Cyrano.

If the production achieves success it will be due to Mr. Herbert's music. It is of exquisite beauty.[77]

But the music was not enough. After four weeks in New York Wilson took the show on tour, and from all reports, as the receipts grew weaker and weaker, his attempts at slapstick became ever more frenetic. To tell the truth, despite two effective trios and a beautiful chorus for men's voices that opens act three, the piece is so flawed in so many ways that its demise must have been a relief for all concerned.

THE SINGING GIRL
Type of work: Romantic Operetta
Premiere: October 2, 1899
Theater: Her Majesty's, Montreal, Canada
Casino, New York (October 23, 1899)

Cast (Major Players):

Duke Rodolph	Eugene Cowles
Count Otto	Richie Ling
Prince Pumpernickel	Joseph W. Herbert
Aufpassen	Joseph Cawthorn
Stephan	John C. Slavin
Greta, The Singing Girl	Alice Nielsen

Major Musical Numbers: "Song of the Danube"; "Love Is Tyrant"; "Clink, Clink"; "The Alpine Horn."

Plot: The Duke, unhappy in love, decrees that henceforth all lovers must be licensed. If they are caught making love without the license they must marry or go to jail for life. The first couple (Greta and Otto) fix things up for everybody, that is, they fix everybody up (including the Duke).

Almost on the heels of *Cyrano*, Herbert produced another vehicle for Alice Nielsen. Perhaps he was hedging his bets. For the theatrical season of 1899–1900 he produced four comic operas. Three were unfortunate efforts, but *The Singing Girl* was a success, largely due to the efforts of the star.

It seems that in this period Smith had grown tired of providing books for comic operas. A glance at the reviews shows why. Although his efforts in this area had met with varying degrees of success, his lyrics were consistently praised. So, with *The Singing Girl*, he again chose to limit his contribution to work as lyricist. The chores of providing a book fell to Stanislaus Stange, a man with a decent track record. Stange set his story in Austria, borrowing heavily from *The Mikado* (kissing/flirting in public without a license is punishable by death/life imprisonment) and *La Perichole* and *The Yeomen of the Guard* (strolling musicians/players as pivots for the plot).

Herbert put some of his best effort into the piece. His favorite number was a grand scena for Nielsen, "The Song of the Danube," really out of place in comic opera. Nielsen sang it beautifully, but the audience yawned. It was a show-stopper in the wrong sense. Producer Frank Perley asked Herbert to compose an alternate number, but Herbert hesitated and begged Nielsen to back him up. She did—for a while—until October 23, 1899, the opening night in New York, when the song was greeted with silence by a confused audience.

That opening was something of a chore for Miss Nielsen. There was another comedy being played in the theater that night in the box to the right of the stage. It might have been titled, "Jesse's Revenge."

> The comedy of the evening was supplied by Mrs. Jessie Bartlett Davis (the favorite of The Bostonians,) who sat in a box. This lady, by her gestures, her smiles, her ostentatious (ahem!) applause and her almost swooning enthusiasm attracted much attention. Of course I know she didn't intend to do so, but she did it. Her extreme love for Miss Nielsen was admirably and scintillantly [sic] shown.[78]

The failure of "The Song of the Danube" forced Herbert to provide a substitute. He tossed off something that he denigrated as a "Dutch Cakewalk." He hoped the audience would reject it. On the first night that Nielsen sang it, the piece got eight encores. The number is "The Alpine Horn, " the best piece in the show. A delicate and delightful "laendler" with yodeling overtones and a charming back-up chorus of village belles in dirndls, it is an absolute knockout. This was a real show-stopper and provided Nielsen with one of her signature encores when, after a brilliant career in grand opera—she studied the score of *Butterfly* with Puccini as he was composing it—she had her greatest triumphs as a concert artist.

Despite the success of "The Alpine Horn," Herbert refused to allow it to be published as part of the vocal score. Witmark published it as a "Tyrolean Song and Dance" and sold it for 50 cents as part of a collections of "vocal selections from 'The Singing Girl'" series. It was warbled in parlors throughout the country and became one of Herbert's biggest hits . . . in spite of him.

Once more the critics fell in love with Nielsen and, incidentally, with *The Singing Girl*. The *Times* was typical.

> It can be said without reservation that "The Singing Girl" is good. . . . Mr. Smith's lyrics are quite as good as any he has given us of late. Mr. Stange's book is as plausible as need be and is narrated clearly. The humor is for the most part humorous. . . . Herbert possesses an inexhaustible fund of pretty melody.[79]

The consensus was that the new piece was bright, tuneful, pretty, and altogether delightful. Boston agreed, but one critic took Herbert to task for his fecundity. "It could be wished that our foremost composer of comic opera could write fewer works, for he cannot do himself justice so long as he continues to send out three or four operas a year.[80]

THE AMEER

Type of work: Operetta Farce
Premiere: October 9, 1899
Theater: Lyceum, Scranton, Penn.
Wallack's, New York (December 4, 1899)

Cast (Major Players):

Iffe Khan	Frank Daniels
Heezaburd	W. F. Rochester
Crackasmile	William Corliss
Blakjak	Will Danforth
Ralph Winston	George Devoll
Lieutenant of the British Guards	Sadie Emmons
Constance	Helen Redmond
Fanny	Norma Kopp
Mirzah	Kate Uart

Major Musical Numbers: None of distinction. Probably his worst score.

Plot: The Ameer is out to marry an American heiress so that he can pay his taxes. She, however, is in love with the local British tax collector. A subplot involves locals who are planning a coup. The American girl and her friend fix things up.

The strictures of the Boston critic are well borne out when we examine Herbert's final two productions of this period. *The Ameer*, another vehicle for Frank Daniels, is probably the worst thing Herbert ever wrote. Kirke LaShelle, former manager of The Bostonians, and Fred Ranken, the man Herbert was said to be grooming to take over the management of the Pittsburgh orchestra, were responsible for the book and lyrics. The show opened in New York, played for two weeks and toured for two years, such success as it enjoyed largely due to Daniels's following. Boston was not amused.

"The word "Ameer" comes, I believe, from the Arabic, the language from which we derive that beautiful word "alcohol," and I should much prefer to write about Arabic and Burton's edition of the Arabian Nights than to discuss this new comic opera . . . a piece that is not a comic opera in any legitimate sense of the word. "The Ameer" is a farce with music . . . music which calls in ensemble for strength of lungs and pectoral endurance rather than for effects or contrast, or delicacy, or any nuancing whatever.

Victor Herbert is a musician of excellent parts. He has written music of worth. He has before this in comic opera, shown that he can be popular and at the same time save his self-respect. I do not understand how he was willing to put his name to this score. For in "The Ameer" he is seldom, if ever, the accomplished musician, and there is not one good, honest tune in the whole piece. . . . His solos are perfunctory and not melodious; his part writing is for once clumsy; the orchestration is thick, as though it had been hurriedly contrived for a room the size of Mechanics' Building.

PHILIP HALE[81]

THE VICEROY
Type of work: Operetta Farce
Premiere: February 12, 1900
Theater: Columbia, San Francisco, Calif.
Knickerbocker, New York (April 9, 1900)

The Viceroy of Sicily	Henry Clay Barnabee
Corleone	William H. MacDonald
Bastroco	George B. Frothingham
Barabino	William H. Fitzgerald
Tivolini	Helen Bertram
Fioretta	Marcia Van Dresser
Beatrice	Grace Cameron
Ortensia	Josephine Bartlett

Major Musical Numbers: "Hear Me"; "Just for Today"; "The Robin and the Rose"; " 'Neath the Blue Neapolitan Skies."

Plot: The comic lead, the Viceroy of Sicily, has gained the throne through illegitimate means. A brigand, Tivolini, is the true ruler. Both the Viceroy and the brigand are in love with Beatrice. Three acts later, Tivolini gains the throne, Beatrice, and agrees to share power with his predecessor—who, it turns out, is also his cousin, twice removed.

The Viceroy was created as a vehicle for The Bostonians. The New York premiere took place on April 9, 1900. The creators as well as the critics tell the story.
Mr. Smith:

"Herbert and I wrote 'The Viceroy' but this one was soon prohibited in America by the fact that audiences were able to restrain their desire to patronize it."[82]

Mr. Barnabee:

"We were then caught with another 'dead one,' 'The Viceroy.' This piece justified the first syllable of its name, so far as the attributes of its leading character went."[83]

Mr. W. R. Sill (the *New York World*):

"Victor Herbert's orchestrations were excellent. . . . There are one or two songs which can be whistled, if you can remember them. I can't, but I have no ear for music."[84]

The *New York Tribune* devoted exactly seventeen lines to the piece, among them:

The moral quality chiefly in exhibition at the production was courage. It required a good deal of the article to write such a book, as much more to compose it, still more to conduct it, as Mr. Herbert did, and more than all to listen to it.

Finally, the *New York Journal* slammed the lid on Herbert's annus not so mirabilis:

This Smith and Herbert emulsion is called comic opera, probably because it isn't comic, but might as well be opera as anything else. It is filled with what Mr. Gilbert calls airy persiflage, dealing with such witty and intellectual topics as corned beef hash, knockout drops, and other pretty fancies. It gives dear old Barnabee a chance to indulge in such screamingly humorous interjections as, "Suffering cats!" "Your grandmother's Dutch uncle" and to remark "You might as well set a hen on a fried egg and expect her to hatch out fricasseed chicken!" Then there are delicious other allusions to fricassee, and also to dumplings. The humor of invective is charmingly indulged in. That choice hyena smile always goes, and Mr. Barnabee gets to call the cast by jovial, rollicking epithets.

This is, of course, comic opera. There is no doubt at all about that. If it isn't comic opera, what is it? Please don't speak all at once. The scenes of this fricassee-dumpling-fried-egg concoction are laid in Palermo, and everybody looks like an animated May pole.

Some of Mr. Herbert's music is catchy. But Mr. Herbert does so much work that he is playing himself out, and gradually sinking to the level of the bandmaster. If I were he I would put my name only to the best. "The Viceroy" is not the best by a very long way.[85]

Thus, a decade which had begun so promisingly in Lillian Russell's drawing room petered out with Herbert embroiled in the high-tension world of his Pittsburgh orchestra career as, for the most part, his theatrical work suffered badly. No, he could not do everything well. All of his shows brought him money, and some of his achievements of this period, *The Serenade*, *The Wizard of the Nile*, and *The Fortune Teller* placed him at the head of his profession. Despite the varying success of his achievements, as the new century dawned his gifts as a theatrical composer, excelling in characterization, word painting and textual illumination, had developed to the point where they matched the purely technical musical skills with which he had entered the decade.

Now he was poised for greatness.

CHAPTER 10

ENTRE'ACTE I: ACE OF CLUBS (1896–1924)

With his jovial personality and his love of camaraderie, it was the most natural thing in the world for Herbert to be an avid club man. He was attracted to the clubby New York world and it, in turn, welcomed him. Participation in that world represented more than recognition of one's professional achievements. The private club was a refuge from the multiple stresses of the urban environment, a place where men of like mind and ability could enjoy themselves in the pleasure of one another's company. At his death representatives of the Lambs, the Friars, the Lotos Club, the Society of Arts and Science, the American-Irish Historical Society, the Friendly Sons of St. Patrick, the Friends of Irish Freedom, the Bohemians and the society he helped found, the American Society of Composers, Authors and Publishers followed Herbert's casket to its entombment at Woodlawn Cemetery. The literally thousands of men who marched in that procession were paying tribute to more than Herbert the musician. As an artist he was held in the highest esteem; but it was the man they had come to love in the environs of the club world who engendered this outpouring of tribute and affection.

Of all the clubs in that line of march, the one closest to Herbert's heart was the Lambs. The club had a distinguished history,[1] both in London and New York. At both venues it gathered together the finest theatrical, musical and literary talents, for purposes of recreation and the cultivation of an informal synergy that gave rise to great achievement in all branches of the arts.

The club had an informal beginning at the London home of Charles and Mary Lamb. These authors of the famous *Tales From Shakespeare* extended hospitality to prominent literary and theatrical luminaries. The brother and sister were held in high esteem and the Lambs, founded in London in 1869, was named to honor their memory.

As more and more prominent British actors emigrated to New York they missed the Lambs, and in 1874 formed their own club. From its earliest days the New York Lambs included both professional and lay members. Actors, musicians, authors, scenic artists and producers attracted attorneys, publishers and other nonprofessionals who looked forward to the stimulating atmosphere at the Lambs. Here was to be found a unique combination of intellectuality with fun and games. This quality set the Lambs apart from other clubs.

In some ways the club was and remains conservative. Coat and tie is still the house rule for gentlemen; ladies dress "appropriately." But beneath the coat and tie a spirit of relaxed friendship has been the invariable house rule. The Lambs is a welcoming place.

In 1874 the American Lambs was informally established in the Blue Room of Delmonico's restaurant at Fifth Avenue and 14th Street. From there it led a wandering life, moving from the Morton House and the Union Square Hotel in 1875 to subsequent clubhouses on Union Square, 16th, 26th, 29th, 31st, 36th, 44th and 51st Streets. The houses at 36th and 44th Streets were elaborate affairs, each of which contained a small theater where experimental dramatic or musical pieces too problematic for public consumption were tried out before audiences of members.

When Herbert was invited to join the Lambs in 1896, the club was on 29th Street, and its members included, in addition to Harry B. Smith, two of Herbert's most important future collaborators: Glen MacDonough and Henry Blossom. Other prominent members were Maurice Barrymore, John Drew, James O'Neil, DeWolf Hopper and David Belasco, as well as Barnabee and MacDonald from The Bostonians. Although there is no hard evidence, the fact that so many of the major players in the story of Herbert's theatrical career were Lambs makes it probable that initial contacts leading to future collaborations were established there.

The Lambs seems to have been the incubator for much of Herbert's best work. Even though house rules discouraged the use of club facilities for business purposes, we know that Herbert did use the Lambs as a business club, most famously with respect to the founding of ASCAP. Although the story is given out that ASCAP began at a meeting at Lüchow's restaurant, the fact is that the process began with Herbert and eight associates meeting at the club, though not in the main rooms. Herbert favored the club's rathskeller for shop talk to the end of his days.

As a composer of national prominence, Herbert was expected to provide special music for Lambs functions. Most famous is "To the Lambs," a choral piece he composed in 1908 for one of the Gambols—fund-raising ventures for the benefit of the club or theatrical charities. It was not his first contribution. Shortly after his election he composed the first Lambs anthem, "Columbia," to a text by Lamb Clay M. Green. Later there was "The Lambs Madrigal," with a text by Lamb Sydney Rosenfeld:

Oh, what imp is this,
That can fill with a gift divine;
Then fill-up-fill-up let us drain the cup
Let's awaken the imp in the wine.
In these can be no spell
To cheer the heart as well
As the spell that's cast
While the cup is passed
By the imp in the heart of the wine.

His final choral tribute to the club, "I Want to be a Good Lamb," closed the first act of the 1909 Gambol.

Beginning in 1898, Herbert provided accompaniments, overtures and interludes for many of the Gambols. His instrumentalists were identical with the members of his 22nd Regiment Band, who were happy to have the extra employment. This employment involved a holiday as well, for the Gambols frequently toured to major cities in a private train equipped with sleepers, parlor cars and two diners loaded with a groaning buffet board and plenty of pilsner, riesling and schnapps. "In every city we paraded in frock coats with hoods, high hats perched on our heads. Victor Herbert and a band of 50 men led the way."[2] These hats were no ordinary hats. They were Irish counemar hats with high, raked crowns and short peaks.

As always, Herbert delighted in his role as drum major. In February of 1898 his band had been selected to lead the parade for the inaugurations of William McKinley and Garret Hobart. He had composed a special quick-step march for that occasion, with a feature not imitated until Glenn Miller picked it up in the 1930s. As the band passed in review, all the musicians stopped playing, turned to the reviewing stand, and shouted, "McKinley and Hobart!" This was followed immediately by a spirited snare drum paradiddle. The shout then repeated, the band and its director moved on. The next time this "band-shout" technique was used was in Miller's "Pennsylvania Six Five Thousand—Pennsylvania Six Five Oh Oh Oh" three decades later. Herbert favored quick-step marches, since they suited his short legs. But the tempo caused problems for his long-legged companions, and often, as a result, the Lambs' line of march was a travesty of military precision.

Nevertheless, the band was a big attraction. The *Hartford Courant* reported that the Lambs' arrival had "looked like a circus day."[3] In Philadelphia the whole city turned out to watch the parade, and at times a platoon of police assembled to lead the procession.[4]

Herbert wasn't the only Lamb who enjoyed marching out in front. David Belasco, the groundbreaking author-producer, often shed his faux clerical collar and joined Herbert in the vanguard, reporting that he "was having the vacation of his life."[5]

Herbert's participation in the Gambols was not limited to providing music from the pit. On one occasion he appeared on stage.

> The number featured twelve composers who were Lambs, among them Irving Berlin, Raymond Hubbell, and Silvio Hein. At the start of the skit eleven were seated at grand pianos as Herbert entered to a huge ovation. The song writers then all began to play at once—each playing his own most famous composition. Herbert called out, "Gentlemen! Gentlemen!" All eleven stopped and stood up. Herbert took his place in front of the twelfth piano and in the best minstrel show style commanded, "Gentlemen—be seated!" They all sat—Herbert missed his stool and fell to the floor. Hugely rotund, he rolled around until his companions helped him up. The audience howled at the sight of the great man taking a ridiculous pratfall. Then all ended the scene playing "The March of the Toys" in unison.

> The problem was that Herbert's fall had not been part of the act. It had been an accident. Try as they might, the Lambs could not convince him that it was worth the laugh to keep the spill in. At every subsequent performance Herbert ostentatiously checked the position of the piano stool—and then and only then did he call out, "Gentlemen, be seated!"[6]

Thus ended Herbert's acting career. From then on he limited his participation in the Gambols to the podium and the composer's desk.

The list of musical satires he created for the Lambs reflects the character of the pieces he wrote in this relaxed atmosphere. When he was not under pressure to create something "artistic" or commercially viable, he did what he wanted and produced pure fun.

In 1899 it was *Hula Lula*—five numbers with a Hawaiian theme, one of which was so raw that it was suppressed. Unfortunately, he was unable to conduct this opus, since about that time the Musical Mutual Protective Union of New York refused to allow its members to work under Herbert. He had been charged with shorting the members of a pick-up ensemble two dollars for a concert at the Mozart Society. Herbert maintained that it was the responsibility of the producers to pay the band. The conflict was eventually settled in his favor, but not in time for him to conduct "Hula Lula" or to prevent uneasy relations developing with the board of the Pittsburgh orchestra, which he was conducting at the time.

In November 1903 Herbert presented a send-up of one of his own works, *Some Babes in Toyland*. It was so successful that its sequel, *Lambs in Toyland*, followed in 1904, with new lyrics provided by Grant Stewart. The year 1906 brought the first benefit Gambol. It was dedicated to the aid of the survivors of the San Francisco earthquake. This was *The Song Birds*, with text by George Hobart, a satire of the war then raging between the Metropolitan Opera Company and Oscar Hammerstein's Manhattan Opera. Opposing groups arrayed in Italian and Germanic costumes and fronted by drag divas Mme. Yellba and Emma Screams held an ear-splitting shout-down contest, to the huge amusement of opera-hating audiences. The piece was so well received that it enjoyed an independent life of its own in "advanced vaudeville," and was produced widely in 1907.[7]

The 1907 Gambol continued the opera theme with a cheeky satire of *La Traviata*: *Miss Camille*. The following year brought *She Was a Hayseed Maid*, featuring a "delightfully refined song and dance by the Ladies Home Journal Octette." The year also brought Herbert's resignation from the club.

Although he had been elected "Boy" (vice president) of the Lambs in 1907, Herbert's short fuse led him out the door by November of 1908. His name had been so closely associated with the club, and his contributions recognized as so essential to its well-being, that news of his resignation made headlines all over the country.

Some years before, shortly after his election to the Lambs, he had proposed his good friend and publisher, Isidore Witmark, for membership. Witmark had been denied admission since, according to the council, music publishers as a group would be objectionable, since they might want to promote their business interests at the club—an activity that was against club policy.

Herbert accepted the decision, and nothing more was said. Fast forward to 1908. Herbert is out of town supervising the tryouts of *Little Nemo* and *The Prima Donna*. Before leaving, he had expressed his opposition to the election of two men, one of whom was a music publisher.

> It's a club matter [he explained to a reporter], and shouldn't be discussed outside of the club. The fact is I tendered my resignation because of certain recent elections that took place in my absence. In the list of men admitted I believe there was one music publisher; but I did not object to him on account of his business. I have every reason to be fond of music publishers, because they pay me royalties.[8]

Herbert felt his wishes had been ignored, and that the council had taken advantage of his absence. Neither of these assertions is correct. According to the by-laws in effect in 1908, *two* objections were needed to eliminate a candidate from consideration. Herbert was alone in his objection, and the council had no choice but to admit the candidates, since they had been seconded by several Lambs.

Although he claimed otherwise, it seems obvious that Herbert's nose was out of joint because of the earlier rejection of his candidate and friend on the grounds of his profession. The fact that Witmark was Jewish was not an issue at the Lambs. The club had welcomed several members who were Jewish, in both the professional and nonprofessional categories. Witmark's election had failed for lack of a second from a member of the council.

Herbert's temper at this period could not have been improved by the fact that, riding his bicycle along 79th Street on the way to his dentist, he had an accident and broke his nose. So his nose was literally out of joint. Then, there were his dental problems. He had terrible teeth, and often complained that he was spending too much time with "the man with the forceps—or was it biceps?" as he put it.

In any event, the vast majority of Lambs pressured him to reconsider his resignation, which he withdrew in time for the club to throw him a celebratory birthday bash. As reported in the *Times*, "Victor Herbert had a wonderful birthday party the other night at which all the celebrities of our set drank his health to the most flattering toasts ever proposed by Augustus Thomas (Shepherd of the Lambs) who, as you know is something of a toastmaster."[9]

The Gambol of 1909 was the most elaborate and successful of all, a double benefit to aid the Actors' Home and to provide funds for a new clubhouse. The tour netted $100,000—$2,000,000 in our dollars.

The evening began with a minstrel show, with the band placed on stage behind the row of end men, bones, and interlocutors. The dialogue was pure vaudeville:

"I just made out mah will. I directed mah wife to marry agin within a yeah of mah death."

"Why'd y' do that?"

"I wanna be sure somebody's sorry I died!"

Rimshot.

All this was followed by a classic routine by Weber and Fields, united for the first time in years after a nasty breakup—just for the sake of helping the Lambs' benefit. Then came a presentation of the forum scene from *Julius Caesar*, played straight. But even with all that talent, "It is safe to say that Victor Herbert was the bright particular star of the whole performance to many in the huge audience."[10] The Gambols continued, off and on through the years, with a highlight being the 1912 production starring DeWolf Hopper as the Village Blacksmith—Hector Hotashes—who sang a lullaby accompanied by an anvil chorus.

For the twentieth anniversary of the premiere of *Babes in Toyland*, Herbert and Glen MacDonough, the original librettist for the show, created *Toyland Today*. It was a double parody of their earlier work and of the much-despised Prohibition. Featuring songs by an ensemble, "The Wandering Spirits," there were solo turns by "Miss Martini," "Señorita Baccardi," the famous tap-dance team, "the Haig Brothers" and, fresh from their triumphs on the vaudeville stage, the comedy kings "Bushmill and Bourbon." This was Herbert's farewell gift to the Lambs.

Just around the corner and down the street from the Lambs was another famous theatrical club, the Friars. Established in 1907, its membership was less eclectic than that of its elder brother. The Friars were all working professionals in the theater. They soon became famous—or infamous—for their "roasts," late-night suppers held to honor prominent men (and later women), largely of the theater, but the list included political and social nabobs as well.

On one of these early occasions Herbert was chosen for roasting. The event was held on Friday, May 3, 1907, at the Café des Beaux-arts. This was a huge establishment, not to be confused with the present Café des

Artistes on Central Park West, which is an excellent but much smaller affair.

> Once more the frockless Friars gathered last night, and Victor Herbert was the guest of honor. The Friars ate, drank and chatted until early this morning and congratulated themselves on getting together the largest number that has so far attended these meetings.

> The big talk of the evening was made by Wells Hawks, the Friar President, but after the cigars were passed there were many other talkers.[11]

As the evening wore on, the time approached for Herbert to respond to these encomiums. Then there was a problem. "Herbert's fear was that he would start stuttering, as was his affliction in such situations. . . . Charles Emerson Cook came up with a solution—when you can't speak it—sing it.[12]

Cook, like all of the New York theatrical world, knew of Herbert's problem with addressing large audiences. Ever since he had been called upon at the premiere of *The Fortune Teller* to respond to the huge ovation and mutely stood at his place and bowed, it was widely known that he could not speak easily in public without stammering. Anticipating the problem, Cook had written a "Hymn to the Friars," which Herbert had composed. Behind the curtain that draped the dias were arrayed a male chorus dressed in monk's robes, as well as a full orchestra. When the time came for Herbert to respond, the curtain parted, and Herbert rose and conducted his composition. The piece was so successful that it was "sung several times to great applause by the entire gathering."[13]

> The Friars of old were a merry old fold
> Care and sadness to them were but folly
> With pipe and with glass and an eye for a lass
> And a quip to defy melancholy.

> Well versed in the stars and in musical bars
> Dispensers of fiction and fable
> And at friendship's command they would pass the glad hand
> With a toast that would ring round the table:
> "Here's to the Friars! Here's to them all!
> Out on the road or here in the hall!
> Raise high your glasses with cheer that inspires

And drink a deep toast
To the boys we love most!
A toast to all other good Friars."

Herbert's reluctance to speak in public may explain something odd that occurred a decade later at the Lotos Club. Herbert was a member from 1898 until his death in 1924. In this period the club was located on 57th Street in an elegant building constructed by Andrew Carnegie. Membership in the Lotos was reserved for the most distinguished men in all the arts and professions, and when, in 1916, it tendered a dinner to Enrico Caruso, it was only natural that Herbert was asked to perform the honorifics.

And what a dinner they tendered! The cover of the souvenir program featured a magnificent etching drawn by Thomas Sindelar that showed Caruso in all of his major roles, blessed by the muse of music. The names of all the operas in which he starred were engraved on a triumphal arch, and the dinner menu was written on the face of Canio's famous bass drum:

Oysters
Turiddu soup
Enzo Grimaldi fish
Radames filet
Lionello sorbet
Samson squab
Cavaradossi salad
Nemorino ices
Rodolfo cakes
Julien coffee

After the repast Herbert rose to speak. And speak he did, without stammer or stutter. For after a few words of welcome in English he said:

A te Caruso, con la tua voce d'oro sollevi all' enthusiasmo piu ardente
e trascini alla commozione piu profonda tutte le folle, alzo il bicchiere
e bevo alla tua salute, alla tua gloria, a quella della tua Italia—grande
nel Pensiero, nell' Azione, immortale nell' Arte. Evviva![14]

To you, Caruso, whose golden voice can arouse the most ardent
rapture and stir up in the crowds the deepest emotion, I raise my glass

and drink to your health, to your glory, and to the glory of your Italy, great in thought, in action and immortal in art. Hurrah!

Although Herbert had prepared a much longer speech, with quotes from Oliver Wendell Holmes and Franz Liszt, he restricted himself to the passage above. Apparently, when he knew that only the guest of honor would understand his words, Herbert had no problem expressing himself. This became an address to a dear friend.

The great tenor responded in his native language and then proceeded to provide some of the caricatures for which he was famous. He started with one of himself, drawn just to the left of the souvenir etching. He then did a few of Herbert. Herbert was delighted for, as he was heard to remark, "He has never drawn me as fat as others."[15]

> Mr. Stanley Adams
> President, A.S.C.A.P.
> Dear Mr. Adams,
> Your letter—and contents—has given me much cause to be happy.
> It is most gratifying to have my dear father remembered for all the effort and physical work he put in to creating ASCAP.
> So well do I recall the hazards entailed—his trips to Washington in all weathers, the rejections, etc. But his determination to insure financial aid for the families of composers won the day.
> My thanks and best wishes to all those involved with this happy project.
> Sincerely yours,
> Ella Herbert Bartlett[16]
>
> DEC. 7th, 1972

Thus the eighty-three-year-old daughter expressed her thanks to the leaders of the American Society of Composers, Authors and Publishers for their efforts to memorialize her father. Reading between the lines, her reference to helping the families of composers was a very personal statement, for when Herbert died he had, as he said he would, spent most of his money. It was only Ella's astute management of the funds that came from the sale of the family home and its contents, including Herbert's personal library and the mementoes of his career, that helped her provide for her mother and herself. Herbert died before he could become beneficiary of all the work he had put into the creation of ASCAP. But with the development of radio, talking pictures and television, not to mention the horrors of Muzak, suddenly a new Aladdin's cave opened its doors to his family and provided wealth far surpassing anything he had earned in his lifetime. ASCAP was his "open sesame!" Here is real irony. The greatest beneficiary of all the effort he made on behalf of his fellow composers turned out to be his own dear daughter.

The project Ella mentions in her letter was the establishment of a Victor Herbert Room at the New York headquarters of ASCAP. The centerpiece of the memorial is Herbert's upright Steinway. At one time it was surrounded by life-size cut-out photographs of many of the most prominent members of ASCAP. On the walls are several mementos of Herbert's career: a formal presentation photograph dated May 1924 with a quotation from *Natoma*, inscribed "To ASCAP from one of its founders"; there is a poster from a London production of *The Enchantress*; another picture of Herbert with the motto written by former ASCAP president Deems Taylor who, as a student at New York University, was mentored by Herbert: "He never wrote a vulgar line"; and finally, a photograph of the "March of the Toys" from the original production of *Babes in Toyland*, dated October 13, 1903.

But perhaps the greatest tribute came from jazz musician and composer Eubie Blake. According to legend around the office, every time Blake entered the room he would face Herbert's picture and bow. When questioned about the action, he explained, "If it wasn't for that man, I'd be nothing. You know, 'tote that barge—lift that bale!' "

That is the truth. Herbert lives on in his music, of course. He lives on in the memoirs of those who knew him. But every American composer, author and publisher who is, or was, a member of ASCAP or its near-cousin, BMI—Broadcast Music, Inc.—stands not only in his shadow, but also in his debt.

ASCAP was founded to make sure that composers, authors and publishers would receive the income they were entitled to under the Copyright Law of 1909, which granted to artists rights in public performances of their works for profit. Herbert was an excellent businessman and, from his experience as both performer and published composer in Germany, he was aware that, whatever composers' rights might be under the law in the United States, in practice they were not protected. As early as 1851 the French had established a society to protect performance rights, and soon similar organizations were established in Germany, Italy, England and Austria-Hungary. These served as Herbert's model.

Before ASCAP, several attempts had been made in the United States to create rights organizations. The Authors' and Composers' League of America had a built-in problem: Herbert served as president, Reginald de Koven as secretary. These two men had cordially despised one another since Herbert had referred to de Koven's magnum opus, *Robin Hood*, as "trash." Soon this group was replaced by another, called the "Society of Authors, Composers and Music Editors." This group was established in 1911, at the time the first International Copyright Agreement had been negotiated. Herbert served as president of an offshoot of this organization, "the Authors and Composers Copyright Association," but efforts to assure benefits to members proved unsuccessful, since the organization was not able to secure collective action by its membership.

In the earliest period of Herbert's career, most income for composers came from the sale of sheet music. With the development of automated devices for the performance of compositions—cylinders, piano rolls, wax records—the sale of sheet music fell precipitously. At the same time, the establishment of cabaret entertainments in restaurants and dance halls gave theatergoers other options for a night on the town, and soon attendance at musical-theatrical performances fell off substantially; shows ran for shorter periods; composers' and authors' royalties declined.

This was a serious situation. These problems were the subject of frequent discussions wherever theatrical artists gathered—especially at the Lambs. While United States Copyright Law specifically recognized "performing rights"—that the right to control public performance for profit belongs to the creator—in the United States these rights had never been enforced. Commercial enterprises made whatever use of copyrighted music they wished. It was this general disregard for copyrights that formed the heart of the discussions.*

When Puccini came to this country to supervise the world premiere of *La Fanciulla del West*, he was astonished to hear his music played in hotels and restaurants when he knew he was receiving nothing for it. He expressed his displeasure to George Maxwell who, as a British subject, was familiar with the much stricter enforcement of copyright laws in Europe. Maxwell was the American representative of Puccini's publisher, G. Riccordi. He was also a friend of Victor Herbert. "Puccini, Herbert and Maxwell discussed the injustice of the situation in America at length."[17]

---

* For a discussion of the issues involved in many of these litigations, see chapter 7.

Shortly thereafter, at Herbert's prompting, Maxwell and he met with seven other interested men at the Lambs. Three were composers: Lambs Gustav Kerker, Silvio Hein, and Raymond Hubbell. Lamb Glen Mac-Donough represented authors; Lamb Nathan Burkan, Herbert's brilliant attorney, provided council. Louis Hirsch and Jay Witmark were guests of the Lambs; along with Maxwell, they represented publishers' interests. This was on February 6, 1914, a bitter cold and snowy afternoon in New York. After a couple of hours the company adjourned to Lüchow's for a continuation of the spirited discussion at dinner.

> Herbert, with his hearty and optimistic nature, was the ideal man to organize a group of temperamental song writers and their publishers into our nation's performing rights society. He had the respect of his colleagues because of his talents, and his robust good humor helped him to bring together people who were strongly individualistic in order that they might get protection for their copyrighted music.[18]

Irving Caesar recalled, "He was a great personality, of course, warm, sympathetic, intelligent, gay."[19]

One week later, on February 13, 1914, a meeting of one hundred composers, authors and publishers was held at the Claridge Hotel, where formal organization was effected. Maxwell was elected president and Herbert was chosen vice president. Both men served until 1924.

The legal basis for ASCAP's program had been the Copyright Act of 1909. Its passage was largely due to the efforts of Nathan Burkan, who was motivated more by a passion for the justice of the issue than for any financial advantages for himself. Burkan brought Herbert, de Koven and Sousa to testify in the bill's favor, but the bill was stalled in committee. The attorney then arranged for Charles K. Harris, composer of "After the Ball" (one of Teddy Roosevelt's favorites) to meet with the president.

> As an author himself Roosevelt was outraged at the situation where creators were deprived of just remuneration. He arranged for Harris to meet with Senator Smoot and Representative Currier, the sponsors of the legislation and also to contact Mr. Solberg of the copyright office so that Harris would have the full facts of the case. When he met with them, with the President's backing, he was able to convince them to pressure their colleagues to report the bill out of committee.[20]

Nathan Burkan worked like a Trojan for that bill, more for the love of the thing than for the money that was in it—for there was not much money in the publishers' treasury at that time. He was pitted against some of the greatest lawyers of the time, representing the mechanical companies—there were a dozen of them—and Burkan worked alone. At the time he was attorney for several New York publishers and became one of New York's most prominent copyright and theatrical attorneys.[21]

Even though Herbert's cause prevailed, there was little payoff at first. From 1914 to 1921, any money that was collected was used to fight others who contested the decisions granting rights to collect for the public performance of music. The dues were ten dollars a year. Some of the more successful composers, like Irving Berlin, Ray Goetz and Herbert, would put in a hundred dollars to pay the dues of some of the delinquent members, in order to keep them in the society. "At the close of 1921 ASCAP had 188 members, divided into four classes. Members in the top class received $600 apiece for the year. Ten years later the top three or four members averaged $50,000 per year."[22]

In 1924 Herbert was in Washington again—fighting for his rights. This time it was to oppose a bill to delete the performing rights section from the 1909 Copyright Law. The attack came from both motion picture companies and radio corporations, who wished to eliminate the language so that they could use copyrighted music without compensation. One network had the gall to put forward this argument: "Radio does not broadcast music, it only emanates electrical energy." Another said: "We make songwriters famous, so why should we pay them?"[23]

A huge contingent of authors, musicians and publishers, including Herbert, Sousa, Harry von Tilzer, Jerome Kern and Irving Berlin descended on D.C. Almost every night you could see them at the Willard Hotel.

> We usually feasted and the trouble was that big hearted Victor always insisted on paying the bill. I told him that I was willing to join him once in a while, but did not always want him to pay the check. He slapped me on the back and said, "My dear C. K. We can't take our money with us; so let's have a good time while we are here."[24]

One evening the delegation was hosted by the members of the National Press Club. In return for the dinner, every composer offered to sing or play for his supper. When Victor's turn came, the club surprised him with a cello, borrowed from a local vaudeville house. He had quite a job tuning it up. Then he began to play his latest hit, "A Kiss in the Dark," but the instrument went out of tune. Embarrassed to be unable to play before his colleagues and the press, he stopped his performance and shouted, "This is a rotten fiddle! Take it away!" This was still the voice of the thirteen-year-old piccolo player from Stuttgart—embarrassed, and mad as hell about it.

The next day, during the committee hearings on the bill, the members were called out for floor votes.

To fill in the time Victor picked up a newspaper and holding it as if it were a piece of music he announced: "Gentlemen, I will now give you an imitation of Charlie Harris singing 'After the Ball' last night at the Press Club." It was a wonderful imitation—a scream. Victor had the congressional staff and witnesses in stitches.[25]

The trip was a success. The Copyright Law favoring composers was left on the books—unchanged.

ASCAP was Herbert's great achievement as a clubman—it was an achievement that is perhaps his most permanent legacy. How wonderful it is that he got the job done as he did it, not with anger, which he reserved for his own shortcomings, but with singing, joking, and good fellowship. Truly this was a man with the heart of a boy.

CHAPTER 11

ACT TWO: SCENE ONE (1903–1905)

During the first decade of the twentieth century, Victor Herbert entered his period of most significant creativity. Most of the major works that date from this time are well known (*Naughty Marietta*, *The Red Mill*, *Mlle. Modiste*), and it was in this period that Herbert sealed his significance as a major force in American theatrical history. But even his lesser-known compositions represented new musical and dramatic achievements. These were, indeed, his finest hours.

BABES IN TOYLAND
Type of work: Fantasy Extravaganza
Premiere: June 17, 1903
Theater: Grand Opera House, Chicago, Ill.
Majestic, New York (October 13, 1903)

Cast (Major Players):

Alan	William Norris
Jane	Mabel Barrison
Uncle Barnaby	George W. Denham
The Widow Piper	Hattie Delaro
Contrary Mary	Amy Ricard
Tom Tom	Bessie Wynn
Jill	Nellie Daly
Bo-Peep	Nella Webb
Red Riding Hood	Susie Kelleher
Miss Muffet	Irene Cromwell
Simple Simon	Virginia Foltz
Peter	Bertha Krieghoff
Tommy Tucker	Doris Mitchell
The Master Toymaker	Dore Davidson
The Moth Queen	Albertina Benson
Mima	Grace Field
The Giant Spider	Robert Burns

Major Musical Numbers: "The Shipwreck"; "Never Mind, Bo Peep"; "Floretta"; "I Can't Do the Sum"; "Barney O'Flynn"; "Go to Sleep"; "The Legend of the Castle"; "The Toymaker's Shop"; "The March of the Toys"; "The Military Ball."

Plot: Evil Uncle Barnaby is eager to gain the inheritance due to the Babes, Alan and Jane. He pursues them through various venues (Contrary, Mary's Garden, the Spider's Forest, the Moth Queens' Palace and Toyland), but the Babes outwit him and joy reigns in Toyland.

> Father dearly loved children. He liked the bright, happy side of life which childhood represents. He liked their songs, and this may be the reason he scattered through his operettas so many delightful children's songs. . . . "Babes in Toyland" is an opera for children.
>
> —ELLA HERBERT BARTLETT[1]

For children—and for their parents. Indeed for anyone who still carries with him in his pockets a bit of his childhood. The recognition that there is a bit of the child in each of us who longs for reawakening was the key to the appeal of Herbert and MacDonough's *Babes in Toyland*. This insight was nothing new. The leaders of the German romantic movement in the nineteenth century had founded many of their creations on the folktales gathered with such success by Jacob and Wilhelm Grimm. The great tradition of the Christmas pantomime, those extravaganzas of dance, song, harlequinade, magic and fantasy that are a staple of the English theater inspired the creators of *Babes* as well. The same appeal to childhood fantasy that was the secret of Herbert's earliest lasting theatrical success is the foundation upon which Disney built his magic kingdom. It is not by chance that Hollywood has thrice attempted to bring Herbert's magic to the screen. Not only that, but elements of the stage *Babes* have influenced other productions. The terrifying monster spider guarding the jewel in the "temple of the all-seeing eye" in Alexander Korda's *Thief of Bagdad* is a direct descendent of the huge tarantula that rules the spider's forest in scene three of *Babes*. Strangely, for all the technical wizardry that Hollywood brought to *Babes*, neither the 1934 Laurel and Hardy film nor the Disney version proved successful. This is a tribute to the inherent theatricality of the material. *Babes in Toyland* is, first and last, a creation for and of the legitimate theater. The piece depends upon the immediacy of the physical presence of an audience—the personal experience of

Herbert's genius for orchestration and musical scene painting; of the comical bounds and sweeps of toy soldiers; of the "songs, dances, processions, toys, spiders, bears, amazing scenic lighting effects, elaborate costumes—all accompanied by music that is one hundred times better than is customary"[2] for its success.

Where did this wonderful composition first see the light of day? Where were audiences first enchanted by Herbert's magical score?

"The Babes in Toyland" music was played in Willow Grove before its New York premiere. The audiences took to the music immediately and it remained a favorite with them from the very first hearing. When I said to Mr. Herbert that I hoped the show that he and Glen MacDonough had written would prove to be as much of a success as the music alone had, he said, 'If it isn't a success,—we'll make it one!' It was that spirit—that will to win—that made him America's most successful comic opera composer."[3]

Produced by Fred R. Hamlin and the director Julian Mitchell—a specialist in musical extravaganzas with dazzling scenic effects—*Babes in Toyland* was scheduled to open at the Majestic Theater in New York, following on the heels of another Hamlin-Mitchell production, *The Wizard of Oz*, which had opened the new theater with fabulous results. *Oz* had a pedestrian score and lyrics that epitomized, in verse, the period's infatuation with puns. The most popular number was "Hoorah for Baffin's Bay."

Avast! Belay!
Hoorah for Baffin's Bay.
A whale began to blubber
He was sorely tried one day.
The boat was cold
(We thought we'd get the grippe)
So the painters put three coats upon the ship!
Hip! Hip! Hip!
Hip, hoorah for Baffin's Bay![4]

Of course the book was incomparable, and *Oz*, which began with the famous tornado, was a scenic triumph that used all the technical resources of the Majestic. Now Hamlin and Mitchell needed something to outdo even that tremendous production. It was clear from the outset that the book of *Babes* could never match L. Frank Baum's creation. It was therefore decided that MacDonough should follow the model of the *Oz* production: begin with a spectacular scenic prologue, introduce an innocent child and lead him or her through a series of adventures, threatened by a wicked adversary. So in place of a tornado there was a shipwreck; for an innocent girl MacDonough doubled up and supplied a couple, Alan and Jane—the "Babes"—to share the adventure. The innocents are led through storybook scenes drawn from the world of Mother Goose and a whole armamentarium of children's fantasy works: Contrary Mary's Garden; the Spider's Forest; the Palace of the Moth Queen; a Christmas Tree Forest; the Master Toymaker's Workshop and finally, the Courtyard of the Palace of Justice.

The score Herbert and MacDonough provided for this fantasmagoria of childhood tales is studded with some of the most effective theatrical music ever created. "The March of the Toys" and "Toyland," of course, stand at the top of any list of Herbert's compositions that can be considered immortal, but there were also "Don't Cry Bo-Peep," "Barney O'Flynn," and the perennial favorite, "I Can't Do the Sum."

And then there were the scenic effects—most memorably the frightening antics of the monster spider. Robert Burns, an acrobat, contortionist, eccentric dancer and comedian, was perfectly cast in the role. Burns crawled up trees, swung on a single line across the stage, spinning a web to snare the Babes, until he was finally destroyed by a bear, who, to the delight of juvenile audiences, stomped on his stomach and crushed the life out of him. In preparation for the role, Burns and Mitchell studied the movements of live tarantulas.

> There is nothing I could do which would better bring into use all the skill of the acrobat and the contortionist. I have to keep my mind constantly on being a spider and move rapidly, for it is only in the rapidity that you would get the smooth crawling motion which is what makes the spider a success."[5]

This example is typical of the detailed effort that lay behind the amazing stagecraft of this production. Julian Mitchell's theatrical genius produced a scenic realization that fully matched Herbert's brilliant score and MacDonough's winning book. From opening night in Chicago, critics heaped praise on the result.

Big and beautiful describes "Babes in Toyland." It was advertised as the most costly production ever presented in Chicago, and without question bears out that claim. It is more gorgeous than its predecessor "The Wizard of Oz" and by far the most magnificent spectacle ever seen here. Full of life and color, handsome girls, beautiful wardrobe, a splendid chorus and a series of wonderful stage pictures, The Babes have captured the town and set a pace that overshadows everything else in the line.[6]

Herbert was in the habit of corresponding with his reviewers. In the midst of his Pittsburgh travails he continued the practice; this note reflects some of the frustration he was experiencing with the critics at that time.

July 12, 1903

My dear Mr. Freiberger

Thank you very much for the most charming criticism on the "Babes in Toyland." Your expressions of approval are doubly pleasing because the article shows the hand of a *keeneyed* [sic] critic who doesn't give everything the devil for h—l's sake, as most of them do nowadays.

I expect to be in Chicago in September before the Babes go to New York and hope to see more of you then.

Thanking you again, I am yours,

Most sincerely,

Victor Herbert.[7]

Herbert needn't have worried about the reception of the piece. After the September 14th opening in Pittsburgh, the critics of the *Pittsburgh Times*, *Dispatch* and *Leader* had only raves for him.

Babes in Toyland is one of the quaintest, most melodious and most gorgeous things in opera since "The Mikado." Since the first night of that work there had not been produced a comic opera which could compete with it until "Babes in Toyland" was written. . . . It has the cleverest light music Herbert has ever written. Half a dozen melodies were being whistled by the gallery last night, so catchy were they.

"Toyland" is a song that is likely to go into the homes of everyone who hears it. Not only was the music that of the nursery in its simplicity and beauty, but the words were worth remembering. With so many gems in the score it would be hard to say "Toyland" was the most beautiful, but it was so appealing that it had to be sung half a dozen times. "Babes in Toyland" was absolutely the best entertainment of its kind ever seen in Pittsburgh."[8]

The *Dispatch* called *Babes* "rich, rare, gorgeous, spectacular," "Herbert's best theatrical work."[9] The *Leader* pronounced it a "dazzling triumph" and remarked that, "Three hours and a half was not too long an evening of the wonderful, so long as the charming music and gorgeous stage effects kept going."[10]

Babes in Toyland opened at the Majestic on October 13, 1903. Rarely has there been such unanimity of praise. The press delivered a producer's dream basket of promotional quotes.

The *Times*:	"A great success. . . . Hugely satisfying . . . full of good things. Nothing more satisfying [than Herbert's music] has been heard here in many a day."[11]
The *Herald*:	"A better show has not been seen in many moons . . . a cure for the blues."[12]
The *Observer*:	"Musically dainty, continually interesting, saturated with bright light-like laughter and permeated with wholesome good nature."[13]
The *Evening Post*:	"The audience insisted upon hearing some of the songs over and over again, and there were no protests."[14]
The *World*:	"In the music which Victor Herbert has written for 'Babes in Toyland' there is an impressive lesson to those who are convinced that music to be tuneful, sprightly, humorous, catchy and popular must be commonplace, trivial and vulgar. There are more of these desired qualities in this exquisite score than in a dozen of the meretricious efforts of the men who are entrusted by the average manager with the task of setting joke and jest to music."[15]

The critics called Mitchell "the Belasco of extravaganza," rated *Babes* "the most dainty and artistic production of extravaganza that the American stage has ever known," and cheered, "*Babes in Toyland* is the biggest, most brilliant and most captivating show of the kind that has turned its rays on the metropolis in a long time."[16]

After a run of almost 200 performances, substantial for its period, the *Babes* company set off and toured for two years. When it finally reached Boston, Herbert's severest critics for the most part proclaimed the production "well worth seeing." The man from the *Globe* distinguished himself not only by his guarded enthusiasm but also by being hoist on the petard of his own erudition almost to the point of incomprehensibility.

> There is music, and although there is a tune in the very first act that sets the gallery to whistling, the music is not really Mr. Herbert's best [!] It is good enough to carry home and keep in mind, for in the weeks to come a good deal of it is likely to be heard. It fits the piece, but after all is said the extravaganza is one to delight the eye. . . .

> Take the female loveliness described by Lucien in his "Images and Choridemus," Xenophon's "Panthea," Heliodorus' "Chariclia," Tacius' "Lucippe," Longus Sophista's "Daphnis and Cloe" [sic], Theodorus Prodomus's, "Rhodanthus," and the beauties favored of Philotratus, Balthasar Castilio, Laurentius and AEneus Sylvius, not to mention the modern poets, and you will find their representatives in the large chorus on the stage of the Boston theater. The girl's the thing and that she is a delight to the eye is not to be questioned.[17]

Only in Boston!

BABETTE

Type of work: Romantic Comic Opera
Premiere: November 9, 1903
Theater: New National Theater, Washington, D.C.
Broadway, New York (November 16, 1903)

Cast (Major Players):	
Babette	Fritzi Scheff
Mondragon	Eugene Cowles
Marcel	Richie Ling
Baltazar	Edward J. Connelly
Vinette	Ida Hawley
Van Tympel	Louis Harrison

Eva	Josephine Bartlett
Captain Walther	Alfred S. Ely
A Court Lady	Mary Smith
Teresa	Emily Montague
Katrina	Florence Belleville

Major Musical Numbers: "Letters I Write"; "I'll Bribe the Stars"; "It's a Way We Have in Spain"; "Where Fairest Flowers Are Blooming."

Plot: Ranging in locale from a rustic Belgian village to the Court of Versailles, this is the story of two patriotic lovers who overcome Spanish tyranny with the aid of a dashing soldier of fortune.

If the story of many of Victor Herbert's greatest stage successes is inextricably linked to the careers of his female stars, none of those divas is more closely identified with Herbert than Fritzi Scheff. Alice Nielsen began her career in operetta and, after *The Singing Girl* left the Broadway stage for further study in Europe. It was a wise choice. Her achievement in grand opera was to surpass anything she had accomplished with Herbert, although she never lost her love and admiration for him and always looked back fondly on their years of association.

Fritzi Scheff, "frisky Fritzi"—the "little devil" of the Metropolitan Opera, followed the opposite career path. Having achieved both notoriety and fame as a talented soubrette at the Met (she felt this was an easy triumph since, as a consummate actress, she had achieved star status on that basis alone with little histrionic competition from the denizens of the old house on 39th Street), when Charles Dillingham, her personal manager, offered her $1,000 per week to appear in operetta, the choice was easy.

> Dillingham belonged to the plush era. He was what we called a swell. Dapper, meticulously dressed, his hat always a little over one eye, he was a unique figure in the theater. He knew more of the important society people than any other producer, but he preferred the company of prize fighters.[18]

"Easy" also describes the time Herbert had had with his first star, Alice Nielsen. He was spoiled by that experience. It was never to happen again. Fritzi had well earned her devilish nickname at the Met—in spades, although she was not the only diva in Herbert's coven to be known as a "little devil." Emma Trentini, the diminutive firecracker star of Hammerstein's Manhattan Opera Company, who created the role of Naughty Marietta, was also identified with that sobriquet—and earned it even more than Fritzi had. But Scheff was the first "little devil" on the block and was probably Herbert's greatest star. He composed four works for her (*Babette* was the first, *Mlle. Modiste* the greatest)—as well as his single-most-enduring song, "Kiss Me Again," with which Scheff was eternally identified. As recently as 1951, on a CBS radio series devoted to the history of the American musical theater, Scheff recalled her success in *Modiste* and—at age seventy-one—sang "Kiss Me Again" brilliantly for a whole new generation of musical theater fans, thus spreading the memory of her charm well into the twentieth century. Even on radio her sparkling personality shines through. One can only imagine what effect she must have made in person.

Scheff was Viennese, the daughter of an opera singer who had become one of the great personalities of the Frankfurt Opera. With such entrée and a shimmering, clear, light lyric coloratura to match her dramatic strengths, she had been hand-picked by Maurice Grau to star in the American premiere of Paderewski's *Manru* at the Met. She earned her nickname during the rehearsals of that work when, in order to break the tension, she had improvised a wild dance macabre with tambourines. This was not inappropriate to an opera with a gypsy theme, but the great pianist was not amused. Neither was the audience, which had to suffer through such lexical gems as:

> He who scorns the gypsy roof
> Holds him from the clan aloof
> Harkens to the gentile woof—
> [as in warp and woof]
> Be he accursed![19]

All this was followed by several pages of choral repetition of the word "accursed."

With such works of textual distinction in her repertoire, it is not hard to understand Scheff's decision to abandon the opera stage. Even the workmanlike texts of Harry B. Smith seemed Shakespearean by comparison. It was more than money that led Scheff to Herbert's world.

Fritzi made her operetta debut on November 16, 1903, in *Babette*, a production that played to her strengths. She had two great coloratura numbers, "It's a Way We Have in Spain," and "Where the Fairest Flowers Are Blooming"—the so called "Butterfly Waltz," which took its name from the costume, one of four changes, that she wore in the last act. There was also a lovely sentimental duet, "I'll Bribe the Stars," which, together with these numbers, allowed her to display all aspects of her volatile, spitfire personality. There was also a quartet, "My Lady of the Manor," which one overly enthusiastic critic proclaimed superior to that in *Rigoletto*.

Babette tried out in Washington one week before its New York opening and made "a decided hit." There were many encores and curtain calls from an audience that included President and Mrs. Theodore Roosevelt, Justice and Mrs. Oliver Wendell Holmes, Jr., Senator and Mrs. Henry Cabot Lodge, and Senator Marc Hanna. The story of a village letter writer who, through a misunderstanding with her lover, runs away to become a strolling player and eventually a singer in the court of Louis XIV, provided the contrasting stage pictures and costume changes that framed Fritzi's debut. Word of her success quickly spread to New York: "Make way for Fritzi Scheff and 'Babette.' They will be with you at the Broadway Theater next Monday night and you are going to like them."[20] The New York opening did not disappoint in production, dramaturgy or musical grace. But the event that set the theatrical world gossiping and provided a lead for every review had nothing to do with Herbert and Smith's material.

During the curtain calls that followed the second act, the traditional place for curtain speeches, Fritzi, whose English was none too strong, began hesitantly:

"I cannot express my thanks. It is hard for me to talk in English. But I am so grateful in my heart (here, a little squeeze) and I hope, as when I was at the opera house, you will come to me here. Won't you?" (This last quickly and with a yearning glance.)[21]

Then came Herbert, who was rarely comfortable speaking in public. But Fritzi pulled him from the wings, and he waded into a little speech. If there were any weak spots in the production, he said, they were his fault. And then—when he struck a snag—Fritzi stood on tiptoe, threw her arms around his neck, and planted a kiss on his cheek. Not a chaste, closed mouth affair—but a real "smack."[22]

The audience went wild. "Her kissing me has got me all fumbled," Herbert stammered. Column after column discussed "the Kiss." Not since Rodin had there been such a kiss! Finally Fritzi lost patience.

I'm dead [sick to death] of that kiss. So much has been said about it. One little, tiny kiss. That is all nuisance. I did not know anything about it. I did not know I was going to kiss Victor Herbert until it was all over. Everybody was so kind and I was so glad and Mr. Herbert he say so many nice things to me.[23]

As for the reviews, they were all variations on the theme of unbridled enthusiasm. Praise for the score, even mild toleration of the book. But for Scheff:

In grand opera she flickered. In operetta she shines resplendently. She has a sense of humor, the faculty of evoking a laugh, finesse of diction and of dialogue, the quality of voice, the skill of singing and above all the inexhaustible fund of vivacity which so few of her competitors possess in union. Last night she sang and acted like one possessed. It was delightful.[24]

And then, after only fifty-two performances, *Babette* closed.

Everything looked rosy for the opera until suddenly Charles B. Dillingham, a young man in the theatrical business who was Miss Scheff's manager decided the public did not like her songs and made up his mind to take it off. Against the wishes of Victor Herbert the piece was taken off and "The Two Roses" by Ludwig Englander substituted. This was short lived and Miss Scheff fell back on Von Suppés' "Fatanitza" which she is now playing in New York, pending the revamping and rehearsing of "Babette."[25]

Thus, at the insistence of the producer, who could have stayed with what looked like a sure thing, but whose knowledge of "the road" was superior to Herbert's, the book was tightened, several characters eliminated, the production costs cut, and the company prepared for a long tour which, in those days as today, was often where the money was to be made. Dillingham's instincts were right on target. He knew that Boston's critics would have something to say—and that as often as not that something was "nay." But this time the sages of Charlestown added something new and unexpected: a touch of personal animus.

Mr. Smith has long since been afflicted with literary prostration caused by a heavy draft on his mental powers. He was not even convalescent when he wrote the book for "Babette.[26]

Mr. Herbert's music is fluent and often plausible; at times it is charming. Mr. Herbert is a true master in operettic [sic] orchestration. We have used the word "plausible" in connection with this music; it may be applied especially to the solo numbers, few of which are of marked distinction.[27]

Nevertheless, *Babette* enjoyed a successful run, thanks to the wisdom of a great producer. Composers, librettists and stars may be more or less brilliant. But a great producer can take them through the tough times and pave the way for greater things to come. If the history of *Babette* has a true star it is, perhaps, Charles Dillingham.

IT HAPPENED IN NORDLAND

Type of work: Musical Comedy–Political Satire
Premiere: November 21, 1904
Theater: New Lyceum, Harrisburg, Penn.
Lew Fields Theater, New York (December 5, 1904)

Cast (Major Players):

Hubert	Lew Fields
Prince George of Nebula	Harry Davenport
Duke of Toxen	Joseph Herbert
Baron Sparta	Harry Fisher
Captain Slivowitz	Joseph Carroll
Princess Aline	May Robson
Dr. Otto Blotz	Julius Steger
Parthenia Schmitt	Bessie Clayton
Hugo von Arnim	Charles Gotthold
Mayme Perkins	"Billie" Norton
Rudolf/Prince Karl	Frank O'Neill
Miss Hicks/Countess Pokota	Pauline Frederick
Katherine Peepfogle	Marie Cahill

Major Musical Numbers: "The Woman in the Case"; "Absinthe Frappé"; "Commandress-in-Chief"; "Al Fresco"; "Knot of Blue."

Plot: Elsa, the Queen of Nordland, has vanished in order to avoid a politically convenient but personally noxious marriage. The kingdom is in turmoil until the American Ambassadress, a ringer for the Queen, agrees to impersonate her. Through the machinations of the court hierarchy led by the Ambassadress, Elsa and her Prince are united and their opponents consigned to their proper places in operetta hell.

It Happened in Nordland is an important work in the history of Herbert's theatrical development. From the standpoint of pure musical achievement, its one lasting contribution to the Herbert canon was Harry Davenport's first-act solo, "Absinthe Frappé," an enduring comic waltz for which Glen MacDonough provided some of his strongest lyrics. But there are many other reasons *Nordland* is important.

It is the earliest Herbert work that is labeled a "musical comedy," and *Nordland* is very much a musical comedy. Its musical elements are simpler, its choral passages less complicated and, as in *The Fortune Teller*, dance movements dominate the score. Such a characteristic is more common in Herbert's "dance operettas," which segue into the dance-dominated musical comedies of his later works. "Knot of Blue," after "Absinthe Frappé" the most successful number of the score, is an elaborate waltz.

Much of this development can be attributed to the influence of Julian Mitchell, the director-choreographer who continued his long and fruitful association with Herbert with the production of *Nordland*. Mitchell was a creative genius whose contribution to the success of many Herbert shows cannot be overestimated. Although severely handicapped (he was extremely hard of hearing), this characteristic may have caused him to focus all the more on the visual elements of his productions and, in fact, may have proven no handicap at all.

Herbert's concern with the musical integrity of his musical comedies was much more relaxed than it was toward that of his operettas. Examination of the program for the original production of *Nordland* reveals two numbers, "Any Old Tree" and "My Hindoo Man," listed with the notation "Interpolated by permission of Victor Herbert." No credit is given to the authors of these numbers, but it is significant that in *Nordland* Herbert specifically sanctioned the inclusion of works by other authors in his score. Although such interpolation was the rule rather than the exception in this period, this was something new for Herbert. It was a precedent he would come to regret. Years later there would be a major flap concerning one of the hit numbers in *The Red Mill.*

The occasion for the production of *Nordland* was the opening of a new theater on 42nd Street, which Oscar Hammerstein had built for the comedian-producer Lew Fields. This smallish house was managed by

Fields in association with Mitchell and Hamlin. A stock company had been engaged for it to produce and tour new musical comedies. Thus the opening was an event of quadruple significance: a new theater, a new ensemble, a new piece, and in it, the first appearance in over twenty-five years of Lew Fields as a single star. (He had originally gained fame as part of the team of Weber and Fields, which had dominated "Dutch comedy" in vaudeville for years.)

But the star of the evening was neither Herbert nor Fields. *Nordland* is first, last and nearly always a triumph for producer Mitchell.

> Such results as he has shown here have never been surpassed on the American stage or probably any other stage. . . . The word magnificent, in its proper sense, is the only one which fits. The production was as elaborate as human ingenuity could make it. From beginning to end there was not a hitch, and the pretty chorus girls were kept busy as bees until the final curtain.[28]

As for those chorus girls,

> With all due deference to the principals of the company, we think those entitled to rank next in order of merit are the great chorus of pretty girls, who are almost constantly in evidence and who did their work with admirable spirit. They appeared as detective girls, Nordland boys (!), and flower girls, water girls, masqueraders, matinee girls, Spanish girls, Dutch girls, Indian maids and their many changes of sumptuous costuming made a tremendous hit. The Indian maids is a particularly effective number, probably the best of all the dances. . . . It was demanded several times.[29]

What sort of vessel had MacDonough constructed to contain this musical comedy froth? One which anticipates the first version of Kaufman and Gershwins' "Strike Up the Band." *Nordland* has surprising resonance for the twenty-first century, although the original satire targeted Teddy Roosevelt's "Great White Fleet."

Lew Fields's character is an assistant to an itinerant dentist and beautician who travels about with a company of beauties displaying his "wares," as it were, a sort of "extreme makeover" routine a hundred years before television discovered its potential. The elopement of the Queen of Nordland is followed by the opportune arrival of the American Ambassadress. She is persuaded to masquerade for a day as the Queen, whom she resembles. Among other gaffes she appoints Fields Secretary of the Navy and, as such, he plans a defense against the threatened attack of the American fleet. He is assisted by his war cabinet, Baron Sparta, the Duke of Toxins, and Prince George of Nebula—all played by outstanding vaudeville comedians. This slight plot, with its strong anti-war overtones leavened by the usual star-crossed love affair, is neatly tied up by a combination of naval bombardment and the final curtain.

Herbert's music was "fittingly, fancifully descriptive . . . giving evidence of his great versatility."[30] MacDonough was said to have provided "an amusing book and some very good lyrics."[31] Indeed he had. *It Happened in Nordland* is a fine and funny show. It played five months in New York, had a successful tour, and returned for another three months in the city. It is more than worthy of reexamination and revival.

MISS DOLLY DOLLARS
Type of work: Operetta–Social Satire
Premiere: August 30, 1905
Theater: Lyceum, Rochester, N.Y.
Knickerbocker, New York (September 4, 1905)

Cast (Major Players):

Dolly Gay	Lulu Glaser
Lord Burlingham	Melville Stewart
Finney Doolittle	R. C. Herz
Samuel Gay	Charles Bradshaw
Mrs. Gay	Carrie Perkins
Guy Gay	Carter DeHaven
Bertha Billings	Olive Murray
Celeste	Elsie Ferguson
Lieut. von Richter	Henry Vogel

Major Musical Numbers: "Ollendorf Duet"; "A Woman Is only a Woman"; "An Educated Fool."

Plot: Miss Dolly Dollars is rich. She wants an English title. Lord Buckingham has a title. He needs cash. In spite of all this they find themselves in love.

"A woman is only a woman, my boy, but a good cigar is a smoke." The line is Kipling's, not Harry B. Smith's, but it is indicative of the atmosphere in which *Miss Dolly Dollars* was created that the most memorable line in the show is borrowed, and that the only hit the piece produced is the song it inspired.

Conceived as a vehicle for Lulu Glaser, a "type of athletic, effervescent American girl, exaggerated but winning, whose delicate tact and ebullient merriment carry her past antagonists and suitors alike,"[32] the production might be viewed as one of the many money-spinners that Smith and Herbert created, relying on the drawing power of their star to fill the coffers.

Dillingham's promotion of the piece described it as "the brightest, wittiest and most up-to-date vehicle she [Glaser] has had since she became a star."[33] This was flack. "*Miss Dolly Dollars* is now finishing a long run in New York, which, beginning in the summer at the Knickerbocker Theater, had to be transferred to the New Amsterdam Theater, the original booking at the former theater proving all too short for the popularity of this star and her new musical comedy."[34] This was pure fantasy. The New York run lasted less than two months. The "Lulu Glaser Opera Company," as the production entity was known in order to give maximum exposure to the drawing power of the star's name, toured briefly and then returned to New York for a revival that lasted all of two weeks.

The negligible plot, which offered Glaser as a super-rich heiress beset by titled fortune hunters who eventually marries the man of her dreams, is one of Smith's most pedestrian creations. Herbert, responding to the uninspired quality of the enterprise and limited by his star's modest vocal abilities, provided very little of interest. A duet that illustrates the difficulties of communication between "lovers" who need to use a language guide to express their emotions is mildly amusing, and "The Moth and the Moon," the star's big solo, was forced to rely for its effect on the fluttering of eight chorines decked out in broad spread-skirts and headdresses that resembled feathered antennae. So much for the female ensemble. The gentleman suitors surrounded her in their own production number—a balletic evocation of a game of badminton.

New York's critical fraternity trotted out all the old adjectives: "charming," "bright," and "catchy" were much in evidence but, for once, Boston got it right.

There was an audience that liked Lulu Glaser and musical shows that are the regular thing in the regular way at the Hollis Street last night, and it applauded both accordingly. Miss Glaser showed all her familiar talents in "Miss Dolly Dollars" but Herbert, who wrote the music, by no means revealed all his. He was doing that in "Babes in Toyland" further downtown at the Boston. . . .

Mr. Herbert had evidently set down the first tune that came into his ear and then "let it run." Once or twice there was a hint of other men's tunes as well. Very seldom was there a hint of Herbert at his best.

Miss Dolly—or Miss Glaser—is very pert, very abrupt, very sure of herself and very good-hearted. She wore a blonde wig—wore a white automobile coat and an evening frock or two. She danced a little and pranced a lot, once or twice agreeably, and she talked a blue streak. It was also a very slangy one. If the show had any particular distinction it was in the incessant talk of American money.[35]

Perhaps in this emphasis Smith, Herbert and Dillingham unconsciously revealed their motivation. By their deed do we know them.

WONDERLAND

Type of work: Fantasy Extravaganza
Premiere: September 14, 1905
Theater: Star, Buffalo, N.Y.
Majestic, New York (October 24, 1905)

Cast (Major Players):

Dr. Fax	Sam Chip
Phyllis	Eva Davenport
Gladys	Aimee Angeles
Hildegarde Figgers	Lotta Faust
Prince Fortunio	Bessie Wynn
Capt. Montague Blue	Charles Barry
James	George McKay
King of Hearts	J. C. Marlowe
Chief of Gendarmes	William McDaniels
Romeo	Marie Franklin

Major Musical Numbers: "Until We Meet Again"; "The Nature Class"; "Jografree"; "Love's Golden Day"; "The Only One"; "When Perrico Plays"; "The Knave of Hearts"; "That's Why They Say I'm Crazy."

Plot: A combination of Alice in Wonderland with The Dancing Princesses has Alice and her Wonderland companions assume the roles of detectives trying to solve the mystery of how the daughters of the King manage to wear out their dancing shoes each evening.

A news item in the *Boston Globe* offered this:

New York March 8, 1902

One of the most important announcements from the music lover's
viewpoint was made today by Julian Mitchell, now with the "Wizard
of Oz" company. Mr. Mitchell, acting for the firm of Hamlin and
Mitchell made a flying trip to Pittsburgh with Glen MacDonough last
Sunday, held a long conference with Victor Herbert, and induced that
composer to sign a contract for the production of Hamlin and
Mitchell's next musical venture.[36]

What had persuaded Herbert to re-enter the field of light opera composition was the prospect that the work would be, as he put it,

... an opera of an entirely new class—a sort of comic opera
extravaganza—but the music will be of a much higher class than the
regular comic opera music. There will be a transformation in the opera
which will give the opportunity for musical effects and lots of chance
for development of themes. . . . I am very happy to have an
opportunity to write a better class of music than any of my former
efforts. I am sure the public will appreciate music of a higher character
and I look forward to the production of this opera as the establishment
of a new era in the realm of light musical production.[37]

The work that resulted from this Pittsburgh conference was *Babes in
Toyland*. But the aesthetic ideal expressed in this statement did not die
with that fully realized work. Herbert loved fantasy. He loved creating
works for children and so, when a few years later Mitchell and MacDonough approached him with the idea for another *Babes*, he was easy to
convince.

Just as the previous success had been based on the Grimms' fairy story
"The Babes in the Woods," so the new work would have as its basis
"The Dancing Princesses." This tale, which presented the riddle of how,
in spite of their father's strictures, twelve princesses were able to wear
out their Capezios night after night, presented huge musical possibilities.
Handsome princes applied at the palace to solve the mystery. If they
succeeded they could marry the princess of their choice. If they failed
they would pay with their heads.

This Turandot-like element was somewhat too bloody for children, so
MacDonough came up with a solution. Introduce Alice—of wonderland

fame—and all her friends as detectives to solve the conundrum. The Mad
Hatter, the Knave of Hearts, the Tweedle Brothers, the Cheshire Cat
would all be there. Thus the wedding of *Alice in Wonderland* with "The
Dancing Princesses" was born as *Alice and the Eight Princesses*. But how
to introduce Alice to the plot? Again, fairytales provided an answer. "The
Little Match Girl" was pressed into service in a prelude that inspired
Herbert to create some of the most beautiful music he ever composed.
Alice is discovered on a snowy Christmas eve in the streets of London,
selling matches until, in a pantomime fantasy, she enters the fairy landscape that provides the setting for the rest of the story. In this way the
various elements of fairyland were combined to produce a huge, extravagant fantasy on fairytales. This is what the audience at the Star Theater
in Buffalo saw on the night of September 14, 1905. They were enchanted.

> Fairy story set to music is gorgeous spectacle. Mr. Herbert's music is
> lovely, dainty, bright, catchy, full of melody characterized by the dainty
> lilt and swing that the composer likes so well.[38]

> The music is delightful, the book is brilliant and Julian Mitchell has
> outdone himself in staging.

Naturally, with a show this elaborate, there were technical problems. The
critic predicted

> ". . . phenomenal success as soon as it is in good running order. Like
> all first night performances it dragged a bit and there was more or less
> unfamiliarity of lines and business. But with a rehearsal today and an
> opportunity to repair the defects it should be well presented
> tonight. . . . Last night's audience was unstinting in its praise of what
> was well done. . . . It is an elaborate, costly production.[39]

Elaborate, costly and nervewracking. After the opening pantomime set in
London, the scenes included: the home of the Tweedle-dums; the looking
glass scene; the Mad Hatter's Department Store (he was a haberdasher);
an enchanted lake (from *Through the Looking Glass*); and the Ballroom
of the Magic Castle. The dreamland atmosphere of the piece was disturbed in performance by mishaps with the scenery changes. Brush-up
rehearsals lasted until 3 A.M. Cuts were made, but the piece still ran over
three-and-a-half hours. Then Mitchell's wife, Bessie Clayton, who had
the role of Alice, lost her voice and by the third performance could hardly
speak. Something had to be done before the Chicago opening planned
for October 8, 1905.

What was done wrecked the production. With the exception of Alice and the Hatter, all the Wonderland characters were eliminated, and in a burst of irony, the show was rechristened *Wonderland*.

How disappointed Herbert must have felt to see some of his most beautiful orchestral music tossed out can be seen in the new music he created. Pedestrian and uninspired, his new score pleased no one, certainly not the man from the *Times*, who wrote of the New York premiere,

> Wonderland is not different enough from its thousand and one predecessors to justify its name, but, if in no way wonderful, it is in many respects just the sort of show to please those gladsome and light hearted souls whose whole idea of enjoyment is centered on pretty girls. . . . It is a very elaborate sort of vaudeville. Once upon a time "Wonderland" was known as "Alice and the Eight Princesses" with a book founded on a fairy tale by the Brothers Grimm. But that time has passed. What remains is just the slenderest sort of thread upon which to hang the specialties.
>
> Victor Herbert provided the music and if it seldom equals his better works it is never quite down to the level which usually prevails in this class of score.
>
> The success of the night was scored by two unnamed actors who represented respectively the front and hind legs of a horse. . . . It literally gave everybody else in the show the horse laugh. . . . All the others showed their faces and mugged and strained and labored, but with hardly a suggestion of real fun.[40]

Thus began two months on Broadway and two years on the road. Herbert took the money and moved on to other things. But something wonderful had been lost. The music he had created for the first version was so effective—so beautiful and haunting—that Mitchell had gone to the extent of depositing copies at the British Museum (now the British Library) in anticipation of securing copyright for a London production. And there it lies to this day. Another Briar Rose, sleeping her beauty away in a far-off castle, waiting to be awakened to new life.

CHAPTER 12

OPERETTA AS SOCIAL DOCUMENT (1905)

MLLE. MODISTE
Type of work: Romantic Comic Opera
Premiere: October 7, 1905
Theater: Taylor Opera House, Trenton, N.J.
Knickerbocker, New York (December 25, 1905)

Cast (Major Players):

Henri de Bouvray, Compte de St. Mar	William Pruette
Capt. Etienne de Bouvray	Walter Percival
Hiram Bent	Claude Gillingwater
Gaston	Leo Mars
General Le Marquis de Villefranche	George Schraeder
Lieut. René La Motte	Howard Chambers
Mme. Cécile	Josephine Bartlett
Mrs. Hiram Bent	Bertha Holly
Fifi	Fritzi Scheff

Major Musical Numbers: "The Time, The Place and the Girl"; "Kiss Me Again"; "I Want What I Want When I Want It"; "The Mascot of the Troop"; "The Nightingale and the Star"; "The English Language"; "The Keokuk Culture Club."

Plot: A shop girl with dreams of something more—a career in the opera—triumphs over all the pressures of the world of the early twentieth century and in the process redefines the role of woman in society.

With *Mlle. Modiste* Herbert and Blossom consciously set out to take American operetta to a new level. Beneath the fluff and furbelow, the work had a serious subtext: the position of women in contemporary society. Gustav Klemm, Herbert's long-time musical amanuensis, testifies to the fact that Herbert had long been frustrated in his attempts to create integrated works. In a letter to biographer Isaac Goldberg, Klemm recalls

Herbert's distaste for "song and dance" compositions and points out the role of publishers as a motive force behind the continuing trivialization of the American musical play.

January 24th, 1931

. . . Reading your book [Goldberg's biography of Gershwin] provokes so many thoughts one hardly knows where to stop. I was reminded at one spot of a long conversation I had with Victor Herbert. . . . He had started writing that string of lesser scores—"Oui, Madame," "The Girl in the Spotlight," etc. What he especially loathed was the fact that the publishers wanted songs that could be lifted out of the action without any difficulty. All his life the old man had been having his songs grow out of the action and occasionally lines would refer to the surrounding situation. But the publishers didn't want this. They just wanted songs—songs that could be lifted out and sung "as is" by Lizzie and her boy friend in the parlor on Sunday night. So Herbert had his instructions to write so many songs—the publishers and the producers would take care of the rest. This, of course, pulled down such productions to the level of the gutter that belched up the popular song and did away with any of the standards established by light opera, etc. Herbert fretted and fumed but, as he said, "After all, I and my family must eat, there must be money . . ." and then he gave one of those significant shrugs of his that expressed volumes. And so we had a drink.[1]

And Herbert, in an interview with the *Philadelphia North American*, specifically underlines Klemm's recollection:

Musical comedies are at present [1914] hodge-podges of totally unrelated actions and songs. A comic opera with any pretense at artistic merit has the two forces so closely related and interwoven that the audience senses them as one and the same thing. Every situation requires some definite sort of music and the song must be logical and part of the natural action.[2]

What were Herbert and Blossom about when they developed *Mlle. Modiste*? Nothing less than presenting on the stage the problems human beings faced because of rigid societal stereotyping. Class distinctions and snobbery engulf royals and commoners alike in the treatment of characters from the nobility, as well as in portrayals of the exploitive roles of employers vis-à-vis their employees. What is more, a proto-feminist agenda is central to the piece: an orphaned female forced to survive on subsistence wages but possessed of a feisty, individualistic spirit triumphs over every type of gender-based restriction to achieve freedom from the highly stereotyped role in which we first see her, to become a fully realized individual, both as artist and woman. At the final curtain she has grown from a poor shop girl to a mature figure who has won recognition and respect and married the man she loves. And she does it all on her own terms.

Mlle. Modiste, written in 1905, is reflective of the social issues of the contemporary world in which it is set. In that respect it is clearly a forerunner of *Show Boat*, with the latter's focus on problems of miscegenation and racial inequities. J. P. Swain almost gets it right when he maintains that "the more serious operettas of Victor Herbert . . . offered the coherent plot and musical integration that the musical comedy lacked," but he gets it wrong when he concludes that the texts "undermined any significant dramatic effect by removing the story far away from the real experience of the audience. They are typically historical fictions or fairy tales . . . and involve disguised heroes, mistaken identities and the like. . . . Audiences were fascinated but seldom moved."

This last is a superficial and inaccurate summary of Victor Herbert's plots and places. Further, perhaps it is time to note, at this umpteenth iteration of the charge that "disguised heroes and mistaken identities" lead inevitably to banality, that no one seems prepared to level that charge at *Cosi fan Tutte*, a work of moving genius whose plot is based on nothing less than a series of disguises and mistaken identities.

Furthermore, as in the case of *Mlle. Modiste*, many other Herbert works are contemporary to their audiences. *Mlle. Modiste*, for example, is set in the Paris of 1905. Its characters dress as its audiences did. The problems depicted are the problems of a contemporary society.

Blossom and Herbert knew what they were doing and, on opening night, their trepidation was fully justified.

> I confess that when I wrote "Mlle. Modiste" it was with a dull dread in my heart that the public would reject it and cast it into ignominious seclusion from which it would never return. On the opening night I felt like a man going to the gallows. I was doubtful that the "dear public" which all playwrights fear and at the same time love, was in the right frame of mind to accept a musical production composed of anything but a conglomeration of vaudeville acts and so-called popular songs woven together with an apology of a plot.[3]

Notice that Herbert refers to himself here as a playwright, not a composer; his thinking was directed at creating a total theatrical experience.

> I cannot express the gratification I felt on the following morning when I awoke and found that I had been deceived by my friends, the public; that after all they had welcomed with outstretched hands the musical play that was a little better than the vaudeville musical atrocities heretofore offered.[4]

H. W. Parker, writing in the *Boston Evening Transcript*, took the full measure of the achievement. It is worth quoting him at length.

> Mr. Herbert did take pains, and, when he does, no American composer writes the music of operetta quite so well as he. Mr. Blossom set human figures—and not the grotesques of musical comedy—on the stage, wove a sentimental tale about them, gave some of them talk that was crisp with dry humor and unexpected retort, and the rest smooth, clicking rhymes to sing.

> It is long since an American operetta has been, from beginning to end, such exhilarating entertainment. Composer and librettist, star and company for once asked us to a musical play without insisting that we leave our intelligence and good taste, our sense of light music and of light humor, at the door.

> Of the three [creators] Mr. Herbert deserves most [praise.] He writes a sentimental tune as simply, flowingly and genially as though he were trained in the school of Strauss. He can patter as lightly, airily and snappingly as though he were an Offenbach or Lecocq. He has Sullivan's gift of musical humor. He knows that three bars for the bassoon or a quirk and a quaver for the flutes will bring a smile as readily as the fall of a "comedian" down a flight of steps, and he dares to use his knowledge and trust his hearers to understand. . . . His American traits are his unfailing animation, the spirited incisiveness of his rhythms, his bright instrumental coloring, and his quick, sure, sharp touch. . . .

> It is time for us to hold our heads fairly high and say boldly that we have an American composer who, when he chooses, can write operetta music as well as it is written in any European capital.

> Most of Mr. Herbert's qualities run through "Mlle. Modiste." He carries a sentimental tune through the operetta. You hear it, and little

else, in the prelude. Fifi sings it offstage when she parts from her lover. Upon it the listening chorus build the finale of the first act. It makes the introduction to the second. It accompanies the girl's musings and memories when she returns, a noted singer. The orchestra plays it as a kind of instrumental postlude. Long before that you have yielded to it. The broad, simple suavity of it is ingratiating. . . . Herbert heightens its appeal steadily by a dozen harmonic and orchestral devices. Fondly you fancy you can hum it as you come out of the theater, but there is that in it that evades you, and what is missing is what made most appeal.

One tune like that has made an operetta, and there are other sentimental melodies besides full-bodied, honest, manly tunes with which a tenor or baritone can look his audience in the face as he sings, and the men who listen not blush for their sex. There are patter songs that are bright with musical humor and gay and musical animation. There are sparkling bits of bravura for Miss Scheff and one or two crisp bits of musical burlesque. The rhythm of the dance snaps. There is a graceful trio or two and a septette for servants that is all musical quips. Almost everywhere there is melody with fancy, lightness and animation in it. Humor and gaiety flavor number after number. There is a genuine musician's practiced hand to make all these qualities tell, until his least musical listener takes joy of them for good entertainment.

Mr. Blossom's book is good entertainment. . . . All the characters wear our own dress. There is not a clown among them or a stick. They are recognizable human figures that still amuse if the librettist can see them a little freshly and animate them with a humor of his own. . . . He keeps his sentiment simple and honest.[5]

In short, Herbert and Blossom achieved in 1905 the theatrical break-through that Kern and Hammerstein reinforced with *Show Boat* two decades later. Gerald Bordman acknowledges that "It can be agreed that he [Herbert] was the first in the great trinity of towering masters our musical stage has produced . . . Herbert, Kern and Rodgers."[6] But Bordman does not acknowledge Herbert and Blossom's achievement as musical dramatists. Arthur Jackson emphasizes that "It is generally accepted that the metamorphosis [from song-and-dance musical to integrated musical] began with 'Show Boat' and goes on to comment that

Show Boat added a new dimension to the musical stage and proved that audiences had the right to expect and demand something more of a musical than the perennial boy-meets-girl plot with its supporting cast of comedians and specialty dancers. . . . Drama, characterization, plot development. . . . Complete integration of the music and libretto in which song advanced the story line were to be the norm in the best musicals of the future.[7]

This is certainly true of the best musicals of the future. But it was equally true of *Mlle. Modiste* and the best of Herbert's works as well.

A decade later J. P. Swain, discussing the reasons for the inability of pre-*Show Boat* musicals to hold the stage, remarks, "The failure was entirely dramatic, a failure of courage, really, on the part of composers, librettists and producers to confront their audiences with real dramatic situations."[8] Swain admits that, after *Show Boat*, Kern and Hammerstein never again attempted musical-dramatic integration on such a large scale. Even in *Show Boat*

Act Two consists of reprises, incidental music and "prop songs," songs sung because the character finds himself in a situation which demands or accommodates singing. . . . The songs are part of the scenery and quite distinct from songs that are expressions of a character's emotions . . . that define character, emphasize emotional state, or bring the action along.[9]

Swain admits that "it took a long time to learn the lessons of 'Show Boat.'"[10] One might add that it took an even longer time to recognize the achievement of *Mlle. Modiste*. Still, Swain concludes,

"Show Boat" is the first American musical that integrates the elements of a musical theater into credible drama. The songs, the instrumental music, the dancing, the crowd scenes *all* arise from events in a rather serious plot. Nothing is extraneous.[11]

With this statement he contradicts his earlier comment, that the second act is, in effect, a series of "prop numbers."

To this point a detailed and technical analysis has been avoided. In order to support the position that in its day *Mlle. Modiste* was as significant as *Show Boat* as a groundbreaking achievement, it is necessary to produce the evidence. For those readers who are already persuaded, the discussion that follows might be skipped. Skeptics are cordially invited to read on.

Mlle. Modiste is a contemporary statement set in the world of 1905. The first scene presents a picture of class distinctions: hat shop girls waiting on a wealthy American woman. The focus of the text is on the superficialities of fashion as well as on the girls' marginal life style:

> Still our wages are but small
> When we are paid, what we have made
> We must quickly spend it all.

The girls fantasize a romantic picture of their life away from the shop:

> It is then we forget
> That the world has a snare or a care. . . .
> That the morning will come that again we sell. . . .
> Ev'ry hat we've got.

while the soloists, who are waiting on the rich American dream of someday being able to afford her finery. This opening presents both a picture of class diversity and poor working conditions for women. Though the mood of the music is sprightly (marked "allegro spumante!"), the focus of the scene is on a social problem, just as "Ol' Man River" serves the same function in *Show Boat*. Herbert was fond of working against type in his settings, frequently surrounding a text with music of an opposite mood. This kind of musical sarcasm is used frequently in *Mlle. Modiste*, especially in the treatment of "Kiss Me Again."

There follows a dialogue between Mme. Cecile, the owner of the shop, and her daughters. Fifi, the *Mlle. Modiste* of the title, is absent because no one expected Mme. Cecile to return to the shop so soon. "I suppose when I'm not here there's *no* work done!" she exclaims. The trio that follows, "When the Cat's Away," reinforces and develops the dialogue and grows naturally from it.

The next scene establishes that Fifi is the best salesgirl in the shop, but has dreams of becoming something more. "I'll wager she's loitering around the opera again, watching rehearsals," Cecile remarks, thus denigrating Fifi's dreams of an opera career. Opera, of course, is a world for the upper classes; shop girls have no place there. Cecile is quick to lay out her plan for Fifi's future: "She's very independent now but all that will be different when I'm her mother-in-law." This is an overt expression of antagonism to her independent streak, and an expression of Cecile's plan to clip her wings through the route typical of the period: marriage; marriage to her son, Gaston: "Once she's safely married then she's *mine*! She shall live right here and I'll pay her *nothing at all*." Cecile's daughters respond that Gaston is an "artist" and mixes in high society. He wouldn't lower himself to marry a simple shop girl. Again class issues are highlighted.

Now Etienne, the love interest, enters, looking for Fifi. He is a soldier, a member of the nobility. But the lyric he is given points to a coming change in the rigid social distinctions of the period:

> I wonder if Cupid
> Is silly or stupid
> Or if the little rascal cannot see?
> For loving and wooing
> Are all of his doing
> And yet he makes it painful as can be.
> *He mixes the stations,*
> *He changes relations. . . .*

Etienne declares his love for Fifi in the beautiful number that follows, "The Time and the Place and the Girl," and declares "I'll take her out of this life as soon as I can afford it," another reference to class and wealth as societal determinants.

After Etienne leaves, Mme. Cecile schemes to get Fifi married to her son as soon as possible. The assumption here is, of course, that Fifi has nothing to say about it. Soon the Count, Etienne's uncle, arrives with Etienne's sister, Marie. These two characters represent high society. Marie is a snob and tells her uncle that Etienne's hanging about a hat shop is "becoming a public scandal." She's also upset that Etienne is bringing her own fiancé to the shop to "mix with these vulgar creatures"—more class snobbery. When she tells the Count that Etienne is in love with Fifi, the Count responds, "We'll put an end to that." Then the two exit, leaving the coast clear for Fifi's first entrance.

As Fifi arrives she meets a new customer, Hiram Bent, an American millionaire. Fifi, the free spirit, feels a natural affinity for this uncultured, self-made man. In fact it is the American millionaire, a man free of all airs and pretense, who doesn't give a damn for class distinctions, who is the true hero of the play. At first the dialogue reflects only Fifi's feisty qualities:

Hiram

I'm sorry to frighten you, Mlle. Modiste. I merely wanted to ask you a question.

Fifi

"No" is the answer.

Hiram

Then you can't tell me . . .

Fifi

Tell you what?

Hiram

The quickest way to the Louvre?

Fifi

The *quickest* way is to *run*.

As Fifi and Hiram become better acquainted, she learns that he is wealthy and that he came up the hard way; that his motto is "never give up." The American becomes her soul mate, and his Horatio Alger model encourages her. But her reply reveals how restricted the role of a woman in the society of 1905 is:

Fifi

Ah, but you are a man, monsieur. You can go out into the world and fight; but a woman—what can she do? Do you think I have no ambition? Do you think that I'm content to sell these things and wait on a lot of people I despise? What chance have I for a future here?

Hiram asks her what she'd rather do, and Fifi tells him of her dream of a stage career. She has confidence in herself, but believes that's not enough: it takes money and influence. Hiram praises her self-confidence, and Fifi replies she has more than that: she has talent.

There follows an elaborate three-part scena for Fifi which, on the surface, seems to be nothing more than a showpiece for a prima donna. Its obvious model is the three-part aria for Adele in the third act of *Die Fledermaus*, where a chambermaid displays her histrionic talents. But in *Mlle. Modiste*, the scena has several layers of meaning. The aria is nothing less than an opportunity for Fifi to do more than display her talent in three types of roles; it is also a chance for her to display her scorn and attitude toward the three strata of society that relate to her experience: the simple farmer's milkmaid daughter, who unhesitatingly accepts her role in a stratified society; a chirping, simpering debutante, whose vapid, spoiled character is perfectly reflected in Herbert's over-the-top polonaise; and finally, the section that has turned out to be the most misunderstood and misinterpreted piece Herbert ever penned, the famous "Kiss Me Again." The melody was so appealing and accessible that it became the hit of the show and one of Herbert's most famous compositions. But that was not what it was intended to be. "Kiss Me Again," with a lyric consciously conceived to be a string of clichés, was a satire of the overtly sentimental Victorian parlor ballad. As set in the show it is designed to reflect Fifi's *un*-sentimental character and her *rejection* of the role of love-sick, cow-eyed female whose sentimentality is mocked in the piece: a woman whose whole life is devoted to finding someone in whose arms, "far from alarms," she can safely be held through the night and kissed "again and again."

The whole scena is an opportunity for Fifi to reject, in song, the three roles society has approved for women. But audiences took "Kiss Me Again" at face value, held it close to their breasts and saw it as a tender and loving expression. This is very different from the context in which it is presented and from the intentions of its creators.

As a footnote to this story, it is fascinating that "Kiss Me Again" finally received the overblown satirical treatment the authors intended. But it took Fanny Brice in the Follies to do the job.

For satire, it is Fanny's special quality that with the utmost economy she always creates the original in the very process of destroying it, as in the numbers which are exquisite, her present opening song in vaudeville with its reiterations of Victor Herbert's "Kiss Me Again" and her "Spring Dance." The first is pressed far into burlesque, but before it gets there it has fatally destroyed the whole tedious business of polite and sentimental concert room vocalism.[12]

Following this scene, Hiram buys several hats, and by a subterfuge arranges for Fifi to accept a substantial loan to help her in pursuing her career. After the millionaire leaves, Mme. Cecile declares, "That minx is getting too independent by half." There is no time to waste in marrying her off to her son, Gaston. Gaston, however, turns out to be a good-for-nothing mama's boy, a lightweight who lives off his mother's generosity. The image of the shallowness of his character is expressed in both the dialogue and the song that follows, "Love Me, Love My Dog."

Cecile

I'm very tired of giving you money to spend on your fine society friends who don't even know your poor old mother exists and wouldn't speak to her if they did! Your father and I have to *work* for our money.

Gaston

Mother! Enough of the people in my set throw that up to me now without your dwelling upon the fact.

Mme. Cecile tells him there'll be no more money unless he agrees to marry Fifi. Gaston tells his mother that Fifi loves Etienne. Cecile replies:

Cecile

What if she does? You're proposing to marry her—to make her your *wife*! You scarcely believe that that nephew of the Count de St. Mar entertains such an idea, do you? With him it's a flirtation!

It is an expression of class snobbery as seen from below, with its overtones of classic exploitation of lower-class girls by upper-class males. Cecile finishes by remarking that Fifi will "jump at the chance of an honorable marriage."

This is followed by a scene between Gaston and Fifi, from which we can see that they are totally impossible as lovers; but they decide that the best thing for both of them would be to remain "Just Good Friends." This number is one of the most charming in the score but, unfortunately, it was cut from the original production. It is nothing less than an outstanding "song and dance" vaudeville turn. Herbert and Blossom had the inspiration to use a superficial musical form to reflect the superficial nature of the relationship. This is a wonderful piece of stagecraft, which cries for restoration to the score.

Now Etienne returns for a private moment with Fifi, in which she expresses her general discontent.

Fifi

I'm tired of everything! I'd like to go away—if I didn't have to take myself along.

Etienne

Don't you love me?

Fifi

Why ask me? What can there ever be between us? You're a Viscount; I'm a shop girl.

Etienne

Someday you could be a Viscountess.

Fifi

Your uncle would never consent.

Etienne

Then let him refuse. I'll marry you anyhow.

Fifi

No. That's impossible.

Etienne

Why?

Fifi

Because such a step would ruin your life. It would cost you your social position—your place in the army—your uncle's favor and your future inheritance.

Etienne

What shall we do?

Fifi

Wait.

Etienne

Wait for what?

Fifi

For the time when I'm no longer a shop girl.

The scene is interrupted by the appearance of the Count and Etienne's sister. The Count angrily demands to meet Fifi. Etienne introduces her as his love. The Count stares at her in disbelief. Fifi is not intimidated by his rudeness.

Fifi

Monsieur! When you've finished your inspection will you kindly state your business?

Count

Ha! As I expected! Self-possessed and independent as well!

Etienne

I won't stand by and hear the woman I love insulted.

Count

What! You dare . . .

Etienne

Yes, I dare, for I mean to make her my wife.

Count

You'll not only *not* do that, but you'll cease your attentions to her at once, or I'll stop your allowance and cut you out of my will forever. (To Fifi) You see, M'lle, that there's nothing to be gained by trapping my nephew into this disgraceful alliance.

So here we have a scene that adds to the negatives the assumption that Fifi's only motivation is that of the gold digger trying to marry up. It's also interesting that Henry Blossom brings out Fifi's admirable qualities by building a drama in which both potential suitors are dependent on their families for their income. Fifi to the rescue:

Fifi

You might be less unkind if you knew that I have told Etienne that I should not marry him against your wishes.

Cecile declares that Fifi is going to marry her son, but Etienne offers to give up all his money and position; he even offers to get a job! Fifi then rejects the traditional role of a wife in marriage.

Fifi

No, Etienne. I can't let you work to support me.

In 1905!

Mme. Cecile again stirs the pot by saying that if Fifi won't marry her son, she's fired. Fifi quits! Mme. Cecile says she was only fooling. Fifi says she wasn't.

Cecile

But where will you go, child? What will you do without money or friends?

Fifi

I'll show you what I'll do!

Which brings us to the decisive first finale. At the beginning of the number, Fifi has a passage that is nothing less than a declaration of independence for a woman unhappy and trapped in a world governed by privilege and social roles determined by gender and class.

Fifi

Oh, how I've dreamed of this day!
The day when the word should be spoken.
For now I am free!
'Twas destined to be:
The spell of the past is broken.

Now I go out in the world.
The future unknown is before me.
But hope is my guide,
What e're may betide
I'll rejoice in knowing my life's my own.

All but the Count and his niece beg her to stay. Fifi leaves, but her voice is heard offstage reflecting on how often she has dreamed of this moment of freedom. She returns to get the hat box, and has a moment of hesitation: "Have I the heart to go?" Here the stage directions in the original script emphasize the power of the moment. "Etienne makes an attempt to embrace her but *she evades him* and runs upstage as the Count steps forward to interfere." Fifi has made her decision before the Count makes his move. She opens the hatbox to find the card with the address to which it is to be delivered. She reads it and finds it is for her; as well as a check for 5,000 francs that Hiram has included to help her reach her goals. The point is that she makes her decision *before* she is aware she has the means to carry it out. She exits in triumph.

This was the original concept, and was the finale as performed at the premiere. Before the publication of the score it was decided that Fifi's declaration of independence was too blatant and incendiary, too much of a feminist statement for audiences in 1906. Blossom revised his text to convey a much more conventional sentiment. Not Fifi, but Etienne is given the first solo:

Etienne
No. She shall not go alone
For I will protect and watch o'er her.
And if she'll repent [!]
And give her consent
I'll wed her—for I adore her.

This patronizing convention is then echoed, Gilbert and Sullivan style, by the chorus. The remainder of the finale is unchanged except for one subtle shift. In the original text, all characters address Fifi in the second person; in the revision all use the third person, thus subtly demoting her image from the personal to that of an object.

In the finale Herbert introduces the music of "Kiss Me Again" as an underscore to Fifi's moment of hesitation. He also uses it as a postlude. By the end of the first act we have heard the music four times as a unifying element for the structure. But this is only part of the story. Herbert's handling of two major themes associated with Fifi is essential to the structure of the operetta and the two poles of Fifi's character: her loving quality and her demand for independence. On the tension between these two the whole musico-dramatic structure depends.

The "Kiss Me Again" theme is used as the basis for the creation of a second theme that represents Fifi's "dream of freedom" or "dream of independence." The three-note diatonic scale-like motif, followed by an upward leap that descends to a lower neighboring tone, is the basic pattern. In "Kiss Me Again," this is all set against an unchanging tonic major.

But in its transformation to the "Freedom" theme, the three-note group is reduced to a triplet.

Sweet sum - mer breeze whis - (pering trees)
G Major -----------------------------------

Ah but in dreams so fair
D Major --

Much of the first finale is a variation of this motif. The transformation of Theme 1 to Theme 2 is accomplished during the passage in which Fifi declares her independence. The metrical shift to 9/8 from 3/4 adds impetus and force to the text.

Oh how I've dreamed of the day

Now I go out in the world

After an extended choral reprise of this thematic transformation, the "Kiss Me Again" theme is introduced as an underscore as Fifi hesitates for a moment at the text, "Have I the heart to go?" It then returns, grandioso, for the closing pages of the finale.

The entr'acte is built entirely on the transformation of the motif. It begins with a maestoso presentation of "Kiss Me Again," which is slowly transformed into the "Dream of Freedom" form, this time marked "lente." We have a conscious identification of the two themes; it is the "Kiss Me Again" melody and harmony dressed in the rhythmic pattern of the "dream of freedom" theme.

E-flat Major --- 3---

Later in the second act, when Fifi returns as a star of the opera, even the bravura waltz song she is given, "The Nightingale and the Star," is not exempt from the pattern associated with her dominant dramaturgical characteristics. The first strain is a variation on both motifs:

Once a young night - in - gale fell to re - pin - ing

A Major-------------------------------E Major-------------E7

The second finale consists of reprises of both "Kiss Me Again" and the march "The Mascot of the Troop." Thus Herbert has consciously used motivic development and dramatic identification of themes to unify the structure of *Mlle. Modiste*. The atmosphere is Herbertian; the method Wagnerian.

Are there exceptions to this striving for unity? Are there "prop numbers" exempt from the advanced role of character illumination and plot development? Of course. The second act of *Mlle. Modiste* can be seen as a series of excellent prop numbers strung together by plot lines. But the same is true of *Show Boat*. Even the most enthusiastic advocates of *Show Boat*'s achievement admit that Kern and Hammerstein outdid themselves in the opening scene and that, although the rest of the act is outstanding in every way, the second act is a let-down from the standard achieved in the first.

Although "prop" elements are introduced in *Modiste*'s second act, the treatment of Fifi is exempt. Her treatment is an exercise in musical portraiture and dramatic development which, with one exception, "The Mascot of the Troop" stands as the first definitive and fully developed musical portrait in the history of American musical theater.

In the second act Fifi returns after achieving great success as an opera singer in London. She has been hired to sing at a charity ball to be given in the Count's residence. It's also revealed that, through Fifi's influence, the Count has managed to gain English financial support for his business ventures. Thus, Fifi is more than a success as an individual; she's also the economic lynchpin of the Count's financial well-being.

With this as background, Fifi and the Count have a confrontation in his study, where she is again given the opportunity to display her feisty independence.

Count

I am pleased to learn that you have done so well for yourself—but you were once a shop girl, Etienne is my nephew and I am . . .

Fifi

. . . . a selfish old aristocrat with the gout—a man who has never worked and couldn't get a job if he tried! Don't you worry—if I ever marry your nephew it will be when you come to me with your hat in your hand and beg me to do so!

Naturally, things work out so that is exactly what the count is forced to do, and the lovers are eventually united on Fifi's terms.

The way in which Herbert used his orchestral technique underlines the dramatic development of the two main motivic elements of his score. The original overture did not even contain these themes; it was a light, buffo introduction for full orchestra. As it became evident during tryouts that "Kiss Me Again" would be important, its melody was added to the overture—but only the final six measures of the refrain were used, the melody that set the words "Kiss me, kiss me again." The orchestration calls for strings, winds, two horns, trumpet, trombone and tympany, with the melody carried by the first violin, piccolo, flute and trumpet playing largo grandioso. After the huge success of the piece, the overture was expanded and the entire refrain introduced twice, the first presentation marked piano, the second, forte. Here the melody is doubled by the winds and brass; during the second repetition the winds play an octave higher.

What these changes signify is that Herbert, in developing his score, was sensitive to the reactions of his audience. Originally he did not expect the "Kiss Me Again" theme to dominate the show; its image and use in the drama was to be a satire of the overly sentimental. As a matter of fact, Herbert expected so little of the passage, he didn't even orchestrate it when working on "If I Were On the Stage." We have a piano score holograph of the scena dated September 7, 1905. The orchestration for the first finale, which contains the "Kiss Me Again" underscore, is dated September 6, 1905. Thus, Herbert orchestrated the finale before he worked on Fifi's scena. In the holograph orchestral score he has a note for the copyist to copy the section of the finale written on September 6 as a guide to the orchestration of "Kiss Me Again" in the scena.

What is the significance of this? Beyond the interesting fact that Herbert did not score his works in textual order, it shows that Herbert intended that the Fifi who expresses her sarcastic, overly sentimental attitude in the scena was the same Fifi who was going to act out her drive for independence and leave the sentimental role society demanded of her far behind. The setting of "Kiss Me Again" at these two spots is marked, Waltz lente. Here is the orchestration: strings play pianissimo dolcissimo, the superlatives themselves implying a bit of camp. The first violin doubles the melody at the singer's pitch, vibrato. The cello does the same, an octave below. The bass plays pizzicato on the first beat of each measure. The violas fill in the harmony, pizzicato, on the first beat of each measure. The second violins complete the harmony on the second beat. At measure seven, the repetition of the theme, solo clarinet is added, pianissimo espressivo, doubled by the flute an octave higher. At measure thirteen, the first and second clarinet sustain the harmony, while the first violins double the melody with a glissando slur introduced for the solo clarinet, to emphasize the satirical character of the setting (text: sleepy birds *dreaming* of love).

At the final measures of the setting Herbert differentiates his orchestration:

As part of the Scena
Tempo: poco diminuendo e rit morendo ppp
Strings: ppp pizzicato
2 mm: Violin 1: ppp rit.
Other strings arco, sul ponticello
Solo flute obligato
Oboe doubles melody
Clarinet: harmonic fill at the 6th

As part of Finale I
(Underscore)
Violin 1 doubles melody with singer
Violin 2 doubles melody with singer
Viola doubles melody with singer
Cello doubles melody *in singer's octave* (!)
    Thus Violin 1 and cello are in unison,
    at "Close to your breast" *molto
    vibrato*
Bass: Root harmony on first beat, pizzicato.
All winds harmonic fill

At the final measures before the stretto

The strings play as at the underscore but Piccolo, Flutes 1 and 2, Oboes, Bassoons and Trumpets double the melody.

Clarinets provide harmonic fill, trombones sustain and tympany and drum are added, *molto pesante.*

All this is a reflection of an entirely *un*sentimental mood as Fifi goes off to seek her fortune, her mind made up!

Herbert's treatment of the "dream of freedom" motif is even more subtle. In the first finale the motif is introduced and then reintroduced three times, each time with an increasing intensity that reflects Fifi's emotional growth from a timorous, dreamlike mood, through hesitancy to increasing resolution to final decisive action.

First presentation:

Strings (Violin 1 and 2 and viola) tremolo
(Cello and bass) arpeggiando
Solo horn—a mournful sound—fills in the harmony
Clarinet in a more soulful quality of sound—dolcissimo—doubles Fifi's melody at the Singer's pitch
Flute—pp—doubles the melody an octave higher
At measures 5–7 the oboe enters to outline the melody
At the final three measures of the section the oboe is again introduced to add new emphasis to the texture.
At this same point the cello, always an important element in Herbert's orchestral thinking, abandons its pizzicato arpeggios and, arco, provides stronger melodic shape and underpinning

First repetition:

The solo horn outlines the *rhythm* of the motif, the upper strings double the melody, molto vibrato, and the lower strings double the rhythmic pattern of the motif, filling in the harmony. The winds sustain the harmony and the bassoon takes up the arpeggiando function that the cello had in the first presentation. This amounts to a stronger, but still delicate orchestral texture.

Second repetition:
The strings are divided and outline the harmony; the winds are doubled. Trumpets and trombones are added, strengthening the texture even more.

Third repetition:
Strings divided, winds and brass all outline the harmony and a cymbal is added to the passage, now marked "tutta forza!"

This short example serves to illustrate how impossible it is to evaluate Herbert's achievement by consulting the piano/vocal score alone. The point is worth repeating: *he thought orchestrally, and his work as a musical dramatist can only be evaluated fairly by reference to the orchestral scores.*

It is significant that Herbert, the orchestral dramatist, chose to emphasize the "dream" motif for the short entr'acte rather than "Kiss Me Again." Here the motif is lined out for the first time in full orchestral texture:

Violin 1, piccolo, flute, oboe, clarinets and trumpets all double the melody in their octave. Horns and trombones sustain and fill in the harmony. Tympany and large drum are added to the texture. On the triplet pickup figure the second violin and viola also double the melody and then play tremolo sostenuto, as does the bass.

At the point where the two motifs are united, where the melody of "Kiss Me Again" is presented in the rhythmic pattern of "the dream," the passage is marked "lento espressivo molto ritardando." Here the solo flute and clarinet play the melody in thirds and the strings fill the harmony "vibrato sostenuto." The "Kiss Me Again" motif *literally becomes part of Fifi's "Dream"* and the final resolution of the drama is anticipated in Herbert's orchestration.

None of this happened by accident. Here is evidence that Herbert was a master musical dramatist who used orchestral texture to illustrate, comment upon, anticipate and enrich the musico-dramatic structure of *Mlle. Modiste.*

In assessing Herbert's achievement, it is also instructive to examine his relationship to the waltz. Mosco Carner, in his definitive monograph,[13] points out that there are many forms of waltzes. Although the dance type is indelibly associated in the popular mind with Vienna, it has a sociological significance beyond its national association.

> It broke down the rigid class distinctions so typical of 18th Century society. Anybody and everybody was free to join in it, irrespective of rank and status. . . . Of all the 19th Century dances it is the waltz that has the merit of satisfying the lowbrow and the highbrow, the layman and the musician, the dancer and the listener.[14]

And it is the waltz that dominates *Modiste*, the operetta whose theme is rigid class distinctions.

In the history of the dance the advent of the waltz was a democratizing event. As such, its use by Herbert as an element of his theatrical composition was very much in line with his often proclaimed goal of creating American operetta. With his European training and journeyman experience as a member of Edouard Strauss's orchestra, the waltz was a natural medium for his expression. Its egalitarian overtones support his Americanization agenda.

Beyond this, Carner points out that the waltz is not a monolithic form. There are many types of waltzes, each with its own characteristics. The melodic and harmonic elements of the Vienna waltz (large skips of the octave, easy chromaticism, a slight anticipation of the second beat in performance) were shaped by the fact that its creators, Lanner and the Strausses, were violinists. In a similar way Herbert's expertise as a cellist shaped his compositional style. We have reports that he often composed on the cello and was fond of introducing his latest compositions to his friends as cello solos. Many of Herbert's most successful waltz melodies can easily be seen as conceived for his natural instrument.

But it was not the Viennese waltz that Herbert composed. It was a form known variously as the "English" or "Boston" waltz. This was much slower and more sentimental than its Austrian cousin. "One of its characteristics is the tendency to suppress the true waltz rhythm by a sarabande-like emphasis on the second beat, or a complete omission of chords on the second and third beats."[15] The "Merry Widow" waltz would seem to fit this definition, but its tempo disqualifies it. The much slower "Kiss Me Again" is a true Boston waltz from a composer who is determined to create American operetta. Moreover, while the Viennese operetta is dominated by waltz movements, the Herbert operetta is not. The vast majority of numbers in most Herbert stage works are in duple meter. This is another reflection of his desire to create an American style.

As Herbert's career developed, his choice of dance music styles reflected the changes in American society. "The machine has taken hold of our lives and is reflected in modern dances. Rigidity of rhythm, mechanics, accentuation of accompaniment, syncopation all yield ragtime, foxtrot and tango."[16] The dance has always boasted long and intimate links with social history. In his flexibility and adaptability to the rapidly changing moods of the decades in which he worked, Herbert created a changing American style. If the works of the 1920s don't sound like those of the 1890s, it is not because Herbert had abandoned his aesthetic or his stated goal of creating American operetta. Herbert changed because America changed. At his best he was as representative of the 1920s as he had been of the 1890s.

The number of stories that have arisen purporting to describe the origin of "Kiss Me Again" are legion, varied and mostly apocryphal. But the variation is so amusing that it is instructive to summarize the litany:

VARIATION 1: THE COMPOSER AND THE HOUSE DICK
Herbert was strolling in the gardens of the Grand Union Hotel in Saratoga Springs after his evening concert.

> The late Tom Winn, while serving as house detective at the Grand Union Hotel was authority for the statement that Mr. Herbert composed the song there. On one particular evening, in the shadows, the composer heard a soft voice say, "Kiss me" and after a pause "Kiss me again." Mr. Herbert gripped firmly the arm of Mr. Winn, stopped dead in his tracks and then they went on. Not until the next year did Mr. Winn recall the incident, when Mr. Herbert sent passes for "Mlle. Modiste" and Mr. Winn heard the song sung by Fritzi Scheff.[17]

VARIATION 2: THE SONG NOBODY LOVED
In the summer of 1905 Henry Blossom arrived at Saratoga with the libretto of *Mlle. Modiste*. He remarked that it needed a great melody for Scheff. He told Herbert to write the music, and that he would find the words to fit the tune. Herbert tried but came up dry, until one night he awoke, turned on the gas and jotted down the melody. Then he went back to bed.

When he later played the music to Dillingham, Blossom and Scheff none of them liked it. Scheff said the B on which it began was too low for her voice. "That was my intention," Herbert responded. "A woman's voice, when low, is always appealing. You don't have to sing it 'open,' just breathe it, very softly." "Well, but I don't really think much of the whole song. I doubt very much if it will get over," Fritzi replied. "Same here," Blossom piped up.

But the stubborn Herbert, spurred on by memories of the haunting tune's determination to be born, was just as determined that it be given its chance. The song stayed in the score. It is Victor Herbert's most popular melody.[18]

VARIATION 3: AN ACTOR REMEMBERS
Lionel Barrymore claimed that Herbert had played the melody for him on his cello at the Players' Club in 1901.[19]

VARIATION 4: A REPORTER REMEMBERS, NO. 1
A reporter friend claimed Herbert had played "Kiss Me Again" for him in Pittsburgh in 1903 and told him he'd use it in an operetta someday.

VARIATION 5: A REPORTER REMEMBERS NO. 2
A reporter who was also a musician was traveling with Herbert to an out-of-town tryout of a show. Herbert got an inspiration for a melody and, not having any music paper with him, wrote it on the cuff of his shirt. The reporter promised to look him up the next day and bring him music paper so he could transcribe it. Herbert went to bed and forgot the whole matter. The next morning the reporter arrived and Herbert, in a panic, realized that he'd sent his shirt out to be laundered. The reporter hurried to the laundry and in the nick of time saved the cuff from being boiled in starch. The melody saved? Of course it was "Kiss Me Again."[20]

What's the truth? Probably none of the above. Herbert always carried a small music notebook with him. He had few friends in the Pittsburgh press corps. Barrymore was a garrulous inventor of tall tales. After his concerts in Saratoga, Herbert invariably held court in the bar of the Grand Union.

The truth lies not in faulty memories or inventions; unfortunately, it is located in the trial transcript of the famous libel suit against the *Musical Courier*, in a piece of evidence entered to support the claim that Herbert was a plagiarist.

Isaac Albéniz is the composer of a piano suite, one of whose movements, "Cordova" (1898), was arranged for cello solo with orchestral accompaniment. Herbert probably knew the work for Albéniz was, inter alia, a composer of much salon music, a type Herbert featured on many of his programs. The opening few measures of "Cordova" are identical with those of "Kiss Me Again," right down to the trill. Beyond that parallel, the way Herbert developed the piece is completely original.

Music history is full of similar instances. The opening measures of Beethoven's *Eroica Symphony* and Mozart's overture to *Bastien and Bastienne* are strikingly similar, and are in the same key. Compare the preludes to Smetana's *Bartered Bride* and Puccini's *Madame Butterfly* and you'll hear the same incipits.

Stung by the evidence at trial, even though he won his suit, Herbert himself may have made up stories and encouraged those who engaged in these fantasies as a way to bury forever any suspicions concerning the originality of what proved to be his most popular composition.

It was apparently Herbert's custom to keep his stars at arm's length. A recent discussion with Doris Eaton Travis, a star dancer at the Ziegfeld Follies, for which Herbert provided ballet music, reveals a strikingly similar profile.

> I was present at three rehearsals when Victor Herbert was in attendance. He did not conduct, but sat next to Mr. Ziegfeld and made suggestions to him. At one point he got up and had a conversation with the director. It was my impression that he was very much involved with the theatrical development of the productions of which he was a part. The only thing he ever said to me was, "Hello."[21]

In addition to her radiant personality and brilliant vocalism, Fritzi made one lasting contribution to the staging of *Modiste*. At one point she appeared as a drummer boy.

> One night she inadvertently rammed the drum stick through the drum skin. She ran to the wings where an attendant strapped another drum to her belt. From that point on she got as many encores as she had strength to break drums. Six or eight were needed for each performance after that.[22]

Fritzi made a career of *Mlle. Modiste*. She toured in it for years. When Dillingham disbanded the company, she formed her own in 1913. On that occasion the *Times* remarked, "[she] had never quite effaced the impression she created in this extremely popular entertainment."[23] Over the years she had grown in the role. And the critics noticed: "Miss Scheff's acting seems to have taken on a deeper tone so that the emotion she expresses has the ring of sincerity."[24]

Years later, Fritzi remembered the good and bad times.

My most distinct memory of Herbert is of his pleasant smile, his sweet manners. Of course, he could be angry. He had his Irish temper, I had my Austrian one. When we clashed there was a little excitement. We would have some differences over the music. It sometimes came to the point when I would refuse to sing the song and he refuse to change it. But eventually I sang it . . . his way."[25]

As usual, Herbert had the last word. In a curtain speech on the occasion of the revival he remarked what a joy it was to be revived—before one was dead.

The achievement of Herbert and Blossom will surely bring fresh joy to new audiences. For *Mlle. Modiste* is not dead. This sleeping beauty of a show will someday be awakened with a kiss—no doubt "again and again!"

CHAPTER 13

ACT TWO: SCENE TWO (1906–1912)

THE RED MILL

Type of work: Musical Comedy

Premiere: September 3, 1906

Theater: Star, Buffalo, N.Y.

Knickerbocker, New York (September 24, 1906)

Cast: (Major Players)

"Con" Kidder	Fred A. Stone
"Kid" Conner	David Montgomery
Jan Van Borkem	Edward Begley
Franz	Charles Dox
Willem	David. L. Don
Captain Doris Van Damm	Joseph M. Ratliff
The Governor of Zeeland	Neal McCay
Joshua Pennefeather	Claude Cooper
Gretchen	Augusta Greenleaf
Bertha	Alleen Crater
Tina	Ethel Johnson
Countess de la Fere	Juliette Dika

Major Musical Numbers: "Mignonette"; "The Isle of Our Dreams"; "Moonbeams"; "The Legend of the Mill"; "Every Day Is Ladies' Day to Me"; "Madrigal"; "Because You're You"; "The Streets of New York."

Plot: Two American vagabonds, stranded in Holland, frustrate the marital ambitions of the Burgomaster and the Governor, and in the process win love and riches for all the juveniles in the cast—and a free trip back home for themselves.

Charles Dillingham had an instinct for success. As an assistant to Charles Frohman, he had learned the formula that might lead to winning the Broadway game: hire famous performers, provide them with top-quality material, and frame the whole package with first-class production values. Any one or two of these elements might guarantee a modest success, but for a super-hit all three were essential. *The Red Mill* is a case in point. It ran for 274 performances on Broadway on its first outing in 1906, and more than doubled that number when it was revived in 1945. It toured, it seemed, forever, and in one form or another it surfaces somewhere almost every season. Whether as a huge extravaganza such as the St. Louis Municipal Opera's production, featuring an ice-skating ballet with interpolated music (not by Herbert), or in cut-down amateur outings by high-school drama departments, the *Mill* turns on and on.

The stars Dillingham chose for the piece were the comedy duo of David Montgomery and Fred Stone. Their most recent success had been in the first dramatization of *The Wizard of Oz*, where Montgomery had played the Tin Woodman and Stone the Scarecrow. But before that they had worked together for fifteen years in vaudeville as eccentric cake-walk dancers. Their first big hit was as partners with Edna May in *The Girl from Up There*, and from that point on they embarked on an international career, a high point of which was a two-year stint in London, capped by a command performance before Edward VII. By 1906 their joint income was said to be "as large as that of the President of the United States"[1] (the statutory salary, since Teddy Roosevelt took no money for his service).

Henry Blossom, who was engaged to create a piece that would showcase the comedians' special talents, had already collaborated with Herbert on *Mlle. Modiste*; he was probably Herbert's best librettist. Glen MacDonough was also gifted, with a talent for fantasy that played to some of Herbert's strengths, and the ever-ready Harry B. Smith could turn out workmanlike, if uninspired, librettos in his sleep. Blossom was something more; he was a real theater man who knew how to shape a show, and he produced books that were more than excuses to introduce musical numbers. His characters were full-drawn, his situations believable, and the humor of his compositions grew out of the events he created. Of course he could write gags—and did; but they were the tinsel on his tree. The solid structure of the book is characteristic of his librettos.

One of Blossom's letters, written from Paris, where he had gone to seek new material, gives insight into his approach to his job as dramatist. He is responding to a suggestion from a producer that he make an adaptation of his novel *Checkers* for the stage.

November 27, '96

My dear Mr. Rhodes—

I have your short but interesting communication regarding my alleged dramatization of Checkers—but candour compels me to say that this is the first I have heard of it.

I can't see enough situation and plot in the story to dramatize well and not being familiar with stage lore—business etc.—I doubt if I could make a success of it in any event.[2]

Even before he embarked on a career of writing for the stage, his instincts were solid; he looked to story rather than business as a basis for a book. Blossom continues:

However the notion pleases me well and as my thoughts come ever slowly, I may in time get an *idea*.

I have been vainly looking for some *new and unhackneyed material* over here but it is as scarce as the *fleas* are thick.

I have done Germany (in one sense) and they have "done" me in another.

I found the Germans very polite (perfunctorily). They are careful to call you "Sie" instead of "du" in conversation, but when it comes to a matter of "stuff" they'll "do" you as quick as they "see" you.[3]

Blossom must have been fond of this wordplay. He used it twice in *The Red Mill* libretto.

In any event, Blossom *did* adapt *Checkers* for the stage, and it proved a substantial success. It was followed by *The Yankee Consul*, a piece that brought him to Dillingham's attention. Hired to provide a libretto for Fritzi Scheff, he supplied Herbert with *Mlle. Modiste*. It proved to be the most historically important work either man created. With such success in hand, it was a natural for Dillingham to try to keep Herbert and Blossom in harness. The composer had put his best effort into *Modiste* and continued to do so when supplied with the *Red Mill* libretto, a first-class piece of work. During the New York run he reminisced about that effort:

I have been to hear "The Red Mill" very many times and, strange to say, I never tire of hearing it, for the reason that I spent more time and study in an effort to make the music of the opera at once tuneful and good. The public can never know the minute and detailed study given to the music of that opera, although it was written in three months.[4]

The flack that preceded the opening of the Buffalo tryout, at the Star Theater on September 3, 1906, emphasized the work of the creators and performers as well as the elaborateness of the production. Blossom was said to have chosen the Netherlands as his setting to provide "a new atmosphere" in which to frame the comedy of Montgomery and Stone, whose success in *Oz* was often mentioned. Dillingham's expenditures included sending scenic artists to Holland to make sketches for the settings. All the creators had been brought to Buffalo. Dillingham was apprehensive about the show, and insisted on strenuous preparations. Perhaps it was because this production was following on the heels of his mega-hit *Modiste*; whatever the reason, the press reported: "All of yesterday afternoon and until midnight was taken up with musical and dress rehearsals."[5] After a dress rehearsal that lasted until the wee hours, the company was exhausted, and Dillingham was convinced that he had a flop on his hands. Only Herbert remained upbeat. In order to raise their spirits he invited the company to a champagne breakfast, featuring his own special cure for the blues: a champagne cocktail with Worcestershire sauce drizzled down the edge of the glass. The potion worked its magic on the cast, but the producer remained gloomy. One reason was purely physical: the physical comedy that was the basis of Fred Stone's performance. Stone recorded it in detail.

> I made my entrance by falling backwards down an eighteen foot ladder and, in the big extravaganza escape scene, swung down a moving wing of a windmill with a girl in my arms, in addition to doing a lot of strenuous dancing and taking a number of parts. By the end of every performance I was so exhausted that I had to divide my twenty-four hours into equal parts, sleeping for twelve of them in order to keep up my work.

> As "The Red Mill" opened, Dave and I were attempting to escape from the inn without paying our bill. Dave knotted a sheet, threw it out the window, slid down, and then got a ladder for me, down which I was to fall backward. It took hours of practice before I mastered that trick. My legs were padded with football shin guards under my pants, and I practiced falling for days before I got it right. The idea was to take two steps down an eighteen-foot ladder, put one foot through a rung, turning backward, execute a back somersault, grip the outsides of the ladder with my legs and slide the rest of the way, doing it so fast that I appeared to fall the whole distance. The first few days of practice there was no illusion about that.[6]

Dillingham's uninsured stars had no understudies!

A second reason was related to tensions that had arisen between Stone, Herbert and Dillingham with respect to personnel. One would think that Dillingham would have had the last word about who would sing in the chorus and who would run the follow spotlights. But it was not that simple. Here is the story in Dillingham's own words.

> Fred Stone loved Baseball and at the time of "The Red Mill" his Red Mill Team and George Cohan's team were bitter rivals on the diamond. Both companies had funny looking male chorus men but they were all good ball players.

> One day, as I watched a matinee of "The Red Mill" when Montgomery and Stone made their entrance as Holmes and Watson the spotlight missed them—it was ten feet away. I hurried backstage thinking Fred would be angry but he was smiling and so I said nothing. At the evening performance the same thing happened and I got angry and I said, "Fred, the light man must be fired at once!"

> "Forget it," Fred snapped. "That's the pitcher!"[7]

Baseball may have taken precedent over lighting effects; that was a matter between Stone and Dillingham. But the influence of our national pastime didn't stop there. Stone takes up the story.

> If a man came around to have his voice tested for the chorus, I would take him outside and try him out for our team. If he could play, I would send him back with a recommendation for his voice. When we were rehearsing for "The Red Mill" I watched out of the corner of my eye while one fellow marched up to the piano where Herbert was testing voices.

> "Mr. Stone recommended me," he said.

> Herbert began to play and the man began to emit strange and horrible sounds. Herbert broke off with a horrible crash of chords and a rush of the profanity for which he was famous.

> "My dear man," he said at length, when he had calmed down, "you have no voice at all."

> "Mr. Stone recommended me," the fellow insisted.

> Victor Herbert came over to me.

> "My God, Fred, that man can't sing a note! He has absolutely no voice."

"Please, Victor," I answered, "He's the best shortstop I ever had!"

"What have we got here?" exploded Herbert, "a baseball team or a musical comedy?"[8]

Strike two! Dillingham was very nervous, for there was also the matter of the dances. Not the dances provided by the choreographer, but the dances provided by the heavyweight champion of the world, "Gentleman Jim" Corbett. One of the best things in *The Red Mill* was a boxing dance that Stone put together in Wood's Gymnasium with Jim Corbett. This was a "stop dance," a routine in which music and dancing break off abruptly every few measures. The dance was used as a special encore for "The Streets of New York" (popularly known as "In Old New York"), a number that always received an enthusiastic reception. It was a boxing bout set to the music of a bowery waltz. While Corbett gave Stone pointers on boxing, which he incorporated into the routine, Stone claimed to have reciprocated. "I taught him a number of dance steps which he did extremely well, but he was always too self-conscious to use them on the stage when he gave exhibition bouts."[9]

And finally, there was the matter of one of the show's biggest hits, "Good-a-bye-John," a number in which Montgomery and Stone appeared as Italian immigrant organ grinders. There has been some question concerning the circumstances under which the piece was brought into the show. Herbert was convinced that he had written an original composition, based on a suggestion that came from David Montgomery. In fact, with the connivance of Dillingham, he had been hoodwinked into using someone else's composition. Dillingham lived in fear that at some point the ruse would be discovered. Who knew what Herbert's hot temper might lead him to? Here is the producer's recollection:

When we were rehearsing "The Red Mill" Montgomery wanted a song by Harry Williams and Egbert van Alstyne interpolated, "Good-a-bye-John." Montgomery and Stone went to Herbert and Montgomery said, "I composed a song myself and you cannot object to my interpolating my own number." Mr. Herbert told him to come up to his house that night and hum the song, and he'd take it down.

The boys went up to the house, and Victor Herbert went to the piano and there was an awful stage wait. Montgomery had forgotten the tune and couldn't hum it. So they went home and sang the song thirty or forty times, and the next day Montgomery was able to hum it for Herbert.

The publisher (Remick) had printed about 1,000 copies of the original song and I bought them all and put them in the cellar of the Knickerbocker Theater. That sale satisfied the authors and they said no more about it.

Can you imagine the scene I had with Victor Herbert some months afterward when he was going through the cellar and he stumbled onto the packages of "Good-a-bye-John" as composed by Williams and Van Alstyne?[10]

By that time the show—with the number intact—had become one of the hits of the season. The score had been published and Herbert's name associated with the number. There was nothing he could do but hurt himself by making a public issue of the matter. Still, with all these forces in play, one can easily understand why Dillingham, for all his vaunted unflappability, was a nervous wreck.

The reviews in the Buffalo press must have eased his mind somewhat.

The play is a bright and sparkling success full of catchy airs and frothy good humor. . . . It abounds with songs that will become favorites and is a continual performance of jokes and frolics. The audience fairly howled its appreciation. . . . Mr. Herbert is at his best and the music and libretto blend delightfully.[11]

There is a laugh in every line and melody in every measure. . . . As lively and snappy a first night as even the managers of the new production could ask for.[12]

The performance was remarkably smooth for a first night and there is no question that "The Red Mill" will make a hit in New York.[13]

Authors, producer and stars were called before the curtain after the first act, and all made characteristic speeches. The Buffalo opening was a triumph.

Back in New York, the Knickerbocker Theater had put up a huge electrified mill in front of the entrance. Its arms slowly rotated high above the sidewalk, the first electrified moving sign in Broadway history. On September 24 the curtain rose, and

From the time the curtain rose on the first act until the closing ensemble the large audience was either beating time to Mr. Herbert's charming music or convulsed with laughter at Messrs. Montgomery and Stone and the humorous lines and situations furnished by Mr. Blossom. "The Red Mill" has a story and a plot which permit comedy to ooze through its entire action without once descending to horse play or vulgarity. The few nit pickers who went to the Knickerbocker expecting to gather a crop of mild faults went home empty handed.[14]

The fog that has enveloped the musical comedy for so long has at last lifted. Thanks to Victor Herbert and Henry Blossom Broadway can now laugh with a clear conscience and cock its ear to music that is really melodious . . . it is a hit.[15]

There is nothing dull about it, not a moment when the audience shows weariness, not a song or a tune that will not bear repetition. . . . It is a steady, satisfying work.[16]

There was even a bow to one of the principal's extra-theatrical activities: "Fred Stone as Con Kidder is even funnier than he was when he caught for the actors' team in the memorable game last Summer."[17] *The Red Mill*, if not Herbert's most artistic or historically significant work, was certainly his greatest triumph.

DREAM CITY AND THE MAGIC KNIGHT
Type of work: Musical Comedy–Social Satire
Premiere: December 25, 1906
Theater: Weber's, New York

Cast (Major Players):

Wilhelm Dinglebender	Joe Weber
J. Billington Holmes	Otis Harlan
Henri D'Absinthe	Maurice Farkoa
Seth Hubbs	Will T. Hodge
Henry Peck	W. L. Romaine
Willie Peck	Lores Grimm
Old Man Platt	Major Johnson
Nancy	Cecilia Loftus
Marie Dinglebender	Lillian Lee
Amanda Boggs	Madelyn Marshall
Mrs. Henry Peck	Cora Tracey
Elsa	Lillian Blauvelt
Ortrud	Cora Tracey
Frederick	Otis Harlan
The King	Frank Belcher
Lohengrin	Maurice Farkoa

Major Musical Numbers: "Oh, the Heat"; "I Don't Believe I'll Ever Be a Lady"; "Down a Shady Lane"; Beautiful Dreamtown"; "Bound for the Opera"; "In Vauderville"; and the *Lohengrin* satire, "The Magic Knight."

Plot: An unsuccessful truck farmer from Malaria Center, Long Island, is hoodwinked into selling his property to real estate developers who promise they will build him a Dream City, complete with Opera House, that will rival New York. The yokels put on finery and airs but when they learn that the price of joining high society is suffering through Grand Opera they explode the deal and return to their favorite pastime, swatting mosquitoes.

The critics were unanimous in their praise—almost.

New York:

"A novelty and a joy. . . . Thoroughly musical and convulsively funny.[18]

"Mr. Herbert's music here rose to the height of genuine travesty and delicate orchestral satire."[19]

Boston:

"Mr. Edgar Smith's book is good and he has been daring enough to exhibit a real, if absurd plot."[20]

"Screamingly funny."[21]

Chicago:

"A poorer entertainment Joe Weber never has offered his Chicago patrons . . . a worthless hodge podge. . . . The music of the show written by Victor Herbert is wanting in inspiration and catchiness. It clearly was penned perfunctorily, with nothing in text or stage business to give its composer interest or spirit."[22]

What happened in Chicago? There had been a blatant theft of Herbert's property. Comedian/producer Joe Weber had contracted with Edgar Smith and Herbert to produce a musical entertainment for his theater in New York. The piece was an attempt to recreate the style and substance of the popular Weber and Fields comedy acts, sorely missed by the public since the two great vaudevillians had parted company. Weber himself would be the star, surrounding himself with an ensemble of funny men and women who would provide an evening of social satire, buoyed by the energy-charged music of Herbert. The New York and Boston critics acknowledged that Weber was successful in creating a show that was new and broke the mold of typical Broadway entertainments. *Dream City* ran for 102 nights, and then set off on tour. Herbert realized substantial financial rewards from the venture, but Weber, apprehensive that satire might not draw as well in the provinces as it had in the East, asked Herbert to reduce his participation from the standard 3 percent of gross to 2½ percent. Herbert declined, whereupon Weber—believing that his contract with Herbert was exclusively for the music (he had made a separate deal with Smith for the book)—ordered the man he had engaged as house composer for the Joe Weber Music Hall, Maurice Levi, to compose a completely new score for Smith's text. This is the show that Chicago heard. Advertised as the New York success, it was logical for the critic to assume that it was Herbert's music. The result of this sleight-of-hand was a disaster.

Herbert immediately repaired to the courts. The details of this litigation are outlined in chapter seven. Herbert won, but the real loss was that one of the most original, satirical musical pieces ever to be produced on the New York stage was abandoned and forgotten amid the hullabaloo. Completely different from anything he or his contemporaries had created, for the first and only time in his career the dramatic material specifically played to one of Herbert's strengths, his delicious musical humor. This aspect surfaced occasionally in his other works; here it is the main focus. *Dream City* represents a turn in the development of American musicals, anticipating the crazy atmosphere of Donald Ogden Stewart's *Fine and Dandy* and the first, anti-war version of George S. Kaufman's *Strike Up the Band*. There is hardly a waltz measure in the score, and Herbert's adaptation of the rhythms of country music and vaudeville buck-and-wing dances to the demands of the book are completely convincing. All this, coupled with a tour de force send-up of Wagnerian pretension (think Leitmoltiven mixed with jigs and "Ach du lieber Augustin"), and you have it.

Dream City is a satire on the land-speculation craze that saw city "sharpies" attempt to swindle "hayseeds" out of their property with promises of untold wealth and society celebrity. The opening act reveals the chorus. But this is not the usual ensemble of leggy chorines and prancing chorus boys. This is the population of Malaria Center, Long

Island, suffering from a terrible combination of scorching heat and mosquito infestation. The only movement on stage is a hilarious choreography of slaps and slams as the suffering inhabitants try to protect themselves from the marauding insects. "Oh, the heat! (slap!) Oh, the skeet! (slam!)," they cry.

The real-estate boom has been circling the village. Ne'er-do-well farmer Dinglebender (Joe Weber), whose survival depends on the meager income provided by the boarding house his wife runs, jumps at the chance when a hustling real estate agent offers to buy his land and build on it a city to rival New York. The old farmer sits in his rocking chair and falls asleep to dream of the way things will be when the Dream City arises on his property.

The second act is a representation of his dream, with all the rural types introduced in the first act trying to live up to their newly acquired wealth. Liveried waiters are given $20,000 tips just for serving a baked apple. A woman stoops to pick up a pearl necklace. "What do you want of that?" her escort remarks. "That only cost $10,000. Come down the street and I'll buy you a good one."

Dinglebender, as the Dream City's wealthiest man, is elected mayor. "What does a mayor do?" he asks. "You stand on the steps of city hall, look like a horse's ass and bray like a mare."

Dinglebender puts up with everything until he is told he must attend the opening of the opera. His daughter, Nancy, is apprehensive. "He went once," she recalls "and got so excited he started yelling at the singers and woke up the whole audience!"

Nevertheless, the company is "off to the opera." The work being performed, *The Magic Knight*, is a travesty of *Lohengrin* that "makes the most hardened operagoer smile broadly. The whole entertainment is interwoven with a wealth of comic detail, in the presentation of which every member of the cast had ample opportunity to shine."[23]

After the performance Dinglebender declares that, if opera attendance is the price of wealth, he'll stay a poor farmer in Malaria Center. He presses a button that sets off a charge of dynamite, and the piece ends with the first scene reconstructed. Dinglebender discovers he has been asleep and is glad it was all a dream. Curtain!

Along with the comic genius of Weber, several outstanding singing comediennes contributed to the fun. Lillian Blauvelt, a concert and oratorio artist with a great sense of humor, and who was not afraid of self-parody, was Elsa in the Wagner satire. Madelyn Marshall played an exaggerated rural girl with short skirts, long legs, a funny laugh and a yen for the men whose song, "I Don't Believe I'll Ever Be a Lady" makes her the undisputed grandmother of *Oklahoma!*'s Ado Annie, who couldn't say, "No." Cecilia Loftus as Dinglebender's daughter almost stole the show (and the reviewers' hearts) in the first act with her double talent as archly comic ingenue and expert imitator. Impressions were very popular in this period, and Loftus laid them in the aisles with her imitations of Ethel Barrymore in "Captain Jinks of the Horse Marines" and Nazimova in "A Doll's House." "I don't know how she got to be my daughter," the short, rotund Weber cried, "but she is it!"

Dream City was "it" as well, a treasure of pure laughter and fun for fun's sake—unquestionably the funniest show Herbert ever wrote. And the most unfairly neglected.

THE TATTOOED MAN

Type of work: Musical Comedy–Farce
Premiere: February 11, 1907
Theater: Academy of Music, Baltimore, Md.
Criterion, New York (February 18, 1907)

Cast (Major Players):

Omar Khayam, Jr	Frank Daniels
Abdallah	William P. Carleton
Algy Cuffs	Harry Clarke
Hashish	Nace Bonville
The Shah	Herbert Waterous
Leila	Sallie Fisher
Fatima	May Vokes
Mutti	Maida Athens

Major Musical Numbers: the Opening Mood Setting; the Persian Dances.

Plot: Omar, Regent of Persia in the Shah's absence, was born with a birthmark so distinctive that the law decrees he must die if he ever meets a man with a similar mark. Fatima, in love with Omar, tattoos this mark on two characters. Omar must keep them alive or die himself. The Shah returns and condemns him to death, or worse, life with Fatima. Omar chooses the latter—after some hesitation.

Joe Weber a hit in *Dream City*? Then why not bring back the glory days of Herbert's first comic success, *The Wizard of the Nile*? So thought

Charles Dillingham, who was on a roll with Herbert shows. The expert manager set out to reassemble his old all-star team: comedian Frank Daniels, librettist-lyricist Harry B. Smith, and Herbert. An attempt was made to build a new success by following the model of the old. If the *Wizard* boasted a recurring line that had caught the imagination of the audience and even entered the slang of the period, "Am I a Wiz?" let's make sure that Daniels has a parallel laugh line built into the text: "Are we downhearted? Nooooo!" Exotic locale—Egypt? How about Persia? And to top it all off hire Julian Mitchell to bring brilliant staging and production values to assure success. *The Tattooed Man*, a two-act recreation of *The Wizard of the Nile*, rests on an equally implausible plot premise involving scarab-like tattoos, aborted beheadings, and a Katisha figure who finally gets her Omar (read Koko) after several harem vicissitudes.

After a week's trial in Baltimore beginning on February 11, 1907, the company opened at the Criterion in New York on February 18, 1907. The man from the *Times* liked Herbert's "catchy" music, Mitchell's "charming" staging and the "girls, glitter and gags." As for Daniels, "in his broad, low-comedy way, he is very funny."[24]

Another critic, less enthusiastic, remarked that "the first act contains all the plot and most of the merriment. . . . The music is of a high grade but it is not Victor Herbert's best," but conceded that "the piece will probably be a popular success."[25]

Both critics were correct. *The Tattooed Man* was not an inspired creation, and lasted less than eight weeks in New York. It did a bit better on the road. Apparently Chicago audiences found sufficient amusement in such lines as "Half a loaf is better than working" and "Uneasy is the tooth that wears a crown" to grant the show another eight weeks of life. Then the production shut down for the summer and refitting. Daniels was given his head. He added his very popular imitations of celebrities and, to the great amusement of the crowds, a burlesque version of the dance of the seven veils from Strauss's *Salome*, which had recently scandalized the opera world. These new elements kept the ticket scalpers happy. Ironically, when the new version of *The Tattooed Man* hit Boston it played in the shadow of its model, for "a sprightly revival" of *The Wizard of the Nile* had just opened across town. Critic Wilder Quint nailed things down neatly.

> Victor Herbert wrote the music. Now there are two Herberts, the one
> of the beauty and flavor of "The Serenade" and "Mlle. Modiste," the

other of the many pot-boilers he has produced with such fatal facility. He of "The Tattooed Man" is mostly of the latter character. The music is better than the best of many other American composers, melodious, dainty and well orchestrated and occasionally wholly charming. Yet that rare individuality and perfection of form that he exhibits at his best is nowhere heard in this work.[26]

All agreed that whatever success the show enjoyed was due to the inspired comedy of Frank Daniels. This was no great achievement for Herbert. But it paid the rent for over two years.

ALGERIA

Type of work: Exotic Comic Opera
Premiere: August 24, 1908
Theater: Apollo, Atlantic City, N.J.
Broadway, New York (August 31, 1908)

Cast (Major Players):

Zoradie, Sultana	Ida Brooks Hunt
General Petitpons	William Pruette
Captain De Lome	George Leon Moore
Millicent Madison, M.D.	Harriet Burt
Ali Kohja	Joseph Carey
Mimi	May Willard
Nella	Grace Rankin

Major Musical Numbers: "The Boulé Miche"; "Rose of the World"; "You'll Feel Better Then"; "Love is Like a Cigarette"; "Twilight in Barakeesh;" "Ask Her While the Band Is Playing."

Plot: The Sultana Zoradie, ruler of a desert tribe, is disguised as Miriam, Mistress of the Bayaderes. She is in love with the poetry of a man she has never met. Captain De Lome, commander of the oasis, is secretly the poet and is in love with a dashing girl of the desert, whom he has never met. Zoradie announces that the only way to avoid war is for her to find her poet. She does, he does, they duet.

THE ROSE OF ALGERIA

Type of work: Exotic Comic Opera
Premiere: September 11, 1909
Theater: Grand Opera House, Wilkes-Barre, Penn.
Herald Square Theater, New York (September 20, 1909)

Cast (Major Players):

Zoradie, Sultana	Lillian Herlein
Millicent Madison, M.D.	Ethel Green
General Petitpons	Eugene Cowles
Capt. De Lome	Frank Pollock
Mimi	Belle Pallma

Major Musical Numbers: See *Algeria*.

Plot: Essentially the same basic structure as that of *Algeria*, with the addition of vaudeville elements à la *Red Mill* (Barnum Sells and Bailey Ringling for Kid Connor and Con Kidder), an American "doctress" with her coterie of nurses, and artists' models to give a New York flavor to the desert proceedings.

If the history of the production of *Algeria* and *The Rose of Algeria* is unique in the canon of Herbert's works, it is not because Herbert was involved in a major revision of the piece. Revisions were commonplace in the development of his theatrical works. But such revisions were normally undertaken on the road, prior to a Broadway opening, and were largely occasioned by the demands of the producers, who had major input into the artistic shaping and content of theatrical works in Herbert's period. The impetus that transformed *Algeria* from a flop into a success, *The Rose of Algeria*, was Herbert himself. For the only time in his career, he assumed the role of both producer and promoter. His *Algeria* material, he felt, was far too strong to be allowed to die aborning, the victim of a MacDonough book that was, in its original format, unrealized in its potential. The fact that Herbert became involved not only as creator but also as financial promoter is strong evidence of the love he felt for this score. Contemporary accounts report that, at home, seated at the piano, he would often play through the score of *Algeria* for his own delight and amusement. Stahlberg reports, "Algeria [was] one of his favorites. In fact, he had so much faith in that score that when the show languished and died, he bought the producing rights, and re-christened it 'The Rose of Algeria.' Then, as a sort of backer's audition, he rented the Criterion Theater and conducted the entire score before an enthusiastic invited audience."[27]

And what a score it was! "Twilight in Barakeesh," one of the most evocative pieces of musical portraiture ever to flow from his pen; "Love is Like a Cigarette," a subtle and insinuating tango with tambourine accompaniment; "Rose of the World," which ranks with the most effective love music Herbert ever produced; and a waltz that set the ballrooms of America aglow and remains one of his most popular compositions, "Ask Her While the Band Is Playing," a piece that received ten(!) encores on the opening night of the revised version. How strongly the composer's melodic stream was flowing when he composed this score! If *The Rose of Algeria* was not his favorite work, one would be hard-put to produce evidence of another claiming that pride of place. Other works achieved greater success and brought him more financial reward, but there was none closer to his heart, not even *Eileen*, which, with its Irish theme, is frequently said to have been his favorite. In fact *Eileen* was not a success, and after its premiere, Herbert essentially abandoned it, although it, too, had gone through a major revision. This was his typical pattern. As soon as a work went into production he began working on his next project. He was the most successful hedge composer Broadway ever knew. Better than anyone, he was aware of the dangers of navigating the shifting rip tides of the New York theatrical waters, and he was reluctant to invest all of his time, and rarely his money, in the fate of a single show. Thus, love is not too strong a word for his feeling for *The Rose of Algeria*. In this case he literally put his money where his art was, and saved his favorite score from the ignominious fate that would have been its lot had he not acted as he had.

As the opening night approached he remarked to Ned Wayburn, the stage director and choreographer of the revised piece, "I'm not kidding myself that I'm a Richard Wagner, but any ass can see that my music has to be conducted carefully."[28] Lack of a competent conductor was the least of the weaknesses that had beset *Algeria* in its first incarnation, as originally produced at the Broadway Theater on August 31, 1908. To tackle the subject of the book first, since so many commentators find it easy to lay the fault for the failure of a Herbert work at the clay feet of the librettist, with *Algeria* it was a case of "damned if you do—damned if you don't." For in creating this piece, MacDonough consciously determined to avoid the cliché: the wonderful music and the execrable book. Here, "The librettist has made a brave effort to get away from the all too familiar musical comedy humor. There is little slang, not many commonplace jokes, and practically no cheap repartee," wrote the solon of the *New York Dramatic Mirror*. "But," he continued, "the book is unequivocally dull."[29]

The story dealt with the complications arising from a native rebellion against the French in Algeria. The romantic theme played over the amours of a young French lieutenant and the female regent of one of the ancient desert tribes. The comedy concerned the mishaps of American soldiers of fortune, deserters from the Foreign Legion. The original production offered some spectacular *coups de théâtre* that roused the critics to enthusiasm. The first finale represented a sirocco sandstorm that got the best notices of anything in *Algeria*. There was also a clever staging of the tenor's "Love is Like a Cigarette," in which half a dozen girls were suddenly metamorphosed into illuminated smoking tables. Above each girl's head a soft, incandescent spot shed mellow light, and on the tables, invitingly displayed, were circlets of liquor glasses. "It is wine, woman and song visualized."[30]

As to the music, the *Sun* was most enthusiastic.

It is a musical play with real musical wit and not an attempt at making popular songs. . . . It goes back a few years and belongs to the period when a musical play had music in it, not a bunch of so-called popular songs from the 28th Street factories [a reference to the Tin Pan Alley publishers].

The music was, in fact, too good. . . . A bit too good for last night's audience . . . a bit over the heads of those who like what they can whistle.

Thus, both MacDonough and Herbert were damned; the librettist for avoiding cliché, the composer for doing his job too well. But the technical aspects of the production met with unanimous praise: even the camel— "The best two-man camel that has been seen in these parts."[31]

The critic of the *New York Dramatic Mirror* led off his review with a comment that both composer and librettist took to heart.

With a rewritten book and a new cast of principals Algeria will pass the Winter with credit to producer and public. As it is, Victor Herbert's fine music and the wonderfully gorgeous scenic and costume effects will scarcely carry it to Christmas.[32]

It is easy to understand why, with so many strong elements, MacDonough and Herbert refused to abandon their creation. They flew back to the drawing board. A new production team was assembled. Lew Fields was brought aboard as producer. Ned Wayburn, a specialist in spectacle, was retained as director. MacDonough's work was doctored by three collaborators, Harry Bulger, Vincent Bryan and Edmond Sylvester. As might be imagined, the rehearsals were tense.

During one rehearsal a dancer wanted Herbert to alter the tempo, claiming it was too fast for him. "What's that?! My music is as good as your dance," Herbert shouted from the pit. "You change your feet instead of wanting me to change my tempo. And while we're at it"—he pointed to the soubrette—"stop holding that high note as long as you do. Where do you think you are—in Italy?!"[33]

Ned Wayburn was just as demanding in his way as was Herbert. During the dress rehearsal he shouted directions at the chorus boys until he had turned them into a mass of quivering sheep. Not noticing the mote in his own eye, Herbert remarked, "Look at those poor fellows. Do you know why they are so incomprehensive? They are broke, that's what's the matter with them. And when a man is broke, his nerve breaks, too. I'll bet there isn't a quarter in the whole bunch." Having said that, during the next rehearsal break Herbert worked his way backstage and, suiting his actions to his words, inconspicuously slipped each chorus member a twenty-dollar bill.

Herbert was so sensitive to the importance of tempo for the total theatrical effect, he asked Wayburn to sit next to him in the pit during the final rehearsals in order to make sure that his musical cues and tempos supported the action. Wayburn recalled his instructions: "He asked me to give him a punch right before the music cues came. Then he added, 'If I conduct too fast just pull my coattail. If I'm going too slow—jab me in the leg.' "[34]

This report is significant, because it shows the composer deferring in musical matters to theatrical concerns. It is a measure of the importance he placed in achieving a perfect premiere for this, his favorite work; it reflects Herbert's gradual transformation from a purely musical creator into a theatrical artist.

The Rose of Algeria opened on September 20, 1909, with an augmented orchestra of fifty players. Herbert's efforts had not been in vain.

> The delightful production of Mr. Lew Fields at the Herald Square Theater is, compared to "Algeria" of last year as the full blown beauty of the rose to the dainty bud. Honor for this evolution is due to the excellent taste of Mr. Fields, the producing manager, to Glen MacDonough, who revamped some of the lyrics and added some new ones, to the musicianship of Victor Herbert, and to Ned Wayburn, who staged the triumphant version. The new production is as rich in original comedy as it is in stirring music.

The critic went on to praise the new cast and the special effects. The sandstorm that had closed the first act was now replaced by its polar opposite.

> The added scenic effect at the end of the first act is a creation of that moving picture genius Frank D. Thomas, and is a sea scene showing a rowboat and the two comedians endeavoring to escape with "moving pictures" breakers and a boiling sea all about them. The effect is startlingly realistic and took repeated encores.[35]

A footnote to the history of technical theater: this is the earliest instance in a Broadway production of the use of rear projections to create moving scenic effects. It anticipates the contributions of the Luenebach projector by almost a half-century.

The Rose of Algeria, having proved itself in New York, set off on tour boosted by encouraging reviews from the city that was historically toughest on Herbert—Boston.

> The best of it was the "Algerian" parts. . . . These were varied and rich in color. They were sensuous, weird and haunting in melody, stirring in barbaric clash or quietly descriptive, by turns. Mr. Herbert has never written more brilliantly. From the musical and scenic points of view, "The Rose of Algeria" is a triumph in what our stage offers us so rarely—genuine comic opera.[36]

LITTLE NEMO

Type of work: Fantasy Extravaganza
Premiere: September 28, 1908
Theater: Forrest, Philadelphia, Penn.
New Amsterdam, New York (October 20, 1908)

Cast (Major Players):

Dr. Pill	Joseph Cawthorn
Flip	Billy B. Van
The Dancing Missionary	Harry Kelly
Little Nemo	Master Gabriel
Morpheus	W. W. Black
An Officer of the Continentals	A. H. Hendricks
The Candy Kid	Florence Tempest
The Little Princess	Aimee Ehrlich

Major Musical Numbers: "Won't You Be My Playmate"; "Valentine Waltz"; "The Cannibal Dance"; "Will O' the Wisp"; "In Dreamland"; "Oh, I Wouldn't Take a Case Like That"; "Give Us a Fleet!"

Plot: Following the outline of Winsor McCay's cartoon, the story tells of Little Nemo's search for his love, the Little Princess, through a series of fantastic locales (St. Valentine's Land, Cloudland, the Ship of Dreams, The Cannibal Island), culminating with a tribute to Teddy Roosevelt's "Great White Fleet" on the deck of a battleship, "manned" by a chorus of female midshipmen.

In the early decades of the twentieth century competition within the New York daily press was fierce. Publishers like Hearst and Pulitzer warred for circulation, and ever since the appearance of Outcoult's "Yellow Kid"—a panel based on scenes of immigrant life in the tenements—the comics had become a major weapon in the circulation wars.

With the appearance of Winsor McCay's "Little Nemo" in the *New York Herald* an element of fantasy was added to the mix. The hero of the strip enjoyed the wildest adventures in his dreams. Accompanied by continuing characters, Flip—a clown with no illusions about life; the Cannibal—a kind of poor soul; Dr. Pill—a satirical portrait of the know-it-all professional; and a dream-girl Princess, Nemo would enjoy fantasy adventures that always wound up with our hero safe at home in bed.

This sort of material was a perfect fit for a composer whose effective evocation of the innocence of childhood, and his ability to produce scores for extravaganzas, had been proven with *Babes in Toyland*. When producers Klaw and Erlanger approached him with an offer to create the first Broadway entertainment based on a cartoon, Herbert accepted enthusiastically, but with certain reservations born of his experience with producers and prima donnas. By 1907, when the contracts were negotiated, he had had his fill of the latter. He therefore insisted on his right to cast approval. This was a power no producer was willing to grant, and the original contract contains a phrase granting that right, which was stricken from the final text. But there were other clauses that reflected Herbert's experience with post-Broadway tours. As soon as box office receipts began to decline, the first move of a producer was to reduce the number of players in the pit orchestra. Herbert had had enough of that technique, and the contract insisted on an "orchestra of at least 23 players in all larger cities." Since Herbert was obviously concerned with protecting the quality of performances—especially in an area in which he was unsurpassed, expressive theatrical orchestration—the producers granted the benefit along with his standard remuneration: $1000 at the signing against 3 percent of the gross receipts.

The choice of a proper librettist for the transformation from strip to stage became complicated. Herbert had written several successful editions of the Lambs Gambols with his brother Lamb George Hobart and, at the outset, Erlanger proposed that the two men collaborate on this project. One of their most popular creations had been *The Songbirds*, a piece poking fun at the rivalry between the Metropolitan Opera and Oscar Hammerstein's Manhattan Opera Company. After its premiere *The Songbirds* had taken on an afterlife as a feature of what was then known as "advanced vaudeville," a kind of nouvelle Americaine theatrical cuisine.

Erlanger had presented the work at many of his houses; that was the basis for his suggestion that Hobart and Herbert would be an ideal team for *Little Nemo*. But before a formal contract was signed, Hobart had a falling-out with Erlanger over the bookings of *The Songbirds*, and Hobart turned the piece over to Erlanger's arch rivals, Keith-Proctor and Percy Williams for future productions. To even the score, the miffed producer approached Henry Blossom as a replacement for Hobart. Blossom was interested but was also a Lamb. Erlanger hadn't reckoned with the loyalty that was typical of the Lamb Brotherhood. When Erlanger removed Hobart from the project, Herbert and Blossom walked. At this point one of the major investors, Frederick Thompson, appeared as honest broker and, after some convincing, Herbert agreed to work with another librettist who was not in the fold. The task fell to the ever-ready Harry B. Smith.

The result of all this was one of the most successful and effective extravaganzas ever produced. It opened on Broadway on October 20, 1908, and played for four months, followed by a national tour of over two years. Little Nemo and his companions were shown in scenes lifted directly from McCay's strips. The playroom of the Princess in the palace of King Morpheus is where the Princess chooses Little Nemo as the one she wants for a playmate. The remainder of the show involves his search for her through a city playground, Little Nemo's Bedroom, the Land of St. Valentine, the Office of the Weather Factory in Cloudland, the Wreck of the Ship of Dreams, an Amusement Park in the Jungle, the Palace of Patriotism on the Fourth of July, and the Deck of a Battleship. Finally, the Princess and Nemo are united in Slumberland. Alongside the major characters of the fantasy there appeared a menagerie of cats, squirrels and teddybears and a coterie of Olympian wrestlers, cannibals, toy soldiers (of course!), naval officers (all played by attractive chorus girls) and special effects. As the program informed patrons, to put them at their ease "The display of fireworks at the end of the 2nd act is obtained by patented electrical and compressed air devices. The effect is produced without emitting sparks."[37]

The show lasted for three hours, but no one seemed to mind. The stage hokum, coupled with Herbert's magical score, kept audiences riveted to their seats. With such an elaborate caravan paraded before them, no one seemed to mind if the libretto didn't amount to much: "The entertainment is just a succession of glittering, melodic pictures, humorous, bright, fantastic and cleverly combined into something like an incoherent, topsy turvy story."[38]

And for once, Herbert's contribution was not seen as a leading factor in the success of the piece: "The contributing factors [to the success] in this production are, first, spectacular effect, second, humor, third, music."[39] The music was, as always, tuneful, evocative and skillful. While he broke no new ground here, there is one ancillary effect significant for the development of the American musical theater. A six-year-old boy was taken to the original New York production and remembered it years later in his autobiography as one of the important influences in his young life. His name was Richard Rodgers.

THE PRIMA DONNA

Type of work: Comic Opera–Social Satire
Premiere: October 5, 1908
Theater: Studebaker, Chicago, Ill.
Knickerbocker, New York (November 30, 1908)

Cast (Major Players):

Colonel Dutois	St. Clair Bayfield
Captain Bordenave	William K. Harcourt
Lieut. Armand	William Raymond
Mons. Beaurivage	W. J. Ferguson
Herr Max Gundelfinger	James E. Sullivan
Mother Justine	Josephine Bartlett
M'lle Athenée	Fritzi Scheff

Major Musical Numbers: "Dream Love"; "A Soldier's Love"; "Everybody Else's Girl Looks Better to Me Than Mine"; "If You Were I"; "What Is Love?"; "The Man and the Maid"; "Espagnola."

Plot: A prima donna of the Paris Opéra Comique performs a song written by an amateur and falls in love with its composer, a Lieutenant in the Guards. His commanding officer falls for the prima donna and tries to use his rank to break up the lovers; but true love wins out.

The Prima Donna was the third piece Herbert created for Fritzi Scheff. Produced by Dillingham, with all the strengths that great theater man brought to his offerings, the show never achieved its potential. Scheff was part of the problem, since the pressures of long tours (two seasons) brought out the "prima donna" in her more than usual: fainting spells and fits of temper were commonplace.

Still, Henry Blossom had provided a serviceable book, and Herbert responded with a score that was far from his weakest effort. Though not equal in inspiration to *The Red Mill*, nor in ground-breaking inventiveness to *Mlle. Modiste*, there was an aspect of the production that was unique in comic opera.

In the case of *The Prima Donna* this concerns the startlingly realistic scene with which the first act closes. The subject of this first finale was nothing less than an attempted rape. Without going into the details of the plot, the Scheff character finds herself alone with a man who has definite designs on her.

> A certain lieutenant attempts familiarities with the wandering prima donna, but is repulsed. Later on, when she is alone, he enters and makes insistent love to her. He is in his cups. It comes to violence between them, and she, lithe and full of pluck, slams him through a door into another room and locks him in. When the others rush in she unlocks the door and after an explanation slashes him across the face and departs.[40]

This was a "thrilling and dramatic finale,"[41] and to support it, "again came Mr. Herbert's musical interpretation . . . deftly fitted to the scene. In the silence of its close, in the sheer melodramatic brutality of its grip, the audience seemed as breathless as the girl upon the stage."[42]

Nothing like this had been seen before in comic opera. Ominous sexual threat as part of a scenario was soon to appear on the American musical stage. *Rose Marie*, *The Desert Song*, *Porgy and Bess*, *Pal Joey*, and *Oklahoma!* all adopted this element. Once again the much underrated Henry Blossom came through with a scene that gave Herbert an opportunity to display his musical theatricality. The New York critics were impressed.

Herbert with John Philip Sousa. (Library of Congress)

THIS PLAQUE IS ERECTED BY
THE AMERICAN SOCIETY OF COMPOSERS,
AUTHORS AND PUBLISHERS

TO THE MEMORY OF THE BELOVED

VICTOR HERBERT

COMPOSER, CONDUCTOR AND CELLIST

BORN IN DUBLIN, IRELAND, FEBRUARY 1, 1859
DIED IN NEW YORK CITY, MAY 26, 1924

IT WAS HERE AT A DINNER AT LUCHOW'S RESTAURANT
IN FEBRUARY, 1914, THAT VICTOR HERBERT AND
EIGHT ASSOCIATES DRAFTED PLANS FOR THE
PERFORMING RIGHTS ORGANIZATION, WHICH BECAME
THE AMERICAN SOCIETY OF COMPOSERS, AUTHORS AND PUBLISHERS

HE SERVED AS DIRECTOR AND VICE PRESIDENT
OF THE SOCIETY FROM ITS INCEPTION IN 1914,
UNTIL HIS DEATH IN 1924.

COMPOSER OF SUCH BEAUTIFUL MELODIES AS
"KISS ME AGAIN", "AH, SWEET MYSTERY OF LIFE",
"GYPSY LOVE SONG", "SWEETHEARTS"
AND MANY OTHERS–

VICTOR HERBERT HOLDS A UNIQUE POSITION NOT ONLY IN
THE HEARTS OF HIS FELLOW COMPOSERS AND WRITERS,
BUT IN THOSE OF ALL LOVERS OF GOOD MUSIC.

NEW YORK CITY – JUNE 27, 1951

Plaque on the façade of Lüchow's Restaurant (recently demolished) commemorating
Victor Herbert and the founding of ASCAP.

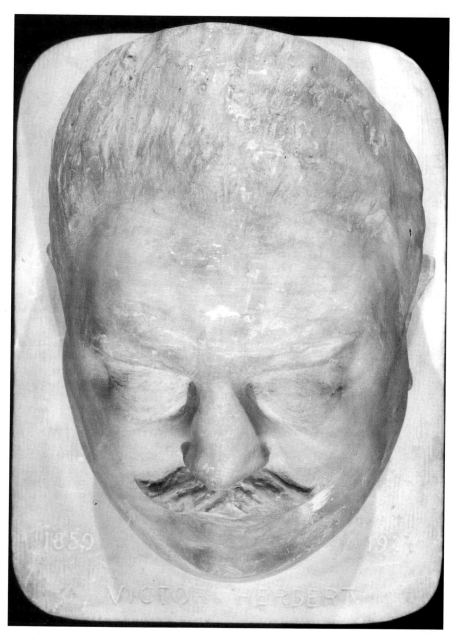

Death mask. (Library of Congress)

"Prosit! Victor Herbert." In his study, where he kept his Bushmill's (for when he worked on Irish music) and his wine (for working on operettas with French settings).

Pittsburgh Orchestra, 1904. Richard Strauss conducting; Victor Herbert on bass.
(Carnegie Library of Pittsburgh)

NELLIE DALY, THE COMICAL "JILL," IN
"BABES IN TOYLAND."—Windeatt.

DAINTY IRENE CROMWELL.
As Little Miss Muffett in
"Babes in Toyland," at
the Majestic.
Windeatt.

CHARLES GUYER AS "GRUMIO" IN
"BABES IN TOYLAND," Windeatt.

IGNACIO MARTINETTI AS JILL IN "BABES IN
TOYLAND."

ALBERTINA
BENSON
As the Moth Queen
in "Babes in
Toyland," at the

Scenes from *Babes in Toyland*.

Alice Nielsen in *The Fortune Teller*. (Museum of the City of New York)

Herbert at home, 321 West 108th Street, New York City. (Library of Congress)

This is a comic opera with a consecutive plot, real music, no vaudeville, and no horse-play. In fact it *is* a comic opera. The book is well built, the humor unrestrained and the dialogue natural. The music is of Victor Herbert's best style, though not the best example of this style. It is restrained, catchy, unobtrusive, and, most of all, fitting.[43]

The critics praised all of Herbert's strengths, his humor in orchestral touches especially. And, of course, there were raves for the prima donna herself.

The little lady was the chief factor in making the play a success. She sings, she beats the drum, she is capricious, she is tantalizing . . . she has a waltz and a bit of bravura, she wears smart evening frocks and the short skirt of the soubrette. Certainly Mme. Scheff's admirers could ask for no more. . . . She shows that the comedienne's arts are hers. . . . To her went the honor of making "The Prima Donna" one of the season's delights.[44]

The Prima Donna is a clean, amusing, intelligent and tuneful comic opera. Why, then, has it been forgotten? First, it is acceptable Herbert but not outstanding Herbert. Then the second act, after the stunning first finale, falls apart. Blossom fell down badly and provided a thin and tenuous dénouement, laced with such hoary gags as this:

Dowager: I'm sorry to hear your wife has run away with the chauffeur.

Comic: Oh yes . . . and he was such an excellent chauffeur.[45]

Nevertheless the show played seventy-two performances in New York and toured for two seasons. The music was pleasant; Fritzi was a delight. But, as George S. Kaufman was wont to say, "anyone can write a first act."

OLD DUTCH
Type of work: Musical Farce
Premiere: November 6, 1909
Theater: Grand Opera House, Wilkes-Barre, Penn.
Herald Square Theater, New York (November 22, 1909)

Cast (Major Players):

Ludwig Streusand	Lew Fields
Liza Streusand	Alice Dovey
Leopold Mueller	John E. Henshaw

Alma Villianyi	Ada Lewis
Joseph Cusinier	Charles Judels
Franz von Bomberg	John Bunny
Rosa von Bomberg	Eva Davenport
Alfred von Bomberg	William Raymond
Hon. Algernon Clymber	Vernon Castle
Little Mime	Helen Hayes

Major Musical Numbers: "Yodeling Chorus"; "U, Dearie"; Ballet Music.

Plot: "Old Dutch," an absent-minded inventor, and his daughter are vacationing in the Tyrol. He mislays his wallet, which contains both his money and his identification papers. A lounge lizard and his disreputable companion, a music hall singer, find the wallet and pretend to be the inventor and his daughter. As the couples are busy straightening things out, Old Dutch's daughter manages to find time to fall in love with the tenor. Curtain.

In 1895 the principals of the venerable vaudeville team of Weber and Fields decided to go their separate ways. The effect of this split on Victor Herbert was to cause him to align himself first with one, then with the other. Herbert was never comfortable in the role of man in the middle, but it was to his advantage to remain on good terms with both personalities, since the success of many of his musical comedies depended on the contributions of the leading comedians. Both Weber and Fields had decided to add theatrical production to their activities, and each was anxious to work with Herbert. Weber got there first.

The contract that he and Herbert executed in 1906 granted Weber rights to produce "a comic opera of which the leading parts are to be played by Joe Weber and his All Star Company" for the term of one year, beginning in December of 1906. Fresh from his problems with interpolations in *The Red Mill*, Herbert insisted on a clause that read

No changes, additions or interpolations of any kind in the music of said comic opera shall be made, and that no musical numbers of any description shall be introduced in the production without the consent in writing of the party of the first part [Victor Herbert].

The following December Weber produced *Dream City*, with all the attendant problems that followed.

Edward Waters, in his biography of Herbert, referenced a contract "signed at Lake Placid on the 19th of June, 1906, describing the production as consisting of two sections as, for instance, a complete comic opera for the first act and a burlesque for the second act. This stipulation was faithfully followed."[46]

Waters claims the contract to have been in the possession of Herbert's daughter. The actual contract, labeled "Exhibit A" and submitted as part of Herbert's complaint against Weber with respect to the subsequent production of *Dream City* without Herbert's music, contains no such description. It was entered into on June 19 and signed on the 21st, witnessed by Herbert's secretary William B. Clayton and his musical associate John Lund. Whether this document referred to *Dream City* or some other work, untitled, it is impossible to know. The fact that the librettist, Edgar Smith, who worked for both Weber and Fields, is not part of the contract, makes it even more problematic to assume that such a detailed description would be included in the absence of a librettist. When Lew Fields approached Herbert with the proposition to compose *Old Dutch*, one can understand that, after the experiences with *Dream City*, Herbert was not enthusiastic about working with Edgar Smith again. His solution was to enlist his fellow Lamb, George Hobart, as lyricist. Herbert would provide songs, and the rest was up to Fields.

The scenario Smith provided played to Fields's strength as a "Dutch" comedian: a German farce backed by a light, pedestrian score. The critics picked up on this to a man:

> Some of the episodes introduced recall the old days when Weber and Fields were together. Everyone remembers the conversations in dialect which used to take place between those two fun makers, conversations now replaced by a talk between "Old Dutch" [Fields] and the hotel proprietor, each speaking in dialect and each misunderstanding each other.

> A word as to Mr. Herbert's music. It is melodious, as one would expect, but he has used the brasses more than he commonly does, and the effect is that some of the numbers are louder and more strenuous than the music which he generally writes in his lighter vein.[47]

The critic of the *New York Dramatic Mirror* also remarked on the "extremely brassy" quality of the music, which "becomes a bit noisy too often," but gave Herbert a pass for a score that was not much above the pedestrian.

As between works which are to bring him fame an artist will turn out a "pot boiler" on the proceeds of which he can live, so it would seem does Victor Herbert lend himself between times to the needs of musical comedy producers who are in a hurry and who are not too exacting. The Herbert scores are never mediocre but they vary in quality of their excellence . . . the impression [is] that it is "hack" work done between really sincere labors.[48]

This is a fair estimate but, amid the darkness of second-rate achievement, one star shone brightly.

The really clever acting of a little group of children who appeared with Mr. Fields cannot be overlooked. They added much to the scenes in which they figured, and one little girl, "little mime," imitated the stage behavior of her elders in amusing fashion.[49]

That "little mime," who gave a silent impersonation of the gestures and gyrations of the prima donna, won the hearts of the critics. At age nine she was already a professional, a veteran of three seasons of stock in Washington, D.C., where she had won notices for her work in *Little Lord Fauntleroy* and *The Prince and the Pauper*. She went on to become the first lady of the American stage. So, whatever else may be said of *Old Dutch*, it provided the launching pad for Helen Hayes, a little genius of a star who, on that dark night of November 22, 1909, outshone both Herbert and Fields in her New York stage debut.

NAUGHTY MARIETTA

Type of work: Romantic Operetta
Premiere: October 24, 1910
Theater: Wieting Opera House, Syracuse, N.Y.
New York Theater, New York (November 7, 1910)

Cast (Major Players):

Simon O'Hara	Harry Cooper
Etienne Grandet	Edward Martindel
Lieutenant Governor Grandet	William Frederic
Sir Harry Blake	Raymond J. Bloomer
Rudolfo	James S. Murray
Marietta d'Altena	Mlle. Emma Trentini
Lizette	Kate Elinore
Adah	Mme. Marie Duchene
Captain Richard Warrington	Orville Harrold

Major Musical Numbers: "Tramp, Tramp, Tramp"; "Naughty Marietta"; "It Never Can Be Love"; " 'Neath the Southern Moon"; "Italian Street Song"; "Live for Today"; "I'm Falling in Love with Someone"; "Ah! Sweet Mystery of Life."

Plot: Marietta d'Altena has left Europe for New Orleans in order to escape an unwanted betrothal. On arrival she meets Captain Dick, a frontiersman pursuing a pirate who has been ravaging the colony. Marietta vows only to marry a man who can successfully complete a melody she has heard in a dream. Captain Dick finds a rival for Marietta's hand in the Governor's son, who actually leads a double life as the pirate. After many complications Captain Dick completes the song, defeats the pirate and wins the girl.

The story of the conception, composition and production of what is arguably Victor Herbert's most famous operetta involves a varied cast of characters—characters in every sense of the word. Among the heavy-weights were Oscar Hammerstein I, impresario extraordinaire, and his son Arthur, impresario wannabe; Emma Trentini, diminutive diva of Hammerstein's Manhattan Opera Company, whom Hammerstein discovered working in a Mantuan delicatessen; tenor Orville Harrold of Indiana, the "American Caruso" and former hearse driver; August Janssen, Boniface restaurateur caterer to the New York "400" and his son Werner, who became an Academy Award–nominated composer; Peggy Wood, in the first stages of her career; William Axt, who became one of the seminal figures in the development of the art of film scoring; and, of course, Victor Herbert.

By 1910 Oscar Hammerstein had established himself as the major force in the New York theatrical world. Years earlier he had built the Olympia Theater and, in choosing the site for it, had defied the established theater world, which in those days was centered around Herald Square. He chose a site far uptown and built an elaborate palace, complete with roof garden, to house his productions. The project bankrupted him financially, but not intellectually. The ultimate risk-taker, he built anew: the Victoria, the Republic, Hackett's Theater, the Philadelphia Opera House and, most famously, the Manhattan Opera House on 34th Street, a successful challenger for the Metropolitan Opera, five blocks to the north.

The Board of the Met feared competition for its vocally stellar but otherwise stodgy productions, for Hammerstein's reputation was built on three things: his ability to discover new talent; the lavish production values of his offerings; and his ability to appeal to a wide public. In an interview, Herbert discussed this aspect of Hammerstein's success.

> Those who study the causes must be impressed with the fact that the success of New York's new opera house was not assured in advance by a subscription list practically oversubscribed. Its patronage came not from wealthy and "fashionable society" but rather from a larger number of less opulent and equally admiring lovers of fine music.[50]

The board had two options: compete with Oscar on his own terms or buy him out. After protracted negotiations, Hammerstein agreed to a deal. He would not produce "grand" opera in New York City for a decade. Oscar took the money and immediately commissioned two "light" operas for his Manhattan house. The first, *Hans, the Flautist*, was a huge success. The second was a work from Victor Herbert, the star to be a little soprano whom Oscar had discovered singing in cabaret in Milan and who had become the leading diva of his company: Emma Trentini.

When the time came to produce the Herbert work, *Hans, the Flautist* was still packing them in at the Manhattan. Hammerstein rented the New York Theater from Klaw and Erlanger for his production. This theater was in fact the old Olympia that had once bankrupted the producer. Since that day he had refused even to walk past the site of his former property. In the years since, the New York theatrical world had followed his lead and moved uptown. The New York Theater stood at the center of that world, and Herbert and Hammerstein's *Naughty Marietta* became its crown jewel.

On opening night the great producer sat in a stage box, his face wreathed in a satisfied smile. When the premiere audience saw him, they cheered and forced him to rise and acknowledge their recognition that he had returned in triumph to the scene of his greatest disappointment. It was the first of many triumphs that night.

Hammerstein's choice of Herbert as a composer was based on more than his reputation. Hammerstein demanded and got what he wanted when he wanted it: the most operatic operetta Herbert ever produced. As early as 1907, Hammerstein had been in negotiation with Herbert for a grand opera for his company. *Musical America* reported that the two had joined forces with James M. Barrie to produce an opera based on *Peter Pan*. When that project fell through, Hammerstein signed a contract with Herbert for the production of an untitled "grand opera"—a contract that would come to haunt both producer and composer a few years later, when Herbert set out to compose *Natoma*. Hammerstein felt that if he engaged grand-opera stars for the new piece, the result would be operatic. Hammerstein stuck to the letter of his agreement with the Met, but in fact produced a work that brilliantly violated its spirit: a grand operetta.

The original title of *Naughty Marietta* was *Little Paris*. That is the first of a series of nicknames by which the setting, New Orleans, was known, long before the city became the Big Easy in the nineteenth century and the Crescent City of the twentieth.

The original production contract was signed in May, 1910. A few weeks later Herbert signed a separate contract with Witmark for the publication of the score. This specifically names Rida Johnson Young as librettist and mentions "Trentini" as part of the production.

Who were these people whom Hammerstein had corralled into a winning team? As noted, Hammerstein had rescued Trentini from the slums of Mantua, where the family lived over a delicatessen, the family business. There were "bare floors and dilapidated upholstery—a bare tile floor in her room—sand on the floor."[51] On weekends Trentini sang in a cabaret in Milan, and Hammerstein, after a grueling day of auditions in which he had found no prospects, went to the cabaret to relax and found his star. This was in 1906. He brought her to New York, and she shone as Musetta, Michaela and, most successfully, as the doll Olympia in *The Tales of Hoffman*. No more than five feet tall, she was a bundle of Italian charm and vivacity. She proved an instant success. Hammerstein paid her $800 per week in her first season, $1000 in her second, $1500 in her third and for the following three seasons. But it was never enough. No matter how much she earned, she could not shake her roots in poverty. If she was owed money (as happened on tour), she became a terror. Money was everything to her. She sent almost all of her money to Gus Schirmer, who would invest it for her in foreign bonds.[52] In the summer she would return to the family home in Mantua to work in the restaurant, waiting on customers alongside her brothers and sisters, to earn a little extra money.[53] Trentini was wonderfully talented, a real natural, but she had a lot of temperament and never lost her connection to her roots—an aspect of her personality that Herbert was later to disparage.

Her partner, Orville Harrold, had an even stranger background. Hammerstein discovered him singing in an amateur theatrical production in Indiana, where his day job was driving a horse-drawn hearse. Hammerstein was impressed by his free, strong, lyric tenor, brought him East for training, and installed him as resident "American Caruso," where he shone as the Duke in *Rigoletto* and Rodolfo in *La Boheme*. Harrold later went on to a career at the Met.

Rida Johnson was a beautiful member of Baltimore society. After graduation from college she went to New York to pursue an acting career, and soon joined E. H. Southern's stock company. There she met and married James Young who, after their early divorce, had a career as a director in Hollywood. Rida found work in the press department of Witmark publishers. She began writing one-act plays for the house and in 1906, with the full-length *Brown of Harvard*, had a major Broadway success. There was a song in the play, "When Love is Young," that had a big sale, and Witmark encouraged her to develop her talent for lyric writing. It was a short step from there to the operetta, and she provided texts not only for Herbert, but for Romberg and Friml as well. Acknowledging her debt to Witmark, she told him, "Your confidence in my ability made me venture farther than I should otherwise have done. You gave me a start when no one else would."[54]

Herbert was fortunate in the conductors who worked with him on *Marietta*. The New York production was directed by Gaetano Merola, who had been musical director of the Manhattan Opera Company. His assistant was William Axt, a native New Yorker who had studied at the National Conservatory and in Berlin. Axt took over the direction of *Marietta* during its second season. By 1919 he was conducting the orchestra at the Capitol Theater in New York, and then went on to a distinguished career at MGM as a composer who developed techniques of musical synchronization for sound films. His most famous scores include those for *Dinner at Eight*, *Grand Hotel* and *Northwest Passage*.

To the right of the entrance door of Herbert's last New York residence at 321 West 108th Street is a plaque that identifies the building as the home of the composer of *Naughty Marietta*. The implication is that many of his works were composed there. We know that Herbert was always working on his music and that, wherever he was, whether at Lake Placid, in his studio above the stage at Willow Grove, in his room at the Grand Union Hotel or on tour, he could work anywhere. We also know that very early in his career in Germany he developed the habit of using the Stammtisch at a local rathskeller as a kind of unofficial work space. This habit he continued all his life, and the story of the composition of *Naughty Marietta* proves it. To understand his choice of compositional venue, we have to take a small detour to the world of another immigrant with a fascinating career in New York that paralleled Herbert's: the world of August Janssen.[55]

Like Herbert, Janssen had a talent for languages. He spoke fluent French, Italian and English, as well as German. He had a love of nature, a sense of inner values, an adventurous spirit and the intuitive personality of an artist. Most of all he had energy, energy to make the impossible become a reality. In all these respects he was a soul brother to Victor Herbert.

As a young man Janssen had a varied career as a tutor, stage hand, line chef, and flautist in a small orchestra that toured Europe. He even became a tour guide for members of the family of Napoleon III. He eventually wound his way to Paris, where he was taken into the home of a great pastry chef who adopted him and taught him his culinary secrets. After many more adventures he landed in New York in 1887, one year after Herbert's arrival. He found employment with a caterer and began a career that, in its field, is unmatched for success. He rose to a position as *maitre de plaisir* of New York through a combination of chutzpah and good luck. He early determined that his way to success lay through the cultivation of New York's "400." But, of course, he had no entrée. So he went to the police and obtained the addresses of many of the leaders of New York society, among them the Vanderbilts and the Goulds.

He decided to visit the Goulds. Calling at the front door of the mansion he spoke—in French—to the butler. The butler did not understand what he was saying, but Janssen refused to stop talking, until eventually Mrs. Gould noticed what was going on and invited the "young Frenchman" in. An hour later, Janssen had a contract in his pocket to cater a party for a thousand guests. The party was a sensation, and from that day he was inundated with contracts from the leaders of New York society.

He was soon arranging twenty-five parties a day. He employed eight hundred waiters and twenty-four orchestras, the most prominent that of Victor Herbert. His business made $10,000 a day in profit for months.

One day he was walking down Broadway and came to a small beer hall at the corner of 30th Street. He entered, liked what he saw, and offered the owner $1,000 for the place. The owner sold it that day. Janssen didn't know that there was a $15,000 mortgage on the property. Three months later, after some renovations, he hung out his banner, "HOFBRAU-HAUS," the first such establishment in America.

It wasn't long before the little Hofbrauhaus became world-famous. It grew into a giant complex of buildings comprising three floors of five separate structures. Thirty-five hundred people ate there every day; 380 waiters served them; after Lüchow's, it was the number-one center for beaux arts New York. Politicians, presidents, both Roosevelts and Taft among them, artists and musicians congregated there. And among these was Victor Herbert.

August Janssen had two sons. One followed him into the business, but the other, Werner, became an Academy award–nominated composer and conductor. Werner left an unpublished memoir, and it is here that we discover how the stories of Victor Herbert, August Janssen and *Naughty Marietta* intersect.

> I can remember being introduced to Victor Herbert; I must have been about ten years old at the time [1910]. Victor Herbert and my father were sitting in one of the small, private dining rooms where they'd been sampling some of Father's best pilsner. There was a small piano in that room and Victor Herbert had taken to using it as his private studio—writing new music. That morning Herbert was working at the keyboard, trying out some themes for a new show—which, according to the composer, turned out to be "Naughty Marietta."
>
> Father interrupted his guest's woodshedding by suggesting that perhaps he might like to hear little Werner play a selection or two. Victor Herbert smiled with avuncular indulgence and slid to one side of the piano bench, while my father instructed me as to what to play.
>
> I thumped out a Liszt showpiece, after which Victor Herbert offered his perfunctory acknowledgment, hoping no doubt to return to his own arpeggios. But Father wasn't finished. While I'd been performing, he'd rushed upstairs to our third-floor dwelling and hurried back with my violin, insisting that I make music on the fiddle as well.
>
> Years later Victor assured me that my father's paternal pride and intrusion upon the composer's concentration were a small price to pay for the privilege of working at the Hofbrauhaus.[56]

Thus Herbert's most famous operetta was written, between drafts of pilsner, on a barroom piano at the Hofbrauhaus at the corner of 30th Street and Broadway. Only in New York.

Auditions for the new work were held "in the dim cavern of the Manhattan Opera House stage one August morning," Peggy Wood remembered.

I sang my scale and was weeded out for the chorus . . . at twenty dollars a week. I was on my way in the role of a "quadroon belle"—the one in yellow—third from the left. The star, Emma Trentini had the usual sound European training of stage and vocal discipline and the others in the cast were either established singers of authority and avoirdupois, or character actors. There were no glamour girls in the chorus that I recall, no stage-door Johnnies barging about backstage. It was all just one big middle-class family.[57]

Rehearsals began in September of 1910. There were 130 in the company in addition to the stars. Herbert was not lost in the crowd.

The person who stands out most clearly of all was Victor Herbert. He usually conducted the first nights of any of his shows. Since he did his own orchestrations and knew what he wanted out of the band and the singers, his orchestral rehearsals and premieres were something to be remembered with mingled delight and agony.

If things went wrong the musicians complained he had such an erratic beat they couldn't tell where they were at, and when that happened his magnificent flow of invective made them wish they weren't where they were.

But they adored him nonetheless and the very sight of him lighted up every face whenever he trotted onto the stage (for he never walked, he moved at a sort of half-run as if in vast impatience to get to the spot where he wanted to be faster than mortal legs could propel him by ordinary procedure). I shall never forget the electricity which seemed to crackle from his immense vitality as he would galvanize any group with chuckling good humor or coruscating criticism.[58]

Although Trentini's musical and histrionic contribution was impeccable, her English was not. She learned her part by rote and, as rehearsals progressed, she managed to keep her famous temper under control. The out-of-town tryout began with three days at the Wieting Opera House in Syracuse, followed by three days in Rochester and a week in Buffalo. Herbert conducted the final dress rehearsal, during which Young was still making revisions to the book. These last-minute changes unnerved Trentini. What is more, the original contract called for six performances per week. When the Syracuse opening occasioned huge ovations for all

concerned, Hammerstein insisted on increasing the number of performances to eight. But Trentini replied that Herbert's music was too demanding; they eventually settled on six plus one matinee. The Wednesday
matinee was pure poison to the star.[59]

Nevertheless, with minimal complications and with the cheers of re-
gional audiences ringing in their ears, the company headed for New York.

As one might expect, the reviewers were unanimous in their praise for
Herbert's achievement. Typical of the notices was that of the *Tribune*,
which called *Marietta* an "instant and distinct triumph," and judged the
score "far and away better than anything Herbert has written in years."
It praised the "real poetry and romance" of the music. Young's book was
roasted on two scores: missed opportunity to build upon the potential of
a work set in the "dreamy, creole atmosphere of two hundred years ago";
and the injection of broad comedy that rudely tore apart what little atmosphere had been created. This also involved the worst kind of ethnic
stereotyping, even in a period of insensitivity to such elements. The
comic relief was provided by a cartoon Irish immigrant maid who indulged in a ludicrous "Salome dance" and by her partner, a stage Hebrew
who, as Simon O'Hara was given a lyric replete with exclamations of "Oi!
Oi!" Photographs of the original production reveal an actor with a false
belly á la Lew Fields and "typical" Hebrew whiskers. It is to the credit
of Arthur Hanmmerstein, who served as the effective producer of the
show, that by the second year of the tour the character's name had been
changed to "Silas Slick" and a good deal of the embarrassing ethnic comedy toned down. Nevertheless, the weakness of the book stood out in
strong relief to the brilliance of the score and the strength of the vocal
performances, which were universally praised.

Oddly enough, Boston was not as put off by the comic elements. While
praising the score and performers to the heights, those normally picky
fault finders were surprisingly gentle on the comedians.

"Those who revel in low comedy were kept laughing by Harry Cooper
and Kate Elmore in weird characters that smacked of amateur night."

"The comedy element pure and simple was a subordinate feature last
night, but Harry Cooper and Miss Kate Elmore supplied the genuine
article."

"Cooper, one of the few good singing comedians was very funny as an
Irish Hebrew. . . . Kate Elmore's grotesque makeup, methods and
conversation kept the audience in good humor."[60]

In sum, the audiences' "riotous and rapturous joy was unconfined" and must have even infected the spirits of those normally captious criticasters of the North. Whatever the weakness of the comedy, Herbert and Trentini carried the day. Almost every number was encored, a fact that proved a very mixed blessing in the long, long run.

For the show rolled on and on. The original tour lasted two years. As the days passed, little problems that had been pushed beneath the surface in the rush of the original production began to rise. Rumors reached New York that Trentini was beginning to cut certain numbers. Although her English was improving, the improvements were limited. "Don't push yourself excited," she was heard to exclaim on one occasion when she attempted to calm things down. There were occasions when she would dry up, and she had been advised that at such times she should fill in the dialogue gaps with the nonsense phrase "Ish Kabibble," a phrase which will have a certain resonance with those who remember the radio programs of Kay Kyser and Eddie Cantor.

Although the second season had a strong opening at the Montauk Theater in Brooklyn, on the road business declined. To save on expenses, Hammerstein made a change and hired inferior performers. Managers in Philadelphia and Chicago were upset by the quality of the production that reached them.

Finally, Trentini refused to continue the tour unless the Wednesday matinees were cancelled. Hammerstein acquiesced, but the diva continued to cut numbers and refuse encores. Knowing how concerned the star was about money, the management began to pay her hotel and dining-room tips in an attempt to keep her happy. Nothing seemed to work.

With all these stories reaching New York, Arthur Hammerstein and his manager, Blumenthal, decided it was time to beard the lioness in her lair. They found her napping in her suite in her dressing gown.

"Haven't I warned you not to leave your door open?" Blumenthal exclaimed, entering her room. Trentini did not stir. "There are strange men who prowl about who could take advantage of you!"

Still no movement.

Finally Hammerstein lit the firecracker.

"Ah," he remarked under his breath, "Who in hell would take a chance?"

Trentini leapt out of bed in a rage.

"What do you mean? Nobody take a chance with me?" she exploded.

Her English had apparently improved.

Looking to the future, Hammerstein had contacted Otto Harbach to see if he could write a new show with Herbert for Trentini. By 1911, Harbach had had a big string of hits, and Herbert wanted to do the project because he "thought it would be a big money maker."[61]

> I traveled with the troupe for about four weeks studying her, seeing what she could do. It was not for nothing that she was called "the little devil of grand opera." She looked better dressed as a boy than she did when dressed in female costume. And she had the most glorious voice you ever heard. Didn't look good, a little monkey—a little comedienne.[62]

But first *Marietta* had to be put to bed. A grand gala performance was arranged for the West End Theatre in Harlem. Harbach was there:

> Herbert was in the pit, to give it éclat. There he was, dressed in his best, leading the orchestra and getting ovation after ovation. As the night wore on Trentini was getting sorer and sorer because there had been two or three encores already—before the Italian Street Song. She sang it and there came this burst of applause. Herbert gave her the stick (he pointed his baton at her—the signal for an encore). She bowed and left the stage. Again he called for an encore—and again she bowed and exited.
>
> I've never seen a man act like that in public. He took his baton, rammed it down, called to Axt to finish the show, turned and walked out of the pit.
>
> At the back of the theater he met Arthur Hammerstein. He said, "Art. Listen! Don't ask me to ever write another note for that woman. I've never been so insulted in my life. She's a peasant!!"
>
> Arthur had many scenes with Herbert, begging him to reconsider and to work with me in a new Trentini show. But he refused.[63]

That was the end of the first production of *Naughty Marietta*. Of course, the show has been endlessly revived. Hollywood did its worst in the '30s; still, it goes on and on.

As for the Harbach show written for Trentini, it was a little piece called *The Firefly*. And the composer who replaced Victor Herbert? A little import from Bohemia who had been hanging around the Witmark offices. His name was Rudolf Friml. And the rest, as they say, is theatrical history.

Type of work: Operetta–Social Satire
Premiere: December 5, 1910
Theater: Court Square, Springfield, Mass.
Daly's, New York (September 14, 1911)

Cast (Major Players):

John Hammond	Frank Belcher
Mrs. Hammond	Josie Intropidi
Victoria	Harriet Standon
Jefferson Todd	William Norris
Stanley Morton	Roy Purviance
The Laird of Loch Lomond	George Ridgwell
Monsieur Beaucaire	Arthur Lipson
Eleanor Bradford	Mable Mordaunt
Mabel Bradford	Belle Taylor
Gridley	R. M. Dolliver

Major Musical Numbers: "In the Golden Long Ago"; "Laughs"; "Sweet Sixteen"; "Reprises."

Plot: Victoria is the daughter of ambitious parents. Her mother wants her to marry into the nobility; her father wants her to marry for money. She wants to marry Stanley, a poor retainer who is actually a would-be novelist looking for experience. The whole bunch are addicted to performing Shakespeare in the California forests and attempt *As You Like It*, with music from Victor Herbert hits.

Camp Joyland

Dear Harry

Enclosed two new Sweet Sixteen numbers. Please have them copied at once so that we can rehearse them at the N.Y. orchestral rehearsal. . . .

Quick work!

Don't you think so?

See you Monday.

Best,

Your

v.h.[64]

"Quick work?" Certainly. A plus? Not really. Herbert had been extraordinarily busy during the years 1910–11. He had created the scores of *Naughty Marietta* and *Natoma* and had arranged for a huge party at Lake Placid to celebrate his twenty-fifth wedding anniversary. Still, he had found time to work with fellow Lamb George Hobart on *Victoria*, later *When Sweet Sixteen*. The actual composition had been in the works for some time. Originally the show was to have been produced by Joe Weber, but the canny producer backed out and had been replaced by the new production team of Harry Everall and Sam Wallach. What those gentlemen could have seen in a book focused on the old plot device of a father who insists his daughter marry for money, a mother who demands she marry a titled Scotsman and a daughter who, of course, wants to marry for love, is easy to see. It had nothing to do with plot and everything to do with Herbert. Fresh from his triumph with *Marietta*, anything he touched looked golden. After three weeks of rehearsal the piece was previewed at Springfield, Massachusetts, on December 5, 1910, with a cast that featured some of Herbert's stalwart performers, including the faithful Eugene Cowles, who dropped out of the cast before the company set off on a tour to Toronto and Chicago. A brief note in the *New York Times*[65] reports that members of the New York Symphony had been transported to Springfield for the premiere, that Herbert had conducted, and that the "song play" had been "well received." But in spite of this, all was not well. Hobart had started out to direct his own book, but by the time the production opened in New York at Daly's Theater on September 14, 1911, he had been replaced by the more experienced R. E. Burnside. Many of the original cast had followed Cowles's lead and left the company. As the letter from Lake Placid suggests, new material was being supplied as late as two weeks before the opening.

Whatever Herbert sent, it could not have been very effective. Nor was the second act (set in a pine grove, i.e., "Forest of Arden"), where a group of amateurs (the first-act principals) gather to attempt a production of *As You Like It*. The classic comedy is spiced up with performances of Herbert's greatest hits from previous shows. In this grotesque plot turn, the fatal influence of *Natoma* librettist Joseph Redding may be detected. Before his move to New York, Redding had actually directed a group of amateurs in Shakespearean productions down among the sheltering redwoods; thus his fatal influence may be seen in the demise of two of Herbert's works.

Whatever the source may have been, the product was praised only in its particulars. A few numbers were singled out, but you know you're in trouble when the orchestration gets the best notices: "There is a very clever use of the drum. . . . The French Horn plays its subtle part. . . . The fife caught many ears."[66] One critic added, "The success of the piece is not quite assured, in spite of the popularity of composer and author, who both suffered from the shortcomings of the cast in several instances."[67]

People speculated on the source of the title. Wags had it that Herbert had composed sixteen numbers and then given up. Others noticed that the cast consisted of sixteen principals. One speculated that the composition had actually begun in 1905, when Herbert's daughter, Ella Victoria, celebrated her sixteenth birthday. None of these assertions can be proven. One thing is certain: with previews, the show lasted sixteen days on Broadway, a not so "sweet sixteen."

NATOMA

Type of work: Grand Opera
Premiere: February 25, 1911
Theater: Metropolitan Opera House, Philadelphia, Penn.
Metropolitan Opera House, New York (February 28, 1911)

Cast (Major Players):

Natoma	Mary Garden
Barbara	Lillian Grenville
Lieut. Paul Merrill	John McCormack
Don Francisco	Gustave Huberdeau
Father Peralta	Hector Dufranne
Juan Bautista Alvarado	Mario Sammarco
José Castro	Frank Preisch

Major Musical Numbers: "Natoma's Soliloquy"; "The Vaqueros' Song"; "Spring Song"; "Daggar Dance"; "Columbia."

Plot: Barbara returns home from school to find waiting for her: Her widowed father, Don Francisco; her childhood friend, the Indian maid Natoma; and her first cousin, Alvarado, who wants to marry her for her money. Enter Paul, a handsome naval officer. Both Barbara and Natoma fall for him, and Alverado hatches a plot to kidnap Barbara. During a fiesta Natoma stabs Alvarado. To assuage her conscience, she enters a convent.

In 1907 *Musical America* announced, "Victor Herbert will compose grand opera for Hammerstein." The article referenced a contractual agreement between the two theatrical giants for a production at the Manhattan Opera House of a new American opera. Hammerstein discussed his motives.

> I have always wished it to be understood that in founding this opera house I had other aims than merely financial profits. . . .
> Fundamentally my aims have been artistic, and will continue so. . . . I want to be an operatic Columbus. It is easy enough to pick up an opera that has been a success in Milan . . . but it is not so easy to voyage the lyric seas on journeys of discovery.[68]

Hammerstein was to play the role of Columbus, and he chose Victor Herbert as his steersman. No captain and crew ever had to navigate stormier or more treacherous seas than those that awaited these two. Like the crew of Jonah's vessel, Herbert attempted to calm the tempest by tossing Hammerstein overboard. The result was an even more furious storm. Herbert himself wound up, if not in the belly of a great fish, then in the mouths of critical sharks who relished tearing his reputation to tatters.

The story of *Natoma* is a history of missed cues and stubborn self-defeating decisions. It's not a pretty story, but is important, not so much because of what Herbert achieved, but because of what it reveals about the attempts to promote opera in English written by American composers in the early twentieth century.

Hammerstein soon put his finger on a basic problem.

> The only difficulty in the way was the libretto. Mr. Herbert has often said he would have written a grand opera if only he could have got the libretto. The way to get a libretto is to ask for it and to pay for it. . . .
> So I offer $1000.00 to the man, preferably an American who will provide a suitable libretto for Victor Herbert.[69]

It is typical of Herbert that, with respect to the composition of *Natoma*, he thought of himself as a co-developer of the book. Thus, some of the responsibility for the weakness of the text must be laid at the composer's door. Herbert was very specific about what he wanted and what he rejected in choosing a libretto.

> I should like to have an American subject and a background of American romance. . . . It is not absolutely necessary that the dramatis

personae be Indians. Indians are not a suitable subject for an opera. The state of the Indians is pathetic, it is true, but in an opera they would not exactly strike the audience seriously.

An American atmosphere is not attained by peppering the score with themes from patriotic songs. I do repudiate absolutely the idea that an infusion of popular or folk songs reproduces the spiritual and intellectual or romantic atmosphere of the country to which these folk songs belong.

The libretto which will satisfy me most is one in which there will be plenty of contrast, diversified action and strong character differentiation.[70]

The irony is that, with all these excellent insights and good intentions, Herbert wound up with an opera based on an American Indian subject, laced with folk themes and devoid of "contrast, diversified action and strong character development." Herewith the roadmap of Herbert's path to hell.

As of September 1909, Herbert was still searching for a suitable book. Hammerstein's office was buried in submissions. David Belasco had been approached about the possibility of using his *Girl of the Golden West*—but he had already assigned that work to Puccini. His *Rose of the Rancho* was also discussed, but nothing came of the project.[71] Whatever the subject, the composer was determined to create a work that gave him opportunity to play to his strengths.

The American people love beauty. In music they demand melody. Always melody. . . . The fundamental musical idea belongs to the American people and the American opera will be the opera of melody. . . . The music, because it is American, should be vivid and stirring like the life of the new continent.[72]

At long last a librettist was selected, an author whose "Charming book suggests wonderful pictures which it is my fault if I fail to paint in the wealth of color and beauty he indicates."[73]

Who was this lucky winner of the Hammerstein prize? For one thing, he was a member of the Lambs, and it was at the club that Herbert had gotten to know him. DeWolf Hopper, another prominent Lamb, remembered him.

Joseph Redding, a brilliant California lawyer and a really fine amateur musician told me he was moving to New York to run away from his

California reputation. "Every lawyer in California admits that I am a great musician, and the musicians agree I am a first class lawyer. In New York I hope to be a lawyer among lawyers."[74]

The *New York Times* provided more specific information about Redding's qualifications as a librettist, noting he was the author of the "grove plays" that the San Francisco Bohemians had performed in the Redwood forests. Redding himself reported:

> Some time ago Mr. Herbert came to me and asked me if I could furnish him with a libretto suitable for a serious opera. He had already gone through some eighty without finding one to his taste. He wanted a book on an American subject and when I suggested the Spanish possession of California he was enthusiastic.[75]

Now with composer and librettist finally at work, one would think Hammerstein's dream production was on target. But it was not to be.

For some time the directors of the Metropolitan Opera had been unnerved by the excellent quality of Hammerstein's productions at the Manhattan Opera House. When Hammerstein and Herbert signed that contract for a new American opera to be sung in English, it was seen as a direct assault on the Met's program to promote the composition and production of opera by American composers. Converse's *The Pipe of Desire*, Parker's *Mona*, and Damrosch's *The Scarlet Letter* had been produced to no great effect, and the prospect of a successful Herbert grand opera produced by Hammerstein was more than the directors could take. Otto Kahn, chairman of the Met board, Clarence MacKay and H. R. Winthrop negotiated a highly lucrative agreement with Hammerstein, according to the terms of which he agreed to refrain from producing grand opera for a period of ten years in any market in which the Met performed. Hammerstein, whose company had been an artistic success but a financial disaster (he was losing $25,000 a week), jumped at the offer. That agreement being duly signed, Hammerstein immediately approached Herbert with the proposition to compose an operetta using the personnel of the Manhattan Opera. The result was Herbert's grand operetta *Naughty Marietta*—a huge success for all concerned. The Met board, thinking they had cleared the decks of possible conflicts in the grand opera arena, now met with Herbert to discuss the possibility of a *Natoma* production under its auspices. But they hadn't reckoned with Hammerstein's animus. The headlines screamed:

"HAMMERSTEIN SAYS HE WILL NOT LET METROPOLITAN PRODUCE 'NATOMA' "

A difference of opinion at present exists between Victor Herbert and Oscar Hammerstein which has resulted in a trial orchestral rehearsal of the composer's new opera, "Natoma," at the Metropolitan Opera House. An orchestra of 60 musicians under the direction of Mr. Herbert played Act II of the score for several of the directors of the Metropolitan company.

"Mr. Hammerstein," said Mr. Herbert last night, "had an option on 'Natoma' for this year [1910] up to January 15th when I told him that the score would be ready. I notified him several weeks before that date that the score would be finished and he was also notified on January 15. However he did not care to exercise his option.

"Now, of course, Mr. Redding, who wrote the words, and I feel that we are free to do as we please about the matter. Consequently we have had a parley with the Directors of the Metropolitan Opera Company. Nothing has been decided as yet, however."

"Option," said Oscar Hammerstein. "I never had an option on the piece. I have a signed and sealed contract with Mr. Herbert, and I am going to hold him to it. If Mr. Herbert attempts to have anyone else produce the opera I will immediately take out an injunction. The Metropolitan will never get it. The contract runs for four years. As yet I have not seen a sheet of music of this opera."[76]

Who was telling the truth? In this case, both men had some of the right on their side. Hammerstein's 1907 contract with Herbert was for a grand opera, necessarily untitled, since at the time of execution no librettist had been secured. The contract did indeed run for four years, and since *Natoma* was not produced until February of 1911, it seems clear that the hold on the production was related to the expiration date contained in the agreement. But Herbert's contention was also valid, since in 1909 a second contract had been negotiated between Hammerstein, Herbert and Redding for the production of *Natoma*—the score to be delivered by January 15, 1910. Whether this second contract contained an option provision is unclear, since the contract has disappeared. Reference to other contracts Herbert executed with respect to his operettas reveals that option provisions were often, but not universally, part of his production agreements. Herbert's attorney, Nathan Burkan, must have been privy to the agreement and, always a wise protector of his client's interests, probably would have insisted on an option. Hammerstein's oath that "The Met will never get it" held true. Andreas Dippel, associate general manager of the company, left in 1910 to assume directorship of the Philadelphia-Chicago Grand Opera, the entity that eventually produced *Natoma* at Philadelphia on February 25, 1911, and a few days later, on February 28, at the Metropolitan Opera House in New York.

In an interview in *Musical America* shortly before the premiere, Herbert embroidered this history with characteristic blarney. " 'Natoma' was written in one year at the request of Oscar Hammerstein, who refused to produce the opera because it was 'too late.' Then it had to be peddled about a bit until the perspicacious Dippel was induced to hear it and constrained to recognize its value."[77]

None of this is true. What *was* true is that in creating *Natoma*, Herbert wrote his heart out. He looked to Mozart, our greatest musical dramatist, as a model in two respects. "In 'Natoma' I have tried to make every character sing differently. My early training has led me to consider Mozart's masterpieces as the most glorious examples of characterization."[78] From Mozart he also took the practice of composing for the talents of specific artists.

> Miss Mary Garden will sing the principal role. I have composed the music with special reference to her voice, which I consider a marvel. She combines more dramatic intensity and skill with a rarer voice than any other person on the stage today. *If anybody can make this opera a success, she can*[79] [italics mine].

This comment, made while the score was still in progress, tips the composer's hand. It reveals that even before *Natoma* went into production—even while Herbert was applying all his skill to the composition—he sensed that what he had written could not stand on its own, but would need a great artist to make it work. His friend, the baritone George Hamlin, who was scheduled to create the role of Paul, spent part of the summer of 1910 at Lake Placid, "climbing, golfing, automobiling, yachting. This relaxation is a necessary part of work, and there is abundant time out in the country for the study of *Natoma*, which is receiving attention of these two great musicians, Herbert fashioning the part to emphasize the strongest qualities of Hamlin's voice."[80] Ominously, by the end of the visit, Hamlin had backed out of the production.

Herbert and Redding frequently discussed the technical aspects of their work—Herbert about his use of Indian materials as leitmotifs for the structure, Redding about his desire to create "real characters" and to put "plenty of action" into the book. Herbert painted his motivation in the broadest terms: "I am not half so interested in the success of my own account as I am for the sake of the cause. I want this work to make such a success that the way of the American composer will be easy, that he will have no trouble in having his works produced."[81]

There was also much talk about the creators' interest in making a success of a grand opera with an English text.

> "We want to show," Redding remarked, "that an opera can be sung in English, and Mr. Herbert is as insistent as I that every word should be understood. The singers already have learned their parts, and every one of them it will be perfectly possible to understand. You will be surprised to hear the clear diction of the foreigners who have taken extra-ordinary pains to perfect their English diction."[82]

Surprised, indeed! John McCormack created the tenor lead in *Natoma*, but his service to his lifelong friend Herbert extended far beyond the reasonable and customary duties of an opera singer.

> Also entrusted to John was the far more arduous task of teaching the English pronunciation to Sammarco, Dufranne, Huberdeau and Armand Crabbé.

> This task took up a great deal of his time. John's sense of humor, if it delayed the proceedings, at least made them go smoothly. Progress was slow, since every time John laughed at some transmogrification of a word his pupils clamored to know what the joke was, and he had to stop and explain. Huberdeau was the most persistent offender. John concluded he was doing it on purpose just to see the effect, but he preserved a poker face throughout.

> Of the four, Sammarco had the greatest difficulty, perhaps because his text was so unkind. One morning he came rushing to John, completely stumped.

> "Giovanni! Nobody can sing this phrase. Not even with your diction you can make understood."

John looked at the score and saw that the unhappy baritone had been asked to sing: "We beg the privilege of a hunt upon the range of your hills."

After hours of hard work, Sammarco succeeded in singing the phrase as, "Wee bag the preveeleedge off a oont upon the raaange off your heels."

In despair John sang it back to him exactly as he had sung it and Sammarco collapsed on a chair and laughed until the tears ran down his cheeks. After this, every time they met, the two would try to see who could get this immortal phrase out first.

McCormack felt that Herbert, a master of operetta had written music that was just so-so. He saw it as an overgrown operetta, bigger, noisier and more bombastic. He felt his part was "more fatuous and stupid than the usual tenor part" and found the music "very high and very ineffective."[83]

The world premiere of Herbert's first grand opera was held on February 25, 1911, at the Philadelphia Metropolitan Opera House. There was an enthusiastic reception, but the major critics passed on the trip to Philadelphia, since the New York premiere was scheduled for the 28th. The only New York critic to attend was Herbert's old bête noire Krehbiel, who apparently couldn't wait for the chance to savage his favorite. To an extent he held his fire for the New York opening, but sent the following telegram to the *Tribune*, whose editors duly published it prominently in the Sunday edition.

> If standards were not different in America and Europe, and if especially professional observers were not rather disagreeably disposed to study the sources of popular demonstrations and measure their sincerity, a success like that which we recently read about as achieved by Richard Strauss' latest opera [*Der Rosenkavalier*] would have to be chronicled for the first production of "Natoma."[84]

Such a communication did not bode well for the fate of the opera at the hands of the New York men. Nevertheless, Dippel's company went to great lengths to create an atmosphere for success for its premiere at the Met. The boxes of the Grand Tier were draped with the national colors, and at the center rear of the house were banners bearing the arms of California and New York. Souvenir programs imparted an atmosphere of unconventionality to the occasion; the first page bore portraits of Herbert, Redding, Dippel and the conductor, Campanini. As for the audience, it was of "unexampled brilliance."[85] The guests included Mayor Gaynor, President Nicholas Murray Butler and Professor Brander Matthews of Columbia University; Walter and Frank Damrosch; Horatio Parker; Vanderbilts, Fishes, Schuylers, Van Rennselaers, Whitneys, Harrisons, Drexels, Belmonts, Otto Kahn, Thomas Edison and Charles Dana Gibson.

Nine curtain calls followed the first act, but the reception was somewhat restrained. The reaction to the second act, which contains some of Herbert's best operetta-style music, was quite different. The audience demanded an encore of the "Vaquero Song" and after the "Dagger Dance" a storm of enthusiasm broke. After the curtain Herbert and Redding acknowledged the cheers and were joined by the full company, conductor and stage director. Wreaths and bouquets showered down upon them.

When the curtain fell on the third act and the cheers had abated, invited guests gathered for a reception at Sherry's on the Grand Tier. Everyone who was anyone was there, including figures from Herbert's past.

It was at the Met's performance of "Natoma." Alice (Nielsen) entered the lobby. Victor was standing surrounded by friends, talking so excitedly as to give Nielsen the impression that he had been imbibing with more enthusiasm than discretion.

Victor had long held it against her that she had abandoned the field of comic opera for grand opera. It was, in a way, an abandonment of Victor. Catching sight of her and with his tongue loosened, he shouted across the room, loud enough for everybody to hear, "Alice, you should never have left comic opera." A dead silence. All eyes were on 'little Alice.'"

Miss Nielsen, incensed, was stung to retaliation. "So, Victor?" she retorted. "Neither should you!"[86]

That remark, brutal in its brevity, summed up the critical reception that followed in the morning papers. Redding's book was justly excoriated:

Its defects are its indefiniteness of form . . . the amateurish quality of its lyrics, which by no stretch of the imagination could be termed poetic, and the stilted and musically unsuggestive dialogue which unites them.[87]

The critics cut Herbert some slack:

> Personally I think that Mr. Herbert has done wonders in writing the
> music he has to a text often so unsuggestive. . . . There are many
> numbers which could be taken out of the score and sung
> independently . . . thus the form and structural character of the work
> is hardly grand opera.[88]

As might be anticipated, the man at the *Musical Courier* had a field day.
He had no need to write his own diatribe, gleefully restricting himself to
quoting the comments of the major critics:

> With redskins on the boards of the Metropolitan Opera House
> primitive emotions patriotically labeled "American" might seem to
> have the right of way. Critics, for one, might let patriotism have full
> sway and raise a chorus of praise over home-grown opera. . . . If
> anyone thought this of Victor Herbert's Indian opera, "Natoma," their
> confidence was misplaced. The critics in this case have taken the role
> of the passengers in the old western days, who sometimes repulsed the
> redskins who tried to board the stage.

> Mr. Gilman [*Harpers Weekly*] calls the construction of the book
> "amateurish to the last degree" with its literary form "incredibly
> fatuous and inane." Mr. Parker [*Boston Evening Transcript*] agrees
> with him with the damaging inclusion of the music, too. "From
> beginning to end, equally in text and music, Natoma is an utterly
> mediocre opera." Parker continues that Natoma must be compared
> with the "best performances of contemporary European opera makers;
> compared with these Natoma leaves no positive impression in the
> mind. It lacks individuality, originality, ideas and no music has value
> unless it possesses one at least of these merits."[89]

Herbert was hurt by these notices as he had rarely been hurt in his
long career composing for the stage. If the critics denigrated one of his
lighter works, he could easily shrug it off. He had run a string of successes
unmatched by any other American composer, and if he ran afoul of the
critics there was always something new coming up. But with *Natoma* he
had put his talent on the line, to be measured against the best production
of his contemporaries: Strauss, Puccini, Debussy. A lingering feeling that
perhaps his facility and genius as an orchestrator and melodist came too
easily to him may have awakened in him the desire to "move up," to face

and meet some greater challenge to his abilities. Perhaps he remembered that evening in Pittsburgh, when Richard Strauss had been a guest in his home and had urged him to expand his scope, and how he had made a joke of the suggestion, remarking that if Strauss expanded his palette any further his scores would have to be written on surfaces the size of the walls of his home. Whatever the motivation, he lashed back at the critics with a fury unmatched in his previous public outbursts. He also unburdened his soul with uncharacteristic frankness.

> Little scribblers on the newspapers! They are the biggest cowards alive. . . . The critics are afraid to say, "It's good." They think that's going to sound as if they don't know much . . . and in most cases they don't! The only man to really see inside a composer's work would be some other man who also had turned the same trick to know the drudgery, the perpetual self-abnegation, the pure love of *deeds* rather than *rewards* that must characterize even the most materially successful of those who devote their lives to creative work. . . . He knows what it has meant in love, labor and sacrifice and exultation to the man who did it.

> But these critics—they have their preconceptions. They always start with some made-to-order point of view. If a success by Wolf-Ferrari [*Donne Curiose* had just been premiered to critical acclaim] was presented and attributed to me—what would be the reception? Can't you see the critics dismissing it with a sneering line or two? as they kept saying of my "Natoma," "proof positive that Mr. Herbert, who can occasionally grind out good little operettas and things for Broadway, should refrain from invading a field for which he is so unfitted both by talent and by training?"

> Your critic chap is the biggest coward alive. He starts with a crystallized popular conception of what a man is, and then tries to say something that will prove his individuality without budging out of line.

> That's my "Natoma." How they've roasted it, grilled it from every possible point of view.[90]

All this in an interview given a full year after the opera's premiere—how he was still smarting!

Of course there had been a grand banquet given in Herbert's honor, full of tributes and praises from colleagues and friends: "All hail, Victor

Herbert," Mary Garden wrote in a letter read at the dinner, "the first writer of American grand opera! May it be the beginning of this great art which America does not yet hold. . . . So lift your glass to [American opera's] glory in the next century."[91]

Natoma was produced over thirty times by Dippel's company throughout the United States—a grand tour ending in California. A copper mine owner from Colorado, A. J. Davis, announced plans for a fall opera season in Paris performed by a company of international artists, with *Natoma* as its chief feature. The plan never materialized.

And Herbert never recovered from his disappointment. In a conversation with composer Jerome Kanner shortly before his death he counseled him,

> Jerum. Never write an opera in English. In English they understand it. Here in America they swallow the most idiotic plot as long as it's in German, French, Italian or anything they can't understand. I still say my "Natoma" is as good as Puccini's "Madame Butterfly." My mistake was not to do it in some American Indian dialect![92]

The voice of Alice Nielsen still echoed through his soul, as it had echoed that night so long before in Sherry's. "Alice, you should never have left the light opera." "So, Victor? Neither should you!"

THE DUCHESS
Type of work: Romantic Operetta
Premiere: March 27, 1911
Theater: Shubert, Boston, Mass.
Lyric, New York (October 16, 1911)

Cast (Major Players):

Aristide Boutonniere	Wilton Taylor
Rose (M'lle Rosita)	Fritzi Scheff
Marianne	Lillian Spencer
Philippe	George Anderson
Adolphe, Comte	John E. Hazzard

Major Musical Numbers: "Cupid, Tell Me Why"; "The Land of Sultan's Dreams"; "It's the Bump"; "Richer than Gold."

Plot: M'lle Rosita works in her father's flower shop. In order to marry money she agrees to a marriage of convenience with Philippe, a minor nobleman. The plan is for her then to divorce him and, with her new title marry Adolphe, a rich Count. But Rose and Philippe inconveniently fall in love and the Count, "a butterfly," as the libretto describes him, is left to his own devices.

The Rose Shop or *M'lle Rosita* or *The Duchess*—or whatever—was the last show Herbert composed for Fritzi Scheff. Despite the star's popularity and Herbert's reputation, nothing could save this production from disaster. The libretto by Joseph Herbert (no relation), with lyrics by Harry B. Smith, did nothing to improve matters. The Shubert brothers were producers of the fiasco, and the troubled tale of their fractious and protracted legal wrangling with Herbert is discussed in chapter seven. The producers must have anticipated a weak reception in New York, for they kept the piece out of town for several weeks. After countless revisions the work opened on October 16, 1911, and after only twenty-four performances in the city, set out on the road in a feeble attempt to recoup losses.

Probably unnerved by the weakness of the material, Scheff made new demands every day. She did not care for her waltz song. Herbert, uncharacteristically, wrote out a new one and sent it off from Placid to Smith, who set words to it. This was "Richer than Gold," the strongest number in the score. Fritzi then demanded a new conductor, one who could communicate with her, since her English had not improved very much. The Shuberts wrote to Herbert, who responded:

August 3, 1911

Dear Mr. Schubert [sic]

I have given Mr. Arthur Lautzenbach a letter to you. He might be the right man for Madame Scheff. He is a fine musician, (he was a member of the Boston Symphony Orchestra), a splendid pianist, and speaks German. He conducted for Grace van Stittiford last year and "made good" from what I hear. All the new "Rosita" numbers are fine and will undoubtedly improve the piece immensely.

Sincerely,
Victor Herbert[93]

The piece, not "immensely improved" despite Herbert's optimistic words, debuted at the Lyric Theater and was the occasion for one of the oddest curtain speeches in the history of the Herbert works. Fritzi stepped before the curtain and begged the audience for help.

You know that since "M'lle Modiste" we have had nothing but bad luck. Help us to make this a success. If you only knew how hard we have worked. Mr. Herbert and the actors and orchestra and everyone else. Mr. Herbert is such a good man that he deserves some encouragement. Please give it to him.[94]

All this *before* the reviews came out. *The Duchess*, based on an old English farce by Madison Morton, was, more or less, *Modiste* redux. Here the hat girl became a flower girl. The male chorus is dressed in the same red-trousered French army uniforms and her suitor wears one of them—just as he did in the Paris of not so long before. Many of the critics noted the similarities, but still paid modified homage to Schiff and Herbert.

> Mr. Herbert has not given us tunes that linger in memory especially.
> . . . His melodies are not up to his best work. . . . The book is not of
> much meriment. . . . Miss Scheff, vivacious and in splendid voice
> dominated every scene and her work fairly radiated with good nature.[95]

The *New York Herald* remarked that "whether 'The Duchess' will cater to the public taste . . . will depend upon how its story affects the operetta going constituency." The *New York Press* praised Fritzi and said she "came off better than any one of less talent would have faired." The *Tribune* agreed. " 'The Duchess' will subsist on her personality and Victor Herbert's score. There is absolutely nothing else to give it the breath of life." Then, responding to Schiff's plea, the newspaper concluded, "If ever an operetta deserved to succeed through the efforts of a single star that operetta is 'The Duchess.' "

All of this was of no avail. One is reminded of John Mason Brown's famous dictum, "I go to the theater to see a play, not the work done on a play."

What a team! Victor Herbert! Fritzi Scheff! The Shubert brothers! And they all struck out!

THE ENCHANTRESS
Type of work: Romantic Operetta
Premiere: October 9, 1911
Theater: National, Washington, D.C.
New York, N.Y. (October 19, 1911)

Cast (Major Players):

Vivien Savary	Kitty Gordon
Marion Love	Nellie McCoy
Princess Stellina	Louise Bliss
Prince Ivan of Zergovia	Harold H. Forde
Troute	Ralph Riggs
Miloch	Harrison Brockbank
Ozir	Arthur Forrest
Prince Zepi	Bertra Fox

Major Musical Numbers: "If You Can't Be as Happy as You'd Like to Be"; "The Land at My Own Romance"; "Rose, Lucky Rose"; "One Word from You"; "All Your Own Am I"; "Ballet Music"; "Art Is Calling for Me."

Plot: The Regent and Minister of War of Zergovia are anxious to retain their power. But Prince Ivan is due to take the throne. If they can arrange for him to marry a commoner, he will forfeit his rights. They produce an enchanting opera singer to charm the Prince. She does, he falls for her—but—at the last minute it is revealed that she has noble blood—love finds a way, and the plotters are foiled.

On June 12, 1911, at its graduation ceremonies, Villanova University awarded Victor Herbert his first—and only—honorary degree: Doctor of Music. The citation, typically hyperbolic, nevertheless seemed to energize the composer beyond even his normal level of activity.

> The greatest musician of this century who has done more for the American music-loving public than has any man in years. The Offenbach of America! How much music lovers and theater goers owe to Victor Herbert, his exquisite melodies and masterly direction of orchestras. Mr. Herbert has a fine, big head and it is full of music and harmony. All honor to the master.[96]

It was a grand moment for Herbert . . . and perhaps a fatal one for *The Enchantress*.

That "fine, big head" rushed back to Lake Placid and plunged into the composition of one of his most beautiful scores. *The Enchantress* had a book by Frederika de Gresac, who had contributed the French dialogue scenes to *The Red Mill*. The author was married to the internationally known baritone Victor Maurel. A resident of Paris and an active member of the haut monde, every fibre of her being was imbued with the world of hereditary privilege that was drawing its last breaths in the polluted atmosphere of pre-catastrophic Europe. In his lyrics, Harry B. Smith tried to capture this spirit. Herbert, for his part, turned out a quintessential Viennese bonbon, full of acceleration waltzes, bittersweet romantic melodies and perky soubretteries.

What is problematic here is that, according to Herbert, he had done no such thing: "I determined to disregard absolutely every foreign impulse. I had determined to write in a frank, American style, full of freshness and vitality."[97] The score is certainly fresh and vital; American, it is not. One wonders if Herbert was promoting the piece for his Buffalo audience when he made those remarks to a reporter from the *Buffalo Commercial*. Even his star, Kitty Gordon, a statuesque British blonde more famous for wearing a golden gown that revealed her gorgeous back than for her voice, was a European type, given to posing and posturing rather than acting. She certainly was no all-American girl after the style of Lulu Glaser or Hazel Dawn. Every aspect of the production, from its voluptuous settings to his elaborate choral writing, smacked of Mitteleuropa.

Joseph M. Gaites's production tried out for a week in Washington, D.C., and then had its New York premiere at the New York Theater. Perhaps this was symbolic, for the venue had been a palace for that typically American art form, the silent film, but for *The Enchantress* it had been re-converted into a legitimate house. There followed a brief run in New York and an extended tour to Rochester, Buffalo, Boston and Chicago. Contrary to his custom, Herbert left the city to conduct the premieres in each of these cities. He gave countless interviews boosting the piece. Perhaps if he had written his score a decade earlier, it would have met with a warmer reception. "The Land of My Own Romance" and the "Champagne Duet" are two of the finest compositions to flow from his pen. "Art Is Calling for Me" has a brilliant lyric and is a perfect musical portrait of the eternal stage-struck teenage girl who "wants to be a prima donna." But on the whole, it was a piece at odds with its time. If ever there was a story that fits the mold of the false image of what a "Victor Herbert Operetta" is, this is it. Princes, imaginary kingdoms, palace intrigue, unfunny comic detectives in oddball disguises—all the kitchy-koo of the pejoratives launched at operetta by its detractors are present in *The Enchantress*—in spades. This was a piece that was old before its time, one of the few creations unredeemable even by a remarkably facile and appealing Herbert score.

The *New York Times* found that score "very agreeable," praised the dancing, "good voices," "very good cast" and pronounced it a musical entertainment "which will appeal to people who do not object to hearing music that is good even if it is light." But the critic must have had his doubts about the chances for overall success, for he concluded, "If people in large numbers do not go to see 'The Enchantress' it will be their loss."[98] People were apparently willing to stay away and take their losses.

The *Herald* stated that Herbert had "written waltzes that would be applauded even in Vienna."[99] Not even, but especially. The *New York Telegraph* praised Herbert for daring "to soar above many of his previous efforts, leaving the jingles and lilts of less talented *native* [italics mine] composers far in the distance."[100] Despite his public claims, Herbert had indeed abandoned his quest for American utterance in the operetta form. And he had done so consciously. It was not only Vienna he had in mind. Bayreuth was calling—to him.

> Victor Herbert says that he has followed the Wagnerian method in his composition of "The Enchantress."
>
> "For the principal theme, I use a Leitmotif which recurs as the story develops and figures prominently in the finale. No matter how tenuous the theme every light opera must have a backbone, otherwise it is an indeterminate thing, which never arrives at a consistent or convincing climax.
>
> "As the plot is to be libretto, so the Leitmotif is to the score, binding the whole composition into a musical whole. Having once settled the form of the score the composer must study the sequence of the numbers, their sentiment and subsequent development. The composition of light opera is no more beneath the dignity of a scholarly musician than comedy is beneath that of a dramatist who can write tragedy."[101]

Besten dank, Herr Doktor Professor Herbert! "A scholarly musician." This is where Herbert tips his hand. This is new. We have seen Herbert the flamboyant, Herbert the joker, Herbert the generous, Herbert the lover, Herbert the bon vivant. But Herbert, the scholar? More typical was this: " 'The Enchantress' will be my masterpiece in every way, for I have never had so many varied inspirations to bring forth the best that I could compose."[102]

What had happened? Perhaps that honorary degree had gone to Herbert's head. Perhaps his subconscious striving to produce something that would be scholarly and respected may have bubbled to the surface. Perhaps fame and financial success were not enough. Whatever the motivation, for the first time, in *The Enchantress*, Herbert's writing may properly be called self-conscious. Ease of expression is abandoned for studied effect. The result is expert, inspired and professional. His "masterpiece" it is not.

THE LADY OF THE SLIPPER
Type of work: Fantasy Extravaganza
Premiere: October 8, 1912
Theater: Chestnut Street Opera House, Philadelphia, Penn.
Globe Theater, New York (October 28, 1912)

Cast (Major Players):

The Crown Prince	Douglas Stevenson
Prince Ulrich	Eugene Revere
Baron von Nix	Charles A. Mason
Atzel	Vernon Castle
Mouser	David Abrahams
Punks	David C. Montgomery
Spooks	Fred A. Stone
Cinderella	Elsie Janis
Romneya	Ellene Crater
Dollbabia	Lillian Lee
Freakette	Queenie Vassar
The Fairy Godmother	Vivian Rushmore
Valerie	Peggy Wood
Première danseuse	Lydia Lopokova

Major Musical Numbers: "Meow, Meow, Meow"; "Like a Real, Real Man"; "The Ride to the Castle"; "The Princess of Far Away"; "A Little Girl at Home"; "Drums of All Nations"; "Halloween."

Plot: This "modern Cinderella" has "Cindy" rise from oppressed drudge to princess with the help of "Punks and Spooks," two friends from the cornfield, a Fairy Godmother, a cat and a gypsy. The original story is updated to include "modern" elements, i.e. labor strikes, and up-to-date dances.

Hurrah! Hurrah! Hurrah! Hurrah!
Great success! Hit of my life!
Everything fine! Packed House!
Everyone of the company fine!
Costumes grand! I guess we are going to be a success this
year—
I hope so

ELSIE JANIS'S DIARY.[103]

There are stars whose performances and personalities are so consistently praised in the press that for those of us who never saw them, the recollections of their contemporaries serve only to heighten our sense that we were born too late. Imagine if all we had of Judy Garland were reminiscences: no films, no recordings, just personal memories. Marilyn Miller is one star who shines on only in memoirs, although we have a few film records of her work. The young John Barrymore as Hamlet and Richard III is another. Elsie Janis is a name less known, but in her time she was as great as any of these and truly an original: a multi-talented, delightful, unegotistical, natural superstar who had the whole theatrical world at her feet. Everyone from Irving Berlin ("Don't wait too long for Elsie Janis") to Dillingham, while he was developing *The Century Girl* in 1915, to that most caustic of critics, Alexander Woollcott, unabashedly worshiped "one of the most entertaining members of the human race."

> There is magic in her mimicry. When she dances the sight is somehow as exhilarating as a cool, fresh wind along an alpine road in May. Here was a comedienne who could go dancing into vaudeville whenever she felt like it or could step into any of the great reviews and shine as she shone in the "Century Girl."[104]

Born Elsie Bierbauer in Columbus, Ohio, in 1889, she early displayed her talent for mimicry, delighting her family with imitations of her minister, her postman, her cook—even her dog. She developed this talent into a fine art, ever encouraged by her mother, who broke the tradition of "stage mother-managers." The two of them loved one another completely, and each recognized the importance of the other for the development of "little Elsie's" career. Mother was "stage manager, prop-man, wardrobe mistress and supporting cast"[105] and there was hardly ever a harsh word exchanged between them. This was not the least of the remarkable things that distinguished Elsie's career.

At the age of five she began professional work with stock companies in Columbus and Cincinnati. "I was a talented, but self-centered, thoughtless brat,"[106] she recalled. In the spring of 1903, she began her association with Victor Herbert when the Aborn Opera Company in New York hired her for a role in a touring revival of *The Fortune Teller*.

"The Fortune Teller" was a great success for Alice Nielsen because she had the loveliest voice of her day. I had, perhaps, the worst. Nevertheless the Aborns bought the touring rights of "The Fortune Teller" for me. I played M'lle Pom-pom, an abandoned hussy.

She was supposed to be an opera singer, but turned out to be the only member of the cast who couldn't sing. . . . I didn't even enter until the end of the second act. I was supposed to upset the morale of the army, instead of which I went into my imitations. . . . I imitated Cohan, Fay Templeton, Eddie Foy.[107]

At this point Charles Dillingham had seen enough of the Aborn production to convince him that Janis was one superstar aborning. He got Herbert's attorney, Nathan Burkan, to break the contract with the Aborns and signed on to manage her—a relationship that lasted for the rest of her career. It wasn't long before "little Elsie" was earning $3,000 a week in vaudeville. "She was a great draw adored by managers, performers and audiences."[108]

Dillingham kept his star on the back burner, slowly developing her reputation in vaudeville while proceeding with other projects on Broadway. One of the most successful had been *The Red Mill*, which starred David Montgomery and Fred Stone, fresh from their triumphs as the Tin Woodman and the Scarecrow in *The Wizard of Oz*. Now the great producer was ready to launch something new for Broadway—an all-star vehicle that couldn't fail. "When in doubt—do Cinderella," is an old theatrical saw. Dillingham followed the tradition with what he called "a modern Cinderella," a retelling of the story in a contemporary setting. With music by Herbert and three of the greatest names in the Broadway world as stars, it could hardly fail. And the high level of casting didn't stop there. The ballet was led by Lydia Lopokova, and there were dance specialties by Irene and Vernon Castle. Dillingham even had a great eye when casting the smaller roles. A maid was a newcomer named Peggy Wood.

It all sounded wonderful, but things did not go smoothly. Dillingham's assumption that Janis, Montgomery and Stone would jump at the opportunity to appear together was a miscalculation. Although Stone later expressed the feeling that "Elsie was a grand little star and a fine trooper as well,"[109] initially he and Montgomery were not anxious to share billing with "little Elsie." Elsie's punctuality had become something of a problem for the company. Whether this was an attempt on her part to assume a bit of the "diva" role isn't clear, but by March the ever-diplomatic Dillingham was forced to write to her.

3/16/11

Dear Elsie

There was some dissatisfaction in the company this morning at the hour wasted before you arrived. They were not unpleasant about it, but naturally would prefer to have an hour set when the rehearsal would surely begin.

Will you think of this when making your call tomorrow.

Yours sincerely,

Ch. Dillingham[110]

Elsie and her mother were also not convinced that an appearance in a show with music by Victor Herbert would do much for a performer with a limited vocal range who, when she sang at all, half-talked her numbers. In this they underestimated Herbert's genius. As he had demonstrated in *The Red Mill*, he was quite able to compose effective music for all sorts and conditions of voices, for he could clothe even the most limited of vocal lines with a patina of harmonic and orchestral richness that made them theatrically effective. Dillingham persisted, and after a lot of discussion Janis agreed to co-star with the two vaudevillians and to do her best with Herbert's score.

The Cinderella story as retold in the book by Laurence McCarty, Anne Caldwell and James O'Day provided Herbert with huge opportunities to expand his musical palette. There was of course a grand waltz for Cindy and her Prince ("The Princess of Far Away"); there were comic trios and duets in vaudeville style ("Like a Real, Real Man," "A Little Girl at Home"); there was an imaginative evocation of Halloween night ("The Games of Halloween"); a wild ride to the castle in a coach drawn by four white ponies; character numbers for Montgomery and Stone ("Bagdad," "The Punch Bowl Glide") and an elaborate ballet. With such a stimulus to his imagination Herbert produced one of his most exciting and varied scores. He played it through for the company at the Globe Theater on the first day of rehearsal.

> There was electricity in the air. Montgomery and Stone didn't want to co-star with me any more than I craved sharing a success with them. At that first rehearsal Dave and Fred were extremely polite. I was rather like an ambitious puppy, striving to please but with one eye on the thickness of my part. The script was read and it was obvious that Fred, Dave and I were to get an even start.

> We started to rehearse and inside of two days Fred, Dave and I were working together like three small time vaudevillians trying to break into the Palace. From the first night in Philadelphia there was little doubt about the success of our "three star circus." Montgomery and Stone were wonderful to work with.[111]

Naturally the stars were expected to perform their "specialties" sometime during the evening. Elsie added to her repertoire of impressions new ones of John Barrymore as Hamlet and, as a pièce de résistance, on opening night, October 28, 1912, in the presence of the great diva, she surprised everyone with an imitation of Fritzi Scheff as Mlle. Modiste! But it was Fred Stone who, for this production developed a routine that remains unequaled.

> I tried to develop a new stunt for each show. In "The Lady of the Slipper" [it was] "The Punch Bowl Glide," a pantomime for which I learned one of the most difficult tricks I ever did on the stage.

> It was worked out on three trampolines. On the landing at the head of three steps leading up to the throne there was a rug about 6 x 8 feet which was a canvas trampoline. Under this was a removable platform. At a given signal the platform was dropped down from beneath the rug. I stepped on the canvas and began to bounce, each time higher and higher. About eight or ten feet in the air I began to turn somersaults and after five or six of these I did a twister out on the landing. I stumbled down the three steps, staggered to a couch, jumped on that—the couch was constructed as a trampoline—then to a table, then to a trampoline mat on the floor—one hard square—which

threw me up six feet through an oil painting, head first, and once out of sight on the other side turned over and landed in a net.[112]

As if all this were not enough, to acknowledge the applause that followed this spectacular performance, Stone entered, grabbed hold of the descending curtain and was pulled up into the fly space, from which he descended—upside down with his head aimed at the apron, only to rescue himself from disaster a split-second before the curtain touched down. The applause went on for five minutes.

David Montgomery's contribution to the three-ring circus is aptly summarized by his partner. "I don't associate Dave Montgomery with anything but laughter. He was never serious in his life. Wherever he went he was joking as though life were one endless party. He was cordial, friendly, and gay, and the most generous man I ever knew."[113]

The initial run of *The Lady of the Slipper* extended from October 28, 1912 to May 17, 1913, and proved to be a bonanza for Herbert. The *New York Herald* reported that "for weeks his check is said to be between $400 and $500 and this is separate from the royalties he receives from the sale of sheet music."[114] The company set off on an extended tour that included stops in Rochester, Buffalo, Chicago, Cleveland and St. Louis.

From the first, critical reception had been unanimously enthusiastic: "Such a combination as Elsie Janis, Victor Herbert's music and the eccentricities of Montgomery and Stone could not help but be a success, but the charming manner in which the parts are molded into a unit is responsible for the emphatic hit the production made."[115] The critic went on to praise the "wonderful spectacle with ever changing pictures, each more elaborate than the last." Of these, the second act finale, "Drums of the World," is one of the most original of Herbert's creations. As Cindy disappears at midnight, the Prince orders all his courtiers, led by Montgomery and Stone in full livery, to search the globe for his princess until she is found. There follows an elaborate balletic search accompanied by percussion instruments representative of all the five continents: American Indian tom toms; African kettle drums; cylander drums from the Indies; gongs from the far east; military drums; Turkish cymbals. It was a finale that was truly grand and remains unique in the annals of theatrical presentation.

Still another commentator called the production "a pronounced and undoubted success," but brought up an important question for those who might consider rescuing *The Lady* from oblivion: "The piece is little more than a vehicle and if it had to rely upon either its book, lyrics or music it would stand little chance of winning public favor, but it offers opportunities for the trio of stars to introduce their specialties and these are always welcome."[116]

What about it? How strong is this book and score? Does *The Lady* demand superstars for success? In 1994 the Victor Herbert Festival presented a production that had neither stars, ballet, elaborate sets nor elaborate finales, and yet the critics and audiences pronounced it a real "find," and the production more than recouped its investment. There is no doubt that this piece, produced on a grand scale with superstar performers, could hold its own with the best of Broadway revivals.

The same critic quoted above also describes in some detail a dance routine whose choreography anticipates the style made famous by Busby Berkeley in 1930s Hollywood.

> Vernon Castle, assisted by a female chorus did a capital number. . . . With swaying dance movement the girls form a line, with Mr. Castle in the centre (he acting as a pivot round which the line revolves). With each half turn a girl joins the line until all of them, about sixteen in all, are in the line. Then, with the same swaying movement the line revolves, and at each half turn a girl leaves the line until Mr. Castle once more stands alone. It is a capital number and one which caught the house.[117]

As an historical footnote it might be added that this routine, while new to the musical stage, was not completely new. Since the eighteenth century it had been part of the performance of the famed Lippizaner white horses of Vienna. Perhaps that is why dancers in Broadway musicals came to be known as "ponies."

Other comments were a producer's dream.

> "Sensational success of the season."
> —*New York Sun*

> "Smashing big hit."
> —*New York Evening World*

> "The best musical show on Broadway since Peter Stuyvesant bought his wooden leg."
> —*New York Herald*

"Children will love it."
—*New York Mail*[118]

The children in particular "loved it," one of whom began a lifelong love affair with the musical theater that ended in a very special way.

During the run of the "Lady of the Slipper" a popular millionaire and his two children occupied the stage box at many Saturday matinees. I used to take the children backstage at the end of the first act where Elsie Janis as Cinderella rode to the ball behind four white ponies. I let the kids ride with Elsie. They were John and Ellin Mackaye. She grew up to become Mrs. Irving Berlin.[119]

The road loved it, too.

"The show is worth $2.50 of any kind of money—even that stored away for a long, cold winter."
—*Chicago American*

"Hurrah! The big show is here!"
—*Chicago Inter-ocean*

"A perfect riot of youth and beauty."
—*Chicago Examiner*

"If some other shows are worth $1.50, 'The Lady of the Slipper' is worth $10.00."
—*Percy Hammond in the Chicago Tribune*

The Boston critics praised both Herbert's music as lovely and sprightly and the wonderful performances of the three stars. With such reviews and such a reception, the company soon became one big, successful family. Montgomery and Stone orchestrated offstage fun and games in which not only the cast but, when the word got around, some of the audience also participated.

For entertainment during the show, Stone set up a projector in a room under the stage to show home movies of his bear hunt in Greenland. One summer he had spent time at his farm in Amityvillle, Long Island, learning to shoot. His teachers were the finest shots in the world: a little Quaker lady known as Annie Oakley and her husband Frank Butler. "I got more pleasure out of breaking 100 straight in a 100 target match than I did out of all our Red Mill notices," Stone recalled.[120]

There were practical jokes as well. A couch set up for observers had been wired by the stagehands, and at a signal the people on the couch got a shock and were thrown off. Word of the special showing got around, and some of the audience each night went below to enjoy the rival attraction. "During the performance of Lady of the Slipper we could hear muffled laughter from below."

It was in Boston that Montgomery and Stone gave the most elaborate of the Christmas parties for which they had become famous.

> We transformed the stage. There were two half-moon tables and several smaller ones, each set for supper. Upstage was a tiny platform with a curtain and footlights. While supper was served we were entertained by vaudeville acts from the Keith circuit. Then the stagehands presented a scene from Hamlet. Elsie Janis gave some of her brilliant imitations and I played the part of a ventriloquist, using a live dummy—a midget from the cast.[121]

With such goings-on we can be sure that of all the Herbert shows, this one delivered the greatest pleasure to cast, creators and audiences alike. It was the sort of experience that was remembered fondly by all. There would be other, more significant productions, but *The Lady of the Slipper* was the last of Herbert's spectacles to appeal to childlike wonder. When it closed, an era that had begun with *The Wizard of Oz* ended.

Woodrow Wilson had been elected the day after *The Lady* opened. Within a year the world was at war. The theater that emerged from that war lost its taste for innocence and charm. More than soldiers died at the Marne.

CHAPTER 14

ENTR'ACTE II: UNCROWNED KINGS (1908–1917)

> *Aside from music and his family there was only one vital interest in his life: the cause of Irish freedom. Even the most casual and slightly derogatory statement concerning the Irish people was sufficient to send him off in a violent burst of temper which would last throughout the day.*
> —*Clifford Victor Herbert, from the* Philadelphia Gazette, *May 13, 1934*
>
> *Every Irishman is an uncrowned king!*
> —*Victor Herbert, from "Yesterthoughts," by Frederick Stahlberg*

While Victor Herbert enthusiastically embraced American music and culture, he never forgot his Irish roots. Of Ireland's music Herbert spoke in the closest personal terms:

Ireland is full of music. It begins at the cradle and does not end at the grave. It is dance music, work music—very typical music: jigs, reels and some very mournful. . . . Ireland would never have survived but for her fairy tales and folk music. . . . Why has Ireland not produced a great national music that would sweep the world with its beauty, its eloquence, its fervor, its grandeur? When Irishmen are transported to freer and better conditions they make themselves felt the world over in art, literature, science and all the practical pursuits of life.

I tell you that in Ireland the Irish would accomplish as much as they accomplish in other parts of the world if they were not suppressed and smothered well-neigh to death."[1]

Herbert promoted Irish music at every opportunity. At his popular Sunday evening concerts at the Broadway Theater, he frequently programmed arrangements of Irish folk songs and the music of other composers of Irish descent; and the annual Feis Coeil Agus Seanachas, a literary and musical festival sponsored by the Gaelic Society at Carnegie Hall, was the occasion for Herbert to introduce Stanford's F-minor Symphony and his own Irish Rhapsody. In 1912 the Gaelic Society presented him with a parchment encomium which used a facsimile of the lettering, coloring and tracery of the Book of Kells in recognition of his work on behalf of Irish causes. Those causes involved much more than advocacy of Irish music and art, for Victor Herbert was a patriot.

In the first fifty years of his life that was a comparatively easy thing for him to be. Born in Ireland, raised by a mother deeply imbued with a love and respect for their Irish heritage, greatly influenced by the example of his prominent forebears on both his mother's and father's sides of the family, Herbert was virulently proud of his membership in what he called "the Irish race." His use of the term "race" was typical for the period in which he lived, a period in which a Western pseudo-science, eugenics, was devoted to the establishment of definitions of "superior" and "inferior" racial characteristics. Since the tradition of German culture in which he had been reared and schooled deeply affected his personal and intellectual development, he could scarcely have avoided racial consciousness. Since 1886 he had struggled to establish his image as 100 percent American, creating and championing the development of the art of music in his adopted land.

But this tripartite loyalty came under serious stress in the first decades of the twentieth century. When in August of 1914 World War I exploded, which tradition would command Herbert's loyalty? Could a loyal Celt support the cause of perfidious Albion against the interests of his Teutonic majesty? And when Wilson led his beloved America into the conflict, and Clifford enlisted and became a hero at the Marne and the Argonne, what was the Irish advocate, the cultural German, the loyal American to do? Truly, patriotism did not come easily to Victor Herbert in the final years of his life. As a celebrity he was active in Liberty Bond drives; he was immensely proud of Clifford's military service, but in his heart of hearts he remained true to his Irish heritage and was a constant supporter of the cause of Irish freedom.

Herbert's earliest association with the organized Irish community in America began in 1908, when he became a member of the Society of the Friendly Sons of St. Patrick in the City of New York. The Society, founded in 1784 during a period when Ireland enjoyed a brief respite from British repression, was a strong supporter of the cause of Irish home rule, not independence. The American-Irish Historical Society, which Herbert joined in 1911, had a broad cultural focus, but in the political arena its aims were exact: it worked to encourage and assist the national independence of Ireland. Herbert's natural leadership qualities quickly advanced him within the ranks of the Friendly Sons. In 1911 he was elected second vice president. In 1913 he established the society's Glee Club, which still exists today. Its program of weekly rehearsals, led by a professional conductor who still uses Herbert's gold-tipped baton at annual concerts, carries on the tradition Herbert established, complete with afterglows. Several of Herbert's arrangements of Irish folk songs are in the club's repertoire, as well as the two anthems he composed for the men: "The Hail of the Friendly Sons," and "The New Ireland." By 1914 he had been elected first vice president, and the following year began two terms as president. On January 26, 1915, in honor of the 131st anniversary of the Society's founding, Herbert conducted the Glee Club in a concert of his own compositions—a high point of his musical association with the group. Separately, he joined the famous Father Duffy in establishing the Irish Musical Society, an organization specifically dedicated to the promotion of music written by composers of Irish descent. But the times they were a-changin', and it soon became evident that cultural activities were no longer sufficient for a man of Herbert's strong loyalties.

The attitude of many Irish-Americans toward freedom for their mother country had changed during the twenty years before World War I. Where once they would have been satisfied with almost any kind of home rule for Ireland, now they were demanding complete independence.

Some were bitterly disappointed with the Home Rule Bill which John Redmond, leader of the Irish party, extorted from the British Parliament in 1914.[2]

As the war dragged on and relations between Ireland and England became strained, a new, strongly political organization, the "Friends of Irish Freedom," was formed at an "Irish Race Convention" held at the Astor Hotel in New York on March 4, 1916. The date chosen and the timing were not coincidental. ~~This was the date of Wilson's second inauguration as president~~, and the convention sent a message, loud and clear, to the man in Washington: support for Ireland and Germany in World War I ~~and opposition to the League of Nations~~. The assembly included

More than 1800 Irishmen from all parts of the United States. . . . It was almost noon before Victor Herbert, President of the Friendly Sons of St. Patrick, standing under a decoration made by twining American flags and the green Irish banner with the golden harp, beat for order.[3]

When Herbert rapped the gavel all stood and cheered. He looked supremely happy at the welcome.[4]

The convention, which moved to the George M. Cohan Theater for its subsequent sessions, declared its loyalty to the United States in the event that "the storm breaks and engulfs our country," but expressed its hope that the United States would not become involved. All agreed on the agenda of the Friends:

> To encourage and assist any movement for the national independence of Ireland and to aid in the industrial development of the country as well as in the revival of the language, the literature, the music and the customs of the Gaels.[5]

A few weeks later, on Easter Monday, April 24, 1916, a huge revolt broke out in Ireland. England put down the uprising with brutal force and hanged sixteen of its leaders. The Irish revolution was a huge embarrassment to those in the power structure who had sought to portray the Irish as 95 percent in favor of the Allied cause. It also frustrated the "sinister propaganda that is being waged from press and platform for the purpose of embroiling the United States in the European strife."[6]

In October Herbert presided at a joint political meeting of Irish and German societies at Madison Square Garden. Its stated purpose was Irish relief efforts, but its agenda was to keep the United States out of World War I. About this time Herbert issued a personal manifesto that detailed his concerns and positions regarding the Irish cause. Although it has been claimed the statement was at least partially written by his friend Judge Daniel Cohalan, a typed copy, prepared on the typewriter used by Ella Herbert, who was serving as her father's secretary, and with written corrections in Herbert's hand, makes it probable that the statement excerpted here and published in the *New York Sun* clearly was composed by Herbert. It is a manifesto, and much of its diction smacks of the revolutionary rhetoric of the time. This is a side of Victor Herbert we have not seen before.

> If England . . . fortunately in the best interest . . . of Ireland, is now fighting against foes whom she cannot frighten or cajole and . . . it has seemed inevitable that the British Empire is doomed and that again we are going to live in a world where there will be liberty and freedom and where the weaker peoples will not have to live in constant dread that their countries and their rights are to be taken from them, such a

result will bring happiness to many lands, but to none other in such measure as to the land of my birth.

The decisive defeat of the English ruling classes . . . is big with promise of immediate good and with the great changes which must follow in the overthrow of their top heavy social system, the proletariat is undoubtedly looking with hope and confidence to the time when a great advance for the better will come to the masses of the people. . . . Nothing but speedy success [in the war] can save England from revolution and even the most optimistic of her rulers no longer looks for that. . . .

Volunteers are today, throughout the whole of Ireland, an armed and disciplined body of men, determined that the manhood of Ireland shall be kept in Ireland to serve Irish interests, and insistent that Ireland has no blood to shed in England's quarrels.

Rural Ireland has remained unmoved by the cries and unswayed by the appeals of the recruiting sergeants. Only those whose necessities have compelled them to do so have donned the hated uniform of England.

Industrial pressure is being brought to bear on Irishmen, to turn them out of work and thus constrain them to join the army. . . . This policy England is pursuing with zeal and energy and help in abundance is required if the men thus thrown out of employment are to be saved and kept in the cradle land of our Race to help it work out its destiny.

Such help was promised at the recent Race Convention and such help will be given as promised. . . . The Friends of Irish Freedom, of which I have the proud honor to be President, is already spreading all over the country and will, I am sure, prove to be a great power for good.

Beset as America is with difficulties in this hour of danger, we are confident that there is no reason and no excuse for the entrance into the World War. . . .

There is here a small but powerful group of men who wish to drag us into war . . . but we are determined to do all that may be necessary to keep the country true to its tradition of peace with all nations and entangling alliances with none. . . .

We see clearly that a broken England means a strong and free Ireland for which we, like our forefathers, hope and pray, and are ready to act.

To that end our hopes are turned; to that end our acts are pledged; and for that end we shall struggle and work in our devotion to the preservation of the free institutions of this glorious land of liberty, and in our hope for liberty and independence for that old land which, through centuries of oppression, has ever hoped to rise, proud and free.[7]

Victor Herbert—revolutionary!

EILEEN

Type of work: Romantic Operetta
Premiere: January 1, 1917
Theater: Colonial, Cleveland, Ohio
Shubert, New York (March 19, 1917)

Cast (Major Players):

Captain Barry O'Day	Walter Scanlan
Sir "Reggie" Stribling	Algernon Greig
Dinny Doyle	Scott Welsh
"Humpy" Grogan	John B. Cooke
Lady Maude Estabrooke	Olga Roller
Eileen Mulvaney	Grace Breen

Major Musical Numbers: "Free Trade and a Misty Moon"; "Tell Me, When Shall I Again See Ireland"; "Eileen"; "When Love Awakes"; "Thine Alone"; "The Irish Have a Great Day To-night."

Plot: Set during the rebellion of 1798, the story tells of the return of Barry from exile to lead the revolt, aided by the French fleet. A price on his head, Barry goes into hiding and falls in love with Eileen, niece of his benefactor. He is captured, the French never arrive, but a new government in an act of clemency grants a general amnesty to all rebels and Barry and Eileen are united in peace and safety.

Herbert's most powerful statement on behalf of the Irish cause was neither a manifesto nor a speech. It was his Irish operetta *Hearts of Erin*, or as it became known, *Eileen*. One critic said as much: "Eileen is more than an opera—it is a bit of propaganda. When we listen to Mr. Herbert's music how could we deny the Irish anything?"[8] Herbert acknowledged his feelings in his curtain speech on opening night in New York on March 19, 1917:

I have spent the best part of my life in the United States. I have been a citizen for many years. I think I am today a good American. But I was born in Dublin and all my forefathers were Irish. It has been the dream of my life to write an Irish opera, one that would add to the glory of its traditions. Now that dream has been realized. You must know how I feel. This is the happiest day of my life.[9]

Hearts of Erin, with a book by Henry Blossom, opened a pre-Broadway tour in Cleveland on New Year's Day, 1917. Set against the background of the historical rebellion of 1798, the book tells the story of Captain Barry O'Day, fighter for Irish Liberty. He hides from the detested redcoats disguised as a groom, falls in love with the young mistress of the estate (Eileen) and after capture and a pardon, wins her hand and proclaims his vision of the day when "Ireland stands among the nations of the world."

The tour reviews augured well for a New York triumph.

"Melody, rhythm, color, spirit, variety in Victor Herbert's best vein."[10]

"The music is the crowning achievement of Mr. Herbert's long and distinguished career."[11]

"Victor Herbert has surpassed himself."[12]

"Mr. Herbert has never publically written in such a vein, nor has he ever done anything which excelled in artistic merit."[13]

During the tour the production was tightened, new numbers added and others revised extensively. A comparison of the scores of *Hearts of Erin* and *Eileen* (as it was called from the time of the Boston run) shows that both Herbert and Blossom were determined to provide Broadway with a critic-proof hit. When the show opened on March 19, as close to St. Patrick's Day as possible, the audience was studded with prominent personalities from the Irish community. Justice Victor Dowling, president of the Friendly Sons, showed up in full regalia with the green scarf and gold badge of his office. Herbert's friend, surrogate Cohalan and his party— Mr. and Mrs. Condé Nast and Mme. Marcella Sembrich—took a stage box. When Herbert came down the aisle to take his place at the head of the orchestra, the scene became electric:

Mr. Herbert's personality and intense enthusiasm constituted so much of "Eileen." One saw him fairly scramble to the orchestra pit the minute the fiddlers appeared from their lair, saw him pick them up with eyes alight, saw his baton darting over them like a living thing, realized that Mr. Herbert was having the time of his life. Much of the man's passionate devotion to Ireland, much of his hatred of England was written into the score of "Eileen"; he conducted with all the ardor of a rebel.

Those delightful bits of music which accompanied outbursts of Irish resentment against British oppression, those harsh and stinging bars which heralded the coming of the Redcoats, were just what one would have expected from Herbert's pen.

Wild Irish yells swayed the drop curtain as Mr. Herbert, mopping a pink brow with a handkerchief edged in green jumped back in the pit doing his best to take Dublin with music that surely would have charmed the bullets of the redcoats out of their courses.[14]

The New York critics were certainly charmed. The *Times* called the premiere a "cause for rejoicing," and found *Eileen* "in Herbert's best vein, bursting with rich melodies of Irish flavor that contribute much to the charm of the score."[15] The one general criticism was one that we have met before. In his enthusiasm Herbert whipped the orchestra into such a frenzy of sound that it tended to drown out the excellent singers. But this was a passing triviality.

Excellent production, first-rate singers, beautiful staging, one of Herbert's finest scores—and the production closed after sixty-four performances. What happened? The world was about to be made "safe for democracy," an agenda that made a paean to the glories of revolution less than box office.

Shortly before *Eileen* opened in New York, Wilson made public a message from the German Foreign Secretary, Arthur Zimmerman, to the Mexican government: if Mexico would join Germany in a war on the United States, she was promised return of her territories lost during the Mexican War—Texas, Arizona and New Mexico. The public outrage was tremendous. That same month the Russian Revolution toppled the Czarist regime in a bloody uprising. Several of the States enacted laws against "criminal syndicalism," ~~which advocated unlawful acts to accomplish political change. Thus Herbert's Irish operetta had become, ipso facto, a hymn to a newly created felony.~~

The show closed its doors, but Joe Weber, the producer, planned a huge two-year tour. He launched it but, shortly thereafter, in Dayton,

Ohio, a mysterious fire destroyed everything: sets, costumes, orchestral parts—even the musicians' instruments. It seemed *Eileen* was finished. But it wasn't. Not yet.

Writing to Judge Cohalan from his vacation retreat at Lake Placid, Herbert actively pursued his interests in the Irish cause, although in a tone we are unaccustomed to finding in his correspondence. His reference to the "unfairness" of things can't be separated from his experience with "the score he loved best of all."[16]

> My Dear Judge—
> Many thanks for sending me the account of the meeting, or hearing before the Committee on Foreign Relations. Its effect ought to be enormous with all just people—but it seems to me that "fairness" is becoming rarer from day to day, especially with those "higher up."
> *You* have really done wonders for the cause and justly have gained the love and admiration of every true Irishman.[17]

The fighting Irish were not to be defeated by something so trivial as a World War. When the dust had settled and the Wilsonian agenda been put to rest, the Irish rose again and formed the Eileen Association, whose purpose was to present a first-class production of the operetta for the benefit of Irish causes. In asking his support Herbert outlined the plan to Cohalan.

> My Dear Judge—
> The following is the route of "Eileen":
> Apr.4–5–6 Dayton
> Apr. 7–8–9 Toledo
> Apr. 10 Cincinnati (one week)
> Apr. 17 Kansas City (one week)
> Apr. 25 St. Louis (one week)
> May 1 Detroit (one week)
> May 8 Milwaukee (one week)
> May 15 Chicago (one week)

As the company is really excellent, and a very beautiful production has been provided, and as the *profits of the entire run are to help swell the Irish Relief Fund,* I hope you will do all you can to interest the leading Irishmen in the above cities in patronizing the performance.[18]

Herbert gave his full support to the tour, conducting opening performances where he could. But why had it been necessary for him to urge

Cohalan to actively support the project? Apparently there had been some factional infighting among the Irish societies, as the following letter from the Cleveland Committee attests. A united front was a prerequisite for a successful tour.

The Eileen Association
Cleveland Committee

My Dear Mr. Herbert:

I write you on a subject which seems to me to be of the utmost importance to the continued success of our presentation of your opera Eileen.

As I told you when you were here last week, we have all endeavored to keep strictly away from anything that might lend an atmosphere of factionalism to the Eileen enterprise. On the theory that we are serving Ireland solely, we at least have not consciously done anything that might offend any American Irish group.

If Eileen is to be successful, it must have the unqualified support of all of these groups. One of the most important of the groups named is the one which is led by Judge Cohalan of New York, whom I understand is a good friend of yours. Barry McCormack told me last week that he had approached Judge Cohalan on the matter of securing his endorsement, and that Judge Cohalan entertained the proposition so seriously, that he promised to have a representative witness the show when it opened here last Monday night for the purpose of reporting to him at least as to what he thought of the performance from the artistic standpoint.

I would deeply appreciate it if you would see the judge and seek to get from him his decision as to whether he can or cannot endorse. You may tell him that if there is any lingering doubt in his mind as to our sincere purpose to employ Eileen as a vehicle for furtherance of the Irish cause without regard whatever to any group, he needs only to consult Attorney James P. Mooney of this association.

Despite the fact that we found it difficult to sell out the tremendously large Masonic Hall during Eileen's engagement here last week, we did make a profit of which we are proud, when we stop to consider the unusual expense involved in getting things running smoothly. We have encouraging reports from Dayton, Toledo and Cincinnati.[19]

Apparently Cohalan was suspicious of the motives of some of the tour promoters, but he eventually came around, and Eileen made a substantial contribution to the cause. Herbert's musical-political statement had at last triumphed at the box office.

The ballot box was another matter. Politics provided a brief coda to this tale. Herbert had been invited to the White House to meet with President Coolidge after Al Smith, "the happy warrior and New York Irishman" had announced his candidacy for the Democratic ticket. Perhaps the photo of Herbert shaking the president's hand was meant to add a Celtic color to the Vermont Yankee's candidacy. At any rate, after Herbert had shaken hands with the president and turned away, he said, for all to hear, "I'm going to vote for Al Smith just the same!"[20]

Was this the voice of the loyal Irish partisan? Or something more? The big issue in the campaign was, after all, Prohibition, the "wets" vs. the "drys." Could it have been a bit of each?

In vino veritas!

CHAPTER 15

ACT THREE: SCENE ONE

In what was roughly the last decade of Herbert's life, he continued his theatrical activities and developed and expanded them in important ways. Although he created seventeen stage musicals in this period, only a few of them were significant achievements in themselves. Their importance lies in more than the quality of Herbert's musical contribution. His output in this period is significant because it represents something new. During his first period Herbert copied and personalized the European operetta tradition; in his second he transformed that tradition into a form that, because of its theatrical and sociological focus, became what he called American operetta; now, in his third period, he worked to develop what may be called the dance operetta. In each of his later compositions it is the dance, in its various forms and movements, that assumes an increased structural importance. More than underpinning the composition, it drives and unifies the work. It is also the vehicle for Herbert's continuing success. The new rhythms of a new century demanded pride of place in the stage musicals of the 'teens and twenties, and this new force continued unabated; the famous influence of George Balanchine for the development of musicals in the thirties and forties, and later of Agnes de Mille's story ballets, were the mature fruit of a tradition that begins with the works of Herbert's third period.

As the dance became an equal player with music and text, it transformed one of the central characteristics of Herbert's works. From the days of his earliest successful composition, Herbert's soprano leads were spunky, independent-minded ladies whose charm for audiences was based on the quirky nature of their characters. Whether it was Smith or Blossom or MacDonough writing the book, all Herbert's heroines shared these qualities. The Nielsen-Scheff-Trentini type became the lynchpin of the Herbert operetta. Now singing and acting ability were no longer enough. The women who portrayed Herbert's new ingenues had to dance. What is more, the best of these, Christie MacDonald in *Sweethearts*, Wilda Bennett in *The Only Girl* and Eleanor Painter in *The Princess "Pat"* brought to their performances a natural, unforced quality that supplants the arch artificialities of their predecessors. Perhaps the new style went hand-in-hand with the ability to dance. Whatever the mechanism of change, change there was: the diva was dead, replaced by the singing danseuse.

Further, Herbert's gift for instrumental theatricality was not lost on his contemporaries. Florenz Ziegfeld hired Irving Berlin to write songs for his Follies, but it was Herbert who supplied the music for his historic dance extravaganzas. Indeed, the last composition Herbert wrote was a sketch for a dance number for the Tiller sisters, slated for the Follies of 1924.

Though his primary activity remained composition for the stage, Herbert's most interesting achievement in this period perhaps lay in his involvement with the developing art of film. Fortunately we have his detailed correspondence with the producers of *Fall of a Nation*. It traces the trial-and-error process through which Herbert developed the compositional techniques needed to provide effective musical underscoring for the silent film. During the same seminal period that saw D. W. Griffith developing the close-up, photomontage, and tracking shot, Herbert, in a parallel activity, broke new ground and showed the way to the generation of film composers who followed in his footsteps. Some of the people who were associated with Herbert became important pioneers in the nascent film industry. William Le Baron, who provided the libretto for *Her Regiment*, became an important producer at Paramount. Werner Janssen, the little boy who "auditioned" for Herbert in his father's rathskeller, went on to compose successful film scores. Max Steiner and William Axt, who became legendary figures in the history of Hollywood as creators of some of the greatest film scores, served apprenticeships with Herbert as road-company conductors. Herbert was very careful in his selection of musical associates and, typically, he saw them as co-creators.

> The musical director is a creator and inventor. He is able to take a completely flat production and animate it so that life oozes from it and turn a hopeless failure into a positive success. He is the white hope of many a composer who could safely leave his treasured work in [a director's] hands who, with his little tricks and nuances often brought such results that the composer did not recognize his own work.[1]

Writing to one of his musical associates, Josef Pasternack, who had been entrusted with making recordings of some of Herbert's most famous songs, the composer did not hesitate to express his appreciation for the conductor's contribution.

> My dear Pasternack:
> Just heard Miss Garrison's "Kiss Me Again" record for the first time. Of course she sings it splendidly—fine little artist that she is—but the accompaniment is so perfect, and the rendition of it so "Herbertian"—if I may say so—in other words "the way it ought to be"—that I must compliment you most highly on your part of it. I greet you as one of the few!
> Most sincerely yours,
> Victor Herbert[2]

In 1922 William Randolph Hearst, whose interest in film was more personal than professional, remodeled a theater on Columbus Circle into a special venue to feature the films of his paramour Marian Davies. He hired Herbert to compose overtures for these films—and to conduct them personally at all performances for the inflated salary of $5,000 a week.

Thus, during Herbert's last decade, the ever-restless workaholic expanded his activities, illuminating both new and familiar territory with special creative brilliance.

M'lle Rosita (The Duchess)

This production, the last score Herbert composed for Fritzi Scheff, was the subject of much contention between composer, producer and star. (The details of the problems that Herbert had with the brothers Shubert are discussed in chapter seven; for production details, please see the entry under *The Dutchess*.) Perhaps if the piece had been more successful, the history of *The Duchess* might have been less strained. But it was not to be. Herbert started the final period of his creative work with a calculated attempt to produce a money maker. It turned out to be a flop. From its first performance, the show received negative critical reception. The formula that had worked, more or less, since *Babette*—Scheff + Herbert + sumptuous production values—yielded only twenty-four performances on Broadway. After a tryout tour and the disastrous New York outing, the show closed for a summer break. Serious revision was required. In July Herbert sent his musical secretary, Harry Florence, a "partly new"[3] first-act finale, and the following month provided "three new numbers including a new waltz for Madame Scheff."[4] But even the normally enthusiastic Herbert seemed less than sanguine about his achievement. As he wrote, "Encl. Waltzes. They're all right, I think."[5]

Fritzi had left the cast after the New York run, pleading poor health. With the new numbers in place the production was relaunched in the fall of 1911, with even less success than before. If this was not the weakest of Herbert's efforts, it was close to it. With few redeeming strengths, *The Duchess* expired, leaving behind her a fog of acrimony and bad feeling that was only dispelled by the success of Herbert's next effort, *Sweethearts*.

SWEETHEARTS

Type of work: Romantic Operetta
Premiere: March 24, 1913
Theater: Academy of Music, Baltimore, Md.
New Amsterdam, New York (September 8, 1913)

Cast (Major Players):

Sylvia	Christie MacDonald
Dame Paula (Mother Goose)	Ethel Du Fre Houston
Mikel Mikeloviz	Tom McNaughton
Franz	Thomas Conkey
Lieutenant Karl	Edwin Wilson
Liane	Hazel Kirke

Major Musical Numbers: "Iron, Iron, Iron"; "Sweethearts"; "Jeannette and Her Little Wooden Shoes"; "The Angelus"; "Every Lover Must Meet His Fate"; "Pretty as a Picture"; "In the Convent They Never Taught Me That"; "Pilgrims of Love."

Plot: Sylvia, as an infant princess, has been carried off to ensure her safety during time of war and left in the care of the owner of a laundry in Bruges. Now that she is grown, the man who brought her to Bruges wants to return her to her country so she may claim the throne from Franz, the heir presumptive. Franz, in disguise, has met and fallen in love with Sylvia, who in turn has been engaged to Karl, a notorious womanizer. All of this gets sorted out and Sylvia and Franz form a dual monarchy.

The history of *Sweethearts* is special, not the least because issues involving the title song became the subject of a landmark Supreme Court decision concerning copyrights as well as rights to public performance for profit (see chapter seven).

For a change, the production process for this work went without a hitch, which must have been refreshing, considering the problems associated with *The Duchess*. The producers, Werba and Luescher, were fortunate to have the amiable Christie MacDonald head a first-class company. With her sweet soprano and a stage presence to match, she appeared in almost every scene and carried the show on her pretty, bare shoulders through an evening of charming and refined lyric excellence.

> She is arch without a bit of calculating coquetry . . . sincere, girlish and untheatrical. . . . Her gestures, her movements, the play of her face are pleasant to watch; not a trace of calculation in them. [There is] a pervading prettiness. . . . She does her parts in a light watercolor, whereas the other women of operetta lay on in broad lines and thick hard tints. Musical plays can be a rather rank garden; Miss MacDonald keeps flowerlike.[6]

The book, by Harry Smith and Frederika de Gresac, with lyrics by Smith's brother Robert, took an old story and gave it a new twist: a princess, kidnapped at birth, finds employment as a laundress; she falls in love with a lothario; a prince, traveling incognito, falls for her; lothario loves another; the princess accepts the prince's suit and, when all is revealed, is restored to her title and estates.

Sweethearts premiered in Baltimore on March 24, 1913, with Herbert conducting. It then moved to Boston for several weeks and settled down in Philadelphia for most of August. By this time the infernal heat had gotten to Herbert. As he wrote to Harry Florence,

> Hotel Walton
> Philadelphia
>
> Sunday [August 31, 1913]
>
> Dear Harry
> . . . I am going to New York tomorrow as I feel that I am wasting time here. . . . I have also decided *not* to go down to the N.Y. opening of "Sweethearts." . . . The piece went fine last night and they don't need me anymore. The heat is *awful*. Tell Clifford not to forget to call for me Wed. morning.
> > In haste
> > Your
> > V.H.[7]

Herbert was headed for Lake Placid, eager to escape the New York scorcher and confident that *Sweethearts* was in good hands. Those hands included a brilliant choreographer, the first to share full credits with director Fred Latham on any Herbert show. This was Charles Morgan, Jr., whose contribution to the success of the evening should not be underestimated. For in developing his score, Herbert, ever sensitive to the theatrical forces driving the contemporary theater, based his music on the rhythms and tempos of a succession of dances. His gorgeous melodic inspiration and piquant orchestration, his nonsentimental waltz melodies and clever choral writing, catch new impetus from the spirit of shifting dance movements that provide the score's underpinning.

The title number is, of course, one of his most famous waltzes, but it is also something new: it is consciously unsentimental and displays the sweep and focus of the great instrumental waltzes of Tchaikovsky. "Jeannette and her Little Wooden Shoes" is an Austrian Laendler; "The Angelus" a perfect pas de deux, which in fact is a double duet for Sylvia and Franz, her prince; "Pretty as a Picture" is a tango; "That Is What She Wanted (But This is What She Got)," a mincing two-step; "The Cricket on the Hearth" is a schottische; and the penultimate quartet "Pilgrims of Love," with its unexpected melodic and harmonic switches, is a comic march in the guise of a liturgical send-up. Compared with the 3/4, 2/4, 6/8 metrical arrangement of even the most successful earlier Herbert scores, this dance-influenced approach is a new and subtly insinuating departure. It is key to the infectious appeal of *Sweethearts*.

The force of Herbert's achievement was not lost on the critics. Boston's H. W. Parker, always a stern critic of Herbert when he felt it appropriate, here gives us a picture of the composer at the top of his game:

No wonder that Mr. Herbert's operettas excel all the rest that American composers of light music write. What they do by halves or by quarters or not at all he does in full measure. Watch him as he led the orchestra . . . how precisely and energetically his stick, his arm, his whole body marked the rhythms; how elastically he kept the melodies moving and expanding; how vigorously and firmly he built up ensembles; how broadly and richly he welled the songful phrases in his tunes; how ingenious he was in suspensive catches in them [rubato]; how alertly and surely he "touched in" his instrumental color. . . . Mr. Herbert conducts with large energy, firm grasp and full command. As he conducts so does he compose. . . . Whatever he sets to music paper he invents and fashions with gusto.

Therein is the outstanding virtue of Mr. Herbert's music. He writes it with such quick and ardent melodic invention, such easy range and command of rhythmic and harmonic means, such apt use of orchestra and voices, with such alert sense of the theater and of the particular play, text, and singer . . . that the expert and the exacting hearer is altogether pleased . . . [Likewise] the average listener, with not a thought in the world except the pleasure of the moment. . . . For both expert and the inexpert is the tireless gusto of the whole.[8]

Sweethearts opened at the New Amsterdam Theater on September 8, 1913, and the critics were unanimous in their praise of both composer and star. The *Sun* praised the music for the usual reasons: rich melody, piquant orchestration.[9] The *Tribune* called it one of Herbert's best and "most melodious and musicianly" scores, praising each number individually and the production as "a beautiful one," the chorus as "one of the best ever heard in this city in works of this kind." It was, at last, "an operetta to rejoice over."[10] MacDonald had found a "vehicle which fit her talents exactly."[11] The *New York Press* loved her "splendid acting and singing" and notes that she had "scored a genuine triumph."[12] Even the book, which had been criticized for wordiness and length on the road, had been trimmed so that it received positive notices.

Robert B. Smith has furnished some excellent lyrics. . . . The story might be considered slightly out of the ordinary, inasmuch as it is a consistent story from start to finish. At no time is it necessary to strain things to haul in a musical number. They all appear to belong just where they are—in fact, they seem almost necessary. The story is a plot of considerable more value than the average light opera. In other words it is of sufficient importance to avoid being lost at any point in the performance.[13]

Sweethearts has enjoyed enormous success. It played 136 nights in New York and toured for years. It was successfully revived in Boston in 1915, and again in New York in 1929, as part of a Herbert retrospective. In 1947, with Bobby Clarke as comic star, it enjoyed its longest Broadway run ever—288 performances.

Sweethearts is Victor Herbert at his most enchanting. No doubt, as performance material becomes available, it will charm new generations of theatergoers with its gentle humor and delicate loveliness.

THE MADCAP DUCHESS

Type of work: Romantic Comic Opera
Premiere: October 13, 1913
Theater: Lyceum, Rochester, N.Y.
Globe, New York (November 11, 1913)

Cast (Major Players):

Renaud	Glenn Hall
Master Hardi	Harry Macdonough
Louis XV	Master Percy Helton
Philip of Orleans	Francis K. Lieb
Watteau	David Andrada
Canillac	Henry Vincent
Adam	Herbert Ayling
Stephanie	Josephine Whittell
Gillette	Peggy Wood
Seraphina	Ann Swinburne

Major Musical Numbers "Aurora Blushing Rosily"; "Love and I Are Playing"; "That Is Art"; "Star of Love"; "Far Up the Hill."

Plot: Prince Renaud and Prince Regent Philip are rivals for the love of the Marquise, Stephanie. Philip banishes Renaud from Paris and, while in exile, Renaud meets a servant girl, Seraphina, at a country Inn. Renaud disguises himself and, to fulfill her theatrical ambitions suggests they join a troupe of strolling players on their way to take up residence at Versailles. Soon Renaud learns that Stephanie is not all he thought she was, and he falls in love with Seraphina. She is no commoner but, in fact "the Madcap Duchess" of the title—and therefore able to accept his proposal.

"There was a large audience and it applauded Mr. Herbert, who conducted the first performance of his most pretentious light opera."[14]

"The Madcap Duchess made her bow last night. A most gracious and elaborate bow it was, too, for the new Victor Herbert comic opera is far and away the most pretentious musical offering."[15]

"Pretentious: making claims to importance; making an exaggerated outward show."

"Pretentious" is a word rarely applied to any Victor Herbert work, whether purely instrumental or theatrical. Herbert's production, whether more or less successful, is never less than an honest and workmanlike job. Certainly because of the pressures his myriad activities put on him, his output at times can be described as less than inspired. But "pretentious"? This story of the Duchess Seraphina, "a merry devil in petticoats" who disguises herself as a male in order to escape from her guardians to win the love of the one forbidden to her, is played out amid the faux finery and "existence a la Watteau" of the Court of Louis XV. Perhaps because Herbert's score reflects the posturing and artificiality of life at Versailles, it was perceived as "pretentious," rather than what it is: apt.

In any case, the artificiality of the whole extended to the text of one of its most successful songs, a text quoted by the critics to epitomize the effect of the piece: "To drink cheap wine as though it were a vintage for a king—that is art!"

The libretto and lyrics are by Justin Huntly McCarthy who, with David Stevens, adapted it from McCarthy's novel *Serafina*. The producer was H. H. Frazee; the star, the up-and-coming soubrette Ann Swinburne. An unknown Peggy Wood played her maid, Gillette, and got some of the best notices. As for the mood of the piece, it was romantic, unrelieved by any attempt at comedy: "No line in the entire libretto of 'The Madcap Duchess' was half as funny as the curtain speech of Mr. Victor Herbert. The programme calls it a comic opera, but it is not comic, except in spots, and then the humor is as mild as weak tea."[16] The *Sun* called it "a comic opera dirge,"[17] described the music of the first act as being in "Mr. Herbert's most treacly and ambitious vein," while reserving such faint praise as it could muster for the music of the second act. Here a madrigal, "Far Up the Hill" and the recurring "Love Is a Story That's Old" seemed to catch the ears of audience and critics alike, as did "Star of Love," and "Love and I Are Playing": "Victor Herbert got an ovation when he walked down the aisle of the theater to take his place as leader of the orchestra"[18] on the opening night. That was before the audience had heard the piece. Two months later the company left New York for the road. The tour ended soon afterward, and in spite of revivals in Boston and Brooklyn the following year, nothing has been heard of *The Madcap Duchess* since. The score is not without its high points, but this is an example of how the framework of a piece, if out of touch with the times, can mortally affect the chances for success of the content, however strong.

Type of work: Opera
Premiere: January 24, 1914
Theater: Metropolitan Opera House, New York

Cast (Major Players):

Madeleine Fleury	Frances Alda
Nichette	Leonora Sparkes
Chevalier de Mauprat	Antonio Pini-Corsi
François, Duc d'Esterre	Paul Althouse
Didier	Andres de Segurola

Major Musical Numbers: "A Perfect Day"; "Didier's Monologue."

Plot: On New Year's afternoon Madeleine, a famous opera singer, receives three of her lovers. She invites each to stay for dinner, but each begs off, since each has always dined with his mother that evening. Didier, an unsuccessful artist and Madeleine's childhood friend, has the same obligation, but invites Madeleine to join him at his mother's home. Madeleine prefers to dine alone, with a portrait of her mother that Didier has brought as a New Year's present.

"Wenn es ihnen nicht gefällt, besser kann ich's nicht. If they don't like it, I can't do any better." Thus said Herbert to his friend Fritz Stahlberg, who visited him the morning following the premiere of his second opera, *Madeleine*. Stahlberg found him in his studio surrounded by the Sunday papers. The notices were uniformly negative. Some of them, like Richard Aldrich's review in the *Times*, were scholarly and well considered. Krehbiel's in the *Tribune* was so laced with animus that it brought the long-simmering negative feelings between the two men to a point of bitterness not seen in Herbert's career since the days of Marc Blumenberg and the *Courier*. Krehbiel, with obvious resort to his thesaurus, proclaimed the work "futile, far-fetched, frivolous, fuliginous [referring to odors emitted by bodily orifices], fumid [murky], fustian in the score and inept, ill devised in the text."[19]

Hoping to cheer his mentor and colleague, Stahlberg reminded Herbert that Wagner, in his autobiography, had mentioned that he had attended the play upon which *Madeleine* was based, "Je dine chez ma mere," in Paris, and had been much impressed with it.

"So," Herbert replied, "it pleased Richard Wagner, but it's not good enough for New York music critics!"[20]

It depends what you mean by "it." Here Herbert may have been betrayed by his cosmopolitanism. Fluent in French, the composer had been charmed by the sentiment, tempered with witty satire, of the original of Decourelles and Thibaud. That was what had attracted Wagner. Herbert's musicalization was another matter.

"I am always looking over old plays," Herbert explained to a visitor, "as you may see from the stack of five-cent editions in the bookcase over yonder. Having found an old French play, which was just what I wanted for an opera story, I made a translation of it and commissioned Grant Stewart to prepare a libretto."[21]

Stewart, a fellow member of the Lambs, was an experienced and successful playwright and lyricist. He was the author of one of DeWolf Hopper's major successes, *Mr. Pickwick*, and had provided the lyrics for two well-received musical plays, *The Gay Hussar* and *Little Boy Blue*. Herbert's choice of librettist was not so ill-considered as it had been in the case of *Natoma*.

But why was this slight comedy of ill manners "just what Herbert wanted"? In it a popular and beautiful prima donna finds herself dining alone on New Year's night. She asks various suitors to keep her company, but each replies that it is his custom to dine with his mother on New Year's. Even her maid refuses the invitation on the same grounds. In the end she dines alone, with only a portrait of her mother for company. What was the attraction that caused Herbert to spend time preparing his own translation of the original, that led him to become so intimately involved with the production that, for the only time in his career, he made specific demands about the scenic elements, even submitting an old French print that "gave an excellent idea of the view to be presented to the audience when the curtains are drawn aside for the premiere of *Madeleine*"?[22] Was there something hidden in the events of the little drama that appealed to this most successful of light opera composers on some very deep level?

> As to the underlying dramatic theme of the opera, it will be found in Madeleine's wistful feeling that in spite of her success, she cannot count on the affection of real friends. . . . Briefly, the story concerns the loneliness of Madeleine.[23]

Perhaps the appeal of the plot was personal. Perhaps at the height of his career, Herbert sought an opportunity to express in musical terms what Stewart had summarized in this text:

Success—the mocking phantom we pursue.

"Come, faint heart, come,
For I am happiness";
And when we grasp it, lo, we find
Too oft the joy has lain in the pursuit
And happiness is just as far away.[24]

The sentiment is far from original, but it appealed to the composer.

Herbert divides his setting roughly into two parts. In the earlier sections, when a succession of suitors come to call on Madeleine, the music is pictorial, "conversational" in style. Yet when Madeleine's final visitor, Didier, a painter and a friend from childhood days, arrives, the mood changes. If in fact Herbert identified with the character of Madeleine, the hugely successful, lonely artist surrounded by superficial friends, then the character of a painter from childhood could be a reflection of his beloved grandfather, Samuel Lover. As the two old friends sit together and recall their youth, a warmth and serenity that contrasts strongly with what has gone before infuses the music. And then a turn of unintentional irony enters the picture.

Didier's solution to Madeleine's problem is to invite her to have dinner in the country with his humble parents. He suggests that, instead of wearing her grande dame attire, she wear one of her maid's dresses so as to make his parents feel more comfortable. Madeleine goes off to change, but while she is gone Didier thinks better of his suggestion and concludes that it would not be right to deceive his parents by having Madeleine adopt an appearance that is unnatural to her. When she returns Madeleine agrees: people must remain true to what they are.

If only Herbert had listened to the wisdom of the text he was setting. Instead, faced with a commitment to produce a "high-class" American opera, he fell into the trap that had ensnared three composers who preceded him in the Met's program designed to promote the development of American opera in English. Converse's *The Pipe of Desire*, Parker's *Mona*, and Damrosch's *Cyrano* had all been failures. The critic of *Town and Country* put his finger on the problem.

> What does disappoint us is that all our composers should strive so
> hard to be what they obviously are not. Art with them seems to be
> entirely a matter of imitation. The composer of "Mona" was
> determined to rewrite Wagner. In "Madeleine" Victor Herbert tries
> his best to be a Richard Strauss. Why not be plain Victor Herbert? As

Victor Herbert, prolific inventor of comic opera melodies, he has never failed to give us some sort of entertainment. . . . He is striking, spontaneous, full of life. If he had attacked "Madeleine" in his own fashion he might have done something. . . . The result would have at least been melodious and genuine. Instead he uses a musical idiom which is entirely foreign to him.[25]

In his defense, Herbert responded:

I have tried to place the drama above everything in my treatment of the story. It seems to me that the operatic composer should make it his aim to give the most adequate representation of the dramatic themes, first of all. Thus I have fashioned the score with the idea of giving the singer a chance to deliver the lines with all the effectiveness of a great actor.[26]

Certainly a noble objective. But in attempting to achieve a declamatory style, Herbert left his melodic gifts behind, as if his most natural means of expression were something to be ashamed of in creating grand opera. His one lapse from the (to him) new aesthetic was a gorgeous aria, "A Perfect Day," which was included at the insistence of Frances Alda, who refused to create the title role without some opportunity to exhibit her lyric gift. It was the only moment at the premiere that evoked spontaneous enthusiasm from the audience. As for the rest,

It seems as if Mr. Herbert had been carefully observing the methods of Strauss . . . but it appears also that he has not the cleverness and the capacity of a Strauss, and the result of his efforts to be not musical but descriptive is a score restless, uneasy, but without a real impression of vivacity or animation, lacking musical beauty and refinement and with a false ring of cleverness. . . . It is not a great showing for American opera.[27]

Or, more bluntly, when someone in the lobby of the Met at intermission remarked that *Madeleine* was the best American opera to date, the reply was heard that this was only because it was the shortest.

Nevertheless, there were sixteen curtain calls for composer and ensemble. The house was packed. For Victor Herbert? Not really. The second half of the program featured *Pagliacci*, with Enrico Caruso!

Smarting from his second defeat as a composer of serious opera, Herbert determined that a change of scene was necessary. Clifford was finishing his junior year at Cornell and had made a good record at the college.

Allowed to follow his own instincts at last, he was successfully completing a degree in mechanical engineering and working summers at the Ford plant in Detroit. He had essentially seceded from the family.

Partly as a distraction, partly as an attempt to find a new direction, Herbert had arranged meetings with managers in London, Paris and Berlin to discuss a series of concerts featuring his own serious compositions; there was even the possibility of a commission for a new operetta.

In early April of 1914 Victor, Theresa and Ella set out on what turned out to be an almost fatal wild goose chase. London had never been kind to Herbert's works, and although Ireland's Easter revolution was still two years in the future, Herbert had made no attempt to hide his Hibernian sympathies. This would have done nothing to endear him to the British public. As for concerts on the Continent, the run-up to the explosion in the Balkans that would plunge the world into total war had created an atmosphere of extreme political tension in the major European capitals— not the best atmosphere for new musical projects to go forward. As it turned out, Herbert was never to see Paris or Berlin again.

Soon after his arrival in London, Herbert was contacted by the director of the Band of the Coldstream Guards, one of Europe's premier military ensembles. Years earlier, when Herbert had been serving as conductor of the 22nd Regiment Band, he had invited Dan Godfrey, the visiting conductor of the Coldstream, to conduct. Now McKenzie Regan, current bandmaster of the Coldstream, invited the family to a rehearsal and surprised them with an "all-Herbert" program, a return of compliment. This was followed by a private tour of Buckingham Palace. During the tour Herbert complained of abdominal pain, and the following day was operated on for acute appendicitis. His condition remained touch-and-go for several weeks. Theresa was shocked, for in all their years together Herbert had never been seriously ill. As soon as he was well enough to travel, she insisted that they return to New York.[28]

On his return, somewhat chastened by his brush with mortality and suddenly aware of his advancing years (he was then fifty-five), Herbert seemed more determined than ever to create something serious. He still harbored bitter feelings about the fate of his grand-opera projects. Like Sullivan before him, while recognizing the value of his light works, he seemed to feel that true greatness lay only in the area of "serious" composition. Again and again, in his public utterances, he returned to the subject of *Natoma*, even at one point defending its indefensible libretto. "There was much talk about the libretto when it [*Natoma*] was first sung here, and the critics had harsh things to say about this verse and that verse. But that doesn't convince me that the libretto was worthless or is worthless."[29]

He went on to blame the failure of American opera in general on a whole litany of causes—anything but the failure of composer or librettist. He claimed the producers refused to revive the works, thus denying the public a chance to become familiar with them. The lack of box-office draw was a flawed argument on the producers' parts, since inferior foreign (read, Italian) works were given repeated hearings (*Montemezzi* and *Mascagni* were the villains here). Even the audience was to blame, since people didn't go to the opera to hear the music, they went to hear the stars; and the stars in their turn were faulted, since Caruso and Ferrar refused to sing in English; finally, "modern" music, which the critics praised, was basically "insincere."

> I could write chords and combinations of notes, orchestrate them in an entirely novel way that would split the ears of the audience and some, I suppose, would say, "wonderful." But I would not be sincere in so doing. And I do not do it. I believe in melody and I maintain that every composer whose work had lasted—from Bach to Wagner—has been a melodist, first of all.[30]

This is where his heart was, still aching from the failures of *Natoma* and *Madeleine*, when an offer arrived that gave him his final opportunity to create a serious theatrical score, an opera manqué.

THE DEBUTANTE

Type of work: Romantic Musical Comedy
Premiere: September 21, 1914
Theater: New Nixon, Atlantic City, N.J.
Knickerbocker, New York (December 7, 1914)

Cast (Major Players):

Elaine	Hazel Dawn
Philip Frazer	Wilmuth Merkyl
Godfrey Frazer	William Darforth
Paul Masson	J. Abbott Worthley
Irma	Zoe Barnett
Armand	Stewart Baird
Ezra Bunker	Will West

Major Musical Numbers: "All for the Sake of a Girl"; "The Golden Age"; "Love of the Lorelei"; "The Music of the Future"; "Call Around Again."

Plot: Philip and Elaine have been reared together, and Philip's father expects them to marry. Philip, however, has fallen for Irma, an exotic Russian dancer. She has also attracted the attention of the father. Thus, father and son become rivals. But Elaine, through a series of plots and plans, manages to snare Philip at last.

December 7 and 8, 1914, are days that will live, if not in infamy, then in the history of the American musical theater. On the earlier date, at the Knickerbocker Theater in New York, Victor Herbert and Harry B. Smith's *The Debutante* had its premiere. The next night, the New Amsterdam Theater saw the first performance of *Watch Your Step*, a "syncopated musical show" by Irving Berlin and . . . Harry B. Smith. Talk about working both sides of the street!

Oh, the critics loved Victor, with his "exquisite music" full of "light and graceful airs, skillful instrumental coloring" with "nowhere anything trite or commonplace" to be heard. There was "warm melodic invention," expressed in such numbers as "All for the Sake of a Girl"—a charming waltz that Herbert used as a leitmotiv to unify the score; and the hit of the evening, "Call Around Again,"[31] a saucy and insinuating duo.

As for Irving Berlin, the critics made short work of him.

His music is without any distinction whatever and is even devoid of his usual whistleable qualities. When one considers that he has written such syncopated masterpieces as "Alexander's Ragtime Band" and "Mesmerizing Mendelssohn Tune," one naturally expects something that will linger in the memory. However, what it lacks in melody it more than suffices in volume.[32]

Nevertheless, the die was cast. The "guns of August" had foretold a fundamental change in all aspects of Western society, from which the American musical theater was not to be excepted. Although Harry Smith bridged the gap between the two styles that Herbert and Berlin represented, and although the critics came down unanimously on Herbert's side, the public cast its vote for the new, infectious rhythms of Irving Berlin, and was eager to abandon the "exquisite." *The Debutante* lasted forty-eight performances. *Watch Your Step* went on and on and on for 175, and then went on an extended tour.

It was not that John Fisher, the producer of *The Debutante*, had not pulled out all the stops. The elaborate production had a beautiful and multi-talented star, Hazel Dawn—who had become the toast of Broadway after her performance in *The Pink Lady*. She was more than an effective personality. She could sing, dance, *and* play the violin. All of these talents were given full play in the piece. And she could act. She scored a great personal success, singing her numbers with "charming effect," and in her dance movements she was a "picture of grace." Boston was kind to *The Debutante*. "Herbert's music is melodious, expressive, dramatic. It always has character and distinction. The liveliness is not vulgarity. In the dance music and in the rollicking ditty there is always the consciousness of a well-graced musician amusing himself, yet respecting his art."[33]

But it seemed that all this was no longer enough. The piece, for all its strengths and graces, was unrelievedly old-fashioned. Even if the dance elements became more and more prominent, they were the wrong dances. All this became clear because of the contrast exposed by the back-to-back debuts of the Herbert and Berlin shows.

Dillingham—the genius producer—had now cast his lot with Berlin, and provided a huge production frame at the New Amsterdam for *Watch Your Step*. Smith's title was well chosen, for the focus of the piece was dance. Not narrative or illustrative ballet; dance rhythms were here to become an equal player with melody in the structure of the new musical review form. Although commentators have remarked that this first big hit of Berlin's career made him the star of the evening, the mechanism of that stellar status was his unique ability to inject into his songs equal parts of evocative melody and infectious dance rhythms. Spicy rhythm—"ginger" in the slang of the period—was the secret of the success of *Watch Your Step*.

For the visual embodiment of the new style Dillingham had chosen the premier ballroom dancers of the era, Vernon and Irene Castle. " 'Watch Your Step' may be classified as a combination rag-time riot and dancing delirium. It is not Irving Berlin but the Castles to whom we must look for the phenomenal success of this entertainment."[34]

Incidentally, both *The Debutante* and *Watch Your Step* featured musical-satirical production numbers in their second acts. Herbert provided a very clever and amusing send-up of "modern music" anticipating the "Ballet Loose" that he later wrote for *The Century Girl*. Berlin went him one better, "An ensemble number in which the ghost of Verdi appears and protests to the dancing revelers against the irreverent syncopation of his 'Rigoletto,' only to be silenced by the reply that ginger is being injected into the opera."[35]

It was the ghost of Verdi who appeared on the New Amsterdam stage, but it might just as easily have been the spirit of Herbert himself. He was not insensitive to the inroads the new dance craze was making in the popular taste of audiences. He himself had produced a ragtime version of "The Streets of New York" as an encore for the second finale of *The Red Mill*. But suddenly the success of *Watch Your Step* and the failure of *The Debutante*—despite the fact that he had provided a superior score for it—just two years after the triumph of *Naughty Marietta*, brought him up short. Harry G. Sommers, business manager of the Knickerbocker Theater has left us a moving portrait of Herbert at this watershed moment of his career. "During the run of 'The Debutante' Victor Herbert lost his exuberant spirits. He used to come into the theater every evening, sit down on the balcony steps and talk moodily of the old times."[36] Still, even though Victor may have been down, he was far from out. He had used dance as a motive force in *Sweethearts*. If it was the new dances that the public craved, that is what he would soon supply. But not until he made a final foray into the world of opera.

CHAPTER 16

AN OPERA MANQUÉ (1915–1916)

When the letter arrived, Herbert was intrigued. Here was an approach from Thomas Dixon, director-general of the National Drama Corporation, suggesting that they meet at the corporation's New York headquarters to discuss the possibility of his providing an original score for a new film, Dixon's *The Fall of a Nation*.

Thomas Dixon was a name well known to Herbert. He was the successful author of twenty-two novels that had sold five million copies, and of nine plays and five screenplays. His novel *The Clansman* had recently been filmed by D. W. Griffith as *The Birth of a Nation*, the first million-dollar movie ever made and the most important serious film to have been created to date. Politician, minister and popular Lyceum speaker, Dixon was a man whose varied accomplishments could rival Herbert's. He was also a man passionately devoted to a political ideal, and this also made him attractive to a man like Herbert. Further, the businessman in the composer must have been excited by the opportunity to work with a man who had created a film that had grossed 18 million dollars on an investment of five hundred thousand.

Dixon's particular political agenda concerned the pacifism that he perceived as a threat to the survival of freedom in the United States. He was devoted to awakening the American people to purported dangers from without and within, and to advocating a spirit of preparedness in the face of the burgeoning threat from European hostilities.

After a preliminary meeting Herbert was sold on the project. A contract was developed and five hundred dollars changed hands to seal the bargain. Shortly thereafter, Dixon sent him a second payment with a letter[1] from the West Coast that detailed the progress being made on the filming. This fascinating document reflects how, from its earliest days, Hollywood was the natural home of hype and hyperbole.

My Dear Mr. Herbert—
We are making fine progress with the outdoor work. I will send you photographs of some of the big 42 Centimetre guns we have built and

put into action. We are putting on the screen now the most thrilling battle the world has ever seen. Our setting looking down on sunlit slopes piled with dead and dying and charging thousands, framed between black, frowning hills wreathed with exploding shells, is something words *can not* convey. Believe me when I tell you that our battle scene will make the Birth of a Nation look like 30 cents compared to a million dollars. . . .

We give you a picture of those great guns lit with the glare of hell at night belching flame 12 feet high with 60 gunners swarming around them like so many demons. The caption is:

THROUGH THE NIGHT THE GREAT GUNS
ROARED THE DEATH KNELL OF A NATION.

We are producing battle effects on a scale unheard of in thrilling power. Combined with your music at its best, we will make a sensation that will shake America and make fortunes for us all.

I want you to come to Los Angeles a little later and see what we have done and are doing. It will be absolutely necessary to give you an idea of the grandeur.

Dixon then got down to specifics:

My scenario expert can give you revised copies of each act as you wish them. The final division into acts is as follows:

THE PROLOGUE	THE MIGHT OF KINGS—12 minutes
ACT I	A NATION FALLS—50 minutes
ACT II	THE HEEL OF THE CONQUEROR—30 minutes
ACT III	THE UPRISING—40 minutes

The novel gives you but a feeble idea of the grip and sweep of the action of the play. . . .

If this play lands as I see it now—with one fourth of it already taken—you should make a royalty of $1500 to $2400 per week the first year in the United States.

Now came the final ploy that hooked Herbert: the first grand opera cinema in history—to be shown at the Metropolitan Opera House—the very scene of Herbert's most wrenching failures. An opportunity for revenge and redemption.

Please do not forget to approach the managers of the Metropolitan Opera House and find if it can be had for our production from May to November. If we can get it we could make this the first grand opera cinema in history.

Herbert was his! Or so he thought. Herbert replied in kind—perhaps with tongue in cheek—for his diction almost matched Dixon's:

December 4th, 1915

My dear Mr. Dixon

Your letter is most interesting and I can very well feel that you are engaged in a work that will astound the world, and surpass even your own expectations!

There is one thing you must do for me: get someone, (who is musical enough to do this) to give me some idea of the *duration* of the pictures—in other words try to send me a book with indications of the "time" of *each page*, or of the period of pictures.

You will remember that I told you, *before* signing the contract, that I couldn't think of coming to Los Angeles—for various reasons—but that must not worry you,—the artist's imagination comes from within, not without—and Schiller never saw Switzerland but nevertheless he was able to write a fairly good "William Tell."

Your 42 Centimeter gun episode will be hard to depict musically—but I will promise you to let loose my wildest imagination on the subject!

I am deeply interested in the work and am working at it daily as hard as I can. (Don't you think it is going to be *very* long?) [Crossed out] It does seem to be rather long, don't you think so? And right here I beg of you to advise me at once of any *cuts* or *alternations*—it takes a long time to write music, especially such complicated music, and you might save me a lot of time by advising me of any possible changes in the book.

In regard to the Metropolitan Opera House idea I will do the best I can and will report to you in due time.

Don't overwork yourself! Please!

Very early on, Herbert was asserting his independence. His instinct demanded specifics. Naturally music—an art which exists in time—must know the dimensions and limits of its framework. Further, Herbert was prescient in intimating that changes, cuts, and so on might create problems for a composer. Already, with this first exchange of letters, Herbert and Dixon had defined two basic elements of film scoring that neither was willing to accommodate: Dixon needed the actual presence of the composer during shooting and editing. This Herbert refused. Herbert envisioned a situation in which filming would proceed in an orderly fashion with few changes, a creative process almost devoid of cutting and editing—another impossibility. Nevertheless, the work went on.

Dec. 10th, '15

My dear Mr. Herbert—

I will give you the acting copy of the play at the earliest possible moment, the first act next week, the second act will follow. I can then give you an approximation of the time. You may be sure that the manuscript which you now have in hand is twice as long as the acting version will be. The only thing you can do with the manuscript in its present form is to get your theme music without reference to duration. . . .

I find that it will be impossible to divide the play into three acts and a prologue. It will be divided into a prologue and two acts as originally planned. . . .

The Birth of a Nation last week reached a highwater mark playing to over $100,000.00 gross, $47,337.00 net profits, which is a pretty good week's work.

P.S. You can figure April 30th as our finishing day on the film. Hope to open in New York May 25.

In late December Herbert responded. He had read the revised shooting script, and his sensibilities had been offended by specific references to America's "enemy." This was the period when the Untied States was nominally neutral with respect to the European hostilities, although President Wilson clearly was sympathetic to the British cause (he had permitted over two billion dollars of wartime loans to England). Herbert's love of Germany was offended by elements in the scenarios, and he did not hesitate to make his feelings clear.

My dear Mr. Dixon—

I was glad to get your letter. Your plan to have a prologue and two acts is certainly a great improvement.

Right here I beg to call your attention to the fact that twice in the 2nd Act you call the attacking army "Germans." I think that the invading force must be an imaginary country's army. You told me it would be when I saw you at your office and I sincerely hope you have not changed your mind. To offend hundreds of thousands of our best citizens in that way would be a great mistake and I sincerely hope that the invading army will remain "imaginary." Anyway to think that the Germans would ever want to invade America is absurd—but even if they did, they would never act as they are made to in your picture. I studied in Germany and although Irish have a soft spot for that country and its people.

The music for the prologue and 1st Act is nearly finished and looks very good to me—but I can't go any further with it until I get the films sent here so that I can *time* the scenes and then begin to *orchestrate*. *That takes a lot of time, and can't be done in a couple of weeks!*"

Herbert then spells out a problem that has been the bane of all film composers, the conflict between the very essence of cinematic art and the requirements of effective musical development.

In composing the music for this wonderful picture I find that the constant changing of locality and atmosphere (the very nature of the moving picture) is the greatest obstacle for the composer. For instance: I have doped out what I consider a (very appropriate) [crossed out] rather beautiful "Love-theme" for Vassar (outside of the individual theme I have given him.) But the 2nd Act is so full of "rumpus" (pardon the word) that I don't seem to get a chance to play it at all—at least not more than three or four bars. Couldn't you squeeze at least a few *lyrical moments* (giving real musical atmosphere) into the 2nd Act?

In other words, Herbert is pointing out that putting a musical score to a film is not just a matter of cutting, pasting and timing. The scenario must be constructed so that due consideration and opportunity is given for the composer to work out his themes in a mature way, in line with the laws of musical development. Thus the composition of the scenario must take into consideration the structural demands of the composer's art.

I fully realize how difficult it may be to do that in this case—but for the musician it is of the greatest importance to bring his main themes to a victorious ending, which he can only do if he is given the proper situation *and time*.

Herbert then turns his attention to practical concerns that Dixon had not considered.

There is also a natural limitation to the powers of the orchestra. No man can saw or blow for an hour without resting a bit—and there seems to be no let up in the second act as it stands now.

I hope you will consider the above suggestions in the spirit they are given in—I am so enthusiastic about the work and have been working so conscientiously on it, that I feel I must give you an idea of my impressions.

Dixon did not respond to Herbert's concerns. He was apparently focused on tying down the Metropolitan Opera House as a venue for the premiere. There had been a split between Giffith, who had directed *Birth of a Nation*, and Dixon, and the auteur had ventured to direct *Fall* on his own. He was determined that Griffith would not beat him to the Met.

TELEGRAM   JAN 6, 1916   3:19 AM
VICTOR HERBERT. OFFER METROPOLITAN SEVENTY THOUSAND
DOLLARS TWENTY WEEKS BEGINNING MAY 29TH. GRIFFITH AFTER IT
FOR HIS NEW PLAY. WE MUST LAND IT WE MIGHT POSSIBLY BEGIN
MAY 15TH DO YOUR LEVEL BEST.

As a ridiculous Hollywood-style fillip he added:

COULD PUT ALL METROPOLITAN DIRECTORS INTO SCENE SAVING
NEW YORK BY RANSOM IF IT WOULD HELP YOU
THOMAS DIXON

The image of Otto Kahn et alia in a silent movie "saving New York by ransom" must be one of the most ridiculous "concepts" ever to emerge from Hollywood. A second telegram followed shortly.

TELEGRAM   JAN 7, 1916   11:15 AM
IN CASE YOU SUCCEEED [sic] IN CONTRACT ARRANGE TO KEEP THE
FACT A PROFOUND SECRET FROM ALL RIVALS AND THE PUBLIC
THOMAS DIXON

Herbert had still not received a clear response to the concerns expressed in his most recent letter. He tried again.

Couldn't you send me another script with your own suggestions as to the general character of the music you would select for the 2nd Act, if you had to select it from music already existing? I mean in regard to the *musical conception* of the various portions of your story of this 2nd Act. In a piece of this magnitude the composer should also receive some consideration—and in this second Act there seems no place for my love themes for the two lover couples! Yet music *demands* lyric moments—and a continued "rumpus" in the orchestra becomes very tiresome after a while. And don't forget that we have had so much of this latter in the 1st Act that we are in danger of an anticlimax in the 2nd Act in regard to the musical possibilities. *Do* let me hear from you soon! I am terribly anxious to have this thing surpass all expectations—but I am worried over this 2nd Act and would like to have a word from you regarding my suggestions.

I hope we will have an answer from the Metrop. people before you receive this!

Herbert soon had the Met's answer.

I find Metropolitan has had offer for some time from concern unknown to me.

They offer for three months beginning May first forty thousand dollars and all expenses.

Better wire me instructions.

At last Dixon responded. The dates the Met offered were not acceptable, and the Liberty Theater (scene of the premiere of *Birth of a Nation*) would be secured. He also sent Herbert "new material." Herbert responded that what was "new" was no improvement on the old, and the political issues now became so irritating that he threatened to resign from the project, although the threat was redacted before his draft letter was sent.

I have your wire and letter containing the new scene. Prologue was much more suitable for musical purposes and more rational than the new one.

As I stated in my last wire there must not be any more radical changes or I could never finish the work on time. You (mention German kings and) [crossed out] promised me that the nationality of the invading army would be absolutely imaginary, but you mention and have inserts about Germany and German princes frequently. I will not be a party to (such nonsense) [crossed out] the violation of our President's proclamation of neutrality. (England is our danger, not Germany and I would not be connected with such a thing for a million dollars) [crossed out].

You promised that your novel was to be the basis of this work and I must insist that you (keep your word or I must refuse to continue) [crossed out] carry out your promise. That was the condition under which I undertook the work.

Herbert's hot letter seems to have caught Dixon's attention at last. He found a musical intermediary who could respond to Herbert's concerns. Herbert reacted in a less fiery tone. But he remained no less demanding.

This is in response to your letters of January 27th and 29th. Mr. Cushing's most intelligent letter and his detailed suggestions as to the remainder of the music were very welcome.

I was much pleased to find that most of his ideas coincided with mine, and what I have already written.

As to coming to Los Angeles and putting the picture on there that is *absolutely impossible*. I told you *before signing the contract* that I couldn't possibly leave N.Y., as I have many other duties and responsibilities here, which I can't leave, no matter how important the complection of this music for your picture is. Even if I could come myself—I would be helpless without my *many* copyists and the needed clerical assistance.

It is a fact that you don't seem to realize that it has taken the greatest composers from 4 to 5 years, sometimes even 10 years ("Louise," for example) to write a grand opera. When you say that you think I can wait with the orchestration until I see the picture you show that you do not realize the time it takes to orchestrate and have copied a composition of this magnitude and scope.

Having great experience composing for the stage, I have *written* all the music so that I can easily cut, simplify, repeat etc. etc. when I see the picture, if the pictures follow your book at all.

But the most important point is this: If you go about changing, as you have done, *the entire character and sequence of some scenes*, getting away from the central idea of your original book, you make it utterly impossible for any man to write and complete *the score in time for delivery*.

It stands to reason that you would set out to make your picture according to your original idea but you seem to change your mind from day to day—then the music *never* could be finished. The Prologue and the 1st Act I have completed and both are fine. Changes in regard to the length or duration of that music can be made in the four weeks you promised me for rehearsal here, but nobody in the world could get ready a completely different version, necessitating different thematic material within that time here or elsewhere.

I must remind you again of your promise not to call the invading force and European potentates by name. That point was one of the first to be discussed and I must hold you to your word. There is no reason for worry or anxiety in regard to the work if you will kindly consider the points I have raised and I am convinced that my work will surpass your fondest expectations when you hear it here.

Then, to his astonishment, Herbert received still another version of the prologue. Imbedded in his reply is the intimation that he is dealing with an improviser—a man flying by the seat of his pants. In other words, from Herbert's point of view, an amateur whose nonprofessional conduct was more than he would tolerate. He quickly retreated to his standard ploy of referring to contractual obligations he had faithfully fulfilled and that, by implication, Dixon had not.

Prologue all finished and orchestrated and partly copied and much of its subject matter I have used throughout the piece.

Am amazed to receive absolutely different prologue today. Do you suppose that I can go on changing continually? I have changed the first Act several times already although you had sent me a script you called the *final revision*. The first Act is all composed and mostly orchestrated, and if you make any radical changes again it would be a physical impossibility for any living man to complete this tremendous task in the given time (even if I was willing to go on with your experimenting) [crossed out.]

My music follows the pictures minutely and it is impossible to keep on changing constantly and I don't propose to do so.

(Honoring the contract you) [crossed out] Under the contract you were to deliver to me the manuscript "not later than September 25th, 1915" I have fulfilled my part of the contract to the letter.

The new material Dixon had sent contained a bathetic episode in which a little immigrant Italian boy is seen in the ruins of the lower East Side, searching for his father. Further, it was suggested that it might be more effective to introduce a Hawaiian tyke at this point, together with a typical island melody. Here is Herbert's reaction.

My Dear Mr. Dixon—

I received the "Aloah" song and also your letter of February 8th. Allow me to tell you that this song is a distinct "chestnut" (here and elsewhere). The Hawaiian singers and instruments finding the public bored to death with it.

I am convinced that something more original will have a better effect. I have already written a plaintive melody in Italian style which will be much more suitable and effective than "Aloah."

If you could see the stack of music I have in front of me and which is nearly all orchestration you would hurry the answer to my lengthy letter.

Across the bottom of the pencil copy of this draft Herbert has scrawled "Hooray Friendly Sons!" No doubt at this juncture Herbert needed a night out with the boys!

Dixon was apparently an inexhaustible source of risible suggestion. He followed his Hawaiian gambit with the idea of adding a chorus to the music of the prologue "just for a few bars." By this time Herbert was so worn down that he could only muster a formal reply. His short fuse, which he had kept under wraps so far, had now been extinguished in a flood of disbelief at the stuff coming out of Hollywood. He dispatched his faithful musical assistant, Harold Sanford, to the coast to "supervise the fitting to the picture of the especially written Herbert music."[2] By now he had decided to keep the whole project at arm's length.

In regard to your idea of having a chorus I am afraid that you have not considered the following points:

To have the chorus sing, and sing only a few bars in the prologue, would create a musical anti-climax not to mention the fact that it is impossible to get musical effects out of a *few bars only*.

Have you thought of the fact that a *chorus* has to consist of at least 40 or 50 people? Have you considered the very considerable expense? And if we had such a chorus why shouldn't they sing again? And if you wanted them to, how could I at this hour remodel the whole scheme?

By May, mirabile dictu, the final cut was complete, the orchestra was in rehearsal, and Victor Herbert was out flacking.

For the first time in the history of American pictorial drama a complete accompanying score will be played that has never been heard anywhere else. When listening to music that marks the flight of cavalry you will not say, "Oh, that is the Ride of the Valkyries" nor in scenes of stress and storm will you be regaled by the strains of "The Hall of the Mountain King." In brief, the musical programme will not be a mosaic or patchwork of bits of Wagner, Grieg, Verdi, Bizet and others, but will be strictly new, as individually written to each particular scene.

And then came the world premiere of *The Fall of a Nation*, dubbed "lively, interesting and sometimes preposterous"—with Herbert's music.

For this motion picture Victor Herbert prepared a special musical accompaniment, and both he and Mr. Dixon were in evidence at the Liberty theater last night. The other members of the large audience found unfolded there an unbridled photo play of the battle, murder, and sudden death species, much of it graphic, and exciting, some of it quite absurd, and all of it undeniably entertaining. . . . "The Fall of a Nation" is full of thrills. . . . The enemy is a debt ridden participant of the present war, a country of incredible efficiency whose commanding officers are given to mustaches strangely like the Kaiser's. . . .

Mr. Herbert's score is effective. It helps a lot. It is easy enough to find miscellaneous musical motifs to accompany a photo play, but here we have a score adjusted also to its rhythms. Of course there are dissonant crashes for the battle scenes. In one scene of lamentation the figure on the screen moves to the measures of a strain that is a blending of "Lead kindly Light" with "Taps." And in the prologue the origins of this country are traced, in scenes which show it as a place of refuge and new life for the variously oppressed of Europe, to a musical accompaniment wherein is woven from time to time the airs of our national anthems. . . .

Like all big spectacular pictures it must face the eternal question, "Is it as good as 'The Birth of a Nation'?" It has not yet been possible to answer this in the affirmative.[3]

In involving himself with the development of a new art form, Herbert lays to rest forever the charge that he was uninvolved with the theatrical elements of the drama for which he created music. We have, of course, pointed out the evidence of how closely he worked with his librettists and directors to create musical scores that were theatrically effective and sensitive to the comedy or drama of which they were to be an integral part. Here, with this exchange of letters, we see just how much a theatrical artist Victor Herbert was. Along the way he defined for those who came after him the processes and techniques needed to create an effective film score. And if his work was not entirely successful, the evidence shows how well he did—considering that he was invading terra incognita with a willful and mercurial collaborator as his guide.

Herbert remained fond of what he had written, even if the result of his final attempt to create a serious theatrical score was not a success. Fritz Stahlberg reports:

> At his home I saw the piano score of this work on his desk and asked him for old times sake to let me have it to play through once again.
>
> "All right, my boy," he said, "but bring it back. Wiedersehen macht Freude."[4]

Stahlberg returned the score, but not with joy, for in the few weeks that followed this conversation Herbert had died.

CHAPTER 17

ACT THREE: SCENE TWO (1914–1924)

The Society of American Dramatists and Composers, an ante-cedent of ASCAP, was founded in New York in 1892. On the occasion of its twenty-first birthday the organization's membership gathered in the upstairs banquet hall of Delmonico's to celebrate the anniversary and to pay tribute to its most illustrious member, Victor Herbert. His image in the profession was reflected in the make-up of the assembly. Over one hundred and fifty playwrights and composers gathered to honor him and to gently roast their guest of honor.

The president of the society, Augustus Thomas, served as toast master and called on many of Herbert's colleagues to speak. Seated at the head table next to Theresa and Ella, Herbert heard himself extolled by Rida Johnson Young and John Philip Sousa, among many others. Thomas himself began with a brief summary of Herbert's career and then called upon the composer to provide a few opening remarks. "I don't want to start any trouble for Victor when he gets home," Thomas concluded, "but I must tell you he shines more at a stag party than he would here."[1] Giggles and guffaws greeted the reference to Herbert's well-known skill as an off-color raconteur. Herbert rose from his seat. "I have a bad mem-ory, which is a good thing for a composer to have. But I know that memory, bad as it is, will retain for the rest of my life the debt of gratitude I owe you for doing me this great honor."[2] Then, turning to Thomas, he likened himself to King Lear and, anticipating the tributes that were yet to come his way, he turned to the audience and concluded with good humor, "Bore on, I will endure."[3]

Endure he did, as the speeches lasted well into the early hours. Less than a month later, on the occasion of his fifty-fourth birthday, his home on 108th Street was besieged by well-wishers. Politicians, opera singers (Caruso among them), bankers, billiard players, amateur card trick ex-perts, librettists, lawyers and even a number of musicians gathered to honor this beloved figure of the American musical stage.

THE ONLY GIRL

Type of Work: Musical Comedy
Premiere: October 1, 1914
Theater: New Nixon, Atlantic City, N.J.
Thirty-ninth Street Theater, New York (November 2, 1914)

Cast: (Major Players)

Alan Kimbrough	Thurston Hall
Sylvester Martin	Richard Bartlett
John Ayre	Jed Prouty
Andrew McMurray	Ernest Terrence
Ruth Wilson	Wilda Bennett
Birdie Martin	Louise Kelley
Margaret Ayre	Josephine Whittell
Jane McMurray	Vivian Wessell
Patrice La Montrose	Adele Rowland

Major Musical Numbers: "The More I See of Others"; "When You're Away"; "Personality"; "Tell It Over Again"; "Connubial Bliss"; "You Have to Have a Part to Make a Hit"; "When You're Wearing the Ball and Chain"; "Equal Rights."

Plot: A librettist is seeking a composer. He finds one in his upstairs neighbor, a talented young woman. They agree to work together—platonically, for he and his bachelor friends have sworn to remain unattached. One by one each falls in love with "the only girl" for him, and eventually librettist and composer follow suit.

The summer of 1913 had been a scorcher. It was so hot Victor Herbert decided not to conduct the opening of *Sweethearts* in New York. Instead, he fled to Lake Placid to enjoy the swimming, boating and hiking that had always provided refreshment and respite from the pressures of his musical and theatrical activities. He spent his down time preparing for the upcoming season at Willow Grove Park and his popular Sunday night concert series at the Broadway Theater with the Victor Herbert Orchestra.

At the same time, his most effective collaborator, Henry Blossom, had escaped in the opposite direction. He owned a summer place in the Pocono Mountains of Pennsylvania. One evening, on a busman's holiday, he decided to attend a summer stock performance of a play he had never seen, *Our Wives*, an adaptation by Frank Mandel and Helen Kraft of a light comedy by Ludwig Fulda, *Jugendfreunde*. As translated and revised by Kraft and Mandel, the play had lasted for only forty performances on Broadway; but Blossom was ever on the lookout for new material, and he saw the play's potential as the basis for a contemporary musical comedy. When he discovered that Herbert's good friend and publisher, Isidore Witmark, owned the copyright, he was encouraged to pursue the project. He called Herbert at Lake Placid and suggested that he read the script. Witmark sent him a copy, and Herbert was fascinated by the possibilities of the plot.

Set in an apartment in a big city, it is the story of a successful librettist and his three friends—all of whom swear to avoid the "ball and chain" of marriage. Still, one by one, his friends fall victim to feminine wiles and desert him as each declares himself to be "the happiest man in the world," since each has found "the only girl" for him. Of course they tell him that marriage will make no difference in their friendship, and that their wives will be bosom friends. The librettist has his doubts, but he has no time for marriage. He is looking for a composer to set his new libretto. He hears an exquisite melody from the apartment above and arranges to meet the musician playing it. To his surprise the composer is a beautiful young woman. With apprehension, he agrees to work with her, but only after she agrees that they will "treat each other as machines" and forget all about romance. So they work together as two machines until they reach the point where they discover sex ex machina. After six weeks the old friends and their wives show up for a dinner party, and it soon becomes clear that marriage is not all bliss. The wives can't stand one another; they say catty things and the party breaks up in a row. Nevertheless, the librettist—ever the optimist—declares that *he* is, in fact the "happiest man in the world" and has found "the only girl" for him, even if the old relationships have been broken up and new ones must take their place.

Herbert jumped at the chance to write a score for a show that was contemporary and completely different from anything he had done before. There was a small cast and no chorus. There was also an unhackneyed plot. Blossom set to work at once, and Witmark lined up Joe Weber as producer. Within a month Herbert had the complete libretto before him. One week later the score was finished in a white heat—a record even for him. And what a score it was! The energy and enthusiasm with which the creators attacked this project shines through every inspired page. Both songs and ensembles advance the plot and reinforce the humorous text. For the melody that first brings the lovers together, Herbert produced one of his loveliest and most enduring creations, "When You're Away." Loving, poignant, warm and subtle, it is a distillation of everything that makes Herbert instantly appealing. Harmonically rich and melodically as original a strain as he ever wrote, it is a summing-up of his style—quintessential Herbert in thirty-two bars. Only Victor Herbert could have written this piece.

With "The Only Girl" Herbert completely abandons his nineteenth-century roots. Here at last is something truly modern. When in the third act the three former bachelors describe their new lives, "When You're Wearin' the Ball and Chain," and are quickly bested by the wives in the trio, "Women's Rights!" we know that Herbert and Blossom are in new territory.

But who was to star in such a natural, unaffected piece? Not a standard operetta diva. Enter again the sweltering summer of 1913. Joe Weber went to Asbury Park, New Jersey, in search of sea breezes. One evening he attended a concert at the Village Hall, "simply because he had nothing to do and was willing to occupy a few hours with anything that was not insufferably boring."[4] There he heard Wilda Bennett, a local belle. She came from a non-theatrical family, indeed from a family that opposed her theatrical ambitions. They were leaders of Asbury Park society, and her life had been full of "bridge parties, charity bazaars and other social pleasures."[5] She had a good voice, enjoyed singing at church, and dreamed of more. At the concert Weber attended she "sang as well as she could—and they seemed to like me."[6] This fresh, unspoiled natural quality was a perfect foil for the self-important, posturing, show-biz figure of the librettist. As soon as Weber heard her, he knew he had found his star.

The company was assembled, Fred Latham hired as director, and, after a pre-Broadway trial, opened at the 39th Street Theater on November 2, 1914. *The Only Girl* was an instant success. There followed ten months—240 performances—on Broadway and two years on the road. There was even a three-month run in London, not Herbert's most welcoming venue. From opening night on, the critics took its measure.

> There are 14 numbers at least one of which will be sung throughout the land. It is the melody, 'When You're Away.' It comes as an intermezzo and runs like a leading motive through the score. . . . What the audience thought of the music is indicated by the fact that every one of the 14 numbers had to be repeated, some of them three or four

times. All are short, appropriate and orchestrated with the skill of a master. . . . One of the merits of these musical numbers is that they grow naturally out of the situations, instead of being dragged on stage by the hair."[7]

It has a libretto singularly free from banal business and hackneyed humor. . . . It is very good fun. The dialog is uncommon. The piece has a sound foundation of amusement in its farce–comedy plot. . . . And there is so much plot that nobody has either time or inclination to notice the absence of a chorus.[8]

"The Only Girl" is one of the brightest and most pleasing musical comedies seen on the local stage in many seasons. The lines are bright, the lyrics in Mr. Blossom's cleverest vein and the music is a sample of Herbert's happiest style, which is to say it is melodious and lilting.[9]

When the show opened in Philadelphia, "They threw bouquets all over Victor Herbert."[10] One critic was perspicacious enough to notice that Herbert's new approach to composition—emphasis on dance movement—was continuing the development that began with *Sweethearts*.

When to this [Blossom's book] is added more than a dozen characteristic melodies by Victor Herbert, ranging from ragtime to a delightful waltz with one-steps and two-steps and a march quartet, there could be little doubt that the result would claim popular favor. . . . The audience laughed until it shook and laughed and applauded. . . . Everybody shared in the jollity.[11]

That included Boston.

Thanks to the good lines supplied by Mr. Blossom, the fluent score of Mr. Herbert and the direction of Mr. Latham it may be said that seldom has a musical comedy "troop" made a better impression. Each of the 16 characters has a part to play; each part calls for intelligent acting and in no instance was it possible to find a weak link in the chain. . . . "The Only Girl" is clean, refreshing and wholly worthy.[12]

Indeed it is—worthy of revival. Worthy to live again!

THE PRINCESS "PAT"
Type of work: Romantic Operetta
Premiere: August 23, 1915
Theater: Cort, Atlantic City, N.J.
Cort, New York (September 29, 1915)

Cast (Major Players):

Marie	Leonora Novasio
Thomas	Martin Haydon
Bob Darrow	Sam B. Hardy
Tony Schmalz, Jr.	Robert Ober
Si Perkins	Alexander Clark
Grace Holbrook	Eva Fallon
General John Holbrook	Louis Casavant
Anthony Schmalz	Al Shean
Princess di Montaldo	Eleanor Painter
Prince Antonio di Montaldo	Joseph R. Lertora

Major Musical Numbers: "Love Is the Best of All"; "For Better or for Worse"; "Neapolitan Love Song"; "I Wish I Was an Island in an Ocean of Girls"; "All for You"; "Two Laughing Irish Eyes."

Plot: Marital boredom among the upper classes leads to almost inevitable infidelities—but not quite. Stratagem and jealousy combine to keep the couples faithful after all.

As rare as are great composers for the musical stage, still rarer are great librettists. "If Herbert had only found his 'Gilbert,'" the cry goes up, "how wonderful his works would be." It is not surprising that he never found his "Gilbert," for the great British genius belonged to that rare company whose numbers can be reckoned on the fingers of one hand: Calzabigi, daPonte, Boito, Wagner. These are the immortals who combined poetic theatricality with originality to produce the greatest works the musical stage has known. There are, of course, many other excellent librettists, and among these "second-string" creators Herbert was fortunate to have found Henry Blossom. Together they created, among others, *Mlle. Modiste*, *The Red Mill*, *The Only Girl* and *The Princess "Pat."* The first of these was revolutionary in the development of Broadway musical entertainment. *The Princess "Pat"* was the most effective dance-operetta Herbert created. The plot, contemporary and structured to allow for a maximum of dance opportunity, was a new departure for a Victor Herbert show. Here he created a little masterpiece. The list of musical numbers reads like a summary of his all-time favorites: "Love Is the Best of All," Pat's stunning entrance waltz quintet; "For Better or for Worse," a duet whose illustrative orchestration is astounding even for Herbert; The Prince's "Neapolitan Love Song," a perfect addition to the canon of "O

Sole Mio," "Musica Prohibita," and "Torna a Soriento"; "All for You," one of his most effective love duets; "I Wish I Were an Island in an Ocean of Girls," which anticipates the dance routines of Eddie Cantor; "Two Laughing Irish Eyes," Pat's tribute to Celtic dance and folk idiom; "Filling the Shoes of Husband Number One," a humorous masterpiece wedding lyric and illustrative orchestration; and the exemplary chorus writing and concerted finales of acts one and two. All this had been inspired by the musical possibilities of Blossom's book.

A wealthy "Yalie," full of booze, meets a young "swell" on Broadway, who takes him under his wing. On a bet they race their car to Easthampton and crash a house party, where the young man's father—a wealthy German—is visiting his fiancée, who is about his son's age.

The Princess "Pat," Irish and married to an Italian Prince, is a guest at the party, visiting her best friend, the perspective bride-to-be. In order to break up the relationship and incidentally to revive her jealous husband's lagging interest, Pat flirts with the old codger. The ruse is successful, and by the final curtain her young friend marries the joy-riding son and the Princess "Pat" is welcomed back to the arms of her Prince. The plot turns on jealousy and, tragically, it was that emotion that stalked the company.

John Cort, who owned and operated his own intimate theater on West 48th Street, was the lucky producer who encouraged Blossom to create something entirely original—something purely American, for he had his eyes on an American girl from the West as a possible star. Eleanor Painter had gone to study in Germany and had made a successful debut in grand opera in Berlin. Andreas Dippel, who had produced *Natoma*, had heard her and brought her to New York to appear in a season of light opera. Her success in *The Lilac Domino* had been an outstanding event of the previous season, and Herbert was especially anxious to engage her for his new piece; for she could not only act and dance, she was a first-class vocalist for whom Herbert would write some of his most challenging music.

Casting went smoothly. An excellent high baritone, Joseph Lertora, was engaged to couple with Painter; Al Shean, soon to headline in vaudeville with his partner Gallegher, singing their famous parodies, was hired as lead comedian. And a newcomer, Angela Palmer (née Pearl Foster) was cast in the role of Pat's best friend and was the perfect ingenue.

The first performances, on August 23, 1915, at the Cort Theater in Atlantic City, were followed by three weeks at the Lyric in Philadelphia. The local critics singled out Painter for special praise and the entire cast for excellence. Herbert's score was "delightful." The show was "one of the best and brightest things [Herbert] has written. . . . One of the best things heard in light opera in many a year." Blossom's lyrics showed him "at his best, for they are humorous in idea and bright in lines."[13]

Singled out for special praise was the first act duet between Painter and Palmer.

> It is entrancingly delicate, sweet and beautiful but is most musicianly as well. . . . The orchestra, with muted instruments, forms a polyphonic background, while the harp adds an obligato. The misses Eleanor Painter and Angela Palmer lent decided grace, delicacy and intelligence to the singing of the number, as well as perfectly blending voices, so they do themselves and the composer full credit and give the audience unlimited pleasure.[14]

"Angela Palmer" had attracted the attention of the critics, was a favorite with the company and, at twenty-five, was on the threshold of a big career. Little Pearl Foster from East 77th Street had come a long way; but not without carrying some baggage in the person of one Herbert Heckler, a sometime operetta tenor. The son of a wealthy Chicago jeweler, Heckler had become infatuated with Angela when the two had appeared in stock a season earlier. He had pressed for an engagement, which Angela resisted. Now firmly on the road to stardom, she returned from Philadelphia, nervous, but ready for her New York debut. Heckler had no better prospects than a job teaching voice at a local music school. Nevertheless, he went up to her room to renew his suit. When he found her suffering from a bad case of opening-night jitters, he suggested that a glass of ale might calm her down and, with a friend, went out to get some. Returning from the store, he unburdened himself. "Something's the matter. I'm losing her love. She isn't the same as she was. She is very successful and ambitious and I think she's forgetting me in her pride in her work. If I can't have her love I don't want to live." Then the distraught lover burst into tears. His friend calmed him down, and Heckler brought the ale to Angela's room.

Soon others in the house heard her laugh. But it was a laugh "in which there was no joy, no humor. It sounded harsh, scornful, cynical as though the girl were amused at Heckler's protestations. . . . And then came several screams."

According to the police report, Heckler shot her twice and then committed suicide. Their bodies were discovered side-by-side on the floor.

Heckler was dead. Angela tried to speak, but lost consciousness and died later that night . . . the night *The Princess "Pat"* was to have opened; the night that would have made Angela a star.[15]

These events sent shock waves through the company. Everything had gone so well until this tragic event. Naturally the opening was postponed and, in true Broadway fairytale fashion, a member of the chorus who had been covering Angela's part was quickly rehearsed. Two days later, on the evening of September 29, *The Princess "Pat"* opened to universal praise:

> The *Times*: "Enchanting. It is Victor Herbert over again, but Victor Herbert at his best."—Alexander Woollcott
>
> The *World*: "Has persistent charm and sparkling vivacity."—Louis V. DeFoe
>
> The *Press*: "A cast of unusually high caliber."—Hamilton Owens
>
> The *American*: "Especially tuneful, splendid cast, handsome costumes."—Charles H. Meltzer
>
> The *Sun*: "A skillful company. Audience delighted."—Lawrence Reamer
>
> The *Herald*: "Has a pungent atmosphere of holiday, melody and fun.
>
> The *Tribune*: "An eminently successful production."—Heywood Broun
>
> *Evening Telegram*: "Easily the most charming of comic operas."
>
> *Evening Journal*: "It is the season's success."—C. F. Zittel
>
> *Evening Sun*: "Charming. Reaches a high water mark."—Stephen Rathbun
>
> *Evening Post*: "Victor Herbert was in his most delightful mood when he wrote 'The Princess "Pat."'"
>
> *Evening Globe*: "Gay, contagious and quite refreshing."—Louis Sherwin
>
> *Evening Mail*: "A Henry Blossom success, a Victor Herbert success and a John Cort success."—Burns Mantle
>
> *Evening World*: "The best American comic opera that has been written in years."—Charles Darnton

Herbert had enjoyed this sort of grand slam before. What was new in the commentary reflected what was new in the production: the role played by the dance.

> Painter's dancing is entrancing. She dances with a natural grace that not all the ballet schools in the world can teach. It is captivating to

watch her tread the measures of the little Irish song Mr. Herbert has reserved for one of the last moments of the evening.

The composer's keen sense of humor is reflected in his modern dance rhythms. . . . The dancing was extraordinary. Katherine Witchie is not only graceful but quite acrobatic. . . . Earlier a most diverting dance number had whetted the audience's appetite for what was to follow. One of the clever divertissements was the dancing of Witchie and Riggs in the last act. . . . They did a dance somewhat different from the usual ones, which won a number of enthusiastic encores. . . . It called forth tremendous applause and deserved it all. Their ballet in the last act was the best liked of all the numbers.[16]

After 158 performances the production moved to the Majestic Theater in Brooklyn, where Eleanor Painter left the company. She was replaced by Ferne Rogers. Rogers was not so strong vocally, and Joseph Lertora, who had sung so beautifully with Painter, decided to leave the company after the Chicago engagement. Now both leads had to be replaced. Herbert traveled with the company to conduct the Chicago opening, and although the strains that had beset the production may have told on others, the excellent reviews were an occasion for rejoicing. Fritz Stahlberg recalled that it was one of only two times he saw Herbert drunk. "The other time was in Chicago, when we celebrated the successful opening of 'The Princess "Pat."' As I remember it on that occasion Mr. Herbert and I had a very serious argument. We couldn't quite decide who was going to take who home."[17]

By the end of April the company had a new lead, Ruth Welch, who apparently filled the bill. She was still starring when the national tour ended a year later in Oakland, California.

Shortly thereafter stock companies started to play the piece, featuring in their casts some members of the original production. For these less elaborate outings, Herbert supplied new numbers to replace the demanding Act 3 dances: a duo specialty for Marie and Tony, "Ragtime Temple Bells," and a solo for the New York "swell," "What's the Matter with You?"

The Princess "Pat," one of Herbert's best, has enjoyed a long, well-deserved popularity. One of the most often reprised works in the Herbert canon, its shining score, attractive book and graceful, humorous dances enchant audiences wherever light opera is cherished.

HER REGIMENT
Type of work: Romantic Operetta
Premiere: October 22, 1917
Theater: Court Square, Springfield, Mass.
Broadhurst Theater, New York (November 12, 1917)

Cast (Major Players):

Colonel Pontsable	Hugh Chilvers
André de Courcy	Donald Brian
Blanquet	Frank Moulan
Eugene de Merriame	Sidney Jarvis
Sergeant Sabretache	Frederick Manatt
Estelle Durvenay	Audrey Maple
Lisette Berlier	Josie Itropidi
Madame Guerriere	Paulina French
Jeanette	Norma Brown

Major Musical Numbers: "Soldier Men"; " 'Twixt Love and Duty"; "Art Song."

Plot: A simple love triangle between André, who has joined the army to escape the consequences of a youthful indiscretion, Estelle, his sweetheart, and the man she is supposed to marry—who is also the Commander of André's regiment, works itself out in Normandy, just before the outbreak of World War I.

Herbert's next piece was *Eileen* (see chapter fourteen). The years 1917–18 were a period of high tension for the composer, whose Irish, German and American loyalties put him in a conflicted position with the nation at war with Germany, and allied with the oppressor of Ireland. A society that expressed its patriotism by banning the word "sauerkraut" from menus in favor of "victory cabbage" could not be expected to exempt the theatrical world from its strictures. Fritz Stahlberg, Herbert's good friend and staff conductor, has left us a vivid recollection of the period.

"Her Regiment" was not an outstanding success in New York [opened November 12, 1917 at the Broadhurst Theater and ran for only forty performances] but proved to be a great attraction on the road. When we played in Detroit the show received very good notices, but one paper spoke of the musical direction being in the hands of "Fritz"

Stahlberg, adding in parentheses, ("what a moniker these days!"). A kind and patriotic management took the hint: the despised, rejected and familiar "Fritz" disappeared from their programs in favor of the more formal "Frederik." [Not only that, but the spelling of his last name was de-teutonized to "Stalberg."]

Mr. Herbert thought, too, that because of the times the change was a good idea, but out of habit he kept calling me "Fritz" against his will. And in the red-hot war days this correcting "Fritz" to "Fred" was sometimes rather embarrassing.[18]

The pressures of bringing out a new piece in wartime told on producer Joe Weber as well. He was determined to offer a light entertainment as far from anything Celtic or Germanic as possible. He enlisted William Le Baron, a young playwright with a French surname, and a reputation as a concocter of what the French might call "boulevard" comedy, to create a libretto set in contemporary, pre-war Normandy.

So far so good. But Le Baron, having no experience creating the books of musical comedies, produced a standard-issue, old-fashioned operetta, which the critics were united in proclaiming "dull." The hackneyed plot, with its commoner lovers who are really royals, its lower-class second couple introduced for comic effect, and its irascible over-the-hill "heavy" who wanted to wed the ingenue, was devoid of invention or charm. The small miracle is that Herbert was able to produce a score of which one of his severest critics wrote, "The sheer zest of the music carries singers and audiences into it."[19] The score contains one gem, the love duet "Some Day," which is one of the most sensitive duos Herbert ever penned.

As to the singers, Weber, realizing that it would be the composer's contribution that would lift all boats, tried to hire Carolina White, an opera star, to carry the musical heft. But she wisely withdrew and was replaced by "Audrey Maple, whose blonde beauty is always pleasant to behold."[20] Thus the female lead was chosen for her extra-musical/theatrical gifts. As for her partner, he looked marvelous in evening clothes: "The principal singing parts are entrusted to persons who either can sing hardly at all . . . or only in a sort of way—not the way of the music that hath charms like blonde Miss Audrey Maple. That constitutes a measurable handicap for any composer's work."[21]

Oh! But could they dance! It is here, in *Her Regiment*, that the new-style "dance operetta" spins out of control. It is one thing to reanimate a theatrical form by increasing the relative importance of the dance element, and quite another to rely entirely on that element to carry the evening. This overemphasis on dance began to have a negative effect since, in casting, all other abilities were sublimated to dance facility. The result was a cast of principals who could neither sing nor act effectively. For the first time in any Herbert work, the chorus was awarded the palm for vocal honors. Still, it was the dancing that captured universal praise and the hearts of critics and audiences.

"One of the features of this performance was the delightful dancing. . . . The dancing won the hardiest applause of the evening."[22]

"[The dances gave] the impression of airiness of movement, carriage of arms and head, sense of flowing line and rhythmic motion, charm of presence and gaiety of spirit. . . . In a dancing dress of blue, bestrewn with roses . . . with her aquiline profile and brown straying hair, in the light flush of her face and the exhilaration of her eyes, she might have descended for the dance from a portrait of youth by Reynolds or Gainsborough at his lightest."[23]

Is this a critic in love? Perhaps; but not in love with Herbert, Le Baron or *Her Regiment*!

THE VELVET LADY
Type of work: Musical Comedy Farce
Premiere: December 23, 1918
Theater: Forrest, Philadelphia, Penn.
New Amsterdam, New York (February 3, 1919)

Cast (Major Players):

Ottilie Howell	Marie Flynn
Susie	Georgia O'Ramey
Bubbles	Minerva Coverdale
Ned Pembroke	Alfred Gerrard
George Howell	Ray Redmond
Vera Vernon	Fay Marbe

Major Musical Numbers: None.

Plot: Ned, infatuated with a dancer (the Velvet Lady) has written her a series of embarrassing letters. He asks his friend George to retrieve them so that he may have a chance to marry Bubbles, George's sister-in-law. George spends so much time on this mission that he neglects his new bride. When he finally returns with the letters in a briefcase there is a mix-up, and he winds up with a similar case filled with jewelry. This is soon retrieved, first by the thief and then by the police. The Velvet Lady finally makes her appearance, and the maid somehow makes it all come out right.

With *The Velvet Lady* Herbert and Blossom finally bowed to the inevitable and created their only work whose leading character *is* a dancer. Dancing title characters were nothing new in musical theater. Carmen and La Muette de Portici were both dancers, but a dancing leading lady was a new emphasis for the Broadway stage. Based on Fred Jackson's farce, *A Full House*, it was essentially a play with musical interludes. Herbert kept his contribution simple. Although he provided a full score, the evening was carried by the play. This was a continuation of a new level of theatrical involvement for Herbert. Since 1916 he had been contributing single numbers to several Broadway pieces, the first of which, *The Century Girl*, produced jointly by Dillingham and Ziegfeld, set a new standard for the musical extravaganza. This type of activity continued for the rest of his career with his compositions for the elaborate numbers of Ziegfeld's "Follies" from 1917 through 1924. As noted, he kept an arm's-length relationship with these productions, limiting himself to private conferences with Ziegfeld and the stage and dance directors. This distancing reached its height in 1924 with the production of *The Merry Wives of Gotham*, for which Herbert provided a single number, "Heart O'Mine," sung by Mary Ellis, who was soon to create the role of Rose Marie in Friml's operetta.

In her memoir Ellis recalled:

Henry Miller, Gilbert's father, asked me to play in "The Merry Wives of Gotham"—a costume play, chiefly concerned with Irish squatters in the nineties in New York. Victor Herbert wrote his last song "Singing in the Rain" for it, which I sang; I'm afraid my brogue was awful, but I did what I could.[24] [The song, not Herbert's last, was titled "Heart O'Mine." The phrase "singing in the rain" was part of the refrain.]

In a telephone interview with the author shortly before her death, Ellis was asked whether she had met Herbert. "Oh, no. We all knew him, of course, and were in awe of him. He just mailed the song in and I sang it with piano accompaniment. He never came to work with me on it."[25]

"Heart O'Mine" is a wistful love ballad in Irish folk style, one of Herbert's most charming creations. He may have merely tossed it off for the money it brought. In any case, this distancing from the nuts and bolts of production was not a good omen. The beginnings of the trend can be found with his work on *The Velvet Lady*.

Nevertheless, the show was a mega-hit. Producers Klaw and Erlanger wisely engaged Julian Mitchell, who had been responsible for such early Herbert successes as *Babes in Toyland* and *The Lady of the Slipper* to supervise the dances, while veteran Edgar MacGregor was entrusted with the staging.

> The show proved to be a great hit from the very first night of its tryout in Philadelphia [Forrest Theater, December 23, 1918]. We played there six weeks instead of the one or two originally planned. Mr. Herbert received higher returns from this show than he had hoped or expected; we ran through the entire season in the New Amsterdam Theatre, New York. [February 3–May 4, 1918]. The next Fall I took "The Velvet Lady" to Chicago where she met the same sort of welcome that New York had given her.[26]

The Philadelphia critics tell the story:

> "The capacity audience almost tore the roof off the house with its enthusiastic applause."[27]

> "Before long it became altogether impossible to meet the demand for encores."[28]

> "So enthusiastic was the applause that the composer was persuaded to make a speech of thanks and he declared that it was the best Christmas present he could have—the generous welcome of the Philadelphia assemblance."[29]

The welcome of the New York critical fraternity was likewise positive, if more tempered. Heywood Broun, in the *Tribune*, was taken with the dancing and praised "several scenes of boisterous fun" as "genuinely amusing."[30] The *Times* critic [not Woollcott] praised Herbert's "dulcet airs" as "alluring and gay as any heard in Broadway in many a day."[31]

The man from the *New York Sun* struck a positive note and attributed much of the success to the ensemble effort, a logical development in a theater piece whose emphasis was the dance. Herbert apparently echoed the sentiment in his opening night curtain speech.

> He thanked the public for his collaborators as well, which was appropriate, since it was not to thank Mr. Herbert alone that he had

been called out. He has written a melodious and graceful score. . . . but Henry Blossom has brightened the new libretto with appropriate witticisms and supplied nimble lyrics. . . . Mr. Herbert struck the right note when he mentioned his fellow workers as entitled to a share of the success of the event.

Una Fleming's graceful participation in a dance stopped the second act. Janet McIlwane issued as a goblin to do a grotesque dance with unusual expertness.

The important and successful chorus blew bubbles into the air with virtuosity, sang a part song unaccompanied, danced with limitless grace and verve and contrived to look lovely all the time, which is sufficient evidence of its qualification to share in the success of "The Velvet Lady."[32]

The road beckoned, audiences responded and, once again, the world was Herbert's oysters Rockefeller!

ANGEL FACE
Type of work: Musical Comedy Farce
Premiere: August 8, 1919
Theater: Colonial, Chicago, Ill.
Knickerbocker, New York (December 29, 1919)

Cast (Major Players):

Tom Larkins	John E. Young
Arthur Griffin	Tyler Brooks
Professor Barlow	George Schiller
Ira Mapes	Bernard Thornton
Slooch	Jack Donahue
Mrs. Zenobia Wise	Eda von Buelow
Betty	Marguerite Zender
Vera	Minerva Grey
Mrs. Larkins	Sarah McVicker
Tessie Blythe	Emilie Lea

Major Musical Numbers: "I Might Be Your Once-in-a-While"; "Angel Face."

Plot: Tessie and Tom are engaged, but Tom's success as a composer of musicals puts him in touch with chorus girls, and this strains their relationship. Arthur is engaged to Vera Wise and is pursued by her younger sister Betty. An eccentric professor with a youth potion believes his formula has regressed Tessie to infancy, since Tessie has disappeared and a baby has appeared. But the baby is a victim of kidnapping, and through the good offices of a correspondence school detective, the mix-up is resolved.

Whenever W. S. Gilbert ran out of ideas for his next comic opera, he would float the concept of a magic lozenge or love potion as the basis for a new topsy-turvy plot. Sullivan's instinct was to consistently reject the idea out-of-hand, and he was right. With the exception of *The Elixir of Love*, which Gilbert had satirized in his *Dulcamara* and, at the other end of the aesthetic spectrum, *Tristan*, the device has not worked. But how many times has it been attempted? It may have been inevitable that, in the course of his long career as a composer of stage music, Herbert would have to deal with the magic potion plot line. In any event, he was willing to accept Harry B. Smith's variation on the theme, and the result was a hodge-podge conflation of plots and musical styles that somehow managed to hold several stages for a little over a year and add to his bank account while, miraculously, subtracting little from his reputation.

As to the reputation of Harry Smith and his brother Robert, who provided respectively the adaptation and lyrics, the critics had long since come to the conclusion that they were sincere, if not especially gifted, hack workaholics who had become fixtures—old fixtures—of the musical theater. Like all old fixtures, they were more or less reliable but difficult to remove. And so the theatrical world humored them, if they were not especially adept at returning the compliment.

Angel Face had been adapted from a play called *Some Baby*; and the rights to the earlier work had already been purchased by Irwin Rosen and Howard Schnebbe. Smith and Herbert had proceeded with the creation of *Angel Face*, and George Lederer produced the adaptation in Chicago, Philadelphia and Boston without first securing the rights to the original.

Lederer should have known better, as he was no newcomer to Broadway. He had produced many noteworthy musical plays, among them *The Belle of New York*, and had made the old Casino Theater the scene of many popular successes. He had an instinct for the mercurial tastes of the public, and it was he who moved Herbert in a new direction. After World War I the public wanted escape—fluff and nonsense—and Lederer satisfied them with a series of farce comedies set to music.

Moving Herbert in a new direction was no easy task. This was, after all, the man who had written *Naughty Marietta* and who, hot from that success, had declared,

> It is generally assumed that good light opera is on the decline. This I deny most emphatically. The public taste is the same as it was years ago. A well constructed, coherent and melodiously composed lyric work is necessary to achieve dignified success. Genuine light opera may be compared to its parallel on the dramatic stage, the romantic play. In the structure of both are nicely balanced the elements of love, romance and comedy.[33]

Keeping Herbert on a new track would be made more difficult if *Angel Face* were derailed by legal maneuvering. The last thing the producer needed was a lawsuit.

When Rosen and Schnebbe contacted Lederer with their claim, Smith was forced to settle, and in August 1920 an agreement was negotiated by which "for the sum of $2500.00—to us in hand paid by Harry B. Smith" the original owners transferred their rights in the property to Smith and Herbert "to the end of the world."

But there were other clouds that hung over this successful polyglot. It was as if the creators, desperate to find success, had determined to create a three-ring circus, to throw all sorts of paint at the canvas and hope something would shtick. In addition to the magic elixir plot, which involves an old professor who has invented an elixir of youth mistakenly supposed to have transformed a grandmother into a baby (this the simplest of more than six subplot lines involving the various couples), the show was said to have been "Cohanized" in its reliance on popular dance routines to carry the action. What else was there? How about a comic "Negro" servant named "Irving" in black face? To top it all off, Herbert, like Sullivan in *Utopia, Ltd.*, tacitly acknowledged a decline in his powers by relying on a number in the last act that reprised some of his greatest musical moments—a cheap theatrical trick calculated to trigger an enthusiastic response from an audience suddenly hit by a burst of nostalgia. Sullivan did it by reprising Captain Corcoran's "What never? . . . well hardly ever" routine from *Pinafore*. Herbert had tried this before in *When Sweet Sixteen* with little success. Now he had his soubrette run through a potpourri of hits from *M'lle Modiste, Babes in Toyland, The Only Girl,* and *The Fortune Teller*, among others. This time the trick pulled applause. One single great new number emerged from all this. "I Might Be

Your Once-in-a-While," an insinuating, lightly syncopated solo that in its sophistication anticipates the Cole Porter of the thirties, took the country by storm.

The first performances at the Colonial Theater in Chicago began on August 8, 1919. The show ran until, with significant changes in cast and a simplified plot line, it continued its pre-Broadway run at the Forrest Theater in Philadelphia in late October; thence to the Colonial in Boston, where it geared up for its New York premiere on December 29, 1919.

On each opening night, Herbert continued his habit of making a grand theatrical spotlighted entrance down the center aisle. As he admitted in a Boston curtain speech, "artists live on applause." He conducted with "great zest . . . and at one time, in the fury of his conducting he gave an unconscious imitation of the "shimmy."[34] Herbert's "shimmy" was appropriate for, once again, it was the dance that carried all before it: "A leading feature of the show was the eccentric dancing of Mr. Donahue—a loose and reckless dancer. . . . His imitations of Russian dancers, of the Isadora Duncan school, and of Ruth St. Denis were remarkably well done, and his 'snake dance' was funny beyond words."[35]

Thus this loyal acolyte of St. Vitus and his accomplices in the beautiful, leggy, high-kicking chorus carried the hackneyed plot and workaday score before them and won Herbert still another success—but at some cost.

"How much of half-forgotten pleasure we owe to Victor Herbert,"[36] Woollcott mused in his review, reflecting on the third act reprise of Herbert's greatest hits. *Angel Face* was a kind of triumph, but a sad one, indeed.

MY GOLDEN GIRL
Type of work: Musical Comedy
Premiere: December 19, 1919
Theater: Stamford, Conn.
Nora Bayes Theater, New York (February 2, 1920)

Cast (Major Players):

Blanche	Dorothy Tierney
Wilson	Robert O'Connor
Arthur	Victor Morley
Peggy	Marie Carroll
Helen	Helen Bolton
Howard	George Trabert

Major Musical Numbers: "Darby and Joan"; "I Want You"; "My Golden Girl"; "A Song Without (Many) Words"; "Ragtime Terpsichore"; "If We Had Met Before."

Plot: Arthur and Peggy, newlyweds, have become bored with one another and spend most of their time with their hobbies, playing the bassoon (Arthur) and playing golf (Peggy). Soon each finds a new lover (Helen and Howard) and decide to divorce. But the lawyers make such a mess of things they decide to stay together; besides, Helen and Howard have themselves fallen in love.

It was 1920, and Victor Herbert was suddenly fighting for his artistic life. Everything seemed to be coming apart. The trappings of success were still in place. The commissions came trooping in; the concerts with the orchestra continued to build in attendance and popularity. Broadway, of course, was changing, and Herbert struggled to keep up, but it seemed that, though his fighting spirit kept him going, the old competitor was losing heart.

Returning home from rehearsals or tours, he met a gloomy reception at 321 West. His Theresa had been diagnosed with diabetes, and spent more and more time in bed. Her years of splendid culinary activity and physical inactivity had at last caught up with her. Her favorite child, Clifford, returned from World War I a hero, but soon found employment as an engineer with Ford, and his fluency in German had landed him a prime post in Berlin. Ella was now triumphantly installed as her father's secretary. She had grown into an astute businesswoman, and used her skills to preserve and further her father's fortune. She shared with Clifford an aversion to marriage; Clifford was enjoying the free and easy pleasures of the Weimar Republic, and Ella, who had inherited a tendency to over-weight from both parents, had her hands full with a semi-invalid mother and a beloved father whose powers were rapidly diminishing.

Herbert could not have been immune to the effects of such an atmosphere, and the depression that seems to have surrounded him now began to show in the quality of his creative output. The man who all his life had been physically vigorous; who loved to stride down Broadway, dressed to the nines in morning coat and walking stick, greeting friends, colleagues and even strangers who recognized him; the man who strode down center aisles to his place on the podium acknowledging the warm applause of audiences; the man who loved to hike with his daughter through the piney woods of the Adirondacks, now found himself chauffeured by her on his daily rounds. The muscles of his short legs began to cramp and become painful. Dr. Baruch, his friend and physician, who had attended the family for years, was an advocate of homeopathy; nevertheless he had supplied him with digitalis to alleviate the intermittent chest pains that he reported with increasing frequency. Still, Herbert strove on, but with negligible result, for the early twenties were a period of small achievement in the face of these odds.

His next show, *My Golden Girl*, has the dubious distinction of being his first production in which the book got better reviews than the music. That was something new for Herbert, and may have resulted in shaking him out of his doldrums. Producer Harry Wardell could not have been encouraged to read this, after the New Haven tryout on January 20, 1920:

> Although the program displays the name of Victor Herbert as the most important factor in "My Golden Girl" the fact remains that the book [by Frederick Arnold Kummer] is better than the score. Mr. Herbert's music is not bad, but it approaches perilously near to being merely adequate. . . . None of these [melodies] strikes the ear as anything particularly novel or distinguished. . . . One expects something more than a middle level from Victor Herbert.[37]

Perhaps the lamb ragout or the service at Kaysey's had been poor that night. But a few weeks later, when the show opened in New York at the Nora Bayes Theater, just six blocks and around the corner from where *Angel Face* was still packing them in, the story was much the same. Although "Mr. Herbert was greeted by a fanfare of trumpets from the orchestra"[38]—a new addition to his customary spotlighted entrance—the new fillip failed to impress the critics. Indeed, considering the quality of the product, it may have served to alienate them.

> Victor Herbert wrote the score, and he cannot hide behind the veil of mediocrity in seeking the plaudits of a public which has known his "Only Girl," "The Enchantress," and "M'lle Modiste." . . . Only the name on the program and the conductor in the pit proved that Victor Herbert was the composer.

> To a thorough admirer of this composer's operettas it seems better to have those delightful, stirring melodies of former successes repeated, as in "Angel Face," than have the creator of "Babes in Toyland" join the ranks of the commonplace. What particularly seems to emphasize the shortcomings of the music is the fact that Herbert has probably the best book in many years.[39]

So there it was again: the book superior to the music. Although some critics were taken with the story and praised the dancing, especially that of a pretty chorine who stopped the second act with her "shimmy," these were the poorest reviews Herbert had received since *The Captive* three decades before.

Clearly, something had to be done.

THE GIRL IN THE SPOTLIGHT

Type of work: Romantic Musical Comedy
Premiere: August 7, 1920
Theater: Stamford, Conn.
Knickerbocker, N.Y. (August 12, 1920)

Cast (Major Players):

Tom Fielding	John Reinhard
Molly Shannon	Mary Milburn
Nina Romaine	June Elvidge
Watchem Tripp	Hal Skelly
Ned Brandon	Richard Pyle
Max Preiss	James B. Carson

Major Musical Numbers: None.

Plot: Show biz Cinderella. When the star (Nina) becomes indisposed, an Irish housemaid saves the show and the career of the composer (Tom), whom she loves.

It was not Herbert, but producer Charles Lederer, who found the solution.

What Lederer did was to touch the right buttons of both audience and composer. The audience part was easy. Once again the old dictum, "when in doubt play Cinderella," worked its wonders. This time the variation on the rags-to-riches theme focused on the world of the theater, where an unknown becomes a star on opening night after the prima donna with the wart-hog personality does herself in. This cliché never seems to fail, and the jump from *The Girl in the Spotlight* to *42nd Street* is a very small one.

But how to revive Herbert's flagging interest? Lederer consulted with librettist Robert B. Smith who, under the nom de plume of Richard

Bruce, hit on the magic twist of plot line: make Cinderella an immigrant Irish maid slaving in a boarding house, where there lives a theatrical composer on the verge of his first big hit. Call her "Molly Shannon" (now, *that's* Irish) and cast unknown Mary Milburn (who was *really* Irish) in the role. Set the scenes in the lodging house, in a rehearsal hall, in the green room and in a garden of orchids, the final scene of the "play within a play." For this milieu Herbert created a score that is among his most theatrically effective. The opportunity for backstage comedy was rich. "Watchem Tripp," the choreographer, had a high old time routining his talentless female chorus line. The critics made much of the clever physical comedy in the dancing, but the highest praise was reserved for Herbert and his new star.

> Miss Milburn is one of the real musical comedy finds of the year. . . . [Her character is] a delectable person, particularly in her grimy costume of the lodging house scene. Big-eyed, youthful and rich voiced she was an altogether captivating colleen, from her drudge in the first act to the star who saved the day in the last.[40]

Milburn saved more than the day. She became Herbert's muse—as he acknowledged in his curtain speech.

> He spoke deprecatingly of his "little musical piece" and pleaded guilty to the charge of having discovered one of the most charming leading ladies seen in New York in some time. . . . In a brogue as rich and musical as the music he has composed Mr. Herbert told the audience that Miss Milburn was a lass having the blood of his own green little isle in her veins and one which he would commend to their enthusiastic consideration.[41]

That bit of blarney notwithstanding, the critics acknowledge that he had produced a score "reminiscent of the very best of the Herbert efforts." Others joined the chorus:

> "The best musical show that has been on Broadway in many summers."
>
> *—Evening World*

> "If we were blind we could sit through and hear it, if we were deaf we could sit and watch it."
>
> *—New York Times*

"The Girl in the Spotlight certainly brightens Broadway."
—*New York World*

"The best music Mr. Herbert has written since M'lle. Modiste."
—*Evening Telegram*[42]

Perhaps it was the heat, but the show lasted only two months in the sweltering Knickerbocker Theater.

The company set out on a national tour with Herbert conducting opening performances in each city visited. Now he seemed to find his only pleasure in the theatrical world that had become his natural environment. It was as if this most theatrical of personalities at last had found his home in the theater. Composer of serious orchestral works, concertizing cellist, conductor of his own orchestra, bandmaster extraordinaire—all these had been roles he had played to the hilt. But as those other activities receded, it was the theater and his work in it that never deserted him and continued to stimulate his creative genius to the end of his life. This theatrical home nourished and supported him for three decades. Now, in his final years, he seemed to acknowledge what everyone had known for so long: that he was first and last a man of the theater. Now in the twilight of his career, with his powers waning, he found in the theater a comfort, support, and inspiration that lifted him to a final burst of glory!

OUI, MADAME

Type of work: Musical Comedy Farce
Premiere: March 22, 1920
Theater: Philadelphia Theater, Philadelphia, Penn.

Cast: (Major Players)

Dick Sheldon	Vinton Freedley
Polly	Dorothy Maynard
Pansy	Georgia O'Ramey
Steve	Harry Kelly

Major Musical Numbers: "Play Her Something I Can Dance To"; "My Day Has Come."

Plot: Dick and Polly want to break into show business. In a borrowed apartment on Riverside Drive, they host a coterie of would-be artistes. When Dick's mother and sister arrive and the owner of the apartment is nowhere to be found, they convince Steve, the super, to portray "Colonel Hutt," the putative owner. Pansy, the maid, is convinced that the "Colonel" is none other than an old lover who jilted her. He claims to be the lover's twin, but an old tattoo gives him away.

World War I had several effects on the American theatrical scene. The disillusionment that followed in the wake of Versailles skewed popular taste in the direction of the frivolous. Light comedy and farce became the order of the day, and nothing that smacked of heavy, overproduced European styles—including operetta—was acceptable. The economic restrictions related to the war also had implications for Broadway. With the exception of the world of Dillingham and Ziegfeld, and perhaps in reaction to that aesthetic, a movement toward "little theater" arose that stressed content over production values.

Jacques Copeau and his "Théâtre de la Vielle Columbier"—a troupe stranded in New York by the hostilities—produced a variety of plays on a simple unit setting composed of levels, arches and step units. Guy Bolton, P. G. Wodehouse and Jerome Kern, in a parallel development, created the small-scale "Princess Theater" musicals. In Philadelphia, Alfred Aarons arranged for a series of similar entertainments to be produced at his 350-seat Philadelphia Theater. The first such musical, which debuted on March 22, 1920, was a collaboration by Victor Herbert and the husband-and-wife team of Robert B. Smith (lyrics) and G. M. Wright (book), entitled, *Oui, Madame*. The continuing dominance of the dance in this period is reflected in the fact that the stars, Georgia O'Ramey and Harry Kelly, were both famous eccentric dancers. Further, although Herbert Gresham was entrusted with the overall direction, "musical numbers were devised and staged" by Julien Alfred.

Herbert entered the world of the "intimate" musical with some trepidation, since the most reliable aspect of his musical gifts—his genius as an orchestrator—might be severely compromised. There is some conflict in the reports of what actually happened with respect to the size of his orchestra. On May 4, 1920. the critic of the *Boston Herald* remarks, "He had a small band, perhaps of 20, but he swayed them as if they were four-score strong," while the man from the *Boston Post*, ostensibly attending the same performance writes, "The orchestra was so greatly enlarged, especially as regards the stringed instruments, that parts of the first row of seats had been removed to make room for the musicians."[43]

The Wilbur Theater in Boston was a small house designed for spoken drama, so it is possible that the removal of a row of seats gave a critic the impression that an "enlarged" orchestra had been installed. The examination of Herbert's production contracts from this period reveals that he insisted that, in road companies of first-class productions, the minimum number of instrumentalists would be twenty-four. It is logical to conclude that the pit band in both Philadelphia and Boston was a balanced ensemble of at least twenty-four players.

The Philadelphia critics agreed that the score of *Oui, Madame* was "not his best music, not his worst music,"[44] but that the aim of those who collaborated on the production, to give an "intimate, cozy character,"[45] had been successful. Not a promising press for the launch of a new, somewhat experimental venture. In any event, whatever happened in Philadelphia did not make Herbert or Aaron happy. Harry B. Smith was brought in as play doctor, several cast changes were arranged and the result was a book that, while still emphasizing the dance and comedy elements, placed more emphasis on the romantic, limited as it was. The plot remained a farcical mix of mistaken identities and impersonations, but the critical reaction was much more positive.

The star, O'Ramey, was praised as agile and genuinely funny as a "black-tulled and tighted Pavlova in uproarious burlesque as a writhing Spanish dancer,"[46] while her new partner, William Kent, stopped the show with his "rapid lapse into mock inebriety" followed by an "exceptionally comic soft-shoe dance.[47] Then in the "humorous apex of the evening" the two "travestied the florid ballad singers and the dancing mediocrities of the cabarets."[48]

As for Herbert's contribution, all agreed that he had consciously created a dance show, as opposed to a song-and-dance show.

> Mr. Herbert, who has such a versatile and sagely musical mind that can turn out anything which savors of rhythm and melody, fashioned a smart dancing score for the first act. . . . In the second act he cut loose and was more himself—resourceful, humorous with laughing notes leaping from the strings and the few reed instruments he employed. . . . His enjoyment of his music was infectious.[49]

But not infectious enough. *Oui, Madame* was withdrawn before a New York premiere could be arranged, and has not been seen or heard from since.

ORANGE BLOSSOMS

Type of work: Romantic Operetta
Premiere: September 4, 1922
Theater: Garrick, Philadelphia, Penn.
Fulton, New York (September 19, 1922)

Cast (Major Players):

Roger	Robert Michaelis
Helene	Phyllis LeGrand
Lawyer Brassac	Pat Somerset
Kitty	Edith Day
Tillie	Queenie Smith
Jimmy	Hal Skelley

Major Musical Numbers: "This Time It's Love"; "A Kiss in the Dark"; "New York Is the Same Old Place"; "Then Comes the Dawning"; "On the Riviera"; "The Lonely Nest"; "A Dream of Orange Blossoms"; "Because I Love You So." "Let's Not Get Married."

Plot: Roger must marry within a year or lose his inheritance. He loves a divorcee, Helene, but his aunt's will forbids such a union. His attorney suggests a marriage of convenience with his goddaughter, Kitty. She will go to Cannes for a year, Roger will get his money, and they will divorce, so he can marry Helene. But when Roger goes to Cannes to finalize the arrangements he and Kitty fall in love. Curtain.

In 1922 Herbert composed his last operetta, *Orange Blossoms*. Based on *The Marriage of Kitty* by Frederika de Gresac, who had supplied the French dialogue scenes for *The Red Mill*, this was an operetta in the grand style. Producer Edward Royce had hired Norman Bel Geddes, one of the great geniuses of contemporary stage design, a man who had not only developed spectacular settings for the Follies but who also was to transform entire theaters into cathedrals for Max Reinhardt (*The Miracle*, 1927) to frame the new work.

Set in Paris and Cannes, the plot is based on the old device of the young man who must marry within a year in order to inherit his fortune. A marriage of convenience is arranged, but the woman in the case turns out to be more than the young man expects; true love rears its lovely head and of course wins the day.

The great number in this score is "A Kiss in the Dark," which revealed that Herbert had not lost his touch. It was so successful that when *Orange Blossoms* closed, Director Ned Wayborn requested it for the Follies of 1923 and built the outstanding scene of that production around the song. It was probably its incorporation in the Follies that accounted for the huge popularity of one of Herbert's gems.

Orange Blossoms was not a success. There was apparently a negative atmosphere surrounding the production. Herbert's friend Gustav Klemm describes it as "The ill-fated 'Orange Blossoms' whose inconsiderate producer caused Herbert so much unhappiness."[50] Nevertheless, there were moments in the first two acts when Herbert still succeeded in wresting a leaden book from disaster, but by the third act it almost seems that even the composer had given up.

The critics loved Bel Geddes' contribution and were respectful of the music. "Pretty music by as able a musician as ever wrote for our stage, this time writing with competence if not with any perceptible amount of inspiration,"[51] was the best Woollcott could muster. The production lost lots of money and closed after ninety-five gorgeous performances.

THE DREAM GIRL
Type of work: Musical Play–Fantasy
Premiere: April 22, 1924
Theater: Shubert, New Haven, Conn.
Ambassador, New York (August 20, 1924)

Cast (Major Players):

Elspeth	Fay Bainter
Wilson Addison	George Lemaire
Aunt Harriet	Maude Odell
Jimmie Van Dyke	Billy B. Van
Jack Warren	Walter Woolf

Major Musical Numbers: "My Dream Girl"; "The Bubble Song"; "If Somebody Only Would Find Me"; "Reincarnation."

Plot: On tour in England, Elspeth dreams she is back in the fifteenth century. She meets Jack, who saves her from an arranged marriage. She awakens to the present to find her lover is still with her.

"Victor Herbert's final score," trumpets the headline introducing Alexander Woollcott's review in the *New York Sun*.[52]

"Victor Herbert left this life on a high note," the man from the *Times* began his piece. "The music of 'The Dream Girl' . . . embraces the last complete score composed by him."[53]

Perhaps the critics had been seduced by J. W. Phillips's account in the *Musical Observer*, in which the reporter fantasizes an interview that presents an unconvincing picture of a temporizing, hesitant composer delaying the start of work on *The Dream Girl* despite the desperate exhortations of his librettist Rida Johnson Young. But early in the story Phillips trips himself up. "Time was moving rapidly. The end of February [1924] had come, and no work had been done. A star had been obtained and her services contracted for. In fact a whole cast had been chosen, re-chosen, and then pruned over again and each part appropriately distributed to the players. But there was no music."[54] On what basis was a star and cast obtained if the musical demands of the score were as yet unknown? Herbert would scarcely have agreed to casting with no input from him. Although the *Observer* story makes good entertainment, it just isn't true. *The Dream Girl* is Herbert's last *produced* work, but not his final score. That honor belongs to *Orange Blossoms*, composed and produced in 1922. That is the score that contains what is in fact Herbert's swan song, "A Kiss in the Dark," one of Herbert's most successful waltzes and a song that, along with "Kiss Me Again," "Ah, Sweet Mystery of Life" and the "Italian Street Song," is most indelibly linked to the composer. In a letter to Phillip James, one of a handful of conductors entrusted with the job of musical direction of the Herbert canon, Herbert reveals the true chronology of these works.

CAMP JOYLAND

August 12, 1923

My dear Mr. James

I am pretty sure that *Max Steiner* has been engaged for the "Dream Girl"—He was really *in line*—as the "Oui Madame" piece closed rather early and another man has been engaged for the road tour of that piece.

If, for any reason, Mr. Steiner should be assigned to some other piece, I shall be glad to suggest *you* for the position.

I wrote the piece two years ago and I'm glad it's going to be done at last.[55]

Thus the *Dream Girl* score had been completed, at the very latest, in August of 1921, before the *Orange Blossoms* music was composed.

Herbert, as always, was very much involved with the development of the dramaturgy of the piece. But his work extended to the shaping of dialogue and lyrics as well. Fortunately there are preserved in the Herbert archive at the Library of Congress some of the work papers for lyrics of *The Dream Girl*. These present a fascinating peek into the composer's workshop and illustrate how Herbert did not hesitate to adjust lyrics to suit his music. In each case the changes Herbert makes lift the lyric's effect from the pedestrian to something ear-catching—through means of his rhythmic shifts.[56]

Bubble Song (Dolly)

Herbert first determined that the lyric would be set as a waltz. He then adjusts it as follows:

Rida Johnson Young	*Victor Herbert*
Line 1 Shh! Shh! Step lightly	Hush! Hush! Step lightly

Herbert has supplied a word with a more singable vowel.

L. 2 Ssh! Ssh! Step lightly	Hush! Hush! Step lightly
L. 3 For someone is dreaming a wonderful dream	
L. 4 A sigh would wake her	
L. 5 A sudden sound shake her	
L. 6 From heights where she rides on a fairy moonbeam.	
L. 7 Ssh! Shh! Be wary	Hush! Hush! Be wary
L. 8 Ssh! Ssh! So airy	Hush! Hush! So airy
L. 9 Fragile and light is the fabric of dream	So fragile and light is the fabric of dream

Herbert has added a word for the upbeat which parallels the early text, i.e., "From heights" = "So fragile, etc."

L. 10   No harm must befall her
L. 11   A touch would recall her
L. 12   From dreamland where nothing is just as it seems.

This line, which repeats the scan of the previous lines 3, 6, and 9, is adjusted to provide a rhythmic contrast that breaks the boring parallelism and provides a segue to the refrain. Herbert first crosses out the text; second, he notates the rhythmic pattern he needs:

along with a dynamic indication: diminuendo.

He then supplies his own text which preserves the thought of
Young's original but fits his rhythmic pattern:

From dreams where nought is as it seems.

This leads gracefully into the

Refrain

L. 13   A bubble, a bubble, a rainbow of mist,
L. 14   That's a dream, that's a dream.
L. 15   From a magical pipe
            By some fairy lips kissed   By a dream fairy kissed

Herbert eliminates the difficult sibilant phrase, "Lips kissed" and
supplies a phrase that is more easily sung.

L. 16   That's a dream, that's a dream.
L. 17   We see in its colors a world of delight,
L. 18 As our ideal appears   As a vision appears

Again, a text change to enhance a more singable text.

            through the shadows of night
L. 19   In vain would we grasp it and pray it to stay
L. 20 One touch and the bubble   One touch—and it's
            is vanished away!   Vanished away!

Here the composer introduces a change that makes the piece. Young's
parallelism (L. 17, 18, 19, 20) is adjusted to provide a kick through the
introduction of a rest—during which the singers can "pop" the bubble.
This small change breaks the repetitiveness of the text and enlivens
the refrain. The resulting pattern is:

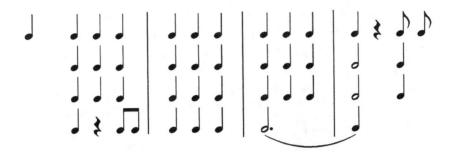

Not satisfied with this rhythmic change Herbert even suggests in a note to himself "different rhythm?" for the dance of the little bubble girl that follows.

Although similar work papers from Herbert's other shows do not survive, we can assume that the technique and approach illustrated by his work on the "Bubble Song" is typical of his compositional process. Herbert was an effective wordsmith, and we can only imagine how much of the effectiveness of many of his compositions can be attributed to his textual and rhythmic contributions.

One final point relating to the date of composition of this work: It is well known that Herbert always carried a small notebook with him in order to jot down melodies as they occurred to him. The only such composer's notebook that survives probably dates from the earliest part of his career, since it was printed in Germany by the publisher Hans Licht. The fact that Licht identifies himself as "Hof-Musicalienhandlung, Leipsig"—dealer of musical wares to the court—places the notebook in a period before 1918, when the Empire was replaced by the Republic. It is likely that the content of the sketchbook also dates from this earlier period, since there would be no reason for Herbert to use an old notebook thirty years after his immigration to the United States. In any case, the book contains a completely realized version of the main waltz from *Dream Girl*, "If Somebody Only Would Find Me." It is in the same key in which it appears in the score, and the articulations, harmonies and tempo indications are exactly as they appear there. Two things are of special interest: We can see that melodies occurred to Herbert in fully realized form. There are very few corrections in this piece, or in any piece in the sketchbook. His inspirations were perfect from the start. But not, apparently, perfect enough for Herbert, for he has drawn an X through the whole piece, rejecting it at some earlier date. When he chose to resurrect it for *Dream Girl*, the music preceded the text. Knowing what we know about Herbert's linguistic strengths, we can assume that Young then fit a text to the melody; or perhaps Herbert himself was responsible for the text. The evidence of the *Dream Girl* material underlines once again the totality of Herbert's contribution to his stage works. Not just a composer with a genius for transforming a theatrical concept into musical utterance, he was a full player in the development of all aspects of these works, music, text and lyrics.

Fay Bainter was engaged by the Shuberts to lead the way through what was originally a romantic fantasy. A group of American visitors to London falls in love with the charm of the city's old monuments, and dreams itself into the world of the fifteenth century. *The Road to Yesterday*, by Beulah Dix and E. G. Southerland, was the basis of Rida Johnson Young's book. The dream world occupies the second act, and it is here that Herbert supplied some of his most effective operetta-style music; sentimental and humorous by turns, it illuminates and refreshes the fantasy world that was often the inspiration for his most effective writing. This was the focus when the show was conceived. But sweetness and light were not enough for the Shuberts, who insisted that the comic element be highlighted. This was accomplished by the addition of Billy Van—a vaudeville comedian—to the cast, in the first act in the role of a "radio addict," in the second as a typical country bumpkin, and in the finale as a vaudeville comic doing his specialties. The addition of this element brought with it such dialogue as this: "The trouble in the Garden of Eden was not caused by an apple; it was caused by a green pair." And at one point "untold wealth" is defined as "income not listed on your tax return." The piece became a work at odds with itself. There was the Victor Herbert operetta fantasy and the musical comedy "relief," a kind of pop *Ariadne*.

After Herbert died in May, the Shuberts indulged in something Herbert would never have permitted. They added songs by other composers and adjusted some of Herbert's own arrangements. Emil Gerstenberger was hired to "extend" one of Herbert's best quartets. Sigmund Romberg was brought in to supply new numbers for the road company version. These were "All Year Round," "Trotting Over London" and a jazz tune, "Dancing All The Way." Thus the show became a hodge-podge of styles.

The version that tried out in Boston eleven days before Herbert died, beginning on May 15, 1924, was rated "above average." There was praise for star and composer, but Bainter got the better notices.

Victor Herbert evidently relished the chance to write sonorous marching songs, sprightly dance tunes and melodious romantic solos that the true operetta quality of the dream permitted. He has not taken kindly to jazz. Even "Saxophone Man" with its tinge of today has something of the older melodious qualities for all its marked rhythms.[57]

H. T. Parker liked the operetta sections of the piece and included in his review the rumor that "Mr. Woolf's tune ["My Dream Girl"] in the first act—amorous, ardent, languorous, waltz-like is the handiwork of Mr. Romberg."[58]

Whatever rumors may have been floating around, the evidence of the sketches and scores in the Library of Congress proves this unfounded gossip, although the Shuberts had Romberg waiting in the wings as backup. Could they have suspected that all was not well with Herbert?

More ominous was the fact that, although Herbert was present on the tour, he allowed his assistant, Goodman, to conduct the opening. After his second act curtain speech, when the audience applauded heartily, he led the orchestra through the introduction to the third act. But that was all. Although his severest critic, Parker, concluded his review, "Vitality yet abounds in Mr. Herbert. Ten of the younger composers have not his single-handed plenty,"[59] in retrospect the comment seems a plaintive "Ave, atque vale." The critic and composer had shared many, many opening nights, and one cannot escape the feeling that somehow both men may have felt this one to have been their last.

The New York reviews were, of course, more valedictory than critical. And, of course, the show went on.

CHAPTER 18

MEDIA VITAE IN MORTE SUMUS (1916–1924)

> Symptoms of heart disease began to show themselves. He was
> still extremely active, his curly hair was thick, though getting
> gray. Heart disease made gradual progress. He was never
> confined to his room, or even to the house. On the last morning
> of his life he arose as usual. He had long known that his end
> was approaching, and had awaited the hour with fortitude and
> resignation.[1]

No. This paragraph does not describe Victor Herbert's finale.
It is an excerpt from an article by his mother in which she discusses the
life of her father, Samuel Lover. But in this, as in so many ways, Victor
Herbert's life mirrored that of his grandfather. The same vigor, the same
dedication to the creative work at hand that characterized Lover was typical of Herbert to the end.

To understand Herbert's decline and death it is necessary to go back
almost to the beginning of his career, to Stuttgart in 1886. This was the
year in which Herbert courted Theresa, and in which they married and
left Europe to continue their careers in New York. It was also the year
when a great friendship began between Herbert and the man who was to
become his physician—a friendship that began at his stepfather's home
and lasted, literally until the hour of his death.

Emmanuel Demarnay Baruch was another of the many fascinating
characters to occupy the stage where the drama of Herbert's life played
out. Born in San Francisco in 1870, he had emigrated to Tübingen, Germany, to earn his medical degree. But his interest in music and drama
was as great as his dedication to the healing profession, and it was this
breadth of spirit that caught the attention of Herbert's stepfather, Dr.
Schmid, a faculty member at the University Medical College. Baruch became a frequent guest at the Schmid home in Tübingenstrasse.

Herbert, though ten years his senior, immediately took to the younger
man, and shortly after Victor and Theresa sailed for New York Baruch
completed his studies and followed them. He enrolled for post-graduate

study at Columbia's College of Physicians and Surgeons and soon became a leader among the medical advocates of homeopathy, specializing in bacteriology and pathology as professor at the New York Homeopathic Medical College (later Flower and Fifth Avenue Hospital). A powerful advocate of the homeopathic approach, "Similia similibus curantur"—the same that causes a disease cures it—he became a strong defender of this approach as science through his extensive publications.[2]

But his writing was not limited to medical matters. He worked avidly to promote the appreciation of German literature in the United States and was elected President of the Goethe Society of America. His drama, *Judith and Arropherius*, was produced in London by Dame Sybil Thorndyke and given a warm critical reception. He was truly a remarkable man.

Baruch once said, "My interest in the stage has been heightened by my work with actors and their ailments. They are difficult as patients because they demand all one's time."[3] Herbert, however, was different. "He had no irritating idiosyncrasies. He was just a big, generous, good natured man, who went through life with a smile. His only hobbies were his music, his friends and his family."[4]

What a roster of patients Baruch treated! His celebrity practice was such that he had to arrange two separate waiting rooms so that the actor Sir Henry Irving, the ballerina Modjeska, and the prime donne Nordica and Sembrich could enjoy privacy. Sarah Bernhardt had no such problem, since she consulted with Baruch by cable from Paris. This was the man, the friend, the physician who cared for Herbert and his family for three decades.

Between 1921 and 1924, generalized arterial sclerosis began the work that culminated in Herbert's death on May 26, 1924. Although his passing shocked the world, there was nothing surprising about it. This was, after all, a sixty-five-year-old man, 5'8" in height, who weighed over 250 pounds. Herbert was not a fat man, although his barrel-chested physique often gave that impression to casual observers. All his life he had been very active, and he was in fact very muscular. Years of vigorous conducting activity would naturally produce that result. His short legs caused him to run when he walked, a characteristic pace that made him stand out when moving among his friends during his frequent strolls through the theater district. He was an avid swimmer and hiker as well. But in the last three years of his life, much of this activity had been curtailed. Herbert was, of course, a heavy drinker. He enjoyed his food tremendously and was a trencherman, par excellence. Given this history, the miracle is that he survived as long as he did.

During the last three years of his life he exhibited symptoms that led Baruch to suspect that his patient might be suffering from chronic endocarditis, an inflammation of the heart's lining membrane especially involving the valves. A wide range of causes has been discovered to result in inflammation, everything from poor dental health (which Herbert suffered)[5] to syphilis (which he did not). At any rate, the condition results in a reduced pumping capacity for the heart muscle, resulting in several symptoms of which Herbert complained: shortness of breath, a feeling of cold even on the warmest of days, poor appetite and uncharacteristic depression. Dr. Baruch seems to have been "an accomplished scientific homeopath" who prescribed digitalis for heart failure, but "the typical homeopathic dosage would have been too weak to have much effect in improving the heart's pumping capacity. Sudden death from occlusion fits with this picture."[6]

In 1924, in a brief conversation with Deems Taylor, one of the many outstanding musicians whom he had mentored, Herbert is said to have remarked, "My day is over. Already they're beginning to forget poor old Herbert."[7] This kind of morose negativism is not typical of Herbert and, although in the last decade of his theatrical activity a new spirit was surely transforming the American musical stage, Herbert's pieces were still in demand, were produced and brought him substantial income. There were disappointments, of course. But there had always been disappointments.

Late in 1919 Herbert wrote to Otto Kahn, Chairman of the Metropolitan Opera Board as well as Managing Director of Kuhn, Loeb and Co., requesting his participation in a project to create a "Victor Herbert Theater." Modeled on the London D'Oyly Carte, the repertory company would produce the best of the Herbert canon, largely the works he had created with Henry Blossom. An earlier attempt to create such a theater, championed by Fred Latham, stage director of some of Herbert's most successful productions, had gone nowhere. Now Alfred Aarons, General Manager for Klaw and Erlanger, encouraged Herbert to try again. He did, writing to Kahn:

> What I ask you is simply a business investment, which will bring you
> splendid returns I am sure, as I feel that my name and my active

participation in the offerings of the Victor Herbert Theater will insure its undoubted success.[8]

This is certainly not the voice of an artist who felt his time was past. Nevertheless Kahn turned him down, in the nicest way.

> The proposition . . . appears to be a very attractive one financially and I should, of course, be gratified to see a Victor Herbert Theater established in New York. I am entirely convinced that your name and your active connection with the undertaking would insure its success.

> However from the business point of view the proposition . . . is not of interest to me. From the point of view of art and of your own personality it is indeed of interest to me but in the field of art I am so swamped with demands and commitments that I do not see any way at present to go beyond my existing obligations and I regret that I must ask to be excused from acting upon your suggestion.[9]

If this reply was disappointing, it was not enough to cause a change in Herbert's personality to one characterized by negativism and depression. But a series of disappointments, coupled with increasing medical problems in the aggregate, might have led to certain personality changes, or rather eruptions of certain negative aspects of his personality that had been present but never dominant throughout his lifetime.

The recurring Victor Herbert Theater project can be understood as an attempt to create a venue where Herbert's most important work might find new life. It was almost as if the old lion was grasping at straws to lift himself out of an undeniable decline, for the failure of the project was not the only disappointment these last years held. His experience with the Irish operetta was also negative. Although *Eileen* was one of his brightest and most inventive scores, it was a financial failure. Little by little these events were adding up to a negative sum total.

Not that Herbert lacked for work. He conducted the Victor Herbert Orchestra, whose annual summer weeks at Willow Grove and appearances at the Broadway Theater and at Lewissohn Stadium were eagerly anticipated. There were special events as well, such as the Carnegie Hall concert celebrating the thirty-fifth anniversary of the Irish Musical and Literary Society, at which Herbert performed Charles Villiers Stanford's F-minor symphony and his own "Irish Rhapsody." But there was even disappointment here, since the audience was only "of moderate size."[10]

It seemed that everything he accomplished was tinged with a bitter aftertaste.

In the theater, in addition to his own shows, Herbert had begun with *The Century Girl* (1916) to supply the orchestral underpinning for the spectacles produced by Dillingham and Ziegfeld.

> Ziegfeld was the first to introduce classical music into reviews in America and he persuaded Herbert to write all the ballet numbers and finales for the Follies as well as the scores for the [designer] Ben Ali Haggin tableaux. Herbert's last effort found on his desk when he died was an unfinished dance for the Tiller girls.[11]

Ziegfeld, of course, used many composers for the Follies, and Herbert shared musical honors with Friml and Berlin.

For *The Century Girl* he worked in tandem with Irving Berlin, and the review format gave him full opportunity to display his talent both for orchestral scene painting and satirical humor. He composed the opening scene, "The Birth of the Century Girl," with its solo for Hazel Dawn, the following song, "Opportunity" for Marie Dressler, and a grand duo, "You Belong to Me." This was followed by an amusing scene, "The Music Lesson," with music and lyrics by Berlin. In this sketch, two actors play the parts of Berlin and Herbert and explore the various strengths of the old and new Broadway musical. Herbert is represented by "Kiss Me, Again," to which Berlin provided a jaunty jazz countermelody, the same sort of thing he did with "I Wonder Why" and "You're Just in Love."

Act Two began with one of the funniest pieces Herbert ever wrote, a send-up of Stravinsky's *Rite of Spring* called *The Ballet Loose*, featuring "Leon Errolovitch" and "Marie Dressleroff" and an ensemble of "cave ladies." This was followed by a nursery scene for which Herbert provided a "Toy Soldiers' Dance" duet à la *Babes in Toyland*. Then a superpatriotic "When Uncle Sam Rules The Waves," an undersea extravaganza with "chorus of mermaids, lobsters, turtles and anemones" and a bouncy number for Leon Errol, "Jumping Jacks" and the sunshine girls, "Romping Redheads."

Fun! Fun! Fun! Money! Money! Money! But the spark is missing from these numbers. These are the serenades of an old man hoping in vain to charm and seduce Thalia and Terpsichore for one last time.

As his frustrations mounted, the negative aspects of Herbert's personality came to the fore: both a tendency toward scatological humor and his famous short fuse became more characteristic. There is a story attributed to Ziegfeld's secretary which is embarrassingly raw. According to the account, when Herbert was first introduced to her he grabbed her breasts and cried, "Oh, nice fresh meat!"[12]

Then there is this:

> One day Herbert was running over a new tune on his cello in the back room [of his publisher's music store]. When a woman buying sheet music out front learned who was playing she hastily bought a copy of "Gypsy Love Song" pushed open the door and asked him to autograph it. He took a fountain pen and as he wrote his name the woman blurted, "It's hard for me to believe that such a *fat* man could write such graceful music. Are you really Victor Herbert?"

> Her rudeness was so uncalled for that Herbert lost his temper. He aimed the pen at the woman, pulled the lever and squirted ink over her white dress. Aghast, she bolted, and he called after her, "Tell your friends the *real* Victor Herbert did that!" As he shredded the autographed music sheet he subsided. "Jerum," he said, "I'm ashamed. But imagine talking to another human being like that!"[13]

More typical of Herbert in this period is his extended correspondence with Gustav Klemm of Baltimore. Klemm had long been an admirer of Herbert and had published a laudatory retrospective in the *Musical Leader*,[14] which he sent to the composer. Klemm was himself a composer, conductor and arranger, and the contact between him and Herbert led to a mutually rewarding professional, and later personal, association.

Writing from Lake Placid in the fall of 1918, Herbert thanks Klemm for his "splendidly written article."[15] "I only hope that I am deserving of the high praise you bestowed on my humble efforts." This was not false modesty, for Herbert often belittled his achievement in this period. His old animus, Krehbiel, surfaces in his mind as he corrects Klemm's information about his birth date—cribbed from one of the critic's books. "I might add that I was born February 1st, (not 8th). That old ass Krehbiel got it wrong in his book—of course!"

By 1921 Herbert was featuring Klemm's arrangements at Willow Grove, making sure that he got proper credit. He had absolute confidence in Klemm's abilities. "Your numbers are on the evening programs of Monday, June 27th. Have been too busy to look at them." Later, when Klemm requested a recommendation, Herbert offered him carte blanche. "If you will send me a sample letter I shall be pleased to recommend your appointment." A passing remark Herbert adds is something new: his only reference in his correspondence to his health. "I am well, thank God, and busy."

Perhaps he protested a bit too much, or tipped his hand about his underlying concern. At any rate, he began to delegate some of his heavy workload. By the end of 1922 Ella had assumed the roles of secretary and driver and was answering most of his correspondence, although when important musical matters were involved Herbert would pick up his pen—especially if the message he had to deliver was negative. In May of 1923 he wrote, agreeing to program one of Klemm's originals but rejecting an assignment to arrange a piece by Cyril Scott. "That Scott thing is a little too 'haarig' [strange, rough] (as the Germans say)—not that it isn't well scored—but it's a little too much for my audiences, I'm afraid." Thus the rejection is clothed in praise for Klemm's work as well as a continuing concern with the taste of his public. This is the Herbert we know. "Terribly busy" is a refrain that runs through his correspondence, as is the constant self-deprecation as he refers to his work again and again as "these little things of mine" and "my little tunes."

As we approach the premiere of *Orange Blossoms*, his hopes again are high in anticipation. "We open tomorrow. The theater is wonderful and ought to be a great success." But *Orange Blossoms* was only a modest achievement, even with "A Kiss in the Dark" as the lynchpin of the score.

Herbert's frustration grew as success continued to elude his new works, and the language that he insisted upon in his production contracts grew more and more specific and controlling. It is easy to read between these lines and conclude that the composer placed the blame for his disappointing results at the door of his producers.

> It is agreed that no alterations shall be made in said score of said opera excepting with the written consent of said Herbert, and it is further agreed that the tempi used in the interpretation of the music shall be those indicated by said party of the first part [Herbert] in the score according to metronome.

And in the margin, Herbert has scrawled "No Interpolations!"[16]

One contract that did not disappoint him, and that made him rich, was the agreement he reached with William Randolph Hearst in the spring of 1923.

The Majestic Theater on Columbus Circle became famous under that name as the home of "The Wizard of Oz" and "Babes in Toyland." It was later rechristened the "Park Theater." Still later Hearst bought it, renamed it the "Cosmopolitan Theater" and turned it into a movie house to feature the films of his paramour Marian Davies.[17]

Herbert was engaged for one year, beginning May 1, 1923, at a salary of $1,500 a week, to conduct an original overture for each film, or a short concert of musical numbers. A typical program featured "America's foremost composer-conductor leading a few Herbert favorites—especially arranged by request for this engagement:

"March of the Toys"
"The Serenade"
"When You're Away"
"Put Down Six and Carry Two"
"I Might Be Your Once-in-a-While"
"I'm Falling In Love with Someone"
"Gypsy Love Song"
"Italian Street Song"
"Kiss Me Again"
"It's a Great Night Tonight for the Irish"

This was followed by the film *When Knighthood Was in Flower*, with incidental music (not by Herbert) conducted by his old colleague Fritz Stahlberg. The performance concluded with Herbert again on the podium to conduct the "Marian Davies March ("especially composed by Mr. Herbert for the premiere of this picture"). Herbert wrote overtures for *Little Old New York, Unseeing Eyes, Under the Red Robe, The Great White Way*, and *Yolanda*. The contract also required Herbert to conduct "in any theater in the United States where Cosmopolitan Films were premiered." The agreement was a letter contract written by Herbert himself. It granted Hearst the option of renewal for another year as of January 1, 1924.[18] This engagement breathed new life into the composer and restored his mood. "Fritz, I have a wonderful contract. It even calls for an ice-box in my dressing room."[19] In fact the contract does not mention an ice-box, but Herbert arranged for one, for his personal comfort and that of his associates, in those days before air-conditioned houses.

His eyes still had that merry twinkle. His wit and tongue were still keen and quick. There were changes, though. His hair was white. And he was quieter,—not as nervous as formerly—more serene. But he was as mischievous as ever.

During the beginning of the season, one evening when I came up after conducting the first part of the show, I found that Mr. Herbert hadn't gone home after the overture as usual, but was waiting for me in the door of his dressing room with a highball in his hand. "Come in, Fritz. This is thirsty weather. I'm better off than you are. I'm through for the night. But I tell you what I'll do, my boy," (his voice sank to a dramatic whisper,) "I'll leave the key to my ice-box in the right pocket of my trousers, under the handkerchief, mind you,—*under* the handkerchief!" And I was never disappointed those hot summer nights after the performance when I looked for the key *under* the handkerchief, mind you.[20]

With the dawn of 1924, Hearst decided not to pick up the option. Herbert's reaction is reported differently by two of his closest associates. Deems Taylor reports that "he took the cancellation very much to heart. He felt that he had been used simply as window-dressing. It was a fearful blow to his pride."[21] This seems a bit extreme. Herbert, who had written the contract himself, was very much aware that Hearst was using him (at an inflated salary and with minimal involvement) to get people to view Davies's films. If he was down, it was probably because of the cancellation of one of the best deals he had ever signed. Fritz Stahlberg's account is more typical, for it shows Herbert concerned with the feelings of his colleagues: "One day in the Spring of 1924, he told me that his contract was not going to be renewed. When he saw that I felt badly about it he explained quietly that the picture was the principal attraction and that the management was trying to cut down the overhead."[22]

Probably the most exciting musical event of 1924, and the last public activity in which Herbert participated, was the famous jazz concert given by Paul Whiteman on February 14 at Aolean Hall in New York. This was the concert that introduced Gershwin's "A Rhapsody in Blue" as well as Herbert's final orchestral effort, "A Suite of Serenades." Whiteman has left us a picture of Herbert during rehearsals that shows him to have been his old self: kind, helpful and always considerate of others' feelings.

I was very proud of the Suite Victor Herbert wrote especially for the occasion. He was a great-souled, wonderful musician and my beloved friend. His encouragement during the weeks we were rehearsing meant a great deal to all of us. I asked him to conduct the Suite, and after he had watched me do it, he almost consented to take my place, because he thought I wasn't getting the most out of his music.

"But I'll wait," he said, his eyes twinkling. "I'll wait, Paul, until you've tried it a little longer and then if I say to you, 'Yes, I'll be pleased to conduct the Suite,' you'll know what I mean." He told me at last that I did very well. "I guess I won't take the stick, Paul," he decided. "There would always be some fool critic to say that I was better than you or you better than me—and it might cause hard feelings."

I am glad that he was alive to sit in a box and bow to the cheers that greeted the playing of his Suite. Writing for a jazz orchestra was new to him and he complained a little about the doubling which he said hampered him when he wanted an oboe, say, and found the gentleman who should play the oboe busy with the bass clarinet.

As to Herbert's feelings about his Suite, Whiteman reports that he remarked, "I respected the rules of the game, and I might even say of this Suite, in the words of the seventh century nun, that even if older people do not like it it pleases me because it is I who did it."[23]

It is well known that Herbert was not a friend of jazz. The raw, improvised nature of the music as it had developed by the early 1920s, as well as the obvious fact that he had no talent or feeling for the idiom, may have been behind this. In any case, the "Suite of Serenades" contains no jazz. It is a series of pieces written for jazz orchestra. Each tries to capture a contrasting national musical style. As for the concept of a concert devoted completely to jazz, Herbert felt it to be a very dangerous move for Whiteman, musically and professionally. He may have been motivated to create the Suite to provide a balance for the program. Whiteman reports on Herbert's original reaction when he heard that the concert would feature a jazz-based concerto.

What! An all jazz concert? Why, my boy, it simply can't be done. You mustn't try it. It would ruin you! You have your future to think of—and your reputation. So far you've been getting on splendidly with your dance music and if you watch your step you will undoubtedly be able to put away a good smart sum while the vogue lasts. But a jazz concerto! Honestly, my boy, I'm afraid you've got softening of the brain. Be guided by me in this and you will never regret it![24]

Even though these were his feelings, Herbert entered into the spirit of the project. We know this because Whiteman gave a series of luncheons for the critics and even took them to rehearsals. One of those critics was Isaac Goldberg, who has left us a fascinating portrait of Herbert at the rehearsals and of his interaction with Gershwin. Goldberg makes a claim for Herbert's contribution to the "Rhapsody" based on his recollection of events during the rehearsals and his conversations with Gershwin, who was a personal friend. "In writing the book I have relied chiefly upon long contact and correspondence with the subject himself [Gershwin]."[25]

The claim of Herbert's input is contained in this passage.

He [Herbert] heard a few rehearsals of the Rhapsody, too, and contributed one valuable suggestion that George was quick to adopt.

The transition to the andantino moderato (the slow melody in the middle section) was originally a single rising passage, rubato e legato, in contrasting motion. This passage Gershwin simply repeated. Why only a sterile repetition [Herbert asked]? Accordingly the passage was changed to the version as printed on page 28 of the piano score, last four bars. The original was but a repetition of the first two bars.[26]

In examining the validity of this claim, it is useful to compare the orchestral score prepared by Ferdie Grofé and used by Whiteman at the premiere with Gershwin's piano score.[27] The two agree up to the D 6/4 chord that preceded the passage in question. The following page in the Grofé is blank, except for a notation at the top, "wait for nod." This is a reference to Gershwin's piano solo—no doubt improvised—that would follow. Grofé's score contains only indications of a cadenza outline.

In Gershwin's score, completed and dated 1/7/24—more than a month before the premiere—there is a full cadenza written out. It consists of rising sequential arpeggios for four measures, followed by four measures of descending triplet figures in parallel octaves, ending on a unison D in octaves. Then follow four measures of rubato chords in contrasting motion, whose function is to provide a *transposition* to the key of E-major, the key in which the andantino moderato is introduced. Since the structural function of the passage in question is to provide a transposition, it is clear that Goldberg's account that Gershwin "simply repeated" the passage cannot be accurate. What is more, the entire passage was written out long before Herbert ever heard it.

However, this does not mean that Herbert made no contribution to the "Rhapsody," only that Goldberg's memory was faulty with respect to which passage he criticized. There is a section in Gershwin's original and in the Grofé score—sixteen measures in length—that was cut at the performance. The passage is for solo piano and consists of two measures of repetitive rising sequences, whose thematic material is that of the clarinet solo with which the "Rhapsody" opens. This is followed by a section marked "slower, increase [in tempo]," and consists of a rising sequence based on a rather dull rhythmic pattern, viz:

There follows a long, descending arpeggio that leads to the pulsating pattern that drives this section to the cadenza.

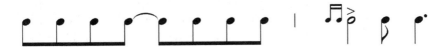

This may be the passage whose pedestrian quality may have led Herbert to suggest an adjustment. In any event, the passage was eliminated.

Shortly after the premiere of his Suite Herbert was back in Washington, D.C., continuing his activities in support of copyright law to prevent radio companies from broadcasting ASCAP music without paying for it. A famous picture posed before the entrance to the old National Press Club shows Herbert at the center of a group of distinguished ASCAP members, among them Irving Berlin and John Philip Sousa, taken just before his appearance before the Senate Committee on Patents. "I have heard one of my compositions, 'A Kiss in the Dark' played eight or ten times in one night over the radio. They play and play and play that ad nauseam. How can you expect anybody to buy it in printed form?" he asked?[28] It was a good thing he did, for after his death his estate received more money from ASCAP royalties based on radio and film usage than he had ever earned during his lifetime.

Herbert's calendar for the last days of his life was characteristically a combination of work and play. The Irish Musical Society he had founded with Father Duffy, chaplain of the famous "fighting 69th" regiment, had arranged for Enid Stoddard to paint a miniature portrait of the composer. It was to have been presented to him on June 1 at a ceremony in the auditorium of City College. Herbert spent Sunday afternoon, May 25, at a last sitting in the artist's studio. He was not pleased with the result. "I'm a very happy person," he remarked, "and refuse to look serious. Humanity can't be put on one dead level. A man is born with a light in his eye, with a song in his heart, with a gift for friendship, or with the power to stamp his personality on others. Nothing can take those gifts away."[29] True enough. Still, the artist had captured something of Herbert in his last hours that belied his remark. There is a visible tension in the face, a staring quality to the eyes that obscures the light and the song. Stoddard had not pleased the composer; she had done her work too well.

From the sitting Herbert hurried to the New Amsterdam Theater for a rehearsal of the Follies that lasted until one in the morning. The next day he arose early and worked on the dance number for the Tiller sisters. At eleven Ella drove him to his first appointment of the day with his music publisher Harms on West 45th Street. That's where she left him as she set off for a day of shopping. May 26 had dawned unseasonably warm, but Herbert dressed in his usual formal morning coat, complete with green tie and vest. From Harms he walked to the Ziegfeld office on 42nd Street. The producer recalled the visit.

> He was here Monday morning going over some things with me. Sat right there in that armchair near the desk. He told me yesterday he never felt better. He was the greatest man in my experience I had dealings with. . . . A very serious man. When he left he said, "I'll be back at 2:30." He had an appointment with Sam Kingston, my General Manager. He never came back.[30]

Kingston was still waiting for him at 4 o'clock, wondering at this unusual failure of promptness in a man who usually was painstaking in his business engagements, when the telephone brought the news.[31]

After his meeting with Ziegfeld, Herbert walked to the Lambs on 44th Street to join his friends for lunch. The main dining room upstairs had been closed during World War I as a result of the national crusade to save food and manpower, but the less formal rathskeller was in full swing—a fitting setting for Herbert's last meal.

Among the Lambs lunching that day was Charlie Harris. His order of wheat cakes had just been brought when he felt two arms around his shoulders. He looked up to see Herbert smiling down at him. "Don't eat those things, C.K.," he recalled Herbert admonishing him. "They're not good for your stomach."

"What's the difference so long as they agree with me," Harris replied.

"Charlie, you and I are getting too old for pancakes."

"That reminds me, Victor. I have some bad news for you." The two had recently been pallbearers for colleagues, among them Glen MacDonough and Gustave Kerker.

"Who is it this time?" Victor asked.

"Poor Teddy Morse. His funeral will be Wednesday."

Victor gave one of his famous grunts, a noise he uttered when he was at a loss for words, and found a seat next to his friend Silvio Hein. He ordered what was to be his last meal: two eggs and bacon, bread and butter and a pot of coffee. As he was about to dig in, Harris came up behind him and threw his arms around his friend. "Don't eat that!" he cried. It will give you indigestion." Herbert smiled and said, "Charlie. I can eat nails."[32]

Yet as he finished his meal he felt discomfort, which he attributed to indigestion. He mentioned it to his lunch companion. "Charlie may have been right. I think I'll get a cab."

Herbert hailed a cab and, instead of heading to the New Amsterdam, directed the driver to take him with all speed to Dr. Baruch's office in East 77th Street. The driver noticed that his passenger was breathing heavily and looked ill, and when he drew up at the curb he opened the cab door and offered his assistance to the composer. They made slow progress across the sidewalk and up the front steps of the brownstone, where Baruch maintained his residence and practice.

Once inside, he was escorted to the private waiting room reserved for the doctor's elite patients. The room was empty, and Herbert preferred not to be alone. The nurse suggested that he go outside in the fresh air and wait for Dr. Baruch to return. Herbert stepped onto the landing in front of the office and fell down the stairs. As he was being carried into the examining room, Baruch returned. Heroic restoratives were administered, but the effort was fruitless. Baruch pronounced his old friend dead at 3:30 P.M. on May 26, 1924.

Within a few minutes of the time Herbert died, a melody of his was sounding through New York in restaurants, radio shops and private homes. This was the hit of *It Happened in Nordland*, "Absinthe Frappé," which was part of a waltz medley played by the pianist Joel Coffey and broadcast over station WEAF 660—NBC's Red network.[33]

When word was sent to Herbert's home, Theresa collapsed—and her world collapsed as well. The man who had been her only love and her reason for being was gone, and she longed for nothing more than to join him in death. From this point on the entire responsibility for what was now the Victor Herbert legacy fell on the capable shoulders of Ella Victoria.

When Ella returned from her shopping trip, she immediately took charge. After cabling Clifford, who was working in Chicago as a stockbroker, she drove across town to Baruch's office, where she remained during the evening beside her father's body. Arrangements were made for a public funeral at St. Thomas' Church at Fifth Avenue and 53rd Street for Wednesday, May 28. Father Stires, Rector of St. Thomas', arranged for the church undertaker to call for the body. Herbert was placed in a plain wooden casket, which was later sealed in a bronze coffin. On Wednesday morning the body was removed to the family residence for a brief private ceremony. Then all proceeded to the church.

Tuesday, May 27, had been a day of frantic preparation. There was little time for grief as the city prepared to honor one of its most beloved adopted sons. As a mark of respect, all the music publishing houses in New York and all their branches throughout the country were closed for the day of the funeral. Rehearsals for the Follies were suspended. Huge crowds filled St. Thomas' and Fifth Avenue as a procession of honor made its way from ASCAP headquarters on 45th Street to the church. First came the New York Police Band and Glee Club, the National Staff Band of the Salvation Army and an orchestra made up of volunteer musicians from all the New York theaters. They played Chopin's Funeral March.

Then came the hearse, with its flower-covered casket. On one side marched an honor guard of soldiers from the garrison on Governors Island; on the other, sailors from the Brooklyn Navy Yard. Next came the family car, with Theresa, Ella and Clifford. Then the delegations from Herbert's beloved club world in order: the Lambs, the Friars, the Lotos, the Friendly Sons of St. Patrick, the Association of Musicians of Greater New York, the American-Irish Historical Society and the Bohemians.

Honorary pallbearers included Augustus Thomas, Gene Buck, John Philip Sousa, Max Dreyfus, Jerome Kern, Nathan Burkan, George Gershwin and Dr. Baruch. The ushers at the church were Irving Berlin, Ray Hubbell, Werner Jenssen, Charlie Harris, Bud da Silva, Earl Carroll, E. B. Mills, Julius Witmark and Otto Harbach.

The family entered the church by a side door as the casket was borne down the nave to its place before the high altar. Dr. Stiles conducted the standard Episcopal service with musical interludes. Nathan Franko played Bach's Air for G-string. The Met's Anna Fitziu sang, "Lead, Kindly Light." Dr. Stires self-effacingly admitted that there was nothing he could say that would improve upon the communication Deems Taylor had published in the *World* and so he read these words:

> Losing Victor Herbert, the musical world loses someone it will never quite replace. He was the last of the troubadours. His musical ancestor was Mozart and the family of which he was so brilliant a younger son numbered Offenbach, Delibes, Bizet, the Strausses and Arthur Sullivan among its elders.
>
> What he had was what they all had, the gift of song. His music bubbled and sparkled and charmed, and he brought the precious gift of gaiety to an art that so often suffers from the pretentiousness and self-consciousness of its practitioners.
>
> The thirty years of his too short career have left us two grand operas and over forty operettas and musical comedies, all distinguished by an unending flow of melodic invention, harmonic and rhythmic individuality and brilliant instrumentations.
>
> Above all he had perfect taste. Herbert's music could be trivial at times but he never wrote a vulgar line in his life. Now that he is gone there is no one left who has quite the combination of effortless spontaneity and endearing light heartedness.
>
> He is not dead, of course. The composer of "Babes in Toyland," "The Fortune Teller," "The Red Mill," "Nordland" and "Mlle. Modiste" cannot be held as dead by a world so heavily in his debt.[34]

Concerning the teeming melodies running through his head that kept him tied to his work table the greater part of every day, he had recently said to a friend, "I often wonder when they will stop coming."

Now the world knew.

The service ended, Theresa and Ella returned to the emptiness of 108th Street. Clifford followed the procession up Fifth Avenue to Mt. Morris Park, east to the Harlem River and across to the Grand Concourse; then north to Woodlawn Cemetery. A firing squad from the 102nd Engineers fired volleys into the damp air as soft rain began to fall. Herbert's body was placed in a holding crypt.

Taps, and a soft stillness. One of God's noblemen was home.

CHAPTER 19

POSTLUDE

But not for long. Few people are comfortable contemplating their mortality; more than half the population of the United States die intestate. Herbert did leave an extensive and detailed will, but made no provision for the ultimate disposition of his remains. Since the suddenness of his death had left Theresa in a state of shock, the immediate decisions fell to Ella. When the undertaker from St. Thomas' Church arrived at Dr. Baruch's office, Ella arranged for her father to be clothed in the formal morning dress—complete with green vest and tie—that he had favored when at work in his studio. Her choice of St. Thomas' Church for the funeral was appropriate. Herbert was Anglican, and St. Thomas' was an excellent setting for the impressive rites that would no doubt ensue. It also had the strongest musical tradition among the major parishes of the New York diocese.

Many of the prominent parishioners of St. Thomas' were buried at Woodlawn Cemetery in what was then a pastoral section of the Bronx. Woodlawn was one of the oldest and most distinguished resting places for prominent New Yorkers, and to this day is favored by the families of many artists and musicians. A coterie of Lambs and Friars were buried there: it was appropriate that Herbert join them.

After the funeral, the body was placed in a holding crypt pending the construction of a suitable mausoleum. In the meantime, the ever-restless Herbert got to rest for only a few days. Sometime between the funeral and the first week in June, ASCAP decided that a death mask and a model of his right hand should be cast. Consequently, on June 4, Herbert's body was removed to the premises of Frank D. Rowe, an undertaker located at 19 West 125th Street, "for the purpose of making a death mask of the features of said deceased on order of Theresa Herbert." The body was then returned to a holding vault to await final disposition on June 10, 1925. The mask and hand remained at the ASCAP offices until June, 1926, when they were shipped to the Library of Congress for safekeeping. The relics wound up on the desk of Edward Waters, Assistant Chief of the Music Division and Herbert's third biographer. Later they were stored with Herbert's papers until 2006 when, in connection with the preparation of this biography, the mask was retrieved for photographic reproduction.

Herbert's will was very specific as to the disposition of his funds and copyrights. He had once joked that he intended to write "an Irish will": "I, Victor Herbert, being of sound mind and body, spent all my money." In any event, this was not far from the truth.

He left $10,000 outright to Clifford, with no participation in any income from royalties: "My reason for this distribution of the property is that my son has received a good education and been the recipient of many benefactions during my life and should be able to provide for himself without any further assistance from me."[1]

Indeed Lawrenceville, Princeton and Cornell had provided Clifford with a first-class education. Ella had been given no such opportunities, and this disparity of treatment may have been one of the roots of her resentment of the brother who she felt had always been her parents' favorite. That status proved a mixed blessing for Clifford; his upbringing as a spoiled rich man's son did not serve him well as an adult. His professional career led from one enterprise to another. At times he worked as an engineer for Ford in Chicago and Berlin; as a stockbroker; as a technical advisor on films based on his father's works, in which he later received copyright under the terms of his mother's will (the disastrous *Babes in Toyland* with Laurel and Hardy among them); as an oil wildcatter in Louisiana; and as a rancher in Texas. In the course of this history he acquired three wives: the first a belle of Troy, Michigan, society who, while honeymooning in Paris, ran away from their suite threatening suicide; the second a New Jersey lady with theatrical ambitions; the third a young woman who survived him and his eccentricities, which included establishing a base for his business activities at the Kickapoo Café at Mansfield, Louisiana, and an attempt to raise cattle in El Paso. Clifford died there on New Year's Day, 1961, and was buried at Forest Lawn Cemetery in the Hollywood Hills among the rich and famous. He left the income from his ASCAP royalties to the Boy Scouts of Pasadena.

This sort of life was off-putting to Ella, who was somewhat straitlaced; but there was more than a conflict of personal style at the root of her disaffection.

RLC Cassell, representing
TRAVELER'S BANK OF PARIS
490 Lexington Avenue, N.Y.

November 16, 1927

Miss Ellen [sic] Herbert
Park Lane Hotel
New York City
    Dear Madame—
    Referring to telephone conversation of yesterday at which time we
read you cable received from our Paris office, which is quoted below
for your confirmation:
    HERBERT BONDS MATTER ENTIRELY SETTLED WITH
    CLIFFORD HERBERT IN HIS OWN NAME NO AUTHORITY
    FROM HIM TO DISCLOSE TRANSACTIONS WOULD
    SUGGEST PARTY INTERESTED GETS [SIC] IN DIRECT
    TOUCH WITH HIM
    Owing to the fact that this transaction has been completed, it will
    be necessary for you to secure any further information direct from Mr.
    Herbert.[2]

Apparently Clifford had secured Herbert bearer bonds, and since these
are redeemable by anyone in physical possession, executed payment in
Paris. No doubt Ella was furious. Although Clifford's actions were technically legal, they certainly contributed to the ill feeling that developed
between brother and sister. The two had contact thereafter, but the interaction was strictly limited to business affairs. Ella disapproved of Clifford,
and her remarks about him were "consistently derogatory."[3] Nevertheless, when he died she flew to Hollywood for the funeral.

    Herbert's will left the family residences at 108th Street and at Lake
Placid and a one-third interest in all copyrights to Theresa. Ella received
two-thirds of the rights. Herbert's gross estate was $94,194, divided as
follows: real estate, $39,000; personal effects, $4,392; bank deposits,
$11,554; the balance attributed to interest in copyrights and musical
works. The gross estate was reduced by debts, administrative costs and
funeral expenses for a net of $58,106, not enough to pay the bequests in
full. Clifford's $10,000 was abated to $1,157. In late 1925 the family home
was sold, and Ella and Theresa moved to the Park Lane Hotel. Presently
Ella married Robert Stevens Bartlett, an old childhood friend whom she
had known since the days of the premiere of Herbert's Easter anthem

"Christ Is Risen" at St. Paul's Cathedral, Buffalo, where Bartlett had sung as a boy chorister. The newlyweds and Theresa then set up housekeeping at 1010 Fifth Avenue.

Herbert's effects and library were auctioned at the Embassy Galleries in 1924 and brought an additional $25,000 to the estate. Gene Buck and Henry Soper were the chief purchasers of Herbert's personal music scores and books. The manuscripts were not included in the sale.

Soon Ella ordered work for a suitable Herbert mausoleum at Woodlawn. The modest structure of "white Dummerston Vermont granite free from cracks, iron, sap and other objectionable substances" has brass doors "of the better type with cross grille rosettes." A Tiffany stained-glass window featuring a green laurel wreath with a red and blue bow was installed, and on June 10, 1925, Theresa, Ella, Clifford and a company of Lambs and Friars brought Herbert to his final resting place. There are six crypts in the structure, three on each side of a central aisle. Herbert rests in the middle one to the right of the entrance, Theresa in the opposite one to the left. Ella is installed above her father, Robert Bartlett beneath him. On the window sill above a marble bench sits a sealed brass urn containing the ashes of Maud Herbert, the third surviving child of Victor and Theresa, who died on June 11, 1894, at the age of eight months. Theresa joined her husband in death on February 24, 1927. She had been ill with pneumonia for just a week. Ella and Clifford were at her side.

It is an indication of just how astute Ella was as a money manager that in the scant three years since her father's death she had increased the value of Theresa's estate to $322,973. The net estate after distributions came to $290,734, of which $279,836 had been invested in bonds, an impressive performance. With all that, Ella still came out on the short end, for Theresa's will left a life interest in $150,000 to Clifford. The balance, a cash bequest of $59,734, went to Ella. Theresa also assigned to Clifford her one-third interest in the copyrights and royalties.

Although executors tend to reduce the value of an estate for tax purposes, one aspect of the court filing is of historical interest. In projecting Theresa's probable royalties from her one-third interest, publishers' affidavits to the court estimated that for compositions written between 1894 and 1898 she would receive no more than $300, and for compositions written between 1898 and 1919 no more than $4,666. Further, the following works were declared economic "failures": *The Debutante, The Madcap Duchess, Sweethearts* [!], *Natoma, My Golden Girl, The Girl in the*

Spotlight, Orange Blossoms, Angel Face, Her Regiment, and Oui, Madame. Only the sheet music for "A Kiss in the Dark" was still being sold. Thus the nadir of Herbert's career was reached in early 1927.

In 1935, under strained circumstances, Clifford and Ella met with Theresa's executors, Gene Buck and Nathan Burkan, to determine the disposition of manuscripts then in possession of Tams-Witmark and at the Manhattan Storage Warehouse. It was agreed that they would choose scores seriatim in the proportion of 2:1, with Ella making first pick. It is revealing which scores each chose:.

Ella's choices:	*Mlle. Modiste, Sweethearts, Algeria, It Happened in Nordland, Prince Ananias, The Tattooed Man, The Viceroy, The Dream Girl, The Prima Donna, The Duchess, The Enchantress, When Sweet Sixteen, My Golden Girl, The Girl in the Spotlight, Madeleine, Old Dutch, The Only Girl, The Captive.*
Clifford's choices:	*Babes in Toyland, Miss Dolly Dollars, Wonderland, Dream City, The Velvet Lady, Her Regiment, Orange Blossoms, The Lady of the Slipper, The Debutante, Miss Camille.*

Other miscellaneous holdings were distributed on a 2:1 basis, and several non-copyrighted items were held for future distribution. Ella claimed sole rights to *The Ameer, The Idol's Eye, The Singing Girl* and *The Serenade*. As soon as these selections were approved by the executors, Ella had the music separated, and that which was Clifford's she intended to deliver to his New York address, but Clifford was anxious to turn his picks into ready cash. He arranged for his manuscripts to be sent directly to the American-Art Anderson Galleries for auction.

Ella took physical possession of her manuscripts and later deposited them in Washington, establishing a memorial archive. She retained ownership until her death, at which time, as she stated in one of her many wills: "I give and bequeath unto the Library of Congress Washington, D.C. all of the manuscripts and other material now on deposit there to be preserved in the archives of said library perpetually in memory of my father, Victor Herbert."[4]

We have already noted Ella's prodigious investment skills. The fact that by the time of her death she was able to build an estate of millions of dollars and that, in May of 1969, those funds were used to establish the Victor Herbert Foundation, is a key to the continuing presence of Herbert as a force in musical theater. Grants from the foundation have enabled many producing organizations, among them The Little Orchestra Society of New York, The New York City Opera, The Ohio Light Opera and The Victor Herbert Festival to keep these works alive for contemporary audiences. It is also informative to examine her work in connection with the management of her father's artistic heritage. Her motivation was certainly to preserve Herbert's legacy for posterity, but what she did and how she did it is significant. The story of Ella's contribution is much more than the story of the activities of a devoted and loving daughter. As early as 1925 Ella recognized the potential of the film medium as a new source of revenue. That year she sold the silent film rights in *The Red Mill* to the International Film Service for $1,215. In 1930 Ella and Clifford granted rights to RKO for a sound film based on *Babes in Toyland* for a substantial sum. Fifty thousand dollars was divided between the authors' heirs; Ella received $11,693.75 and Clifford $9,918.75. The travesty that resulted, a farce-comedy, one of the weakest of the Laurel and Hardy series, so outraged Ella that when, in 1936 she arranged through her agent to sell the film rights to MGM for a series of film musicals based on *The Red Mill, Algeria, Sweethearts*, and *Eileen*, she insisted that the contract contain the following language: "No opera is to be 'burlesqued' nor done by [Hal] Roach with Laurel and Hardy, or a like team."[5]

Each of the four works was assigned to MGM for $50,000, again the sum split equally between the heirs of the authors. Ella received $45,300 and Clifford $45,000.

At about the same time Ella was negotiating a contract with Paramount for a Herbert biography. This is a story that deserves separate discussion. Ella was actively engaged as a technical advisor on the film, and her extensive correspondence with producer, director and authors is revealing. What Ella wanted kept and what she demanded be eliminated from the script tells volumes about the image of her father she promoted, and aspects of his personality she wanted hidden from the public. In the meantime, her agreement with MGM reserved certain rights to Paramount.

All operas excepting "The Red Mill" to be subject to conditions of the Paramount contract [February, 1935] granting rights to use certain music in their one picture based on the life of Victor Herbert.

All rights covering licensing of single numbers from these operas for use as individual music in *other* motion pictures remain with the sellers.[6]

And the lady meant what she said. When in connection with the filming of *Sweethearts* the producers decided to convert a famous Herbert instrumental number, "Badinage," to a vocal number, they unwisely neglected to obtain Ella's permission. She demanded—and received—$3,333.30 for copyright infringement and insisted that MGM sweeten the pot with a payment of $30,000 [!] for recording rights. MGM should have known better.

In 1928 an old friend wrote to Ella. He had attended a concert that featured a performance of a song called "Coming Home," by Charles Willeby (music) and D. Eardley-Wilmot (text), which was so similar to "Ah, Sweet Mystery of Life" as to be of interest to her. Ella immediately contacted Witmark, whose attorneys landed on the John Church Company, publisher of "Coming Home." Shortly, both authors acknowledged that the song was "sufficiently similar" to Herbert's composition as to constitute copyright infringement. Witmark accepted a royalty of three cents per copy on each copy of the sheet music, settled from January 1, 1928. Ella's three-fifth's share amounted to $200. Not much, but it proved to anyone interested in Victor Herbert music that Ella was minding the store. In 1931, when Witmark wanted to republish "All For You," the duet from *The Princess "Pat"* with a new text and a refrain in 3/4 time rather than the original 6/8, they were careful to get Ella's permission. Later, after the production of the Herbert biopic, the publisher requested permission to reprint a song from the film based on "Rose of the World" with a new lyric. Ella approved the text and gave her okay, "subject to the same royalties." She had good taste. The verse was by a young man who was beginning his Hollywood career as a film lyricist. He had not yet started to write music. That would come later when he created *Where's Charley?*, Guys *and Dolls, The Most Happy Fella*, and *How to Succeed in Business.* Thus was born "Rose of the World," by Frank Loesser and Victor Herbert.

Ella was forever checking on the present state of Herbert copyrights, and in 1935 wrote to one of her father's old collaborators, a letter that brought this touching reply.

December 23, 1935

Dear Ella

I have not been able to write to you before. I have been and still am pretty sick. The operas in which I have sold my interest are Fortune Teller, Viceroy, Wizard of the Nile, Cyrano, Idol's Eye, Babette, Dolly Dollars, Serenade.

Excuse haste and bad pen. The haste is owing to heart condition, but the bad pen is my own fault.

With the season's greetings.

Your aged friend,

Harry B. Smith[7]

In 1940 Ella sent a note to Glen MacDonough's son, detailing still another adventure in copyright protection: "Sonja Henie used 'Babes in Toyland' music for about nine nights [in her ice show] trying again to get away without royalties—but we stopped her!"

But the greatest triumph of the daughter of ASCAP's founder was achieved in 1944. In conjunction with Clifford and Alan MacDonough, she filed suit in U.S. District Court against the Columbia Recording Company, Decca Records and RCA, charging copyright infringement. The defendants had illegally sold more than one million copies of "The March of the Toys." The companies settled out of court and the kids, once again, were rich.

Ella also recognized the importance of public relations. In 1930 Witmark reported that he had found the manuscript piano-vocal score, solo parts and chorus arrangements of a show called *Three Little Widows*, with text by Rida Johnson Young. This was one of three "unknown" Herbert works that Ella periodically announced had been "discovered." Between 1930 and 1935 the discovery of *Seven Little Widows*, *The House That Jack Built*, and *The Lavender Lady* was repeatedly noted in the press, keeping Herbert's name in the public eye just at the time that MGM was starting to release the series of films that were part of a 1930s Herbert renaissance. This was no coincidence. She even got to Louella Parsons, who reported:

Mike Todd Lists "Secret" Operetta of Victor Herbert

The dynamic and resourceful Mike Todd unearthed an unpublished score by Victor Herbert and kept it under wraps for over a year. He refused $350,000 for it because he believed he had something special. And this is what happens. He has signed Jeanette Macdonald to star in the operetta, which he says will be his greatest producing venture.[8]

Nonsense! It never happened.

Each time Ella made a gift of new material to the Library of Congress, it was news of a sort. But she was inventive in using gifting to preserve her father's memory in other ways. She gave $3,600 to the Sisters of Mercy Building Fund at Lake Placid for a room memorialized in the name of Victor Herbert. In 1951, at the University of Pennsylvania, "The Victor Herbert Collection established by his daughter Ella Herbert Bartlett" was completed with the donation of a rare copy of the piano-vocal score of *Prince Ananias.* This remains the only complete collection of the Herbert operetta scores at any university library.

Perhaps the most exciting story in connection with the building of the Herbert archive at the Library of Congress is the hunt for the manuscript of *Babes in Toyland.* By 1955 the collection was substantially complete, with the exception of this major item. The manuscript had been Clifford's first pick when the materials were divided, and since its sale in 1935 nothing had been heard of it. Robert Bartlett wrote to Waters early in 1955 that he thought he "had a line on it." Indeed he had. Ironically, the manuscript had surfaced in London, where Herbert's works had never been particularly successful. Sotheby's planned to include it in the catalogue of an upcoming sale. Bartlett wrote to the auction house immediately and received this reply:

> Dear Sir—
> We thank you for your letter concerning the manuscript score of "Babes in Toyland."
> This will be included in one of the later sales of the collection and we fear that at this moment it is not possible to let you know the date.
> It is however unlikely to go before the end of the year. We will certainly send you a copy of the catalogue with our appraisal and should of course be very pleased to execute a bid on your behalf.[9]

Waters emphasized to Bartlett, "We must do everything possible to bring it to the national collection." Ella was successful in her bid, and *Babes in Toyland* was repatriated to Washington.

Ella's efforts to keep the memory of her father's achievement in the forefront of the American consciousness were very successful, but she was only one of the forces operating to achieve that goal. Herbert's activities and associations had been so varied that it was natural for many hands to be involved in the work of memorializing him.

On the first anniversary of his death the managers of the Keith-Orpheum vaudeville circuit arranged for his music to be featured in all of their 300 theaters throughout the nation. One year later, radio had become a presence in many homes, and a Herbert memorial concert was broadcast from the Ritz-Carleton Hotel in New York to an estimated 18 million listeners.

Baltimore had been associated with Herbert's career in many ways. *Sweethearts* had its world premiere there, and Herbert frequently concertized in the city with the 22nd Regiment Band and, later, with his own orchestra. Two of his most important colleagues, librettist Rida Johnson Young and composer-arranger Gustav Klemm, were Baltimore natives. It is not surprising that Herbert composed his "Baltimore Centennial March" to honor the city that had been so important in his career.

Baltimore's German heritage may have been at the root of the popularity of his music there. But the city's beery burghers, from Mencken on down, no doubt also fondly remembered his widely publicized comments on Prohibition.

> Prohibition was brought about by fanaticism and hypocrisy. Do you know the reason the laboring man is not happy—is not contented? He does not have his beer. You cannot take away something from people that they actually want.
>
> Why 200 years ago in Russia the punishment for smoking was to have one's nose cut off. But it didn't stop smoking, did it? Prohibition is one of the greatest farces of today.[10]

In 1936 an all-Herbert memorial concert was held at Baltimore's Homewood Stadium. Eighteen thousand loyal fans attended. The city had not forgotten a favorite son.

In 1939, the first year of the New York World's Fair, whose theme was "the world of tomorrow," Herbert was honored with a retrospective of his world of yesterday. The Gaelic Musical Society promoted "Victor Herbert Night" and for the occasion assembled a special orchestra composed solely of men who had played under Herbert. It was a night of great music and greater emotion.

The next year, on May 13, a commemorative three-cent stamp honoring the composer went on sale. Fifty million stamps were issued, and 108,000 first-day cachets were made available at 9 AM to the 1,500 people gathered at the General Post Office in New York City. The crowd was entertained with a Herbert concert played by the Post Office Band under the direction of Edwin Franko Goldman. There were speeches by Postmaster Albert Goldman and Gene Buck, president of ASCAP. At the end of the program the Glee Club of the Friendly Sons of St. Patrick sang some of the original works Herbert had composed for them while he served as their director. The coverage in the *New York Times* sounded a faintly elegiac tone that reflected the contrast between the happy days when Herbert ruled Broadway and the anxieties of 1940s America:

> Thousands still whistle and hum the tunes of The Fortune Teller, M'lle Modiste and Naughty Marietta. [These] represent an unforgotten New York. Victor Herbert adopted Broadway with a whole-heartedness that made him one of the kindliest myths of that romantic street. . . . His work was only operetta, but no one can say that slightingly, for it had a lilting melody. Today it is heard almost as often over the radio and from the sound screen as when Fritzi Scheff and other stars were popularizing it on the stage. Victor Herbert's days were pleasant days in New York. A stamp dedicated to him brings a flood of pleasant memories when they are needed most.[11]

When World War I broke out, Herbert had lent his name to the effort. In 1943, years after his death, a Liberty Ship, one of those great, gray bare-bones utility vessels used to transport men and materiel to the World War II battle front, was commissioned the S.S. *Victor Herbert*.

It was also during the war years that Ella turned her attention to promoting an area of her father's music that had been neglected, his liturgical and patriotic compositions. As her husband described the effort, "I have chosen a different city each year and have requested one of the leading Episcopal Churches of that city to include Mr. Herbert's anthem in one of their Easter services."[12] This effort had first borne fruit at Trinity Church, Buffalo, on Easter Sunday, 1944, probably because the work in question, "Christ Is Risen," a huge cathedral anthem for mixed choir with solists, had had its premiere there at St. Paul's Cathedral in 1908. The next year Trinity Cathedral in Cleveland performed the work, and soon after Bartlett wrote suggesting they consider performing the final section of Herbert's Cantata, "The Call to Freedom"—"God Shall Guide Us." This religio-patriotic composition, with text by Herbert, was composed during the final days of World War I, but its message seemed as appropriate in 1945 as it had been in 1918. It would be pleasant to report that these works were neglected masterpieces, but that is surely not the case. Although they were sincere efforts and acceptable achievements, there is little to distinguish them from the vast number of pedestrian choral works that were turned out for the consumption of churchgoers in the first half of the twentieth century—a vast if uninspired repertoire.

February 1949 saw a month-long exhibit at the Library of Congress. Curated by Edward Waters, it presented some treasures of the Herbert memorial archive. Ten years later, for the centennial of his birth, a second and more elaborate exhibition was arranged, featuring photographic materials and manuscripts. Across the street in the Capitol building, members of the House and Senate rose to memorialize the man who had appeared there so many times in support of legislation protecting the copyrights of creative artists. The commissioners of the District of Columbia proclaimed February 1 "Victor Herbert Day in memory of the man whom people throughout the world honor as one of the greatest musicians and composers of his time."

In September of 1935 Ella shipped to the ASCAP offices in New York the piano Herbert had used at Lake Placid. This is the instrument now installed in the ASCAP reception hall. It was ASCAP that took the lead in orchestrating the centennial of its founder's birth; on the actual anniversary, ASCAP placed a wreath at the foot of the statue on the mall in Central Park, which it had given to the city in 1927. Deems Taylor, Otto Harbach and Irving Caesar were among the prominent guests of President Paul Cunningham, who addressed the Lambs, Friars and Friendly Sons assembled for the occasion. Mayor Robert Wagner proclaimed the first week of February Victor Herbert Week in New York City in recognition, among other things, of the "Beautiful melodies and operettas which have given so much pleasure to generations throughout the entire world." Herbert's old haunt, Lüchow's, featured Herbert music all week. Even the New York Athletic Club—not famous for its musical activities—presented a special concert at the urging of Clifford, who was a member.

Of all the tributes a grateful posterity provided, surely the one that would have pleased Herbert most was the "Victor Herbert–ASCAP Scholarship Awards." Funded by that organization, it was established to honor and encourage students and junior composers. The program gained national press coverage and helped "stimulate continued interest in the wonderful music of your father," as Stanley Adams, President of ASCAP, wrote to Ella.[13]

In 1950, twenty-five years after his death, Herbert became eligible for a place in New York University's Hall of Fame. The only other musicians with membership at that time were Stephen Foster and Edward Mac-Dowell. The electors for 1950 turned Herbert down.[14]

Physical memorials are important, of course, but the most important memorial to any theatrical artist is the continuing life of his work on the stage. In 1929 the Shubert Organization, original producers of *Little Nemo*, *Old Dutch*, *The Duchess* and *The Dream Girl* formed "the Jolson Theater Musical Comedy Company," whose purpose was to test the waters for operetta. After a decade when musical theater had been transformed by scores reflecting modern tastes in musical style, was there still gold to be mined from the vast treasures of the light opera repertoire—or was the vein played out? A visit in 1927 by the D'Oyly Carte had attracted sold-out houses of Gilbert and Sullivan aficionados, and perhaps a similar company might be organized to present a related repertoire.

The Shubert series included *The Prince of Pilsen*, *Robin Hood*, *The Chocolate Soldier*, *The Merry Widow* and *The Count of Luxembourg*. But the focus of the series was Herbert: *Sweethearts* with Gladys Baxter, *M'lle Modiste* with Fritzi Scheff, *Naughty Marietta* with Ilse Marvenga, *The Fortune Teller* with Eleanor Painter, *Babes in Toyland* and *The Serenade*. All the productions were directed by Milton Aborn, who strove to preserve the integrity of Herbert's material. "The music has not been tampered with—not one note. Even the instruments called for by Mr. Herbert in the original productions are used. . . . The only changes that have been made at all were in the book [of *Babes in Toyland*]. . . . But the music is unchanged, believe me."[15]

On September 22, 1929, on the occasion of the series' premiere, a revival of *Sweethearts*, John Mason Brown, no friend of operetta found the music "truly engaging."[16] The notice of the *New York Tribune* was more typical:

> Greeted by applause, hearty and frequent and interspersed with outbursts of laughter . . . the season of Victor Herbert operetta was launched and the hand of a master of comic opera was evident. After the fall of the curtain on the first act Father O'Callahan, one of the officers of the Victor Herbert Memorial Association expressed on its behalf appreciation of what the Shuberts had done to bring the operetta of Victor Herbert again before the public. He then announced that the original "Sylvia" in the first presentation of "Sweethearts" was in the house. He asked Miss Christie MacDonald if she would kindly stand up. An outburst of applause greeted her as she stood bowing and smiling.[17]

One month after the series was launched the stock market crashed, ushering in what was subsequently known as the "great depression." Operetta lovers hardly noticed.

Success has attended the revival of various of his operettas at Jolson's Theater this season. Jazz has not blotted out of the appreciation of the American public the kind of music which Victor Herbert created.

Could Mr. Herbert return to the flesh long enough to stand for a few minutes in the box office of Jolson's he would find proof conclusive of just how great the interest in his musical compositions still is. . . . He might even feel justified in feeling that his works were immortal.

"Sweethearts," "M'lle Modiste," "Naughty Marietta" and "The Fortune Teller" were all financial successes and now that "Babes in Toyland" is about to be presented the ticket-selling force reports that not only is the advance sale the biggest of the season, but that it is the biggest pre-opening sale in the history of Jolson's Theater.

It was either rank ignorance or base subterfuge to assume that the public would not appreciate good things.[18]

Such appreciation was not limited to New York audiences. When the series at the Jolson ended because the theater had a previous commitment, the company was transported to the Shubert Theater in Newark, New Jersey, and the same cycle was repeated with the same success.

"The revivals . . . have proved by the incontrovertible logic of the box office receipts the existence of a vast audience for the music of the American master."

"Six companies are on tour in pieces heard earlier this season. The theater is a commercial proposition; the tours would scarcely be continued if they were not profitable."

"The season here [Chicago] originally announced for but ten weeks has stretched thus far to twenty-two of which eleven have been devoted to Herbert. It goes on and on with no end in sight."[19]

On and on indeed, to the Majestic theaters in Boston and Chicago. Fritzi Scheff formed her own company, and *Mlle. Modiste* with Scheff is past its 20th week on tour.[20] Still, this huge success was playing to an audience that had known Victor Herbert in his prime. They were revisiting—perhaps with their children—the theatrical glories of their youth.

What of the future? Fast forward to 1947—to the 46th Street Theater in New York, where Paula Stone, Fred Stone's daughter, and Hunt

Stromberg, Jr., took a chance on Herbert once again with *The Red Mill*. They faced a new audience that had no sentimental memories of Herbert's golden days. Eddie Foy, Jr., and Jack Whiting played the roles created by Montgomery and Stone in the original, and the mill kept churning out gold, surpassing its original run of 275 performances. It was the same story with the second production, Bobby Clark in *Sweethearts*. Hollywood took notice.

The first impetus for the creation of a Herbert film biography came from Benjamin Glazer. This multi-talented playwright and producer shared an Irish heritage with Herbert. Born in Belfast, he was raised and educated in Philadelphia, where he later worked as a music critic. It was in this capacity that he became a Herbert devotee, and in 1935, having resettled in Hollywood, he prepared a scenario based on Herbert's life.[21] The two-time academy-award winner (for *Seventh Heaven* and *Arise My Love*) fashioned a delightful outline that closely followed the details of Herbert's American career. The first scene shows him and Theresa crossing the Hudson on a ferry shortly after their arrival. Herbert's main concern is finding a decent glass of beer on board, and he disappears in search of a brew. Theresa locates him comfortably ensconced in the ferry salon, enjoying his drink and sitting in with the house orchestra on his cello, surrounded by a group of new friends. In this one scene Glazer captured three aspects of Herbert: his conviviality, his musicality and his love of good beer. Unfortunately, the powers that be at Paramount never picked up on Glazer's project. It had been a labor of love and went into that Bermuda triangle called turnaround, from which so many film projects have never emerged. Still, to a biographer, Glazer's scenario offers many treasures. It was written by a theatrical professional whose early career in New York as a playwright was contemporaneous with Herbert's last decades. Glazer knew Herbert's career intimately. This is reflected in the monologue he assigns to Herbert at the very beginning of his treatment.

I'll compose. I'll conduct. I'll start an orchestra—a string quartet—a band. I'll write operettas for every theater in town. I'll even write something dull enough for the Met if I have to. I'll make Broadway doff its hat to me. I'll make America sing along.
(Flash scenes follow Herbert's career monologue. Herbert conducting the Pittsburgh Orchestra, the 22nd Regiment Band, The Victor Herbert Orchestra. Theater marquees with names of his hits.)

Perhaps the most valuable insight Glazer's treatment provides lies in the section that deals with the subject of Herbert's fidelity. This is a lovely sequence in which an affair between the Fritzi Scheff character and Herbert is hinted at. It begins with Herbert and "Leni" at dinner, where he prepares his famous champagne cocktail for her.

(He takes the wine glass, tilts it, pours in a few drops [of Worcestershire sauce] rolling the glass until it is half covered with the dark liquid. He pours in champagne.)

Herbert: Under its spell pessimism flies. *One* gulp and all the earth's round face puts on a silken fool's cap. *Two*—and each cloud in the sky takes the form of a fair lady. *Three*—and M'lle Modiste will be the love of all New York's lifetime—the darlin' of its middle age—as Leni is of mine.
(He takes out one of his cigars, lights it expansively and settles back, his hand finding an affectionate place on Leni's on the table.)
(Leni tells him she likes his cigars.)

Leni: It is a wise woman who knows her hero's favorite brand. Has your wife no interest in smoking?

Herbert: What? No. Not very much. I wouldn't expect her to.
(Learning that Theresa won't be at her opening Leni invites Victor to a small party at her apartment after the premier.)

Leni: Just a few people. But they won't stay long. You have never been to my apartment. It's very cosy.

Herbert: I'm sure it must be.

Leni: And I'll have cigars for you.

Herbert: Big, dark strong ones. That's what I like.
(There follows a short sequence in Herbert's study. Theresa is brushing his dress suit. She puts cigars and a note "Good luck to my Victor" in his pocket. She wraps the note around a cigar and secures it with her wedding ring.
Segue to finale of "M'lle Modiste" on opening night. Curtain calls. Herbert and Leni hold hands. Herbert bows to her. Leni gives him a big kiss. She puts one of the roses from her bouquet in his lapel.)
(Relaxing backstage with Leni Herbert takes out a cigar and finds the wedding ring.)

Leni: Oh, Victor. I'm afraid your wife does take just a little interest in your—smoking.

Herbert:	So it seems. Perhaps I'd better. . . .
Leni:	I understand. (She looks at the ring.) She must have a very big hand.
Herbert:	It only hints at the size of her heart. Good night, my dear Leni.
Leni:	Good bye, my dear Victor.

(Leni leaves. Victor remains.)

This scene segues to a scene at the stage door where Victor invites a few friends to his home. His protégée, Hal, is surprised at the late invitation.

> *Victor* (to Hal): You chaps can't understand how important friends are. If you were married you'd understand what I'm talking about. Marriage means the greatest friendship—and the greatest love of them all!

Although this scene is fictitious, the subject of Herbert's fidelity was often discussed in theatrical circles. He was a man who took his pleasures seriously; food, drink, career. The "kiss" had been the talk of Broadway, although it happened at the premiere of *Babette*, not of *Modiste*, and in fact Herbert's reaction to it was embarrassment. This sequence, coming from the pen of a theater man whose career was contemporary with Herbert's, is strong if indirect evidence that philandering was not one of Herbert's vices. This is a scene that could have played out differently. It was, after all, part of a scenario that was never filmed, and therefore not limited by the film restrictions of the late 1930s. Glazer could have intimated a delicate indiscretion or even ended the sequence with the famous kiss, and left the rest to the audience's imagination. That he chose to show Herbert's fidelity in the face of temptation is the surest evidence we have that this was in fact the truth. Temptation was all around him, but it was food, drink and career that received his indulgence.

The film that Paramount eventually produced was based on an entirely fictional treatment by Robert Lively and producer-director Andrew Stone. It was written by Lively and Russel Crouse. Ella was contracted

> To perform services as a technical advisor. . . . Services to include advice on all matters pertaining to the life of Victor Herbert and incidents therein, as well as all matters relating to the story and music of the production; to read all scripts and to give the Corporation the benefit of her recommendations, suggestions and comment thereon; if

required to advise with the writers, directors, artists etc. and to give them the benefit of her knowledge, experience and background of the life of her father.[22]

Ella took her responsibilities seriously. In the months that followed, she engaged in an extended correspondence with the producers and authors of the film, objecting vigorously to a script that in its initial form painted Herbert as a beer-swilling, short-tempered gourmand. She was also concerned with the physical image of her father that Walter Connolly might project.

> I have seen Mr. Connolly in pictures . . . and I feel that he is now just about the same size as father, except in height. I thought I would suggest that nothing be done to make him look any heavier. Some people have the idea that father was a big man and "fat." This is *not* so, although, because of his broad well developed shoulders he might have appeared so to some who did not know him well. He was an imposing man, but he did not carry one ounce of excess weight considering his height.[23]

For the most part Lively and Crouse accepted Ella's comments and revised the image of Herbert so that nothing that was offensive to her is included in the shooting script. There was a section, key to the drama, in which Herbert is shown to be concerned with the weakening success of his later stage works. Ella fought that tooth and nail, but because the sequence was essential to the dramatic development, the authors refused to yield. As a compromise, Ella insisted on a disclaimer being run at the end title:

> No attempt has been made to depict in this picture the actual life of the immortal Victor Herbert. Many of the episodes, incidents and characters are entirely fictitious. A careful effort has been made however to preserve the character and mood of the great composer whose music serves as the inspiration for this picture.

The greatest conflict arose concerning the proper title for the film. The original, *The Life and Melodies of Victor Herbert*, was inexplicably changed to *The Gay Days of Victor Herbert*. Ella lodged a vigorous protest.

> Your title is misleading and untruthful and it infers that there were licentious or racy incidents in father's life and that you have chosen

these on which to base your picture. This title will seriously adversely affect father's reputation and character and for this reason I ask that you return to the original title, or one that is not libelous and damaging.[24]

The film, now titled *The Great Victor Herbert*, was released in December, 1939, and received many positive reviews as an "elaborate picture of a florid yesterday." But no reaction was more positive than Ella's. She loved it. So her husband wrote to Andrew Stone:

> You may be interested to know that we are going to see "The Great Victor Herbert" for the third time on Thursday. . . . It is a picture which grows on one and the more we see it the better we like it. We watch with great interest the success of it as reported each week in "Variety" and we are sure you must be gratified with its records. . . . Your musical director . . . did a wonderful job in arranging and directing the score.[25]

Another Hollywood happy ending.

To the films based on the Herbert operettas, the statement of film historian Michael Druxman may be applied—in spades! "With few exceptions, most film musical adaptations of the '30s and '40s bore scant resemblance to their stage originals. Sometimes the plot was completely changed; on other occasions, all but the major hit tunes were dropped in favor of new material."[26]

The earliest film was the 1934 travesty of *Babes in Toyland* already mentioned. It was followed by the two most famous Herbert films. These starred Jeanette MacDonald and Nelson Eddy: *Naughty Marietta* (1935) and *Sweethearts* (1938). MacDonald brought six years of prior film experience to her roles, and was a charming screen presence. Eddy was another in a line of "voices" that Hollywood had been showcasing since the earliest days of sound film. With the exception of Lawrence Tibbett, none of these (Grace Moore, John McCormack, Dennis King, Nino Martini) brought much distinction to the dramatic aspect of the productions. Eddy had an instrument that blended well with MacDonald's lyric coloratura, and for a while the duo was one of Hollywood's most reliable box-office attractions. But the unreality of the fairytale settings and plots that these films offered served to create an image of the "Victor Herbert musical" from which it has never recovered. Mention the name Victor Herbert to

90 percent of the contemporary audience and the reaction—if any—will be, "Oh, yes . . . Jeanette McDonald and Nelson Eddy"; the image that most often comes to mind is of a romantic-sentimental cloud-cuckoo-land—irremediably old fashioned—festooned with a few nice tunes. And the tunes in these films were not always Herbert's! In a contract for a second *Babes in Toyland* film (1945) Ella granted the right

> To use, arrange, adapt, change, transpose, add to and subtract from said operetta, its words and music, lyrics, limiting the right to interpolate additional musical numbers (i.e. musical numbers not contained in said operetta) to two numbers. . . . The Licensee shall have the right to interpolate in the overture, entre'actes or finales such additional music as is needed.[27]

The result is reflected in Edward Waters's comment to Bartlett:

> One parting shot *re* Naughty Marietta. . . . My contention is that anyone seeing it would not learn very much about the operetta itself, at least musically. To be sure the most famous solos were in it, but most of the music in the film was composed by Herbert Stothart for which I thought there was no excuse at all.[28]

Hollywood's success (*Sweethearts* proved one of the biggest box office grossers of 1938) was purchased at the cost of a lasting false image of Herbert's works, an image that only productions based on a close and extensive examination of the original materials can lay to rest.

In 1924, the year Herbert died, 190,000 American homes had radios. By the end of the 1920s the number had grown to just under five million. Herbert missed personal participation in the wonders of the new medium, but his music was the fuel that drove the new engine of mass entertainment. "Radio cut its musical eye teeth on Victor Herbert. . . . There was hardly a program in those early days that did not include a Herbert melody. 'All Herbert' programs were as common as static."[29]

This phenomenon was not restricted to the United States. The archives of ASCAP reveal that between April and June of 1924 radio in Great Britain programmed twenty-four performances of Victor Herbert favorites. And Radio Luxembourg, in the same few months, featured six Herbert programs. Naturally the majority of Herbert radio performances were American. Smack in the middle of the Jazz Age, when Herbert's melodies were supposed to have been too old-fashioned and sentimental for modern tastes, their popularity with the American public was undiminished.

All of this free exposure increased the sale of Herbert recordings and sheet music, and, in combination with the Shubert revivals and Hollywood films, resulted in a Herbert renaissance. We are fortunate to have reminiscences of the early radio era from one of its stars, Jessica Dragonette:

> The program was "The Musical Comedy Hour." It was broadcast Saturday nights on the "New England Network" and again on Sunday in New York. Harold Sanford, who had worked closely with Herbert was our musical director. He told me exactly the way every phrase, every role had to be played according to Victor Herbert.

> Then we launched two and a half years of the "Philco Hour of Theater Memories." Herbert's daughter came to the studio every time we did one of her father's operettas. She was very silent, but oh so touched. We tried to do all the Victor Herbert ones and they were always popular. She was very nice to me. She said, "Oh, if my father could only have heard you."[30]

In 1959, on the one-hundredth anniversary of Herbert's birth, radio went all-out to honor the occasion. The Peter Lind Hayes show on ABC featured music and an interview with ASCAP President Paul Cunningham. NBC's "Monitor" interviewed Deems Taylor, Cunningham and Ella. CBS featured a similar interview with Taylor. Herbert was the subject of a special feature on the Metropolitan Opera Broadcast of January 31. And television was not to be left out of the festivities. Lawrence Welk, Dinah Shore, Vincent Lopez and even Milton Berle did their part to honor the memory of the great man. But it was Mike Wallace in 1951, on a CBS radio series, "50 Years of Musical Comedy," who mined the crown jewel of Herbert radio recollections. He managed to snare an interview with Fritzi Scheff (no easy task) and to get her to talk about "Kiss Me Again." Here from the diva's own lips is the most authentic version of the events associated with the premiere of Herbert's greatest hit.

> I did sing it the first two days of rehearsals. But it was so low—it annoyed me.

Herbert said, "No, no Fritzi. You have wonderful low notes. That's the only way I can make you use them."

I threw the song out for twelve rehearsals. Victor Herbert said, "It's my best number, Fritzi." Henry Blossom said, "It's my best lyric."

So I said, "I'll sing it—as a Christmas present."

Mlle. Modiste premiered on Christmas night 1905. Fritzi's performance was the best Christmas present Herbert had ever received.

At the end of the interview with Mike Wallace, Fritzi sang "Kiss Me Again" for the radio audience, and for posterity. When she finished, she remarked wistfully to Wallace, "If I die and go to heaven St. Peter will let me in. He'll say, *'You're* the one who sang "Kiss Me Again." How do you do? In you go!'"[31] No doubt Herbert was waiting there to welcome her to the company of the immortals.

CHAPTER 20

FEBRUARY 1, 2003

February 1, 2003, was a warm day in Central Park. The night before, a light snow had fallen, and the warm air moving across the icy landscape gave rise to a mist that obscured the mall where, on summer nights, hundreds of music lovers gathered. In recent years the Goldman Band had performed there, carrying on a tradition established by the great bandmasters of the past: Gilmore, Sousa and Victor Herbert.

From a distance of a hundred feet the image of Victor Herbert's statue was also shrouded in mist. Approaching the hillock where it stands, a visitor joins a small group of people gathered to commemorate his birthday. The Victor Herbert Foundation, under the chairmanship of Herbert P. Jacoby, arranged for the Central Park Conservancy to place an elaborate floral display by the statue, the colors of spring flowers incongruous amid the snow-covered fences and benches. One of the visitors was a living link to Herbert's past—some to his future. Jacoby had been Ella's attorney and had been instrumental in creating the Foundation. Representatives of organizations responsible for the continuing renaissance of the Herbert operettas—the Little Orchestra Society of New York and the Victor Herbert Festival—were also there.

No one spoke. Perhaps the silence was more eloquent than any speech, for there had been speeches aplenty. The mist-shrouded statue called to mind the first time it stood covered, February 1, 1927, the day ASCAP presented it to the city of New York. To the imagination, the spirits of the men and women who had gathered that day were easy to make out through the swirling fog: Irving Berlin, Harry Von Tilzer, Sigmund Romberg, Julius Witmark, Eddie Cantor, John Golden, Arthur Hammerstein, Joe Weber, Charles K. Harris, Nathan Burkan, H. T. Burleigh, Ella and Clifford. Gene Buck, President of ASCAP had made the formal presentation to Mayor Jimmy Walker.

As President of ASCAP, and spokesman for every author and composer in America I am presenting this monument as a symbol of affection and esteem for a man and a great composer. He had

547

technique and taste. No greater, better, more lovable or admirable composer has graced our generation. His music had originality, force, simplicity and charm. And that is why his music lives.

To which Mayor Walker replied:

Valuable as this spot is, it is made richer by the presence of this statue. You'll find statues of men great in war, science and the arts in this great park, but none can overshadow Victor Herbert.

I remember Victor Herbert when he was leader of the band of the old 22nd Regiment, when I was just a New York kid. We boys used to think it the finest band in the world. As long as the human voice shall sing, as long as human hearts respond to melody the genius of Victor Herbert shall exist. Here where the people of the world come to make their home Victor Herbert brought all the romance and imagination of his heritage.

And then Mayor Walker surpassed himself and paid Herbert the greatest tribute of all: "Herbert would have been a great man even without his music." True enough. In every aspect of his life—his work, his generosity, his caring for the welfare and enhancement of others, his patriotism, his concern for his family he was "great" as only great souls can be. The music was a bonus through which he lives on, rich, varied, soulful, sweet, funny and—dare we say it in an age when scatology is accepted and this next is reviled—sentimental?

What's wrong with sentiment? Herbert's legacy is that—a gift that our brittle, sterile world can ill-afford to reject.

In 1927 Ella pulled the chord—the shroud fell—and Herbert's bronzed face looked upon these transient scenes for the first time.

The few gathered in 2003 slowly dispersed. And then, through the hanging mists, we heard a melody. A street musician—a black man whose solo saxophone playing has become an icon of the world of Central Park—began to play "Indian Summer." And we turned back, amazed, caught by the haunting phrases and we looked up at Herbert's idealized face.

Through the mists of that day—and of time—he was smiling. That smile, that melody are enduring gifts to all of us, born of his rare artistry and even rarer humanity.

STAGE COMPOSITIONS BY VICTOR HERBERT

OPERAS

Madeleine (1913): lyric opera, one act. Text by Grant Stewart. New York: G. Schirmer, Inc.

Natoma (1911): opera in three acts. Text by Joseph D. Redding. New York: G. Schirmer, Inc.

Musical Numbers:

"Beware of the Hawk"; "My Baby" ("Indian Lullaby"); "Dagger Dance"; "Grand Fantasia"; "Great Manitou"; "Habanera"; "I List the Trill in Golden Throat"; "In My Dreams"; "Indian Invocation"; "Indian Lullaby"; Introduction; "Lonely Am I"; Minuet; "Natoma Serenade" ("When Sunlight Dies"); "Panuelo"; Prelude; "Paul's Address"; "Spring Song"; "Vaquero's Song" ("Who Dares the Bronco Wild Defy?").

OPERETTAS AND MUSICAL COMEDIES

The Ameer (1899). Text by Frederic Ranken and Kirke LaShelle. New York: M. Witmark and Sons.

Musical Numbers:

"Ah! Woe Is Me"; "The Ameer"; "Cupid Will Guide"; "Fancies, Only Fancies"; "Fond Love, True Love"; "I'd Like It"; "In Old Ben Franklin's Day"; "Lanciers"; "Little Poster Maid"; "Old Maids Are Willing to Please"; "Soldiers All"; "Sweet Clarissa" ("Darky Love Song"); "Tell Me Pray."

Angel Face (1919). Text by Robert B. Smith. New York: Harms, Inc.

Musical Numbers:

"Call It a Day"; "Everybody's Crazy Half of the Time"; "How Do You Get that Way?"; "I Don't Want to Go Home"; "I Might Be Your Once-in-a-While"; Lullaby ("Bye, Bye, Baby"); "My Idea of Something to Go Home to"; "Someone Like You"; "Those Since-I-Met-You Days"; "Tip Your Hat to Hattie."

Babes in Toyland (1903). Text by Glen MacDonough. New York: Witmark and Sons.

Musical Numbers:

"Angels Over the Fields"; "Babes in Toyland"; "Barney O'Flynn"; "Beatrice Barefacts"; "Before and After"; "Birth of the Butterfly"; "Contrary Mary"; "Country Dance"; "Don't Cry Bo-Peep"; Finale (Act 2); "Floretta"; "From Heaven on High"; Gavotte; "Go to Sleep, Slumber Deep" (Lullaby); "Hail to Christmas"; "Hang March"; "He Won't Be Happy 'Till He Gets It"; "The Health Food Man"; "I Can't Do the Sum"; "In the Toymaker's Workshop"; "Jane"; "John Johnson"; "Lancers"; "Largo"; "A Legend"; March And Two-Step; "March of the Toys"; "Melodramatic Music"; "Men"; "Mignonette"; "Military Ball"; "The Moon Will Help You Out"; "Never Mind Bo-Peep, We Will Find Your Sheep"; "Our Castle in Spain"; Overture; "Song of the Poet";

Spanish Basque Carol; "Spiders' Den"; "Toyland"; Waltzes; "Winter Song"; "With Downcast Eyes."

Babette (1903). Text by Harry B. Smith. New York: Witmark and Sons.
Musical Numbers:
"Babette" (March); "Be Kind to Poor Pierrot"; "Entrance of Babette"; "He Who'd Thrive Must Rise at Five"; "Hear the Coachman Crack His Whip"; "Here In Pleasure's Favorite Court"; "I'll Bribe the Stars"; "It's a Way We Have in Spain"; "Let Hope of Thee My Guardian Be"; "Letters I Write All Day"; "Life of a Bold Free Lance"; "My Honor and My Sword"; "My Lady 'Tis for Thee"; "The Lady of the Manor"; "On the Other Side of the Wall"; "On the Stage"; "Story of Babette"; "There Once Was an Owl"; "To Sound of the Pipe and Roll of the Drum"; "Tony the Peddler"; "We're Very Highly Polished at the Court Don't You Know"; "What Is Love?"; "Where the Fairest Flowers Are Blooming."

The Century Girl (1916). Text by Harry B. Smith. New York: Harms, Inc.
Musical Numbers:
"You Belong to Me"; "The Birth of the Century Girl."

Text by Henry Blossom. New York: Harms, Inc.
Musical Numbers:
"The Century Girl"; "Humpty Dumpty"; "The Romping Redheads"; "The Stone Age"; "The Ballet Loose"; "The Toy Soldiers"; "Under the Sea"; "When Uncle Sam Is Ruler of the Sea."

Cyrano de Bergerac (1899). Text by Harry B. Smith. New York: M. Witmark and Sons.
Musical Numbers
"Cadets of Gascony"; "Diplomacy"; "I Am a Court Coquette"; "I Come from Gascony"; "I Must Marry a Handsome Man"; "I Wonder"; "The King's Musketeers"; "Let The Sun of Thine Eyes"; "Over the Mountain"; "Ragueneau's Café"; "Since I Am Not for Thee"; "Song of the Nose"; "Those Were the Good Old Times"; "In Bivouac Reposing."

The Debutante (1914). Text by Robert B. Smith. New York: G. Shirmer, Inc.
Musical Numbers:
"All for the Sake of a Girl"; "Baker's Boy and the Chimneysweep"; "Call Around Again"; "Debutante One-Step"; Entr'Acte; "Fate"; "Gay the Life"; "Golden Age"; "Love Is a Battle"; "Love of the Lorelei"; "Never Mention Love When We're Alone"; "On a Sunny Afternoon"; Overture; "Peggy's a Creature of Moods"; "Professor Cupid"; "Springtime of Life Is Fairest"; "Take Me Home with You"; Waltzes; "When I Played Carmen"; "Will o' the Wisp"; "The Music of the Future."

Dream City and The Magic Knight (1907). Text by Edgar Smith. New York: M. Witmark and Sons.
Musical Numbers:
"Down a Shady Lane"; Entr'Acte; "A Farmer's Life"; "Hannah"; I Don't Believe I'll Ever Be a Lady"; "I Love You"; "Improvements"; "In Vaudeville"; "Lancers Waltz"; "Love by Telephone"; "Nancy, I Fancy You"; "An Operatic Maiden"; "Ravenous

Rooster"; "Shy Suburban Maid"; "Ta Ta My Dainty Little Darling"; "The Volunteer Fireman"; Waltzes; March.

The Dream Girl (1924). Text by Rida Johnson Young. New York: Harms, Inc.
Musical Numbers:
"At the Rainbow's End"; "Bubble Song"; "Cling"; "Gypsy Girl"; "If Somebody Only Would Find Me"; "My Dream Girl" ("I Loved You Long Ago"); "My Hero"; "Stop, Look, Listen."

The Duchess (1911) (previously called *Rosita, Mademoiselle Rosita, The Rose Shop* and *Mademoiselle Boutonniere*). Text by Harry B. Smith and Joseph Herbert. New York: M. Witmark and Sons.
Musical Numbers:
"The Coryphee"; "Cupid Tell Me Why"; "The Duchess"; "Entrance of Rose"; Finale Act I; Finale Act II; Finale Ultimo; "Girlie-Land"; "Hunting Song"; "If I Should Dream of You"; "I'm Such a Romantic Girl"; "Isn't It Nasty of Papa"; "It's the Bump"; "Lane of Maidens' Charms" (March Song); "Land of the Sultan's Dream"; "Latest Society Pet"; "Let Me Be Free"; "Life Is a Riddle"; "Old Noblesse"; Opening Chorus; Opening Chorus Act II; "Play the Game"; "Sally"; "Sham"; "Teach Me to Forget"; "Upsi-Daisy"; Waltzes; "What's the Use of Moonlight?"

Eileen (1917) (previously entitled *Hearts of Erin*). Text by Henry Blossom. New York: M. Witmark and Sons.
Musical Numbers:
"Cupid the Cunnin' Paudeen"; "Dinny's Serenade"; "Eileen"; "Entrance of Humpy Grogan"; "Erin Slanthogal Go Bragh"; "Erin's Isle" ("In Erin's Isle"); Finale; "Free Trade and Misty Moon"; General Dance; "Glad Triumphant Hour"; "I'd Love to Be a Lady"; "If Eve Had Left the Apple on the Bough"; "In the Name of the King"; Introduction (Act 3); "Ireland, My Sireland"; "The Irish Have a Great Day Tonight"; "Jig"; "Life's a Game at Best"; "Love's Awakening" ("When Love Awakens"); "A Man that Can Die like a Soldier"; "My Good Friends of Erin's Isle"; "My Little Irish Rose"; One-Step; Opening Chorus (Act 3); Overture; Prelude; Reveries; "Stars and Rosebuds"; "Thine Alone"; "Too-Re-Loo-Re" ("A French Pavanne"); "When Ireland Stands among the Nations of the World"; "When Shall I Again See Ireland."

The Enchantress (1911). Text by Harry B. Smith and Frederika de Gresac. New York: M. Witmark and Sons.
Musical Numbers:
"All Your Own Am I"; "Art Is Calling for Me"; "Come Little Fishes"; "Come to Sunny Spain"; "Dreaming Princess"; "Duo"; Entrance of the Regent; Entrance of Vivien and Song; Finale; "Gold Fish Song"; "If You Can't Be as Happy as You'd Like to Be, Just Be as Happy as You Can"; "I've Been Looking for the Perfect Man"; "Last Little Girl Is You"; "Lover Come Back"; March Chorus; March of Prince's Regiment; "One Word From You"; "Rose, Lucky Rose"; "That Pretty Little Song"; "They All Look Good When They're Far Away"; "The Land of My Own Romance"; "When the Right Man Sings Tra-La-La"; "When You Look in Her Eyes."

The Fortune Teller (1898). Text by Harry B. Smith. New York: M. Witmark and Sons.
Musical Numbers:
"Always Do as People Say You Should"; "Czardas" ("Romany Life"); "Champagne Song"; Chorus of Hussars; Entrance of the Count; "The Fortune Teller" ("Slumber On, My Little Gypsy Sweetheart"); "Guten Morgen, Buon Giorno, Bonjour; "Gypsy Jan"; "Ho! Ye Townsmen"; "Hungaria's Hussars"; "The Lily and the Nightingale"; "Maestoso"; "Only in the Play"; Opening Chorus (Act 2); Opening Ensemble (Act 1); Overture; Prelude; "The Power of the Human Eye"; "Serenades of All Nations"; "Signor Mons. Muldoni"; "Sing to Me Gypsy"; "Where'er in Thick of Fight"; "With Lance at Rest."

The Girl in the Spotlight (1920). Text by Richard Bruce (Robert B. Smith). New York: Harms, Inc.
Musical Numbers:
"Catch 'Em Young, Treat 'Em Rough, Tell 'Em Nothing"; "Girl in the Spotlight"; "I Cannot Sleep without Dreaming of You"; "I Love the Ground You Walk On"; "I'll Be There"; "It Would Happen Anyway"; "Marry Me and See"; "Only You"; "Somewhere I Know There's a Girl for Me"; "There's a Tender Look in Your Eyes."

The Gold Bug (1896). Text by Glen MacDonough. New York: Schuberth.
Musical Numbers:
"One for Another"; "The Owl and the Thrush"; "Gold Bug March."

Her Regiment (1917). Text by William Le Baron. New York: Harms, Inc.
Musical Numbers:
"American Serenade"; "Art Song"; "As the Years Roll By"; "Girl behind the Gun"; "If Things Were What They Seem"; "Little Farm in Normandy"; "Nerves"; "Oh, My"; "Soldier Men"; "Someday"; "Superlative Love"; "'Twixt Love and Duty"; "Vive la France."

The Idol's Eye (1897). Text by Harry B. Smith. New York: Schuberth.
Musical Numbers:
"Absent-Minded Maid"; "Captain Charlie Chumley"; "Fairy Tales"; "Lady and the Kick"; "Lancers"; "Letter Duet"; March; "Mindin' the Baby"; "Only for Thee"; "Pretty Isabella and Her Umbrella"; "Priestess' Song"; "Talk about Yo' Luck"; "The Tattooed Man"; "Tom and Jack"; Two-Step; Waltzes.

It Happened in Nordland (1905). Text by Glen MacDonough. New York: M. Witmark and Sons.
Musical Numbers:
"Absinthe Frappé"; "Al Fresco"; "Bandana Land"; "Commanderess-in-Chief"; "Folly Is Our King"; "Friends That Are Staunch and True"; "Goodbye My Love"; "Governor of Guam"; "I Brought Them Home to Mother"; "Jack O' Lantern Girl"; "Knot of Blue"; "Little Class of One"; "Love Is Like a Cigarette"; "The Man Meant Well"; March and Two-Step; "Matinee Maid"; Melodramatic Music; "My Catamaran"; "Oyaneetah" ("Seminole Love Song"); "Potpourri"; "Saturday Saidee"; "She's a Very Dear Friend of Mine"; "Slippery James"; "The Woman in the Case."

The Lady of the Slipper (A Modern Cinderella) (1912). Text by L. M. McCarty and A. Caldwell. Lyrics by James O'Dea. New York: M. Witmark and Sons.
Musical Numbers:
"At the Bal Masqué"; "Bagdad"; Ballet Suite; Entrance of Cinderella and Princess of Far Away; Fairy Music; "Fond of the Ladies"; "Games of Halloween"; "Garden Party"; "Jack O' Lantern Love"; "Just Love Me all the Time"; "Just You and I in Dreamland"; "Like a Real, Real Man"; "Little Girl at Home"; "My Russian Girlski"; "Princess of Far Away"; "Put Your Best Foot Forward, Little Girl"; "Punch Bowl Glide."

Little Nemo (1908). Text by Harry B. Smith. New York: M. Witmark and Sons.
Musical Numbers:
"Give Us a Fleet"; "Happy Land of Once Upon a Time"; "The Hen and the Weathervane"; "I Guess I Talk Too Much"; "I Want to Be a Naughty Little Girl"; "I Wouldn't Take a Case Like That"; "If I Could Teach My Teddy Bear to Dance"; "In Happy Slumberland"; "March of the Valentines"; "Remember the Old Continentals"; "There's Nothing the Matter with You"; "They Were Irish"; "What Fools We Mortals Be"; "When Cupid Is the Postman"; "Will-o-the-Wisp"; "Won't You Be My Playmate"; "Won't You Be My Valentine."

The Madcap Duchess (1913). Text by David Stevens and Justin McCarthy. New York: G. Schirmer, Inc.
Musical Numbers:
"Aurora Blushing Rosily"; "Babette of Beaujolais"; "Canzonetta"; "Do You Know"; "Far Up the Hill"; "Love and I Are Playing"; "Love Is a Story"; "Oh Up, It's Up"; "Star of Love"; "Sweethearts' Waltzes"; Three Favorite Airs; "To Paris"; "Tweedledum and Tweedledee"; "Winged Love."

Mlle. Modiste (1905). Text by Henry Blossom. New York: M. Witmark and Sons.
Musical Numbers:
Ballet; Charity Bazaar; Chorus of the Footmen; "Dear Little Girl Who Is Good"; Entr'Acte; Finale (Act 1); "Furs and Feathers"; "Hats Make the Woman"; "I Should Think that You Could Guess"; "I Want What I Want When I Want It"; "If I Were on the Stage"; "I'm Always Misunderstood"; "In Dreams so Fair"; Introduction; "Just Good Friends"; "Keokuk Culture Club"; "Kiss Me Again"; "Love Me, Love My Dog"; "Mascot of the Troop"; "The Nightingale and the Star"; Opening Chorus (Act 1); Overture; Servants' Chorus; "The Time, the Place and the Girl"; "When the Cat's Away the Mice Will Play"; "Ze English Language."

Miss Dolly Dollars (1905). Text by Harry B. Smith. New York: M. Witmark and Sons.
Musical Numbers:
"American Heiress"; "'Tis Better than Old Parsifal to Me"; "Barney Maguire"; "Dolly Dollars"; "Educated Fool"; Entrance of Dorothy; Entrance of Friendly Rivals Club; "A Woman Is only a Woman, but a Good Cigar Is a Smoke" (Puff, Puff, Puff); "It Keeps Me Guessing all the Time"; "Just Get Out and Walk"; "Life's a Masquerade"; "Moth and the Moon"; "My Fair Unknown"; "No One Will Steal Him"; Ollendorf Duet ("It's All in the Book, You Know"); Overture; "Queen of the Ring"; "Self-Made Family"; "Walks."

My Golden Girl (1919). Text by Frederic Arnold Kummer. New York: Harms, Inc.
Musical Numbers:
"Darby and Joan"; "I Want You"; "I'd Like a Honeymoon with You"; "If We Had Met Before"; "In Venice"; "Little Nest for Two"; "My Golden Girl"; "Name the Day"; "Oh Day in June"; "Ragtime Terpsichore"; "Shooting Star"; "Song Without (Many) Words."

Naughty Marietta (1910). Text by Rida Johnson Young. New York: M. Witmark and Sons.
Musical Numbers:
"Ah! Sweet Mystery of Life"; "All I Crave Is More of Life"; Barn Dance—Schottische; Dance; Dance of the Marionettes; "Dream Melody" (Intermezzo); Finale (Act 1); Finale (Act 2); "If I Were Anybody Else but Me"; "I'm Falling in Love with Someone"; "It Never, Never Can Be Love"; Italian Street Song; "It's Pretty Soft for Simon"; "Lancers"; "Live for Today"; "Loves of New Orleans"; March; "Mr. Voodoo"; "Naughty Marietta"; "'Neath the Southern Moon"; "New Orleans Jeunesse Dorée"; Opening Chorus; Overture; Prelude (Act 2); "Sweet Bye and Bye"; "Taisez Vous"; "Tramp, Tramp, Tramp" (We've Hunted the Wolf in the Forest); "You Marry a Marionette."

Old Dutch (1909). Text by George V. Hobart. New York: M. Witmark and Sons.
Musical Numbers:
"Algy"; Barn Dance; Entrance of Lew Fields with Children; Fantastic Dance; "Honor the Brave" (Finale, Act 2); "I Love ze Parisienne"; "I Want a Man to Love Me"; "If You Ever Want a Favor Mention Me"; March and Two-Step; "Mrs. Grundy"; "My Gypsy Sweetheart"; Overture; "Pourquoi"; "Pretending"; "Rich Man, Poor Man, Beggar Man, Thief"; Russian Duo and Dance; "Sweet Wireless Whispers"; "That Is Love"; "U, Dearie."

The Only Girl (1914). Text by Henry Blossom. New York: M. Witmark & Sons.
Musical Numbers:
"Antoinette"; "Be Happy Boys Tonight"; "Compact"; "Here's to Health, Here's to Wealth"; "Here's to the Land We Love, Boys!"; "Hesitation"; "Husbands! Husbands! Husbands!"; "I Love Not One, But All"; "More I See of Others, Dear, the Better I Like You"; "The Only Girl"; "Personality"; "Tell It All Over Again"; Valse Hesitation; "When You're Away"; "When You're Wearing the Ball and Chain"; "Why Should We Stay Home and Sew"; "Women's Rights"; "You Have to Have a Part to Make a Hit"; "You're the Only Girl for Me."

Orange Blossoms (1922). Text by B. G. DeSylva. New York: M. Witmark and Sons.
Musical Numbers:
"Because I Love You So"; "Dream of Orange Blossoms"; "I Can't Argue With You"; "In Hennequeville"; "I've Missed You"; "J. Flynn"; "Just Like That"; "A Kiss in the Dark"; "Legend of the Glowworm"; "Let's Not Get Married"; "Lonely Nest"; "Moonshine and Ballet"; "New York Is the Same Old Place"; "On the Riviera"; "Quite a Nifty and Effective Detective Am I"; "Then Comes the Dawning"; "This Time It's Love"; "Way Out West in Jersey."

Oui, Madame (1920). Text by Robert B. Smith. New York: Harms, Inc.
Musical Numbers:
"Every Hour Away from You Is Sixty Minutes Lost"; "He Wanted to Go and He Went"; "If I Saw Much of You"; "My Day Has Come" (words by Irving Caesar); "Over the

Garden Wall"; "Play Me Something I Can Dance To"; "When You Know Me Better"; "Where Were You?"; "Wooing of the Violin."

The Prima Donna (1908). Text by Henry Blossom. New York: M. Witmark and Sons.
Musical Numbers:
Ballet-Waltz; Band behind Scene; "Dream Love" ("'Twas only Dreaming"); Ensemble; "Espagnola"; "Everybody Else's Girl Looks Better to Me than Mine"; "The Game of Love"; "Ha! Ha!"; "Here's to My Comrades and Me"; "If You Were I and I Were You"; "I'll Be Married to the Music of a Military Band"; "The Jolly Cuirassier"; "Love Light"; "The Man and the Maid"; March and Two-Step; "O! Mia Speranza" (words by Signor Ciucicini); "Oh! Oh! Oh!"; "One You're Looking For"; Orchestra on Stage; "Soldier's Life Is Never Long"; "Soldier's Love"; "Something Always Happens When It Shouldn't"; "Think of Me"; " 'Twas Different Years Ago"; "Twenty Years Ago!"; "What Is Love?"; "When Girls Command the Army"; "You'd Be Surprised."

Prince Ananias (1894). Text by Frances Neilson. New York: Schuberth.
Musical Numbers:
"Ah, Cupid, Meddlesome Boy"; "His Highness"; "Love Ne'er Came Nigh"; March; Polka; "Regal Sadness Sits on Me"; Schottische; Two-Step; Waltz; "Who Might You Be? An Author-Manager Am I."

The Princess "Pat" (1915). Text by Henry Blossom. New York: M. Witmark and Sons.
Musical Numbers:
"All for You"; "Allies"; "Flirting"; "For Better or for Worse"; Fox Trot; "I Need Affection"; "I Wish I Was an Island in an Ocean of Girls"; "I'd Like to Be a Quitter but I Find It Hard to Quit"; "I'd Like to Have You Around"; "In Day Dreams"; "In a Little World for Two"; "Love Is the Best of All"; "Make Him Guess"; March and One-Step; Melodrama; "Neapolitan Love Song" ("Sweet One How My Heart Is Yearning") ("T 'amo"); "Shoes of Husband Number One as Worn by Number Two"; "There's a Message of Love in Your Eyes"; "Two Laughing Irish Eyes."

The Red Mill (1906). Text by Henry Blossom. New York: M. Witmark and Sons.
Musical Numbers:
"Beautiful Isle of Our Dreams"; "Because You're You"; Dance; "Every Day Is Ladies' Day to Me"; Finale; "Go While the Goin' Is Good"; "Good-a-Bye John"; "Gossips' Song"; "I Want You to Marry Me"; "If You Love But Me"; "I'll Ring the Bell"; "I'm Always Doing Something I Don't Want to Do"; "The Legend of the Mill"; "Mignonette"; "Moonbeams"; Overture; "Streets of New York"; "Teach Them What to Say"; "Wedding Bells"; Wedding Entrance; "When You're Pretty and the World Is Fair"; "Whistle It"; "A Widow Has Ways"; "You Can Never Tell about a Woman."

The Serenade (1897). Text by Harry B. Smith. New York: Carl Fischer, Inc.
Musical Numbers:
"All for Thee"; "The Angelus"; "Cupid and I"; "Don Jose of Sevilla"; "Dreaming, Dreaming"; Entrance of the Duke and Dolores ("Who Can This Be?"); Entrance of Yvonne, Colombo and Gomez; "For I'm a Jolly Postillion"; "The Funny Side of That" ("Although a Duke of High Degree"); "Gaze on This Face"; "Here Merrily Bide the Bandit Tribe" ("When Day's Honest Work Is Done"); "I Envy the Bird"; "I Love Thee,

I Adore Thee"; "In Attitudes Alert"; "In Fair Andalusia"; "In Our Quiet Cloister";
March; "The Monk and the Maid"; "Peering Left, and Peering Right" ("For We Are the
Duke's Bodyguard"); "The Serenade"; "The Singing Lesson"; "Song of the Carbine";
"Woman Lovely Woman."

The Singing Girl (1899). Text by Harry B. Smith. New York: M. Witmark and Sons.
Musical Numbers:
The Alpine Horn ("Tyrolean Song"); "Chink, Chink"; "Don't Talk to Me of Marriage";
"Do You Follow Me?"; "If Only You Were Mine"; "Lancers"; "Love Is Merest Folly";
"Love Is a Tyrant, So I Bid You Beware"; "Love, the Marvelous Magician"; Mazurka;
"Our Native Land"; "The Singing Girl"; "Siren of the Ballet"; "Song of the Danube";
"To Be a Little Singing Girl"; "Well Beloved."

The Rose of Algeria (a revision of *Algeria*) (1909). Text by Glen MacDonough. New York:
M. Witmark and Sons.
Musical Numbers:
"Ask Her While the Band Is Playing"; "Bayaderes"; "Bohemia, Good-Bye"; "The Boule
Miché"; "Go Happy Bride"; "He Was a Soldier, Too"; "I'll Dream of Thee" (words by
Vincent Bryan); "In Jail"; "I've Been Decorated"; "Little Bird of Paradise"; "Love Is
Like a Cigarette"; March; "My Life I Love Thee" ("Rose of the World"); "Only One of
Anything"; "Same Old Two"; "Thanksgiving Day" (words by Vincent Bryan); "Twilight
in Barakeesh"; "You'll Feel Better."

Sweethearts (1913). Text by Robert B. Smith. New York: G. Schirmer, Inc.
Musical Numbers:
"The Angelus"; "The Cricket on the Hearth"; Entrance of Sylvia; "Every Lover Must
Meet His Fate"; Finale ("Pretty One"); "Hail Franz of Zilania"; "I Don't Know How I
Do It but I Do"; "In the Convent They Never Taught Me That"; "The Ivy and the
Oak"; "Jeanette and Her Little Wooden Shoes" (Sabot Dance); March and Two-Step;
"Mother Goose"; "On Parade"; Overture—Opening Chorus ("Iron, Iron, Iron");
"Pilgrims of Love"; "Pretty as a Picture"; "Sweethearts" ("If You Ask Where Love Is
Found"); "Talk about This, Talk about That"; "There Is Magic in a Smile"; "Waiting
for the Bride"; "What She Wanted—and What She Got"; "Welcoming the Bride."

The Tattooed Man (1907). Text by Harry B. Smith. New York: M. Witmark and Sons.
Musical Numbers:
"Awfully Nice to Love One Girl"; "Boys Will Be Boys and Girls Will Be Girls";
Entrance of Arabs; Entrance of Omar (Oriental March); Entrance of Shah; Floral
Wedding; "Hear My Song of Love" (Serenade); "I Say What I Mean, and I Mean What
I Say"; "I'm Not So Particular Now"; "The Land of Dreams"; "Legend of the Djin";
"Never, Never Land"; "Nobody Loves Me"; "Omar Khayam"; "Sleep Sublime and
Perfect Poet"; "Take Things Easy"; "There's Just One Girl I'd Like to Marry"; "Things
We Are Not Supposed to Know"; "Watch the Professor"; "Wedding of the Lily and the
Rose"; "Kitten that Couldn't Be Good."

The Velvet Lady (1919). Text by Henry Blossom. New York: M. Witmark and Sons.
Musical Numbers:
"Any Time New York Goes Dry"; "Bubbles"; "Come Be My Wife"; "Fair Honeymoon,
Shine On"; Fox-Trot; "Girl and Boy"; "I've Danced to Beat the Band"; "Logic"; March

and One-Step; "Merry Wedding Bells"; "Merry Wedding Dance"; "Scandal"; "Spooky Ookum"; "There's Nothing Too Fine for the Finest"; "Velvet Lady"; "What a Position for Me."

The Viceroy (1900). Text by Harry B. Smith. New York: M. Witmark and Sons.
Musical Numbers:
"All Men Have Their Troubles"; "Eyes of Black and Eyes of Blue"; "Hear Me"; "I'm the Leader of Society"; "Just for Today"; "Love May Come, Love May Go"; "'Neath Neapolitan Skies"; "Robin and the Rose"; "Since I Am Queen of the Carnival"; "Viceroy"; "We'll Catch You at Last"; "With Military Pomp."

When Sweet Sixteen (1910). Text by George V. Hobart. New York: M. Witmark and Sons.
Musical Numbers:
"Dear Old Fairyland"; "Fairies' Revel"; "Frolic of the Fairies"; "Ha! Ha! Ha!"; "Hearts Are Trumps"; "I Love to Read the Papers in the Morning"; "I Want to Be a Wild, Wild Rose"; "I'm Not a Bit Superstitious"; "In Fairyland"; "In Society"; "In So-So Society"; "In the Golden Long Ago"; "Island of Sweet Sixteen"; "Lancers" (Finale Ultimo); "Laughs"; "Little Fifi"; "Mah Honey Love"; "Man's a Man for a' That"; "Mary Drew"; "My Toast to You"; "Oh! Mary! You're Contrary"; "Oh, the Things They Put in the Papers Now-a-Days"; "Oh, Those Boys"; "People Will Talk, You Know"; "Pourquoi"; "Rosalind"; "Since Papa Became a Billionaire"; "Superstitious"; "That's Boys"; "There's a Raft of Money in Graft! Graft! Graft!"; "There's None So Sweet as Rosalind"; "They Follow Me Everywhere"; "While the Big Old World Rolls Round"; "Wild Rose."

Wizard of the Nile (1895). Text by Harry B. Smith. New York: Schuberth.
Musical Numbers:
"Am I a Wizard?"; Cleopatra's Aria; Entrance of Cleopatra ("Pure and White Is the Lotus"); Entrance of Kibosh ("I've Appeared Before Crowned Heads"); "Gaze on this Face"; "If I Were King"; "In Dreamland"; "Know Ye the Sound"; "Lancers"; "My Angeline"; Oriental March; "Cleopatra's Wedding Day"; "Starlight, Star Bright" ("Starlight Waltz"); "Stonecutter's Song"; "That's One Thing a Wizard Can Do"; "To the Pyramid"; "What Is Love?"; "When the Bugles Are Calling."

Wonderland (1905) (previously titled *Alice and the Eight Princesses*). Text by Glen MacDonough. New York: M. Witmark and Sons.
Musical Numbers:
"Companions of the Blade"; "Crew of the 'Peekaboo'"; "Hallowe'en"; "How to Tell a Fairy Tale"; "Hunting of the Cock"; "I Myself and Me"; "It's Hard to Be a Hero"; "Jografree"; "The Knave of Hearts"; "Little Black Sheep"; "Love's Golden Day"; "Nature Class"; "No Show Tonight"; "The Only One"; The Oriental Dance; "The Ossified Man"; Overture; "Popular Pauline"; "Princess's Song"; "Tale of a Music Box Shop"; "That's Why They Say I'm Crazy"; "The Voice for It"; "When Perrico Plays"; "With Frame, Two Forty-Nine"; "Woman's First Thought Is a Man"; "Your Heart If You Please."

PUBLISHED INSTRUMENTAL, CHORAL, AND MISCELLANEOUS

WORKS

A

"À la Muzurka" (before 1893).

"À la Valse." See Two Pieces for Violin.

"Ah Love Me!" See Three Songs, Op. 15.

Air de Ballet. New York: G. Schirmer, 1912.

"Al Fresco." New York: M. Witmark and Sons, 1904.

"All Hail To You, Marines!" Words by Richard J. Beamish. July 14, 1918.

"All the Vogue." New York: M. Witmark and Sons, 1915.

Alma Mater Song of the Catholic University of America. Words by Robert H. Mahoney.
    Washington, D.C.: Washington Catholic University, 1921.

"Amaryllis" (1894).

"American Fantasia" (1898).

"The American Rose." Waltz. New York: M. Witmark and Sons, 1917. (Dedicated to the
    American Rose Society.)

"Aschenbrödel March" (1910).

Auditorium Festival March. For orchestra—composed 1901 for the 12th anniversary of the
    Auditorium, Chicago. See Festival March.

Aus "Liedern eines fahrenden Gesellen," Op. 20, No. 2. Berlin: Luckhardt, 1890.

B

"Badinage" (1895).

Bagatelle (before 1890).

Baltimore Centennial (1896). (Also for band; composed for the Baltimore Centennial, 1897.)

"The Bards of Ireland." Folk songs arranged for voice and piano. (Privately printed by the
    composer, 1908.)

"Belle O'Brien." Words by John Ernest McCann. New York: Harms, 1895.

"The Belle of Pittsburgh" (1895).

"Benamela." Finale to Carlo Brizzi's romantic opera or ballet, 1894. (Later used in *The Idol's
    Eye*.)

Berceuse. New York: M. Witmark and Sons, 1912.

"Bird-Catching." See "Vogelfang."

"The Birthday of the Dauphin." Scene in the Ziegfeld Follies, 1921.

"Blümlein am Herzen", Op. 4. Stuttgart: Zumsteeg, 1884.

"Bring on the Girls." Scene and song in the Ziegfeld Follies, 1922.

"Butterfly Ballet." In Jerome Kern's *Sally*, 1920.

C

"The Call To Freedom." A patriotic ode. Lyric: Victor Herbert. New York: Oliver Ditson Co., 1918.

"Cannibal Dance." New York: C. Fischer, Inc., 1926.

"Can't You Hear Your Country Calling." Lyric by Gene Buck. From the Ziegfeld Follies, 1917. New York: Harms, 1917.

"The Captive." Dramatic cantata for soli, chorus and orchestra, Op. 25. Text by Rudolph von Baumbach. Translated: Victor Herbert. Berlin: Luckhardt, 1891.

"The Championship of the World." Scene in the Ziegfeld Follies, 1921.

"Chant d'Amour." Written for Marcel Dupré, 1924.

"Chiffon Fantasie." Scene in the Ziegfeld Follies, 1920.

"Christ Is Risen: An Easter Anthem." New York: M. Witmark and Sons, 1908.

"The Cinderella Man." See "Out of His Heart He Builds a Home."

"The Circus Ballet." Scene in the Ziegfeld Follies, 1919.

"Columbia." Anthem. Words by Clay M. Greene (1898).

"Columbus." Suite for orchestra, Op. 35 (1903).

Concerto for cello and orchestra, Op. 8. (1894).

Concerto No. 2 for cello and orchestra, Op. 30. (Dedicated to the New York Philharmonic Society). New York: Schuberth, 1898.

"Confession." See "Geständnis."

"Consecrated Spot." See "Geweihte Stätte."

"La Coquette." New York: M. Witmark and Sons, 1900.

"Cosmopolitan March." New York: Leo Feist, 1935 (composed 1923).

"Creation." Scene in the Ziegfeld Follies, 1920.

"The Crucible's Toast." Words by Arthur G. Burgoyne.

"The Cruiskeen Lawn" (Old Irish). New York: G. Schirmer, 1913. (Dedicated to Clarence Dickinson and the Mendelssohn Glee Club of New York.)

D

"The Dancing School—Her First Lesson." Scene in the Ziegfeld Follies, 1920.

Danse Baroque. New York: C. Fischer, Inc, 1925. (Composed 1913.)

"Day Is Here." Words by Lorraine Noel Finley. New York: G. Schirmer, Inc., 1940.

"Defendam March." New York: M. Witmark and Sons, 1919. (Written for the 22nd Engineers, N.Y.N.G., and dedicated to Col. H. H. Treadwell by Lieut. Victor Herbert.)

"Der Liebsten Namen schrieb ich in Sand." See "Mein Herz ist treu."

"Der Schöheit Krone", Op. 5. Stuttgart: Zumsteeg, 1884.

"Devotion: A Love Sonnet for Piano." New York: Harms, 1921.

"Dodge Brothers March." With lyric refrain by Maxwell I. Pitkin. New York: Jerome H. Remick and Co., 1920. (Dedicated to Horace E. Dodge.)

Dramatic Overture. See "Under the Red Robe."

"Dream On." Words by B. G. DeSyva. New York: Harms, 1922. (Adaptation of "Indian Lullaby.")

"The Dream Song." See "Farewell, Lovelight."

"Du ahnst es nicht", Op. 21, No. 1. Berlin: Luckhardt, 1891.

Duo. For 2 violins. New York: Harms, 1923.

E

"An Easter Dawn." Words by Glen Macdonough. A new Easter song composed especially and exclusively for the *New York Evening World*. New York: M. Witmark and Sons, 1907. (Composed 1905.)

"Einsamkeit." Op. 18, No. 2. Berlin: Luckhardt, 1889.

"Eldorado." March. Boston: Oliver Ditson Co., 1894.

L'Encore. New York: M. Witmark and Sons, 1910.

"The Equity Star." Lyric by Grant Stewart. New York: Harms, 1921.

"Estellita: Valse Pathétique." New York: M. Witmark & Sons, 1915. (Also used in *The Princess "Pat."*)

"Eventide." See "Aus Liedern eines fahrenden Gesellen."

"Exile's Haven." Words by Lorraine Noel Finley. New York: G. Schirmer, Inc., 1940.

F

"The Faded Rose." See Three Songs, Op. 15.

The Fall of a Nation. Symphonic score for motion picture, 1916. Excerpts published: "Piano Love Theme" (New York: Witmark, 1916); for orchestra (New York: C. Fischer, 1925 and 1926); "Devastation"; "Entrance of the Heroes"; "Forebodings"; "Heart Throbs"; "Karma"; "The Knight's Tournament"; "Little Italy"; "Mystic Rider"; "Punch and Judy"; "The Rabble." Arrangement by Harold Sanford.

"Falling Leaves." Ballet in *Miss 1917*.

"Fanshastics." See "Heart O' Mine."

Fantasia on Mascagni's Cavalleria Rusticana.

Fantasie on "The Desire" of Schubert. For cello and orchestra.

"Farewell." Words by Edward Locke. New York: Harms, 1919. (Written for the play, *The Dream Song*.)

"Farljandio." Scene in the Ziegfeld Follies, 1922.

"The Fawn and the Wood Nymph." Ballet. Ziegfeld Follies.

"Fencing" Number. Scene in the Ziegfeld Follies, 1923.

"Fernher tönte Cicadensang." See "Die versunkene Stadt."

Festival March. New York: C. Fischer, 1935. See also Auditorium Festival March.

"The Fight Is Made and Won." Words by Thomas J. Vivian. W. R. Hearst, The *New York Journal*, 1898.

"The Finest." March. New York: Music Printing Co., Inc., 1918. (Dedicated to the Police Band, City of New York.)

"The First Kiss." See "Geweihte Stätte."

"Fleurette." Valse lente. New York: M. Witmark and Sons, 1903.

"Fliege fort, du klein Waldvögelein", Op. 18, No. 1. Berlin: Luckhardt, 1891.

"Flower of My Heart." See "Blümlein am Herzen."

"Fly Away, Little Bird." See "Fliege fort, du klein Waldvögelein."

"For 'Franz's' Wedding." For cello and organ. (Composed 1903.)

"For the Flag He Loved So Well." Words by Vincent Bryan.

"Forget-Me-Not." No. 2 of Three Compositions for String Orchestra. New York: G. Schirmer, 1912.

"Fowling." See "Vogelfang."

"The Friars." Words by Charles Emerson Cook. New York: M. Witmark & Sons, 1907.

"Frieden." See "Peace."

Frühlingslied, Op. 14, No. 1. Luckhardt, 1889.

G

"A Garden—The Beauty Contest." Scene in the Ziegfeld Follies, 1924.

"Gate City Guard." March. New York: E. Schuberth and Co., 1895.

"Der Gefangene." See "The Captive."

"Das Geheimnis", Op. 14, No. 4. Berlin: Luckhardt, 1889.

"Geständniss", Op. 13, No. 1. Berlin: Luckhardt, 1889.

"Get Together." New York: M. Witmark and Sons, 1915.

"Geweihte Stätte", Op. 13, No. 2. Berlin: Luckhardt, 1889.

"Ghazel." New York: M. Witmark and Sons, 1900. (The first of a set of six pieces.)

"Give Me That Rose." Words by Booth Tarkington.

"Give Your Heart in June-time." New York: Harms, 1925. (Used in *Sky High*, a musical production by Harold Atteridge and Harry Graham.)

"God Shall Guide Us!" New York: Oliver Ditson Co., 1944. (From *The Call to Freedom*.)

"God Spare the Emerald Isle." Words by William Jerome. New York: Harms, 1923.

"Golden Days Overture." See "The Great White Way."

"The Great White Way." Overture. Composed for motion picture (1923). (Published in 1939 by G. Schirmer, Inc., of New York as "Golden Days Overture.")

H

"The Hail of the Friendly Sons." Words by Joseph I. C. Clarke. New York: G. Schirmer, 1913.

"Hamlet of Fancy" (*Prince Ananias*). New York: Schuberth, 1894.

"Hast ein Blaublümelein einst mir gegeben." See "Blümlein am Herzen."

"Heart O' Mine." An Irish song, as sung in Henry Miller's production of *Fanshastics* (also called *Merry Wives of Gotham*). Words by Laurence Eyre. New York: Harms, 1924.

"Heimweh." See "Home Sickness."

"Hero and Leander", Op. 33. Symphonic poem.

"Home Sickness." New York: Schuberth, 1896.

"The Host's Daughter." See "Wirthstöchterlein."

"Hula-Lula." A "Territorial Operetta" written for the Lambs' annual gambol, 1899. Words by L. J. B. Lincoln.

Humoresque (arrangement of Dvorák).

"Humpty Dumpty" (*The Century Girl*). New York: Harms, 1916.

I

"I Love the Isle of the Sea." Words by Louis O'Connell. Chicago: Keithley, 1935.

"I Love Thee." See "Ich liebe dich."

"I Want to Be a Gambling Man." See "Miss Camille."

"I Want to Be a Good Lamb." Words by George V. Hobart. New York: Famous Music Co., 1940. (Composed 1909.)

"Ice-Water Gallop."

"Ich liebe dich", Op. 14, No. 2. Berlin: Luckhardt, 1889.

"I'd Love to Waltz through Life with You." Words by Gene Buck. New York: Harms, 1923. (From the Ziegfeld Follies, 1923.)

"If Love Were What the Rose Is." Words by Algernon Charles Swinburne. New York: M. Witmark and Sons, 1907.

"If You but Knew." See Three Songs, Op. 15.

"I'll Be There." Words by Robert B. Smith. New York: Harms, 1921. (Used in *The Girl in the Spotlight*.)

"In Khorassan." Words by Gene Buck. New York: Harms, 1921. (From the Ziegfeld Follies, 1921.)

"In the Folds of the Starry Flag." Words by Paul West. New York: M. Witmark and Sons, 1904.

"In the Sweet Bye and Bye." Words by George V. Hobart. (Composed 1906.)

Inauguration March. See "McKinley Inauguration."

"Indian Lullaby." (Composed 1922; title subsequently changed to "Dream On.")

"Indian Summer." An American Idyl. New York: Harms, 1919. (Later, with words by Al Dubin, 1938.)

"Irish Rhapsody." New York: G. Schirmer, 1910. (Composed 1892.)

"It Needs No Poet" (*Prince Ananias*). New York: Schuberth, 1894.

J

"Janice Meredith." Overture. (Incomplete; completed by Deems Taylor.) (1924.)

"Jenny's Baby." Words by John Ernest McCann. New York: Schuberth, 1895.

The Jester's Serenade. New York: C. Fischer, Inc., 1925. (Composed 1908.)

"Just For Fun." New York: C. Fischer, Inc., 1950. (Composed 1895.)

K

"Kiss Me Again." Words by Henry Blossom. New York: M. Witmark and Sons, 1915. (Words and music of the stanza different from those in *Mlle. Modiste*.)

L

"Lady of the Lantern." Words by Gene Buck. New York: Harms, 1923. (From the Ziegfeld Follies, 1923.)

"Lambs in Toyland." Words by Grant Stewart. (A skit written for the Lambs, 1904.)

"The Lambs' March." (Written for the Lambs, 1914.)

"The Lambs' Star Gambol." March. (Written for the Lambs, 1912.)

"The Legend of the Cyclamen Tree." (Scene in the Ziegfeld Follies, 1921.)

"The Legend of the Golden Tree." Words by Gene Buck. New York: Harms, 1921. (From the Ziegfeld Follies, 1921.)

"Légende." For cello and orch. (Composed before 1894.)

"Legends of the Drums." (Scene in the Ziegfeld Follies, 1923.)

"Liebesleben." See "Three Songs, Op. 15."

"Liebeslied." See "Love-Song."

"Little Old New York." Overture. (Composed for motion picture, 1923.)

"Little Old New York." Words by William Le Baron. New York: Harms. (Scene and song in the Ziegfeld Follies, 1923.)

"The Little Red Lark." Old Irish. New York: M. Witmark and Sons, 1917.

"Lora Lee." Words by Joseph I. C. Clarke. New York: Harms, 1922. (Dedicated to the Glee Club of the Friendly Sons of St. Patrick, New York, and its director, G. H. Gartlan.)

"The Love Boat." Words by Gene Buck. New York: Harms, 1920. (Scene in the Ziegfeld Follies.)

"Love Is Spring" (Op. 15). Berlin: Luckhardt, 1894.

"Love Laid His Sleepless Head." Words by Algernon Charles Swinburne. New York: M. Witmark and Sons, 1907.

"Love-Song." New York: Schuberth, 1896.

"A Love Sonnet." New York: C. Fischer, Inc., 1925. (Arr. By Harold Sanford.)

"Lovelight." Words by Edward Locke. New York: Harms, 1919. (Written for the play *The Dream Song*.)

"Love's Hour." Words by Rida Johnson Young. New York: G. Schirmer, 1912. (Composed for Luisa Tetrazzini.)

"Love's Life." See "Three Songs, Op. 15."

"Love's Oracle." Words by Edward Peple. New York: M. Witmark and Sons, 1909. (Dedicated to Billie Burke.)

"Love's Token." See "Three Songs, Op. 15."

M

McKinley Inauguration. March. (Dedicated to President McKinley.) New York: Schuberth, 1897.

"Mädchen ging im Feld allein." See "Schnelle Blüthe."

"A Maiden Went into the Field Alone." See "Schnelle Blüthe."

March of the 22nd Regiment, N.G.N.Y. New York: Schuberth, 1898.

"The Marion Davies March." New York: Harms, 1922. (Composed for the motion picture *When Knighthood Was in Flower.*)

"Mary Came Over to Me." Words by Irving Caesar. New York: Harms, 1922.

"Mary's Lamb." Words by Edward E. Kidder. (Dedicated to the Lambs.) New York: Schuberth, 1898.

"Mazuma." See "The Song Birds."

"Me and Nancy." See "Sweet Nancy."

"Mein Blick ruht gern auf dir." See "Du ahnst es nicht."

"Mein Herz ist true." Op. 21, No. 2. Berlin: Luckhardt, 1891.

"Mein Schätzlein, froh sing ich dir." See "Der Schönheit Kron."

Mélodie. For cello and piano. (Composed 1893.)

"Merry Wives of Gotham." See "Heart O' Mine."

"Mirage." See "Two Pieces for Violin."

Miss Camille. A musical burlesque. Words by George V. Hobart. New York: M. Witmark and Sons, 1907. ("My Toast to You," "I Want to Be a Gambling Man," "The Spanish Serenade.") (Composed for the Lambs, 1907.)

Miss 1917. A revue. (The composer supplied music for the following: "The Mosquitos' Frolic," "The Society Farmerettes"; "Falling Leaves"; "The Singing Blacksmith of Curriclough"—the last-named a medley of airs by Samuel Lover.)

"Molly." Words by Rida Johnson Young. New York: M. Witmark and Sons, 1919.
(Dedicated to John McCormack.)

"The Mosquitos' Frolic." Scene in *Miss 1917*.

"The Mountain Brook." New York: M. Witmark and Sons, 1900.

"My Heart is True." See "Mein Herz ist treu."

"My Toast to You." See *Miss Camille*.

N

"The New Ireland." Words by Joseph I. C. Clarke. New York: G. Schirmer, 1914.

"Nina" (Undated).

Nocturne. For cello and piano.

"Nur du bist's." See "Three Songs, Op. 15."

O

"Ocean Breezes." New York: Schuberth, 1898.

"O'Donnell Aboo! The Clanconnel War Song." A.D. 1597, by M. J. McCann. Air: Roderich Vich Alpine dhu. New York: G. Schirmer, 1915.

"Old Fashioned Garden." Scene in the Ziegfeld Follies, 1923.

"Old Ireland Shall Be Free!" Words by John Jerome Rooney. Traditional air: Boys of Wexford. New York: M. Witmark and Sons, 1915.

"On the Promenade." New York: M. Witmark and Sons, 1900.

"On Your Way." New York: M. Witmark and Sons, 1915.

"Only You." See "Three Songs, Op. 15."

"The Orange, White and Blue." Words by John P. Pine. New York: G. Schirmer, 1916.
(Dedicated to the schoolchildren of New York.)

"Out of His Heart He Builds a Home." Words by Edward Childs Carpenter. New York: M. Witmark and Sons, 1916. (Composed for the play *The Cinderella Man*.)

P

"Pan-Americana." Morceau charactéristique. New York: M. Witmark and Sons, 1901.

"Peace." New York: Schuberth, 1896.

"Pensée amoureuse." Paris: G. Ricordi et Cie., 1906.

"Persian Dance." New York: C. Fischer, Inc., 1926. (Arr. by Harold Sanford.)

Persian March. New York: C. Fischer, Inc., 1926. (Arr. by Harold Sanford.)

"Petite Valse." Paris: G. Ricordi et Cie, 1906.

Two Pieces for Violin with Piano Accompaniment: (a) "Mirage," (b) "À la Valse." New York: G. Schirmer, 1915. (Dedicated to Fritz Kreisler.)

Polonaise de Concert, in A. (Composed before 1887.)

Prelude ("The Two Marys," by Rev. Joseph P. Herbert). For orch. (Composed 1923.)

"The President's March" (1898). (Dedicated to President McKinley.)

"The Princess of My Dreams." Words by Gene Buck. New York: Harms, 1921. (From the Ziegfeld Follies, 1921.)

"Punchinello." New York: M. Witmark and Sons, 1900.

R

"Remembrance." Words by Fanny Lover (from the German of Carl Weitbrecht). New York: G. Schirmer, 1915.

"Remembrance." (Published in orchestral arrangement as "Souvenir," by C. Fischer, Inc., New York, 1925.)

"The River Song." Words by Lorraine Noel Finley. New York: G. Schirmer, Inc., 1940.

"Romance." Paris: G. Ricordi et Cie., 1906.

"Romeo, Juliet, Johnny and Jane." (Used in *Round the Town*, a revue, 1924.)

"Rose-Briar Waltz" (Undated).

"Rosemary." Waltz. New York: Harms, 1917.

Round the Town. See "Romeo, Juliet, Johnny and Jane."

"Royal Sec, a Champagne Galop" (1885).

S

"Sally." See "Butterfly Ballet."

"Salute to America." March.

"Salute to Atlanta." March. Atlanta: Phillips, 1895.

Scherzino (1892).

"Schnelle Blüthe," Op. 18, No. 2. Berlin: Luckhardt, 1891.

"Secrecy." See "Das Geheimnis."

"The Secret." Words by James Russell Lowell. New York: Appleton, 1895.

Serenade. See "Ständchen."

Serenade für Streichorchester, Op. 12, Berlin: Luckhardt, 1889.

"She Was a Hayseed Maid." (Composed 1908.)

"The Silent Rose." See "Three Songs, Op. 15."

"The Singing Blacksmith of Curriclough." See *Miss 1917*.

"Sky High." See "Give Your Heart in June-time."

"The Society Farmerettes." See *Miss 1917*.

"Soixante-neuf (69)." (Composed 1902.)

Some Babes from Toyland. A skit for the Lambs, 1903.

The Song Birds. A musical skit. Words by George V. Hobart. New York: M. Witmark and Sons, 1907. ("Mazuma," "Yankee Land.")

"A Song of Spring." See "Frühlingslied."

Two Songs, Op. 10. See "Wirthstöchterlein" and "Vogelfang."

Two Songs, Op. 13. See "Geständniss" and "Geweihte Stätte."

Four Songs, Op. 14. See "Frühlingslied"; "Ich Liebe dich"; "Ständchen"; and "Das Geheimnis."

Three Songs with Piano accompaniment, Op. 15. ("The Silent Rose"; "Love's Token"; "Ah Love Me!") New York: Schuberth, 1888.

"Souvenir." See "Remembrance."

"Souvenir de Saratoga." See "Under the Elms."

Spanish Rhapsody.

"The Spanish Serenade." See *Miss Camille*.

"Ständchen," Op. 14, No. 3. Berlin: Luckhardt, 1889.

"Star of the North." Overture. (For motion picture, 1923.)

"Die Stille Rose." See "Three Songs, Op. 15."

"Success Is Work." March. (Composed for the dedication of the new Witmark Building, Aug. 4, 1903.)

Suite, Op. 3 Stuttgart: Zumsteeg, 1884.

A Suite of Serenades. New York: Harms, 1924. (Composed originally for Paul Whiteman's Orchestra; also arranged for Symphony orchestra.) Chinese, Cuban, Oriental, Spanish.

"Suite romantique," Op. 31. Berlin: Simrock, 1901. (Dedicated to the Pittsburgh Orchestra.)

"The Sunken City." See "Die Versunkene Stadt."

"Sunset." No. 3 of Three Compositions for String Orchestra. New York: Schirmer, 1912.

"Sweet Harp of the Days that are Gone (To the Irish Harp)". Words by Samuel Lover. New York: Schuberth, 1898.

"Sweet Nancy." Words by John Ernest McCann. New York: Harms, 1895.

T

The Tale of a Lamb. A musical skit. (Composed for the Lambs, 1921.)

"The Old-Fashioned Garden of Mine." Words by Gene Buck. New York: Harms, 1923. (From the Ziegfeld Follies, 1923.)

"The Three Solitaires." Polka. New York: M. Witmark and Sons, 1915.

"Time Will Come." Words by Fred Dixon. New York: Schuberth, 1895.

"To the Irish Harp." See "Sweet Harp of the Days that are Gone."

"To the Lambs." Words by Augustus Thomas. (A new club song of the Lambs, 1906.)

"To Thee, My Queen of Beauty." See "Der Schönheit Krone."

"The Toy Soldiers." New York: Harms, 1916.

"Toyland Today." A fantasy, words by Glen MacDonough. (Composed for the Lambs, 1923.)

"Trinity Blue." Words by Judge Joseph Buffington.

"Twenty-second Regiment March." See "March of the 22nd Regiment" N.G.N.Y.

"The Twirly Little Girlies at the End of the Line." Words by Rida Johnson Young. New York: M. Witmark and Sons, 1912.

"The Two Marys." See "Prelude (The Two Marys)."

U

"Under the Elms" ("Souvenir de Saratoga"). New York: M. Witmark and Sons, 1903.

"Under the Red Robe." Overture. (Composed for motion picture, 1923; published as Dramatic Overture by G. Schirmer, Inc. of New York, 1938.)

"Under the Sea." New York: Harms, 1916.

V

"Valse à la Mode." New York: M. Witmark and Sons, 1915.

"The Veiled Prophet." March. New York: Schuberth, 1896.

"Die Versunkene Stadt," Op. 20, No. 1. Berlin: Luckhardt, 1890.

The Village Blacksmith. A musical skit. Words by George V. Hobart. (Composed for the Lambs, 1912.)

"The Vision of Columbus." (See "Columbus Suite.")

"Vogelfang," Op. 10, No. 2. Berlin: Luckhardt, 1889.

W

"The Water Sprite." Ballet (1922). Ziegfeld Follies.

"Weaving." Scene in the Ziegfeld Follies, 1922.

"Weaving My Dreams." Words by Gene Buck. New York: Harms, 1922. (From the Ziegfeld Follies, 1922.)

"Wedding." Scene in the Ziegfeld Follies, 1923.

Wedding Music, composed expressly for Viola Cahn and Isidore Witmark, 1908.

"Wenn im Purpurschein." See "Aus 'Liedern eines fahrenden Gesellen.'"

Western Overture. New York: C. Fischer, Inc., 1940.

What Twenty Years Will Do (to Some People and a Tune). A musical skit. Words by George V. Hobart. (Composed for the Lambs, 1914.)

"When Knighthood Was in Flower" (Waltz Song). Words by William Le Baron. New York: Harms, 1922. (The musical theme of the motion picture of the same name.)

"When the Frost Is on the Punkin" (in Junior Laurel Songs). New York: Birchard, 1916.

"When the Maytime Comes Again" (in Junior Laurel Songs). New York: Birchard, 1920.

"When the Right One Comes Along." Words by Gene Buck. Song in the Ziegfeld Follies, 1920.

"When the Sixty-ninth Comes Back." Words by Gene Buck. Song in the Ziegfeld Follies, 1920.

"When Uncle Sam is Ruler of the Sea." New York: Harms, 1916.

"Whispering Willows." New York: M. Witmark and Sons, 1915.

"Widow Machree." (From the song by Samuel Lover). New York: G. Schirmer, 1915.

The Willow Plate. A Chinese shadowgraph play by Tony Sarg. New York: Harms, 1924. ("The Mandarin's Garden"; "The Little Gardenhouse"; "Chang, the Lover"; "Kongshee, the Mandarin's Daughter"; "The Wedding Procession".)

The Winning of the West. A spectacle or pantomime. (Composed for the Lambs, 1916.)

"Wirthstöchterlein,' Op. 10, No. 1. Berlin: Luckhardt, 1889.

"Woodland Fancies," Op. 34. Suite for orch. New York: G. Schirmer, 1928–29. (Composed 1901.) (Contains: "Morning in the Mountains"; "Forest Sylphs"; "Twilight"; "Autumn Frolics".)

"The World's Progress." March. New York: M. Witmark and Sons, 1916. (Dedicated to the Associated Advertising Clubs of the World.)

Y

"Yankee Land." See "The Song Birds."

"Yesterthoughts." New York: M. Witmark and Sons, 1900.

"Les Yeux bleus." (1890?)

"Yolanda." Overture. (For motion picture, 1923.)

"You Belong to Me." New York: Harms, 1916.

Z

The Ziegfeld Follies. Music for the productions of 1917, 1919, 1920, 1921, 1922, 1923, 1924.

ABBREVIATIONS

ALS   Autograph letter, signed

ASCAP   ASCAP Archive, New York

BPL   Boston Public Library (Brown Collection)

COH   Columbia University Oral History Collection

CL   Carnegie Library of Pittsburgh

CVL   Clifford Victor Herbert File, Lawrenceville School, Lawrenceville, N.J.

DH   Dartmouth College Special Collections, James G. Huneker File

HLC   Victor Herbert Archive, Library of Congress

HTC   Harvard University Theater Collection

HUM   Harvard University Music Library

LOC   Library of Congress

MH   Margaret Herrick Library of the American Academy of Motion Picture Arts
           and Sciences

NYPL-LC   New York Public Library of the Performing Arts–Lincoln Center

NYPL-R   New York Public Library, Rare Book and Manuscript Division

POC-CL   Pittsburgh Orchestra correspondence, unpublished and catalogued,
           1897–1903, Carnegie Library of Pittsburgh

TA   University of Texas at Austin, Ransom Humanities Research Center

TL   Typed letter

TLS   Typed letter, signed

VCR   Vassar College Archive, Ferdinand Louis Ritter Collection

CHAPTER 1. IRELAND, MY SIRELAND

1. "Victor Herbert," *New York Review* (October 3, 1909).

2. Karl Marx to Richard Froelich, ALS (November 2, 1964); ASCAP.

3. F. H. Martens, "A Little Talk with Victor Herbert," *Musical Observer* 18, no. 4 (April 1909).

4. *New Jersey Telegram* (November 20, 1906).

5. Janice McWilliams, interview with the author (December 12, 2000).

6. Frederik Stahlberg, "Yesterthoughts," unpublished memoir of Victor Herbert, Yale University Music Library.

7. Cornelia Dyas, "Victor Herbert, Musician," *Metropolitan Magazine* (November 11, 1899).

8. Herbert's first attempt at stage music was an operetta, *La Vivandiere*, written for Lillian Russell. She eventually decided not to appear in the piece and plans for a production were dropped. In a letter dated 1893 from Herbert to the librettist Harry B. Smith, stored in the Smith archive at TA, he writes, "I have sent you the 'Vivandiere' material." A search of the archive does not reveal the presence of the missing score.

9. Stanley Olmstead, "The Boy Who Played Cello," *New York Morning Telegraph* (December 13, 1914).

10. Ibid.

11. Olmstead, "The Boy Who Played Cello."

12. Isaac Goldberg, *American Mercury* (October 1930).

13. "Interview with Victor Herbert," *Broadway Magazine* (March 1915).

14. Ibid.

15. *Jenkintown* (Pa.) *Post* (July 2, 1937).

16. Ibid.

17. William Armstrong, "In Musicland," *Amalie Magazine* (September 1910).

18. Ibid.

19. Ibid.

20. Ibid.

21. Ibid.

22. Ibid.

23. Abbott Eames, in *Entertaining* (n.d.)

24. Ibid.

25. Unidentified newspaper clip, HLC (January 28, 1885).

26. M. F. Schlesinger, unpublished memoir, HLC.

27. Loc. cit.

28. The mention of a "joint contract" comes from a biographical article, approved by Ella V. Herbert Bartlett, in the ASCAP file. An archivist of the Metropolitan Opera Association, noting that the archive contains no contracts from this period, remarks that to his knowledge there are no "joint contracts" in any of the extant files.

Note: The letters and poems contained in this chapter are the author's translations of holographs in HLC.

CHAPTER 2. IN OLD NEW YORK

1. "Interview with Victor Herbert," *Christian Science Monitor* (December 4, 1915).
2. Francis Neilson, *My Life in Two Worlds* (Appleton, Wisc.: Nelson, 1952).
3. James G. Huneker, "Notes on New York City," *Sun* (May 8, 1910).
4. Unidentified clip, Herbert Scrapbook, HLC.
5. James G. Huneker, *Steeplejack II* (New York: Scribners, 1922).
6. Ibid.
7. Isidore Witmark, *From Ragtime to Swingtime* (New York: Furman, 1939).
8. Victor Herbert to James G. Huneker, ALS in BMI Archive, New York.
9. Heinrich Haas to F. L. Ritter, VCR, box 1.
10. Ibid.
11. *American Musician* (April 12, 1890).
12. A. S. Crockett, *Peacocks on Parade* (New York: Sears, 1931).
13. "Places in New York," *Century Magazine* 53, no. 4.
14. Ibid.
15. Lily Lehmann, *My Path Through Life* (New York: Putnam, 1914).
16. M. F. Schlesinger, unpublished memoir, HLC.
17. *New York Herald* (October 25, 1886).
18. Lehmann, *My Path Through Life*.
19. Douglas Gilbert, *American Vaudeville* (New York: McGraw, 1940).
20. David Mannes, *Music Is My Faith* (New York: Norton, 1938).
21. Municipal archives of the City of New York: box 88—G. H.; box 41—J (Koster and Bial's).
22. Mannes, *Music Is My Faith*.
23. VCR, box 11.
24. *American Musician* (April 12, 1891).
25. Lehmann, *My Path Through Life*.
26. Ibid.
27. *American Art Journal* (January 22, 1987).
28. A. Steinberg, in the *Worcester Festival Program* (1889).
29. *New York Herald* (October 18, 1887).
30. H. T. Finck, *My Adventures in the Golden Age of Music* (New York: Funk, 1926).
31. C. L. Purdy, *Victor Herbert—America's Music Master* (New York: Messner, 1944).
32. *Musical Courier* (October 1887).
33. DH.
34. Ibid.
35. Joseph Kaye, *Victor Herbert* (New York: Watt, 1931).
36. *Baltimore Sun* (December 27, 1931).
37. *New York Times* (May 20, 1924).
38. *Souvenir Program, Brighton Beach Concert Season* (1889).
39. At this time, 1891, Mrs. John G. Curtis was beginning her support of music education. Her philanthropy sponsored an orchestra of men, women, boys, and girls that performed a regular series of concerts at Chickering Hall in New York City.

40. *American Musician* (April 1891).

41. VCR, box 3.

42. Finck, *My Adventures in the Golden Age of Music.*

43. Franko, Sam, *Chords and Dischords* (New York: Viking, 1938).

44. Op. cit.

45. ALS in HLC.

46. Huneker, op. cit.

47. Franko, *Chords and Dischords.*

48. *New York Tribune* (January 9, 1887).

49. *New York Tribune* (December 2, 1888).

50. *Buffalo Tribune* (January 22, 1892).

51. *Buffalo Daily Courier* (January 22, 1892).

52. J. Meyer, proprietor of Schuberth Co., in COH.

53. Arlene Zeier, interview with author (October 18, 2001).

54. Mary Ellis, interview with author (October 2001).

55. Robert Kimball, interview with author.

56. COH.

57. Franko, *Chords and Dischords.*

58. Witmark, *From Ragtime to Swingtime.*

59. Crockett, *Peacocks on Parade.*

60. All figures converted to year 2000 values.

61. *American Musician* (June 22, 1889).

62. *Kansas City Star*, newspaper clip, HLC, n.d.

63. Loc. cit.

64. A. P. Hughes, *Music Is My Life* (Cleveland: World, 1947).

65. J. Mason, "Memories," HLC.

66. *New York Sun* (December 8, 1887).

67. *New York Tribune* (December 8, 1887).

68. *Musical Courier* (December 26, 1888).

69. Kaye, *Victor Herbert.*

70. *New York Times* (December 10, 1891).

71. Kaye, *Victor Herbert.*

72. Ibid.

73. *New York Sun* (February 3, 1894).

74. *American Musician* (June 22, 1889).

75. Loc. cit.

76. Loc. cit.

77. Purdy, *Victor Herbert—America's Music Master.*

78. Eames, in *Entertaining.*

79. Owen Hackett, "The Genius of the Opera," *Munsey's Magazine* (June 1892).

80. Purdy, *Victor Herbert—America's Music Master.*

81. *American Musician* (August 11, 1888).

82. *New York Tribune* (January 21, 1889).

83. Lehmann, *My Path Through Life.*

84. Franko, *Chords and Dischords.*

85. W. J. Henderson, *New York Times* (December 11, 1887).

86. *New York World* (December 11, 1887).

87. *New York Herald* (December 11, 1887).

88. VCR, box 1.

89. *New York Times* (January 21, 1889).

90. *Worcester Festival Program* (1889).

91. *Spy* (Worcester, Mass., September 25, 1890).

92. *Worcester Evening Gazette* (September 25, 1890).

93. *Worcester Telegram* (September 27, 1889).

94. Loc. cit.

95. Raymond Morin, "Worcester's Mixed Emotions about Victor Herbert," newspaper clip in Worcester Public Library Festival file, n.d. [1890].

96. John Carter Glenn collection (New Haven, Conn.: Yale University).

97. *Worcester Evening Gazette* (September 25, 1890).

98. *Worcester Telegram* (September 26, 1890).

99. Morin, "Worcester's Mixed Emotions."

100. *Worcester Telegram* (September 24, 1891).

101. Ibid.

102. *Worcester Gazette* (September 24, 1891).

CHAPTER 3. OH, MY NAME IS VICTOR HERBERT—I'M THE LEADER OF THE BAND

1. "Hollywood Recalls Some Gossip About Victor Herbert," unidentified newspaper clip in MH (Victor Herbert file, 1939).

2. Joseph Kaye, *Victor Herbert* (New York: Watt, 1931).

3. James F. Cooke, "Herbert, The Wizard of Melody," typed manuscript of article [not published] intended for publication in *Etude*, Shubert Archive, New York.

4. "Famous Bandmasters," *The Scrapbook of Henry Woelber—Bandmaster* (1934) in BPL.

5. Ibid.

6. Ibid.

7. *New York World*, newspaper clip, Bartlett Scrapbook, HCL, n.d.

8. Ibid.

9. DH, file A.

10. "Opera Sung by Americans," prospectus, BPL, n.d.

11. "Opera in English by Americans," unidentified newspaper clip, BPL.

12. My discussion of the history of brass bands in the United States is based on the following sources: "A History of Popular Bands Before 1890," *New York Times* (June 29, 1979); *Historical Register of the Centennial Exposition at Philadelphia, 1877*, program, 19 and 123; Margaret Hazen and Robert Hazen, *The Music Men* (Washington, D.C.: Smithsonian, 1987); Marwood Darlington, *Irish Orpheus* (Philadelphia: Oliver, 1956); Victor Herbert, "Artistic Bands" in *The Music of the Modern World,* ed. Anton Seidel (New York: Appleton, 1895–97); and H. L. Mencken, *Heathen Days* (New York: Knopf, 1943).

13. Henry Woelber, "Famous Bandmasters," *Cleveland Musician* (September 1933).

14. Loc. cit.

15. Ibid.

16. *American Muscian* (March 7, 1889).

17. Mencken, *Heathen Days*.

18. Richard Aldrich, unidentified newspaper clip, HUM, n.d.

19. *New York Evening Post* (November 11, 1893).

20. *New Yorker Staats-Zeitung* (November 23, 1893).

21. *New York Home Journal* (November 20, 1893).

22. *Musical Courier* (November 22, 1893).

23. *New York World* (November 27, 1893).

24. *New York Herald* (February 5, 1894).

25. *New York Herald* (March 26, 1894).

26. Rudolph Aronson, *Theatrical and Musical Memoirs* (New York: McBride, 1913).

27. Bartlett Scrapbook, HLC.

28. *Baltimore American* (March 17, 1895).

29. *Baltimore Herald* (March 20, 1895).

30. *Knoxville* (Tenn.) *Journal* (March 20, 1895).

31. *Atlanta Commercial* (March 21, 1895).

32. *Augusta* (Ga.) *Herald*. Newspaper clip in Bartlett Scrapbook, HLC.

33. Ibid.

34. *Jacksonville* (Fla.) *Citizen* (March 25, 1895).

35. Ibid.

36. *St.Paul* (Minn.) *Globe* (April 19, 1895).

37. *Chicago Times-Herald* (April 25, 1895).

38. Ibid.

39. *Kalamazoo News* (April 26, 1895).

CHAPTER 4. PITTSBURGH—HEAVEN AND HELL

1. W. N. Frew, letter, February 10, 1898, POC-CL.

2. *Pittsburgh Post* (December 4, 1903): "Mr. Herbert entered upon his present position here on 11/3/98, as successor to the late Frederick Archer, and in rivalry with Emil Mollenhauer."

3. Haysleys to Wilson, n.d, POC-CL.

4. Frew to Herbert, January 31, 1898, POC-CL.

5. Frew to Burnham, February 8, 1898, POC-CL.

6. Loc. cit.

7. Frew to guarantors, January 10, 1898, POC-CL.

8. Frew to Herbert, March 17, 1898, POC-CL.

9. *Musical Courier* (February 16, 1898).

10. *Musical Courier* (March 26, 1898).

11. Loc. cit.

12. Loc. cit.

13. W. B. Clayton to Wilson, August 27, 1898. This earlier letter asks Wilson to arrange for "a suite of four rooms for himself [Herbert], Mrs. Herbert, two children and nurse." Apparently Wilson acted upon the earlier request. In POC-CL.

14. Frew to Herbert, February 11, 1889, in POC-CL.

15. Frew to Herbert, February 18, 1889, in POC-CL.

16. Frew to Herbert, February 19, 1889, in POC-CL.

17. Frew to Herbert, September 10, 1889, in POC-CL.

18. Frew to Herbert, October 3, 1889, in POC-CL.

19. Herbert to Members of Pittsburgh Orchestra, October 12, 1898, in Victor Herbert Collection, miscellaneous correspondence file, Library of Congress.

20. Herbert to Wilson, March 22, 1898, in POC-CL.

21. Wilson to Herbert, April 26, 1898, in POC-CL.

22. Herbert to Wilson, May 1, 1898, in POC-CL.

23. Original, corrected in Herbert's hand, in POC-CL.

24. Herbert to Wilson, May 8, 1898, in POC-CL.

25. Wilson to Herbert, June 10, 1898, in POC-CL.

26. Loc. cit.

27. Wilson to Herbert, September 20, 1898, in POC-CL.

28. Wilson to Herbert, November 8, 1898, in POC-CL.

29. Herbert to Wilson, October 26, 1898, in POC-CL.

30. *Pittsburgh Post* (December 29, 1900).

31. Frederik Stahlberg, "Yesterthoughts," unpublished memoir of Victor Herbert, Yale University Music Library.

32. *Pittsburgh Press* (n.d.), in clipping file of Pittsburgh Orchestra correspondence, Carnegie Library.

33. Wilson to Herbert, memo, n.d., POC-CL.

34. *Pittsburgh Press* (November 4, 1898).

35. Loc. cit.

36. Loc. cit.

37. *Pittsburgh Dispatch* (November 4, 1898).

38. *Pittsburgh Leader* (November 4, 1898).

39. Loc. cit.

40. "Symphonie-Konzert," *Pittsburgher Volkblatt* (November 4, 1898).

41. *Pittsburgh Leader* (November 4, 1898).

42. Frew to Herbert, November 7, 1898, POC-CL.

43. Frew to Guarantors, January 12, 1899, POC-CL.

44. *Pittsburgh Press* (January 14, 1899), in POC-CL.

45. *Pittsburgh Times* (January 14, 1899).

46. *Musical Courier* (February 23, 1898).

47. Frew to Herbert, April 6, 1899, in POC-CL.

48. Frew to Herbert, June 5, 1899, in POC-CL.

49. Frew to Herbert, June 12, 1899, in POC-CL.

50. *Pittsburgh Dispatch* (October 20, 1899).

51. *Pittsburgh Dispatch* (November 5, 1899).

52. HLC; ALS.

53. *Pittsburgh Leader* (December 3, 1899).

54. *Pittsburgh Press* (n.d.).

55. Loc. cit.

56. Frew to Herbert, December 29, 1899, POC-CL.

57. Herbert to Wilson, September, 1899, in POC-CL.

58. *New York Journal* (January 24, 1900).

59. The excerpts from the *New York Herald* and *New York Tribune* are quoted in the *Pittsburgh Commerce Gazette* (January 25, 1900).

60. The excerpts from the *New York Times* and the *Musical Courier* are from scrapbooks of musical clippings relating to the out-of-town concerts of the Pittsburgh Orchestra, 1896–1901, Carnegie Library, Pittsburgh, Pa.

61. *Pittsburgh Leader* (February 18, 1900). This article is the source of all information on the subject of both The Caribou Hunters Dinner and the question of American repertoire for the orchestra.

62. Loc. cit.

63. Wright to Wilson, n.d., POC-CL.

64. Frew to Wright, February 10, 1900, POC-CL.

65. *Pittsburgh Press* (n.d.), in scrapbooks of musical clippings, Pittsburgh Orchestra, 1896–1901, Carnegie Library.

66. Loc. cit.

67. Wilson correspondence, in POC-CL.

68. *Pittsburgh Press* March 8, 1900, POC-CL.

69. Loc. cit.

70. *Musical Courier* (February 3, 1900).

71. *New York Times* (February 27, 1900).

72. Frew to Guarantors, February 16, 1900, POC-CL.

73. Press release, March 8, 1900, POC-CL.

74. Loc. cit.

75. Agreement between Art Society and Victor Herbert, season 1900–01; POC-CL.

76. Herbert to Wilson, July 10, 1900, POC-CL.

77. Parsons to Wilson, August 21, 1900, POC-CL.

78. Herbert to Wilson, June 9, 1900, POC-CL.

79. Herbert to Wilson, July 11, 1900, POC-CL.

80. ALS: Herbert to Wilson, September 20, 1900, POC-CL.

81. Zeisler to Herbert, October 6, 1900, POC-CL.

82. Zeisler to Wilson, October 27, 1900, POC-CL.

83. Loc. cit.

84. *Pittsburgh Leader* (October 22, 1900).

85. *Boston Journal* (October 28, 1900).

86. Loc. cit.

87. *Pittsburgh Dispatch* (October 30, 1900).

88. *Pittsburgh Post* (November 5, 1900).

89. Clayton to Wilson, November 12, 1900, POC-CL.

90. Frew to Herbert, November 6, 1900.

91. Herbert to Wilson, January 27, 1900, POC-CL.

92. *New York Herald* (January 27, 1900).

93. *New York World* (January 19, 1901).

94. *New York Evening Post* (January 19, 1901).

95. *New York Times* (February 13, 1901).

96. Statement of Orchestra Committee, March 1, 1901, POC-CL.

97. *Richmond* (Indiana) *Sun* (April 3, 1901).

98. Stahlberg, "Yesterthoughts."

99. Frew to Herbert, July 3, 1901, POC-CL.

100. *Pittsburgh Dispatch* (May 3, 1901).

101. *Pittsburgh Leader* (May 12, 1901).

102. Frew to Herbert, July 1, 1901, POC-CL.

103. Frew to Herbert, July 3, 1901, POC-CL.

104. Herbert to Wilson, September 25, 1901, POC-CL.

105. Herbert to Wilson, November 6, 1901, POC-CL.

106. Stahlberg, "Yesterthoughts."

107. Herbert to Wilson, September 7, 1901, POC-CL.

108. Loc. cit.

109. Herbert to Wilson, September 24, 1901, POC-CL.

110. Herbert to Wilson, October 7, 1901 and November 6, 1901, POC-CL.

111. Fenelson B. Rice to Wilson, July 18, 1901, POC-CL.

112. Herbert to Wilson, October 7, 1901, POC-CL.

113. A. P. Hughes, *Music Is My Life* (Cleveland: World, 1947).

114. Herbert to Wilson, October 7, 1901, POC-CL.

115. Hughes, *Music Is My Life*.

116. *Chicago American* (December 10, 1901).

117. "The American Musical Theater," Museum of Radio and Television archival tape, WABC (CBS) (October 1953).

118. Borsch to Wilson, n.d., POC-CL.

119. Borsch to Buchanan, March 4, 1903, POC-CL.

120. *Pittsburgh Dispatch* (March 8, 1903), POC-CL.

121. *Pittsburgh Leader* (May 15, 1903), POC-CL.

122. Harrison Gravely to Wilson, March 3, 1903, ALS; POC-CL.

123. Herbert to Buchanan, November 26, 1903, POC-CL.

124. Loc. cit.

125. Smith and Buchanan to Herbert, December 3, 1903, POC-CL.

126. *Pittsburgh Leader* (December 4, 1903).

127. *Pittsburgh Dispatch* (December 4, 1903).

128. Loc. cit.

129. *Pittsburgh Dispatch* (December 3, 1903).

130. Loc. cit.

131. *Pittsburgh Leader* (December 3, 1903).

132. Herbert to Schenk in Sibley Library of the Eastman School of Music: Special Collections; ALS.

133. HLC.

134. J. B. Oliver to J. B. Park, POC-CL.

135. Members of Pittsburgh Orchestra to Orchestra Committee, POC-CL.

136. Wilson to Buchanan, February 17, 1904, POC-CL.

137. Arthur W. Tams to Wilson, February 26, 1904, ALS; POC-CL.

138. HLC.

139. Stahlberg, "Yesterthoughts."

140. *Pittsburgh Gazette* (March 6, 1904).

141. *Pittsburgh Post* (March 8, 1904).

142. Buchanan to Herbert, memo, POC-CL.

143. Hall to Buchanan, March 17, 1904, POC-CL.

144. *Pittsburgh Dispatch* (March 19, 1904).

145. *Pittsburgh Dispatch* (March 20, 1904).

146. *Pittsburgh Dispatch* (March 19, 1904).

147. *Pittsburgh Dispatch* (March 20, 1904).

148. *Pittsburgh Gazette* (March 20, 1904).

149. *Pittsburgh Dispatch* (March 19, 1904).

150. Loc. cit.

151. Loc. cit.

152. *Pittsburgh Dispatch* (March 20, 1904).

153. Document in POC-CL.

154. Loc. cit.

155. Frew interview, *Pittsburgh Gazette* (March 20, 1904).

156. Loc. cit.

157. Loc. cit.

158. "Remembering Victor Herbert," *Coronet* (March 1963).

159. *Pittsburgh Leader* (March 25, 1904).

160. *Pittsburgh Leader* (March 27, 1904).

161. Memo, in POC-CL.

162. W. J. Dunham to Wilson, POC-CL.

163. Hughes, *Music Is My Life*.

164. *Musical America* (August 21, 1906).

165. Stahlberg, "Yesterthoughts."

166. Wallace Munro, "The Victor Herbert I Knew," *Lambs Script* 21 (January–February 1952).

CHAPTER 5. CODA BRILLIANTE

1. *New York Times* (December 14, 1903).

2. Prospectus for the Grand Union Hotel Season, 1894, Saratoga Springs Public Library, Saratoga Springs, N.Y.

3. George William Curtis, *Lotos Eating—A Summer Book* (New York: Harper, 1852).

4. Clarence H. Knapp, "The Passing of the Grand Union Hotel," *Saratogian* (December 5, 1952).

5. Edward B. Marks, *They All Sang* (New York: Viking, 1934).

6. Ibid.

7. George Waller, *Saratoga: Saga of an Impious Era* (Englewood Cliffs, N.J.: Prentice-Hall, 1952).

8. Gustav Klemm, "Victor Herbert As I Knew Him," *Musical America* (March 10, 1939).

9. Arthur Wise and Mary-Margaret Eitzler, "Victor Herbert's Philadelphia Love Affair," *Music Journal* (July 1972).

10. Alice Gordon Hogan, "Victor Herbert Talks of Music," *Philadelphia Record* (June 12, 1901).

11. Deems Taylor, unpublished memoir, Yale University Music Library.

12. Frederik Stahlberg, "Yesterthoughts," unpublished memoir of Victor Herbert, Yale University Music Library.

13. Klemm, "Victor Herbert As I Knew Him."

14. Thomas Stearns, "Victor Herbert, Composer and Man," *Caxton*: American-Irish Historical Society (n.d.).

15. Ibid.

16. H. T. Finck, *My Adventures in the Golden Age of Music* (New York: Funk, 1926).

17. *New York Times* (September 10, 1905).

18. "Catholic Taste in Music," *Standard* (June 9, 1905).

19. Stahlberg, "Yesterthoughts."

20. *Philadelphia Record* (April 19, 1911).

21. *Atlanta Journal* (May 15, 1911).

22. *Musical America* (July 13, 1911).

23. Stahlberg, "Yesterthoughts."

24. *New York Telegraph* (June 18, 1907).

25. *Toledo Blade* (June 8, 1911).

26. *New York Telegraph* (June 13, 1911).

27. *Pittsburgh Post* (September 22, 1907).

CHAPTER 6. PATERFAMILIAS

1. TLS (July 14, 1939); NYPL-LC case file.

2. Unidentified newspaper clip, *Baltimore Sun* (c. 1920).

3. "Hollywood Recalls Some Gossip about Victor Herbert," MH.

4. Frederik Stahlberg, "Yesterthoughts," unpublished memoir of Victor Herbert, Yale University Music Library.

5. ALS; TA.

6. Stahlberg, "Yesterthoughts."

7. "Reflections," loc. cit.

8. "A Study of Herbert," *Pittsburgh Press* (1902).

9. Joseph Pasternack, "Memories of Victor Herbert," unidentified clip, ASCAP.

10. Stahlberg, "Yesterthoughts."

11. Told to the author at a rehearsal of the of the glee club of the Friendly Sons of St. Patrick, New York (January 2002).

12. Mary Mackenzie, "Yesteryears," *Lake Placid News* (July 31, 1980).

13. ALS; CV.

14. Joseph Kaye, *Victor Herbert* (New York: Watt, 1931).

15. Much of the description of Herbert's residences is drawn from an article in the *New York Telegraph* (January 21, 1907) and from unidentified clips in the Carnegie Library of Pittsburgh.

16. James Francis Cooke, "A Musical Giant," Shubert Archive, New York.

17. Stahlberg, "Yesterthoughts."

18. Helene Reinhardt-Thimig, *Wie Max Reinhardt Lebte*. Starnberger See: Schulz, 1973.

19. Alice Nielsen, "Remembering Victor Herbert," Robinson-Locke Scrapbooks, NYPL-LC.

20. Ibid.

21. Kaye, *Victor Herbert*.

22. Author interview with Herbert P. Jacoby, Esq. (Mr. Jacoby was attorney for Ella Herbert Bartlett.)

23. Bartlett Scrapbook 2, LOC.

24. "A Study of Herbert," loc. cit.

25. Jacoby interview.

26. Baptismal records of St. Agnes Chapel of Trinity Parish, N.Y.

27. Stahlberg, "Yesterthoughts."

28. Pasternack, "Memories of Victor Herbert."

29. "A Study of Herbert," loc. cit.

30. "Son of Noted Composer with No Love for Music," *Detroit News* (February 18, 1914).

31. Gustav Klemm, "More Herbertiana," *Musical Courier* (January 4, 1923).

32. Stahlberg, "Yesterthoughts."

33. "Victor Herbert's Daughter Tells How He Got His Ideas," *New York Times* (c. 1930).

34. Mackenzie, "Yesteryears."

35. ALS; CVL.

36. ALS; CVL.

37. TLS; CVL.

38. TLS; CVL.

39. ALS; CVL.

40. ALS; CVL.

41. ALS; CVL.

42. TLS; CVL.

43. TLS; CVL.

44. Telegram, CVL.

45. TLS; CVL.

46. TLS; CVL.

47. ALS; CVL.

48. ALS; CVL.

49. ALS; CVL.

50. TLS; CVL.

51. TLS; CVL.

52. Loc. cit.

53. Loc. cit.

54. Loc. cit.

55. ALS; CVL.

56. TLS; CVL.

57. *Detroit News* (February 28, 1914).

CHAPTER 7. OYEZ! OYEZ! OYEZ!

1. *Amalie Magazine*, op. cit.

2. *Atheneum* (June 14, 1856), 752.

3. Ibid., 787.

4. *New York Tribune* (January 9, 1887).

5. *Atheneum*, 818.

6. Ibid.

7. London *Times* (July 5, 1856).

8. Arnold T. Schwab, *James Gibbons Huneker* (Stanford, Calif.: Stanford University Press, 1963).

9. A. J. Goodrich, "Marc Blumenberg Obituary," *Musical Courier* (May 21, 1913).

10. *The New York Sun* (February 5, 1906).

11. All quotations concerning Huneker and Blumenberg are in DH, MS 299, 1. Apparently Diggs followed Blumenberg's suggestion and forwarded the entire memo to Huneker.

12. *New York Times,* n.d., 5, NYPL-LC, Robinson-Locke Scrapbooks.

13. "Victor Herbert Feted and his Detractor Denounced," *Concert Goer* (November 1902).

14. *Musical Courier* (October 22, 1902).

15. *Victor Herbert v. Musical Courier Company* (Walton, N.Y.: Reporter Co., 1904) is the source of all quotations regarding the trial record.

16. *New York Sun* (February 05, 1901).

17. Frederik Stahlberg, "Yesterthoughts," unpublished memoir of Victor Herbert, Yale University Music Library.

18. Ibid.

19. Schwab, *James Gibbons Huneker.*

20. *Musical Courier* (November 15, 1902).

21. Ibid.

22. *Buffalo Evening News* (November 22, 1902).

23. *Concert Goer* (November 1902).

24. *Musical Courier* (November 29, 1902).

25. Ibid.

26. *Musical Courier* (November 5, 1902).

27. Ibid.

28. *Musical Courier* (November 26, 1902).

29. Ibid.

30. Lazar Ziff, *The American 1890s* (Lincoln: University of Nebraska Press, 1966).

31. Harry B. Smith, "Canned Music and the Composer," *American Mercury* (August 1924).

32. Ibid.

33. Campbell B. Casad, "Song Writers Fighting for Life," *Show World* (January 5, 1908).

34. *Joint Hearings Before the Committees on Patents on S. 2328 and H.R. 10353,* 69th Congress, First Session (Washington, D.C.: U.S. Government Printing Office).

35. Casad, "Song Writers Fighting for Life."

36. Ibid.

37. Ibid.

38. Booklet advertising Shanley's Restaurant (1917), Collection of the New-York Historical Society.

39. *Decisions of the United States Courts Involving Copyright: 1914–1917,* Copyright Office Bulletin 18 (Washington, D.C.: U.S. Government Printing Office, 1918).

40. *United States Supreme Court Records and Briefs*, vol. 242, pp. 591ff.

41. Ibid.

42. *Decisions*, p. 210.

43. Ibid.

44. *New York Telegraph* (September 24, 1907).

45. All correspondence from file 430, Shubert Archive, New York.

46. *Philadelphia Inquirer* (April 25, 1920).

47. *New York World* (October 23, 1912).

CHAPTER 8. A THEATRICAL MUSICIAN AT WORK

For many of the insights in this chapter I am indebted to the following sources, referenced in the text: Bruce Kerle, *Unfinished Show Business: Broadway Musicals as Works in Progress* (Carbondale: Southern Illinois University Press, 2005); Edith Boroff, "Origin of Species: Conflicting Views of American Musical Theater History," *American Music* (Winter 1984); and Raymond Knapp, *The American Musical and The Formation of National Identity* (Princeton, N.J.: Princeton University Press, 2005).

CHAPTER 9. ACT ONE

1. TA.

2. *New York Times* (January 30, 1902).

3. "The Opera of the People," *Etude* (January 1912).

4. "The Future of Our Opera," VCR box 2.

5. A. S. Crockett, *Peacocks on Parade* (New York: Sears, 1931).

6. Rudolph Aronson, *Theatrical and Musical Memories* (New York: McBride, 1913).

7. DeWolf Hopper, *Once a Clown, Always a Clown* (Boston: Little, Brown, 1924).

8. ALS; HLC.

9. Gustav Klemm, "More Herbertiana." *Musical Courier* (January 4, 1923).

10. Francis Neilson, *My Life in Two Worlds* (Appleton, Wisc.: Nelson, 1952).

11. H. T. Finck, *My Adventures in the Golden Age of Music* (New York: Funk, 1926).

12. "Victor Herbert's Last Words," *Philadelphia Democrat-Gazette* (July 13, 1934).

13. Neilson, *My Life in Two Worlds*.

14. Ibid.

15. *Musical Courier* (January 1, 1894).

16. Neilson, *My Life in Two Worlds*.

17. "Interview With Francis Wilson," *New York Sun* (1891).

18. Neilson, *My Life in Two Worlds*.

19. *Portsmouth, Historic and Picturesque*, unpublished manuscript, Portsmouth, N.H., Public Library (n.d).

20. "Biographical Sketch of a Popular Musical Artist and Humorist," *Boston Times* (June 23, 1978).

21. "A Shock Caused by Their Disbandment," newspaper clip, HTC.

22. H. C. Barnabee, *Reminiscences*. Boston: Chapple, 1913.

23. "Early Triumphs of the Famous Bostonians," *Boston Sunday Globe* (October 30, 1904).

24. Neilson, *My Life in Two Worlds*.

25. Unidentified newspaper clip, HLC.

26. *New York World* (November 21, 1894).

27. Ibid.

28. *New York Recorder* (November 21, 1894).

29. *New York Tribune* (November 21, 1894).

30. *New York World* (November 21, 1894).

31. *Boston Advertiser* (February 26, 1895).

32. Frederik Stahlberg, "Yesterthoughts," unpublished memoir of Victor Herbert, Yale University Music Library.

33. N. M. Strang. *Celebrated Comedians* (Boston: Page, 1901).

34. "Interview with Harry B. Smith," *Boston Transcript* (April 11, 1896).

35. Ibid.

36. ALS, n.d.; TA.

37. Ibid.

38. Unidentified newspaper clips, HTC.

39. *Chicago Daily News* (October 22, 1895).

40. *New York Herald* (November 5, 1895).

41. ALS; TA.

42. HLC.

43. *Stage* (September 7, 1897).

44. Ibid.

45. Barnabee, *Reminiscences.*

46. Witmark, *From Ragtime to Swingtime.*

47. "Alice Nielsen—Born to Sing," *Colliers Magazine* (July 2, 1932).

48. ALS; HLC.

49. Loc. cit.

50. *Boston Herald* (September 21, 1897).

51. *Colliers Magazine*, loc. cit.

52. *Chicago Tribune* (March 2, 1897).

53. *Chicago Chronicle* (March 2, 1897)

54. *Colliers Magazine*. loc. cit.

55. Ibid.

56. Ibid.

57. *New York Dramatic Mirror* (March 21, 1897).

58. *New York Sun* (March 17, 1897).

59. *New York Mail and Express* (March 17, 1897).

60. *New York Herald* (March 17, 1897).

61. *Hartford Times* (September 17, 1897).

62. "Article by Hillary Bell," *Stage* (September 1897).

63. *Boston Record* (September 21, 1897).

64. *Boston Globe* (September 21, 1897).

65. Ibid.

66. *Boston Herald* (September 21, 1897).

67. *St. Louis Globe-Democrat* (January 4, 1898).

68. Ibid.

69. Ibid.

70. *Los Angeles Record* (February 28, 1899).

71. Unidentified newspaper clip, BPL.

72. *New York Evening Post* (October 26, 1897).

73. "The Idol's Eye," *Boston Globe,* n.d., clip in HTC.

74. Ibid.

75. *Pittsburgh Leader* (April 10, 1901).

76. Gustave Kobbé, *The American Stage and Those Who Have Made It Great* (New York: Gervic, 1901).

77. Unidentified newspaper clip, HTC.

78. Kaye, op cit.

79. *New York Times* (October 24, 1899).

80. Unidentified newspaper clip, HTC.

81. *Boston Transcript* (February 11, 1899).

82. Smith, op cit.

83. Barnabee, op cit.

84. *New York World* (April 10, 1900).

85. *New York Journal* (April 11, 1900).

CHAPTER 10. ENTR'ACTE I: ACE OF CLUBS

1. "A History of the Lambs," *Chicago Herald-Record* (May 23, 1909).

2. Ibid.

3. *Hartford Courant* (May 26, 1909).

4. *Philadelphia Times* (May 27, 1909).

5. *Pittsburgh Morning Telegraph* (May 28, 1909).

6. Frederik Stahlberg, "Yesterthoughts," unpublished memoir of Victor Herbert, Yale University Music Library.

7. *New Jersey Democratic News* (May 18, 1907).

8. *New York Telegraph* (November 10, 1908).

9. *New York Times* (February 7, 1909).

10. *Hartford Courant*, loc. cit.

11. *New York Telegraph* (May 4, 1907).

12. Barry Dougherty, *The New York Friars Book of Roasts* (New York: Evans, 2000).

13. *New York Telegraph*, loc. cit.

14. HLC.

15. Wallace Munro, *Lambs Script* (January 2, 1952).

16. TLS; ASCAP.

17. TLS; ASCAP.

18. Charles K. Harris, *After the Ball* (New York: Frank, 1926).

19. COH.

20. Loc. cit.

21. Paul Cunningham, "Address on the Occasion of the Victor Herbert Centenary," ASCAP (January 1, 1959).

22. Stahlberg, "Yesterthoughts."

23. HLC.

24. Harris, *After the Ball.*

25. Ibid.

CHAPTER 11. ACT TWO: SCENE ONE

1. Victor Herbert and Ella Bartlett, *Victor Herbert's Music for Children* (New York: Schirmer, 1942).

2. James G. Huneker, *New York Sun* (October 14, 1903).

3. Frederik Stahlberg, "Yesterthoughts," unpublished memoir of Victor Herbert, Yale University Music Library.

4. Vincent R. Bryan and Charles Zimmermann, "Hurrah for Baffin Bay," in *Songs of the Gilded Age* (New York: Golden Press, 1960). (This number was added to the Sloane-Tietjens score for *The Wizard of Oz.*)

5. Eleanor Ames, "How They Make a Human Spider in 'Babes in Toyland,'" *Boston American* (November 19, 1905).

6. *Chicago Mirror* (June 22, 1903).

7. ALS; HTC.

8. *Pittsburgh Times* (September 15, 1903).

9. *Pittsburgh Dispatch* (September 15, 1903).

10. *Pittsburgh Leader* (September 15, 1903).

11. *New York Times* (October 14, 1903).

12. *New York Herald* (October 14, 1903).

13. *New York Observer* (October 14, 1903).

14. *New York Evening Post* (October 14, 1903).

15. *New York World* (October 18, 1903).

16. Unidentified newspaper clips, HTC.

17. *Boston Globe* (November 13, 1905).

18. Fred Stone, *Rolling Stone* (New York: McGraw, 1945).

19. I. J. Padereswki, *Manru* (Berlin: Bote und Bock, 1901).

20. *New York Dramatic News* (November 9, 1903).

21. *New York World* (November 17, 1903).

22. Ibid.

23. Unidentified newspaper clip, HTC.

24. *New York World* (November 17, 1903).

25. *New York World* (January 1, 1904).

26. *Boston Herald* (January 12, 1904).

27. Ibid.

28. New York premiere; unidentified newspaper clip, HTC.

29. Boston premiere; unidentified newspaper clip, HTC.

30. Ibid.

31. Ibid.

32. *New York Dramatic Mirror* (September 5, 1905).

33. Advertisement in Hollis Street Theater Program, Boston; HTC.

34. Ibid.

35. *Boston Globe* (November 14, 1905).

36. Unidentified newspaper clip, Robinson-Locke Scrapbooks, NYPL-LC.

37. Ibid.

38. *Buffalo American-Express* (September 15, 1905).

39. *Buffalo Inquirer* (September 15, 1905).

40. *New York Times* (October 25, 1905).

CHAPTER 12. OPERETTA AS SOCIAL DOCUMENT

1. ALS; NYPL-R.

2. J. P. Swain, *Broadway Musical* (New York: Oxford, 1990).

3. "Interview with Victor Herbert," *Tone* (April 1908).

4. Ibid.

5. *Boston Evening Transcript* (October 17, 1905).

6. Gerald Bordman, *American Operetta* (New York: Oxford, 1981).

7. Arthur Jackson, *The Best Musicals* (New York: Crown, 1977).

8. Swain, *Broadway Musical*.

9. Ibid.

10. Ibid.

11. Ibid.

12. Gilbert Seldes, "The Demoniac in the American Theater," *Dial* (September 1923).

13. Mosco Carner, *The Waltz* (London: Parrish, 1948).

14. Ibid.

15. Op. cit.

16. Op. cit.

17. Jean McGregor, "Chronicles of Saratoga," unpublished manuscript in Saratoga Springs Public Library, N.Y.

18. Gustav Klemm, "Victor Herbert as I Knew Him," *Musical America* (March 1939).

19. "Some Friends Recall Stories about Victor Herbert," unidentified newspaper clip, MH, "The Great Victor Herbert" file.

20. Unidentified newspaper clip, CL.

21. Author interview with Doris Eaton Travis (October 28, 2004).

22. Joseph Kaye, *Victor Herbert* (New York: Watt, 1931).

23. Newspaper clip in Robinson-Locke Scrapbooks (1913), NYPL-LC.

24. Loc. cit.

25. Kaye, *Victor Herbert*.

CHAPTER 13. ACT TWO: SCENE TWO

1. *Buffalo American-Express* (September 2, 1906).

2. ALS; HTC.

3. Ibid.

4. Unidentified newspaper clip, HTC.

5. *Buffalo Daily Courier* (September 3, 1906).

6. Fred Stone, *Rolling Stone* (New York: McGraw, 1945).

7. Charles Dillingham, unpublished memoir, Burnside Collection of Musical Theater Manuscripts, NYPL-R

8. Stone, *Rolling Stone*.

9. Ibid.

10. Dillingham, unpublished memoir.

11. *Buffalo Inquirer* (September 4, 1906).

12. *Buffalo American-Express* (September 4, 1906).

13. *Buffalo Evening News* (September 4, 1906).

14. Unidentified newspaper clip, HTC.

15. Unidentified newspaper clip, HTC.

16. *New York Dramatic Mirror* (September 27, 1906).

17. Ibid.

18. *New York Tribune* (December 26, 1906).

19. *New York Sun* (December 28, 1906).

20. Unidentified newspaper clip, HTC.

21. Unidentified newspaper clip, HTC.

22. *Chicago American* (May 20, 1907).

23. Unidentified newspaper clip, HTC.

24. *New York Times* (February 19, 1907).

25. Unidentified newspaper clip, HTC (March 2, 1907).

26. Unidentified newspaper clip, HTC (September 1897).

27. Frederik Stahlberg, "Yesterthoughts," unpublished memoir of Victor Herbert Yale University Music Library.

28. Joseph Kaye, *Victor Herbert* (New York: Watt, 1931).

29. *New York Dramatic Mirror* (December 1908).

30. Unidentified newspaper clip, HTC.

31. *New York Sun* (September 1, 1908).

32. *New York Dramatic Mirror,* loc. cit.

33. Kaye, *Victor Herbert.*

34. Thomas Stearns, "Victor Herbert, Composer and Man," *Caxton*, American-Irish Historical Society (n.d.).

35. "The Rose of Algeria," *New York Dramatic Mirror* (October 1909).

36. *Boston Globe* (November 2, 1909).

37. *Colonial Theater Program* (February 15, 1909).

38. Unidentified newspaper clip, HTC.

39. *Boston Herald* (January 26, 1909).

40. *New York Dramatic Mirror* (December 1908).

41. *Boston Evening Transcript* (March 2, 1909).

42. Ibid.

43. Unidentified newspaper clip, HTC.

44. Unidentified newspaper clip, HTC.

45. HLC.

46. Edward Waters, *Victor Herbert: A Life in Music* (New York: Macmillan, 1955).

47. Unidentified newspaper clip, HTC.

48. *New York Dramatic Mirror* (November 23, 1909).

49. Ibid.

50. "Have American Composers a Chance in Grand Opera?" *New York Telegram* (March 31, 1907).

51. Joseph Blumenthal, *My Sixty Years in Show Business* (New York: Osberg, 1936).

52. Ibid.

53. Ibid.

54. Isidore Witmark, *From Ragtime to Swingtime* (New York: Furman, 1939).

55. The information on the biography of August Jenssen is based on an article in *Der New Yorker*, kindly supplied by Mrs. Werner Janssen.

56. Werner Janssen, unpublished memoir, courtesy of Mrs. Werner Janssen.

57. Peggy Wood, *How Young You Look* (New York: Farrar, 1941).

58. Ibid.

59. Blumenthal, *My Sixty Years in Show Business*.

60. Unidentified newspaper clips, HTC.

61. Otto Harbach [Hauerbach] in COH.

62. Ibid.

63. Harbach tape, The Institute of the American Musical, Inc., Los Angeles.

64. HLC.

65. Robinson-Locke Scrapbooks (December 5, 1910), NYPL- LC.

66. Unidentified newspaper clips, HTC.

67. Unidentified newspaper clips, Theater Collection of the Museum of the City of New York.

68. *Musical America* (April 12, 1907).

69. Ibid.

70. *New York Times* (April 18, 1907).

71. Ibid.

72. *Musical America* (February 11, 1909).

73. "M'lle Manhattan Gossip." Robinson-Locke Scrapbooks (February 11, 1909), NYPL-LC.

74. DeWolf Hopper, *Once A Clown, Always A Clown* (Boston: Little, Brown, 1927).

75. *New York Times* (February 4, 1911).

76. *New York Times* (n.d.), in Robinson-Locke Scrapbooks, NYPL-LC.

77. *Musical America* (February 11, 1911).

78. Ibid.

79. *New York Telegraph* (July 19, 1909).

80. *Musical Herald* (September 1911).

81. *New York Times* (January 22, 1911).

82. Ibid.

83. L. A. G. Strong, *John McCormack* (New York: Macmillan, 1941).

84. *New York Tribune* (February 24, 1911).

85. *New York Times* (March 1, 1911).

86. Dillingham, unpublished memoir.

87. *New York World* (February 26, 1911).

88. Ibid.

89. *Musical Courier* (April 5, 1911).

90. *Musical America,* HLC.

91. HLC

92. Jerome Kanner, "Those Wonderful Days with Victor Herbert," *Coronet* (March 1963).

93. ALS Shubert Archive, New York.

94. "The Duchess Promising," *Billboard* (October 17, 1911).

95. Unidentified newspaper clip, HTC.

96. Quoted in the *Toledo Blade* (June 13, 1911) and the *New York Telegraph* (June 13, 1911).

97. *Buffalo Commercial* (February 28, 1912).

98. *New York Times* (October 19, 1911).

99. *New York Herald* (October 21, 1911).

100. *New York Telegraph* (October 21, 1911).

101. Unidentified newspaper clip, Robinson-Locke Scrapbooks, NYPL-LC.

102. *Rochester Post* (February 12, 1912).

103. Elsie Janis, *So Far, So Good* (New York: Dutton, 1932).

104. Alexander Woollcott, *Enchanted Aisles* (New York: Putnam, 1924).

105. Ibid.

106. Janis, *So Far, So Good.*

107. Ibid.

108. Douglas Gilbert, *American Vaudeville* (New York: McGraw, 1940).

109. Stone, *Rolling Stone.*

110. Dillingham, unpublished memoir.

111. Janis, *So Far, So Good.*

112. Stone, *Rolling Stone.*

113. Ibid.

114. *New York Herald* (April 20, 1913).

115. Unidentified newspaper clip, HTC.

116. Unidentified newspaper clip, HTC.

117. Ibid.

118. Various newspaper clips, HTC.

119. Dillingham, unpublished memoir.

120. Stone, *Rolling Stone.*

121. Ibid.

CHAPTER 14. ENTRE'ACTE II: UNCROWNED KINGS

1. "Victor Herbert Talks of Music," *Philadelphia Record* (March 12, 1908).

2. Carl Whittle, *The Irish in America.*

3. *New York Times* (March 17, 1916).

4. *Gaelic American* (March 19, 1916).

5. *New York Times* (March 17, 1916).

6. Ibid.

7. Typescript of article from the *New York Sun* (n.d.), HLC.

8. *Musical America* (March 24, 1917).

9. Unidentified newspaper clip, HTC.

10. *Boston Evening Transcript* (n.d.), HTC.

11. *Boston Herald* (n.d.), HTC.

12. *Boston Journal* (n.d.), HTC.

13. *Boston Post* (n.d.), HTC.

14. Unidentified newspaper clip, HTC.

15. *New York Times* (March 20, 1917).

16. Frederik Stahlberg, "Yesterthoughts," unpublished memoir of Victor Herbert, Yale University Music Library.

17. Daniel C. Cohalan, *Papers*, box 17, folder 3, American-Irish Historical Society, New York.

18. Cohalan file.

19. Cohalan file.

20. Charles K. Harris, *After the Ball* (New York: Frank, 1926).

CHAPTER 15. ACT THREE: SCENE ONE

1. Isadore Witmark, *From Ragtime to Swingtime* (New York: Furman, 1939).

2. *Chicago Tribune* (September 2, 1933).

3. ALS; HLC.

4. ALS; HLC.

5. ALS; HLC.

6. *Boston Evening Transcript* (May 5, 1913).

7. HLC.

8. *Boston Evening Transcript* (May 6, 1913).

9. *New York Sun* (September 9, 1913).

10. *New York Tribune* (September 9, 1913).

11. Unidentified newspaper clip, HTC.

12. *New York Press* (September 9, 1913).

13. Bide Dudly, "Review," HTC (n.d.).

14. *New York Herald* (October 14, 1913).

15. *New York Times* (November 12, 1913).

16. *New York Herald* (November 12, 1913).

17. *New York Sun* (November 14, 1913).

18. *New York Herald*, loc. cit.

19. *New York Tribune* (January 25, 1914).

20. Frederik Stahlberg, "Yesterthoughts," unpublished memoir of Victor Herbert, Yale University Music Library.

21. "Foretaste of New Herbert Opera," *Musical America* (March 29, 1913).

22. Ibid.

23. Ibid.

24. Victor Herbert and Grant Stewart, *Madeleine* (New York: Schirmer, 1914).

25. *Town and Country* (January 31, 1914).

26. *Musical America*, loc. cit.

27. *New York Times* (January 25, 1914).

28. *New York Times* (April 4, 1914, April 25, 1914).

29. *Musical America* (April 5, 1919).

30. Ibid.

31. Unidentified newspaper clips, HTC.

32. *New York Dramatic Mirror* (December 16, 1914).

33. *Boston Transcript* (January 19, 1915).

34. *New York Dramatic Mirror* (December 16, 1914).

35. Ibid.

36. Joseph Kaye, *Victor Herbert* (New York: Watt, 1931).

CHAPTER 16. AN OPERA MANQUÉ

1. HLC.

2. Frederik Stahlberg, "Yesterthoughts," unpublished memoir of Victor Herbert, Yale University Music Library.

3. *New York Times* (May 3, 1916).

4. Stahlberg, "Yesterthoughts."

CHAPTER 17. ACT THREE: SCENE TWO

1. *New York Sun* (January 7, 1913).

2. Ibid.

3. Ibid.

4. Unidentified newspaper clip, HTC.

5. Ibid.

6. Ibid.

7. *New York Evening Post* (November 3, 1914).

8. *New York Globe and Advertiser* (November 2, 1914).

9. Unidentified newspaper clip, HTC.

10. Unidentified newspaper clip, HTC.

11. Unidentified newspaper clip, HTC.

12. *Boston Herald* (November 29, 1915).

13. Unidentified newspaper clips, HTC.

14. Unidentified Philadelphia publication (September 1, 1915), HTC.

15. *New York Times* (September 27, 1915).

16. Conflation of reviews, New York and Boston, HTC.

17. Frederik Stahlberg, "Yesterthoughts," unpublished memoir of Victor Herbert, Yale University Music Library.

18. Ibid.

19. Horatio T. Parker, article, in *Boston Evening Transcript* (February 5, 1918).

20. *New York Times* (November 13, 1917).

21. Philip Hale, article, in *Boston Traveler* (February 12, 1928), HTC.

22. Ibid.

23. Parker, Ibid.

24. Mary Ellis, *Those Dancing Years* (London: Murray, 1982).

25. Author interview (January 2001).

26. Stahlberg, "Yesterthoughts."

27. *Philadelphia Telegraph* (December 26, 1918).

28. *Philadelphia Ledger* (December 26, 1918).

29. *Philadelphia Record* (December 16, 1918).

30. *New York Tribune* (February 5, 1919).

31. *New York Times* (February 4, 1919).

32. *New York Sun* (February 3, 1919).

21. MH.

22. MH.

23. TLS; NYPL-LC.

24. TLS; NYPL-LC.

25. TLS; NYPL-LC.

26. Michael Druxman, *The Musical from Broadu* 1980).

27. NYPL-LC.

28. TLS; HLC.

29. Warren Emmett, "Intimate Portraits of the I *Etude* (March 19, 1939).

30. COH.

31. "Fifty Years of Musical Comedy," Museum of I

33. *New York Dramatic Mirror* (July 26, 1911).

34. *Boston Traveler* (n.d.), HTC.

35. Ibid.

36. *New York Times* (December 30, 1919).

37. *Christian Science Monitor* (January 21, 1920).

38. Unidentified newspaper clip, HTC.

39. Unidentified newspaper clip, HTC.

40. Various newspaper clips, HTC.

41. Ibid.

42. Ibid.

43. *Boston Herald* and *Boston Post* (May 4, 1920).

44. *Christian Science Monitor* (March 23, 1920).

45. Ibid.

46. *Boston Globe* (May 4, 1920).

47. *Boston Herald* (May 4, 1920).

48. Unidentified newspaper clip, HTC.

49. *Boston Herald*, loc. cit.

50. *New York Times* (September 20, 1922).

51. Klemm, op cit.

52. *New York Sun* (August 21, 1924).

53. *New York Times* (August 21, 1924).

54. Unidentified clip, *Musical Observer*, HTC.

55. ALS; HTC.

56. HLC.

57. Unidentified clip (May 15, 1924), HTC.

58. *Boston Evening Transcript* (May 11, 1924).

59. Ibid.

CHAPTER 18. MEDIA VITAE IN MORTE SUMUS

1. Fanny Lover Schmid, "The Author of Rory O'More," *Century Magazine* 53, no. 4.

2. Along with many monographs laced with quotations from German literature, his most important publication was *The Relation of Antitoxins to Homeopathy* (New York: Boeriche and Runyon, 1899).

3. *New York Times* (July 2, 1935).

4. Robert Gartland, "Victor Herbert Dies," *Baltimore American* (May 27, 1924).

5. Unidentified newspaper clips, Robinson-Locke Scrapbooks, NYPL-LC.

6. Author interview with Dr. Curt Brieger, Johns Hopkins School of Medicine, Baltimore (September 29, 2005).

7. Deems Taylor, unpublished memoir, Yale University Music Library.

8. TLS, Otto Kahn Papers, box 105, Princeton University Special Collections.

9. Copy TL. Ibid.

10. *New York World* (March 1924).

11. Eddie Cantor and David Friedman, *Ziegfeld* (New York: King, 1934).

12. Laurence Bergreen, *As Thousands Cheer* (New York: Viking, 1990).

13. "Those Wonderful Days with Victor Herbert," *Coronet* (March 1963).

14. ALS; HLC.

15. Ibid.

16. NYPL-LC.

17. Taylor, unpublished memoir.

18. HLC.

19. Frederik Stahlberg, "Yesterthoughts,"
University Music Library.

20. Ibid.

21. Taylor, unpublished memoir.

22. Stahlberg, "Yesterthoughts."

23. Paul Whiteman and Mary Margaret Mc

24. Ibid.

25. Isaac Goldberg, *George Gershwin* (New

26. Ibid.

27. Gershwin Archive, Library of Congress.

28. *New York Times* (May 27, 1924).

29. "Victor Herbert and the American Ope
HLC.

30. *Pittsburgh Musician* (May 27, 1924).

31. *New York Telegraph* (May 27, 1924).

32. Charles K. Harris, *After the Ball* (New Y

33. *New York Times* (May 27, 1924).

34. *New York World* (May 28, 1924).

CHAPTER 19. POSTLUDE

1. Edward Waters, *Victor Herbert: A Life in*

2. TLS; NYPL-LC.

3. Jacoby interview (December 11, 2000).

4. Waters, *Victor Herbert: A Life in Music*.

5. MH.

6. Ibid.

7. TLS; HLC.

8. *Pittsburgh Sun-Telegraph* (September 2, 19

9. TLS; HLC.

10. Newspaper clip, *Baltimore Sun* (n.d.), HL

11. *New York Times* (May 14, 1940).

12. TLS; HLC.

13. TLS; ASCAP.

14. ASCAP.

15. Milton Aborn, Shubert press release, Shub

16. *New York Evening Post* (September 23, 1929

17. *New York Tribune* (September 23, 1929).

18. *New York Tribune* (December 22, 1929).

19. HLC.

20. Ibid.

21. MH.

22. MH.

23. TLS; NYPL-LC.

24. TLS; NYPL-LC.

25. TLS; NYPL-LC.

26. Michael Druxman, *The Musical from Broadway to Hollywood* (New York: Barnes, 1980).

27. NYPL-LC.

28. TLS; HLC.

29. Warren Emmett, "Intimate Portraits of the Life of a Widely Loved Composer," *Etude* (March 19, 1939).

30. COH.

31. "Fifty Years of Musical Comedy," Museum of Radio and Television, New York.

Alda, Frances. *Men, Women & Tenors*. Boston: Houghton, 1937.

Aronson, Rudolph. *Theatrical and Musical Memoirs*. New York: McBride, 1913.

Barnabee, Henry Clay. *My Wanderings*. Boston: Chapple, 1913.

——. *Reminiscences*. Boston: Chapple, 1913.

Bergreen, Laurence. *As Thousands Cheered*. New York: Viking, 1990.

Block, Goeffrey. *Enchanted Evenings*. New York: Oxford, 1997.

Blumenthal, George. *My Sixty Years in Show Business*. New York: Osberg, 1936.

Bordman, Gerald. *American Operetta*. New York: Oxford, 1981.

Boroff, Edith. "Origin of Species: Conflicting views of American Musical Theater History."*American Music* (Winter 1984).

Bradle, Hugh. *Such Was Saratoga*. New York: Doubleday, 1940.

Bryan, Vincent R., and Charles Zimmerman. *Songs of the Gilded Age*. New York: Golden Press, 1960.

Cantor, Eddie, and David Friedman. *Ziegfeld*. New York: King, 1934.

Carner, Mosco. *The Waltz*. London: Max Parrish, 1948.

Crockett, A. S. *Peacocks on Parade*. New York: Sears, 1931.

Curtis, George. *Lotos Eating*. New York: Harper, 1852.

Darlington, Marwood. *Irish Orpheus*. Philadelphia: Oliver, 1950.

Dougherty, Barry. *The New York Friars Book of Roasts*. New York: Evans, 2000.

Druxman, Michael. *The Musical from Broadway to Hollywood*. New York: Barnes, 1980.

Ellis, Mary. *Those Dancing Years*. London: Murray, 1982.

Finck, H. T. *My Adventures in the Golden Age of Music*. New York: Funk and Wagnalls, 1926.

Fischer, W. A. *Music Festivals in the United States*. Boston, 1934.

Franko, Sam. *Chords and Dischords*. New York: Viking, 1938.

Gilbert, Douglas. *American Vaudeville*. New York: McGraw, 1940.

Goldberg, Isaac. *George Gershwin*. New York: Simon, 1931.

Grau, Robert. *Forty Years' Observation of Music and Drama*. N.Y.: Broadway, 1909.

Harris, Charles K. *After the Ball*. New York: Frank, 1926.

Hazen, Margaret, and Robert Hazen. *The Music Men*. Washington, D.C.: Smithsonian, 1987.

Herbert, Victor. *Artistic Bands*. In *The Music of the Modern World*. Ed. Anton Seidl. New York: Appleton, 1895–97.

——. *The Call to Freedom*. Philadelphia: Ditson, 1917.

Herbert. Victor, and Grant Steward. *Madeleine*. New York: Schirmer, 1914.

Herbert, Victor, and Ella V. Bartlett. *Victor Herbert's Music for Children*. New York: Schirmer, 1942.

Hopper, DeWolf. *Once a Clown, Always a Clown*. Boston: Little, Brown, 1927.

Hughes, A. P. *Music Is My Life*. Cleveland: World, 1947.

Huneker, James Gibbons. *Steeplejack II*. New York: Scribners, 1922.

Inman, Felix. *Weber & Fields*. New York: Boni, 1924.

Jackson, Arthur. *The Best Musicals*. New York: Crown, 1977.

Janis, Elsie. *So Far, So Good*. New York: Dutton, 1932.

Kaye, Joseph. *Victor Herbert*. New York: Watt, 1931.

Kerle, Bruce. *Unfinished Show Business: Broadway Musicals as Works in Progress*. Edwardsville: Southern Illinois University Press, 2005.

Knapp, Raymond. *The American Musical and the Formation of National Identity*. Princeton: Princeton University Press, 2005.

Kobbé, Gustave. *The American Stage and Those Who Have Made It Famous*. New York: Gevic, 1901.

Kreuger, Miles. *Show Boat: The Story of a Classic American Musical*. New York: Oxford, 1977.

Leavitt, M. B. *Fifty Years of Theatrical Management*. New York: Broadway, 1912.

Lehmann, Lily. *My Path Through Life*. New York: Putnam, 1914.

Mannes, David. *Music Is My Faith*. New York: Norton, 1938.

Marks, Edward B. *They All Sang*. New York: Viking, 1934.

Mason, William. *Memories of a Musical Life*. New York: ALMS, 1970.

Mencken, H. L. *Heathen Days*. New York: Knopf, 1943.

Morell, Parker. *Diamond Jim*. New York: Garden City, 1934.

Nielson, Francis. *My Life in Two Worlds*. Vols. 1 and 2. Appleton, Wisc.: Nelson, 1952, 1953.

Paderewski, I. J. *Manru*. Berlin: Bote und Bock, 1901.

Purdy, C. L. *Victor Herbert—America's Music Master*. New York: Messner, 1944.

Reinhardt-Thimig, Helene. *Wie Max Reinhardt Lebt*. Starnberger See: Schulz, 1973.

Schwab, Arnold T. *James Gibbons Huneker*. Stanford, Calif.: Stanford University Press, 1963.

Smith, Cecil. *Musical Comedy in America*. New York: Theater Arts, 1950.

Snyder, Robert. *The Voice of the City*. New York: Oxford, 1989.

Stone, Fred. *Rolling Stone*. New York: McGraw, 1945.

Stebbins, Lucy Poate, and Richard Poate Stebbins. *Frank Damrosch: Let The People Sing*. Durham, N.C.: Duke University Press, 1945.

Strang, N. M. *Celebrated Comedians*. Boston: L. C. Page, 1901.

Strong, L. A. G. *John McCormack*. New York: Macmillan, 1941.

Swain, J. P. *The Broadway Musical*. New York: Oxford, 1990.

Thompson, Oscar. *The American Singer*. New York: Dial, 1937.

Waller, George. *Saratoga: Saga of an Impious Era*. Englewood Cliffs, N.J.: Prentice-Hall, 1952.

Waters, Edward. *Victor Herbert—A Life in Music*. New York: Macmillan, 1955.

Weinstein, Gregory. *The Ardent Eighties*. New York: International, 1929.

Whiteman, Paul, and Mary Margaret McBride. *Jazz*. New York: Sears, 1926.

Whittle, Carl. *The Irish in America*.

Witmark, Isidore. *From Ragtime to Swingtime*. New York: Furman, 1939.

Wood, Peggy. *How Young You Look*. New York: Farrar, 1941.

Woollcott, Alexander. *Enchanted Aisles*. New York: Putnam, 1924.

Worden, Helen. *The Real New York*. Indianapolis: Bobbs, 1932.

Ziff, Lazar. *The American 1890s*. Lincoln: University of Nebraska Press, 1966.

INDEX